W9-CZM-922

THE URBAN LAND INSTITUTE

REAL ESTATE DEVELOPMENT

Principles and Process

Mike E. Miles · **Emil E. Malizia** · **Marc A. Weiss** · **Gayle L. Berens** · **Ginger Travis**

ABOUT ULI–THE URBAN LAND INSTITUTE

ULI–the Urban Land Institute is a nonprofit education and research institute that is supported and directed by its members. Its mission is to provide responsible leadership in the use of land in order to enhance the total environment.

ULI sponsors educational programs and forums to encourage an open exchange of ideas and sharing of experience, initiates research on emerging land use trends and issues, and publishes a wide variety of materials to disseminate information on land use and development.

Established in 1936, the Institute today has nearly 17,000 members and associates representing the entire spectrum of the land use and development disciplines. They comprise developers, builders, property owners, investors, architects, public officials, planners, real estate brokers, appraisers, attorneys, engineers, financiers, academics, students, and librarians. ULI members contribute to higher standards of land use by sharing their knowledge and experience from the United States and other countries. The Institute has long been recognized as one of the nation's most respected and widely quoted sources of objective information on urban planning, growth, and development.

David E. Stahl
Executive Vice President

ULI Project Staff

Rachelle L. Levitt
Staff Vice President, Education

Frank H. Spink, Jr.
Staff Vice President, Publications

Gayle L. Berens
Project Director

Nancy H. Stewart
Managing Editor

Barbara M. Fishel/Editech
Manuscript Editor

Helene Y. Redmond
Manager, Computer-Assisted Publishing

Betsy VanBuskirk
Art Director

Kim Rusch
Artist

Jeff Urbancic
Artist

Diann Stanley-Austin
Production Manager

Recommended bibliographic listing:

Miles, Mike E., et al. *Real Estate Development Principles and Process*. Washington, D.C.: ULI–the Urban Land Institute, 1991.

ULI Catalog Number: R23
International Standard Book Number:
 0-87420-712-6
Library of Congress Catalog Card Number:
 90-72027

© 1991 by ULI–Urban Land Institute
625 Indiana Avenue, N.W.
Washington, D.C. 20004

Printed in the United States of America. All rights reserved. No part of this book may be reproduced in any form or by any means, electronic or mechanical, including photocopying, recording, or any information storage and retrieval system, without written permission of the publisher.

Dedication

This book is dedicated to the memory of Jim Graaskamp—
dynamic, insightful, slightly opinionated,
and one helluva guy.

ABOUT THE AUTHORS

Mike E. Miles

Mike Miles, PhD, SRPA, CPA, is Foundation Professor of Urban Development in the School of Business at the University of North Carolina at Chapel Hill. Along with this textbook and *Modern Real Estate*, a textbook now in its fourth edition, Miles is the author of over 50 journal articles, cases, and monographs on various aspects of the real estate development process. His previous experience includes vice president of finance of Alpert Investment Corporation, a real estate development firm; accountant with Peat Marwick Mitchell and Company; and faculty member of the Schools of Business of the University of Wisconsin, University of Hawaii, and University of Texas. Miles received a BS from Washington and Lee University, an MBA from Stanford University, and a PhD from the University of Texas at Austin. He is the academic adviser to the National Council of Real Estate Investment Fiduciaries and a fellow with the Urban Land Institute, serving on ULI's education committee.

Emil E. Malizia

Emil E. Malizia, PhD, is professor of real estate and economic development in the Department of City and Regional Planning, the University of North Carolina at Chapel Hill. After earning his BS from Rutgers University, he received his MS and PhD from Cornell University. He was on the faculty at the Georgia Institute of Technology and received a Fulbright scholarship to study in Bogota, Colombia. During the past 20 years, he has authored and researched over 50 publications on urban, rural, and regional development. His professional experience includes real estate market research for a major life insurance company and federal contract administration. He has also analyzed projects and secured financing for commercial developers. His current research focuses on the economic fundamentals that influence long-term space demand in commercial real estate in U.S. metropolitan areas.

Marc A. Weiss

Marc A. Weiss, PhD, is research director and associate professor of real estate development in the graduate School of Architecture, Planning, and Preservation at Columbia University. He is the author of *The Rise of the Community Builders*, a book about the history and political economy of large-scale real estate development. Currently he is writing *Own Your Own Home*, a book on the real estate industry, homeownership, and national housing policy. In addition, he has written numerous articles and research monographs on urban development and the history of development. Weiss was a fellow of the Lincoln Institute of Land Policy, Cambridge, Massachusetts, and a faculty member at MIT. He received his undergraduate degree from Stanford University and his PhD from the University of California at Berkeley.

Gayle L. Berens

Gayle L. Berens is senior associate for university education at the Urban Land Institute. She taught English at Georgetown University, Northern Virginia Community College, and Nuremburg Gymnasium, West Germany, and worked previously in education at the National Architectural Accrediting Board, the National Association of Home Builders, and the American Society of Landscape Architects. Berens received her undergraduate degree from the University of Wisconsin and an MS from Georgetown University. She is a doctoral candidate at Georgetown.

Ginger (Virginia) Travis

Ginger Travis is a professional writer and editor in Chapel Hill, North Carolina. She earned an MBA from the University of North Carolina, spent five years in commercial and industrial real estate appraisal, and has edited three editions of *Modern Real Estate*.

REVIEWERS

The authors would like to thank the following people for reviewing one or more chapters of *Real Estate Development Principles and Process*.

Ralph Basile
Principal
Basile Baumann Prost & Associates, Inc.
Annapolis, Maryland

J. Miller Blew
Adjunct Professor of Real
  Estate Development
Harvard University
Cambridge, Massachusetts

Jay M. Brodie
Executive Director
Pennsylvania Avenue
  Development Corporation
Washington, D.C.

Stephen W. Chamberlin
Regional Partner
Rouse & Associates
Union City, California

Donald Chisholm
President
Vernon Development Company
Ann Arbor, Michigan

James J. Didion
Chair and CEO
Coldwell Banker Commercial Group
Los Angeles, California

Bernard J. Frieden
Professor
Massachusetts Institute of Technology
Cambridge, Massachusetts

John J. Griffin, Jr.
Managing Partner
Rackemann, Sawyer & Brewster
Boston, Massachusetts

E. Eddie Henson
President
Henson-Williams Realty, Inc.
Tulsa, Oklahoma

David R. Jensen
President
David Jensen Associates, Inc.
Denver, Colorado

Gadi Kaufmann
Managing Partner
Robert Charles Lesser & Company
Beverly Hills, California

M. Leanne Lachman
Managing Director
Schroder Real Estate Associates
New York, New York

Robert W. Lisle
Chair and CEO
Farnham Corporation
Dallas, Texas

James M. Luckman
President and CEO
The Luckman Partnership
Los Angeles, California

John W. McMahan
President and CEO
Mellon/McMahan Real Estate Advisors
San Francisco, California

Ehud G. Mouchly
Principal
Kotin, Regan & Mouchly, Inc.
Los Angeles, California

Peter O. Muller
Professor and Chair
Department of Geography
University of Miami
Coral Gables, Florida

Dowell Myers
Associate Professor
University of Southern California
Los Angeles, California

Arthur C. Nelson
Associate Professor
Georgia Institute of Technology
Atlanta, Georgia

Harry Newman, Jr.
Chair
Newman Properties
Long Beach, California

Patricia Nicoson
Senior Transportation Planner
Department of Public Works
Arlington, Virginia

Hugh O. Nourse
Professor
University of Georgia
Athens, Georgia

Jay Parker
Executive Vice President
HOH Associates, Inc.
Alexandria, Virginia

Russell J. Parker
Vice President/Leasing
JMB Properties
Los Angeles, California

Lynne Sagalyn
Associate Professor
Massachusetts Institute of Technology
Cambridge, Massachusetts

Robert W. Siler, Jr.
Chair and CEO
Hammer, Siler, George Associates
Silver Spring, Maryland

Eric Smart
President
Bolan Smart Associates
Washington, D.C.

Lewis H. Spence
Lecturer and Public Policy Analyst
Kennedy School of Government
Harvard University
Cambridge, Massachusetts

John E. Stefany
President
Architectural Consultants Corporation
Tampa, Florida

William Webb
William Webb Associates
Jacksonville, Florida

J. Michael Welborn
Vice President
The Prudential Acquisition & Sales Group
Los Angeles, California

Preface

The impetus for writing this textbook on the real estate development process was twofold: 1) real estate development has an enormous—and increasing—effect on many aspects of our society; and 2) entering the 1990s, no single textbook is designed to give future decision makers a total look at the complex process of development, even as the number of students in university-level development programs increases steadily. While many popular basic real estate textbooks are available, very few deal with the development process itself. Instead, textbooks focus on narrower issues, such as real estate finance, land planning, and affordable housing; no single publication adequately covers the complete process of development.

Yet development provides shelter, one of the three basic needs fundamental to every human being's survival. As such, it constitutes a very large portion of gross private domestic investment, which represents our nation's investment in the future. More important, development today determines in many respects how we will live in the future. Development affects everybody as it shapes the built environment.

The inherently interdisciplinary nature of the real estate development process and its entrepreneurial nature give develop-ment a special status and create a decision-making environment best suited to a well-rounded person. Though many activities related to development now take place under the corporate or institutional umbrella, the activities themselves still bear a distinctive entrepreneurial stamp.

Real estate development is also unusually dynamic, with rapid changes occurring in the links among construction, regulation, marketing, finance, management, and so on. The dynamic nature of the process contributes a factor of extra excitement and makes development the most challenging aspect of the real estate industry, particularly in the rapidly evolving environment of the 1990s, replete with more and more complexities.

This textbook captures an understanding of the development process in eight distinct segments, called the "eight-stage model of real estate development." The activities that collectively constitute the process are the academic portion of development. With knowledge of this process firmly in hand, the reader can then proceed to do the additional detailed studies of product types and local markets necessary to develop buildings successfully.

The book is divided into seven parts. Part I, Introduction, lays out the general framework of the development process in the eight interactive stages, describing the primary players in the development process, and the magnitude of dollars, land, and labor necessary for development. The introduction also includes a brief review of the financial tools necessary for understanding the process. Certainly other books do an excellent, detailed job of describing real estate finance and investment; this review is intended to highlight how the financial markets work as a source of development capital and how the logic of discounted cash flow can help all the players make better decisions about development.

Successfully anticipating the future and generating the numbers needed for the discounted cash flow analysis are best done by first studying the past. Thus, Part II, The History of Real Estate Development in the United States, thoroughly reviews the evolution of development in this country from colonial days to the present. This historic picture is clearly one of a dynamic relationship between public and private players. The players' exact roles have changed over time, but it has always been and always will be true that the public sector is a partner in all private development.

With the historical evolution clearly stated, the book moves on to the consideration of ideas for specific development projects. Part III, Ideas, discusses the sources of ideas and how those ideas are refined as the developer starts to move through the initial two stages of the development process.

Part IV, Planning and Analysis: The Public Roles, deals with the public perspective of development. Chapter 10, by Douglas R. Porter, focuses on the increasing importance of impact fees and the related financing of infrastructure. Chapter 11, by Rachelle L. Levitt, discusses codevelopment and a more proactive role for public sector players. Chapter 12, by Diane Suchman, deals with affordable housing, an increasingly important political issue as our generally affluent society continues to leave certain people behind. That chapter is included partially as food for thought for future developers, who will be faced with social issues as they change the face of the environment.

Part V, Planning and Analysis: The Market Perspective, moves from the public to a private perspective. The chapters in this section deal with feasibility studies and market analyses that will facilitate making decisions and building the development team. The developer, as team leader, is responsible for seeing that all the pieces add up to the whole and that collectively the enterprise is worthwhile, but all the players in the process have a role in the feasibility study.

Part VI, Making It Happen, deals with everything from contract negotiations to construction to the formal opening. Thus, it reviews the legal aspects of putting the team together as well as the critically important management of the construction phase of development. Chapter 16 includes a considerable section on the environmental issues facing developers, particularly hazardous waste and how it affects contracting and management of the development process.

Part VII, Continuing to Make It Work, looks at the concerns that continue once the building is completed. Developments in the 1990s seldom occur without planning for the project's operation. Chapter 18 deals with asset management, the umbrella term encompassing traditional property management as well as institutional and corporate portfolio management. Chapter 19, authored primarily by William Webb, deals with marketing, sales, and leasing. And Chapter 20 deals with the future, reviewing what has passed and how development decision makers combine an analysis of today's market conditions with projections of future market conditions to establish cash flows that justify a project. Developers must anticipate many different aspects of the future, for existing trends can lead developers to predict reactions and interactions and to consider different risks and opportunities, all in the expectation of developing better buildings.

This text is intended for university students in schools of business, planning, architecture, engineering, and law. It is also a useful beginning point for individuals shifting careers, either into development or between roles in development. While the text certainly does not guarantee success and financial reward, it does introduce readers to a process that is both enjoyable and rewarding. Once bitten by the development bug, few people want to return to less challenging environments.

Many people had a hand in producing this book, including academics from several different fields, practitioners from across the country, and numerous members of ULI's staff. The practitioners are cited throughout the text in the profiles. On ULI's staff, we are particularly indebted to Rachelle L. Levitt for her unrelenting effort and backing. Dana Heiburg, Marie Vinciguerra, J. Thomas Black, David Salveson, Frank Spink, Jr., Karen Bradbury, and Geraldine Bachman contributed many hours. Members of ULI's education com-mittee provided assistance and support throughout the textbook's lengthy germination. In particular, the authors would like to thank Harry Newman, Jr., John Griffin, Jr., John McMahan, J. Miller Blew, and Bernie Frieden.

Mike E. Miles
Emil E. Malizia
Marc A. Weiss
Gayle L. Berens
Ginger Travis

November 1990

Contents

PART III. IDEAS

xii

PART V. PLANNING AND ANALYSIS: THE MARKET PERSPECTIVE

PART I
INTRODUCTION

Chapter 1

Introduction to Real Estate Development

All of us who inhabit the built environment, whether consumer, citizen, or real estate professional, need to understand the development process. It is this development process that creates the houses we live in, the publicly assisted apartment project in our town, the 25-story office tower downtown, the warehouse that stored the paper this book was printed on, and the fast-food restaurant on the commercial strip.

Both public and private participants in real estate development share compelling reasons for understanding the development process. The goals of participants from the private sector are to minimize risk while maximizing personal and/or institutional objectives—usually profit but quite often nonmonetary objectives as well. Few business ventures are as heavily leveraged as traditional real estate development projects, magnifying the risk of ruin but also increasing the potential for high returns to equity. Large fortunes can be made and lost in real estate development.

The public sector's goal is to maximize good development, seeing that buildings constructed are attractive and safe and located to help the town or city function well. Good development means balancing the public's need for constructed space and economic growth with the public responsibility to provide services and improve the quality of life. The public and private sectors are involved as partners in every real estate development project. A key tenet of this book is that all players enjoy a higher probability of achieving success if they understand *how* the development process works, *who* the other players are, and *where* everyone fits.

This book was written for people who need to understand real estate development from the private and public perspectives. Its aim is to be useful to present and future developers, city planners, legislators, regulators, corporate real estate officers, land planners, lawyers specializing in real estate, architects, engineers, building contractors, marketing analysts, and leasing agents/brokers. Readers are assumed to have already acquired the fundamentals of real estate and/or city planning. This book builds on but does not repeat basic information about real estate law and finance, urban economics, and land planning and design.

Throughout, the book includes profiles of successful developers and professionals who work with developers. Their career paths are always interesting and often surprising. Their perspectives on development are especially valuable because they have lived the process described at a time when development has become more difficult to undertake profitably, and their insights can help put the development process in human terms.

In addition to the profiles, the book focuses on one developer, Whit Morrow of Fraser Morrow Daniels, and one development, the Europa Center. That project, a 95,000-square-foot Class A office building, was being developed while this book was being written. Mostly through Morrow's own words, readers can follow his idea for an office project from conception through planning, permitting, financing, and construction to completion, leasing, and ongoing management.

This chapter introduces the development process and its many players, including:
- Defining real estate development;
- The eight-stage model of real estate development;
- Characterizing developers;
- The development team;
- The public/private partnership;
- Market studies and feasibility studies;
- Design; and
- Developers and their partners.

DEFINING REAL ESTATE DEVELOPMENT

Development is an idea that ends in bricks and mortar. Land, labor, capital, management, and entrepreneurship bring that idea to fruition, realizing value by providing space over time with certain associated services. While the definition of real estate development remains simple, the activity grows more and more complex. Today, development requires more knowledge than ever before about prospective markets and marketing, patterns of urban growth, law, local regulations, public policy, conveyances and contracts, elements of building design, site development and building techniques, financing, controlling risk, and managing time, the project, and assets.

Greater complexity in real estate development has resulted in more specialization. As more affiliated professionals have begun to work with developers, the size of the development team has increased and the roles of some professionals have changed. Although greater complexity generates better-educated developers (educated both in book knowledge and hard knocks), it does not change the steps they usually follow in the development process (or the personality traits that most developers share).

THE EIGHT-STAGE MODEL OF REAL ESTATE DEVELOPMENT

Developers follow a sequence of steps from the moment they first get an idea to the time when they complete the project and either move the tenants in and sell the project or manage it through its life cycle. While various observers of the development process may delineate its sequence of steps slightly differently, its essence does not vary substantially. This text is based on the eight-stage model depicted in Figure 1-1. Succeeding chapters detail all the activities that collectively make up this eight-stage model of the development process.

Before proceeding further with the model, a few points about development must be emphasized. First, the development process is messy. A flow chart like that shown in Figure 1-1 can freeze the discrete steps and help one understand development, but it cannot capture the constant repositioning that occurs in the developer's mind or the nearly constant renegotiation between the developer and all the other participants in the process.

Second, development is an art. It is creative, often very complex, partly logical, and partly intuitive. Studying the components of real estate development can help all players make the most of their chances for success; developers themselves can learn from studying the process. What cannot be taught are two essential ingredients in the successful real estate developer/entrepreneur: creativity and drive.

Third, at every stage, developers should consider all the remaining stages of the development process. By doing so, they ensure that the development plan and its physical implementation come closest to being optimal over the whole process and, equally important, over the project's long expected life.

FIGURE 1-1
THE EIGHT-STAGE MODEL OF REAL ESTATE DEVELOPMENT

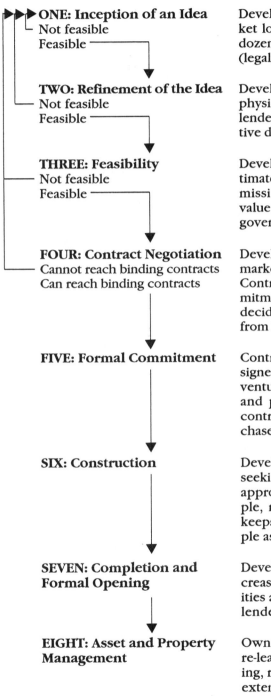

ONE: Inception of an Idea
Not feasible
Feasible

Developer with background knowledge of the market looks for needs to fill, sees possibilities, has a dozen ideas, does quick feasibility tests in his head (legal, physical, financial).

TWO: Refinement of the Idea
Not feasible
Feasible

Developer finds a specific site for the idea; looks for physical feasibility; talks with prospective tenants, lenders, partners, professionals; settles on a tentative design; options the land if the idea looks good.

THREE: Feasibility
Not feasible
Feasible

Developer commissions formal market study to estimate market absorption and capture rates, commissions feasibility study comparing estimated value of project to cost, processes plans through government agencies.

FOUR: Contract Negotiation
Cannot reach binding contracts
Can reach binding contracts

Developer decides on final design based on what market study says users want and will pay for. Contracts are negotiated. Developer gets loan commitment in writing, decides on general contractor, decides general rent requirements, gathers permits from local government.

FIVE: Formal Commitment

Contracts, often contingent on each other, are signed. Developer may have all signed at once: joint venture agreement, construction loan agreement and permanent loan commitment, construction contract, exercise of land purchase option, purchase of insurance, and prelease agreements.

SIX: Construction

Developer switches to formal accounting system, seeking to keep all costs within budget. Developer approves any changes suggested by marketing people, resolves construction disputes, signs checks, keeps work on schedule, brings in operating people as needed.

SEVEN: Completion and Formal Opening

Developer brings in full-time operating people, increases advertising. City approves occupancy, utilities are connected, tenants move in. Construction lender is taken out, and permanent loan is closed.

EIGHT: Asset and Property Management

Owners oversee property management, including re-leasing; longer-term owners oversee reconfiguring, remodeling, remarketing space as necessary to extend economic life and enhance performance of asset; corporate management of fixed assets and considerations regarding investors' portfolios come into play.

It is a huge mistake to underrate the importance of asset management and property management after the project is built or to overlook them during design and construction. Operating "smart" buildings requires technical competence beyond the general management skills that all property managers need. In addition, asset managers need to remarket space continually and upgrade or remodel the building periodically to keep the space competitive in an evolving market. Institutional investors and corporate owners are also keenly aware of the periodic need for and cost of major remodeling to prolong the economic life of buildings. Careful planning during stages one to seven should enable developers to find ways to minimize the frequency and cost of retrofitting buildings. Whether developers manage the property for the long term or not, they are responsible for considerations involving asset management during the first seven stages.

It is also imperative to remember that the development process is inherently interdisciplinary. It is not a game that is won by having exceptional depth in one particular area, say, electrical design. Rather, it is a complex process that demands attention to all the different aspects of creating the built environment—political, economic, physical, legal, sociological, and so on—as well as good management of the interaction.

Finally, U.S. real estate development is global in perspective. Financing is increasingly provided by international sources, tenants are served globally, and international building firms offer the full gamut of construction services. Most important, immigration is changing the consuming public, which changes the types of cities where people want to live. As different ethnic groups settle in U.S. cities, the configuration of cities and needs of citizens change. Developers must be prepared to respond to those changes.

CHARACTERIZING DEVELOPERS

Developers are above all entrepreneurs. They put a product on a site and sell it for a profit. An entrepreneur's willingness to tolerate variability in returns (though not necessarily more risk from his or her perspective) in pursuit of a larger return to equity (both capital and sweat) is an important distinction between the entrepreneur and public and private sector professionals who simply receive salaries or clock billable hours. As later chapters show, this entrepreneurial spirit is still essential, even when major corporations and large pension funds take an active role in real estate development.

In other preferences and traits, developers may differ strikingly from each other, and it is a big mistake to assume that all developers are alike. Some, for example, develop only one type of property, such as single-family houses; others will develop anything commercial or industrial. Some developers carve out a niche in one city and refuse opportunities outside it; others work regionally, nationally, or internationally (although "national" developers, such as Trammell Crow Company, often resemble an association of local developers doing business together). The company in this book's case study, Fraser Morrow Daniels, was founded to develop real estate in the Carolinas. Its focus was geographic, its products office, residential, and hotel space.

EUROPA CENTER

THE DEVELOPMENT COMPANY

Name:
Fraser Morrow Daniels & Company (four partners).

Founded:
1985, in affiliation with other ventures by Charles E. Fraser.

Purpose:
To develop real estate in the Carolinas, initially in the Research Triangle (Raleigh, Durham, Chapel Hill) of North Carolina.

Projects under way or completed from 1985 to 1989:
1. ***Park Forty Plaza:*** *Class A office building, 125,000 square feet, Research Triangle Park, completed, still leasing, approximate cost $12 million.*

2. **Spring Hill:** *Residential community on 65 acres in Research Triangle Park, 25 single-family houses and 100 condominiums completed out of 600 housing units projected.*
3. **Rosemary Square:** *In-town hotel, Chapel Hill, projected to contain 188 suites/rooms, 22,000 square feet of commercial space, and 516 parking spaces. Estimated cost $30 million. Designed but marketing delayed by litigation until September 1987 in North Carolina Supreme Court. The project absorbed over $2 million, and in 1989 the company decided not to build the project.*
4. **Europa Center:** *Class A office building, 95,000 square feet in Phase I, Chapel Hill.*

Some developers run extremely lean organizations, hiring outside help for every function from design to leasing; others maintain needed expertise in house. In between are many gradations. While on average the reputation of developers may be poor, developers range from those who put reputation above profit to those who fail to respect even the letter of the law. Likewise, in ego and visibility, developers vary enormously. Some name buildings for themselves; others cherish anonymity.

Private developers/entrepreneurs must balance an extraordinary number of requirements for completing a project with the needs of diverse providers and consumers of the product. As Figure 1-2 shows, developers first need the blessing of local government and neighbors around the site. Often to obtain public approval, developers are required to redesign the project. Second, developers need tenants or buyers who will pay for space if they provide the right product at the right price. Third, they lead an internal team of specialists who depend on them for their livelihood and recruit external players whose business is contracting with other developers. Fourth, developers demonstrate the project's feasibility to the capital markets and pay interest or give equity positions in return for funding. In every one of these interactions, developers practice some form of risk management,

initiating and managing this complex web of relationships from day one through at least stage seven of the process.

The developer's job description includes shifting roles as creator, promoter, negotiator, manager, leader, risk manager, and investor, adding up to a much more complex vision of an entrepreneur than a person who merely buys low to sell high. They are more innovators—people who realize an idea in the marketplace—than traders skilled at arbitrage. Balancing roles is part of the developer's art, something that can be described but not taught. Equally important and equally unteachable is the drive that makes developers persevere through problems and obstacles to the desired end. Developers tend to be single-minded; they do not like to stop. This quality, perhaps more than the profit motive, accounts for the negative public view of some developers. Yet the same single-mindedness can lead to the design and construction of innovative projects.

This book refers many times to the "development team" that designs and builds the developer's idea. It is worth noting that probably only 1 percent (perhaps fewer) of the people in real estate development are actually developer/entrepreneurs. The other 99 percent include a wide range of professionals and building tradespeople who are indispensable players. Clearly, challenging work abounds in real estate development for all participants, not just the developer.

THE DEVELOPMENT TEAM

If developers consistently play one role throughout the development process, it is that of a leader of people who help them realize their vision of what is possible. Developers almost never work in isolation. To design, finance, build, lease or sell, and manage their dream, they must use the services of many other experts, public and private, some of them professionals and others entrepreneurs themselves.

Developers vary in the technical expertise they bring to the team. Earlier in their careers they might have been architects, lawyers, contractors, brokers, land planners, or lenders; almost all started elsewhere. Consequently, developers must

FIGURE 1-2
THE DEVELOPER'S MANY ROLES

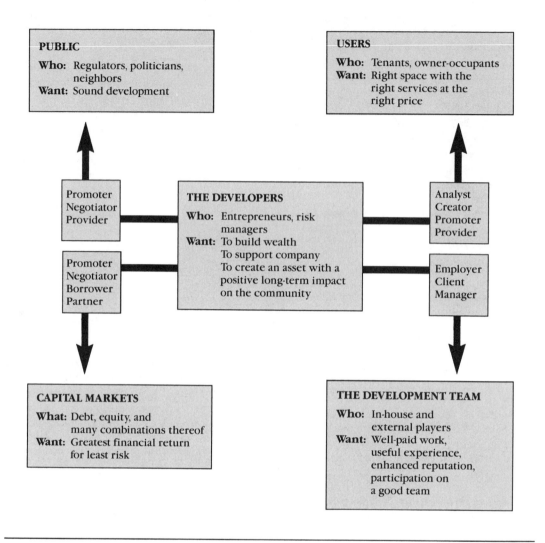

PUBLIC

Who: Regulators, politicians, neighbors
Want: Sound development

USERS

Who: Tenants, owner-occupants
Want: Right space with the right services at the right price

Promoter
Negotiator
Provider

THE DEVELOPERS

Who: Entrepreneurs, risk managers
Want: To build wealth
To support company
To create an asset with a positive long-term impact on the community

Analyst
Creator
Promoter
Provider

Promoter
Negotiator
Borrower
Partner

Employer
Client
Manager

CAPITAL MARKETS

What: Debt, equity, and many combinations thereof
Want: Greatest financial return for least risk

THE DEVELOPMENT TEAM

Who: In-house and external players
Want: Well-paid work, useful experience, enhanced reputation, participation on a good team

hire the expertise they lack—whether they keep their experts on the payroll or contract with outside help. In lieu of paying cash for services, developers occasionally put together a joint venture with certain specialists. Regardless of the financial arrangement, however, developers must be able to find the right people, keep them motivated and on schedule, and ensure that their work is acceptable—or the project may not get done successfully.

Often developers, like any team leader, motivate players with incentives other than money—with pride in the proj-

ect, with the hope of future work, and with fear of the consequences of not performing. Knowing when and with whom to use different incentives is part of leading the development team.

Developers spend a large part of their time managing other people when design and construction first start. Earlier, when developers shape and sell an idea to get commitments from others, they are promoters foremost. They have both the plan and the responsibility for making it happen, something like being a quarterback, a coach, *and* a team owner rolled into one.

Photo courtesy of The City Market

City grants and below-market loans are two ways in which the public sector works with the private sector in the development process. Such grants and loans were among the techniques used to finance the rehabilitation of Raleigh, North Carolina's historic City Market.

THE PUBLIC/PRIVATE PARTNERSHIP

Private sector real estate developers have a public sector partner in every deal—no exceptions—whether they choose to recognize the partner or not. *Government*—federal, state, and local—permeates the U.S. system of capitalism in which private developers operate. And real estate development itself is a highly regulated process. Taxes, labor law, property law, public infrastructure, financial markets, zoning, permits, and impact fees all issue from legislation, regulations, and public policy. In some cases, the public sector even enters the development process directly as equity partner of a private developer to pursue a public goal, such as redevelopment of the downtown.

Developers should recognize their public partners, especially local govern-ment, and the neighbors that will be directly affected by the project. Time *is* money in real estate development; overlooking or antagonizing public partners ultimately costs a developer time in interest payments and other costs. Furthermore, the public sector can slow down a developer, and the public can change the rules in the middle of the game. For these reasons, it pays for private developers to treat the public sector as partners or as equals in the process.

MARKET STUDIES AND FEASIBILITY STUDIES

Textbooks on marketing and market research seldom cover real estate. Likewise, when real estate textbooks discuss market research, typically they do so quite specifically, without drawing connections to the broader principles of marketing. Developers, planners, public officials, lenders, and investors, however, can use fundamental concepts of marketing to make better decisions about real property. This discussion will be useful to business students who are taking real estate courses after having studied marketing. It should also be helpful to students of law, planning, or design who have previously studied real estate and now want to understand the developer's role in conceiving ideas that actually become buildings and then serve the community profitably.

One important trend in development today is that developers increasingly use market studies for decision making at several steps in the development process rather than simply as a sales tool to convince lenders. Large developers are constrained by huge oversupplies of certain types of space in many large markets—for example, Class A office space in Houston and Denver. Small developers usually face oversupplies in their local markets as well. And today all developers are dealing with more skeptical lenders. It no longer works as often for developers to rely on instinct to decide what to build or on optimism to assure prospective lenders that the project *will* capture market share from competitors. A rigorous market study early in the process stimulates development ideas, improves initial concepts, and serves as a device to control initial risk.

Developers can use a market study of a projected design on a specific site to answer several questions: What is the anticipated household growth in the market area? What is the best configuration and size of housing units for the proposed residential subdivision? How many units will the market absorb, at what price, and over what period of time? What percentage of that demand can this project capture and why? How should housing units be marketed to the appropriate consumers? The bottom line of the market study is how much operating income over what period of time the developer can expect a particular project to generate, given market conditions and expected competition.

Equally important, the developer can use a market study to determine what will gain the support of public participants. In a sense, development creates "public goods" by putting long-lived products on the land, and the public must live with the products for many years. The analyst's research into the market area should include both regulatory requirements and the attitudes of neighbors and other "publics." Not only will research guide the project's size and design; it will also indicate ways for the developer to win public approval and/or various entitlements.

Furthermore, market studies are versatile in that they can accomplish other objectives. They can, as noted, be used to help obtain financing. After a project is financed, they can also be used as a marketing guide for the sales or leasing staff. To be salable, a project needs an identity in consumers' minds; the market study should provide the competitive analysis and identify a market niche so that advertising and promotion can be properly targeted.

A feasibility study completes the rest of the equation: the project is feasible if its estimated value exceeds costs, value being a function of projected cash flow and a market-derived capitalization or discount rate (defined in Chapter 3). Cost means total cost to develop the project (including losses during leasing if it is slow).

Local real estate markets are moved by regional, national, and international trends, be they development of interstate highways, changes in the U.S. tax code, the collapse of oil prices, or fluctuations in the value of the dollar on world markets. A thorough market study looks beyond the primary market area at wider trends affecting local supply and demand. Ultimately, the project's revenues will reflect these trends. Furthermore, sharp developers look for fresh design and marketing ideas outside local markets. Thus, developers must understand their local markets as well as relevant global trends (which may be easier said than done).

Information has a cost. The more data an analyst gathers and the more time spent manipulating them, the higher the price tag on the study. The developer has to weigh the cost of each device to control risk in relation to expected returns from the project. In market studies, cost depends on the level of detail, on who performs the analysis, and on how much certainty a developer wants (or is forced by lenders or regulators) to pay for.

The future is not a straight-line extrapolation from the past. Although the market analyst scrupulously examines past performance and is very exacting in determining current market conditions, the future is what matters most to real estate developers. They must look for indications of the kind of space that will satisfy society's needs over the long expected life of the project. The future is not just the one year or five years that it takes to develop a project: it is the entire useful life of the project, which may last 30, 50, 100, or 200 years. No one can fully anticipate the future, yet the developer's challenge is to be at least a few steps ahead.

DESIGN

Good design has never been more important than it is today. Taking a cookie-cutter design off the shelf and setting it on an available site is not the winning strategy in saturated markets or in markets where needs for space are changing. Serious attention to the market—which means to the people who will use the project—can show developers and their architects and planners how to capture market share from competitors or to build for a new niche. Needs for space change over time, and existing oversupplies may *never* be absorbed without expensive modifications.

Design has emerged as a versatile method of establishing contact with and discriminating between specific market segments. Buildings have images that send direct messages, and architects who want to contribute successfully to development teams have had to become proficient in creating the right design message. At the same time, it is important to remember that for some uses and certain tenants, the right image is pure functionality—that is, the most functional bay sizes and core elements covered with a skin whose operating costs are low.

Proficiency in design is hard won, for the right image is frequently elusive. Each player in the development process brings some idea of what the finished development will be. For example, public sector players might bring intimate images of desired interactions with surrounding areas intended to maintain their town's character. Members of the development team might have visions of the project ranging from minimalist to cosmetically dazzling. In the final analysis, the developer/entrepreneur charges the architect (and other design professionals) with solving the design problem and resolving the diversity of pictures into a single, coherent image.

The design of the Europa Center was intended to bring big-city, Class A office space to a small but sophisticated town that had nothing exactly comparable. Not by coincidence was it located next door to the town's first luxury hotel.

EUROPA CENTER

A SUMMARY OF THE PROJECT

Location:
Chapel Hill, North Carolina (population 35,000), home of The University of North Carolina; 12 miles from Durham (population 100,000), home of Duke University; 10 miles from Research Triangle Park; 28 miles from Raleigh, the state capital and home of North Carolina State University; 18 miles from Raleigh-Durham airport, site of an American Airlines hub.

Land:
7.3 acres, zoned for office and industrial use, fronting U.S. 15-501 (four lanes, the main route to Durham, and, two miles farther east, a heavily developed commercial strip), Europa Drive (site of Hotel Europa), and Legion Road.

Land cost:
$2.1 million, $1 million allocated to Phase One, remainder to Phase Two.

Building:
Phase One: Five-story, 95,000-square-foot Class A office, poured-in-place reinforced concrete structure with glass curtain wall. Atrium lobby, marble, granite, and fabric panel finishes. Adjoining three-level parking deck.
Phase Two: Projected to contain roughly 100,000 square feet.

Project cost:
As of January 1987, projected at $9.3 million. Revised June 1987 to $10.5 million (construction very close to budget, about $250,000 in construction changes, the remainder to fund slow leasing).

Initial chronology:
Land purchased: November 1985
Site preparation began: April 1986
Building construction began: Summer 1986
Building certificate of occupancy: November 1987.

Joint venture shares:
50 percent: **Centennial Group** *buys land for $2.1 million.*
35 percent: **Fraser Morrow Daniels** *contributes up to $100,000 worth of research, planning, negotiating, staffing, which is only partially reimbursed by joint venture.*
15 percent: **Centennial Group** *(a joint venture partner during construction) guarantees $1 million if needed to fund protracted leasing; this amount becomes additional equity in 1987 when Centennial is acquired by the construction lender and the entire financing is renegotiated to handle the slow leasing period.*

Configuring the built environment to create specific images has a long and instructive history. Early merchandisers knew that building a massive single structure sent a message of abundance that a profusion of small branches could never achieve. In a similar vein, books of house plans containing Greek revival designs sold particularly well at the beginning of the 19th century. It was not the floor plans or efficient space that were popular but the strong identification with the image of an earlier democracy that attracted homebuilders. Today, most travelers can readily identify the quality and cost of a motor hotel simply by the image that the building projects. Creating a formal image that becomes a vital, interactive component in a project's success is neither accidental nor mysterious. It results from careful consideration of design criteria during *all* eight stages of the real estate development model—not just exterior design but also all the functional aspects of interior design that are so critical to tenants' efficient use of constructed space. (Later chapters show how integrating both exterior and interior design criteria during the eight stages produces an effective structure.)

Finally, the implications of successful design go far beyond creating an effective structure. Architects, like the other players in the development process, have ethical obligations. They understand space and urban design far better than lay people. If architects do not see it as their responsibility to innovate and move the state of the art forward, then society will not live up to its potential, at least not in improving the built environment.

DEVELOPERS AND THEIR PARTNERS

The remainder of this chapter introduces the major participants in the development process, each of which makes different contributions and has different goals or reasons for becoming involved in real estate development.

The Developer

As a project's primary decision maker, developers seek the maximum possible return with a minimum commitment of time and money. This return consists of several components:
- The development fee, the stated direct compensation for developing the project;
- Profits on any sale to long-term investors (i.e., sale price less cost to construct and finance);
- Possibly a long-term equity position (for which the developer may or may not put in cash), in which case their goals are similar to those of passive investors (discussed later);
- Personal and professional satisfaction in advancing a new concept or improving the urban environment;
- Enhanced reputation, which creates future opportunities for development.

Whit Morrow, developer for Fraser Morrow Daniels, speaks throughout this book about the development of Europa Center.

Developers' commitment of time is usually the length of the development period. Although the other equity interests discussed later also wish to minimize the time of their involvement, they are not selling their time, as do developers. Other professionals either get paid by the hour or are involved in only a portion of the development process; they are thus less sensitive to the overall length of the development period.

Private developers may also profit through ownership of entities that sell services to the development: insurance agencies, mortgage banking firms, leasing companies, management companies, or even general contracting firms. To the extent that these arrangements are made at arm's length and represent clearly understood agreements, developers are simply being compensated for performing additional functions. On the other hand, if compensation for outside activities in which developers have an interest are above standard, any excess should be considered an addition to the development fee.

Private developers' financial exposure arises in two different ways. First, developers spend time and money before being assured that the project will be built (i.e., before stage five, formal commitment, in the sequence). Naturally, developers seek to minimize such expenditures. Second, in addition to a developer's own equity position (both contributed capital and debt for which the developer is personally liable), the developer might guarantee a certain project cost or a certain initial occupancy level to the investors or lenders or both. As *primary risk bearers,*[1] developers are exposed over a certain time period (usually stage six of the sequence) in the amount of their direct financial commitment plus the magnitude of any guarantees and the likelihood of their being called on.

Developers' personal qualities are also a vital element in the process. This chapter referred earlier to the drive and creativity that developers seem to have in common. Many have arrived at their life's work from fairly diverse starting points, as the profiles of different developers show. On the other hand, Whit Morrow knew early in life that he wanted to develop real estate. The accompanying segment of the case study describes his decision to pursue a career in real estate development and his surprise at the complexity of the process.

EUROPA CENTER

THE DEVELOPER SPEAKS FOR HIMSELF

I want you to hear about real estate development from someone who is up to his eyeballs in alligators right now in the marketplace. You should know how we started, how we got to where we are now, and how we're going to get out of it and make a profit at some point.

I grew up in Albemarle, North Carolina, a small town with about 10,000 people. My grandfather owned a third of the office buildings in town, which you could probably crowd into one room, so I was vaguely aware of real estate at a young age. When I was older, I had a job making change in the old hardware store building. They had pneumatic tubes that went from the cash registers back to the central office where they kept all the money, and

13

that was where I sat making change. That was the extent of my exposure to business before college, when I was trying to decide what I was going to do. When I headed off to college (Davidson College, 40 miles away, near Charlotte), I didn't even know what an architect was.

At Davidson College, the subject that fascinated me most was the readings we had on utopias—ideal communities. Davidson College had about 1,000 students and sat in the middle of the countryside, the most pristine Walden II *setting you've ever seen. One of the books I read was* Walden II, *of course, about how B.F. Skinner made the ideal community, designing everything the way it ought to be, with all the people fitting into his community. So I decided during my college days that I wanted to go out there like Alexander the Great and build cities. Or be an industrialist and build Hershey, Pennsylvania. I thought that was the greatest thing you could possibly do.*

Coming out of college with my BA degree, I was a little naive, and my advisers said I should go to business school. For me, going to Harvard Business School was like being drafted into the Marines. The first day or two of class when I talked about why I was there and what I wanted to do, they burst my bubble. So you want to go out and build cities, huh? Do you know what a REIT is? Do you know what a second mortgage is? I wasn't exposed to any of those things, even at college. I was totally shocked by all the intricate details that go into building a house or an office building or a street. But I survived Harvard Business School, and after learning the details, I thought I knew a lot more and got a job with the Sea Pines Company.

Public Sector Developers

Private developers must be distinguished from public sector developers. Increasingly, the public sector engages in real estate development in pursuit of goals for community housing and economic development. A new breed of professional is emerging who could be referred to as a "public entrepreneur."

The term "public entrepreneur" is reserved for those public development professionals who plan, design, and structure the financing for large-scale projects of such importance to the community that the government not only shares in their costs but may also assume some of the risk. Unlike private developers, public entrepreneurs are usually salaried employees. Their compensation is generally higher than that of other planning professionals for two reasons. First, they have unusual financial and analytical skills. Second, they are very valuable to their cities, because properly structured transactions help make projects happen at minimum cost to the city while stimulating additional private investment at less public cost.

Museum Tower at the Museum of Modern Art in New York City rests on top of the museum's west wing. Proceeds from the sale of air rights were used to finance renovation and expansion.

14

Significant public/private ventures are being developed throughout the United States and are not limited to large projects like, for example, a private, 56-story luxury condominium tower adjacent to the Museum of Modern Art in New York that makes payments in lieu of taxes to support the museum's operating deficits. Another project in which the public sector has assumed a major portion of the risk is the Old City Market in downtown Raleigh, North Carolina, a $6 million commercial project involving historic rehabilitation that includes a combination of city grants for on- and off-site improvements, a city loan at below-market interest that is subordinated to a first mortgage financed by tax-exempt bonds, syndicated "tax-oriented" equity, contributions from the developer/general partners, and a city-financed operating deficit account to carry early negative cash flows. In exchange for its substantial and multidimensional front-end commitment and role as backstop, the city will take a share of the cash flow after a threshold return on investment is reached.

Architects and Engineers

Architects and engineers are critical to the development process from the perspectives of physical safety, political risk, and market risk. As stated earlier, these professionals translate ideas into specific plans that must meet the requirements of political players as well as the users. In large-scale and some small-scale projects, land planners and landscape architects are part of the design team. In the marketplace, a structure that lacks eye appeal or efficient operations (elevator travel times, the location of bathrooms, and so on) will be difficult to lease, possibly even leading to the developer's bankruptcy. Both the financial and human loss can be even greater, however, if architects and engineers, or contractors, fail in their primary duty to deliver a safe product. They are collectively responsible for ensuring users' health, safety, and welfare.

The naive view of an architect is of someone who simply draws the developer's idea and produces a set of specifications to be used for obtaining construction bids and guiding the builders. In fact,

architects offer a menu of services to developers and, like other players, may work as external professionals or as in-house, salaried members of the team.

Besides preparing drawings and specifications for a project, architects can support developers in a variety of ways: 1) by developing alternative concepts for a site and heading the land use team; 2) by helping pick a site for a specified use; 3) by negotiating with the public sector (because architects are licensed under the state's health and safety laws, they theoretically have an ethical obligation to the state and often do in reality enjoy a better working relationship with local planners than the developer); 4) by balancing size and cost of a projected structure; 5) by employing the structural engineer, who in turn employs the geotechnical (formerly soils) engineer; 6) by supervising construction; and 7) by verifying to the lender that the work is being done as specified. How and when the developer uses an architect depends on the complexity of the project and on the developer's own expertise. In complex projects, architects and engineers are generally brought in early to test a project's feasibility and to help shape the developer's idea.

Do developers always need an architect and an engineer? States vary in legal requirements for the use of architects, and architects' and engineers' infringement on each other's turf is common. As a practical matter, a developer who builds several hundred thousand square feet of strip shopping centers may forgo an architect and put an engineer on salary to adapt a standard plan to different sites. While it should save money on design, it is not always wise. What works in Peoria may not work exactly the same in Omaha. And as the public becomes more sensitive to design, developers must respond appropriately. Developers should never underestimate the value of good design. It can improve the public's perception of a project and increase its desire to lease space or purchase units where comparable but less-well-designed projects fail.

Engineers usually work with an architect to ensure that plans are structurally sound and that mechanical systems will serve the project adequately. Engineers are

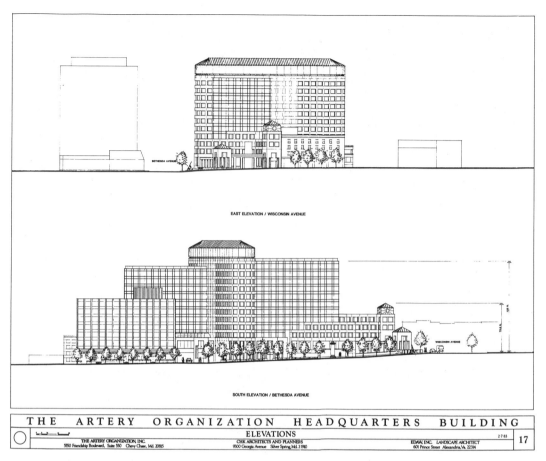

THE ARTERY ORGANIZATION HEADQUARTERS BUILDING

ELEVATIONS

EAST ELEVATION / WISCONSIN AVENUE

SOUTH ELEVATION / BETHESDA AVENUE

THE ARTERY ORGANIZATION, INC.
5550 Friendship Boulevard, Suite 550   Chevy Chase, Md. 20815

CHK ARCHITECTS AND PLANNERS
9500 Georgia Avenue   Silver Spring, Md. 2 5910

EDAW, INC.   LANDSCAPE ARCHITECT
601 Prince Street   Alexandria, Va. 22314

2-7-83   17

A typical architectural rendering of elevations for a proposed building, in this case, for The Artery Organization's headquarters building in Bethesda, Maryland.

responsible for determining the soil's bearing capacity, the required depth of footings, stress, and related items. Working with mechanical subcontractors, engineers also specify necessary air-conditioning systems and other mechanical capacities.

In more complex developments, engineers might also be used as construction managers, supplementing the architect in supervising construction. Construction managers, unlike architects, are on the construction site continually and serve as the developer's representative to the general contractor. "Construction manager" is not a controlled title like architect or engineer. Whereas architects and engineers are licensed by the state, a developer can designate anyone as construction manager.

Both architects and engineers bear the legal liability for their plans and specifications for years (the term varies with the state) in contrast to contractors, whose standard liability is one year. The duration of liability fits with the seriousness of the undertaking and the timing of recognizing defects: shoddy construction and shoddy design both can cost dollars and lives. Shoddy construction is usually visible sooner, however. Not surprisingly, architects and engineers are licensed under health and safety laws, contractors under the commercial code.

Architects and engineers take a particular job with a developer for a range of motives, including, but not limited to, money. Hiring and being hired is a two-way street; architects and engineers want to work for ethical clients whose notions of good development are compatible with their own. The concept of "fit," used to describe corporate culture in relation to individual workers, also applies to the real estate development team. In real estate development, the origin of a team's "culture" is extremely simple to trace: it derives from the developer, whose ethical standards, preferences regarding risk, profit motive, personality, and affinity for design determine the type of people he chooses and who choose him.

Land Use Professionals

In addition to architects and engineers, land planners, geotechnical engineers, landscape architects, and many other design professionals may be involved in any particular project. On larger land developments, the land planner is a critical team member charged not only with locating the various uses on the site and specifying traffic patterns between them but also with making the best use of the land, given the market value of the different potential sites. As the accompanying profile of David Jensen suggests, land plan-

ners can significantly affect the profits of complex developments.

Geotechnical engineers perform initial tests of the soil's bearing capacity, evaluate drainage, and may engage in elaborate planning to fit the desired project on a complex site. Landscape architects from the beginning can help the design team work out the ideal finished product. At the end of the project, they may be called on to offset errors others have made and help the project achieve its desired impression. They must carefully complement and enhance the building or the project with landscaping. More than one project has benefited from a landscape architect who brings all the elements together or provides a striking landscape design that piques the public's interest.

Increasingly important on the developer's design team are environmental engineers. Environmental engineering at one time was fairly simple, usually dealing with water and soil runoff onto surrounding properties. In the 1980s, however, the discovery that asbestos in existing buildings was a hazardous substance led to

---

PROFILE: **DAVID R. JENSEN**
President, David Jensen Associates, Inc.
Denver, Colorado

Background: David Jensen is a land planner, one of the professionals hired by developers to contribute expertise in the early stages of the development process. He has a broad range of expertise in urban planning and design, planning mixed-use developments, and commercial, industrial, and residential planning, having worked on numerous projects throughout the United States. Starting with a background in economics, Jensen then earned a master's degree in landscape architecture from the University of Illinois.

Back to the basics: In addition to his role as a land planner, Jensen conducts numerous seminars on the development process, where he reminds developers that a developer's role is to create communities where buyers and tenants achieve their objectives. Developers do not just put up structures; they also fill people's need for good investments (whether a house or an industrial building). Jensen notes also that developers create the potential for profit at three different stages in the process before the sale of the finished product: 1) when land is purchased (by influencing the amount and terms of the sale); 2) during master planning and design (by ensuring the site is used to its full potential); and 3) during the acquisition of government approvals. Jensen believes that tomorrow's entrepreneurs will be the people who can implement the public/private process in innovative ways.

costly renovations in some cases, creating a new, growing industry of environmental professionals who test sites to detect asbestos and determine when and how to remove it. Today it appears that the industry, primarily rehabilitation development, is moving toward a reconciliation of what is legally required and what is scientifically possible regarding asbestos. At the same time that this environmental issue appears to be coming under control, however, a new set of environmental problems related to toxic waste and a much wider range of concerns have arisen, requiring environmental impact analysis.

Throughout, the text talks about the emerging area of law, ethics, and development that is troubling the entire population. From the perspective of development, the Superfund legislation in 1980 and its reauthorization in 1986[2] have created very significant additional legal and financial considerations for developers. Under Superfund, liability is strict, joint, and almost unlimited in scope. Cleaning up waste is an issue society will have to deal with, one that has a dramatic impact on the potential for development of many sites. As shown in detail later in the text, it is not enough to know the environmental conditions of a particular site; developers must also know of any problems with toxic waste surrounding the site.

Contractors

Contractors are builders and managers of builders who turn ideas on paper into enduring physical forms: houses, apartments, warehouses, stores, offices, public buildings. In our highly specialized society, constructed space and its providers are often taken for granted, yet without builders, each of us would face a simple choice: build our shelter ourselves or do without.

General contractors typically execute a contract with the developer to build the project according to the plans and specifications of the architect and engineer (or, on a very small scale, with the user or homeowner who orders a house built). They then divide the contract among different *subcontractors* to perform different tasks: excavation, pouring and finishing

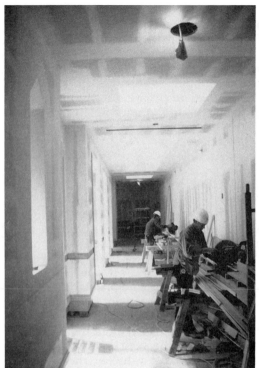

Photo courtesy of David M. Schwarz Architectural Services

Subcontractors at work on the Cook–Fort Worth Children's Medical Center.

concrete, rough carpentry, installing mechanical, electrical, and plumbing systems, finish carpentry, and so on. General contractors schedule subcontractors' work and monitor its quality to ensure that their performance will satisfy the general contractor's obligations to the developer. While the general contractor's contract is with the developer, subcontractors' contracts are with the general contractor, who pays them when the work is completed.[3]

Besides the obvious motivation of money, both general contractors and subcontractors work for a variety of nonpecuniary reasons: to add to experience, to enhance their reputations, to be their own boss, and to do physical work they enjoy. The contractor submitting the lowest bid is not always the best choice; the best player for the team may have other more critical attributes, such as the necessary experience or complete reliability. In some cases, developers with expertise in building serve as their own general contractors and make contracts directly with subcontractors.

Joint Venture Partners

Any individual or institution providing the developer with equity funding during the development period in return for a share of development profits can be called a *joint venture partner*. (The term "joint venture" is not a precise legal term.) The joint venture partner's contribution of equity often bridges a portion of the gap between the project's cost and available debt financing for construction. (The remainder of the gap, if any, must be filled by the developer's equity.)

Joint venture partners attempt to achieve the maximum possible share of returns from development based on the minimum possible financial commitment. Partners' return is based primarily on the difference between the project's value and the project's cost and therefore indirectly on the amount and terms of any additional debt financing. The risk to joint venture partners is a function of the size of their contribution, assuming no personal liability, or the size of their contribution plus the amount of debt, in the case of personal liability. In either case, partners are interested in their obligations (especially if the project nosedives) and in the developer's talent and financial strength, because all these factors relate to the project's solvency.

Construction Lenders

Construction lenders (frequently commercial banks) are responsible for financing during a project's construction and for seeing that the developer completes the project on time and within budget according to the plans and specifications. Their primary concern is not the project's long-term economic viability so long as a permanent loan commitment (the takeout commitment) has been obtained. With such a commitment in hand, construction lenders are assured of being repaid when the project is completed, so long as the work has been done according to plan. Construction lenders generally certify the degree of completion before each payment, or *draw*, under the construction loan.

Construction lenders face the risk that construction costs will exceed the amount of the permanent loan, forcing recourse to equity interests or the developer to cover the difference. If the developer is unable or unwilling to do so, construction lenders usually have the option of foreclosing the property or taking a long-term loan position as a remedy. Construction lenders weigh the cost of these undesirable outcomes against the expected return in interest (including loan origination fees) to be earned by lending the funds.

Permanent Lenders

Permanent lenders, like construction lenders, seek a secure loan while achieving the maximum possible return. Because permanent lenders, unlike construction lenders, have no takeout commitment, the market value of the completed project is critical, as it serves as collateral for the loan. The project's value will be a function of the expected cash flow, market capitalization rates (i.e., the relationship of value to operating cash flows), and the project's expected economic life (i.e., how long the operating cash flows will continue before major renovation is needed).

In addition to charging interest on the permanent loan, long-term lenders frequently receive a form of "contingent" interest. Sometimes referred to as "income" or "equity" kickers, contingent interest allows the lender to participate in the project's overall success. *Income kickers*, for example, may stipulate that the lender will receive a portion of gross income over some minimum, perhaps 15 percent of gross rent over the first year's estimated gross rental receipts. In the case of *equity kickers*, the lender participates in a portion of the capital gain received when the project is sold.

Like other players on the development team, lenders may also have nonpecuniary motives for participating. Some lenders have an interest in serving particular social needs (for example, the development of low-income housing), while others are particularly attracted to innovative design and construction. Almost everyone enjoys being associated with a high-class winner, and lenders are no exception. Successful developers bring to their team a lender whose nonpecuniary interests as well as its preferences for risk and return fit the proposed development.

Long-Term Equity Investors

Long-term equity investors may or may not be involved during construction. They might contract to purchase the completed property before construction (basing the price on preconstruction estimates of value) or wait until the project is completed. In the first case, the contract usually is signed before the point of commitment—the time immediately preceding the beginning of construction. Whatever the time of sale, the price is often not payable until completion, and so the funds are not available to the developer. A purchase commitment before construction may substitute for or supplement the permanent loan commitment as a takeout for the construction lender, however.

Long-term equity investors are often *passive investors* during the development period and do not share development risks. On completion of the project, investors want the maximum possible operating returns (sometimes guaranteed by the developer for an initial period of one or more years) for the least possible price. These returns normally are lower than those accruing to investors during the development period, because the latter assume more risk; that is, they bear the uncertainties of construction (and possibly of leasing).

In the past, tax deductions allowed during the construction period (primarily for interest and real estate taxes) encouraged early participation by long-term equity investors. The Tax Reform Act of 1976 substantially reduced the tax incentive for early investment, however, by requiring most of those costs to be capitalized and written off over 10 years. The Tax Reform Act of 1986 delivered the latest in a long series of blows to tax shelters by requiring the amortization of all construction costs (including construction interest and property taxes) over far longer periods (27½ to 31½ years). Further, the 1986 tax law created three classes of income and prohibited the use of real estate losses (termed "passive income") to affect earned income (salary). Although early commitments for equity have become more difficult to obtain,

developers' incentive for preselling long-term equity interests remains. The sale enables developers to avoid or to minimize the market risks associated with changing estimates of value over the development period. Preselling equity might also make it easier for developers to procure permanent financing.

Final Users

A description of participants in the development process would be incomplete without a mention of the final users of the space. Final users are the direct consumers of the finished product. Developers anticipate their needs in articulating the original idea for the project. The market study further specifies the idea and guides developers in reaching their intended market(s). Architects and engineers produce plans consistent with final users' needs, and contractors build the space. The final users determine the success of the project by accepting or rejecting the finished product as it is presented in the marketplace.

Users often contract for space before construction is completed. Working through the developer's marketing representative, final users may interact with the developer's financial and construction representatives during actual construction of a project. In this way, they can make sure that their needs will be met by the finished product. In so doing, they become active participants in the development process.

Brokers/Leasing Agents and Property Managers

Beyond the market analysts who do the initial market and feasibility studies (often outside consultants who work with the developer's staff), marketing people present the product to final users. Leasing usually begins well before construction is complete, so these people are part of the process before stage eight. Their function, particularly in leasing large industrial and commercial spaces, is one of the most complex financial operations in the development process. Leasing agents should balance all of the different users' needs with the developer's needs and with public policy and regulations. Clearly, leasing involves more than quoting the number of square feet at a price per square foot. Leasing requires setting the long-term price per square foot, including specifying who bears the different operating costs, and it requires identifying any of the user's special needs, such as extra electrical or heating, ventilation, and air-conditioning capacity.

Once construction of a project is completed, the project enters the final stage of the development process—management of the asset over time (see Chapter 18). During this stage, appropriate services must be provided to make the space efficient for the user (janitorial services and monitoring mechanical systems, for example). Ongoing management also includes re-leasing and thus remarketing the space. Remarketing can be quite complex if the space must be reconfigured to suit the evolving needs of current users or new users. Ongoing management must also position the project properly, given long-term investors' need for a return on their investment (see Chapter 18).

Regulators: Public Sector Partners

Theoretically, public regulation of the development process should produce a more fair, efficient, flexible, and certain system of allocating land use and higher-quality developments than that produced under a purely private system.[4] Locally, developers must comply with zoning requirements and subdivision regulations and must often obtain approvals for site plans and special use permits—all before development can begin. Once the project is under way, another host of regulations and regulators come into play to ensure safe construction, in the name of the public welfare. On the regional, state, and national levels, additional regulators abound. Their functions range from environmental and consumer protection to oversight of financial intermediaries, mortgage instruments, and lending practices.

In reality, the various rules and regulations often conflict. Rather than producing more harmonious, well-designed projects that the community and the developer can be proud of, such policies sometimes elicit uninspired projects that manage to meet all codes and other regulations but nothing more.

If society's needs are to be met through the private sector's development process, rule makers and regulators must learn how to protect the public's interest without erecting roadblocks to well-designed, creative projects that respond to the market's needs. The development process has become so complex that the only way to enhance the quality of the finished product is for the developer to view and treat the public sector as an active participant of the development team.

Lawyers and Accountants

Because of legally complex interactions between buyers and sellers, lenders and borrowers, contractors and subcontractors, brokers and users (and even among partners), lawyers and accountants are important in the development process. Attorneys also sometimes serve as the developer's chief liaison with regulators. (Developers who stay involved themselves, however, tend to have more credibility, particularly with neighborhood groups.)

The great development lawyer is not the great litigator. With the intense time pressures of the development process, the great attorney is the one who anticipates problems and then structures legal documentation to minimize the necessity of resolving differences in court. As just one aspect of a complex transaction, for example, the loan agreement for a major real estate project is usually several hundred pages long. The agreement cannot be pulled straight out of a lawyer's form book; rather, it must be carefully designed for the particular deal. It is often good practice for developers to put legal and accounting experts on the team early in the process.

Corporate Real Estate Officers

In the last several years, corporate real estate officers have risen considerably in the hierarchy as corporations have realized the magnitude of their real estate investment (nearly $2 trillion total, according to Salomon Brothers). With new ways to own, control, and finance real estate evolving constantly, corporate real estate officers

21

have been challenged to balance the traditional needs of the right space and future flexibility with the overall corporate financial structure. While not a member of most development teams, corporate real estate officers often represent the major space user and thus are a key contact for the development team.

SUMMARY

This chapter has briefly described the development process and the players, highlighting the importance of appropriate design, of a good market study and feasibility analysis, and of explicit recognition of the real partnership between public and private interests. The details of these concepts are more fully developed in Chapters 7 through 20 in the sequence shown in the eight-stage model of the real estate development process. First, however, Chapter 2 sets the scope of development in the U.S. economy, Chapter 3 reviews key financial concepts, and Chapters 4, 5, and 6 present the history underlying the framework laid out in this section of the book. While development looks forward, a brief review of where we have been is helpful in anticipating where we are going. With history informing the broad framework, the reader will be ready to explore the stages of the development process in an organized and coherent manner.

The case study of the Europa Center continues. As you follow its progress, note the ways that this project fits, as well as departs from, the description of the development process. And note the complexity of a developer's work even in a relatively small, straightforward project such as the Europa Center. Specifically, as you read about the Europa Center, note several factors: 1) how important it is to understand your own goals and abilities and to realistically assess those of your competitors; 2) the costly time and effort meaningful research requires; 3) how ideas can change dramatically before anything gets built; 4) the way the rules made by the public sector can change in the middle of the game; 5) the necessity to plan for contingencies and to expect the unexpected; 6) correctly structured financing as the key to survival; and 7) how developers decide where they will take risk and/or how much extra they will pay to avoid it.

NOTES

1. It is certainly possible for investing lenders and/or city officials to err in underwriting and end up the primary risk bearers, but that is not usually their intent in traditional situations. In more complex developments, risks may be shared in many creative ways, as shown in later chapters.

2. The 1980 legislation creating the Superfund is known as the Comprehensive Environmental Response, Cleanup, and Liability Act (CERCLA), the 1986 legislation as Superfund Amendments and Reauthorization Act (SARA). See Chapter 16 for more detail.

3. As will be shown in a later chapter, this organizational arrangement is most common; many different combinations and permutations are possible.

4. For a critique of the regulatory system, see, for example, Douglas W. Kmiec, *Zoning and Planning Deskbook* (New York: Clark Boardman Company, 1986), Chap. 1.

Chapter 2

Land and Demographics in The United States Today

Since World War II, the United States has enjoyed unparalleled prosperity. And except in rural areas, the familiar surroundings are mostly highly developed real estate—shopping malls, interstate highways, government complexes, condominiums, office buildings—and, of course, land and buildings being bulldozed for more construction. Expansion and development have always accompanied the American dream of having more than a subsistence living, of having plenty.

Most of us take for granted not only our developed surroundings but also the governmental agencies that undergird, promote, and constrain development. This chapter suggests that citizens not take so much for granted, that we begin to search for future opportunities by taking a fresh look at changing demographic and economic indicators. Understanding the recent past and present can help people better imagine future changes. Furthermore, the understanding of national and regional forces should help guide development of a particular site in the market.

This chapter sketches an overview of U.S. real estate in two parts:
- Where we are—a demographic and economic picture of real estate development in the United States today; and

- How we got here—a brief discussion of visible structures in our built environment (cities, buildings, transportation networks) and the less visible structures of our institutional environment.

This background and the rest of the first six chapters provide the foundation on which to build a greater understanding of the real estate development process in subsequent sections of the book.

LAND, WEALTH, AND POPULATION IN THE UNITED STATES

Is Land Scarce?

The United States contains 3,618,770 square miles (2.3 billion acres) of land supporting a population of about 250 million people. Canada and China are both slightly larger than the United States; the Soviet Union, with 8,649,496 square miles (although much of it frozen), is almost two and one-half times as large. Brazil is slightly smaller.

In contrast to countries where overall land use is intensive, such as the Netherlands, the United States has extensive and relatively unused deserts, mountains, dry plains, tundra, and swamps—roughly 336 million acres, or 15 percent of the land area.

23

In fact, more than 70 percent of U.S. citizens live on 1.5 percent (35 million acres) of the land. Adding highways, airports, railroads, and state institutions, highly developed land takes about 3 percent, or 63 million acres, of the total land area. The present land-to-people ratio in the United States is a little over nine acres per person.[1]

In addition to vast rural lands, huge land reserves are available even in metropolitan areas of the United States. These reserves have resulted from leapfrog suburban development[2] (although now much less common than from 1950 to 1970), from abandoned or dying central city neighborhoods, and from lower density in new urban areas.[3] The high cost of infrastructure and decreasing federal funds to cities for extending services have constrained leapfrog development, however. As a result, demand for developable land—that is, land with the necessary infrastructure in place and properly zoned—has driven up land costs sharply in some areas, producing somewhat higher-density commercial and residential land use.[4]

Who Owns the Land and How Is It Used?

The federal government is the largest single landowner in the United States, with 762 million acres (about one-third of the total 2.3 billion acres); in fact, Uncle Sam owns more than 50 percent of five states: 98.6 percent of Alaska (over 360 million of 365 million acres);[5] 85.7 percent of Nevada (over 60 million of 70 million acres); 66.0 percent of Utah (35 million of 53 million acres); 64.1 percent of Idaho (34 million of 53 million acres); and 51.6 percent of Oregon (32 million of 62 million acres).[6] State and local governments collectively own another 6 percent of the nation, leaving private landowners and Native Americans on trust lands to share the remaining 60 percent of the pie (Figure 2-1).

Although forest products industries and railroad companies in particular own extremely large institutional land holdings in the United States, real estate is still widely owned by individual citizens, a legacy of the 17th through early 20th centuries. The first immigrants arrived in the New World hungry to own land as individuals. Later waves of migrants pushed West, still in quest of land, buying it cheaply or staking claims under liberal government programs. For social and political reasons (and not merely because of the huge land mass), people of little wealth but healthy ambition could acquire land here cheaply and easily. Government at all levels has actively promoted private ownership throughout U.S. history.[7]

FIGURE 2-1
LAND OWNERSHIP IN THE UNITED STATES

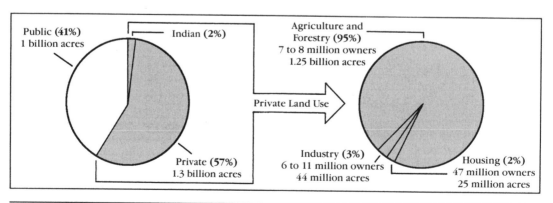

Source: Charles H. Wurtzebach and Mike E. Miles, *Modern Real Estate*, 4th ed. (New York: John Wiley & Sons, 1991), p. 6.

24

Among the more obvious ways that government promotes private ownership of real estate in this century are the Federal Housing Administration's mortgage insurance program and the Veterans Administration's mortgage guarantee program (which revolutionized home mortgage lending in the 1940s and 1950s), the federally facilitated secondary mortgage market for home loans, tax legislation benefiting not only homeowners but also private investors in commercial and industrial real estate, and, most important, the provision of the infrastructure—roads, utilities, and so on—needed to make private ownership viable.

Many more governmental agencies are of course now in place than 200 years ago, engaging in much more regulating and restraining than formerly. Collectively, these agencies make a convenient whipping boy, offering politicians a platform (or at least a plank) to "get government off the people's back." But what should not be forgotten is that the federal government acts as the single most powerful promoter of widespread, private ownership of real estate in the United States.

Today, 64 percent of all U.S. householders own their home. Furthermore, the ease of acquisition that U.S. citizens take for granted strongly attracts foreign investors to U.S. real estate. In many other developed nations, real estate markets are *much* smaller, and laws dramatically restrict foreign investment in real estate.

Real Estate, the GNP, Wealth, And Employment

It should come as no surprise that real estate development, construction, and investment are highly promoted and regulated by government at all levels, considering their central importance in the U.S. economy. The gross national product (GNP) now runs around $5 trillion a year—roughly $20,000 per person.[8] Of this total, individuals consume about 64 percent, the government purchases another 21 percent, and the private sector invests 15 to 16 percent. This investment determines the nation's future productive capacity, which must grow if society's wealth is to increase.

Private investment must be sufficient to replace depreciated assets and must provide for new and more productive investments.

Over half of annual domestic private investment is in real property assets, and about half of that amount (one-quarter of the total) is usually in housing. As just one example, in 1988, owners of existing residential property (all types) in the United States spent $101.1 billion for improvements, repairs, additions, and alterations, including $12.5 billion on painting alone. Owner-occupants of single-family housing accounted for $60.8 billion of the total invested in improvements.[9] (These figures do not include governmental investment in real property.) Clearly, private investment in the GNP is substantial, and real estate is the largest component of gross private domestic investment.

A second way to get a feel for the relative importance of the real estate industry is to look at national income, which is essentially GNP minus depreciation and indirect business taxes. The different components of national income are as follows:

- Compensation of employees, which represents about 76 percent of the total and has been increasing over the past two decades.
- Corporate profit, which today represents about 6 to 8 percent of the total GNP and has been decreasing over the past two decades.
- Proprietor's income, which represents about 5 to 6 percent of the total and also has been decreasing.
- Rent, which is about 1 to 2 percent and decreasing.
- Interest, which is about 8 to 11 percent and increasing.

The relationship between rent and interest is instructive. Two decades ago, rent was nearly three times interest, while today, interest is four times rent. One reason is that interest rates have risen more rapidly than rents; another is that over the past quarter century borrowed capital has increased as a percentage of the total financing for real estate investment. For both reasons, more of the total cash flow is going to lenders. As a result, lenders have gradually obtained a more active voice in making decisions affecting the real estate industry. (Total mortgage debt, residential and

FIGURE 2-2
TOTAL WORLD WEALTH[a]
(1980 = $27,680.5 Billion)

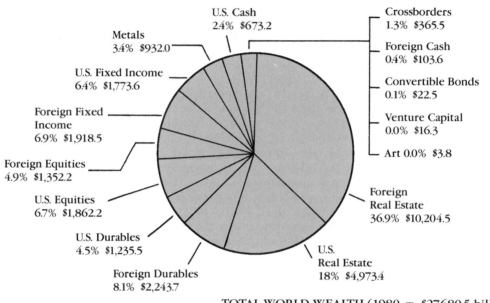

U.S. Cash
2.4% $673.2

Crossborders
1.3% $365.5

Foreign Cash
0.4% $103.6

Convertible Bonds
0.1% $22.5

Venture Capital
0.0% $16.3

Art 0.0% $3.8

Metals
3.4% $932.0

U.S. Fixed Income
6.4% $1,773.6

Foreign Fixed
Income
6.9% $1,918.5

Foreign Equities
4.9% $1,352.2

U.S. Equities
6.7% $1,862.2

U.S. Durables
4.5% $1,235.5

Foreign Durables
8.1% $2,243.7

U.S.
Real Estate
18% $4,973.4

Foreign
Real Estate
36.9% $10,204.5

TOTAL WORLD WEALTH (1980 = $27,680.5 billion)

[a]Individual figures in millions of dollars.
Source: Charles H. Wurtzebach and Mike E. Miles, *Modern Real Estate*, 4th ed. (New York: John Wiley & Sons, 1991), p. 17.

commercial, is approaching $3 trillion, and new mortgage debt represents about 30 percent of the total funds raised in the United States each year.)[10]

For individuals, real estate is an extremely important component of wealth. Besides providing shelter and psychic benefits like pride and security, a house, if owned, probably constitutes the biggest portion of an individual's net worth. In fact, according to the 1980 Census, home equity represented 41 percent of the net worth of the median U.S. family.[11]

Finally, the significance of real estate in terms of total world wealth can be seen in Figure 2-2. Roger Ibbotson, Lawrence Siegel, and Kathryn Love calculated real estate in the United States to constitute 18 percent of total world wealth ($4.97 trillion out of $21.49 trillion in 1980). All other real estate constitutes 37 percent of the world's total wealth. The dollar value is difficult to imagine, but the implications are clear: any-

thing of such great value and productivity must be of vital concern to individuals and to governments.

The importance of the real estate industry in the United States can also be seen in national employment figures. Approximately 125 million civilian workers are employed in the U.S. labor force. Of the total, 1.2 million are classified as in the real estate business and another 5 million in construction, which is certainly part of the real estate development industry.[12] Thus, about 5 percent of the nation's employment is in real estate development and sales, suggesting another reason why the federal government encourages new construction of real estate projects.

An interesting sidelight to total employment figures deals with the number of people actively marketing real estate. In 1969, fewer than 100,000 people were entitled to be designated "REALTOR®" (a designation limited to members who have sat-

26

isfied specified requirements of the National Association of Realtors, the leading real estate trade association in the United States), but 20 years later, the number had risen to nearly 800,000.[13] The tremendous rise in the number of people in the service functions associated with real property illustrates the extraordinary growth of real estate transactions in the 1970s and early 1980s.

It would be a mistake to note the size of employment in the real estate industry without also recognizing its cyclic nature. Employment in the industry shrinks and swells in concert with construction starts, which in turn tend to move broadly up and down with interest rates. The employment figures for construction in Figure 2-3 show how workers may enter and leave this industry, depending on opportunity. In 1983, slightly fewer people were employed than in 1973. And the growth of 700,000 jobs in just three years from 1975 to 1978 preceded a decline of 400,000 jobs in two years (1980 to 1982). Construction, particularly by location, is a volatile, boom-or-bust segment of the real estate industry. In good times, skilled tradespeople are in short supply and a laborer can call himself a carpenter after three months and a finish carpenter after six. In bad times, when the less skilled are laid off, they often take up other work, while the more skilled—or committed—workers try to hang on.

Population Growth in the United States

Population growth alone does not ensure a strong, steadily growing economy; witness sub-Saharan Africa, where some countries are increasing in population by 3 percent per year while their economies stagnate or deteriorate. But population growth and growth of the work force are two powerful engines in expanding economies. (The U.S. population expanded at 3 percent per year for seven decades—1790 to 1860—and thereafter at over 2 percent for 50 years. At the same time, agricultural and industrial output kept pace.) Jobs are critical. Real estate development increases when people with *purchasing power* increase in number. Development may also occur without much or any net increase in

FIGURE 2-3
CONSTRUCTION WORKERS EMPLOYED: 1970 TO 1990

Year	Millions of Workers	Percentage Change from Previous Year
1970	3.588	–
1971	3.704	3%
1972	3.889	5
1973	4.097	5
1974	4.020	–2
1975	3.525	–12
1976	3.576	1
1977	3.851	8
1978	4.229	10
1979	4.463	6
1980	4.346	–3
1981	4.188	–4
1982	3.905	–7
1983	3.948	1
1984	4.383	11
1985	4.673	7
1986	4.816	3
1987	4.967	3
1988	5.125	3
1989	5.300	3
1990	5.234[a]	–1

[a]Preliminary.
Source: U.S. Department of Commerce, Bureau of the Census, *Employment and Earnings*, vol. 36, no. 6, June 1989, Table B-1, p. 61.

population when land uses are reallocated, as in Manhattan and San Francisco; however, in general, development opportunities expand with growth in population.

How do national and regional populations grow? As Figure 2-4 shows, they grow in just two ways: more people are born than die and more people immigrate than leave. In the very early days of our country, immigration was the larger source of population growth, later overtaken by natural increase. Today in some areas, immigration (legal and illegal) again surpasses natural increase. Immigration is a very important local factor in the economies of California, Florida, and Texas. As detailed in Sections II and III, real estate players must understand the national and regional impact of immigration. Locally, immigration represents opportunities for players who see new needs and ways to fill them, such as the Hispanic supermarket chain in Los Angeles that offers not only special foods and assistance by Spanish-speaking clerks but also check cashing and other needed services completely unrelated to food.

In the United States today, net population growth (natural increase plus immigration minus deaths) is very slow: less than 1 percent per year. (At that rate, compounded annually, it would take our population 98 years to double in size, according to the Population Reference Bureau.) In the language of product life cycles, the population could be characterized as being in its mature phase. Figure 2-5 shows how the United States grew more than 55 times, from 3.9 million people at the first census in 1790 to 226.5 million in the 1980 Census, and the growth rate for the decade.

Regionally, population growth of the 1980s saw sharp differences from the national average. For example, Figure 2-6 captures dramatically generalizations about the Sunbelt's growing at the expense of the Frostbelt. With the exception of New Hampshire, unusual growth occurred *only* in the South and West (Florida, Arizona, Nevada, and Alaska) between 1980 and 1989. Nevada took top honors with 38.8 percent growth over that period.

Population grows fastest where jobs grow (and stagnates or declines in ailing economies). Toward the end of the 1980s, signs of economic change appeared that will be reflected in the 1990 Census. New England's economic boom of the 1980s turned into a recession entering the 1990s. States heavily dependent on income from petroleum were depressed, notably Texas, Oklahoma, Colorado, and Louisiana. Texas, however, aggressively courted corporations and industries and began to show

FIGURE 2-4
COMPONENTS OF POPULATION CHANGE: 1960 TO 1987

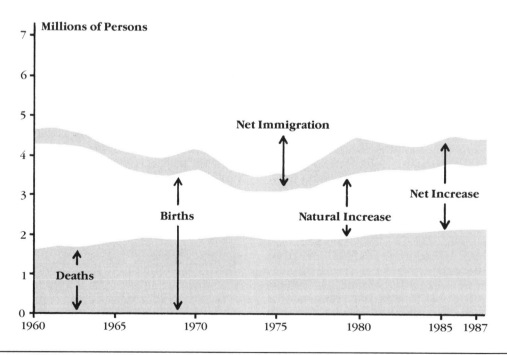

Source: U.S. Department of Commerce, Bureau of the Census, *Statistical Abstract of the United States, 1989,* Figure 1-1, p. 6.

FIGURE 2-5
POPULATION GROWTH IN THE UNITED STATES: 1790 TO 1990

Census	Number of People	Percent Increase over Previous Decade
1790	3,929,214	–
1800	5,308,483	35.1%
1810	7,239,881	36.4
1820	9,638,453	33.1
1830	12,866,020	33.5
1840	17,069,453	32.7
1850	23,191,876	35.9
1860	31,443,321	35.6
1870	39,818,449	26.6
1880	50,155,783	26.0
1890	62,947,714	25.5
1900	75,994,575	20.7
1910	91,972,266	21.0
1920	105,710,620	14.9
1930	122,775,046	16.1
1940	131,669,275	7.2
1950	151,325,798	14.9
1960	179,323,175	18.5
1970	203,302,031	13.4
1980	226,545,805	11.4
1990[a]	250,000,000	10.3

[a]Authors' estimate.

Source: U.S. Department of Commerce, Bureau of the Census, *Statistical Abstract of the United States, 1989*, Table 1, p. 7.

some signs of recovery going into the 1990s. One easy lesson for real estate players is that the speed of economic change can significantly affect development prospects in relatively undiversified economies. In the accompanying profile, developer E. Eddie Henson discusses the role of timing in developing mixed-use projects in Denver's depressed, overbuilt market.

Even population figures for metropolitan statistical areas (MSAs) underscore the Frostbelt/Sunbelt dichotomy of the 1970s and early 1980s.

Heilbrun notes that "all of the large MSAs in which population declined in the 1970s were located in the Northeast and Midwest. . . . The six largest all lost numbers (New York, Chicago, Philadelphia, Detroit, Boston, Washington, D.C.). In every case there was a sharp drop in central city population. . . . On the other hand, in the South and West, the six largest MSAs continued to grow during the 1970s, though usually at a slower pace than before."[14]

The numbers in Figure 2-7, taken from 1985 census data, not only show regional disparities but also reveal tremendous population shifts within metropolitan areas, that is, shifts between central cities and outlying areas, or suburban flight. For example, Atlanta's central city population declined 14.1 percent from 1970 to 1980, while population in the outlying area grew 45.8 percent. Raw population data can be a source of ideas about opportunities for real estate development for the private sector and about the expected future tax base and requirements for services for planners. The figures represent change, and almost all changes result in new possibilities in the marketplace.

Heilbrun also notes another recent trend in U.S. population: smaller metropolitan areas grew fastest in the 1970s and continued to do well in the first half of the 1980s (see Figure 2-8). One result has been that as big-city markets have become saturated, large office and industrial developers like Trammell Crow Company and Lincoln Properties have moved into smaller but possibly more dynamic "second-tier" metropolitan markets. Entering the 1990s, large developers have helped overbuild several second-tier markets and retrenching is in process, indicating again the dynamic nature of real estate development.

This chapter earlier emphasized economic opportunity in the form of landownership as the attraction drawing early immigrants to the colonies and later migrants west across the country. Early in this century, migrants from rural to metropolitan areas sought jobs offering a higher income (not land directly) and found them in the city; for example, southern African-Americans moved north to Chicago, Philadelphia, New York, and Washington, D.C. Post-1970s migration patterns are harder for economists to explain in classic monetary terms, because the South has become a very popular migration spot, even though

FIGURE 2-6
PERCENT CHANGE IN STATE POPULATIONS: 1980 TO 1989
(Total U.S. Change = 9.6 Percent)

Under 5% (n=20)	5–10% (n=11)	10–15% (n=7)	15–20% (n=6)	Over 20% (n=6)
Connecticut	Alabama	Colorado	Georgia	Alaska
Illinois	Arkansas	Delaware	Hawaii	Arizona
Indiana	Idaho	Maryland	New Mexico	California
Iowa (-2.5)	Kansas	North Carolina	Texas	Florida
Kentucky	Maine	South Carolina	Utah	Nevada
Louisiana	Minnesota	Vermont	Washington	New Hampshire
Massachusetts	New Jersey	Virginia		
Michigan	Oklahoma			
Mississippi	Oregon			
Missouri	Rhode Island			
Montana	Tennessee			
Nebraska				
New York				
North Dakota				
Ohio				
Pennsylvania				
South Dakota				
West Virginia (-4.8)				
Wisconsin				
Wyoming				

Source: U.S. Department of Commerce, Bureau of the Census, *State Population and Household Estimates,* July 1, 1989, Table 1.

the average income there is still well below the level in the other three regions, and because smaller MSAs have grown faster than the largest ones, even though per capita income is generally higher in the larger metropolitan areas.[15]

How do economists reconcile these real-life anomalies with theories? How do they explain migrants' turning their backs on higher income and moving where their monetary rewards, on average, will be lower? Perhaps nonpecuniary returns to living in large cities are negative (crime, pollution, crowding), and income differences by city size that remain after adjusting for differences in the cost of living can be interpreted as "compensatory payments" to city workers needed to offset the net, nonpecuniary disadvantages of urban living, which increase with city size.[16]

The real estate industry, like any other producer of goods and services, profits by satisfying buyers' needs and wants. The developers, builders, and salespeople who pioneer new products and techniques do so by spotting trends early and betting they can make money on them. Looking at broad demographic data is useful to developers and planners: the data not only give the big picture of the United States and its regions but also stimulate obvious questions—is the same trend happening in my market, will it continue in the future, what opportunities does it represent?

A current widely recognized trend is the aging of the U.S. population; older people are beginning to constitute a bigger portion of the population and will do so for some time to come. One reason is the large bulge of post–World War II babies now approaching middle age. Another is that life expectancy has also increased. Thus, from 1960 to 1985 when the number of people in the United States aged 65 to 74 increased by almost 50 percent, the number aged 75 and older doubled. (In the same period, the total population of all ages increased by only 25 percent.)[17]

While this trend increases the burden on medicare and social security, it provides

---

PROFILE: **E. EDDIE HENSON**

President, Williams Realty Corp.
Tulsa, Oklahoma

Background: Henson is an Oklahoman whose grandfather joined the land rush. After receiving his undergraduate degree from Texas Tech and MBA from Harvard, Henson started work with an oil drilling contractor in 1963. His second day on the job, his new employer loaned him to the governor of Oklahoma to organize the state's exhibit for the 1964 New York World's Fair. When Henson returned from New York a year later, he took charge of a shopping center project for his old employer and this time stayed 10 years. In 1973, he left to develop a mixed-use project and has done them ever since.

Denver: How did Denver get so tough? At the same time it become overbuilt (like almost every other large U.S. city), its oil-based economy got very sick. In January 1986, oil in the spot market was $28.50 a barrel; in May, it was $9.00. When oil rebounds, so does Denver. In mid-1987, office space in Denver was 30 percent vacant, giving developers the choice to give a project to lenders or to sweat it out. In such a market, Henson says, you position your project to be on everybody's short list when their subleases end and they're looking for space again. Leasing is everything.

Henson's company finished Tabor Center (550,000 square feet of office space, 120,000 square feet of retail space, and a 450-room hotel) in 1984, just in time to catch a deteriorating market. His leasing strategy has successfully targeted tenants who will pay an extra $1.00 per square foot for the quality a good mixed-use project offers, even in a depressed market.

Market research: The key to developing successful mixed-use projects is proving demand for each of the proposed uses. The tough part is that it takes so long to develop mixed-use projects—three to five years—that simultaneous demand for all of the uses may no longer exist when the doors open. Time and demand do not stand still.

The future: Henson cites the advantage of marketing to niches: Double Tree's Capri Hotel, for example, is oriented to female business travelers and doing a booming business. The potential for mixed-use development is finite in central business districts, but the village concept that mixed-use projects promote may find a wider market on sites for regional shopping centers.

One major Williams Realty project includes Denver's Tabor Center, a mixed-use development of retail, office, and hotel space.

FIGURE 2-7
POPULATION INSIDE AND OUTSIDE CENTRAL CITIES OF MAJOR METROPOLITAN AREAS: 1984[a]

Six Largest Metropolitan Areas in North and East[b]	Population in 1984	Change (Percent)		
		1980–1984	1970–1980	1960–1970
New York City/New Jersey	9,221,200	1.1	-8.6	4.6
New York City	7,164,700	1.3	-10.4	1.5
Outside Central City	2,056,500	0.4	-1.4	18.2
Chicago	7,215,900	1.6	1.8	12.1
Chicago City	2,992,500	-0.4	-10.8	-5.1
Outside Central City	4,223,400	3.0	13.7	35.0
Philadelphia/New Jersey	4,768,400	1.1	-2.2	11.1
Philadelphia City	1,646,700	-2.5	-13.4	-2.6
Outside Central City	3,121,700	3.1	5.4	22.8
Detroit	4,184,800	-3.9	-1.8	12.3
Detroit City	1,089,000	-9.5	-20.5	-9.3
Outside Central City	3,095,800	-1.7	7.8	28.1
Boston/Lowell/Brockton/ Lawrence/Haverhill	3,695,300	0.9	-1.3	10.5
Inside Central Cities	872,700	1.4	-8.2	-4.3
Outside Central Cities	2,822,600	0.7	1.1	16.6
Washington, D.C./ Maryland/Virginia	3,219,000	5.2	5.2	37.1
Washington City (D.C.)	622,800	-2.4	-15.6	-1.0
Outside Central City	2,596,200	7.2	12.5	58.5
Aggregate of Six MSAs in North and East	32,304,600	0.9	-2.5	11.2
Inside Central Cities	14,388,400	-0.9	-11.9	-1.9
Outside Central Cities	17,916,200	2.1	7.0	28.3

opportunities to develop products that will suit this growing market segment—or bundle of segments—but only with careful research and planning. Congregate-care facilities, for example, have proven more expensive to market and slower to sell than many developers anticipated. One survey found that only 20 percent of homeowners aged 55 and over plan to move in the next five years. The housing market for the elderly may prove to be much more segmented than developers originally be-

lieved, consequently offering a wider range of opportunities but with more risk.

For real estate players in all markets, large or small, understanding the present and past is the first step in projecting future opportunities. Life, however, has a way of confounding the forecasters who lay a straight edge down and draw a line through two points in the past to project the future. The future cannot simply be extrapolated from the past, for many changes are unforeseen. The surprising net migration from

FIGURE 2-7 (continued)

Six Largest Metropolitan Areas in South and West[c]	Population in 1984	Change (Percent)		
		1980–1984	1970–1980	1960–1970
Los Angeles/Long Beach	7,901,200	5.7	6.2	16.6
Inside Central Cities	3,475,500	4.4	5.0	12.3
Outside Central Cities	4,425,700	6.7	7.1	20.4
San Francisco/Oakland	3,413,300	5.0	4.6	17.4
Inside Central Cities	1,064,700	4.6	-5.5	-2.8
Outside Central Cities	2,348,600	5.2	9.9	31.8
Dallas/Fort Worth	3,403,300	14.4	25.1	36.8
Inside Central Cities	1,388,800	7.7	4.2	19.5
Outside Central Cities	2,014,500	19.5	47.9	62.4
Houston	3,350,300	15.4	45.3	39.5
Houston City	1,705,700	6.9	29.3	31.5
Outside Central City	1,644,600	25.6	71.0	55.6
Atlanta	2,262,100	11.5	27.2	36.5
Atlanta City	426,100	0.3	-14.1	1.6
Outside Central City	1,836,000	14.4	45.8	61.5
Anaheim/Santa Ana/ Garden Grove, California	2,075,800	7.4	36.0	101.9
Inside Central Cities	588,166	7.7	23.2	53.5
Outside Central Cities	1,487,634	7.3	41.8	135.6
Aggregate of Six MSAs in South and West	22,406,000	8.9	17.2	27.8
Inside Central Cities	8,648,966	5.4	7.1	15.8
Outside Central Cities	13,757,034	11.3	25.1	39.1

[a]For each metropolitan area except Boston, boundaries of the MSA as defined for the 1980 Census were carried forward to 1984 and backward to 1960. Thus, boundaries of MSAs are held constant. Boundaries of central cities (and therefore outside central city boundaries) in some cases changed as a result of annexation. All data for Boston refer to the Boston/New England County metropolitan area, as defined for the 1982 economic census.

[b]Corresponds to Northeast and Midwest census regions plus Maryland and Washington, D.C.

[c]Corresponds to South and West census regions minus Maryland and Washington, D.C.

Source: U.S. Department of Commerce, Bureau of the Census, *Census of Population, 1980,* and *Current Population Reports*, Series P-25, No. 976, October 1985. In Heilbrun, *Urban Economics*, Table 3.3.

metropolitan to nonmetropolitan areas in the 1970s did not continue in the 1980s; the phenomenon may have been only a blip. Few people foresaw the decline in oil prices that crippled cities like Houston in the 1980s. The lesson to real estate players is to stay well informed yet never become complacent. Every player should assume that the unforeseen is always just around the corner—and he or she should be ready to meet it.

Over time, uncontrollable and unforeseen shifts in the economy have wrought changes in the real estate industry. At the end of Whit Morrow's experience in Chapter 1, he had just accepted a position with

FIGURE 2-8
POPULATION GROWTH IN METROPOLITAN AND NONMETROPOLITAN AREAS, BY REGION, SIZE, AND PERCENT COMMUTING: 1970 TO 1984

	Change in Population (Percent)	
	1980 to 1984	1970 to 1980
All MSAs	4.5	10.6
Northeast	1.1	–1.0
Midwest	0.4	2.7
South	8.1	21.8
West	8.2	22.7
Over 5 Million	3.4	3.4
2.5 To 5 Million	4.5	10.9
1 To 2.5 Million	4.9	11.9
500,000 To 1 Million	5.3	14.2
250,000 to 500,000	4.8	15.6
Fewer than 250,000	5.3	17.7
All Nonmetropolitan Counties	3.4	14.3
15 Percent or More Commuting	4.6	18.3
10 to 14 Percent Commuting	3.3	15.4
5 to 9 Percent Commuting	3.4	14.9
Less than 5 Percent Commuting	3.2	13.3

Source: U.S. Department of Commerce, Bureau of the Census, *Current Population Reports*, Series P-25, No. 976, Table 8, October 1985. In Heilbrun, *Urban Economics*, Table 3.7.

the Sea Pines Company. As the Europa Center case study continues, Morrow describes the development field's peak in the early 1970s and the rapid changes in the culture of the real estate industry that occurred as oil prices and interest rates skyrocketed.

EUROPA CENTER

WHIT MORROW'S FORMATIVE YEARS IN THE DEVELOPMENT INDUSTRY

My first job at the Sea Pines Company was assistant to the president. In 1972, the business environment for real estate was at its highest peak in history. Banks were flush with money, giving it away as fast as they could to anybody who had a little bit of success. My employer, Charles Fraser at the Sea Pines

Company, enjoyed enormous success over 10 or 15 years—first building the Sea Pines Resort, Hilton Head Island, and Sea Pines Company. He had a great tradition of building things very well, hiring the best architects, the best landscape architects. One of my first jobs with the firm, because our company was growing so fast, was to hire 20 more MBAs just like me to manage 10 or 12 proposed new projects.

Then in 1973, the Arabs decided $6.00 for a barrel of oil was too low, raised it to $20.00 a barrel, and started an embargo. There was no oil, and because there was no oil, there were no resort vacationers because they had no gas for their cars. At the same time, bankers figured out how to adjust interest rates, moving away from the fairly stable interest rates of 6.5 to 7 percent across the board for years. In the previous business environment where oil was cheap, travel was cheap, enthusiasm abounded, and money moved easily around the country at very stable rates, we were able to borrow $200 million to $400 million with the prospect of actually paying it off from sales of houses, lots, and commercial tracts.

All of that came to a grinding halt when the business environment changed from steady low interest rates to rapidly fluctuating rates, going from 9 percent to 22 percent interest. With all the loans tied to the prime rate, 2 percent or 1 percent above the prime (which was great when the prime was 4.5 percent but not so great when it was 18 percent) and the Arabs' shutting off the oil, the number of sales within the Sea Pines empire went from 100 to three almost instantly. And the interest rate rose to 22 percent on $250 million to $350 million of debt.

I learned very quickly the meaning of the word "leverage." One of the big brokerage houses in New York City recently came up with a word for the kind of mortgage that was developed during that period: the neutron mortgage—the one that explodes, blows up the developer, but leaves the project intact. All of our nice landscaping and streets and houses were perfect—but we were blown to bits. Twenty MBAs from Harvard and Wharton and even the Carolinas are no longer at Sea Pines. Some of them have since become presidents of other real estate businesses. But that kind of leverage, that kind of activity, that kind of sexy real estate development during the mid-1970s was killed, gone forever. Now when developers try to recruit people for jobs, they have to say that they can hire only one person this year—and maybe not this year. It might be next year, and if the bank's interest rate goes up half a point, you'll probably have to work on the sales force and sell houses or on the leasing staff and lease office space. That's the difference from when I came out of business school and they told me in six months I'd be in charge of a $200 million project on 5,000 acres.

So as a result of that early experience at Sea Pines, I'd say the most important

Photo courtesy of Sea Pines Plantation

The Sea Pines Plantation, begun in 1957, is a 4,500-acre resort and residential community covering 25 percent of South Carolina's Hilton Head Island.

FIGURE 2-9

WHY DO FOREIGN INVESTORS INVEST IN U.S. REAL ESTATE?

Foreign investors in U.S. real estate include banks, pension funds, construction companies, life insurance companies, and individuals. They invest in the United States for the following reasons, some of which, like strength of the foreign currency relative to the dollar, can change rather rapidly.

1. **Political stability:** Thorsten Ulrich Beyer, a West German investor, shares a widely held perception: "The United States is the last politically stable country. It can ensure that private property is honored."

2. **Familiarity:** Foreign companies often invest in manufacturing first and real estate later. The Germans, for example, invested in textile manufacturing in the Carolinas and then invested in real estate because they already knew the area. Japanese real estate investment has been concentrated in New York City, Los Angeles, San Francisco, the Boston-to-Washington corridor, and Hawaii—areas with which the Japanese have become familiar for a variety of reasons.

3. **Size of market:** The United States is the world's largest single market. According to *Office Network*, 12.7 million square feet of office space was absorbed in Western Europe in the first half of 1986, compared to 31.8 million square feet absorbed in the United States for the same period. Because of the size of the United States and its culture, land here changes hands more easily than in most of Europe or, in particular, Japan.

4. **Return on investment:** Return is often greater in the United States. Salomon Brothers reports that office buildings in Tokyo currently yield 1 percent, compared with 7 percent in major U.S. cities.

5. **Relative strength of other currencies to the dollar and the supply of dollars in foreign hands:** Because of their huge trade surplus with the United States, the Japanese have dollars to spend, and the same is true of other U.S. trading partners. Mike Almond, an international investment lawyer, says, "They all

---

thing to do in real estate and development is to judge the business environment accurately. While we like to think that we have control of our destiny, the business environment really dictates what can be done. And it's complex.

Foreign Ownership of Real Estate in the United States

Today real estate receives only about 10 percent of total foreign direct investment in the United States annually—in 1987, $24.5 billion out of a total of $261.9 billion invested here. Both total foreign direct investment and real estate's share of it more than doubled between 1982 and 1987, however. Land in the United States attracts foreign investment for several reasons (see Figure 2-9), the most powerful being the country's perceived political stability, the huge size of the market, potential for long-term economic growth, and the foreign trade deficit. Our trading partners with surplus dollars have invested heavily in selected commercial real estate. As of mid-1988, nearly two-thirds of the office space in downtown Los Angeles, for example, was owned by foreign investors. In Chicago, foreign investors owned 20 percent of downtown office space, in Washington, D.C., 23 percent, and in downtown Manhattan, 21 percent (see Figure 2-10). These figures prompted Roger Lowenstein to remark, "The U.S., it would seem, is

FIGURE 2-9 (continued)

have a fascination with landownership. They all see this land and are quoted the prices and think there's a mistake in the money they've been quoted."

6. **Different ways to invest in U.S. real estate:** Direct purchase of real estate is the obvious way, but a joint venture with an established U.S. developer and purchase of U.S. construction and development companies with real estate holdings are other methods of entering the U.S. market.

7. **Protection of wealth from runaway inflation:** U.S. real estate attracts capital from countries in South America, where enormous inflation rapidly erodes the value of currency.

8. **Wide variety of property types and locations:** Different property types, from raw land to houses and condominiums to commercial buildings, dispersed among many local markets, allows foreign investors, just as it does U.S. citizens, to diversify risk.

9. **Higher population growth in the United States:** Relative to countries with low growth rates, notably Great Britain and West Germany, the more vigorous U.S. economy attracts long-term investors like pension funds.

10. **Absence of government restrictions on foreign ownership of real estate and repatriation of earnings:** Many countries exercise very strict control over foreign ownership of real estate and over foreign exchange. The United States is extraordinarily open in this regard, adding to the political liquidity of funds invested here.

Sources: LuAnne Nelson, *Business: North Carolina*, August 1987, pp. 42–49; and Peter DeWitt, "Foreign Direct Investment in U.S. Real Estate," *Real Estate Review*, Winter 1987, pp. 66–71.

trying to balance its trade by exporting its land, or at least the underlying deeds."[18]

Aggressive Japanese buying, particularly of very large office buildings in big cities, began receiving attention from the media in 1986 when Shuwa Investment Company reportedly spent almost $1 billion acquiring Arco Plaza in Los Angeles and the ABC Building in New York City. The contractor, Kumagai Gumi, was also reported to have spent $1.2 billion in Manhattan since the early 1980s, including a $500 million office and condominium project on the former site of Madison Square Garden.[19] Then in 1989, the Japanese bought the famed Rockefeller Center, an acquisition that generated much publicity and some concern.

The inflow of Japanese capital in particular should not be a surprise. The Japanese enjoyed a huge trade surplus with the United States in the 1980s; investment in U.S. stocks, bonds, and real estate gives them a use for their dollars. Furthermore, their own real estate market is small and rates of return minuscule by comparison. When the Japanese finally relaxed their restrictions on overseas investing in the mid-1980s and, at the same time, developed a network of their own financial institutions abroad, their dollars came flooding in, as shown in Figure 2-11.[20]

The last wave of foreign investment in real estate to attract as much attention from the media was in the late 1970s, when Arab petrodollars flowed back to the United States for investment in farmland. In response, Congress in 1978 directed the Department of Agriculture to take an annual inventory of foreign-owned land, and considerable public discussion of the dangers of foreign ownership ensued. Although some states eventually enacted restrictions,

FIGURE 2-10
FOREIGN INVESTMENT IN DOWNTOWN OFFICE SPACE
(As of November 1988)

	Percent
Los Angeles CBD	64%
Washington, D.C., CBD	23
Chicago CBD	20[a]
Phoenix CBD	7
Atlanta CBD	25
Honolulu CBD	50[b]
Houston CBD	39[c]
New York (Downtown) CBD	21[c]
New York (Midtown) CBD	7[c]
San Francisco	17[c]

[a]Includes 9 million square feet planned.
[b]Approximate figure.
[c]As of September 1987.
Source: Foreign Investments in U.S. Real Estate: Status, Trends, and Outlook, 1988 (Chicago: National Association of Realtors and MIT Center for Real Estate Development, 1988).

the federal government did not, and today the U.S. market for all types of real estate remains open to foreign investors.

How much land do foreign investors own? At the end of 1989, they held approximately 1 percent of U.S. farm and forest land, a total of 12.9 million acres (the area of Vermont and New Hampshire). Slightly under 50 percent of foreign holdings is forest land. At the end of 1988, Maine had the largest foreign ownership of any state, 1.8 million acres largely owned by Canadian paper companies. Oregon, Texas, and California reported more than 800,000 acres each under foreign ownership, Louisiana, Florida, and Georgia over 500,000 acres each.[21]

As might be expected, the countries that invest the most in U.S. real estate are our major trading partners, typically those with large dollar surpluses. Canada at one time was the largest foreign owner, but entering the 1990s the Japanese have moved into first place.[22] Other major investors in the 1980s were West Germany, the United Kingdom, the Netherlands, and the

Photo courtesy of the Hyatt Regency, Atlanta

The dramatic 22-story atrium of the Hyatt Regency in Atlanta, designed by John Portman.

FIGURE 2-11
JAPANESE INVESTMENT IN U.S. REAL ESTATE

Japanese investment in U.S. real estate soared 30 percent in 1988, even though the average purchase price paid by Japanese investors for U.S. properties declined, according to a study by Kenneth Leventhal & Company. Investments in office and mixed-use developments increased, while hotel investments declined.

Including investments made before 1985, Japanese investment in U.S. real estate totaled $42.9 billion at the end of 1988, a 63 percent increase from the $26.3 billion at the end of 1987. "By the end of 1990, Japanese investment in U.S. real estate may exceed British and Dutch investments," said Jack Rodman, managing partner of the Los Angeles office of Kenneth Leventhal & Company, at a seminar in Tokyo on Japanese investment in U.S. real estate sponsored by Nomura Securities, Eastdil Realty, and Kenneth Leventhal & Company.

In 1988, the Japanese invested $16.5 billion in U.S. real estate, half of it in office buildings. Office investments jumped 60 percent, to $8.3 billion. The other type of property that claimed a significantly greater share of Japanese investment in 1988 was mixed-use properties, which accounted for 15 percent of total investment, or $2.4 billion.

Hotel investments declined 22 percent in 1988, to $3.6 billion. Japanese investment in hotel properties in Hawaii dropped 70 percent in 1988 to $753 million, partly because of reduced opportunities for investment in a market where the Japanese are heavily invested.

Japanese investment in residential real estate development in the United States declined in 1988 to $702 million, from $1.3 billion the previous year, mainly because no large projects were started in Hawaii and Arizona, two of the states where the Japanese have been most active in residential development.

Billions of Dollars

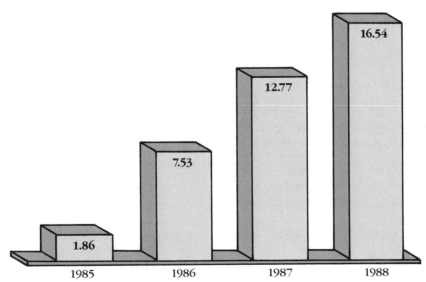

1.86	1985
7.53	1986
12.77	1987
16.54	1988

Source: Kenneth Leventhal & Company, *Real Estate NEWSLINE*, March 1989, p. 1.

39

Netherlands Antilles (a large offshore banking center).

When the impact of foreign investment on development is weighed, two important issues must be considered. First, some of this investment is coupled with immigration. In that case, the impact on development patterns is naturally more pronounced. New citizens in our land bring with them their cultures, and different cultures require different things of their cities. As the ethnic mix of U.S. cities changes, the type of space and appropriate services change over time as well. It is important to recognize that immigrants are not simply Asian or Hispanic or European; rather, they are many different varieties of Asian, Hispanic, or European. Just as the original European settlers of the country brought Northern European, and later Southern and Eastern European, ideas to U.S. cities, the new Hispanic and Asian immigrants bring a rich mix of ideas. Hispanic immigrants to Miami tend to be very different from Hispanic immigrants to Texas; thus, cities in those two states tend to respond differently.

These new international influences on our cities are also entering the development process. Foreign investors and foreign tenants, as well as new immigrants to the United States, may be members of the development team. It is incumbent on developers to remember that ethnic differences occur in decision making just as different nationalities claim different cities of origin. The Japanese tend toward group decisions, multiple reviews, and extensive due diligence. The ethnic Chinese, a very different Asian group, tend toward a patriarchal process, with the eldest male in the family the key decision maker. In both cases, titles that are so important in the United States, such as chief executive officer or chief operating officer, are less important, with group decision making and family relationships, respectively, much more important.

Today, with many U.S. markets substantially overbuilt, some large U.S. developers are looking for opportunities overseas. London may already be overbuilt (thanks to changes brought by U.S. and Canadian developers and U.S. investment bankers), but Germany and France look ripe for new development. Both countries are still using many vintage office properties built in the 1950s that are clearly substandard in today's more technical environment. While U.S. developers do have some of the skills to exploit such market opportunities, most choose to undertake joint ventures with politically sophisticated local organizations to obtain the most effective development teams.

THE WAY WE WERE

History offers more than just examples of past mistakes to avoid repeating. Understanding how and why cities, buildings, and institutions evolved can stimulate innovation. John Portman, for example, who became famous for designing hotels with dramatic atrium lobbies, brought the vibrant spectacle of street life *indoors* in central cities where crime, pollution, and automobiles had made the streets uninviting. Portman captured the best of street life by understanding the appeal of cities like New York and Paris that grew up before the automobile. Portman's genius was to understand that people love to watch the color and movement of other people—vendors, shoppers, diners, spectators, and passersby—and that bringing such a spectacle indoors would attract customers to a hotel. His understanding of the history and future of cities provided information for his imagination to use in new ways.

The Shape of Our Cities

All cities exist because they create possibilities, and one of the original possibilities was trade. As people move to cities, where they no longer grow their own food, they import food from the countryside. In return, they export manufactured goods or services like distribution and banking or medical care; some cities also export "order," that is, government, which provides defense, law, and administration. Early cities tended to locate at "economic transport points: at seaports, on navigable lakes and rivers, or at junctions of overland trade routes."[23] Obviously, some transport points (or breaks in transportation) have been determined by natural features like deep water ports. But other U.S. transport points grew up in the 19th century after canals and railroads were built; points along those transport routes immediately gained a cost advantage over other routes served only by horse and wagon. As a result, those points attracted industry and often evolved into manufacturing cities. In fact, Heilbrun asserts, railroads "proved to be the most powerful agglomerative invention of all time"; that is, railroads more than anything else made cities grow.

Transportation also dictated the shape and density of U.S. cities. The classic old city was mononuclear; that is, it had one extremely dense center with a business district at the hub and residential and manufacturing neighborhoods tightly surrounding the core. Density was high because people and goods moved by "hoof and foot." Before the 1870s, workers could not live beyond walking distance of jobs. Between 1853 and 1900, horse-drawn streetcars first, then electric ones, radically transformed patterns of housing. Like spokes of a wheel, streetcar lines radiated out from the mononuclear city center, carrying workers to and from houses in the new suburbs. But people still worked downtown, where business and manufacturing remained centralized because horses and wagons moved freight for short hauls; that is, the cost of moving freight was higher than the cost of moving people. In the old hub-and-spoke pattern, spokes (streetcar lines) converged at the center rather than connecting laterally or at the perimeter. The high point of center city development, according to Heilbrun, was from 1900 to 1920.

The automobile brought the next radical change to urban development after 1920, when its use became widespread. The automobile overcame more easily than the streetcar what urban economist Robert Murray Haig called in 1929 "the friction of space." The newer cities of the South and West (age roughly correlated with region) grew up relying on auto transport rather than urban mass transit, and because people with rising incomes also purchased more space around them wherever they could, the population of younger cities is *much* less dense than that of older cities, as the numbers in Figure 2-12 reveal. And because short-haul freight now moved by

FIGURE 2-12
POPULATION DENSITY IN MAJOR U.S. CITIES
(As of 1986)

	Population per Square Mile
Old Cities	
New York	24,089
(Borough of Manhattan)	(66,577)
Boston	12,153
Chicago	13,194
San Francisco	16,142
New Cities	
San Antonio	3,093
San Diego	3,086
Atlanta	3,216
Denver	4,728

Source: U.S. Department of Commerce, Bureau of the Census, *Statistical Abstract of the United States, 1989*, Table 39, p. 33.

truck and efficient manufacturing assembly dictated single-story plants, manufacturing began moving to cheaper land away from the center city and nearer the suburbs. In new outlying locations, manufacturing firms could lower production costs and still remain accessible to customers and suppliers. Eventually, department stores followed their customers to the suburbs, too. Today, retail trade in many younger cities takes place almost exclusively in suburban malls and strip centers rather than in the center city. And in many middle-sized U.S. cities, more office space now exists in outlying areas than in downtowns.

The growth of suburban activity centers has changed some typical commuting patterns. Suburban communities no longer must focus their transportation planning on the trip from the suburbs to the central business district (CBD). Instead, roadways connecting suburbs must be planned to accommodate the increasing number of workers who now live in one suburb and work and shop in another.

The suburb-to-suburb commuting pattern is one of the most significant changes in U.S. cities. The advent of expressways

41

The suburb-to-suburb commuting pattern is one of the most significant changes in transportation in metropolitan areas. Traffic jams are no longer confined to rush hour commuters trying to get in and out of downtown. Instead, suburban dwellers drive to different suburbs for work, for shopping, and for entertainment.

changed patterns of travel and housing and altered the idea of "best location." No longer were the best locations in the CBD. Instead, freeway intersections—most accessible to more people—became some of the most desirable locations for commercial development.

The automobile has not killed the center city. Visually, the structure of cities since the advent of automobiles still looks like a hub with spokes, but now the spokes are connected by more lateral lines and often by one or more perimeter rings. In all cities, some functions remain at the core. Raymond Vernon, who headed the famous New York metropolitan regional study in the 1960s, characterized them as functions that require face-to-face contact in the daily conduct of business: nonroutine activities whose speed is crucial to their success. They include government, banking, law, advertising, broadcasting, and the corporate headquarters of large companies.[24]

That growth has often been at the expense of lower-income families, however. Gentrification of older, formerly working-class neighborhoods has forced many lower-income residents into homelessness or relocation. These families are often the ones who had previously lived in working-class city neighborhoods and worked in manufacturing jobs located in the city. The cost of urban land and services has pushed many manufacturers to the edge of the MSA, eliminating a source of income for many of those urban dwellers.

As a place of residence, most older central cities lost population in the 1970s, but a few reversed that trend and grew again, quite slowly, in the 1980s. For developers and planners alike, central cities with large pockets of decay present a challenge and an opportunity in revitalization. Detroit has many healthy, growing submarkets, yet the core area near Renaissance Center still needs substantial redevelopment.

A new force for dispersion from the city is communications, particularly overnight mail, facsimile machines, and computer modems. Such devices let people do business from remote areas, even businesses that require frequent and fast communication. Southern New Hampshire, an area of small farms and villages, has grown rapidly as a result of the spillover of high-tech businesses around Boston. Communications, interstate highways, and commuter airlines have made growth possible in such semirural areas.

The Evolution of Modern Buildings

Any central business district in a moderately sized U.S. city today boasts at least one fairly flashy office tower, usually with the biggest bank in town occupying street level. What is perceived as modern about the building, though, is usually just skin—the fashionable covering of the moment. The really significant innovations in structure took place near the end of the 19th century, and what has been built for the last 75 to 100 years has improved on the past in terms of comfort systems, communications (smart buildings), and cosmetics.

Skyscrapers

Until the late 1800s, multistory buildings usually had solid masonry, weight-bearing walls and rarely exceeded six stories. New York brownstones and New England brick mill buildings are well-known examples. Then two innovations took the lid off the structural limits on building height: steel frame construction and the passenger elevator. Elisha Graves Otis demonstrated his passenger elevator in 1853 at the Crystal Palace Exposition in New York. And in 1885, the 10-story Home

---

FIGURE 2-13
"HOW HIGH CAN YOU MAKE IT SO IT WON'T FALL DOWN?"

In an old photograph, an office building begins to rise on an ordinary, big-city construction site; the first two stories of steel H- and I-beams are in place, floor pans are down, and third-story steel is going up, all surrounded by a wooden construction fence against the backdrop of adjoining skyscrapers. You have almost certainly driven past an identical steel frame, emerging on a downtown lot in any of 100 U.S. cities, sometime this year.

In this photograph, the unremarkable steel structure shows how humble even great buildings look at the very beginning—and how little things have changed in 60 years. Painted on the construction fence is a rendering of the building-to-be with a caption: "EMPIRE STATE, ready for May 1931 occupancy."

That was how, in 1930, you constructed what was then, and for a long time after, the world's tallest building (102 stories, 1,250 feet). On top of the poured concrete foundation, your crew hoisted into place, bolted, and riveted beams of steel, attaching stone panels as a skin on the outside. Today, to build the world's tallest building—or just a five-story office structure in Wichita—you'd do it the same way, with a minor difference: your crew would bolt the steel members together and weld some of the joints. Riveters are out of business.

When complete, the Empire State Building's skeleton consumed 57,000 tons of steel. The finished building contained 51 miles of pipe, 17 million feet of telephone cable, and seven miles of elevator shafts. Today, it is very difficult to believe that construction of this monster skyscraper was completed in only one year and 45 days and that total time, including planning and design, was only 18 months. (Because of the depression, the project also came in under budget, at $41 million instead of $50 million.)

The physical achievement of the Empire State Building obscures the fact that, like today's projects, it too had to meet legal and financial requirements for feasibility. John Jacob Raskob, one of five partners in the development, asked his architect, William Lamb, "Bill, how

Insurance Company Building was completed in Chicago, the first tall building in the country erected with an iron-and-steel frame rather than masonry weight-bearing walls. (The last tall masonry building in Chicago was the 16-story Monadnock Building, constructed in 1891. At street level, its walls were six feet thick to support the tremendous load above. But for this technology, it was the end of the line.)

Changes over the years in methods of connection and increasingly sophisticated engineering have lightened the materials necessary to support a structure safely. Architectural styles have also come and gone. But as Figure 2-13 reveals, *the* way to put up a tall building, years after the Home Insurance Company "skyscraper," still is with steel beams.

Industrial Buildings

Until the 1920s, goods were still moved on short hauls by horse and wagon; suppliers, manufacturers, and long-distance transport stations usually needed to be close together. Multistory manufacturing buildings made the most of crowded, expensive, central city sites. Two innovations changed this pattern of development. First, trucks made short-distance freight hauling economical after World War I, freeing manufacturers to relocate from downtown sites to outlying areas with cheap, plentiful land. Subsequently, the interstate highway system also allowed manufacturers to leave the suburbs—even the region—to locate near cheap labor in rural areas. The 41,000-mile, limited-access in-

---

FIGURE 2-13 (continued)

The "hat" tops off the Empire State Building in 1931.

high can you make it so it won't fall down?" The real question was, how high and still profitable? The answer de-

pended on a stipulation in New York's 1916 zoning ordinance that above the thirtieth floor, a building could occupy no more per floor than one-fourth of the total area on its lot. With two acres of ground, the Empire State tower could cover half an acre. Lamb determined that 36 million cubic feet would be a profitable size; he then began playing with alternatives. The sixteenth iteration (Plan K) was it: an 86-story tower. His client Raskob declared, "It needs a hat," and in a creative burst suggested a mooring mast for a dirigible. The 200-foot mast, intended to be an international arrival point for lighter-than-air craft, extended the building's total height to 1,250 feet. Because of high winds, the mast never worked as intended, but it was eventually used for observation (in fact, during the depression, income from the observation platform offset large office vacancies and kept the Empire State Building in business).

Source: Eastern Airlines, *Review*, April 1981, pp. 55–58 and 88–94.

terstate system, mostly built between 1956 and 1972, has given long-distance freight hauling by trucks the competitive edge over railroads, ultimately dispersing manufacturing plants throughout the country.

Second, the most efficient materials-handling and assembly methods now require a one-story plant, usually feasible only on cheaper, outlying land. As a result, the old multistory buildings of the central city became obsolete for manufacturing but sometimes found new economic life with new uses, like the shops, offices, and apartments occupying converted brick mill buildings and lofts in the 1980s.

Dwellings

No structural innovation has occurred in housing comparable to the steel frame in commercial buildings. Suburbanization, begun in the 19th century when streetcars came into use, revolutionized the location and density of housing. By the middle of the 20th century, the automobile had pushed suburbanization even farther. Housing in the streetcar suburbs was dense by today's standards although still less dense than in the central city, where land was scarce and more expensive and, as a result, people lived in apartment houses. In the suburbs, single-family houses were in demand. As automobiles made it possible for people to live farther from work and from each other and as suburbs pushed farther into the countryside, lots grew in proportion to people's appetite for space and ability to pay for it. The size of suburban lots has probably peaked because of high land development costs (although, as noted earlier, some former city workers have gained more land by moving beyond the suburbs to live in the country and either commuting long distances or working from home). Houses themselves have changed in style and have grown larger, on average, over the years (to a median size of 1,850 square feet for newly constructed houses in 1989), but the *structure* of the wood-frame house has not really changed in principle from colonial times.[25] The 19th century U.S. house,

In many major metropolitan areas, more office space now exists in suburbs and outlying areas than in central business districts.

however, with the balloon wood frame, was a substantial change from the European house with load-bearing masonry walls. The American version may not last as long, but it is far faster and less expensive to build.

An innovation that has fallen short of expectations in the 20th century is prefabrication. What seems in theory such a good idea turns out to be very limited in use. Some say it is because of expensive transportation (and varying local government regulations). Others say it is because the building industry has not embraced prefabrication into its longstanding method of building houses. Exceptions exist, however. Small parts of buildings, like wooden roof trusses, that can be hauled with regular trucks on any roads have gained wide acceptance, as have mobile homes. But larger manufactured houses have not met expectations in terms of total units sold.

The Public/Private Partnership: Zoning, Subdivision Regulations, Licensing, Planning, and Capital Markets

The public/private partnership among real estate developers and players, government at all levels, and neighbors and users of real estate projects pervades *every* aspect of development. Chapters 4, 5, and 6 discuss the evolution of this partnership more fully; this section sketches its outlines to flesh out the conceptual framework of the real estate development process.

A study of early land developers contends that the private sector recognized its need for some governmental controls on real estate development in the first three decades of this century and lobbied for them.[26] The study shows that large, influential private players, acting in their own interest, pioneered applications of city planning and often led the campaigns for state and local government controls on development: zoning, subdivision ordinances, comprehensive planning, and real estate licensing laws, all of them taken for granted today.

The transportation revolution of the 19th century stimulated the growth of cities, including the streetcar suburbs after 1870. Suburbs meant subdivisions, and a new era in U.S. land speculation opened. In the late 19th century, the real estate industry was still extremely fragmented, with little coordination among subdividers, builders, and salespeople. In the first place, subdividers only bought land and platted lots; they did not, like today, actually construct the streets or extend water and sewer lines. Furthermore, even in the early 20th century, builders put up most houses as well as commercial buildings on contract for users rather than speculatively as is often done today. As a result, lots in subdivisions were marketed to individuals who bought them as users or as speculators. Subdivision of land was virtually unregulated, barriers to entry were low, and anyone could act as a sales agent. As subdivision boomed, the public became enthusiastic buyers and speculators; cycles of boom and bust in lot sales went on for decades up to the Great Depression. Because very few subdividers provided infrastructure, it was left to municipalities to build streets and extend water, paying for these improvements by levying special assessments on the lot owners.

In some areas, abuses were enormous. "Land butchers" platted lots and streets with no regard for connection with existing streets, and "curbstoners" hawked lots to passersby on the streets and at train stations. With some justification, the public came to hold subdividers and salespeople in low regard. At the same time, a few well-capitalized developers were creating large subdivisions for high-income buyers; in fact, they were creating communities. In contrast to most subdividers of the time, the "community builders" took land development farther than platting. They offered amenities like parks and well-laid-out streets, and, above all, they enforced overall development standards with private deed restrictions. The community builders recognized that more value could be created by the character of a neighborhood as a whole than by the features of any individual lot.

The community builders, in concert with engineers, landscape architects, and building architects, worked out such features of subdivision design as "the classification and design of major and minor streets, the superblock and cul-de-sac, planting strips and rolling topography, arrangement of the house on the lot, lot size and shape, setback lines and lot coverage restrictions, planned separation and relation of multiple uses, design and placement of parks and recreational amenities, ornamentation, easements, underground utilities, and numerous other physical features . . . later adopted as rules and principles by public planning agencies."[27] Furthermore, private deed restrictions, the community builders' vehicle for enforcing standards for lots, "served as both the physical and political model for zoning laws and subdivision regulations."[28]

At the time community builders were trying these innovations (at the end of the 19th and beginning of the 20th centuries), the concept of a "residential" subdivision was fairly novel, and "subdividing land exclusively for residential purposes presupposed a level of planning and control that was certainly not the norm for American urbanization."[29] The planning and controls of the community builders were described as "private innovation preceding

---

FIGURE 2-14
LEGISLATIVE MILESTONES IN REAL ESTATE

1908 Los Angeles adopts the first major zoning ordinance in the nation, creating three broad use districts. The Los Angeles Realty Board pushes the ordinance.

1909 Wisconsin passes the first state subdivision planning enabling law, authorizing Wisconsin's cities to regulate width and alignment of streets proposed for public dedication. Similar legislation follows in California in 1913 and 1915.

1913 Washington state requires subdividers filing plats of subdivisions near major cities to dedicate small public parks.

1913 The California Real Estate License Bill passes in the legislature with realtors' vigorous support; the governor vetoes it.

1916 New York City passes the nation's first comprehensive zoning ordinance.

1919 California, Michigan, and Oregon pass licensing laws regulating the sale of real estate. By 1929, 27 states require licensing, regulating 115,000 brokers and 150,000 salespeople.

1923 Chicago passes a zoning ordinance; the bill is largely written by the Chicago Real Estate Board.

1924 NAREB, comprising private sector players, organizes the National Association of Real Estate License Law Officials.

1927 NAREB and ACPI (the American City Planning Institute) issue a joint statement after two years of work that becomes the basis for the U.S. Department of Commerce's Standard City Planning Enabling Act.

1934 Congress passes the National Housing Act, creating the Federal Housing Administration, in the depths of the depression "to bring the home financing system of the country out of a chaotic situation." NAREB lobbies for the bill. Almost all of FHA's staff is hired from the private sector. FHA encourages large-scale building with "conditional commitments" to lenders and justifies insuring high loan-to-value ratios and long terms (80 percent for 20 years, subsequently increased to 90 percent for 25 years) with detailed appraisals and uniform standards for underwriting.

Source: Marc A. Weiss, *The Rise of the Community Builders* (New York: Columbia Univ. Press, 1987).

public action."[30] Larger land developers and salespeople organized real estate boards early in the 20th century to promote themselves as members and to reduce competition by lobbying for licensing laws. These boards and their national body, NAREB (the National Association of Real Estate Boards, founded in 1908), were the forerunners of the National Association of Realtors. Figure 2-14 lists some of the legislation private players lobbied for and other institutional initiatives.

From the 1930s through the 1950s, community builders moved into housing for moderate-income families, integrating their operations: not only subdividing large tracts of land but also building the houses and selling them to the owner-occupants. Today integrated development is taken for granted, but at the time (the 1930s through 1950s), it "constituted a dramatic change from the speculative subdividing and 'lot selling' practices of the preceding generation."[31]

Two final points about the public/private partnership: First, the contention that the community builders of 75 years ago were de facto private city planners is echoed today by large land developers working in rural areas outside sophisticated city planning jurisdictions. Even now, community builders in those areas sometimes take land planning beyond the scope of zoning and subdivision regulations already in place—for example, when they seek approval for planned unit developments (PUDs) but the ordinance has no provisions for them. Second, the governmental interventions that have been most popular with the private sector have been those that facilitated, more than they restrained, private activities;[32] notable examples are the FHA's mortgage loan insurance and the federal secondary market makers—the Federal National Mortgage Association (Fannie Mae and its siblings Ginnie Mae and Freddie Mac)—providing liquidity to mortgage lenders (see Appendix A).

Private and public interests have often been adversaries. What should be recognized, however, is how often in the history of the real estate industry various private players have sought government intervention to promote their own interests. The partnership has a long, complex history and still evolves, often not smoothly.

SUMMARY

Throughout, this book stresses that the real estate players who best anticipate the *future* will reap the greatest rewards, in this chapter describing the present and recent past as a means of demonstrating that smart players do not take the world as it is for granted. Technologies, tastes, values, modes of financing, government interventions, demographics, and structures of economies evolve—at times very slowly, at other times rapidly in response to crisis.

Since 1973, the economic setting of the real estate industry has become much more volatile than in the 1950s and 1960s. In the early 1980s, certain real estate markets experienced the deepest recession since the Great Depression (in some places even worse than the early 1930s). In the mid-1980s, huge investments of institutional capital in real estate resulted in grotesquely overbuilt markets in some cities. In 1990, not only small players—the carpenter turned contractor and the part-time real estate agent—but also large players occasionally became casualties. In April 1987, in the fifth year of economic expansion in the business cycle, the tenth largest homebuilder in the United States declared bankruptcy. Robert Campeau's combination real estate and retailing empire began missing debt service obligations in 1989, and in 1990 the $3 billion Trump hotel, casino, and condo empire was unable to meet its financial commitments.

Understanding the scope of the built environment, the institutions that support it, and their history will not guarantee surviving recessions or reaping big profits in boom times. But a sense of perspective puts one a step ahead of the slower players and will be an absolutely basic requirement for working with (or competing against) the best. Chapters 4, 5, and 6 provide historical detail and clearly show that government has always been the developer's partner.

NOTES

1. Peter Wolf, *Land in America* (New York: Pantheon Books, 1981), pp. 24-25.

2. See Chapter 4 for a discussion of leapfrog development, skipping over undeveloped but expensive land in the existing city for less expensive land in the hinterland.

3. Wolf, *Land in America*, p. 25.

4. On the other hand, despite talk among builders of smaller houses in the early 1980s, U.S. citizens have demanded, and gotten, more interior living space: the median single-family house grew from 1,385 square feet in 1970 to 1,595 square feet in 1980 (the decade when the energy crisis and high inflation first hit) and continued at virtually the same level in 1984 and 1985 (1,605 square feet). A significant corollary to less-land-more-house is the steadily increasing proportion of houses with two or more stories: 17 percent in 1970, 31 percent in 1980, 36 percent in 1983, 40 percent in 1984, and 42 percent in 1985. U.S. citizens, in the aggregate, are selective as to how they compromise. The perception that more living space with less land but still *some* land around the house is better than no land seems to explain U.S. residents' tenacious demand for single-family detached housing and thus for relatively low-density, owner-occupied residential development. *Source* of figures: U.S. Department of Commerce, Bureau of the Census, *Statistical Abstract of the United States, 1989* (Washington, D.C.: U.S. Government Printing Office, 1989), Table 1273, p. 706.

5. The federal government *and Native Americans* own over 360 million acres under the recent settlement of a long-standing Indian claim.

6. Wolf, *Land in America*, p. 549.

7. While government has continuously promoted private ownership, the degree of government regulation of that private ownership has been increasing for reasons explained in Chapters 3, 4, and 5.

8. U.S. Department of Commerce, Bureau of Economic Analysis, *Survey of Current Business* (Washington, D.C.: U.S. Government Printing Office, April 1990).

9. U.S. Department of Commerce, Bureau of the Census, *Expenditures for Residential Upkeep and Improvements*, Report C50 (Washington, D.C.: U.S. Government Printing Office, 1988).

10. Charles H. Wurtzebach and Mike E. Miles, *Modern Real Estate*, 4th ed. (New York: John Wiley & Sons, 1991), pp. 14–15.

11. As reported in *The Wall Street Journal*, 1980 Census figures on median net worth speak eloquently of the distribution of wealth in the United States: net worth of the median family in the United States is $32,667, of the median white family is $39,135, of the median Hispanic family is $4,913, of the median African-American family is $3,397, and of the median household headed by a woman is $13,890.

12. U.S. Department of Commerce, *Statistical Abstract of the United States, 1989*, Table 657, p. 399.

13. In the early 1970s, sales associates became eligible for the title "REALTOR® Associate." Accordingly, the number of Realtors increased immediately by about 450,000 and then grew more gradually. The number as of January 1990 was 796,800.

14. James Heilbrun, *Urban Economics and Public Policy*, 3d ed. (New York: St. Martin's Press, 1987), p. 56.

15. Ibid., p. 59.

16. Ibid., p. 60, citing Irving Hoch.

17. U.S. Department of Commerce, *Statistical Abstract of the United States, 1989*, Table 13, p. 14.

18. Roger Lowenstein, The Wall Street Journal, September 18, 1987.

19. Kenneth R. Sheets, "Landlords from the Far East," *U.S. News & World Report*, April 7, 1986, pp. 53–54.

20. Kenneth Leventhal & Company, *Real Estate NEWSLINE*, p. 1.

21. J. Peter DeBraal, *Foreign Ownership of U.S. Agricultural Land through December 31, 1989* (Washington, D.C.: U.S. Department of Agriculture, Economic Research Service, Resources & Technology Division, 1990).

22. Lowenstein, *The Wall Street Journal*, September 18, 1987.

23. Heilbrun, *Urban Economics and Public Policy*, p. 8-11. This section draws heavily on Heilbrun's lucid explanation of the evolution of U.S. cities. See especially Chapters 2 to 4.

24. In the 1980s, however, even some large corporations deserted the center city for a suburban "office campus" or left one big city altogether to move to another. J.C. Penney's moving its headquarters from New York City to Plano, Texas (near Dallas, in a park with other corporations) is not unusual.

25. In Europe, load-bearing walls are far more common than the less expensive stick-built construction typically seen in the United States. So over the centuries, some progress has occurred.

26. Marc A. Weiss, *The Rise of the Community Builders* (New York: Columbia Univ. Press, 1987).

27. Ibid., p. 3.

28. Ibid., p. 4.

29. Ibid., p. 1.

30. Ibid., p. 3.

31. Ibid., p. 2.

32. Weiss, *Rise of the Community Builders*.

Chapter 3

A Brief Review of Financial Concepts and Investment Tools

*T*he mechanics of real estate finance are well covered in numerous texts, and this text does not attempt to repeat them all here. The underlying concepts of finance are so important to the logic that governs development, however, that they bear review in this introduction to real estate development.[1]

Developers need to see and understand the whole picture. This brief review looks at the total picture and provides references so readers can pursue individual parts on their own. Consequently, it does not cover much basic real estate finance terminology or the fundamentals of important real estate calculations. The chapter does, however, talk about the relationships between time, rate, and risk, which are critical to the determination of when a wraparound mortgage makes sense and why the mortgage loan constant is important.

The financial review is covered in the following sequence:
- Financial concepts: Capital markets, the financial officer's job, obtaining the best possible financing, finding the right loan officer, loan terms, and critical financial ratios.
- Discounted cash flow logic: Mechanics of discounted cash flow, distinctions in value, a simple illustration of discounted cash flow, and managing the development process using discounted cash flow.

FINANCIAL CONCEPTS

Capital Markets

The capital markets aggregate and allocate savings, or, simply put, they bring together those who save money and those who invest it. While certain physical locations are synonymous in many people's minds with capital markets, such as Wall Street, "capital markets" is a concept, not a place. They bring together the portion of the gross domestic product not immediately consumed (savings) and then allocate those savings to investments that presumably will benefit society in the long run. Capital markets are important to development companies when their chief financial officers seek financing.

Capital markets are comprised of three components: savers, financial intermediaries who operate the capital markets themselves, and investors. Savers include individuals, businesses, life insurance companies, and pension funds. Financial intermediaries include commercial banks, bank trust departments, S&Ls, mutual savings banks, credit unions, life insurance companies, real estate investment trusts, mortgage bankers, investment bankers, venture capitalists, finance companies, investment managers, syndicators, and the government, among others. Investors include the government, mortgagors, corporations, and individuals.

Both the aggregation and the allocation of capital are based on the quality of the potential investment. Savers want high *expected* returns with low associated risk. Consequently, the higher the investment's prospective return and the lower its related risk, the more likely it is to be financed on attractive terms. "Attractive terms" means both a low rate and few restrictions, such as limits on the activities that the borrower or user of the funds may engage in. (Common restrictions include maintaining minimum loan-to-value ratios, debt service coverage ratios, and the like.)

The real savers, those in our society that consume less than they produce, think of themselves as investing their savings, but they are different from the "real" investors. Real investors are those groups or individuals who have more ideas than funds—the ones who will put savings to use in terms of equipment and bricks and mortar.

By far the largest source of savings in the U.S. economy today is pension funds; by 1995, their total value is expected to exceed $3 trillion. The second largest source of funds is life insurance general accounts. People save for retirement, and they save for their heirs. In both cases, this money needs to be invested, eventually in real assets so that the beneficiaries will receive more than the amount initially set aside. In addition, some people are sufficiently frugal to save money; collectively, they constitute a large pool of savings. And finally, particularly after the Tax Reform Act of 1981, some corporations are net savers.

Over the last decade (and probably for several years more), the largest single user of savings has been and will be the federal government—as a result of a deficit brought on by a government that spends more than it collects in tax revenues. During the Reagan administration, for example, the deficit in several years was over $200 billion a year, a rather large drain on the limited pool of savings. The second largest use

of savings is in mortgage finance. Nearly 64 percent of U.S. citizens own houses, and over 67 percent of those houses are mortgaged. And many growing corporations and individual investors have a greater need for funds than they can generate or have ideas that exceed their financial capacity. In this simplistic view of the capital markets, most developers would probably place themselves in the last category. Because capital markets allocate funds based on expected return and associated risk, developers are usually last in line for a portion of the funds.

The government is the lowest-risk borrower and gets money cheaper and faster than all other debtors. Mortgage finance, particularly for single-family houses, is also low risk, not only because borrowers personally guarantee the debt and the house serves as collateral but also because in many cases the federal government provides additional guarantees (see Chapter 2).

The financial intermediaries who operate the capital markets engage in varied endeavors. S&Ls in the 1980s financed a great deal of development, but they made a series of investment errors, including investing in speculative development and, worst of all, in junk bonds. Most analysts predict that S&Ls will finance very little development in the 1990s, particularly with new capital adequacy rules that require financial institutions to have more capital for high-risk loans than for low-risk loans. S&Ls, because of past losses, have very low capital bases to start from and thus will find it difficult to invest in high-risk real estate projects.

Mutual savings banks are similar to S&Ls but have slightly different regulations and are concentrated mostly in the Northeast. While they have some of the problems of the S&L industry, they have generally been more conservatively managed and will probably have a bigger impact on development financing in the 1990s.

Commercial banks are different from S&Ls. Their primary source of funds is shorter-term demand deposits rather than savings accounts (the primary source of S&Ls' funds), and thus they tend to invest in shorter-term assets. Many commercial banks got into trouble in the 1980s, however, by investing too much of their money in risky ventures (particularly loans to third-world countries and leveraged buyouts). And as rents declined in many markets in the late 1980s, what were originally good real estate loans became problems as the projects' net operating incomes declined when leases were rolled over and previously solid projects became unable to carry their debt service.

Mortgage bankers make loans and then resell them in the secondary market. They might make a series of individual loans from capital borrowed from a commercial bank, then resell those loans to individuals (possibly through some type of government pool, as detailed in Chapter 2) or to pension funds or life insurance companies. The proceeds of the sale would be used to pay back the commercial bank and provide for the mortgage banker's own profit and overhead.[2]

Venture capitalists and investment bankers are not traditional sources of real estate capital, but they are critically important in the overall capital markets and are increasingly becoming involved in the business of real estate. Traditionally, venture capitalists provided financing to small, startup operations, nurturing those operations with financing as well as advice about management until the company was ready to go public. The investment banker would then handle the public offering, selling shares to the general public under the Securities and Exchange Commission's regulations. As shown in later chapters, the lengthening timetable for development has created a need for something akin to venture capital. And the same investment bankers who helped securitize the residential loan market now offer securitized commercial loans to developers of larger projects.

Finance companies are yet another financial intermediary but with a different source of funds and thus a different attitude toward the allocation of those funds. Major finance companies—GE Capital, Westinghouse Credit, General Motors Acceptance Corporation, for example—might well begin to provide some higher-risk real estate capital now that the S&Ls and many commercial banks have been forced into a more conservative position.

This simplistic view of the capital markets nevertheless lends perspective on how development is financed. In the modern world of global finance, most major life insurance companies allocate their internal funds as well as manage funds for other savers, particularly the pension funds. Thus, such major life insurance companies are both financial intermediaries and savers. A developer who borrows money from a life insurance company, for example, may end up with the insurance company's own funds or funds that it is managing for various pension funds.

Likewise, major global banks, domestic and foreign, are involved in many different aspects of finance. Citicorp, for example, holds more mortgage loans in this country than any other nongovernmental financial institution. While Citicorp is a traditional commercial bank in the sense of having demand deposits that need to be put into relatively short-term investments, its holding company has many other sources of funds and is thus able to provide a full supermarket of financing alternatives. (Figure 3-1 provides the aggregate amount of mortgage loans outstanding by type of lender.)

The Financial Officer's Job

A development company's chief financial officer has three jobs: obtaining funds as inexpensively as possible with as few complicating restrictions as possible, finding the right place to put the money (picking the right type of property, the right city, and the right amenities to add to a project), and frequent reporting of the development company's financial activities and about particular projects. This endeavor has always been complicated, because development involves a complex set of interrelated activities. Traditionally, financial officers dealt with a local construction lender as the project was built. With more institutional financing of real estate projects today, the reporting job becomes even more important.

Obtaining the Best Possible Financing

Capital markets finance projects based on prospective return and associated risk. A primary responsibility of a financial

FIGURE 3-1
MORTGAGE DEBT OUTSTANDING: CUMULATIVE 1988, CUMULATIVE 1989, AND FIRST QUARTER 1990[a]
(Millions of Dollars, End of Period)

Type of Holder and Type of Property	1988	1989	1990 (Q1)
All Holders	3,243,371	3,524,474	3,593,640
1- to 4-Family	2,172,161	2,384,076	2,440,682
Multifamily	286,356	306,652	311,573
Commercial	698,064	747,277	756,670
Farm	86,791	86,468	84,714
Selected Financial Institutions	1,805,691	1,919,269	1,916,241
Commercial Banks[b]	669,237	756,786	783,100
1- to 4-Family	317,585	358,652	376,616
Multifamily	33,158	36,994	39,202
Commercial	302,989	343,841	350,473
Farm	15,505	17,299	16,809
Savings Institutions[c]	903,629	921,410	883,628
1- to 4-Family	657,591	675,891	649,537
Multifamily	108,003	108,534	103,025
Commercial	137,384	136,343	130,443
Farm	651	641	622
Life Insurance Companies	232,825	241,073	249,513
1- to 4-Family	15,299	13,531	14,173
Multifamily	23,583	26,646	28,182
Commercial	184,273	191,369	197,621
Farm	9,671	9,527	9,537
Finance Companies[d]	37,846	50,728	45,808
Federal and Related Agencies	200,570	212,370	216,961
Government National Mortgage Association	26	24	22
1- to 4-Family	26	24	22
Multifamily	0	0	0
Farmers Home Administration[e]	42,018	42,080	8,045
1- to 4-Family	18,347	19,091	18,419
Multifamily	8,513	9,168	9,199
Commercial	5,343	4,463	4,310
Farm	9,815	9,358	8,997
Federal Housing and Veterans Administrations	5,973	6,220	6,215
1- to 4-Family	2,672	3,009	2,977
Multifamily	3,301	3,211	3,291
Federal National Mortgage Association	103,013	110,970	112,353
1- to 4-Family	95,833	102,863	103,300
Multifamily	7,180	8,107	9,053

FIGURE 3-1 (continued)

Type of Holder and Type of Property	1988	1989	1990 (Q1)
Federal Land Banks	32,115	30,788	29,325
1- to 4-Family	1,890	1,889	1,197
Farm	30,225	28,899	28,128
Federal Home Loan Mortgage Corporation	17,425	22,289	19,823
1- to 4-Family	15,077	19,182	16,772
Multifamily	2,348	3,107	3,051
Mortgage Pools or Trusts[f]	810,887	931,619	981,265
Government National Mortgage Association	340,527	374,650	378,292
1- to 4-Family	331,257	362,865	366,300
Multifamily	9,270	11,785	11,992
Federal Home Loan Mortgage Corporation	226,406	266,407	281,736
1- to 4-Family	219,988	259,443	274,084
Multifamily	6,418	6,965	7,652
Federal National Mortgage Association	178,250	216,600	246,391
1- to 4-Family	172,331	207,765	237,916
Multifamily	5,919	8,835	8,475
Farmers Home Administration[e]	104	79	75
1- to 4-Family	26	23	20
Multifamily	0	0	0
Commercial	38	22	25
Farm	40	34	31
Individuals and Others[g]	426,223	461,216	479,172
1- to 4-Family	258,639	285,966	301,573
Multifamily	78,663	83,299	84,873
Commercial	68,037	71,239	72,136
Farm	20,884	20,711	20,589

[a]Based on data from various institutional and governmental sources, with some quarters estimated in part by the Federal Reserve. "Multifamily" refers to loans on structures of five or more units.

[b]Includes loans held by nondeposit trust companies but not bank trust departments.

[c]Includes savings banks and savings and loan associations. Data reported by FSLIC-insured institutions include loans in process and other contra assets (credit balance accounts that must be subtracted from the corresponding gross asset categories to yield net asset levels).

[d]Assumed to be entirely 1- to 4-family.

[e]FmHA-guaranteed securities sold to the Federal Financing Bank were reallocated from FmHA mortgage pools to FmHA mortgage holdings in the fourth quarter of 1986 because of accounting changes by the Farmers Home Administration.

[f]Outstanding principal balances of mortgage pools backing securities insured or guaranteed by the agency indicated. Includes private pools not shown as separate line items.

[g]Other holders include mortgage companies, real estate investment trusts, state and local credit agencies, state and local retirement funds, noninsured pension funds, credit unions, and other U.S. agencies.

Source: Federal Reserve Bulletin, July 1990, p. A38.

officer in a development firm is to obtain low-cost financing. The best way to obtain the best financing is to understand the motives of prospective lenders, decide who the right lender is for a particular project, and then package the deal to suit the lender. What do lenders want? Basically, to pay back their source of funds, to cover profit and overhead, and to avoid being fired, declaring bankruptcy, or going to jail for making serious errors.

When all three of these desires are put together, distinct groups emerge among the different lenders regarding types of loans. These groups are based partly on history and partly on regulation. And the groups contain distinctions based on the self-image of lenders and their technical competence in different fields.

For financial officers seeking the best possible loan, knowing a lender's source of funds tells a great deal about the length of loan they can make. The size of the difference between their yield on assets and the cost of their funds—the spread—tells something about the amount of in-house analytical capability they possess. A lender with a small spread would be unlikely to become involved in a complex financing deal. And legal issues tell something about exposure to risk. Pension funds, for example, are both morally and legally obligated to undertake low-risk loans. With the application of modern portfolio theory and the benefits of diversification, pension funds are not prohibited from involvement in activities that are individually risky. Collectively, however, they are more averse to risk than other lenders.

Assume, for example, that a development team has found a particularly attractive 5,000-acre parcel that it wishes to develop over the next 10 years into a high-income residential community with multiple golf courses and other amenities. One member of the team suggests to the financial officer that pension funds would be a good source of financing. What is the astute financial officer's response?

First, the financial officer notes that this source of funds is oriented toward the long term, which fits with the 10-year development plan. On the question of spread, the astute financial officer notes that some pension funds have large in-house staffs and extensively use outside investment advisers as well. Such groups would have the capability to analyze projects as complex as a 5,000-acre high-income residential development. Considering the question of risk, however, elicits a clearly negative perspective. Pension funds prefer low-risk investments, which a 5,000-acre residential development clearly is not. Although some pension funds would invest in such a project, pension funds in general are probably not a logical source of funds.

Finding the Right Loan Officer

Once financial officers have determined the right group of institutions to finance a particular development, they must also decide whom to approach within the financial institution. Most financial institutions have several loan officers, and the one to select depends on the riskiness of the loan as well as the loan officer's qualifications. A complex loan would do best with a "rising star," an officer who wants to increase the volume of business in the future. A standard low-risk loan that will not provide repeat business would probably not be a high priority for an up-and-coming loan officer and might be more successfully handled by an experienced officer approaching retirement. Such considerations might sound simplistic, but they can make the difference between success and failure. The good judgment needed to choose the appropriate loan officer often comes with experience and is just one more example of the role of sound judgment in successful real estate development.

Loan Terms

Successfully negotiating loan terms involves a great deal more than simply knowing the definitions and understanding the underlying economics. But while loan terms are critical, their successful negotiation is probably more a function of experience than academic study.

It is fair to say that a shift occurred during the 1980s in the negotiation of loan terms. In the 1970s, typically terms were negotiated, the participants went to closing, and they signed a set of agreements that had been negotiated over a long time.

Today, increasingly, people renegotiate terms until the last minute. Because the right terms are critical to successful financing, financial officers now expect negotiations to be long and difficult.

Critical Financial Ratios

Lenders typically begin to measure their exposure in any real estate loan with two well-known ratios: the debt service coverage (DSC) ratio and the loan-to-value (LTV) ratio (see Figure 3-2). The debt service coverage ratio equals net operating income (NOI) divided by debt service. The debt service, in turn, is the product of the mortgage loan constant (MLC) times the amount of the loan. The mortgage loan constant is the constant amount that must be paid each period, so that by the end of the term of a fully amortized loan, the entire principal debt plus the stated rate of interest have been repaid. Thus, the mortgage loan constant increases as the interest rate increases and decreases as the term of the loan increases. In like fashion, debt service increases if either the mortgage loan constant or the loan amount increases.

The debt service coverage ratio can be measured over any time period but is typically measured in years. Thus, it is usually annual net operating income divided by annual debt service. While most lenders use the next year's projected operating income in this calculation, some conservative lenders use the previous year's net operating income or the current month's net operating income annualized.

Clearly, this ratio measures the likelihood that the property itself will be able to service the debt. A ratio of 1.0 indicates that expected net operating income will exactly equal the debt service. Anything less than 1.0 indicates that a shortfall will occur even if anticipations are met. Lenders are typically very reluctant to make loans when the debt service coverage ratio is below one, even in early years, unless the borrower is personally liable and has sufficient resources to cover the anticipated shortfall. The most common situation is for the lender to expect a debt service coverage ratio larger than one.

The more risk the lender sees in a loan, the higher the debt service coverage required. And the less certain lenders are of the projected net operating income, the more they will require a high ratio to be sure that their debt service is paid. The ideal situation for lenders is that the debt service always is paid by the property, regardless of whether the loan is covered by the borrower's personal liability.

In real estate development, debt service coverage ratios of 1.05 and 1.10 are not uncommon in conservative, low-risk loans on structures preleased on a triple net basis to very good credit risks. On the other hand, purely speculative buildings in untried neighborhoods with new combinations of features, functions, and benefits may involve debt service coverage ratios of 1.5 or higher (if a lender can be found at all).

From the financial officer's perspective inside the development company, the debt service coverage ratio the lender requires is critical, because it determines the maximum amount of the loan. Because a first lienholder typically charges a lower rate than any second lienholder or equity investor, the desire is usually to get the largest loan possible from the first lienholder. The formula for the debt service coverage ratio shown in Figure 3-2 can easily be rearranged to calculate the maximum amount of the loan. In this algebraic restatement, the maximum loan is seen to be the net operating income divided by the debt service coverage ratio times the mortgage loan constant. Thus, a property can typically obtain a larger loan the higher the net

---

FIGURE 3-2
MEASURING EXPOSURE IN A LOAN

Debt Service Coverage Ratio

$$\text{DSC Ratio} = \frac{\text{NOI}}{\text{Debt Service} = (\text{MLC} \times \text{Loan Amount})}$$

Therefore, using algebraic substitutions:

$$\text{Maximum Loan} = \frac{\text{NOI}}{\text{DSC Ratio} \times \text{MLC}}$$

Loan-to-Value Ratio

$$\text{LTV Ratio} = \frac{\text{Loan Amount}}{\text{Appraised Value}}$$

operating income, the lower the debt service coverage ratio (i.e., the lower the risk), and the lower the mortgage loan constant (i.e., the longer the term and the lower the interest rate).

The second critical ratio is the loan-to-value ratio. It is typically less important in commercial properties than the debt service coverage ratio, because it represents the lender's fallback position. The lender would prefer to never have to foreclose on a loan, but the loan-to-value ratio is a measure of the lender's safety should foreclosure be necessary. As shown in Figure 3-2, the calculation is the loan amount divided by the appraised value. The riskier the loan from the lender's perspective, the lower the maximum loan-to-value ratio allowed. Further, conservative lenders tend to be more restrained in the allowed appraised value. Therefore, this case really involves two variables—the loan-to-value ratio itself and the conservatism of the appraised value.

Lenders typically require a specific debt service coverage ratio and permit no more than a certain loan-to-value ratio for any loan, given its expected risk. The debt service coverage ratio is the more critical of these two ratios, because it is usually the first to come into play. Covering debt service with net operating income is easier for the lender than recovering the amount of the loan in foreclosure. Second, with relatively high interest rates and soft rental markets, most developers find that their maximum loan is constrained more by the debt service coverage ratio than by the loan-to-value ratio.

DISCOUNTED CASH FLOW LOGIC

It is safe to say that a person seriously involved in business will use the discounted cash flow logic to make decisions. It is probably also safe to say that the use of this fundamental business tool is far more an art than a science.

Discounted cash flow logic is useful because it allows the user to bring everything that can be known about a particular investment down to a single dollar amount at a particular time. From the perspective of development, doing so means that everything that can be known about future occupancy, cost of operations, physical wear and tear on the building, and additional factors can be put in a consistent format and reduced to one number, today. This number, the *present value*, can then be compared with the cost to see whether the project is feasible.

The Mechanics of Discounted Cash Flow

The easiest way to understand discounted cash flow and present value is to think about compound interest. Assume a person has $100 to invest at 6 percent for one year. At the end of one year, the investor has $106. Extend the question slightly. If the investor has $100 to invest for two years at 6 percent, at the end of two years, he or she has not $112 but $112.36. The $.36 represents 6 percent interest on $6, interest on interest or "compound interest."

Figure 3-3 illustrates both these calculations. If the future value is equal to the present value times one plus the interest rate and investors are interested in calculating a present value given their expectation of a certain future value, then the calculation of present value is a straightforward algebraic rearrangement of the formula for future value. As shown in the figure, present value is the future value divided by one plus the interest rate.

By extension, the present value for multiple years is equal to the sum of the present values of the future values in all future years. The Σ indicates summation from the first year to the nth year in the multiyear formula for present value. It is the summation of the future value in every year divided by one plus the interest rate, now raised to a power equal to the number of years into the future before the value is realized.

The present value will be higher if the expected future value is higher and if this future value is received sooner. It will also be higher the lower the rate of interest.

The only difficult part in moving from compound interest to present value is the handling of risk. Again, as shown in Figure 3-3, when risk is added, one does not have a certain future value. Rather, one has an

FIGURE 3-3
CALCULATING PRESENT AND FUTURE VALUE

$$\text{Future Value (FV)} = PV(1 + i)$$
$$x = \$100 (1 + .06) = \$106$$

$$\text{Present Value (PV)} = \frac{FV}{(1 + i)}$$
$$x = \frac{\$106}{(1 + .06)} = \$100$$

$$\text{Two-Year FV} = PV(1 + i)^2$$
$$x = \$100 [(1.06)(1.06)] = \$112.36$$

$$\text{Two-Year PV} = \frac{FV}{(1 + i)^2}$$
$$x = \frac{\$112.36}{(1 + .06)(1 + .06)} = \$100.00$$

$$\text{Multiyear PV} = \sum_{i=1}^{n} \frac{FV_n}{(1 + i)^n}$$

$$\text{With Risk, PV} = \sum_{i=1}^{n} \frac{ECF_n}{(1 + r)^n}$$

where:

i = real return + inflation premium

$r = i$ + risk premium.

---

expected cash flow (ECF) in each future year. The algebra is the same with the same summation of values, yet it is no longer a known future value.

How do financial officers obtain the ECF? This question is critical, and several issues are involved. First, by examining comparable properties (similar properties in a particular market) and adjusting for different features, functions, and benefits, the analyst estimates current (year one) net operating income. Then by examining relevant trends (global to local neighborhood), the analyst projects net operating income as far into the future as possible. Finally, when the net operating income is assumed to have reached some stable level (that is, as far into the future as logic allows), the analyst assumes a sale. The expected cash flows are then each year's ex-

pected net operating income plus the final year's estimate of proceeds from net sales.

Because an expected cash flow rather than a definite future value is involved, the discount rate must include a risk premium. The interest rate on a savings account is simply the real return plus the inflation premium. The real return is the net increase in purchasing power to the saver (the paper investor). This saver has come to anticipate inflation and thus, in addition to compensation for deferred compensation, wants an adjustment for the declining value of the dollar. Thus, i equals the real return plus the inflation premium.

In a typical investment that involves risk, the risk premium must be added to i. Thus, the discount r is i plus the risk premium. The critical question then becomes, how big is the risk premium?

The size of the risk premium is a function of the quality of the estimate of the expected cash flows. Note that it is the expected cash flow that is discounted, not accrual income. The easiest way to think about it is that expected cash flow is the periodic change in the bank account if the only thing happening in this bank account is the particular project or participation in the particular project. Thus, cash rents, not accrual rents, are most important, for free rent is zero in the discounted cash flow model.

If expected cash flows are very certain, then the risk premium will be low. Likewise, if estimates of expected cash flow are at best dubious, then the risk premium will be high. Just because expected cash flows are dubious, however, does not mean that the investment is necessarily a bad one. The question is risk in combination with expected return. More risk requires more expected return for the investment to be a good one. But high-risk investments can be very attractive if the prospective return is sufficient.

In mid-1990, most institutional investors were looking for a total return of about 11 percent on the highest-grade equity real estate investments, which is not the required return on investments made during the development process. It is the return on investments in completed projects of high quality, in the right locations, and with the best tenants—in other words, the lowest end of the risk spectrum. Thus, r would be 11 and because i (the return on government bonds of a similar maturity) was between 8 and 9 percent in mid-1990, the risk premium would be between 2 and 3 percent on the highest-quality real estate investments.

Compared to the historic return on common stocks, the risk premium for real estate is lower, because the highest-quality real estate investments are perceived to have less risk than an investment in a diversified portfolio. As various financial researchers have shown, over the last 50 years the risk premium (that is, the return in excess of the government rate) has been between 6 and 7 percent on a diversified portfolio of common stocks.

Moving away from the safest real estate investments to riskier investments, the risk premium continues to rise. A vacant office building in suburban Austin, Texas, for example, with a 36 percent vacancy rate probably has a nearly infinite risk premium. It is simply impossible to find financing because the future looks bleak.

Distinctions in Value

Level one in value distinctions is the project level: the cash flows to be discounted are the project's annual net operating incomes, regardless of how it is financed. Level two is the participant: the flows to be discounted are the annual cash flows to each particular participant. The lender gets origination fees plus interest and repayment of principal, the architect is paid fees, the leasing broker is paid commissions, and so on. In both level one and level two, the discounted cash flow mechanics are the same but the expected cash flows are different, and the risks are probably different so that the discount rates (r) also vary.

Discounted cash flow is a useful tool. For more complex projects, a distinction is often made between the project's present value and the present value to any individual participant in the project. Probably the best illustration of this point is the situation that owner-operators of S&Ls found themselves in in the 1980s.

Entering the 1980s, a large number of S&Ls would have had a negative net worth if all of their loans, their assets, had been carried at their market value instead of face value, because the loans had been made for a long period of time at a fixed rate of interest and interest rates had risen. Recognizing this problem but being unwilling to provide the financing necessary to cover the situation, the federal government allowed S&Ls (with 1980 and 1982 legislation) far greater freedom to invest beyond their local markets and to move out of loans for single-family houses and into commercial loans. This diversification supposedly reduced their risk and certainly, with investments that matured in a shorter time, such as development, would reduce their exposure to rising interest rates, the cause of their current dilemma.

In the mid-1980s, there was no logic to simply liquidating the enterprise, because the federal government was guaranteeing future deposits and it was relatively easy to raise funds. Not many good investment opportunities were available, however, and other lenders had more history and expertise in lending money for development than S&Ls. Hence, the only opportunities to invest any new funds were in high-risk development projects with less experienced developers, usually on a nonrecourse basis. (In other words, either the developer had no personal assets or would do business with the S&L only if the S&L agreed to look solely at the property in the event of default.)

In such a situation, a clear difference exists between the present value of a prospective development and an S&L's present value of participating in that development. Consider, for example, a project whose prospective rents do not justify the cost. In other words, the present value of owning and operating an office building is expected to be less than the cost of developing it. Thus, at level one (the project level), it is infeasible. It may be, however, that for both the developer and the lender, individual present values are positive.

Again, consider an S&L that is already broke but has the opportunity to raise money because its deposits are insured by the federal government. While the project has a negative present value, a nonzero chance exists that the project value will exceed its costs. Thus, the S&L is better off making the loan, generating origination fees today and having a 20 or 30 or 40 percent chance that it will work than simply closing the doors and going broke today. While the project has a negative present value, participation in it from a lender's perspective (given its initial condition) has a positive present value.

The developer's position is similar. Because the development fee is taken out at the front end and the developer has no personal liability if the project defaults but participates if it succeeds, the developer has a positive present value. Money now and a nonzero chance of positive equity in the future equal a decision by the developer to go ahead with the project.

A Simple Illustration

Assume that detailed market analysis leads to a proposed development whose features, functions, and benefits are expected to yield the annual net operating cash flows shown in Figure 3-4. Assume that initial leases are projected to roll over at the end of three years, and the cash flow during the fourth year represents the project's long-term potential.

The project is expected to take two years to build, with all costs (including hard construction, interest, marketing, and so on) totaling $3 million. The $3 million cost includes a $200,000 development fee over and above recovery of the developer's overhead during the construction period. After examining the current capital market, the developer obtains the following "optimal" financing.

A six-year miniperm loan with an S&L for $2.5 million has been established. Construction interest for the first two years is included in the $3 million total cost. For operating years 1 through 4, interest only, at 10.5 percent, will be paid.

At the end of six years (four years of operation), the developer believes the project can be sold to a pension fund at an 8 percent capitalization rate (that is, at 13.3 times the fourth year's net operating cash flow).

Such a development is fairly risky, and the market usually requires a 15 percent return on such investments. The developer has no personal liability on the loan beyond

FIGURE 3-4
CASH FLOW FOR A PROPOSED DEVELOPMENT

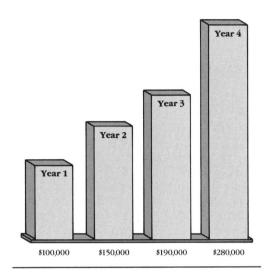

| $100,000 | $150,000 | $190,000 | $280,000 |

a guarantee that construction will be completed on budget and possibly a guarantee of the first two years of operating debt service. He is risking $500,000 (the projected cost less the amount of the loan) plus possibly two years of interest payments ($2.5 million × 10.5 percent = $262,500 per year); considering construction and operating risks, the developer wants a 20 percent return on the investment.

At level one, the value of the project using discounted cash flow is as shown in Figure 3-5. Everything suggests that upon completion, the project will be worth $2,481,000, which is less than its projected total cost of $3 million. At level two, however, the present value of the developer's participation in the proposed project is $574,400 without the guarantee of the first two years' debt service. This amount exceeds the equity of $500,000, so without any required guarantees on the loan, the developer might want to proceed despite the negative present value at level one. If, however, the S&L requires the debt service guarantees on the loan, the developer will not want to proceed.

The projected cost of the guarantees to the developer is $525,000 (two years'

FIGURE 3-5
DISCOUNTED CASH FLOW MODEL

	Present	End of Year 1	End of Year 2	End of Year 3	End of Year 4	End of Year 5	End of Year 6
Level One							
NOI		0	0	$100,000	$150,000	$190,000	$280,000
Sale Price ($280,000/.08)							$3,500,000
Total Cash Flow		0	0	$100,000	$150,000	$190,000	$3,780,000
Discount Factor $=\dfrac{1}{(1+r)^n}$							
Discount Rate = 15%				.87[a]	.76[a]	.66[a]	.57[a]
Total Present Value at Start of Year 3			$2,481,000				
Level Two							
Developer's Cash Flows without Loan Guarantees							
Development Fee	$100,000	$100,000					
Sale Price Less Loan Repayment							$1,280,000
Total Cash Flow to Developer Assuming No Guarantee	$100,000	$100,000					$1,280,000
Discount Factor $=\dfrac{1}{(1+r)^n}$							
Discount Rate = 20%		.83[a]	.69[a]	.58[a]	.48[a]	.40[a]	.33[a]
Present Value of Developer's Position at Start of Year 1	$574,400						
Cost of Guarantees				($162,500)	($112,500)		
Present Value of Developer's Guarantees	($148,250)						

[a]Rounded to two places.

debt service), less the project's NOIs of $250,000 for the first two years of operation, which should be available to service the debt. The present value of making these guarantees is $148,250 ($162,500 at the end of year three plus $112,500 at the end of year four, both discounted at 20 percent). Therefore, the developer's total projected outlay in terms of present value is $500,000 plus $148,250, or $648,250. If the developer must guarantee the first two years of debt service, then the present value is negative ($648,250 exceeds $574,400), and he does not proceed.

The remainder of this text focuses on estimating cash flows properly (at both level one and level two), because it is far more difficult than the mechanics of discounted cash flow. In real life, any such decision would be modeled to facilitate sensitivity analyses on a computer. In computerized sensitivity analyses, the software and hardware allow the developer to very quickly and easily test tradeoffs at level one in marketing or design using the logic of discounted cash flows. It also allows the developer to examine the attractiveness of participating in the development for each participant at level two. Consequently, it is very useful in loan negotiations as well as in feasibility analyses.[3]

Managing the Development Process Using Discounted Cash Flow

The critical decision about a project's feasibility involves the concept of present value. If the present value of the expected cash flow exceeds the cost, then the project is feasible. This step is not the end of the association of present value with the development process, however. The developer's role moves from initiator and promoter to manager over the course of a development. As manager of the process, the developer must continually monitor the position of all the different participants in the process.

The successful manager of the development process stays close to all of the partners and realizes that the present value of the project may be very different from the present value to them of participating in the project. By anticipating how changes over the course of the development affect the present value to each participant, the manager of the development process can anticipate problems. This flexibility has tremendous value—and it is available by applying discounted cash flow to each major participant's position in the project.

SUMMARY

This chapter has presented an overview of some fundamental financial concepts and illustrated the concept of present value or discounted cash flow. Looking at the whole picture, it is critical to remember that capital markets allocate funds based on expected return and the associated risk. Some member of the development team must find the right loan for a particular project. The best way to do so is for the development team's financial officer to determine which lender wants which loan and how that loan should be structured to make it most attractive to the lender.

The discounted cash flow method of determining a project's feasibility allows everything that one can know about a particular investment to be brought down to one number at one time. It is critical in the final decision and in the ongoing management of a real estate development project.

NOTES

1. For readers who are untrained in finance, a helpful discussion is Charles Wurtzebach and Mike E. Miles, *Modern Real Estate*, 4th ed. (New York: John Wiley & Sons, 1991). Other helpful books and articles that define concepts and explain calculations are listed in the accompanying bibliography for Section I.

2. Mortgage brokers are distinguished from mortgage bankers in that they do not take title to loans but facilitate commercial mortgage lending.

3. A complete description of lenders and their operations is found in William B. Brueggeman and Leo D. Stone, *Real Estate Finance*, 8th ed. (Homewood, Ill.: Richard D. Irwin, 1989). The Salomon Brothers Real Estate Research Series also provides more sophisticated and contemporary analysis of new capital market instruments. Similar descriptions are available from Goldman Sachs Real Estate Research for its real estate–oriented capital market innovations.

Bibliography

Part I. Introduction

BASIC REAL ESTATE AND PLANNING TEXTS

Barnett, Jonathan. *An Introduction to Urban Design*. New York: Harper & Row, 1982.

Bjork, Gordon C. *Life, Liberty, and Property*. Lexington, Mass.: Lexington Books, 1980.

Bloom, George F., Arthur M. Weimer, and Jeffrey D. Fisher. *Real Estate*. 8th ed. New York: John Wiley & Sons, 1982.

Bookout, Lloyd W., Jr., et al. *Residential Development Handbook*. 2d ed. Washington, D.C.: ULI–the Urban Land Institute, 1990.

Burrows, Lawrence B. *Growth Management: Issues, Techniques, and Policy Implications*. New Brunswick, N.J.: Rutgers Univ., Center for Urban Policy Research, 1978.

Catanese, Anthony, and James C. Snyder. *An Introduction to Urban Planning*. 2d ed. New York: McGraw-Hill, 1988.

Chapin, F. Stuart, Jr., and Edward J. Kaiser. *Urban Land Use Planning*. 3d ed. Champaign: Univ. of Illinois Press, 1979.

De Chiara, Joseph, and Lee E. Koppelman. *Time-Saver Standards for Site Planning*. New York: McGraw-Hill, 1984.

DeGrove, John M. *Land, Growth, and Politics*. Washington, D.C.: Planners Press, American Planning Association, 1984.

de Neufville, Judith I., ed. *The Land Use Policy Debate in the United States*. New York: Plenum Press, 1981.

Ficek, Edmund F., Thomas P. Henderson, and Ross H. Johnson. *Real Estate Principles and Practices*. 4th ed. Columbus, Ohio: Merrill Publishing Co., 1987.

Getzels, Judith, and Charles Thurow, eds. *Rural and Small Town Planning*. Chicago: ASPO, 1980.

Godschalk, David R., et al. *Constitutional Issues of Growth Management*. Rev. ed. Chicago: Planners Press, American Planning Association, 1979.

Goodman, William I., and Eric C. Freund, eds. *Principles and Practices of Urban Planning*. 4th ed. Washington, D.C.: International City Management Association, 1968.

Graaskamp, James A. *Fundamentals of Real Estate Development*. Washington, D.C.: ULI–the Urban Land Institute, 1981.

Greer, Gaylon E., and Michael D. Farrell. *Contemporary Real Estate: Theory and Practice*. Chicago: Dryden Press, 1983.

Harwood, Bruce. *Real Estate Principles*. 4th ed. Englewood Cliffs, N.J.: Prentice-Hall, 1985.

Healy, Robert G., and John S. Rosenburg. *Land Use and the States*. 2d ed. Baltimore: Johns Hopkins Univ. Press for Resources for the Future, 1979.

Heilbrun, James. *Urban Economics and Public Policy*. 3d ed. New York: St. Martin's Press, 1987.

Kau, James B., and C.F. Sirmans. *Real Estate*. New York: McGraw-Hill, 1985.

Lefcoe, George, ed. *Urban Land Policy for the 1980s*. Lexington, Mass.: Lexington Books, 1983.

Lynch, Kevin. *A Theory of Good City Form*. Cambridge, Mass.: MIT Press, 1981.

Lynch, Kevin, and Gary Hack. *Site Planning*. 3d ed. Cambridge, Mass.: MIT Press, 1984.

McHarg, Ian. *Design with Nature*. Garden City, N.Y.: Natural History Press for the American Museum of Natural History, 1989.

McMahan, John. *Property Development*. 2d ed. New York: McGraw-Hill, 1989.

Marsh, William M. *Environmental Analysis for Land Use and Site Planning*. New York: McGraw-Hill, 1978.

Ring, Alfred A., and Jerome Dasso. *Real Estate Principles and Practices*. 10th ed. Englewood Cliffs, N.J.: Prentice-Hall, 1985.

Shenkel, William M. *Modern Real Estate Principles*. 3d ed. Homewood, Ill. Richard D. Irwin, 1984.

Shirvani, Hamid. *The Urban Design Process*. New York: Van Nostrand Reinhold, 1985.

Smith, Halbert C., Carl J. Tschappat, and Ronald L. Racster. *Real Estate and Urban Development*. 3d ed. Homewood, Ill.: Richard D. Irwin, 1987.

So, Frank S., et al., eds. *The Practice of Local Government Planning*. Washington, D.C.: International City Management Association, 1987.

Unger, Maurice A., and Georgia R. Karvel. *Real Estate Principles and Practices*. 8th ed. Cincinnati: South-Western Publishing Co., 1987.

Urban Land Institute. *Management and Control of Growth*. Occasional series. Washington, D.C.: ULI–the Urban Land Institute, 1975 forward.

Whyte, William H. *The Social Life of Small Urban Spaces*. Washington, D.C.: Conservation Foundation, 1980.

Wofford, Larry E. *Real Estate*. 2d ed. New York: John Wiley & Sons, 1986.

Wolf, Peter M. *Land in America*. New York: Pantheon Books, 1981.

Wurtzebach, Charles H., and Mike E. Miles. *Modern Real Estate*. 4th ed. New York: John Wiley & Sons, 1991.

More specialized publications are available from textbook publishers and from the following sources:

American Institute of Real Estate Appraisers
430 North Michigan Avenue
Chicago, Illinois 60611
(312) 329-8559

Building Owners and Managers Association
1201 New York Avenue, N.W., Suite 300
Washington, D.C. 20005
(202) 408-2662

Commercial-Investment Real Estate Council
Realtor's National Marketing Institute
430 North Michigan Avenue
Chicago, Illinois 60611
(312) 329-8624

International Council of Shopping Centers
665 Fifth Avenue
New York, New York 10022
(212) 421-8181

Mortgage Bankers Association of America
1125 15th Street, N.W.
Washington, D.C. 20005
(202) 861-6500

National Association of Home Builders
15th & M Streets, N.W.
Washington, D.C. 20005
(202) 822-0200

National Association of Industrial and Office Parks
1215 Jefferson Davis Highway, Suite 100
Arlington, Virginia 22202
(703) 979-3400

National Association of Realtors
430 North Michigan Avenue
Chicago, Illinois 60611
(312) 329-8200

National Council of Real Estate Investment Fiduciaries
276 Fifth Avenue, Suite 902
New York, New York 10001
(212) 532-6440

Realtors National Marketing Institute
430 North Michigan Avenue, Suite 500
Chicago, Illinois 60611
(312) 670-3780

Society of Industrial and Office Realtors
National Association of Realtors
777 14th Street, N.W., Suite 400
Washington, D.C. 20005
(202) 383-1150

ULI–the Urban Land Institute
625 Indiana Avenue, N.W., Suite 400
Washington, D.C. 20004
(202) 624-7000

INVESTMENT REFERENCES

Alexander, Gordon J., and William F. Sharpe. *Investments*. 4th ed. Englewood Cliffs, N.J.: Prentice-Hall, 1990.

Allen, Roger H. *Real Estate Strategy*. 3d ed. Cincinnati: South-Western, 1988.

Amling, Frederick. *Investments: An Introduction to Analysis and Management*. 6th ed. Englewood Cliffs, N.J.: Prentice-Hall, 1989.

Armfield, W.A. *Investment in Subsidized Housing: Opportunities and Risks*. New York: Pilot Books, 1979.

Atterbury, William. *Modern Real Estate Finance*. 3d ed. New York: John Wiley & Sons, 1984.

Baker, D. Richard, and Rick Stephan Hayes. *A Guide to Lease Financing*. New York: John Wiley & Sons, 1981.

Beaton, William R. *Real Estate Finance*. 2d ed. Englewood Cliffs, N.J.: Prentice-Hall, 1982.

Brueggeman, William B., and Leo D. Stone. *Real Estate Finance*. 8th ed. Homewood, Ill.: Richard D. Irwin, 1989.

Case, Fred E. *Investing in Real Estate*. Englewood Cliffs, N.J.: Prentice-Hall, 1988.

Cooper, James R., and Steven Pyhrr. *Real Estate Investment: Strategy, Analysis, Decision*. 2d ed. New York: John Wiley & Sons, 1989.

Copeland, Thomas E., and J. Fred Weston. *Financial Theory and Corporate Policy*. 3d ed. New York: Addison-Wesley Co., 1988.

Creedy, Judith, and Norbert F. Wall. *Real Estate: Investment by Objectives*. New York: McGraw-Hill, 1979.

Dasso, Jerome, and Gerald Kuhn. *Real Estate Finance*. Englewood Cliffs, N.J.: Prentice-Hall, 1983.

Dennis, Marshall. *Mortgage Lending Fundamentals and Practices*. 2d ed. Englewood Cliffs, N.J.: Prentice-Hall (Reston), 1983.

Dougall, Herbert E., and Jack E. Gaumnitz. *Capital Markets and Institutions*. 5th ed. Englewood Cliffs, N.J.: Prentice-Hall, 1986.

Epley, Donald R. *Basic Real Estate Finance and Investments*. 3d ed. New York: John Wiley & Sons, 1988.

Epley, Donald R., and James A. Millar. *Basic Real Estate Finance and Investments*. 2d ed. New York: John Wiley & Sons, 1984.

Greer, Gaylon E., and Michael D. Farrell. *Investment Analysis for Real Estate Decisions*. 2d ed. Chicago: Longman Financial, 1988.

Henning, Charles, et al. *Financial Markets and the Economy*. 5th ed. Englewood Cliffs, N.J.: Prentice-Hall, 1988.

Hines, Mary Alice. *Real Estate Finance*. Englewood Cliffs, N.J.: Prentice-Hall, 1978.

Hoagland, Henry E., and Leo D. Stone. *Real Estate Finance*. 8th ed. Homewood, Ill.: Richard D. Irwin, 1989.

Irwin, Robert. *The New Mortgage Game*. New York: McGraw-Hill, 1982.

Jaffe, Austin, and C.F. Sirmans, *Fundamentals of Real Estate Investment*. 2d ed. Englewood Cliffs, N.J.: Prentice-Hall, 1989.

Lyons, Paul. *Investing in Residential Real Estate*. Englewood Cliffs, N.J.: Prentice-Hall (Reston), 1981.

Messner, Stephen D., et al. *Marketing Investment Real Estate: Finance Taxation Techniques*. 3d ed. Englewood Cliffs, N.J.: Prentice-Hall, 1986.

Meyers, Myron. *Foreign Investment in United States Real Estate*. Homewood, Ill.: Dow Jones–Irwin, 1982.

Miles, Martin J. *Real Estate Investor's Complete Handbook*. Englewood Cliffs, N.J.: Prentice-Hall, 1982.

Morton, Tom. *Real Estate Finance: A Practical Approach*. Glenview, Ill.: Scott Foresman & Co., 1983.

Reilly, Frank K. *Investment Analysis and Portfolio Management*. 3d ed. Chicago: Dryden Press, 1989.

REIT Fact Book. Washington, D.C.: National Association of Real Estate Investment Trusts, 1990.

Ross, Stephen A., and Randolph W. Westerfield. *Corporate Finance*. St. Louis: Times Mirror/Mosby College Publishers, 1988.

Seldin, Maury. *Real Estate Investments for Profit through Appreciation*. Englewood, Cliffs, N.J.: Prentice-Hall (Reston), 1980.

Seldin, Maury, and Richard H. Swesnik. *Real Estate Investment Strategy*. 3d ed. New York: John Wiley & Sons, 1985.

Shapiro, Alan C. *Multinational Financial Management*. 3d ed. Boston: Allyn & Bacon, 1989.

Sirmans, C.F. *Real Estate Finance*. 2d ed. New York: McGraw-Hill, 1988.

Stegman, Michael A. *Housing Finance and Public Policy*. New York: Van Nostrand Reinhold, 1986.

Stevenson, Eric. *Financing Income-Producing Real Estate*. 2d ed. Washington, D.C.: Mortgage Bankers Association, 1988.

Sweat, Ray, et al. *Mortgages and Alternate Mortgage Instruments*. New York: Practising Law Institute, 1981.

Unger, Maurice A. *How to Invest in Real Estate*. Rev. ed. New York: McGraw-Hill, 1984.

Unger, Maurice A., and Ronald W. Melicher. *Real Estate Finance*. 2d ed. Cincinnati: South-Western, 1984.

Van Horne, James C. *Financial Management and Policy*. 8th ed. Englewood Cliffs, N.J.: Prentice-Hall, 1989.

Vernor, James D. *An Introduction to Risk Management in Property Development*. Washington, D.C.: ULI–the Urban Land Institute, 1981.

Weidemer, John P. *Real Estate Investment*. 4th ed. Englewood Cliffs, N.J.: Prentice-Hall (Reston), 1988.

Periodicals

Federal Home Loan Bank Board Journal (monthly). Atlanta: Federal Home Loan Bank Board.

Federal Reserve Bulletin (monthly). Washington, D.C.: Board of Governors of the Federal Reserve System.

Financial Analysts Journal (bimonthly). New York: Financial Analysts Federation.

Financial Management (quarterly). Tampa: College of Business Administration, Univ. of South Florida.

Freddie Mac Reports (monthly). Reston, Virginia: Federal Home Loan Mortgage Corporation.

Housing Finance Review (quarterly). Philadelphia: Whitmore Publishing.

Institutional Real Estate Letter (monthly). San Francisco: Institutional Real Estate.

International Real Estate Journal (quarterly). Scottsdale, Arizona: International Real Estate Institute.

Investment Research Review (monthly). London: Richard Willis Research.

Japanese Investment in U.S. Real Estate Review (monthly). Phoenix, Arizona: Mead Ventures.

Journal of Real Estate Finance and Economics (quarterly). Boston: Kluwer Academic Publishers.

Market Profile (quarterly). New York: Baring Institutional Realty.

Mortgage Banking (formerly *Mortgage Banker*) (monthly). Washington, D.C.: Mortgage Bankers Association of America.

Mortgage and Real Estate Executives Report (bimonthly). New York: Warren, Gorham, and Lamont.

National Council of Real Estate Investment Fiduciaries Report (quarterly). Washington, D.C.: NCREIF.

National Real Estate Investor (monthly). Atlanta: Communications Channels, Inc.

National Thrift News (weekly). New York: National Thrift News.

REIT Report (bimonthly). Washington, D.C.: National Association of Real Estate Investment Trusts.

Resolution Trust Reporter (weekly). New York: Dorset Group.

Savings Institutions Sourcebook (annually). Chicago: U.S. League of Savings Institutions.

Savings and Loan News (monthly). Chicago: U.S. League of Savings Institutions.

Secondary Mortgage Markets (quarterly). Washington, D.C.: Federal Home Loan Mortgage Corporation.

The Stanger Register: Partnership Profiles (monthly). Shrewsbury, N.J.: Stanger & Co.

PART II
THE HISTORY OF
REAL ESTATE DEVELOPMENT
IN THE UNITED STATES

Chapter 4

The Colonial Period to The Late 1800s

Real estate has been a part of the American tradition for quite some time. To paraphrase Calvin Coolidge, the business of the United States is real estate. More than any other country, the ownership of land and buildings in the United States is widespread; millions of people own, buy, and sell real property. Mass participation in the real estate market has been a fundamental characteristic of the economic life of this country since its origins.

The settlers and colonists who migrated here from many parts of the world came in search of greater freedom and prosperity—and owning land was essential to attaining both goals. Throughout the 18th and 19th centuries, Americans fought for greater legal rights and opportunities to become property owners. They battled for changes in the laws and administration of colonial governments, and later, after the successful war for independence, they lobbied the federal government and state and local governments for basic reforms to establish and protect private property rights, to make it easier and safer to obtain and develop land.

No institution or practice was left untouched by this sweeping movement: legislatures and the courts established and enforced new laws and definitions of the rights inherent in property and contracts,

land was physically surveyed and real estate market mechanisms organized to facilitate sales, a vast array of subsidies was granted to prospective settlers to enable them to afford to own land, and enormous public investments in improved transportation and infrastructure helped make the land accessible and productive. All of these actions were designed to increase property values for the new private owners, and in many cases they succeeded.

The story of how these changes came about and how modern attitudes toward land evolved begins in this chapter and continues through Chapters 5 and 6. This chapter covers the history of real estate development from the colonial period to the late 1800s (although the chapters overlap somewhat), including:

- Real estate as an American tradition;
- Land subdivision and residential development; and
- The role of railroads and railroad barons in real estate development.

REAL ESTATE AS AN AMERICAN TRADITION

The extensive privatization of U.S. land is a remarkable story, if only because the settlers initially held land in a highly centralized pattern of ownership and control. During the colonial period, most land was in the hands of the various governors by authority of the English crown and other sovereign powers; it was purchased or violently appropriated from the Native American tribes that inhabited the continent when the European settlers first arrived, beginning in the 17th century.

In the early 1600s, settlers were brought to this country to farm land owned by the Virginia Company; they were paid in money and shares of stock for their labors. The early settlers quickly rebelled against this practice, however, insisting on ownership of the land they were farming. In 1616, the Virginia colonial governor acquiesced, granting free and clear title to a minimum of 100 acres for each farmer—an action that set an important precedent for patterns of settlement in the country.

Colonial governors had many different methods of spreading the ownership of land. Outright grants were given for farming land, settling the frontier, serving in the military, a religious order, or as an educator, and having political connections. Large parcels of land were sold to investors, speculators, land developers, and settlement ventures. In Massachusetts and other New England colonies, governors granted and sold land to groups for establishing towns.

Once independence was achieved and the colonies formed the United States, the federal and state governments together still owned the overwhelming majority of all the land. Much more land was added to the public domain during the next century through the Louisiana Purchase, the annexation of Texas, the war with Mexico, the purchase of Alaska, and several treaties with Spain and Great Britain. Much time and effort were expended dispensing this land from public to private ownership. Of the total current U.S. land area of 2.3 billion acres, only 20 percent of it was never in the public domain. The federal government disposed of more than 1 billion acres through land sales and land grants to veterans, homesteaders, railroads, and state governments. The states in turn sold or granted much of their public lands to private individuals and companies.

At first, public land was put into private ownership mainly through sales of large numbers of acres to individual inves-

tors. The sales occurred as a result of negotiated deals, public auctions, and fixed prices per acre set by Congress. This approach reached its peak in 1836, when the federal government sold 20 million acres, most of it for $1.25 an acre. The problem with this technique was that many prospective frontier settlers could not afford to pay even the minimum government price to purchase federal land, let alone the often much higher prices of the private speculators who bought public land wholesale and attempted to resell it retail. The huge numbers of land-hungry pioneers were also voters, however, and they rebelled in the mid-19th century as their forebears had done two centuries earlier in Virginia.

Fee Simple Real Estate Transactions

In 1862, Congress responded to this political "Free Soil Movement" by passing the Homestead Act, enabling settlers who did not already own sufficient land to be granted title to 160 acres for each adult in the family simply by living on and improving the "homestead" for a period of five years. No cash payments were required, thereby opening up ownership to a wide segment of the population that had previously been excluded. The system was also subject to a great deal of fraud and abuse, allowing large landowners and wealthy investors to obtain substantial public acreage at bargain prices.

Despite the abuses, the Homestead Act was extremely popular, and it was followed in the 1870s by additional federal laws granting free 20- and 40-acre parcels to settlers engaging in mining and cultivating trees. In all, the government gave away nearly 300 million acres of public land at no charge to private owners through the various homesteading programs—almost as much land as through cash sales.

The creation of the fee simple system of complete property rights through private ownership, including the ability of one private party to convey those rights to another through sale, lease, or trade, generated a vibrant real estate market that attracted substantial amounts of investment capital. In the early years, the money moving into and out of real property was extremely volatile and subject to wide fluctuations in amounts and prices. By the late 18th century, land speculation had already become a main preoccupation of U.S. citizens. Legendary fortunes were made and lost as the steady influx of immigrants entered the new nation. Rapidly rising prices frequently led to a mania for land gambling. Many people, like Charles Dickens's character Martin Chuzzlewit, got caught up in the excitement and the greed and were swindled in the process, while countless others were eventually disappointed when the inevitable financial panic led to a drastic fall in prices. Every time new territory was opened for settlement and land was subdivided for sale, these speculative cycles of boom and bust were repeated. Many colorful books and articles have recounted tales of glory and grief in American "land bubbles," both before and after they burst.[1]

"Land-jobbing" or "town-jobbing" by obtaining land and selling it through promotional schemes to speculators and settlers was one of the principal means of accumulating wealth in the early history of the United States, and all of the major business and government leaders—from Benjamin Franklin to George Washington—engaged in it. Indeed, the father of our country was a professional land surveyor in addition to being a planter, general, and president, and he was an energetic entrepreneur in the real estate business who was heavily involved in one of the country's first big development deals—the establishment of the District of Columbia as the nation's capital.

Developing the District Of Columbia

The selection of the site for and the development of the District of Columbia as the Federal City was based on President Washington's plan for encouraging private land sales and trading. Speculative real estate activity in the nation's capital got so overheated before it crashed that a visiting French dignitary, the Duke de La Rochefoucauld, wrote in 1797:

> In America, where more than in any other country in the world, a desire for wealth

TERMS of SALE of LOTS in the CITY of WASHINGTON, the Eighth Day of *October*, 1792.

ALL Lands purchased at this Sale, are to be subject to the Terms and Conditions declared by the President, pursuant to the Deeds in Trust.

The purchaser is immediately to pay one fourth part of the purchase money; the residue is to be paid in three equal annual payments, with yearly interest of six per cent. on the whole principal unpaid : If any payment is not made at the day, the payments made are to be forfeited, or the whole principal and interest unpaid may be recovered on one suit and execution, in the option of the Commissioners.

The purchaser is to be entitled to a conveyance, on the whole purchase money and interest being paid, and not before. No bid under Three Dollars to be received.

Advertisement for the public auction of lots in Washington, D.C., in 1792, where the lowest acceptable bid was $3.00.

is the prevailing passion, there are few schemes [that] are not made the means of extensive speculations; and that of erecting the Federal City presented irresistible temptations, which were not in fact neglected. . . . The building of a house for the President and a place for the sittings of Congress excited, in the purchasers of lots, the hope of a new influx of speculations. The public papers were filled with exaggerated praises of the new city; in a word, with all the artifices [that] trading people in every part of the world are accustomed to employ in the disposal of their wares, and [that] are perfectly known, and amply practiced in this new world.[2]

Both the federal and state governments used land sales as a primary method of raising revenues to pay for public improvements. Washington, D.C., was also to be developed on this basis, with both President Washington and future presidents Thomas Jefferson and James Madison among the private bidders for purchase of subdivided urban lots at the initial public auction in 1791. Only 35 lots were actually sold at that time, leading to additional promotional efforts that culminated in the wholesale purchase on credit of 7,235 lots by a syndicate headed by Robert Morris, a Philadelphia merchant, well-known Revolutionary War financier, and major real estate investor in Pennsylvania and New York. Morris and his two partners, James Greenleaf and John Nicholson, promised to bring needed capital for land development and building construction into the Federal City, starting with the "Morristown" project, 20 two-story brick houses near the Capitol. George Washington also built several for-sale row houses in the same area.

President Washington had commissioned Major Pierre Charles L'Enfant in 1791 to design a long-term plan for development of the entire Federal City, including arrangement of the street system and the public buildings. Though little of

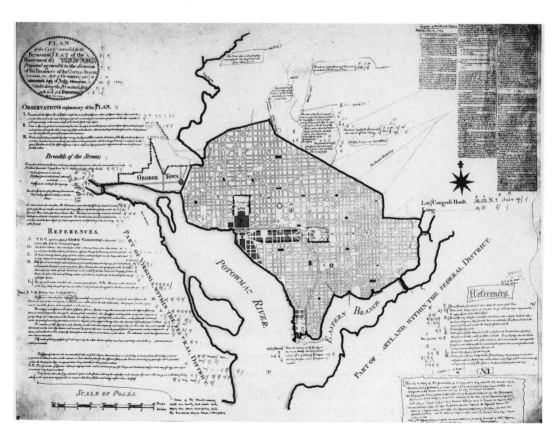

L'Enfant's 1792 plan for the Federal City. Although it was implemented slowly, two centuries later much of L'Enfant's original plan for a majestic city to rival any of the great European capitals is now complete.

L'Enfant's scheme was immediately adopted, much of his grand conception was eventually realized over the next two centuries. In the 1790s, the federal government tried to stimulate new investment and economic and population growth by requiring all those who purchased lots to construct permanent, good-quality, two-story brick or stone buildings, with minimum and maximum prescribed heights to ensure uniformity in the appearance of the streetscape.

Unfortunately, Robert Morris's syndicate defaulted on its payments for the Washington lots and failed to complete construction of Morristown, and all three principals were sent to debtors' prison. Land prices fell precipitously, and the federal district remained for decades what Charles Dickens called "the City of Magnificent Intentions."[3] Nevertheless, the city named for George Washington eventually proved him right—that extensive public and private investment, good planning, quality development and construction, desirable location, a sound economic and employment base, and a growing population would ultimately produce a healthy real estate market with rising long-term values.

The Holland Land Company

While the story of the promotion of U.S. land and town sales is full of get-rich-quick hype and broken promises and dreams, it is also a story of the basic fundamentals of real estate development, as an entire continent was steadily improved with productive economic uses for rural and urban land. One example is the Holland Land Company, which bought 3.3 million acres of land in western New York State from Robert Morris in 1792. Morris had purchased the vast property on credit, hoping that rising prices would yield huge profits through quick turnover.

The Holland Land Company, a group of Dutch financiers and wealthy investors, acquired the immense territory with the intention of breaking it up into large parcels and rapidly dispensing them wholesale to major investors. A serious downturn in property markets brought on by the financial panic that ensued after the collapse of Robert Morris's syndicate in Washington,

D.C., however, led the Holland Land Company to reassess its strategy. The principals decided out of necessity to engage in long-term, value-added investment and development. Land would be sold retail to new settlers who could be induced to migrate to the region only through the development of infrastructure and services that would make both the farmland and the sites for towns physically accessible and economically viable as locations for commerce, industry, and permanent residence.

In 1797, the Holland Land Company hired Joseph Ellicott, an experienced Pennsylvania land surveyor, to serve as chief land agent and to direct its operations in upstate New York. For the next two decades, Ellicott implemented a comprehensive long-term plan for the development of the territory and the retail sale of land. Included in the company's holdings was the city of Buffalo, which Ellicott laid out at the western boundary of the territory along Lake Erie. Ellicott began in the late 1790s by conducting a massive survey of the region and devising a geometric system of subdividing land into six-mile-square townships so that lots could be easily and clearly identified and transferred. Small lots of 40 to 160 acres were surveyed and targeted to prospective farmers and artisans. Low prices and easy credit terms were tailored to appeal to the numerous potential clients. Ellicott also developed an extensive marketing network of land agents to promote retail sales. The federal government later adopted his path-breaking work in surveying when selling public lands in 40-acre parcels. Improving the process of facilitating transactions has always been crucial to the evolution of U.S. real estate development.

Ellicott's long-term development strategy included the construction of hundreds of miles of roads through the wooded wilderness and the building of towns at strategic points along the newly developed transportation routes. The company's land offices were located in the towns, and Ellicott engaged in a wide variety of promotional activities to stimulate population growth and settlement in the towns and in the hinterland. In addition to building long-distance roads, the Holland Land Company assisted in the construction of sawmills, gristmills, distilleries, and potash refineries to stimulate regional economic activity that would enhance demand for land sales and leasing. Further, when a town center was first platted and opened for development, the company frequently subsidized the pioneering private owners of general stores, inns, taverns, grain mills, ironworks, smithies, and other providers of essential goods and services. They also donated land for schools, churches, and public squares.

Joseph Ellicott successfully sold a great deal of land and within a decade had brought more than 200,000 new settlers to the Holland Land Company's vast territory, prompting the president of Yale College to write in 1810, "It is questionable whether mankind had ever seen so large a tract changed so suddenly from a wilderness into a well-inhabited and well-cultivated country."[4] Unfortunately, most of the settlers who had bought land on credit with little or no down payment found themselves unable to meet the credit terms to complete their purchases. Thus, they became essentially tenants of the Holland Land Company, and in 1820, the company attempted to bail out of the situation by reselling all its land to the state of New York. The legislature refused to buy, and the company was forced to squeeze more cash from the settlers or repossess their holdings.

Neither approach proved economically or politically worthwhile, and in 1830, the company helped organize the New York Life Insurance and Trust Company, which began to refinance Holland Land's creditors by converting the unpaid sales contracts into first mortgage loans. A powerful local businessman and politician, William H. Seward, arranged in 1836 for Wall Street and European investors to purchase the loans, a popular act that helped elect him governor of New York in 1838. As Seward put it, "In less than eighteen months, four thousand persons whom I found occupying lands, chiefly under expired and legally enforceable contracts of sale, and excited and embarrassed alike by the oppression and uncertainty of ever obtaining titles, became freeholders."[5]

The Holland Land Company had sold its property to a New York investment syndicate in 1835 for $1 million, leaving the continuation of the massive enterprise for large-scale land development to a new group of real estate entrepreneurs. Fortunately for the Dutch owners of Holland Land, they managed to sell their holdings before the major economic depression of 1837. But the enduring heritage of their nearly four decades in the land development business was not the record of financial deals; it was Joseph Ellicott's establishing a prominent national role model as an early American "community builder."

John Jacob Astor

An alternative model to either short-term speculators or long-term land developers of for-sale properties is the "Astor method," based on the real estate career of John Jacob Astor, one of the country's richest and best-known businessmen in the first half of the 19th century. Astor, who had started as a fur trader in the Pacific Northwest, owned a tremendous amount of real estate, including numerous land parcels and buildings in Manhattan that he began accumulating in 1810. His philosophy of real estate was to purchase land at low prices and wait patiently for the market to change and for urban growth to eventually drive values exponentially higher. While waiting for these long-term increases, he collected substantial rental income from his extensive commercial and residential real estate holdings.

Astor was always eager to buy properties when he could get a bargain, and he rarely sold except when he needed money to purchase more real estate or occasionally when values skyrocketed. During the crash of 1837, for example, Astor acquired numerous lots and buildings at "distress sale" prices and foreclosed on hundreds of properties on which he held or obtained the mortgages. He seldom invested in any significant improvements, preferring to lease properties and earn profits primarily from rental income. By 1840, Astor was the country's wealthiest man, with an estate worth more than $20 million, attributable largely to the tremendous growth in the value of his urban real estate assets. Shortly before his death in 1848, he declared, "Could I begin life again, knowing what I now know, and had money to invest, I would buy every foot of land on the island of Manhattan."[6]

Times Square, 1910. To the right of the well-known Flatiron Building is the Hotel Astor, designed in Second Empire style by Clinton and Russell and once one of New York's finest hotels.

Capital Improvement Projects

Just as the Holland Land Company discovered it had to invest in infrastructure to enhance the value of its real estate assets, the federal, state, and local governments engaged in wide-ranging development of roads, canals, ports, and a host of other facilities to enable them to turn public lands into private and, most important, to promote growth in population and employment. "Boosterism" and public investment went hand in hand. Often such capital improvement projects were financed through borrowing by issuing bonds, to be repaid from user fees like bridge, highway, and canal tolls or rail and transit fares combined with revenues from the sale or lease of nearby land that had increased in value because of the new infrastructure. For over 200 years, private developers have used this same model when installing major improvements. Private utility, transit, railroad, and other companies similarly used these methods, sometimes with public powers of land acquisition or even outright grants of public land. In other cases, taxpayers voted to sell bonds for improvements to be repaid through increased property taxes, anticipating that future population growth would increase the tax base and property values so that both the public treasury and private landowners who purchased local real estate would benefit through "boosting" the area with expensive new government-financed construction.

The public sector's role was crucial in facilitating successful development and widespread ownership. Forms of intervention ranged from the ubiquitous rectangular survey that opened up the western lands to regulations like the legal protection of property transactions, building codes, and land use controls that have enhanced the physical environment, public safety, and property values. Further, the role of financing has been essential to the success of real estate ventures, as the saga of the Holland Land Company demonstrates. As noted in the first two chapters, governments, through controls on currency, regulatory oversight of publicly chartered financial institutions, and macroeconomic policies, have played a major role in encouraging and monitoring the apparatus of money and credit that has enabled U.S. real estate development to thrive and grow.

LAND SUBDIVISION AND RESIDENTIAL DEVELOPMENT

While the disposition of public lands involved millions of acres sold or granted by the federal and state governments and resold by private investors and developers, the nature of land subdivision fell into two different categories: larger acreage for farming or other essentially rural uses and smaller lots for towns and urban uses. As cities grew in the 19th century, more and more land was subdivided into building lots within existing urban areas and in the open countryside to establish new cities. Many of the latter enterprises never succeeded, leaving ghost towns in their wake, but some did grow from modest beginnings. Chicago, for example, grew in a brief seven decades from a tiny hamlet inhabited by a few hundred pioneers in the 1830s to the fifth largest city in the world by 1900. The biggest single use of land in these metropolitan communities was for housing the steadily growing population. Land and in some cases buildings were continually carved up to provide dwelling units for new residents.

An enormous amount of urban housing in the United States consisted of single-family detached dwellings because of the abundance of cheap land, inexpensive construction materials, and a constant stream of innovations in transportation technology that made residential dispersion possible. In the older and more crowded cities of the early 19th century, attached row houses (typically constructed in block groups by speculative builders) and multi-family dwellings converted from spacious mansions accommodated a higher-density population that walked to work in areas where available space was limited. Later in the century, a number of other dwelling types made their debut, including luxury apartment buildings, squalid tenements, and structures housing two to four families with modest-income owners often living in one of the units and in some cases constructing the building themselves.

Unlike most other countries, the U.S. urban real estate market allowed for mass participation. Vacant building lots were frequently sold on credit with small down payments required, making it relatively affordable for a wide range of potential purchasers. Millions of people bought lots, including families who wanted to build their own houses, entrepreneurial builders who wanted to construct dwellings for sale or rent, and investors who wanted to turn over the land for a fast profit or hold it for long-term gain. Many of these subdivisions had only the most rudimentary improvements, such as unpaved streets, and lacked basic amenities like sanitary and storm sewers, a supply of fresh water, or curbs and sidewalks. In higher-income communities, developers sometimes installed key improvements in advance of sales and added those costs to the prices of lots; more common was for infrastructure and amenities to be built and provided after initial sales of land, to be paid for by individual lot owners through special tax assessments. Subdivisions intended to house the working classes generally did without many amenities to reduce the costs of property ownership for people of limited means. Often they lacked basic features like sewers and paved streets as well. Just like building and housing codes, society's minimum acceptable standards for neighborhood development are much higher today than a century ago.

In the 19th century, most urban subdivisions, whether already built-up and inhabited or new and vacant, also lacked any significant land use controls. Mixtures of lot size and shape and of building density, height, bulk, form, occupancy, and use were typical and could be limited only through actions by private owners. Deed restrictions as private contracts were the one regulatory device available to developers and property owners, but they were difficult to establish and enforce and were used mostly in a small number of new, high-income neighborhoods. By the 1920s, the extensive use of private deed restrictions and the introduction of public controls through zoning and subdivision regulations brought new elements of stability and order to residential real estate development.

Not only was it possible for the first time for millions of people to become urban property owners, but many were also actively engaged in the real estate business. Selling one's own or someone else's property as an agent was a completely unregulated activity in the 19th century and occupied the time and energy of a substantial segment of the population, especially during boom times. Regrettably, some of these vendors indulged in unethical, fraudulent, fly-by-night practices that at times lent sales agents, developers, and landlords an unsavory image and later led to calls for reform by angry private citizens, concerned industry leaders, and progressive public officials.

In addition to ownership, sales, and property management, building construction was also a widespread endeavor. Most contractors and subcontractors, particularly in the residential field, were very small-scale operators, often shuttling back and forth between contractor and laborer. The vast majority of houses were built under contract to the owner-users, with a signifi-cant segment actually built by the owner-users with the help of family and friends. Stock architectural plans could be easily obtained, and only a minority of houses, mainly for the wealthy, were truly custom-designed by professional architects. By the early 20th century, the Sears catalog was even selling many different models of pre-fabricated houses that came in pieces with a manual explaining how to put them together, like today's Swedish furniture. Contract work was the principal mode, but many large and small builders also constructed houses as speculative investments, though generally just one or two and seldom more than five such houses per year. Merchant homebuilding, as this method came to be known, did not really begin to dominate the housing industry until the 1950s. The standard approach for even sophisticated real estate developers was primarily to sell finished building lots, not completed houses.

Advances in Transportation And the Rise of Suburban Development: Llewellyn Park, New Jersey, and Riverside, Illinois

The ability to plan and develop large-scale urban, primarily residential, neighborhoods and communities depended on new advances in transportation technology that enabled residents to reach their places of employment without being confined to the tight boundaries, high densities, and mixed uses of the "walking city." By the early 19th century, the population of cities began to spread out and to differentiate uses by location. Commuter ferry service by steamship across rivers and other bodies of water served as one means of circulation. Ground transportation started with the omnibus—a horse-drawn urban stagecoach—for short in-city trips and the steam railroad for longer, inter- and intracity travel. Later, horse-drawn passenger cars running on rail rights-of-way, cable cars, electric streetcars or "trolley" cars, elevated and subway rail transit, electric rail, and finally the gasoline-powered automobile all helped turn the landscape into its present vast, low-density suburban world of houses, highways, in-

Sears, Roebuck and Co. had a booming homebuilding business in the early part of this century. On the cover of this catalog of houses from 1929, Sears advertises itself as the world's largest building materials dealer, a different Sears from the one we know today.

Downtown Philadelphia, 1897, where streets are clogged with horse-drawn carriages, trolley cars, and pedestrians.

dustrial and office parks, shopping malls, and parking lots.

The first generation of major residential land developers was spawned by the coming of long-distance railroads in the 1840s and 1850s. Their developments were essentially elite, upper-middle-class suburbs in pastoral settings, located on railroad lines connected to large central cities. Two of the earliest and best known of these suburbs are Llewellyn Park, New Jersey, and Riverside, Illinois.

Llewellyn Haskell, a successful New York merchant, together with eight partners, purchased 400 acres of land near West Orange, New Jersey, in the 1850s. The location was only 13 miles from Manhattan and directly on a railroad line into the city. Haskell was attracted by the natural beauty of the site, with its hills, streams, woods, and views of a mountain to the north and New York to the east. His aim was to create a model community for "the wants of citizens doing business in the city of New York, and yet wishing accessible, retired, and healthful homes in the country."[7] To further this goal, Haskell hired as his chief planner Alexander Jackson Davis, a well-known architect of luxurious and romantic country estates and author of *Rural Residences*, one of the bibles of stylish residential architecture.

Haskell and Davis worked together to make the most of the appeal of this parklike environment. Missing was the familiar grid-iron pattern of straight streets meeting at right angles; instead, roads and lanes curved to the natural contours of the land. The use of curvilinear streets later became a standard feature of suburban residential land development, but in 1856 it was a bold innovation for a new real estate venture. The developer and his architect-planner also created "the Ramble," a 50-acre natural park that followed a stream at the side of the mountain. The Ramble was left in its natural state except for the addition of some curving pedestrian paths. Haskell established a property owners' association to hold title to and maintain this common area, establishing another important precedent for new community projects—open space and recreational facilities dedicated by the developer.

Haskell also wrote restrictions into the deeds prohibiting industrial and commercial uses of the land, requiring large minimum lots (three acres), and barring fences on people's property—these and other rules all designed to preserve Llewellyn Park as a quiet and green paradise for wealthy residents, who entered the exclusive private community through a security gate house. Haskell and Davis both moved there, the lots sold at high prices, and the partners earned an excellent return on their investment. The suburb's attractiveness as an elite enclave was so well conceived and executed that, more than a century later, it remains as Haskell originally envisioned it.

Riverside is more familiar to many urbanists because it was planned by the famous American landscape architects Frederick Law Olmsted and Calvert Vaux, the designers of New York's Central Park. Emery Childs and a group of investors acquired 1,600 acres of undeveloped land on the Des Plaines River and formed the Riverside Improvement Company in 1868 to build a new suburban community combining "the beauties and healthy properties of a park with the conveniences and improvements of the city."[8] The site was located nine miles west of downtown Chicago on the Burlington railroad line, and Olmsted and Vaux were impressed by its attractive natural features, calling it "the only available ground near Chicago [that] does not present disadvantages of an almost hopeless character."[9]

Olmsted and Vaux planned a central 160-acre park along the river and numerous smaller parks and recreation areas. The streets were laid out in a naturalistic curvilinear pattern, and numerous other innovations in high-quality community planning and design were included in the development of this commuter suburb. Deed restrictions covered an impressive array of issues, requiring everything from mandatory 30-foot setbacks, minimum costs, and design review for houses to prescribed rules for maintaining private lawns. Olmsted and Vaux also proposed a limited-access parkway from Riverside to downtown Chicago, an unrealized idea in 1868 that was a half century ahead of its time for American suburban development.

The Riverside Improvement Company hired William LeBaron Jenney, Chicago's leading architect, to review house plans of those who bought lots and to design the Riverside Hotel (built in 1870) overlooking the river. Jenney also built his own house in the new community and helped set a tone for the kind of style the developers and landscape planners desired.

Unfortunately, Emery Childs's and the Riverside Improvement Company's luck was not as good as Llewellyn Haskell's and his partners'. The costly improvements installed to develop Riverside were not supported by vigorous land sales in the first few years. Many people still considered it too far away from the city. Market demand, access to capital, and lot prices all fell dramatically after the 1871 Chicago fire, and the company went bankrupt during the national depression of 1873. By the 1880s, however, sales of lots and construction of houses in Riverside increased substantially. Despite the early disappointments, Riverside, which today is a historic district, was eventually built as a middle-class suburb according to Childs's visions, Olmsted and Vaux's plans, and Jenney's designs. It served as an important early model for many later suburban developments from Roland Park in Baltimore to the Country Club District of Kansas City.

While the elite suburbs based on commuter railroad service came first in terms of the development of large-scale residential subdivisions, further advances in transportation technology later in the 19th century enabled people of more modest means to move to suburban-style neighborhoods and travel by electric transit to their jobs. "Streetcar suburbs" began to appear on the outskirts of growing cities. Often these new subdivisions started as unincorporated areas that were later annexed to the central city and now exist as urban neighborhoods.

The development of subdivisions during this period was tied to the availability of mass transit. Sometimes the private transportation company was also the land subdivider, with the enormous profits on land sales helping to pay for an initially money-losing transit operation that used cheap promotional fares to encourage people to buy lots and build houses in a sparsely settled community. Real estate entrepreneurs of this type ranged from Boston's Henry M. Whitney, the leading subdivider of Brookline, Massachusetts, to F.M. "Borax" Smith, the largest land developer in Oakland, California. Developers who did not own transit companies usually had to pay subsidies to induce a transportation firm to extend its operations to outlying locations. These subsidies were an essential business cost for the developer, because without transit service, there would be no market for the subdivided land.

Samuel E. Gross

Most subdividers were small-scale real estate dealers, though some, especially the transit and utility companies and other large landowners, often sold a high volume of building lots. Rarely did any subdivision developer build more than a handful of houses, usually just enough to help establish the character of the community and give it a more lived-in image. One exception to this general pattern was Samuel E. Gross, a flamboyant residential subdivider who built thousands of houses in the Chicago area in the 1880s and 1890s, mainly inexpensive and affordable houses for skilled blue-collar and white-collar workers with moderate incomes.

Samuel Gross had gone bankrupt in the Chicago real estate business during the 1873 panic, but after working as a lawyer and a playwright, he reentered the real estate market in 1880. By 1892, he had sold 40,000 lots and built and sold 7,000 houses in the Chicago metropolitan area. Many of his subdivisions were in nearly 20 new suburbs he developed. The best known is Brookfield, originally called Grossdale, located adjacent to Riverside.

This popular developer engaged in extensive and dramatic advertising campaigns, emphasizing his easy-payment financing plan with a 10 percent down payment, low monthly installments, and generous refinancing for delinquent borrowers. Where he built houses, he charged a single price to sell the house and lot together. He always made sure that a major transit line ran through his subdivisions, sometimes by working in partnership with Charles T. Yerkes, Chicago's "traction king."

Gross also included major utilities and infrastructure in his developments and added special touches of quality to the residential atmosphere. The houses ranged from a modest four-room cottage that he sold for $1,000, charging $100 down and $10 a month, to larger and more expensive houses, such as a nine-room model selling for $5,000. Most of the houses were built from orders and down payments taken from customers, though Gross also maintained a small inventory available for immediate sale. He built from stock plans but provided touches to individualize the design and trumpeted this fact in his advertising.

Gross was aided in his production of inexpensive houses by the development of the balloon-frame method of construction in Chicago during the 1830s and 1840s. This technique, which used light wooden two-by-fours hammered together with machine-made nails rather than heavy timbers and elaborate joints, saved a tremendous amount of construction time, labor, and materials. By the time Gross entered the real estate business, the balloon-frame house had revolutionized homebuilding in the United States and, together with cheap land, made homeownership much more affordable in the United States than in Europe.

Samuel Gross's somewhat bigger houses and more extensive amenities were reserved for middle-income subdivisions, such as Grossdale. His explicitly working-class subdivisions marketed the small houses and a very modest environment designed to keep down the cost of the lots. Even in the most moderate subdivisions, however, Gross always planted a lot of trees. His basic real estate development and marketing activities, involving small, inexpensive houses and lots sold on easy credit, were so well received that Gross was nominated for mayor of Chicago in 1889 by the Workingman's Party. He declined the honor, but two years later the city's *Real Estate and Building Journal* crowned Samuel Eberly Gross "the Napoleon of home builders."[10]

The Growth of Inner-City Slums

While new housing was being built for the upper class, the middle class, and the more skilled working class, unskilled, low-income workers were still being crowded into inner-city neighborhoods called "slums." Close to plants and distribution centers that were the major sources of employment for people who still walked to work, slums had the worst housing, the greatest overcrowding, and the highest rates of disease. In 1890, journalist and social reformer Jacob Riis had attempted to arouse the conscience of the country with his photographically documented book, *How the Other Half Lives*,[11] and four years later, Carroll Wright, the U.S. Commissioner of Labor, systematically documented the deplorable conditions in his study of the slums of Baltimore, Philadelphia, New York, and Chicago.[12]

Even though the individuals and families living in the slums had low incomes, often the landlords packed so many rent-paying customers into a building and spent so little money on maintenance that slum properties could be highly profitable. Not only were older structures constantly converted to house greater numbers of the cash-poor immigrants flocking to the central cities in search of economic opportunity, but new tenements and other forms of high-density residences were also frequently built. Many of even the newest structures lacked such basic necessities as indoor plumbing and windows that brought light and air into all the rooms. Lot coverage was extremely high, with little open space around buildings and no place

This photo, taken by Jacob Riis in 1888, depicts the living conditions of some of New York City's slums.

for people to congregate and recreate other than the streets and alleys, both of which were frequently covered with mud and littered with garbage.

In cities from New York to San Francisco, housing reform movements during the late 19th and early 20th centuries began to organize for stricter laws to regulate the minimum quality and standard features of new residential construction and existing housing. Unfortunately, these movements frequently met with stiff resistance from elements of the real estate industry. Where the movements did succeed, they often encountered the fundamental problem that many of the slum tenants could not afford to pay the higher rents necessary to finance the major physical improvements needed.

Another strategy was to encourage philanthropic capitalists to build housing for workers under limited-profit financial arrangements to reduce rents. These efforts were intended as both physical models of better construction and design and economic and social models to stimulate more extensive investment. Some real estate developers became involved in these efforts, such as Alfred T. White's City and Suburban Homes Company of New York. Most of the leaders in this movement were from business and professional fields not directly related to the real estate industry. All together, these efforts did not produce enough units to make even a dent in the immediate problem, though in the long run they had important symbolic value in helping to raise minimum standards and educating developers about better methods of planning and building low-cost housing.

A third approach was to form settlement houses led by middle-class social workers in the slum neighborhoods. These professionals provided public health and educational services to the local residents to improve their living conditions and their opportunities. Workers in the settlement houses also assisted members of the community to organize labor unions and to agitate for economic, political, and social reforms from business and government. Often the same people who contributed to the work of the settlement houses also were involved in various attempts to publicly regulate slum housing and to promote the private, limited-dividend construction of new low-income dwelling units. The problem of housing the poor has a long history in this country, with many serious attempts at remediation that have not yet achieved a long-term solution (see Chapter 12).

THE ROLE OF RAILROADS AND RAILROAD BARONS IN REAL ESTATE DEVELOPMENT

The coming of the railroad in the mid-19th century profoundly affected life in the United States. Railroads quickly became the prime mover of people and goods around the nation, into and out of cities and towns. The existence of transportation routes by water had made some land accessible, and many towns of the 18th and early 19th centuries developed mainly because of their location near navigable bodies of water. In the first half of the 19th century, man-made canals expanded the number of accessible sites for land development. But canals were nothing compared to the railroads. Track could be laid almost anywhere, and the volume of land potentially available for development thus expanded tremendously. This expansion led to feverish speculation at times, because no investors could predict with certainty which sites with access to rail transport would be in demand and at what price.

Once the railroads became the principal mode of long-distance passenger and freight transportation, areas depended on access to service for growth and, in many cases, even for survival. In the early years, some municipalities organized their own short-haul rail corporations; later, many towns went deeply into debt paying huge subsidies to private railroad firms for providing service to their communities. Once regular rail service was established, local citizens bought land and marketed it to newcomers. Railroads and real estate development were twin forces for change in many growing areas.

The giant railroad corporations, the country's first truly big businesses, were intimately involved in the real estate business. The interstate long-distance carriers

The growth of land speculation brought a frenzy of railroad construction, including this line connecting Houston and New Orleans, circa 1880.

obtained their franchises and their capitalization through the federal government's grant of not only rights-of-way but also millions of acres of land along their proposed routes. Between 1850 and 1871, the federal government granted 130 million acres of public land to railroad companies. They were given about half of the land within six to 40 miles of the right-of-way, with the government retaining the other half. The land was divided by sections, 640-acre parcels, and the railroads were granted every other section. Public officials argued that once the railroad was built, the government could sell its remaining sections for at least twice as much as it could have otherwise, though it did not always work out that way in practice. After the tracks were laid, the railroads and the government went into competition with each other over subdividing and selling their alternate sections.

Railroads entered the real estate promotion business in an enormous way. In addition to selling land, many companies held onto their vast acreage, mortgaging it to bankers and bond buyers to obtain capital. Indeed, when some politicians and citizens tried to force the railroads to sell their publicly granted land, the companies responded that the assets were tied up as collateral and that they could not sell the land without permission of their lenders—an argument upheld by the U.S. Supreme Court.[13] Over the years, railroads have retained ownership of immense quantities of rural and urban land. They have sold it, leased it, and developed it. It has been used for agriculture, forestry, mining, recreation, and commercial, industrial, and residential developments. In many cities today, railroads are still the biggest private landowners, and some have formed real estate development divisions to earn a greater return on these assets, such as Santa Fe-Southern Pacific's proposed Mission Bay, a large mixed-use project near downtown San Francisco.

The Effect of the Railroads On Industry

The railroads completely reshaped the industrial landscape of cities. Originally, in the preindustrial era of older cities, everyone was packed together within walking distance of the center, and artisan workshops were frequently inside or next to people's homes. Later, as cities expanded and manufacturing grew in importance, much of it took place in separate multistory "loft" buildings with high ceilings and open floor space. As demand for this type of space increased, supplying it became an important branch of the real estate business. Small manufacturers still needed to be crowded near the center of the city, which was where the port facilities—the lifeblood of the transportation system—were located. Once the railroads came, however, manufacturing and warehousing could spread out to many possible sites along the rail lines, and rail spurs and feeder lines were built to connect local shippers to the main, long-haul trunk lines.

By the latter part of the 19th century, large factories and factory complexes with workers' housing could be built on new sites through the cooperation of the railroads' bringing in raw materials and shipping out finished products. In addition to entire factory towns for large manufacturers, such as the new steel mill cities of Gary, Indiana, and Birmingham, Alabama, decentralized industrial parks began to appear on the outskirts of large cities and in nearby suburban locations. Unlike the giant factories, these parks were primarily speculative real estate ventures. In some cases, the early industrial parks were partially owned and financed by the railroad firms to promote more intensive use of their developed land and transportation services.

By the early 20th century, Chicago real estate developers had established both the central manufacturing district and the clearing industrial district. Each was located on the southwest side, far from the central business district, from which many manufacturing and warehouse firms were relocating to take advantage of cheaper rents, larger one-story floor spaces, easy access for cars and trucks to load and unload shipments and to park, proximity to mass transit for workers, and, most important, excellent connections to railroad sidings. These industrial parks were professionally managed, with low-rise and low-density buildings, newly developed and well-maintained grounds, clean sites, and, compared to the older loft neighborhoods and downtown railyards, more attractive landscaping. While this type of industrial development did not become really prominent in the United States until the 1950s, the earliest models in various cities were established in the 1910s and 1920s.

Railroad Barons as Real Estate Developers

Two railroad barons played a crucial role in shaping the patterns of real estate development and urbanization for entire regions: Henry M. Flagler on the east coast of Florida and Henry E. Huntington in southern California.

Henry M. Flagler and the Growth Of Southern Florida

Henry M. Flagler was one of John D. Rockefeller's original partners in the petroleum business, becoming extremely wealthy through the growth of the Standard Oil Company. By the early 1880s, Florida was experiencing one of its periodic land booms. St. Augustine, where Flagler vacationed in 1885, was considered to have a very healthful climate. Flagler became captivated by the town and decided to develop it into a premier resort city for the upper classes, creating a southern version of Newport, Rhode Island. Flagler hired two young New York architects, John Carrere and Thomas Hastings, to design the massive and luxurious Spanish-style Hotel Ponce de Leon, named for the man who had searched in St. Augustine for the fountain of youth. The Hotel Ponce de Leon opened in 1888 and proved so successful that by the following year, Flagler built the Alcazar, a large entertainment center that included midpriced hotel rooms. He also purchased a new, small luxury hotel called Casa Monica, which he renamed the Cordova. In addition, he built 14 expensive cottages for winter guests. The Alcazar contained ballrooms, theaters, swimming pools, and an array of other facilities, including Roman, Russian, and Turkish baths.

In the process of arranging for goods to be shipped to St. Augustine and in marketing his hotels in the northeastern states, Flagler discovered that transportation to the site was a problem. To alleviate that problem, he began to acquire and reorganize local railroad lines. Eventually, he consolidated them and created the East Coast Lines, laying tracks southward along the coast toward Daytona Beach and gaining thousands of acres of public land grants from the state for his railroad-building activities. When Flagler's lines reached the Lake Worth area, he created the new resort community of West Palm Beach, starting with The Royal Poinciana, which, with 1,500 rooms, was the world's largest hotel when it opened in 1894. Two years later, he built Breakers, a 500-room hotel. Palm Beach soon eclipsed St. Augustine. The elite from New York, Philadelphia, and Chicago traveled on Flagler's trains to this winter pleasure palace, and by 1900, it had truly become the "Newport of the South."

During 1894 and 1895, Florida suffered from a series of winter freezes, and Flagler decided to extend his rail lines farther south, where the winter weather was even warmer. He settled on Dade County and negotiated thousands of acres in land grants from private landowners in exchange for promising to bring rail service to a little town called Ft. Dallas on the Miami River and the Biscayne Bay. When the railroad reached the site in 1896, the town was incorporated as Miami, and Flagler built a huge hotel there, the Royal Palm, which opened in 1897. He also built a rail terminal, an electric plant, a sewage system, a water works, docks and wharves, and a harbor for ocean vessels, having dredged the Miami River. In addition, he laid out miles of streets, donated land for a civic center, public buildings, schools, parks, and churches, and started a newspaper called the *Miami Metropolis* at a time when the city had only a few hundred year-round residents. By 1910, fast-growing Miami was already the state's fifth largest city, with a population of 11,000 and hotel accommodations for 100,000. Flagler took advantage of his extensive holdings to subdivide a tremendous amount of land for highly profitable sales and to develop more hotels and other properties.

In addition to the various railroad land grants, Flagler had acquired several large landowning companies in Florida, including a former canal promoter, consolidating

The lobby of the luxurious 500-room Breakers hotel, built in 1896 in Palm Beach.

them all into his Florida East Coast Canal and Transportation Company, which also became the holding company for his railroad lines. Flagler made enormous profits by the timely linking of his land sales and development activities to the provision of rail service. In 1897, he added shipping to his transportation and development plans, founding the Florida East Coast Steamship Company to offer improved access from Miami to Havana, Nassau, and Key West, again building hotels and other projects, and selling land in Nassau and Key West. His final project was extending the railroad to Key West, a major engineering achievement. Henry Flagler rode the inaugural train 225 miles over land and sea from his home in West Palm Beach to Key West for the grand opening in 1912. When he died a year later, the hotel, railroad, and land baron left an enduring legacy on the form and pattern of development and growth in the Sunshine State.

Henry E. Huntington and Southern California's First Boom

At the same time that Henry Flagler was building the Hotel Ponce de Leon on the Atlantic Coast, southern California, across the continent on the Pacific Coast, was in the midst of a wildly speculative land boom brought on by the arrival of transcontinental railroad service. Los Angeles was a small pueblo community of fewer than 6,000 inhabitants when it first began negotiating in the early 1870s for the Southern Pacific to extend its railroad lines to the town. The Angelenos offered free land, an ownership share in their local railroad, $600,000 in cash borrowed through municipal bonds, and other subsidies to the Southern Pacific before its chief executive, Collis P. Huntington, finally agreed to expand to Los Angeles during the 1880s.

The Atchison, Topeka, and Santa Fe Railroad was also building a new line over the mountains to terminate in Los Angeles, and by 1887, the Santa Fe and the Southern Pacific were fighting a rate war to establish dominance in the market for coast-to-coast travel to southern California. At one point, they cut fares so low that passengers could ride all the way from Kansas City to Los Angeles for one dollar. The rate war brought in vast numbers of tourists, and the existence of the new rail connections to the East and Midwest set off a subdivision boom that lasted for one frenzied year and then quickly crashed. In Los Angeles County, 1,350 new subdivision maps were recorded in 1887, whereas just 10 had been recorded in 1880 and 70 in 1890. Real estate transactions in the city of Los Angeles topped $100 million in 1887; only New York and Chicago had more that year. Prices for acreage and for subdivision lots rose 10 to 20 times higher within the year, only to drop back down again by 1888.

In all, the 60 new cities and towns covering 80,000 acres that were laid out and marketed in 1887 and 1888 contained enough land to house several million people at low densities, yet by 1889 fewer than 3,500 people were living in those communities. Though Los Angeles itself grew to a population of 50,000 by 1890, other boom towns disappeared as ghost towns, such as Border City on the Mojave Desert that Simon Homberg platted on land bought from the federal government. He sold lots that cost him about 10 cents each to East Coast investors with great fanfare for $250; when the buyers found out the true nature of their nearly worthless purchase, the market dried up like the desert air.

While the land speculation boom and bust in 1887 and 1888 left the Los Angeles real estate market in a somewhat weakened condition during the 1890s, and the national depression of 1893 added to the difficulties, the long-term prospects for Los Angeles's growth turned out to be very strong. Even during the 1890s, the population doubled in size, and by 1901, the city was poised for a major revival of real estate activity. The most important figure in this revival was Henry Huntington, vice president of the Southern Pacific Railroad and nephew of its president, Collis Huntington.

When Collis Huntington died in 1900, his nephew Henry inherited an enormous fortune. He did not succeed in gaining control of the Southern Pacific, however, and left his position to embark on an entirely new venture in urban development using interurban railroads. Huntington moved from San Francisco to Los Angeles and incorporated the Pacific Electric Railway in 1901. Earlier he had acquired the Los Angeles Railway, a downtown-oriented commuter service. The Pacific Electric, on the other hand, reached far out into the suburbs and to sparsely settled and mostly undeveloped areas of the vast metropolis.

Huntington laid out a transportation network over southern California that stretched from the San Fernando and San Gabriel valleys of Los Angeles County all the way to Newport Beach on the Pacific Coast in central Orange County. By 1910, his various railway companies together covered more than 1,300 miles, making Huntington the owner of the largest private interurban transit system in the world. Many of the communities of southern California owed their rapid growth in the first two decades of the 20th century to Huntington's rail service. By 1920, the population of Los Angeles city was 576,000, and Los Angeles County contained nearly 1 million people. The landscape of the metropolitan region was so strongly shaped by Huntington's rail network that many of today's freeways follow the old Pacific Electric rights-of-way.

The normal practice for streetcar extensions before Huntington was for landowners to pay the transit company for capital costs, in anticipation of the appreciation in property values once service was instituted. Huntington did not bother to pursue such an incremental strategy. He had his own capital and easy access to lenders and investors. Besides, he was his own biggest landowner along most of the suburban transit routes. The Huntington Land and Improvement Company and several other entities bought, subdivided, and sold real estate wherever the Pacific Electric's "big red cars" rolled along their tracks. Huntington brought rail service to areas he considered ripe for land development, even when the existing ridership was minimal. In many cases, those areas did grow rapidly once they became accessible to the regional mode of electric transporta-

Downtown Los Angeles lined with streetcars and automobiles in the midst of a southern California real estate boom that would result in extensive rail service to outlying areas.

tion. Huntington developed a wide variety of residential subdivisions, with lots of different sizes and prices and different deed restrictions, landscaping, street plans, and utilities, depending on the target market.

In subdividing and selling land, Henry Huntington often worked closely with one of Los Angeles's leading real estate brokers and developers, William May Garland. Huntington also was a partner in the powerful syndicate headed by the owners of the *Los Angeles Times* that made an estimated $100 million profit on the purchase of 108,000 acres of arid land in the San Fernando Valley and the subsequent subdivision and reselling of that same newly irrigated land after the completion of the 238-mile Owens Valley Aqueduct paid for by the taxpayers of Los Angeles (a story immortalized in the motion picture *Chinatown*).

Huntington's real estate developments ranged from very exclusive upper-class areas in Pasadena and San Marino, where his own house was located (which is now the Huntington Museum and Li-

brary), to middle-class communities like South Pasadena, Huntington Beach, and Redondo Beach, to working-class suburbs like Alhambra, where Henry Huntington developed industrial land and even established his own large factory to promote industrialization in addition to new homesites. Huntington Beach and Redondo Beach had oil wells, and though residential development was the primary focus of his subdivisions, many Huntington projects also included commercial development, particularly retail stores and hotels, and some involved industrial land uses, including power stations.

Another element of Huntington's ambitious regional real estate development strategy was to get into the utilities business as a way of providing necessary services to enhance the value of the land he was selling and to take advantage of his ownership of the transit system and of so much land. The Los Angeles Railway and the Pacific Electric were major users of electricity, so Huntington established the Pacific Light and Power

Company to provide hydroelectric and steam power to his transit operations and to the areas that he was busy developing. By 1913, Pacific Light and Power was supplying 20 percent of the region's electricity and natural gas as well as all the power for Huntington's streetcars. Having bought so much rural land to obtain a source of water to generate power, Huntington also organized the San Gabriel Valley Water Company to supply fresh water to San Marino, Alhambra, and the entire greater Pasadena area.

The interrelationship of transportation, infrastructure, utilities, and real estate development that Henry Huntington exemplified on such a grand scale is neatly illustrated by a local joke from 1914. A mother was taking her daughter on a trolley ride to the beach. The daughter asked, "Whose streetcar are we riding in?" Her mother replied, "Mr. Huntington's." Passing a park, the girl asked, "What place is that?" "Huntington Park," responded her mother. "Where are we going, mother?" "To Huntington Beach," was the answer. Finally arriving at the sea, the child ventured one more query: "Mother, does Mr. Huntington own the ocean or does it still belong to God?"[14]

SUMMARY

This chapter reveals how real estate in the 1800s began to become a very strong part of the country's overall economic growth. The railroads' twofold involvement in real estate—as transporters and as land developers and owners—strongly promoted speculative land development.

As less and less land was left in the government's control, speculation became the great American pastime. At the same time that large tracts of land were exchanging hands and being subdivided and developed, the public sector was also becoming more involved in regulating those activities. It was also looking to the real estate industry for new sources of public revenue. Thus, the period saw the beginning of government intervention and the creation of large private fortunes made hand-in-hand with government support.

The next chapter explores the industry's continuing evolution from the late 1800s through World War II.

NOTES

1. See, for example, A.M. Sakolski, *The Great American Land Bubble: The Amazing Story of Land-Grabbing, Speculations, and Booms from Colonial Days to the Present Time* (New York: Harper, 1932); Glenn S. Dumke, *The Boom of the Eighties in Southern California* (San Marino, Cal.: Huntington Library, 1944); and Homer B. Vanderblue, "The Florida Land Boom," *Journal of Land and Public Utility Economics,* May 1927, pp. 113–31, and August 1927, pp. 252–69.

2. Sakolski, *The Great American Land Bubble*, pp. 147, 164.

3. Larry Van Dyne, "The Making of Washington," *Washingtonian*, November 1987, p. 172.

4. Sakolski, *The Great American Land Bubble*, p. 82.

5. Ibid., pp. 84–85.

6. Kenneth T. Jackson, *Crabgrass Frontier: The Suburbanization of the United States* (New York: Oxford Univ. Press, 1985), p. 134.

7. Ibid., p. 77.

8. Ann Durkin Keating, *Building Chicago: Suburban Developers and the Creation of a Divided Metropolis* (Columbus: Ohio State Univ. Press, 1988), p. 73.

9. Jackson, *Crabgrass Frontier*, p. 80.

10. Keating, *Building Chicago*, p. 76. See also Gwendolyn Wright, *Moralism and the Model Home: Domestic Architecture and Cultural Conflict in Chicago, 1873–1913* (Chicago: Univ. of Chicago Press, 1980).

11. Jacob Riis, *How the Other Half Lives: Studies among the Tenements of New York* (New York: Scribner, 1890).

12. Carroll D. Wright, *The Slums of Baltimore, Chicago, New York, and Philadelphia.* Seventh Special Report of the Commissioner of Labor (Washington, D.C.: U.S. Government Printing Office, 1894).

13. *Platt* v. *Union Pacific R.R. Co.*, 9 U.S. 48 (October 1878).

14. William B. Friedricks, "A Metropolitan Entrepreneur Par Excellence: Henry E. Huntington and the Growth of Southern California, 1989-1927," *Business History Review*, Summer 1989, p. 354.

Chapter 5

The Late 1800s to World War II

In the latter half of the 19th century, a massive wave of industrialization took place in the United States, much of it concentrated in cities. Urban areas became magnets for an immense migration of population from rural areas at home and abroad, of people looking to start their own businesses or to work in the factories, stores, and offices of the expanding metropolis. Adna F. Weber's landmark 1899 study, *The Growth of Cities in the Nineteenth Century*, fully documents the rapid urbanization, which he called "the most remarkable social phenomenon."[1] As cities grew in population, they also spread out over a great deal of additional territory, with technological and organizational improvements by the public and private sectors in transportation, utilities, infrastructure, and urban services encouraging the mass movement of industry and residences away from the crowded center of the city. All but the very rich and the very poor moved to outlying neighborhoods in search of newer and better housing and in many cases homeownership on cheaper land. Factories and warehouses moved along with the workers to industrial districts where space cost less, facilities were more modern, and it was easier to ship goods.

This chapter looks at the change in the growth of cities and the increasing involvement of government and regulators in real estate development through the early 1900s. It was a volatile time, encompassing two world wars and the Great Depression. The chapter covers several topics:

- CBDs and commercial development;
- The beginning of the modern role of the public sector;
- The real estate boom of the 1920s;
- Finance; and
- The Great Depression and World War II.

CENTRAL BUSINESS DISTRICTS AND COMMERCIAL DEVELOPMENT

What was left behind in the city center as people began moving farther and farther out of the city? High-volume, high-value activities that represented both the new concentration of wealth and power and the rise of the new administrative and consumer-oriented society. The central business district, or "downtown," was the region's focal point for the largest banks, insurance companies, corporate headquarters, newspaper publishers, governmental functions, professional offices, general and specialty retailing and wholesaling, hotels, cultural activities, and much more. The main railroad and streetcar lines all termi-

Pittsburgh's downtown experienced remarkable growth in the late 1800s. Liberty Avenue, circa 1910, was one of the main streets leading to the convergence of the Allegheny and Monongahela Rivers.

nated in and radiated out from downtown, bringing in (and taking home) the majority of the metropolitan population every day and week to work, shop, obtain services, and be educated and entertained.

As land values rose in the central core, many industrial and residential land uses were outbid, forced out, torn down, and replaced by an incredible building boom for commercial owners and tenants. In Pittsburgh's CBD, for example, more than 400 new buildings were completed in just a five-year period in the late 1880s and early 1890s, and nearly as many were completed over the next decade.

The Growth of the Skyscraper

No symbol of the prosperous new corporate-commercial city and its growing CBD was more potent than the tall building, or "skyscraper." Most skyscrapers were office buildings that replaced church spires as the highest points of reference (though perhaps not reverence) for the entire urban community and its rural hinterland.

By the 1880s, a workable electric elevator had been invented, making it possible for buildings to rise above the previous six stories that represented the limit of how many flights of stairs people were willing to walk on a daily basis. Indoor plumbing, electric lighting, and other inventions made the interiors livable and functional, while the advent of structural steel-frame construction enabled builders to transcend the physical height constraints imposed by traditional masonry construction. Instead of thick, heavy load-bearing walls that could support only so much weight and volume, the new steel skeletons with light masonry curtain walls and plate-glass windows allowed buildings to soar hundreds of feet in height in the 1880s and eventually to top 1,000 feet half a century later.

Life insurance companies erected many of the earliest and most prominent office buildings. The largest of these firms had substantial long-term capital to invest in real estate, needed their own headquarters, and desired to communicate visually their financial strength to the millions of current and prospective policyholders. In New York in the late 19th century, Manhattan Life, Mutual Life, Equitable, Prudential, Metropolitan, and others warred to build the tallest and most impressive structure. A similar battle took place among major metropolitan newspaper publishers, who desired the symbol of a distinctive office tower as a marketing device to boost circulation, advertising revenue, and public prestige. Again in New York, the *Tribune* and the *Evening Post* buildings took the early lead but were soon eclipsed in 1892 by publisher Joseph Pulitzer's *New York World* Building, which at 309 feet was the first structure in the city taller than the steeple of Trinity Church. Not to be outdone, the *New York Times* fought back a decade later with the 362-foot Times Tower.

Two years later, the Singer Sewing Machine Company, a manufacturing corporation whose consumer products were distributed globally, stunned both the insurance and newspaper businesses by announcing plans to construct a headquarters building more than 600 feet tall. The Singer Building on Broadway in lower Manhattan, designed by the distinguished architect Ernest Flagg, when completed in 1908 was twice as high as nearly all of New York's and the world's other skyscrapers—and 40 feet taller than the Washington Monument in the nation's capital. The *New York Times* called a 34-story building under construction at the same time "a comparative dwarf alongside the Singer Tower"; 10 years earlier this "dwarf" would have been the world's tallest building.[2]

Singer, however, was rapidly overshadowed by the Metropolitan Life Tower, which was finished in 1909 and was nearly 100 feet taller. Some city residents became so alarmed by the perceived negative impact of the new towers on urban overcrowding, sunlight, and safety that they lobbied municipal authorities to impose limitations on building height. By the 1890s, Boston and Chicago passed such restrictions, to be followed by Washington,

D.C., Los Angeles, and numerous other cities; in most cases, the maximum permitted building heights were between 100 and 200 feet. But by the 1920s, many of these regulations were lifted or modified to allow continued vertical expansion.

Though corporations put their names on the skyscrapers for the advertising value and in most cases also owned their headquarters buildings, they definitely did not occupy all of the office space. A great deal of it was leased to a variety of business and professional tenants. The CBD spawned a specialized real estate industry in architecture, construction, brokerage, and property management. The demand for office space was sufficiently strong that real estate developers and investors also put up purely speculative buildings to compete with the large company headquarters structures. In New York, Singer's neighbors included the Trinity Building and the United States Realty Building, both built speculatively without an anchor or "name" tenant. A more famous example is the attractive and unusual triangle-shaped Flatiron Building on

Once New York's most famous skyscraper, the Flatiron Building (originally known as the Fuller Building), at the intersection of Fifth Avenue and Broadway, was built in 1902. The facade is rusticated limestone, with French Renaissance details.

Fifth Avenue and Broadway, designed by the well-known Chicago architect Daniel Burnham and completed in 1903. The Flatiron was occupied primarily by wholesalers and many other small firms.

The most important early commercial office building developers were the Brooks brothers from Boston. Peter and Shepherd Brooks were Boston property investors who in 1873 acquired the seven-story Portland Block, Chicago's first office building equipped with a passenger elevator. From this initial investment, the Brookses developed many of the key structures that pioneered the world-famous Chicago school of architecture in the design and construction of large commercial buildings during the late 19th century. The Portland Block, completed in 1872, was designed by William Le Baron Jenney, who later served as architect for the Home Insurance Building, considered by many to be the first modern skyscraper because of its pioneering use of steel-frame construction. The Portland, which was also the first building where every office had direct sunlight, paid off handsomely for the Brookses and was completely occupied from the 1870s until its demolition in 1933. Peter and Shepherd Brooks hired Owen Aldis, an attorney, to manage the Portland Block and serve as their real estate agent in Chicago. By the turn of the century, Aldis was managing 20 percent of the office space in downtown Chicago. He and his nephew, Graham Aldis, became national leaders in commercial building investment and management.

In 1881, the Brookses decided the downtown Chicago real estate market was robust enough to support the construction of the city's first 10-story building, the Montauk Block. Peter Brooks wrote Owen Aldis that "an office building erected to suit modern notions, thoroughly equipped with modern appliances, would fill up with modern tenants, leaving the old and unremodeled houses to the conservative fogy."[3] Brooks wanted a building whose modern construction techniques, attractive, simple design, and quality materials, methods, and maintenance would project a businesslike image of efficiency and strength: "The building throughout is to be for use and not for ornament. Its beauty will be in its all-adaptation to its use."[4] The

partners Daniel Burnham and John Wellborn Root were the architects of this project plus two other Brooks-Aldis office buildings of the 1880s, the Rookery and the Monadnock Block. Brooks and Aldis teamed up to develop two other major Chicago office structures in the 1890s, the Pontiac Building and the Marquette Building, both designed by another famous architectural firm, Holabird and Roche.

The Brooks brothers' and Owen Aldis's guidelines for the design of their numerous buildings included "height sufficient to warrant the use of elevators, as much light as possible, easy maintenance, high percentage of rentable space, and ornament sufficient to avoid absolute plainness."[5] Aldis also wrote rules for building management when the Marquette was completed in 1894, with the basic thrusts of the eight points being that building first-class space and providing first-class service are the best investments. It certainly turned out that way for Peter and Shepherd Brooks, who earned a substantial return on their investment in developing and owning Chicago office buildings. Aldis too did extremely well financially from his investments and fee income. The buildings developed by Brooks-Aldis were fully rented when they opened in the 1880s and 1890s, and though the Montauk was demolished in 1902, the others maintained high occupancy rates all the way through the mid-1960s. Interestingly, Aldis's leasing strategy was to "arrange [a] typical layout for intensive use." He went on to note:

> A large number of small tenants is more desirable than large space for large tenants because: a) a higher rate per square foot can be added for small tenants; b) they do not move in a body and leave the building with a large vacant space when hard times hit; c) they do not swamp your elevators by coming and going by the clock.[6]

The Growth of Downtown Hotels, Apartment Buildings, And Department Stores

While high-rise office buildings were among the most distinctive new features of the rapidly growing CBDs, they were joined by other prominent new structures and land uses. Large hotels, many of them also rising many stories in height, were an increasingly vital feature of downtowns, attracting business customers and the rapidly increasing tourist trade for meetings, social functions, entertainment, and, most important, the thousands of new guest rooms. Henry Flagler's thriving Florida hotel operations, though winter resorts, also served to anchor the downtowns of several growing cities, particularly Miami. In New York, the heirs and descendants of John Jacob Astor built the luxurious Waldorf-Astoria Hotel in the 1890s on the site of their parents' mansions. Elsewhere, Potter Palmer in Chicago, Henry Huntington in southern California, and other developers built similar "grand hotels."

Another emerging central city innovation of the late 19th century, related to the residential hotel, was the apartment house. As land values rose in the central area, it became increasingly uneconomical to build or maintain single-family detached houses or attached town houses other than as mansions for the very wealthiest people. Spacious apartments, complete with the latest physical amenities and a wide assortment of extra services, provided an attractive alternative for many upper- and middle-class urbanites desiring to live close to the business and entertainment world of downtown. Some of the buildings with the most services and facilities, including dining rooms, were even called apartment hotels. This vertical lifestyle had already become popular in Paris by the mid-19th century, and when first transplanted to the United States, the units were often referred to as "French flats."

The original American prototype for the French flat was the fashionable Stuyvesant Apartments in Manhattan, developed by a rich socialite, Rutherford Stuyvesant, in 1869. Richard Morris Hunt, the first U.S. architect to be trained at the Ecole des Beaux Arts in Paris, designed the Stuyvesant. By 1900, apartments were an increasingly important use of land in New York, Chicago, Boston, San Francisco, Washington, D.C., and a few other cities. Luxury apartments and working-class tenements were located in separate neighborhoods close to the CBD, and middle-class multi-

The Waldorf-Astoria Hotel, built in the late 1890s by the descendants of John Jacob Astor in Second Empire style.

family dwellings were built farther out from downtown, along the many avenues and boulevards traversed by streetcar lines.

The other major innovative urban land use was massive, multistory facilities for retail trade, originally called dry goods or general stores and, by the late 19th century, department stores. These massive structures, often designed as "pleasure palaces" with ornate exteriors and lavish interiors, catered especially to women shoppers with service-oriented sales personnel and special events and promotions. The first major department store was Alexander T. Stewart's elaborate Marble Palace dry goods center, which opened in 1846 on Broadway and Chambers Street in New York. Later in the century, larger and more spectacular department stores covering entire city blocks and serving as major downtown institutions flourished in many cities, including Filene's in Boston, Rich's in Atlanta, Marshall Field's in Chicago, The Emporium in San Francisco, Dayton's in Minneapolis, Hudson's in Detroit, Robinson's in Los Angeles, and numerous others. In every case, these stores acted as magnets for the real estate market. When Marshall Field's changed locations in Chicago from Lake Street to State Street in 1867, its new site became the "100 percent corner" almost immediately.

One of the greatest of all the department store ventures was Wanamaker's in Philadelphia. John Wanamaker and his partner Nathan Brown opened "Oak Hall," their original men's and boys' clothing store, on the ground floor of a six-story building on Sixth and Market Streets in central Philadelphia in 1861. Their business philosophy, which Wanamaker elaborated throughout

The grand atrium of Wanamaker's downtown Philadelphia store in 1911. This neoclassic, 13-story building was a block long.

his long retailing career, included selling good-quality merchandise at one, everyday low price and guaranteed money-back returns on all goods. Wanamaker emphasized a democratic, egalitarian ethic with his slogan "no favoritism."[7] Every customer was to be treated with equal respect, to be charged the same low prices, and to be properly served. In the early years, Wanamaker's made only cash sales, refunded only cash, and paid its workers daily in cash.

By the 1870s, the store proved so successful that Wanamaker purchased an abandoned rail depot from the Pennsylvania Railroad and built the world's largest department store, a huge two-acre dry goods emporium on Thirteenth and Market Streets. Perhaps foreshadowing today's successful retail centers in former train stations, such as St. Louis's Union Station, Wanamaker dubbed his store "the Grand Depot." The new store opened in 1876 in the midst of the centennial celebration of the Declaration of Independence, which brought 10 million visitors to Philadelphia over a six-month period for a grand exhibition in Fairmount Park. And one of the big tourist attractions was Wanamaker's Grand Depot. A year later, Wanamaker was already expanding, building an addition on Chestnut Street that connected through a stylish arcade to the main store. The Chestnut Street store, with its own separate and ornate entrance, was designed to specialize in "ladies' goods," which eventually became an even bigger business for Wanamaker's than its already brisk trade in men's and children's clothing, hats, and shoes. Linens, appliances, housewares, furniture, pianos, and everything else imaginable were eventually added to various departments in the acres of space. Sales reached nearly 100,000 items on a single day in December 1896, breaking all previous records.

For many years, John Wanamaker's at Thirteenth and Market, with its distinctive clock tower, was known around the world as one of Philadelphia's central landmarks. In 1908, the Chestnut Street store was demolished and replaced by a much larger, block-long structure, complete with its own subway station. In 1896, Wanamaker acquired A.T. Stewart's flagship store, built in 1862 at Tenth and Broadway in Manhattan as an "uptown" branch of the Marble Palace, and reopened it as Wanamaker's New York store. After a decade of growing sales, Wanamaker constructed a huge 16-story structure next to the old A.T. Stewart's building, creating again one of the world's largest shopping complexes, with three separate stores: The Woman's Store, The Man's Store, and the Wanamaker Galleries of Furnishing and Decoration. (The latter included "The House Palatial and Summer Garden," which brought in 70,000 shoppers on opening day.) By the time John Wanamaker died in 1922, Wanamaker's, like other major department stores, was beginning to build suburban stores at prime locations near commuter train stations. Regardless of the subsequent decentralization, the role of Wanamaker and the other central city department store owners in the creation of the modern commercial downtown is an enduring legacy.

THE BEGINNING OF THE MODERN PUBLIC ROLE

As cities grew larger and more complex in the late 19th and early 20th centuries, governments became increasingly involved in providing municipal services, promoting the development of public infrastructure, and regulating private real estate development. The advent of industrialization reinforced the urban trend away from the "walking city" and toward a spreading separation of work and residence so that commuting, traffic congestion, and transportation technology all became more important public concerns. As greater numbers of people migrated to cities, issues ranging from overcrowding to pollution to public health and safety to the need for light, air, and adequate recreation all were hotly debated. They led to various proposed solutions, to new forms of public intervention in the "private markets," and to the rise of urban and metropolitan planning.

Industry and trade brought rising prosperity to the cities, though many citizens also disliked the unpleasant side effects like filth and noise. In response and to celebrate their new wealth and power and the success of U.S. democracy, municipalities launched "City Beautiful" campaigns to construct attractive and often monumental public buildings—city halls, libraries, museums, and schools. Another element of this movement was the establishment of public parks, both large "pleasure gardens" and smaller neighborhood parks and playgrounds. New York established its massive Central Park during the 1850s, and the principal designer, landscape architect Frederick Law Olmsted, then spent the next four decades designing parks and parkways in many cities across the country, including San Francisco's Golden Gate Park, Brooklyn's Prospect Park, and park systems for Boston, Chicago, and Buffalo.

Along with civic centers and parks came parkways, wide streets that coursed through parks or other natural settings, and boulevards, tree-lined thoroughfares bordered by buildings and other urban scenery. While these roads initially were intended for leisurely promenading in carriages or automobiles, many of them later turned into principal transportation arteries overflowing with traffic. The constant need to expand and upgrade the roadways preoccupied local governments, because 30 to 40 percent of the land in a typical city was used for streets and highways. Further, local governments assumed responsibility for franchising, regulating, financing, building, maintaining, planning, and coordinating the movement of goods and people around and through urban areas. Structures like docks, port facilities, bridges, and tunnels for cities on water, railroad lines and railway terminals for every city, streetcars, subways, and mechanized transit lines, and trucking all came under the purview of the public sector. These new areas of activity added to already expanding demands for the public provision of infrastructure and utilities, such as water and sewer systems, and the burgeoning growth of essential services, from police protection to street cleaning.

A good example of this expansion of government and private initiative is the 1909 Plan of Chicago sponsored by the Commercial Club, a powerful downtown business group, and authored by a group of businessmen and professionals led by architect Daniel Burnham. The purposes of the plan were to firmly establish the central area as a modern corporate and commercial downtown, to reclaim the lakefront for recreational use and development of luxury housing, and to encourage suburban growth through radial highways emanating from the CBD and by the designation of forest preserves to maintain open space. Nearly $300 million in public expenditures was spent during the first two decades to implement the plan, supplemented by a great deal of private investment and massive promotional campaigns by the Commercial Club and the Chicago Plan Commission. The plan had a wide-ranging effect:

- Downtown rail lines were covered over and the air rights developed for parks, office buildings, and consolidated passenger terminals.
- The wholesale produce market was relocated to accommodate construction of the bilevel boulevard-style Wacker Drive along the Chicago River.
- Building the Michigan Avenue Bridge opened up the Magic Mile retail and office district and the Gold Coast residential neighborhood on the near north side.
- Other new bridges built over the Chicago River improved access to downtown.
- Chicago's "front yard" was redeveloped and filled in with attractive new lakefront parks like Grant Park and Burnham Park, museums, cultural institutions, a waterfront pier, and expanded and improved existing lakefront parks.
- Numerous major streets were widened and new thoroughfares developed.
- Suburban regional parks were created.

Public works proved to be a strong stimulus for private commercial and residential development, and Chicago citizens who voted for the many bond issues were pleased with the results.

One problem of urban living was the threat of fire from so many wooden buildings so close together. Major portions of Boston, Baltimore, Chicago, and San Francisco had been destroyed by conflagrations in the late 19th and early 20th centuries, and smaller fires were a common occurrence in cities everywhere. To safeguard the dense urban environment, cities not only organized fire departments but also increasingly promulgated building codes to improve the safety of urban structures. By the late 19th century, some municipalities prescribed limits in the center city, requiring all new buildings to be made of brick.

Building codes, in addition to focusing on fireproof materials, also regulated building materials and methods of construction to increase the safety and longevity of structures. Because building codes regulated only general construction, many cities also developed specialized housing codes to require minimum standards of habitability for dwelling units.

Also in the latter part of the 19th century, cities began to limit to certain areas within the city those hazardous but necessary business and industrial activities that might cause fires or expose people to disease, harm, or bad smells. Selective prohibition of these noxious uses by geographic location was an early form of land use zoning. The first local government to initiate a very broad zoning law was Los Angeles, which in 1908 divided the entire city into residential and industrial districts. Many cities, including Los Angeles, also imposed limitations on building heights, with Boston and Washington, D.C., establishing differential height districts to allow taller buildings in the downtown than in the rest of the city. By 1916, New York combined height and use restrictions with regulations on lot coverage and building bulk to create "comprehensive zoning." A series of U.S. Supreme Court decisions between 1909 and 1926 essentially validated this new form of public limitation on private property rights, and by the end of the 1920s, most large cities and many smaller towns and suburban villages (more than 1,000 in all) had zoning ordinances in effect and planning agencies to implement the new regulations (see Chapter 10 for more detailed information about zoning practices).

Why did property owners agree to abridge their rights and exchange laissez-faire laws for stricter government supervision? In some cases they did not agree, and a great deal of protest and controversy ensued. But overall, the private sector—not just community groups but also many real estate entrepreneurs—strongly favored the growing number of public laws and codes regulating urban development and land use. They supported zoning restrictions to stabilize real estate markets, increase property values, and encourage new investment, because the restrictions enabled them to build or buy property with less risk

Built in 1900, the 15-story Continental Building in downtown Baltimore, a classic early skyscraper in the Chicago style.

of unfavorable change on the adjoining lots and the surrounding neighborhoods. They welcomed subdivision controls for introducing a level of coordination that enabled both private developers and local governments to more efficiently plan, finance, and construct the new infrastructure and amenities that were essential to the success of development projects.

Real estate owners and developers had already created their own system of private restrictions written into property deeds as contractual obligations, before the introduction of zoning and other types of governmental controls. Deed restrictions were a private form of land use regulation that evolved in the late 19th century, establishing the precedents and models later used in establishing the public sector's development regulations. Several state and local governments supported the application of these privately negotiated restrictions on property owners by publicly enforcing them in civil courts. More direct and extensive public intervention came in the 20th century after leaders of the real estate industry recognized that greater

powers and flexibility for local governments were needed to regulate urban property and land uses more broadly and extensively than private efforts had been able to accomplish without active public involvement and authority.

THE ROARING TWENTIES

After a relative dry spell in the period immediately before, during, and after World War I, the construction of downtown office space burgeoned in the 1920s, in structures of all shapes, sizes, and heights. Near the end of the decade, the Thompson-Starrett Company of New York, one of the world's largest private construction firms that specialized in building skyscrapers, surveyed the country's 173 largest cities and found nearly 5,000 buildings 10 stories or higher, many of them built during the 1920s. This list included hotels, department stores, manufacturing lofts, civic centers, and other private and public structures, but private office buildings made up by far the predominant category.[8]

While New York had more than three-fifths of the total for the entire country, many other cities had significant and growing numbers. New York, Chicago, Los Angeles, Philadelphia, Detroit, and Boston all had more than 100 buildings taller than 10 stories. St. Louis, Pittsburgh, Kansas City, San Francisco, Cleveland, Seattle, Baltimore, Minneapolis, Tulsa, Dallas, and Houston each had at least 30 buildings 10 stories or higher. The growth in the height and bulk of these structures had been made possible by new building technology but was fueled by the increasing economic productivity and urban wealth of the 1920s and the tremendous expansion of cities both outward and upward. By the late 1920s, financing was flowing freely from institutional lenders, equity syndicators, and mortgage bond houses, further encouraging the construction of speculative office space. New organizations and methods of equity financing through the sale of stocks, such as the Fred F. French Investing Company or Harry Black's United States Realty, and debt financing through the likes of the S.W. Straus mortgage bond company fed

FIGURE 5-1
THE STORY OF THE EMPIRE STATE BUILDING

The site of the Empire State Building was attractive to its investors because a very large land parcel, 197 by 425 feet, was available. The old Waldorf-Astoria Hotel, which sat on that parcel, was slated to be demolished when the new hotel on Park Avenue was completed. After developer Floyd Brown, who had bought the site in 1928, defaulted on his mortgage payments, the property was sold to the Empire State Company, and the hotel was demolished just a few weeks before the stock market crashed in October 1929. Despite the crash, Empire State Company, partially owned by the du Pont family and headed by former New York Governor Al Smith, decided to move forward with the project in the face of what it incorrectly perceived to be a brief economic downturn. The company invested a total of $45 million to acquire the site, demolish the hotel, and design and construct the world's tallest building, all in less than 18 months! The actual construction, managed by the general contracting firm of Starrett Brothers and Eken, took less than a year. At the peak of activity, 3,500 construction workers were adding one story a day. By the official opening on May 1, 1931, the building stood 1,250 feet tall, with 85 floors of offices and the equivalent of another 17 floors devoted to the magnificent mooring mast and observation decks.

One reason for the speed of construction was that in those days commer-

The completed Empire State Building in 1931—the symbol of New York for over 50 years. The facade is of limestone, granite, aluminum, and nickel, with a hint of Art Deco ornamentation.

cial leases in New York expired on April 30, and if the Empire State Building were not ready for occupancy on May 1, the company would have to wait an entire year to attract tenants—a costly delay. The rationale for building it so tall was

the rapid private development of high-rise commercial and residential buildings.

Of the buildings listed in the census of skyscrapers, 377 were more than 20 stories high, and 188 of them were in New York, including what was then the world's tallest, the 55-story, 792-foot Woolworth Building, constructed in 1913 by the Thompson-Starrett Company. This neogotic "cathedral of commerce" was a corporate head-

quarters for the F.W. Woolworth Company, and its owner, Frank Woolworth, had paid $13 million in cash to build a monument to his empire of retail stores. The building had no mortgage, and though it advertised the Woolworth name, most of the office space was actually leased to other firms.

By the late 1920s, office buildings were going up so fast and American business tenants, investors, and real estate de-

FIGURE 5-1 (continued)

that the syndicate had paid record high prices for a location at 34th Street and Fifth Avenue that was less than ideal for a quality office skyscraper: the principal office districts were at 23rd Street near Madison Square, 42nd Street near Grand Central Station, and downtown around Wall Street. The Empire State Building stood alone in the middle of a low-rise section of hotels, department stores, shops, and loft buildings, relatively far from the Grand Central and Pennsylvania Railroad Stations, and several blocks from the nearest subway lines. The extreme height and distinctiveness of the building were designed to serve as an advertising beacon to attract office tenants.

Similarly, key architectural features were intended to maximize the net revenue that could be generated by the rentable space. For example, the building is less bulky than was permitted under the zoning laws because by designing almost the entire building as a setback tower over a wide, five-story base, the developers increased the rents per square foot by offering offices that were quieter and had more natural light. By building shallow floors with window access for every office, the developers also took away the disadvantage of their location relative to the other tall buildings, offering prospective tenants panoramic and unobstructed views. In this design, constructing less space per floor made each square foot more valuable. Similarly, rather than building a simple

flat rectangular structure that would have produced four corner offices on each floor, the Empire State Building was recessed in the north and south towers so that the extra angles of the structure would yield eight to 12 corner offices per floor, adding significantly to the potential rent.

Unfortunately, all of the developer's sophisticated planning and marketing strategies designed to cope with the basic circumstances of no pre-leased tenants, a bad location, and a terrible office market during the Great Depression were in the short run to little avail. The building stood mostly vacant throughout the 1930s, widely nick-named "The Empty State Building." With the return of full employment and prosperity in the 1940s, however, the building filled up and has proven successful. Rather than being a symbol of a corporation, government, educational, medical, or cultural institution, the Empire State Building stands after more than a half century as a symbol of commercial real estate development.

See also Carol Willis, "Form Follows Finance: The Empire State Building and the Forces That Shaped It" (Social Science Research Council, Committee on New York City, 1990) and two teaching cases—Empire State A by Stephen Roulac from Stanford Business School and Empire State B by Mike Miles and Brian Webb from the University of North Carolina at Chapel Hill—for greater detail on this property from inception through 1982.

velopers were all in such a confident mood that several new structures, including the 77-story, 1,030-foot, art deco Chrysler Building, far surpassed the Woolworth Building in height and prominence. The building that was to become the world's tallest for more than four decades, the Empire State Building, was not a corporate headquarters like some of the other giant skyscrapers, but a purely speculative office

building built quickly in what was considered to be a poor location (see Figure 5-1).

The Rise of Urban Apartment Buildings

One of the most notable trends of the 1920s was the tremendous increase in the construction of apartment buildings. Earlier waves of urbanization in the United States, outside of New York and a handful of other major cities, had been based on a relatively low-density pattern of small, detached single-family houses, attached row houses, or duplexes. Some cities, like Boston, had triple deckers, and in many cities, large older houses were subdivided into multiple units. This pattern began to change dramatically during the 1920s. Real estate investors, developers, lenders, and contractors all became active participants in the production of new apartment buildings. The apartments were built primarily as rental units, though in a few cities, some of the buildings were sold to occupants for cooperative ownership. These new structures, built mainly with brick or stucco exteriors, ranged from very fashionable luxury residences with doormen and other services to more modest housing, and from individual six-unit buildings to high rises and to large complexes equipped with schools, parks, and community centers.

Perhaps the largest private rental project of the decade was the 2,125-unit, moderate-income Sunnyside apartment complex in Long Island City, New York, with rents subsidized through a 10-year property tax abatement. The Metropolitan Life Insurance Company developed the apartments in 1922 to help ease New York's severe shortage of housing. As an experiment in direct ownership and management of rental housing, it proved economically successful and later induced the insurance firm to build many larger projects across the country during the 1930s and 1940s.

Living in apartments suddenly became more fashionable in the Parisian sense for many middle- and upper-income people and a cost-effective form of housing for people across the spectrum of incomes. Rents were relatively high because of the lack of supply as a result of the low level of new residential construction during and immediately after World War I. With the growth in postwar demand, apartments thus became a good investment. The volume of apartments increased steadily throughout the decade, remaining at a near peak of new starts through 1928. Starts of single-family housing, by contrast, peaked in 1925 and dropped sharply thereafter.

Nearly 40 percent of all the dwelling units built during the 1920s were multifamily units. Further, the annual percentage of total residential construction devoted to multifamily dwellings rose from approximately 25 percent in 1921 to more than half of all residential building permits issued in 1928. In every region of the United States and in all urban areas, the absolute number and relative percentage of apartments significantly expanded.

New single-family houses were also built in record numbers during the 1920s. The peak year, 1925, established an all-time high for starts of new housing that was not surpassed until 1950. The level of U.S. nonfarm homeownership escalated by more than 5 percentage points from 1920 to 1930. Urban decentralization and suburbanization spread in all directions across the metropolitan landscape, the number of private automobiles increased by the millions, disposable income and savings for the middle class rose substantially, and land subdividers carved up an astonishing amount of acreage on the periphery of cities into lots for sale. Massive land speculation and wild price escalation ensued in many rapidly growing areas of the country, helping to induce an unfortunate degree of mismanagement and fraud. In Florida alone, enough lots were subdivided, many of them in swampland or literally under water, to house the entire U.S. population.

At the height of the boom, new suburban subdivisions entered the market daily along the country's "crabgrass frontier." While most of them were only modestly improved with basic infrastructure and amenities, a small but significant group of community builders was increasingly developing large-scale, well-planned, fully improved subdivisions complete with extensive landscaping, parks and parkways, and shopping centers. This pattern of development, with roots in the 19th century, was becoming more common and growing in scale of operations and degree of capital investment during the 1920s. The most eloquent representative of this trend was Jesse Clyde Nichols of Kansas City, Missouri, developer of the world-famous Country Club District and a founder of the Urban Land Institute (see Figure 5-2).

FIGURE 5-2
J.C. NICHOLS AND THE DEVELOPMENT OF KANSAS CITY, MISSOURI

Jesse Clyde Nichols returned home to Kansas and entered the real estate business upon graduating from Harvard University in 1903. He started as a small, speculative homebuilder, building and selling single-family houses on vacant lots in a partially improved subdivision. Two years later, he acquired a 10-acre subdivision just south of the city limits of Kansas City, Missouri, and began to plan his vision: the long-term development of a large and high-quality urban community. By 1908, with capital from a group of wealthy investors, he had gained control of more than 1,000 acres on Kansas City's south side, calling it the Country Club District to emphasize its proximity to the Kansas City Country Club. Eventually, those 1,000 acres would contain 6,000 houses, 160 apartment buildings, and 35,000 residents.

By the 1920s, J.C. Nichols had already established the Country Club District as one of the most attractive and expensive communities in the region. The J.C. Nichols Company employed the well-known landscape architect George Kessler, who had previously designed a "City Beautiful" plan for Kansas City that included an elaborate park and parkway system, to do the initial planning and landscaping of the new development. Later, S. Herbert Hare became the Country Club District's chief landscape designer. Nichols worked with the city to extend and build two of the new parkways, the Ward and the Mill Creek, through the Country Club District, giv-ing it excellent transportation connections to the downtown and a vital community amenity. Ward Parkway became among the most fashionable addresses in Kansas City.

Nichols extensively used long-term deed restrictions to control the design, cost, and uses of all private property in the District. For years, he advertised the Country Club District as "the one thousand acres restricted." Nichols invested heavily in a wide range of community facilities from landscaped parks to public art and in an ambitious program of community activities from pageants and regattas to flower shows. In addition, he was one of the first developers to establish a mandatory homeowners' association that collected fees to help legally enforce, revise, and renew the restrictions, finance and maintain the facilities and activities, and establish an active, participatory community identity.

J.C. Nichols engaged in practices that were unusual for real estate developers in his day and was generally ahead of his time. He regularly installed first-rate infrastructure in advance of development, adding its costs to the prices of the lots for sale. He engaged architects to design model homes and built many houses both on a speculative basis and under contract with lot purchasers. Finally, Nichols saw the potential for developing and owning retail centers as a profitable enterprise and as a strategy for building community atmosphere, and over the years he developed and owned

The Spread of the Garden City

Part of what inspired Nichols to build his ideal of a stable, family-oriented, and beautifully landscaped community was his exposure to the European Garden City movement during his college years. Sir Ebenezer Howard in 1898 had published the first edition of his international classic, *Garden Cities of Tomorrow*, and the following year he founded in London the International Garden City Association.[9] By 1904, Letchworth, the first of the English garden cities, was under construction. The garden city movement was a response to the rapid growth and overcrowding of the

FIGURE 5-2 (continued)

J.C. Nichols's Country Club District promised "spacious grounds for permanently protected homes, surrounded with ample space for air and sunshine."

many neighborhood centers. His flagship was a regional retail and office complex in the heart of the District called the Country Club Plaza, developed beginning in 1922 and generally recognized as the first suburban shopping center. Designed with a unified Moorish-Spanish architectural theme and controlled by a centralized management, the Plaza provided both on- and off-street parking, was well located for public transit, and drew a walk-in trade from residents of apartment buildings and workers in office buildings that Nichols developed nearby. Both the District and the Plaza are even today the in places to live and shop in Kansas City.

The restrictive covenants unfortunately discriminated against racial, ethnic, and religious minorities, as was standard on most deed restrictions before the U.S. Supreme Court ruled such provisions legally unenforceable in 1948. And the District in general catered primarily to upper-income people, though beginning in the 1930s and 1940s, Nichols shifted some of the newer subdivisions to smaller houses and lots for a middle-income clientele. Yet for creative and successful real estate entrepreneurship over half a century, Nichols's achievement stands out. He provided leadership to the real estate community as an officer of the National Association of Realtors, to the urban planning community as a founding member of the American Planning Association, and to large-scale developers in particular as the first chair of the Urban Land Institute's Community Builders Council.

grimy, unsanitary, and crime-ridden industrial cities of the west. Howard envisioned balanced, self-contained, and modestly sized communities, each with an adequate economic base for manufacturing employment near workers' housing, democratically self-governing with public ownership of land and community facilities, physically well planned with plenty of greenery, open space, and easy transport, and all part of a regional system of small cities separated by a permanent greenbelt of agricultural land.

The philosophy of garden cities as it spread around the world contained four elements: environmental reform, social reform, town planning, and regional planning. Many of the actual development efforts, including J.C. Nichols's Country Club

District, were motivated primarily by interests in environmental reform and town planning, with far less concern for the other two elements.

The most ambitious attempt to translate the full expression of Howard's ideas in the United States was the City Housing Corporation (CHC) of New York, headed by Alexander Bing. Bing, who along with his brother Leo was a successful developer of luxury apartment buildings in Manhattan, became more public-spirited during his service as a housing consultant to the federal government during World War I, and after the armistice, he was determined to embark on a path of social reform. Linking up with a group of visionaries called the Regional Planning Association of America headed by critic Lewis Mumford and architects and planners like Clarence Stein, Henry Wright, and Catherine Bauer, Alexander Bing attracted sufficient investment capital to establish the City Housing Corporation with the intention of building a garden city in the United States. After developing one successful preliminary project called Sunnyside Gardens in New York, the CHC bought a large parcel of land in Fair Lawn, New Jersey, within commuting range of Manhattan, and began in 1928 developing Radburn, "a town for the motor age."

Planned and designed mainly by Clarence Stein and Henry Wright, Radburn contained many innovative features, such as the separation of vehicular and pedestrian traffic through the use of bridges, underpasses, and footpaths and the use of extra large "superblocks" with interior parks and culs-de-sac to create common open green space, keep automobile through traffic away from houses, and significantly economize on the typical costs of land and infrastructure for conventional development. Radburn also modeled new ways of establishing an unincorporated self-governing community through strict, comprehensive deed restrictions and an active and well-funded homeowners' association. While Radburn received global publicity and many of its planning ideas were widely imitated, it ran into the economic crisis of the 1930s, and only a small portion of the original scheme was actually completed. The CHC encountered serious cash flow problems and was eventually forced into

bankruptcy. Yet its development of Radburn remains one of this country's best known and most admired experiments in for-profit, speculative community building by a private real estate developer.

The Birth of Industry Trade Associations

The vigorous spirit of reform and modernization that characterized the early 20th century was married with the tremendous growth and institutional development of the real estate industry through the movement for "professionalization." Many elements of the flourishing business organized trade associations to upgrade standards of practice, to isolate, ostracize, and where possible eliminate unsavory activities, and to cooperate with the public sector and other segments of the business world and the general public to protect the interests of real estate and enhance its political stature and economic viability.

The National Association of Realtors (NAR), for example, was established in 1908 to seek government licensing of the brokerage business. Operating through local boards of Realtors, the NAR lobbied for public regulation of all participants in the larger industry combined with self-policing of the smaller and more select groups of members. NAR promoted education and research about real estate and played a role in many public policy issues, from urban planning to property taxation. Its Home Builders and Subdividers Division was a national leader in the formation of federal housing policy in the 1920s and 1930s.

Two other groups that started in this period were the Building Owners and Managers Association (BOMA International) and the Mortgage Bankers Association of America (MBAA). BOMA represented the owners and property managers of the rapidly growing numbers of skyscrapers and other large commercial buildings in central cities and later in suburbs. The focus was on professional training for management combined with providing a voice for relevant public policy issues. The MBAA was originally called the Farm Mortgage Bankers Association but changed to an urban focus and a new name during the early

1920s. At that time, mortgage bond houses and mortgage lending companies allied with real estate brokers and developers and life insurance companies were rapidly evolving and expanding the variety of capital financing instruments available to acquire and develop property. The MBAA later increased its national prominence with the advent of the federal government's new housing credit system during the 1930s and 1940s.

FINANCE

In real estate more so than in most other investments, capital costs are generally high relative to current incomes, so the means of financing always is a critical factor in the ability to engage in transactions and in the success or failure of projects. To compensate for the first problem, real estate is normally a valuable physical asset that makes excellent collateral for securing loans. Thus, while cash equities have always been important in financing real estate, increasingly during the past two centuries, new institutions were created and methods devised to establish real estate as a highly leveraged form of enterprise operating chiefly on borrowed funds. Easily available credit has usually fueled real estate booms as well as excessive speculation and overbuilding. Conversely, when lenders turn off the spigot, tight money becomes the bane of the industry, leading at times to decreasing supply, declining sales, falling prices, rising defaults and foreclosures, and illiquid markets—as was the case in mid-1990.

An important source of credit has always been the sellers, including landowners and building owners, subdividers, and speculative builders. Sellers "taking back paper" in the form of land contracts, purchase money mortgages, second mortgages, assumables, and a host of other instruments of "creative financing," enabling purchasers to buy now and pay later, has been a significant feature in the history of U.S. real estate markets. Beginning in the 1880s, subdivider William E. Harmon launched what became a successful enterprise selling subdivision lots with as little as 5 percent down and the rest due in small monthly installments.

Before the advent of the FHA and Veterans Administration mortgage insurance and guarantee programs, "builders' mortgages" were an essential component of the sales of one- to four-unit housing. Developers acquiring acreage from farmers and other rural landowners often negotiated complex transfers of ownership and repayment schemes in an attempt to bridge the gaps of time and cash flow. Brokers also entered the field, with many real estate sales firms maintaining mortgage and loan departments as a service to their clients and to help generate a greater volume of sales (and thus sales commissions) and additional profits from the loan business itself.

Another traditional supplier of funds for real estate has been networks of local investors, ranging from direct financing from friends, relatives, and wealthy individuals to lending through the vehicle of a trust company or mortgage company to providing equity capital by forming or joining syndicates and limited partnerships. Richard Hurd, most famous today for writing the classic *Principles of City Land Values* in 1903, headed for many years the Lawyers Mortgage Company in New York, gathering money from prosperous investors and then making first mortgage loans on commercial and residential real estate, strictly limited to high-quality rental buildings or "income properties" in the best locations.[10] Hurd's instincts for good value and his low-risk strategy led to a successful track record in loan safety and relatively high yields.

In contrast to Richard Hurd, mortgage bond houses like S.W. Straus flourished during the 1920s, selling securities backed by frequently overinflated values of new office and apartment buildings. Before the 1929 stock market crash, funds flowed into mortgage bond sales, and securities dealers arranged for highly speculative new construction simply as some minor detail needed to issue and sell more bonds. After the crash, even the most optimistic appraiser had to admit that the buildings were grossly overvalued; not only did the borrowers default for lack of sufficient tenants to generate cash flow but the bond houses themselves also went bankrupt and left vast numbers of investors with little or nothing of what had often been promised as a guaranteed high yield and timely return of principal and interest.

Throughout the 19th century and up to the 1920s, the main source of financing for home mortgages was private individuals, operating mainly through the various methods described earlier. Since that time, financial institutions have played the dominant role in all types of real estate finance; the growth of these institutions is an important part of the story of real estate development. Chapter 3 examined how these financial intermediaries operate today. This chapter looks at their histories to obtain a clearer perspective on their contemporary decision making.

Commercial banks are the oldest of the institutions that have been involved in making both construction loans and mortgage loans. These banks have been heavily involved in real estate lending, often to the point of insolvency during periods of economic and financial crisis. Financial "panics" and banking problems were so common in the 19th century that when the federal government introduced national bank charters in the 1860s, urban real estate mortgage lending was expressly prohibited. State-chartered commercial banks were under no such constraints, however, and they continued to be major real estate lenders. National banks were permitted to get back into urban mortgages beginning in 1916, and they expanded lending significantly during the 1920s.

Because commercial banks relied primarily on short-term deposits for funds, they generally preferred and were often required to lend for short terms, either through construction loans or through mortgages on properties for as little as one year. Most bankers considered a three- to five-year mortgage loan long term and risky well into the 1930s. Normally such short-term mortgages were renewable; in fact, the borrowers counted on being able to keep rolling them over for extended periods. When the market turned down and the banks got into trouble, however, they called these loans or refused to refinance them, often forcing borrowers into default and foreclosure. Historically, the system of real estate credit has been far more unstable than it is in today's volatile world.

Life insurance companies have always been important players in real estate, both as owners and as lenders. Since the mid-19th century, 25 to 50 percent of life insurance companies' portfolios has been in real estate assets. Life insurance companies have traditionally been involved in financing and purchasing large-scale projects, such as office buildings, shopping centers, and apartment complexes. Beginning in the 1920s, some insurance companies also entered the home mortgage field.

Mutual savings banks have also been major real estate lenders. Most of them are located in the northeastern United States, and in some cities, they have been major institutions. Nationally, however, their role and influence in residential lending was eclipsed by savings and loan associations. Also called building and loan associations, homestead associations, and cooperative banks, S&Ls were developed in the mid-19th century specifically to promote homebuilding and homeownership for people of modest incomes. Savings were pooled through monthly savings plans, and money was loaned for the construction or purchase of one- to four-family dwellings. Though S&Ls charged higher interest than other mortgage lenders to pay a higher return to their depositors, their loan terms were more favorable in two ways: 1) higher leverage—they lent up to 75 percent of the property's appraised value when most other lenders advanced only 40 or 50 percent on first mortgages; and 2) longer terms—S&Ls used amortized monthly loan repayment plans for up to 12 years, while most other lenders used nonamortized balloon mortgages with semiannual interest payments and the entire principal due in one to five years.

By the 1920s, S&Ls had emerged as the leading residential lender among financial intermediaries, particularly for one- to four-family houses. Life insurance companies and commercial banks dominated commercial and industrial real estate lending. While syndications, mortgage companies, and a variety of other noninstitutional lenders remained important, the major trend in real estate lending was the increasing role of financial institutions, especially in the field of housing. For example, the institutional share of residential mortgage debt increased from less than half during the 1890s to 66 percent by 1912. The total percentage of owned houses that were mortgaged rose from 25 percent in 1890 to nearly 40 percent in 1920 and more than half in New England and the Middle Atlantic states, where the larger financial institutions were concentrated. More and more, "sweat equity" was being supplanted in real estate by a debt-driven system encompassing entrepreneurial producers and institutional financiers.

THE GREAT DEPRESSION AND WORLD WAR II

The long boom of the 1920s came to an abrupt end when the stock market crashed in October 1929. Though most people believed that the economic downturn was only a temporary setback—that prosperity was just around the corner—in fact the Great Depression was the longest and worst in our nation's history. Starting in 1929, output and employment steadily fell for four straight years, finally hitting bottom in 1933. At the low point, one out of every four people was out of work, desperately seeking but unable to find any kind of job.

The bubble had burst on the real estate boom even before the stock market crash, though many eager speculators had not quite realized that they were in for such a hard landing. Most real estate markets had reached their peak in 1926, the same year that the Florida land boom collapsed. Investment in real estate, construction, sales, and values had been slowly spiraling downward since 1926. Activity, though declining in most markets, was still at a very high level relative to the early 1920s or the previous decade, and in certain categories, such as construction of new urban office and apartment buildings, the markets still appeared to be flourishing.

By the late 1920s, the speculative craze for subdivision lots was abating, and many of the legions of people that had bought on credit in anticipation of rapid and profitable resales were defaulting on their loans and property tax assessments. A major disaster loomed. Soon most of the mortgage bond issues were in default and foreclosure, with many bondholders losing

Soup lines formed in major cities across the country to feed the many unemployed workers after the Great Depression.

their capital, leading to widely publicized investigations of fraud and corruption during the 1930s, similar to the S&L scandals of 1990. As banks increasingly faced a crisis of liquidity, they refused to make new real estate loans or refinance existing ones, often calling in loans to be repaid immediately. That approach was self-defeating, as it further collapsed markets, thousands of banks failed, and millions of their depositors lost much or all of their savings.

Through 1931, new investment, development, sales, and leasing continued in many markets, and real estate entrepreneurs kept hopes alive; in the following year, however, everything began grinding to a halt, and bankruptcy became the normal state of affairs. Financing was unavailable, and real estate plummeted in value. Much of the market was frozen, flooded with properties for sale or lease that no one wanted, even at heavily discounted prices and rents. By 1933, nearly half of all home mortgages were in default and 1,000 properties a day foreclosed. Annual starts of new housing had dropped by more than 90 percent, from the record-breaking peak of 937,000 units in 1925 to the dismal trough of 93,000 units in 1933.

Into this escalating crisis stepped the federal government, at first gingerly under President Herbert Hoover with considerable prodding in 1931 and 1932 from the Democratic Congress and then forcefully under the New Deal of President Franklin Roosevelt. Failing banks and securities markets were reorganized and stabilized, with federal deposit insurance and a new regulatory apparatus helping to restore the public's and investors' confidence. Public works programs were initiated on a massive scale that dwarfed any previous peacetime federal budget, with billions of dollars spent to employ millions of jobless workers, building and rebuilding the nation's infrastructure—roads, bridges, tunnels, highways, dams, power plants, airports, waterways and ports, fixed-rail lines and terminals, parks, playgrounds, schools, health clinics, community centers, civic administration buildings, low-rent housing, and a host of other popular facilities.

The ever-changing and -expanding alphabet soup of federal agencies—the RFC, PWA, CWA, WPA, TVA, and many others—played key roles in financing, contracting, and mobilizing state and local government and the private sector. Collectively, this effort built a better economic future while putting people immediately to work and stimulating the rebirth of economic activity and growth. In many real estate markets during the worst years of the 1930s, government-supported development and redevelopment projects were the only action in town. These mainly federal public works initiatives helped encourage two forms of entrepreneurship that flourished during the New Deal: the powerful public works manager, best symbolized by New York's Robert Moses (see Figure 5-3), and the large-scale private contractor, exemplified by California's Henry J. Kaiser (see Figure 5-4).

Bailing Out the Financial Institutions

Public works was only one of the strategies New Dealers used to revive the general economy and one of its most important sectors, construction and development. The field of private housing had by 1933 suffered an almost complete collapse, and the entire system of residential financing that had grown so rapidly during the 1920s with its crazy quilt of land contracts, second and third mortgages, high interest rates and loan fees, short terms, balloon pay-

---

FIGURE 5-3
ROBERT MOSES

Robert Moses directed the construction of parks and parkways for the state of New York beginning in the 1920s. In 1933, Mayor Fiorello LaGuardia appointed him parks commissioner for New York City. During the New Deal, LaGuardia lobbied in Washington for billions of dollars in federal public works funds, and Moses built many of the projects, including the complex and expensive Triborough Bridge, which opened in 1936. As chairman of the Triborough Bridge Authority, Moses discovered that semi-independent public authorities could amass considerable long-term power so long as the authority's management continued to control an activity that generated sufficient revenue to repay debt and accumulate a surplus. These authorities could successfully finance their operations through the sale of bonds (in the early days of the Triborough, the federal Reconstruction Finance Corporation was the only willing buyer, though private investors later bought the bonds) and then retire those bonds through a dedicated source of revenue, such as bridge tolls. Moses's extensive multibillion dollar development activities as head of several authorities for more than three decades helped establish public authorities as critical organizations in the real estate field. During the early 1970s, for example, under the leadership of Austin Tobin, one of Robert Moses's most powerful competitors among public authority chief executives, the Port Authority of New York and New Jersey built the massive twin office towers of the World Trade Center in lower Manhattan, at that time the world's tallest buildings.

FIGURE 5-4
HENRY J. KAISER

Henry J. Kaiser was a general contractor who built public works. Initially a road builder for governments in the western United States and Canada, in 1930 he put together a consortium of six large construction firms, including Bechtel and Morrison-Knudsen, and successfully obtained the federal contract to build the massive Hoover Dam on the Colorado River in southern Nevada.

Beginning in 1933, Kaiser established a close working relationship with U.S. Secretary of the Interior Harold L. Ickes, who was one of a handful of key New Deal officials who controlled the federal public works purse strings and dispensed billions of dollars in government contracts. During the 1930s, Kaiser-led teams won the contracts to build both the Bonneville and the Grand Coulee Dams in addition to doing part of the work on the San Francisco–Oakland Bay Bridge and constructing Oakland's Broadway Tunnel and several other large projects. Headquartered in Oakland, California, Kaiser achieved national recognition as a shipbuilder during World War II and as a manufacturer of cement, gypsum, aluminum, chemicals, steel, automobiles, cargo planes, and jeeps.

During the war, Henry Kaiser built a substantial number of emergency housing units for the workers who were flocking to Richmond, California, Portland, Oregon, and Vancouver, Washington, to construct his "liberty ships" for the U.S. Navy. After the war, Kaiser became interested in mass-producing houses and formed, in 1945, a partnership with Fritz Burns, a major southern California developer. Their new company, Kaiser Community Homes, built thousands of small, inexpensive, two- and three-bedroom single-family detached houses on the West Coast until they ceased production in 1950. In the mid-1950s, Henry Kaiser retired as chief executive of Kaiser Industries, remarried, and moved to Hawaii, where he became a major developer of resort hotels, recreational subdivisions, houses, shopping centers, golf courses, and convention facilities until his death in 1967 at the age of 85.

ments, and various other high-risk and speculative practices had come crashing down like a house of cards. In the wake of this panic of defaults and foreclosures, the federal government intervened to transform structurally the rules of the financial game and to help move private housing sales and construction out of the doldrums.

The first federal actions in housing finance focused on bailing out the savings and loan associations. S&Ls had mortgaged 4.35 million properties during the 1920s, lending out more than $15 billion to homebuilders and purchasers. By the early 1930s, thousands of these institutions were insolvent as a result of bad loans, overvalued properties, and inability to raise sufficient new capital. President Hoover and the Congress responded to the crisis by establishing the Federal Home Loan Bank System in 1932, which merged and reorganized bankrupt S&Ls, encouraged the creation of new federally chartered S&Ls that would be better capitalized and more strictly regulated, and, most important, provided vitally needed liquidity for federal- or state-chartered thrifts, helping to free them from their traditional dependence on short-term commercial bank credit. Two years later came the Federal Savings and Loan Insurance Corporation, which greatly strengthened the attractiveness of S&Ls to savers by insuring deposits and by helping to standardize management of thrift institutions. S&Ls also were granted a series of income tax and regulatory benefits in exchange for the requirement that they continue to lend money primarily for residential mortgages (a requirement that remained in force until the Reagan administration's monetary "reforms" of 1980 and 1982).

Other dramatic structural changes occurred in the 1930s. The federal government created the Home Owners' Loan Corporation (HOLC) in 1933 and the FHA in 1934. The HOLC refinanced more than $3 billion of shaky or defaulted mortgages and introduced long-term (15-year) self-amortizing loans to many borrowers who were not familiar with the idea.

The Rise of the Federal Housing Administration

While the HOLC was a temporary bailout operation that stopped making loans in 1936, the FHA was a permanent program that launched a revolution in financing housing. FHA's mutual mortgage insurance system reduced the investment risk for lenders and brought the twin S&L principles of long-term amortization of mortgage loans and high loan-to-value ratios into the world of commercial banks, life insurance companies, mutual savings banks, and mortgage companies—institutions that had not previously used such underwriting practices. FHA's initiatives encouraged lenders to extend the first mortgage loan-to-value ratio to an unprecedented 80 to 90 percent, to extend the length of the loan repayment period to 20 and 25 years, to eliminate second mortgages, and to significantly lower interest rates and total loan origination fees.

Among its many reforms, FHA rationalized, standardized, and improved methods and practices of appraisal, universalized the use of title insurance, required the lender's monthly collection of property taxes and property insurance as part of the loan payments, and helped popularize other methods for stabilizing real estate transactions and financing procedures. Its insured mortgages became a standardized product and a safe investment that helped establish a nationwide mortgage market in place of the previously idiosyncratic and localized submarkets. The entire home mortgage lending system began to shift from lending primarily on the security of the property in the event of foreclosure to lending mainly based on the borrower's projected income and ability to repay without default. It was a major conceptual change.

FHA also promoted cost-efficient production of small houses and affordable homeownership for middle-income families. The FHA's conditional commitment enabled developers and merchant builders of subdivisions to obtain debt financing for large-scale construction of new residential neighborhoods and communities, complete with finished houses and full installation of improvements, ready for immediate occupancy by people who were able to buy with modest savings because they qualified for FHA-insured mortgages. The FHA model of real estate development represented a dramatic advance over previous methods of subdividing and selling unimproved lots that had been fairly common in the 1920s.

FHA's property standards and neighborhood standards helped to improve the minimum levels of quality in the design, engineering, materials, equipment, and methods of land development and housing construction. FHA's Land Planning Division encouraged private planning by developers and builders and public planning by state and local governments to coordinate accessible transportation, recreational facilities, utilities, services, and land uses through comprehensive plans, official maps, zoning and requirements for setbacks, and regulations for subdivisions. The Land Planning Division played a key national role in reshaping the design of suburban housing tracts, upgrading the use of deed restrictions for private planning and development, and reorganizing and extending the role of local and metropolitan public planning.

FHA also introduced new techniques for analyzing market demand and using underwriting to limit overbuilding and excessive subdividing. This element of market control was explicitly aimed at eliminating curbstone subdividers and "jerry-builders" and replacing them with community builders. More sophisticated market analysis and greater market control became necessary as a result of FHA's primary emphasis on long-term financing of large numbers of housing units in newly developed neighborhoods. FHA underwriters needed to know before development began that a sufficient number of potential buyers for the houses existed and that purchasers' incomes, market demand, and house values would either be stable or rise over the 25 years the mortgages would be insured. FHA's "risk-rating system" included consideration of factors affecting the supply of and demand for housing, such as patterns of urban employment, distribution of income, population growth, changes in the housing stock, formation of households, the locational dynamics of residential neighborhoods, and future land uses and values.

Within two years of its creation, new federal and state laws to stabilize and restructure the commercial banking system and the establishment of the Federal Deposit Insurance Corporation in 1933 enabled commercial banks to participate in the FHA's program. Life insurance companies and mutual savings banks also took advantage of FHA insurance, enabling them to act as primary lenders and to purchase and sell the standardized and relatively low-risk FHA-insured loans. The existence of FHA mortgages made it possible to start the Federal National Mortgage Association (Fannie Mae) in 1938. Fannie Mae, capitalized by the Reconstruction Finance Corporation, initiated a strong secondary market for FHA-insured mortgages, purchasing loans from primary lenders to provide them with the liquidity to make new loans plus additional income through retention of servicing fees. This national secondary mortgage market helped to smooth out fluctuations in real estate business cycles and geographic differences in availability of mortgage funds. Fannie Mae was particularly vital to the growth of the modern mortgage companies, many of whom started their high-volume businesses in the 1930s and 1940s based mainly on making FHA loans for resale to Fannie Mae or to a life insurance company, a savings bank, or another group of lenders and investors. (See Appendix A for more detail on the public sector's secondary mortgage activities.)

FHA's underwriting guidelines strongly favored new housing over used, suburban locations over central-city sites, whole subdivisions over scattered units, single-family houses over apartments, and Caucasians over African-Americans. For older cities and racial minorities, these policies were inequitable, discriminatory, and disastrous. But for the growth of white, middle-class suburbia, they were of crucial importance. Though FHA did insure mortgages on suburban garden apartments, its overall thrust helped reverse the trend of the late 1920s toward increased construction of apartments and significantly boosted large-scale homebuilders and suburban homeownership.

By the late 1930s, the economy and housing markets were reviving, and FHA was insuring more than one-third of all new houses; 98 percent of FHA's insured mortgages were on single-family detached houses in new suburban subdivisions. Even the J.C. Nichols Company was building relatively inexpensive, modestly sized FHA-insured houses on the outskirts of Kansas City, and the principal landscape architect for the Country Club District, S. Herbert Hare, wrote in 1939 that "the greatest value of the Federal Housing Administration regulations has been in raising the standards of design in districts for less expensive houses."[11]

FHA's highest volume was in California, where the country's suburban future was already under construction in the late 1930s. Fred Marlow, who headed FHA's southern California office from 1934 to 1938, and Fritz Burns formed a private development company and, beginning in 1942, built more than 4,000 FHA-insured small houses in a new southwest Los Angeles subdivision called Westchester. The purchasers of the houses were primarily workers in the nearby and rapidly growing aircraft industry. Westchester, located adjacent to what is now Los Angeles International Airport, consisted of more than 3,000 acres—so big that the Marlow-Burns Development Company divided the project among three other residential development firms, who built an additional 10,000 houses. The four companies in partnership also developed a major shopping center at the intersection of La Tijera and Sepulveda Boulevards. Westchester became a model for postwar suburban tract housing, and Fred Marlow and Fritz Burns both served as presidents of the National Association of Home Builders.

Housing after the Great Depression

While starts of new houses finally began rising after the long slump, much of the older housing stock was badly deteriorated and getting worse as a result of overcrowding, lack of maintenance, and other direct effects of the Great Depression. In 1937, President Roosevelt declared in his second inaugural address that "one-third of a nation [was] ill-housed, ill-clad, and ill-nourished."

In 1919, Edith Elmer Wood, a talented housing reformer with a Ph.D. in political economy from Columbia University, had written *The Housing of the Unskilled Wage Earner*, an eloquent book documenting the problems of low-income shelter and arguing for government subsidy as part of a positive solution. In 1935, the federal Public Works Administration under Harold Ickes published Wood's *Slums and Blighted Areas in the United States*, in which she demonstrated in considerable detail that more than 36 percent of the American people were living in very substandard housing. In her 1919 book and in *Recent Trends in American Housing*, published in 1931, Wood described various private, philanthropic, and public sector efforts to build decent and affordable low-rent housing in many areas of the country.[12]

Except for New York and a handful of other cities, however, substantial government involvement did not begin to emerge until the early 1930s. The collapse of the housing industry opened the way for public subsidies and programs to stimulate employment and economic activity in urban real estate development.

Starting with RFC loans for limited-dividend housing companies building apartments at moderate rentals, the federal government established the PWA Housing Division in 1934 and the U.S. Housing Authority in 1937 to support the removal of the worst slum dwellings and their replacement with brand new public housing. Under USHA's formula, local governments owned the housing, which was built by private contractors. Local authorities borrowed the funds by selling 40-year tax-exempt bonds to private investors, and the federal government repaid the principal and interest on the bonds through annual contributions. Operating costs of the housing were to be paid by the local government

Postdepression housing in Washington, D.C., circa 1937.

through rents collected from the tenants. By the time that World War II interrupted and changed the nature of the public housing program to providing temporary shelter for war workers, USHA and its predecessors had already generated more than 100,000 units of decent, safe, and sanitary dwellings in low-rise buildings, well constructed and attractively landscaped, providing a welcome new environment for many low- and moderate-income families.

Nathan Straus, the chief administrator of USHA from 1937 to 1941, had been an early pioneer of private, limited-dividend housing development in New York. During 1934 and 1935, he developed Hillside Homes in the Bronx, which was the largest private housing project built with a federal loan from the PWA. Clarence Stein served as the architect for Hillside Homes, and Starrett Brothers and Eken were the general contractors. The 26-acre project consisted of low-rise and garden apartments for 1,400 families and included landscaped interior garden courts, a public school, a large central playground, clubrooms, a nursery school, a community center, and other recreational facilities. Straus, though initially a private developer, authored *The Seven Myths of Housing* in 1941, a spirited defense of the public housing program.[13]

Rockefeller Center

One private development that tore down several blocks of older tenement housing was Rockefeller Center in New York, one of the few major projects during the 1930s that was not publicly funded or subsidized. Rockefeller Center stands as the forerunner of today's large-scale urban mixed-use developments and continues to be among the best-known and most successful of such projects.

The original parcel of land between Fifth and Sixth Avenues and 48th and 51st Streets belonged to Columbia University, which leased it for 46 years to John D. Rockefeller, Jr., in October 1928 at an annual rent of nearly $4 million—10 times the existing rental yield from the site. The Rockefeller family lived on 53rd Street near Fifth Avenue and already owned a great deal of property in the neighborhood. In autumn 1928, New York City was in the midst of the real estate boom that preceded the stock market crash, and Rockefeller was very optimistic about his prospects for redeveloping the area. He originally planned to build a new Metropolitan Opera House on the site, because the directors of the opera company wanted to relocate from their 45-year-old facility at 40th and Broadway, which had recently become surrounded by the garment industry. Ironically, the opera company eventually turned down Rockefeller's many appeals to become the centerpiece of his ambitious real estate venture, preferring to remain in place until the mid-1960s, when it finally moved to a new opera house built as part of the massive urban renewal project called the Lincoln Center for the Performing Arts.

The Sixth Avenue portion of Rockefeller's site was considered a blighted area in 1928 because of the elevated railroad tracks running along the avenue. By 1939, a new Sixth Avenue subway was constructed and the elevated tracks removed, opening up new opportunities for private redevelopment. The Rockefeller Center site was very large, and it was highly uncertain how all the land could be redeveloped and space occupied in the market-wide context of economic depression, falling rents, and rising vacancies. Teams of architects worked for several years on many different schemes, both with and without the opera house as a focal point. The buildings were planned in a relatively unified architectural theme of style and materials, enhancing the new and unusual image of a mixed-use center of activity within a single development project. Innovative design features included the addition of private streets to cut up the long east-west blocks and the creation of the first privately developed public plaza in the city, which today houses the world's most famous outdoor ice skating rink.

Lacking the high culture of opera, Rockefeller turned to mass culture as his best prospect for attracting commercial tenants to this untested location. By the mid-1930s, he had filled the 70-story RCA Building (now called the GE Building), his main high-rise office tower, with entertainment businesses from radio, motion pictures, and vaudeville that were thriving even during the depression, including

Everything comes together in Rockefeller Center, one of the forerunners of more recent mixed-used developments. Completed in 1940, this fine example of a large-scale urban complex is based in traditional Beaux Arts principles and is rich with much-admired Art Deco detail.

RCA, RKO, and NBC. He also developed on Sixth Avenue his own entertainment facility for the general public, the Radio City Music Hall. Magazine, news service, and book publishers also gravitated to new office buildings in Rockefeller Center. On the Fifth Avenue side, he constructed low-rise structures for international tenants, taking advantage of proximity to prestigious retailers across the street. By the early 1940s, the project had clearly succeeded as a desirable location for corporate office space, and since the 1950s, Rockefeller Center has expanded to the west across Sixth Avenue, with tall office buildings and major tenants ranging from Time-Life to McGraw-Hill to the Rockefeller family's own Exxon. At the same time, travel agents at street level, below-ground retail shops, and a tightly controlled and well-maintained environment all helped turn what was initially a risky, speculative, expensive, money-losing venture into the premier private project of the depression decade.

The Professionalization of Real Estate Development

Two new organizations, both spin-offs from the National Association of Realtors, also emerged out of the crucible of economic crisis and political reform that characterized the 1930s. The Urban Land Institute started as a small, elite organization, primarily of big commercial and residential developers. ULI was intended to focus on education and research, concerned with affecting public policy issues as well as improving standards and practices of private development. Initially, ULI organized into two key subgroups. The Central Business District Council sponsored a series of studies on urban decentralization and urged federal, state, and local government officials to establish and provide funds for urban renewal, urban highways, and other programs to physically redevelop and economically revitalize the commercial core of the older central cities. The Community Builders Council, which sponsored ULI's *Community Builders Handbook* beginning in 1947, concerned itself with promoting high-quality, large-scale residential and commercial development in suburban areas.[14]

The National Association of Home Builders (NAHB) was formed in 1943 to lobby the federal government during wartime to allow the continuation of private development of housing for sale or rent financed with the aid of FHA mortgage insurance. Some government policymakers favored limiting new housing to public construction and ownership during the wartime emergency, arguing that such an approach would be more cost-efficient and easier to manage in the context of allocating scarce resources for the war effort. The Home Builders Emergency Committee, led by Hugh Potter, a former lawyer and judge who developed River Oaks in Houston, fought for publicly subsidized housing for war workers to be built and owned by the private sector. In the end, a compromise was reached involving housing of both types. In the process, the Home Builders and Subdividers Division of NAR split from the parent organization and merged with a completely separate group called the National Home Builders Association. Together, the two groups became the NAHB, with Fritz Burns of Los Angeles as the founding president of the new organization, which grew from an initial 1,300 members to more than 25,000 in less than a decade.

During World War II, the real estate industry in certain locations received an enormous economic boost from the surge of demand for new construction, for land, and for space in existing buildings. Yet many ventures not directly related to the war economy were put on hold for the duration, and some entrepreneurs were anxiously waiting for peacetime to reappear. Many people were apprehensive, fearing a replay of the Great Depression after the soldiers and sailors were sent home and the production of so many new guns, tanks, ships, and planes was no longer necessary. Others were more optimistic, seeing a wave of growth precipitated by the rising disposable incomes and pent-up consumer demand that was accumulating during the war, when most people were earning much more than the previous decade but were unable to spend their new wealth because a great deal of U.S. production capacity was diverted to the global battlefields. By 1948, the optimists were proven correct in their predictions, and the postwar suburbs depending on the automobile, suburban homeownership, and a consumer boom were in full swing.

SUMMARY

Expansion in the real estate industry characterizes most of the period from the end of the 1800s through the first half of the 1900s. Aggressive commercial development and movement to the suburbs changed the face of the city.

The further involvement of the public sector altered the way development was done, and the changes in lending policies brought about by the creation of the FHA made residential development easier and increased the number of homeowners in the United States.

Chapter 6 takes a look at postwar development trends and how the real estate industry evolved into its present situation.

NOTES

1. Adna Ferrin Weber, *The Growth of Cities in the Nineteenth Century: A Study in Statistics* (New York: Macmillan, 1899), p. 1.

2. Paul Goldberger, *The Skyscraper* (New York: Alfred A. Knopf, 1981), p. 7.

3. Kenneth Turney Gibbs, *Business Architectural Imagery in America, 1870–1930* (Ann Arbor, Mich.: UMI Research Press, 1984), p. 45.

4. Ibid.

5. Ibid., p. 54.

6. Earle Shultz and Walter Simmons, *Offices in the Sky* (Indianapolis: Bobbs-Merrill, 1959), pp. 33–34.

7. *Golden Book of Wanamaker Stores* (Philadelphia: John Wanamaker, 1911), p. 47.

8. Thompson-Starrett Company, "A Census of Skyscrapers," *The American City*, September 1929, p. 130.

9. Ebenezer Howard, *Garden Cities of Tomorrow* (London: Faber & Faber, 1945). See especially the introductory essays by Lewis Mumford and Frederic Osborn.

10. Richard M. Hurd, *Principles of City Land Values* (New York: Real Estate Record and Guide, 1903).

11. Marc A. Weiss, *The Rise of the Community Builders: The American Real Estate Industry and Urban Land Planning* (New York: Columbia Univ. Press, 1987), p. 157.

12. Edith Elmer Wood, *The Housing of the Unskilled Wage Earner* (New York: Macmillan, 1919); *Recent Trends in American Housing* (New York: Macmillan, 1931); *Slums and Blighted Areas in the United States*, Public Works Administration, Housing Division Bulletin No. 1 (Washington, D.C.: U.S. Government Printing Office, 1935).

13. Nathan Straus, *The Seven Myths of Housing* (New York: Alfred A. Knopf, 1941).

14. Community Builders Council, *The Community Builders Handbook* (Washington, D.C.: ULI–the Urban Land Institute, 1947).

Chapter 6

Post–World War II To the Present

For the duration of World War II, most new private construction was put on hold except for industrial and residential development directly related to the war. On the heels of a decade-long economic depression, most U.S. real estate markets by 1945 were badly *under*built. Housing was a pressing need. Eleven million servicemen and women were returning home to communities where very few unoccupied houses were available. By 1947, more than 5 million families were either living doubled up with other families in overcrowded dwellings or occupying temporary shelters. Starts of new houses quadrupled to a half million units in 1946, but production was far below the demand, and the newly deregulated housing prices were skyrocketing upward. After a bumpy start, the homebuilding industry eventually rose to the challenge. With government assistance through mortgage credit financing, new highways and infrastructure, permissive zoning and planning, and other tools, housing starts reached an all-time high of more than 1.5 million new units by 1950, mostly single-family houses to accommodate the new suburban baby boom.

Against this backdrop of postwar economic growth, this chapter explores the evolution of the real estate industry since World War II, examining:

- Suburbanization and the postwar boom;
- Urban renewal;
- The expansion of interstate highways and the growth of the suburbs;
- The urban crisis in race, housing, and neighborhoods; and
- The 1970s to the 1990s.

SUBURBANIZATION AND THE POSTWAR BOOM

In 1944, Congress prepared for growth after the war by passing the Servicemen's Readjustment Act—the "GI Bill"—which established both the Veterans Administration (VA) and the VA home loan guarantee program. Under this program, an eligible veteran could obtain a low-interest, highly leveraged mortgage loan to buy a house, in some cases with no down payment at all. In the original legislation, homeownership loan guarantees were available only to veterans for the first two years after returning to civilian life, but by 1946 the housing shortage became so severe that Congress soon extended the program for 10 years. Billions of dollars were authorized for FHA, VA, and Fannie Mae during those postwar years, most notably in the landmark 1949 Housing Act, which declared as a national goal "a decent home and a suitable living environment for every American family."

The production of housing reached an unprecedented volume. Fifteen million units were started in the 1950s, more than double the number in the 1940s and more than five times the total in the 1930s. Two-thirds of this housing was being constructed in the rapidly expanding suburbs, while many central cities began losing population after 1950. Formerly agricultural land was being subdivided into suburban tracts on a grand scale all over the United States, with the greatest growth in the Sunbelt states, especially California, Texas, and Florida—new centers of what President Eisenhower called "the military-industrial complex."

FHA's and VA's promotion of large-scale homebuilding and the availability of mass financing through life insurance companies, S&Ls, mutual savings banks, and other sources led residential developers to grow rapidly in size as the entire industry dramatically increased its total production. By 1949, 10 percent of the builders constructed 70 percent of the houses, 4 percent of the builders constructed 45 percent of the houses, and just 720 firms built 24 percent of the houses. These figures represented a drastic change from before the war, and they were to continue changing during the 1950s with increasing expansion in size, scale, and volume by the big homebuilders. Part of this change in the real estate industry after the war can be attributed to the experiences during the war, when the federal government encouraged and subsidized residential developers to quickly mass-produce private housing for war workers.

The biggest of all the homebuilders immediately after the war was Levitt & Sons, developers of Levittown, New York. Levittown was the country's largest private housing project at the time. The first houses were completed in fall 1947, and by the early 1950s, Levitt & Sons had built 17,500 houses on 4,000 acres of potato fields in Hempstead on central Long Island, about 30 miles east of New York City. *Time* magazine devoted a cover story to Levittown in July 1950, calling the firm's presi-

dent, William Levitt, "the most potent single modernizing influence in a largely antiquated industry."[1] The Levitts priced most of their newly built houses at $7,990—$1,500 less than any of their competitors—and still managed to earn $1,000 profit on every house sold.

Abraham Levitt and his two sons, William and Alfred, started in the housing business on Long Island in the late 1920s, building individual luxury houses and later a small subdivision called Strathmore-at-Manhasset. During World War II, the Levitts' firm received government contracts to construct 2,350 houses for war workers in and around Norfolk, Virginia; what they learned about high-volume methods of production became the basis for their postwar planning and development. At Levittown, William Levitt turned the entire development into a mobile assembly line, with teams of workers moving from house to house to perform 26 specific, repetitive tasks. Everything was carefully programmed and tightly controlled. The Levitts bought materials in bulk, producing them to their own specifications. Subcontractors were required to work only for them; Levitt specially trained and managed construction crews. Materials were preassembled in central facilities and delivered to each construction site just in time for that day's set of repetitive assignments. The emphasis was on speed, and at the peak, houses in Levittown were completed at the astounding rate of 35 per day.

With an advance commitment from the FHA to insure mortgages on thousands of houses, the Levitts were able to obtain the credit they needed to construct the houses and to develop roads, sewers, parks, schools, swimming pools, a shopping center, and other facilities. Levitt simplified the transaction of selling houses to two simple, half-hour steps, making it easy for people who had never before owned a house. Many of the purchasers were veterans who could move in with no down payment other than $10 in closing costs and then pay $56 a month for principal, interest, taxes, and insurance, considerably less than the monthly rent for a comparable apartment. The two-bedroom houses came already equipped with modern appliances, and the quarter-acre lots contained plenty

The inexpensive two-bedroom Levittown houses made it possible for homebuyers to make a purchase with little money down and low monthly payments—a real boon to war veterans who were starting over.

of room for expansion. The Levitts regrettably restricted their American Dream to whites only. Before the civil rights movement of the 1960s, this practice was unfortunately common among most new housing developments, and even the FHA and VA, two agencies of the federal government, actively supported discriminatory policies against racial minorities.

Levitt & Sons built two other Levittowns, both in the suburbs of Philadelphia: in Bucks County, Pennsylvania, in the early 1950s and in Willingboro, New Jersey, in the late 1950s . They built the last of their very large housing projects, Belair, in Bowie, Maryland, during the early 1960s. The Levitt style of mass-produced community development had its share of critics, who disliked both the architectural and the social conformity, best captured during the 1950s by John Keats's *The Crack in the Picture Window* and William H. Whyte's

The Organization Man.[2] The latter book is a sociological study of Park Forest, Illinois, a 2,400-acre postwar Chicago suburb developed, beginning in the late 1940s, by an appropriately named firm, American Community Builders. Philip Klutznick, who had served during the war as head of the federal Public Housing Authority, was the lead developer of Park Forest, which, like Levittown, included thousands of FHA- and VA-financed middle-income houses. Klutznick later founded the Urban Investment and Development Company, which constructed downtown office buildings, hotels, retail space, and mixed-use complexes, including Chicago's Water Tower Place and Boston's Copley Place. While many other big developments flourished and large builders operated during the postwar years, the original Levittown in Hempstead, Long Island, still stands as a cultural symbol of America for all of them.

The American Dream—a typical FHA-financed subdivision in San Diego, circa 1964.

URBAN RENEWAL

Though suburbanization hit the country like a tidal wave in the 1950s, the movement of population and employment away from the central cities was already evident three decades earlier. While downtown development flourished in most cities during the 1920s, the neighborhoods surrounding the central business district, sometimes called "the zone of transition," had stopped growing and started deteriorating. Once the depression hit, development in most central cities ground to a halt, a condition that continued in the commercial core through the war and immediately after it. By the mid-1950s, many U.S. cities had not seen a single new office building constructed in nearly 30 years. Most of these cities were also losing large numbers of manufacturing jobs after the growth spurt induced by the war. Railyards, factories, and warehouses were being abandoned, with little demand for new occupancy. Many old houses and apartments in the zone of transition were in terrible physical condition and lacked tenants. Offices, retail stores, hotels, and restaurants all suffered

from declining markets and vitality. Civic leaders feared that the heart of the city would die a slow economic, political, and cultural death.

The remedy proposed by many downtown business, real estate, and civic groups was first called district replanning, then urban redevelopment, and, finally, urban renewal. The idea was to rebuild centrally located slums and blighted areas—clearing away the old and underused commercial and industrial structures, moving out the poor and minority residents, and tearing down their housing—and replace them with shiny new office towers, convention centers, hotels, shopping malls, and luxury housing. Local governments would use powers of eminent domain (condemnation) to acquire the land, then demolish the structures, replan and redevelop the land with new infrastructure and public amenities, and sell the land at a discount to private developers who, with tax subsidies and other financial inducements, would invest in and construct new private facilities.

Initially state and local governments operated these programs. One of the most ambitious efforts was the Pittsburgh "Renaissance" fostered by a coalition of corporate executives headed by Richard King Mellon, the scion of a family that owned Gulf Oil, Alcoa, and Mellon Bank, and Mayor David Lawrence, an energetic New Deal Democrat. Working through the Allegheny Conference on Community Development, state and city officials and private sector leaders devised a master plan that guided the rebuilding of downtown's "Golden Triangle" as well as part of the nearby Lower Hill neighborhood, largely populated by African-Americans. Several new high-rise office buildings, a state park, two parkways, a convention center, a sports arena and stadium, luxury apartments, and a mixture of other new public and private development projects replaced the older buildings that had previously occupied this strategic site.

The main obstacle to extensive state and local redevelopment was the high public cost. Local taxpayers balked at the price tag of full-scale renewal, although sometimes a subsidy in the form of tax abatement proved sufficient incentive for a large investor to bear the direct expenses, as in Metropolitan Life Insurance Company's Stuyvesant Town and Peter Cooper Village, two massive private residential redevelopment projects on the east side of Manhattan built during the 1940s. The experience of the 1930s, when the federal government had for the first time granted billions of dollars for public works to state and local governments to rebuild the infrastructure and amenities of central cities, led to many key lobbying groups' demanding that Washington pay for urban renewal through a federal grant program. Title I of the 1949 Housing Act brought such a program into existence, and it was strengthened and modified in the 1954 Housing Act and on many subsequent occasions. Under Title I, the federal government paid anywhere from two-thirds to three-fourths or more of the "writedown," the total direct public cost minus the revenue from the sale of the land to the private redevelopers.

By the 1960s, one could see the impact of Title I in the form of new private and public buildings in numerous central cities. Many of these projects brought needed new investment into the urban economy, creating jobs, increasing the tax base, improving the physical, cultural, and recreational environment, modernizing the use of urban land, and adding attractive structures as well as public open spaces.

Some efforts at clearance, however, brought holes in the ground but no new development; projects like St. Louis's notoriously nicknamed "Hiroshima Flats" cleared sites that failed to attract bids from private developers and became a more blighting influence on the community than the buildings that had been demolished. Urban renewal projects also brought a great deal of displacement of small businesses and low- or moderate-income residents. Unless they owned property, those who were displaced received no compensation and in most cases little or no relocation assistance, either money or new facilities or dwellings. Even when relocation housing was available, it was seldom in the same neighborhood. Between 1949 and 1967, for example, 400,000 residential units were demolished through Title I, but only 10,000 new public housing units were built on urban renewal sites. By the middle 1960s, such statistics led to outcries of "Negro removal" and a vast amount of controversy, with the program first substantially improved during 1968 to 1970 and then abolished in 1974.

Lenders, investors, and users of downtown space were generally a cautious lot during the 1950s and early 1960s, with the powerful suburban trend and the long period of downtown stagnation uppermost in their minds. As a result, even with all the incentives, most local governments found it difficult to attract private developers to participate in efforts at renewal. One successful high-risk developer who bucked the conservative mood and plunged headfirst into the urban renewal program in cities all across the country was William Zeckendorf (see Figure 6-1).

In the early days of urban renewal, the largest investors, lenders, and in many cases joint venture developers of projects were the country's leading life insurance companies. They had emerged from the war with tremendous amounts of cash to invest, and real estate assets appeared to offer a good economic return. Companies like Equitable, which developed the Gateway Center office complex in Pittsburgh's

FIGURE 6-1
WILLIAM ZECKENDORF

As head of Webb & Knapp, William Zeckendorf was America's best-known national developer in the 1950s and 1960s, buying and selling land and existing buildings in and near many large cities and building major projects from Mile High Center and Court House Square in Denver to Roosevelt Field Mall on Long Island to Place Ville-Marie in Montreal to Century City in Los Angeles. He had assembled the land for the site of the United Nations in New York, and he achieved distinction in urban design through the work of his chief architect, I.M. Pei. His most aggressive efforts were in developing urban renewal projects. Beginning in the 1950s, Webb & Knapp built L'Enfant Plaza, a mixed-use office complex, and Town Center apartments and shopping center in southwest Washington, D.C. In Philadelphia, Zeckendorf developed the Society Hill Towers and town houses near the waterfront of the historic city and restored many of the old nearby colonial row houses in the Society Hill neighborhood. Webb & Knapp, using the talents of I.M. Pei and his architectural partner, Henry Cobb, won the contract to redevelop Society Hill through a design competition. They also won design competitions to build the University Gardens apartment complex in the Hyde Park neighborhood of Chicago and an even larger project in Pittsburgh's Lower Hill area. In New York, where Webb & Knapp had its headquarters, Zeckendorf and Pei teamed up to do three major Title I residential development projects, all in Manhattan: Park West Village, Kips Bay Plaza, and Lincoln Towers. And Zeckendorf was also involved at some point in urban renewal planning in Cincinnati, St. Louis, San Francisco, Cleveland, and Hartford.

Golden Triangle, New York Life, developer of Chicago's Lake Meadows racially integrated middle-income apartments, Prudential, which built and occupied the main tower in Boston's Prudential Center, plus Metropolitan Life and John Hancock were all players in the urban renewal game in a variety of cities, involved in corporate office towers, shopping facilities, and residential complexes.

THE EXPANSION OF INTERSTATE HIGHWAYS AND THE GROWTH OF THE SUBURBS

Though urban renewal was controversial for displacing residents and businesses and received much attention for its efforts to reshape central cities, it was dwarfed by the impacts of the interstate highway program on the urban landscape. Downtown corporate interests lobbied heavily for the federal interstate program, which was started in 1956, to bring the highways into the heart of the cities. It was to be the last hope for downtown, with new expressways radiating out in all directions from the central core, bringing in workers, shoppers, tourists, and middle-class residents while simultaneously reducing the traffic congestion on city streets and improving speed and accessibility. In the process of building this grand and expensive automobile-based transportation system, inner-city communities were decimated by displacement and many new patterns of land use established. "One Mile," Robert Caro's dramatic chapter on the Cross-Bronx Expressway in *The Power Broker*, paints a vivid portrait of the human story behind a small portion of the vast network of urban highways.[3]

Ironically, the downtown expressways turned out to be two-way streets, allowing city businesses and residents to leave as well as enter the center city, and thus disappointed the most ardent advocates of urban renewal. Together with the beltways and highways that surrounded and bypassed the urban core, the radials opened up a new frontier of suburbanization, and many hallmarks of downtowns—office buildings, department stores, and hotels—moved or expanded to rapidly growing developments near the intersections of two or more major suburban transportation arteries.

The Growth of Suburban Shopping Centers

Even before the federal interstate program was launched, state and local highways in the suburbs offered promising locations for a new type of large-scale development project, the shopping center. By 1954, total retail sales in suburban centers already exceeded total sales volume in major central cities. Though antecedents to the modern shopping center existed before the war, such as J.C. Nichols's Country Club Plaza in Kansas City, Hugh Prather's Highland Park Shopping Village in Dallas, and Hugh Potter's River Oaks Center in Houston, they were mostly built to serve existing communities. It was only after World War II that the first freestanding regional shopping centers were built that drew patrons from a wide geographic area and were not tied to any specific residential development.

By the early 1950s, shopping centers were springing up on the periphery of cities everywhere, from Cameron Village in Raleigh, North Carolina, to Poplar Plaza in Memphis, Tennessee, to Shopper's World in Framingham, Massachusetts, near Boston. One of the most widely heralded of the new suburban malls was the Northgate Shopping Center, about 20 miles from downtown Seattle. Developed by Allied Stores and opened in 1950, Northgate provided a large Bon Marché department store as the anchor tenant. Smaller stores were lined up along what at that time was considered a major innovation in design: a central outdoor ground-level pedestrian mall with an underground truck tunnel to hide deliveries and removal of refuse. Surrounding the mall was the necessary sea of parking spaces, and it was considered a bold step to turn the mall storefronts away from the automobile traffic and parking lots. In 1954, Northland Center outside Detroit, developed and anchored by J.L. Hudson's department store, opened as the largest regional shopping center to that date and the first to offer attractive open space and amenities. *Architectural Forum* even compared Northland, which was designed by Victor Gruen, America's leading architect of shopping centers, to Rockefeller Center.[4]

Two years later, another department store company, Dayton's of Minneapolis, built Southdale, the first fully enclosed, heated and air-conditioned, suburban shopping mall, in Edina, Minnesota. Southdale was also designed by Gruen, who had won critical acclaim for Northland and later went on to design nearly 100 other malls. To block the threatened construction of a nearby competing mall and reduce the risks

Before 1956, Southdale, Minnesota, was farmland. But in 1956, Dayton's opened Southdale Center, the first fully enclosed, heated, and air-conditioned suburban mall.

on its expensive project, Dayton's broke with previous development practices for shopping centers by inducing another department store, Donaldson's, to come to Southdale as a second anchor. Southdale set new standards for the design, construction, leasing, and management of shopping malls. Other department store chains and speculative shopping center developers quickly followed these new trends. The year after Southdale opened, James Rouse, an independent developer, built the fully enclosed Harundale Mall in the Baltimore suburbs. In 1961, Rouse and Victor Gruen teamed up to design and develop Cherry Hill, a 78-acre shopping center in the Philadelphia suburb of Delaware Township, New Jersey. The shopping center became such a successful focal point and symbol of the suburban area's economic and cultural life that the township residents later voted to change the community's name to Cherry Hill.

Many of the early shopping centers proved to be highly popular and profitable, and those with available land expanded the square footage of retail space, number of stores, and number and size of department store anchors over the past three decades. Equitable now owns Southdale and has purchased, built, or financed many other malls. The total number of shopping centers in the United States has grown exponentially, from a relative handful at the end of the war to 7,000 at the beginning of the 1960s to 35,000 by 1990, including several hundred very large regional malls and a host of different types of smaller centers. In 1954, the International Council of Shopping Centers was formed to represent developers, owners, and managers of this innovative suburban phenomenon and in 1990 represented about 28,000 members.

The Growth of Suburban Industrial Parks

The decentralization and suburban growth fostered by the new highway system was not limited to just housing and retail centers. Industry and commerce also began moving to suburban locations near major transportation arteries. Manufacturing plants that had previously depended mainly on railroad lines now relied more heavily on trucking, finding highway-accessible suburban sites, where land costs and rents were cheaper than the inner cities, to be increasingly attractive for expansion or relocation. In the 1950s, industrial parks, office parks, research and development parks—with full utilities, plenty of parking, access roads, attractive landscaping, and occasionally nearby services—sprouted across suburbia, particularly near the interstate freeways. Cabot, Cabot & Forbes Company of Boston earned a national reputation for successfully developing many of these projects.

Cabot, Cabot & Forbes was an old-line real estate investment management company for Boston's Brahmin elite. In 1947, 26-year-old Gerald Blakely convinced the senior partner, Murray Forbes, to hire him to develop suburban industrial parks. The role of MIT and Harvard in pioneering new science and technology for the war effort suggested that the Boston area could become a significant center of research and manufacturing for electronics and related industries. Blakely also assumed that engineers and scientists then moving to the expanding residential suburbs farther out from the city would appreciate shorter commuting times to nearby industrial and office parks. He focused his development strategy on Route 128, a circumferential state highway then under construction west of Boston in a semicircle about 12 miles from the center of the city.

Blakely acquired land in two suburban towns on Route 128, Needham and Waltham. It took several years to raise the necessary private financing, win support from local governments for the required zoning changes, and convince the state government to build the appropriate highway interchanges and access roads. In the mid-1950s, Cabot, Cabot & Forbes finally opened three large facilities, the Waltham Industrial Center, the Waltham Research and Development Park, and the New England Industrial Park in Needham. All three centers were soon fully occupied, and CC&F was soon searching for more sites to capture a major share of the rapid economic growth then taking place around Route 128.

By the mid-1960s, Cabot, Cabot & Forbes had built 13 of the 19 industrial parks along Route 128. It also developed the 800-acre I-95 Industrial Center farther away from Boston near Route 495, Technology Square in Cambridge near MIT, industrial parks in Pennsylvania and California, and several office buildings and shopping centers. Gerald Blakely became a millionaire, and CC&F acquired assets worth hundreds of millions of dollars, all from an initial investment of several hundred thousand dollars for land acquisition and site planning. In 1967, the National Association of Industrial and Office Parks was formed to represent developers, owners, and managers of such parks.

With manufacturing come distribution and wholesale trade; for developers, that means warehouses and showrooms. Trammell Crow, the country's largest developer of the postwar period, started out as a specialist in providing space for industry's needed storage and wholesaling facilities, building millions of square feet of warehouses and trade marts in his hometown of Dallas and across the country. As the U.S economy grew, especially in the Sunbelt, so did Crow's ambitious development, construction, and leasing activities (see Figure 6-2).

FIGURE 6-2
TRAMMELL CROW

Initially a leasing agent for existing warehouse space, Trammell Crow began in 1948 building new warehouses in Dallas's 10,000-acre Trinity Industrial District along the Trinity River. A federally funded flood control construction program in 1946 had rendered an area formerly considered an undesirable floodplain ripe for development when Crow first approached the industrial district's owners, John and Storey Stemmons, to negotiate a deal to obtain land. The Stemmons brothers decided to go into partnership with Trammell Crow. With financing from several local banks and from life insurance companies like Pacific Mutual and Equitable, Crow and the Stemmonses over the next two decades developed more than 50 warehouses. Crow, working with different partners, built another 40 warehouses in the Trinity Industrial District and branched out to Denver, Atlanta, and many other cities, where he built numerous warehouse projects with various partners. Crow has been a partner in constructing tens of millions of square feet of warehouse space—more than any other single developer—ranging from speculative multitenant facilities to custom-built, single-tenant projects.

In his travels to find tenants for his rapidly expanding inventory of warehouse space, Crow became fascinated by Chicago's massive 24-story Merchandise Mart, built by Marshall Field in 1934 as the world's largest wholesale showroom facility, with more than 4 million square feet of space. By the mid-1950s, Crow launched a new plan to build trade marts in the Trinity Industrial District. Over the next three decades, the Dallas Market Center became Crow's largest and best-known development. The project became feasible in 1955 when the Stemmonses donated 102 acres of land to the state of Texas for a planned interstate highway with service roads for the Trinity District, making the site for Crow's trade center just two blocks from an on/off ramp and a short 10- to 15-minute commute to downtown Dallas and the airport. The highway (I-35), known in Dallas as the Stemmons Freeway, opened in 1959.

Rather than build one gigantic, multipurpose structure like the Merchandise Mart, Crow's strategy was to build an entire complex of attractive and modern buildings that would specialize in specific product lines, one building at a time. In partnership with the Stemmonses, Crow started with the Dallas Decorative Center in 1955 for decorators and the design trade, then developed the Homefurnishings Mart in 1957 for the furniture and fixtures business, the Trade Mart in 1960, the Apparel Mart

FIGURE 6-2 (continued)

in 1964, the World Trade Center in 1972, and the Infomart in 1984 for the high-tech information industry. He also built the Market Hall in 1963, which was the largest privately owned exhibition hall in the United States, and the 1,600-room Loews Anatole Hotel, which opened in two stages in 1979 and 1981. The hotel had so many amenities and facilities that it helped turn the Dallas Market Center into a focal point for nighttime activity and added to its attractiveness as a location for conducting business and holding conventions and trade shows.

Crow entered the hotel business through his association with architect-developer John Portman of Atlanta. The two teamed up in 1960 to build the Atlanta Decorative Arts Center and over the next two decades codeveloped two huge urban renewal projects, Peachtree Center in Atlanta and, together with David Rockefeller, Embarcadero Center in San Francisco. Both projects involved the construction of multiple high-rise office buildings and the development of a large Hyatt Regency Hotel. Crow had included large indoor atrium lobbies in his projects, beginning in 1960 with the Trade Mart in Dallas, and it has become a standard feature of his wholesale market centers, office buildings, apartments, industrial parks, and hotels ever since. Portman, as chief architect, achieved public recognition for the large atrium lobbies in the Atlanta and San Francisco Hyatt Regency Hotels, and the ensuing publicity accorded this innovative hotel design helped set off a wave of similar projects during the boom in downtown and suburban hotel construction that ebbed and flowed during the 1970s and 1980s.

Source: Robert Sobel, *Trammell Crow: Master Builder* (New York: John Wiley & Sons, 1989).

Trammell Crow and architect Martin Growald modeled Infomart, an information industry showplace, after the Crystal Palace Exposition of 1851. Crow thought the warm Victorian style with wooden floors and potted plants would contrast well with the coldness of the computer age.

Hotel and Motel Development

The growth of the interstate highway system and the wave of postwar suburbanization also dramatically affected the hotel business. Before the late 1940s, most hotels were located in the center of cities and towns, except for resort hotels near lakes, rivers, oceans, mountains, and other vacation spots. Large hotels almost always fit this pattern, from the Astor family's Waldorf-Astoria in Manhattan to Henry Flagler's Royal Poinciana in Palm Beach. When the primary mode of transportation was by rail, hotels served travelers through their proximity to train stations.

Beginning in the 1920s, "roadside inns" grew in popularity along major thoroughfares to accommodate automobile drivers, but this type of lodging was usually quite small and nearly always a local mom-and-pop business. And this type of lodging quickly acquired a seedy image, denounced by FBI Director J. Edgar Hoover in 1940 as "dens of vice" whose main clientele was the "hot pillow trade."[5]

In 1952, Kemmons Wilson and Wallace Johnson opened the nation's first Holiday Inn "hotel courts" in Memphis, with clean rooms, free parking, modest prices, and a respectable family image bolstered by the widely advertised offer of free accommodations for children under 12 when accompanied by their parents. The Holiday Inn hotel chain expanded rapidly during the 1950s and 1960s, initially building the inns along highways and taking advantage of key locations along the new interstate system. The chain later moved into urban areas and resort communities, becoming the world's largest hotel chain by the 1980s.

The earliest hotel chains like the Hilton and the Sheraton were based on large downtown hotels, with a few major hotels in big cities and most of them generally independently owned and managed. With the 1950s and the explosion of motels, motor hotels, motor inns, and the like springing up along newly developed freeway exits and interchanges and near airports, chains like Ramada Inn, Howard Johnson's, and TraveLodge quickly proliferated, as did cooperative referral organizations like Best Western and Friendship Inns for large groups of independently owned hotels and motels. By 1954, the number of motel rooms exceeded the number of hotel rooms for the first time, and by 1972, the United States had twice as many motel as hotel rooms.

Not only did the focus of new development shift from the center of town to the

A typical motel outside Washington, D.C., in the early 1950s.

outskirts: much more of the growth occurred in the Sunbelt states and the intermountain West than in the Northeast and Midwest, where, in 1948, more than half of all hotel rooms in the country were located. By 1981, the South Atlantic states stretching along the coast from Virginia to Florida had nearly one-quarter of all U.S. hotel rooms, with another 40 percent in the rest of the Sunbelt and the Rocky Mountain states. Hotels and motels grew steadily larger in size: between 1948 and 1981, the number of properties decreased slightly, while the number of rooms grew by 35 percent. The different types of product also proliferated, with hoteliers offering conference centers, budget motels, residence suites, and a multitude of other new categories. Unfortunately for the industry, all of this expansion and competition led to a dramatic decline in average occupancy rates, which fell from 85 percent in 1948 to 65 percent in 1990.

Probably the most important changes in the lodging industry were the entry of investors into the business and the reemergence of many large chains, such as Hilton, Hyatt, and Sheraton, as contract management firms. The many new and complicated methods by which hotels and motels are owned and operated created an opening for real estate developers in speculative hotel development, both single buildings and as part of mixed-use projects. Some developers also own and operate hotels, motels, conference centers, and resorts as a business on a long-term basis, but many more are involved on a shorter term in the construction and sale of such properties. Today, hotels are considered a key sector of the real estate development industry, and most of the growth and interest in investment have taken place in the last 45 years, since the dawn of the postwar suburban age.

THE URBAN CRISIS: RACE, HOUSING, AND NEIGHBORHOODS

In 1957, the editors of *Fortune* magazine published a book called *The Exploding Metropolis*. The title referred primarily to the burgeoning postwar suburbs, but the volume also included articles on downtowns, central cities, and rising racial conflict. A chapter on "the enduring slum" concluded with a rather ominous statement: "One way or another, we will continue to pay plenty for our slums."[6] Written at the time of the bus boycott in Montgomery, Alabama, led by the Reverend Martin Luther King, Jr., and the first stirrings of the civil rights movement for racial justice and equal opportunity, these words proved a perfect introduction to the 1960s and the title of the book a presage of the events that occurred in our cities during the decade. Along with the migration of white middle-class homeowners to the suburbs, another massive urban migration was taking place: African-Americans were moving to central cities in record numbers. The black population in northern and southern cities was growing rapidly, and, particularly in many of the older industrial cities of the north, the new immigrants from the rural south overflowed the boundaries of the established and highly segregated ghetto areas. Three million African-Americans migrated from the south to the north and west in the 1940s and 1950s; by 1960, two-thirds of that population was concentrated in the 12 largest cities. The percentage of blacks in Chicago, for example, jumped from 8 percent in 1940 to nearly 25 percent in 1960 (and 40 percent in 1980).

The unfortunate legacy of racism cast a cloud over this dynamic process of urban growth and change. Newly arrived African-Americans were forced in many cases to live in overcrowded, overpriced, poor-quality housing, because they were restricted from buying or renting in many white neighborhoods. Often when they attempted to break through the "color line," they were met with verbal intimidation and physical violence. In response, many metropolitan areas launched interracial anti-discrimination movements for "open housing." At the same time, most cities were beginning to lose industrial jobs, either to the suburbs or from the entire region, so new unskilled migrants in the 1950s and thereafter had fewer economic opportunities than their predecessors. The competition for jobs with existing residents intensified, also contributing to racial tensions. Finally, most city government agencies, bu-

Washington, D.C., after the 1968 riots. The destruction of the inner city was extensive, and evidence of it remains more than 20 years later.

reaucracies, and politicians proved unreceptive to these newcomers, who were often denied access to adequate municipal services and political representation. Schooling in particular became a volatile issue, with numerous battles fought over issues of racial desegregation and involvement by citizens.

Other groups of "new minorities" also became more prominent in some cities during this period, most notably Puerto Ricans in New York, Cubans in Miami, and Mexican-Americans in many communities, especially in Texas, Arizona, Colorado, and California. By the 1970s and 1980s, a wide variety of Hispanic-Americans from many countries of Central and South America and Asian-Americans, including Chinese, Japanese, Korean, and Vietnamese, had become major forces in urban life in the United States. What came to be called the "urban crisis" of the 1960s, however, revolved mainly around the economic and social inequality and lack of civil rights for African-Americans.

The battle grew increasingly heated throughout the 1950s and 1960s, with violent skirmishes in the 1950s exploding into full-scale rebellion during the 1960s. Local police or white workers and community residents directed much of the early violence against blacks. Later, blacks fought back, battling in the streets with law enforcement officials, including the National Guard, looting stores, and burning or vandalizing buildings and cars, usually in their own neighborhoods. Long hot summers of riots descended on U.S cities, from New York's Harlem in 1964 and Los Angeles's Watts in 1965 to Detroit and Newark in 1967 and dozens of places in 1968 in the wake of Martin Luther King's assassination. In all, nearly 200 people were killed and 20,000 arrested, with the estimated property damage in the hundreds of millions of dollars.

Eventually, many people mobilized to address the interconnected set of problems that had helped spawn the dissatisfaction and disorder. The most obvious inequity was the overt legally and officially sanctioned segregation and discrimination that had existed for so long. The powerful political coalition and moral force of the civil rights movement finally began to sweep away many of these barriers through a series of federal, state, and local laws and court decisions, beginning in the 1940s.

President John F. Kennedy issued an executive order banning racial discrimination in federal housing programs in 1962, and after his assassination the following year, President Lyndon B. Johnson carried through on a host of successful legislative efforts, including the Civil Rights Act of 1964 and the Voting Rights Act of 1965.

Legal rights had to be supplemented by economic and social action to solve the real problems, however, and beginning in 1960, the Ford Foundation launched its Gray Areas Program to foster the revitalization and redevelopment of communities in minority areas, simultaneously trying to improve housing, social services, job training and opportunities, crime prevention, and schooling. These pilot projects later helped initiate a vast array of public efforts, from the many programs and organizations grouped under the War on Poverty starting in 1964, to the comprehensive neighborhood-based Model Cities Program of 1966. One of the most innovative private/public partnerships was the creation of community development corporations (CDCs), entrepreneurial institutions that attempted to combine the best features of business investment and management with government services and citizen participation. The Ford Foundation worked with U.S. Senators Robert F. Kennedy and Jacob K. Javits to establish the Bedford-Stuyvesant Restoration Corporation in a predominantly black neighborhood of Brooklyn, New York, in 1967. A combination of public and private nonprofit funding plus for-profit activity has helped a variety of other CDCs grow and mature since the 1960s in a wide variety of neighborhoods, representing many different ethnic and religious groups. Today, hundreds of CDCs and neighborhood development organizations (NDOs) exist in U.S. cities and rural areas, building and managing subsidized and affordable housing, health clinics, shopping centers, office and industrial parks, and providing preschool education, child care, job training and placement, and a host of other services. Much of today's political, business, and philanthropic leadership has emerged from these organizations and movements. Esteban Torres, who founded The East Los Angeles Community Union in the 1960s to serve a rapidly growing Hispanic population, was elected to serve as a U.S. Congressman from east Los Angeles in 1983. Franklin A. Thomas, who headed the Bedford-Stuyvesant Restoration Corporation for many years, was named president and chief executive of the Ford Foundation in 1979.

The Government's Response To the Urban Crisis

One of the focal points of response to the urban crisis during the 1960s was the creation of a federal government cabinet-level Department of Housing and Urban Development (HUD) in 1965. Robert C. Weaver, a lifelong activist for better-quality affordable housing and a strong opponent of racial discrimination, was appointed secretary of HUD, becoming the first African-American member of a U.S. President's cabinet. President Kennedy previously had appointed Weaver in 1961 to head the Housing and Home Finance Agency (HHFA), HUD's predecessor. Before then, he had served as the New York State Rent Administrator. Under Weaver's direction as HHFA administrator and then as HUD secretary, federal involvement in subsidized housing changed dramatically. The main emphasis since the 1930s had been on mortgage insurance and guarantees and the secondary market, mostly for middle-income homeowners but also for middle-income suburban garden apartments. These activities all encouraged private development and had active support from the real estate development industry. The other emphasis at that time was on public low-rent housing for low-income people. It was a small program nationwide, mostly concentrated in the larger cities, and was extremely unpopular within the real estate community. Some of the original base of support in the 1930s and 1940s had dwindled, the result of rising affluence and racial tensions. Catherine Bauer, one of public housing's most famous advocates, wrote in 1957 that "public housing, after more than two decades, still drags along in a kind of limbo, not dead but never more than half alive."[7]

By the late 1950s, the incredible postwar demand for new suburban single-family houses had largely been satisfied, and builders and developers began searching for new products and markets. One potential market yet to be tapped was households whose incomes were still too low to pay for new housing priced at the low end of the market. These people could be served by the private sector if public subsidies were available. Proponents of low-income housing began to view the subsidized public/private approach as a way to break what Catherine Bauer called "the dreary deadlock of public housing."[8] On the other side of the barricades, the National Association of Home Builders, recognizing the economic potential of this new approach for its membership, changed its position and became a key supporter of federal subsidies to produce privately owned housing for moderate-income individuals and families.

With NAHB's backing, new housing programs were launched in Washington in the 1960s, including the Section 221(d)(3) program (below-market interest rates), the Section 202 program (housing for the elderly), and a variety of others. These programs generally served a somewhat higher-income market than public housing and by the 1970s were producing a much greater volume of new units. Further initiatives occurred in 1968 with the passage of the landmark National Housing Act, which set the enormously ambitious goal of building 600,000 subsidized units a year for 10 years. The 1968 act included both a program to encourage production of rental housing (Section 236) and a subsidy to cover mortgage interest for low-income homeowners (Section 235). Both programs expanded very rapidly in the early 1970s and ran into problems ranging from poor management to outright fraud to the economic recession and inflated oil prices of 1973. In 1974, the so-called 236 program was replaced by yet another variant, Section 8. (The Section 8 program is also discussed in Chapter 12.)

Particularly during the 1960s and 1970s, these programs helped produce literally hundreds of thousands of units of new housing, many of good quality. Unfortunately, the federal government drastically cut back these programs during the 1980s, eliminating some entirely and reducing others by as much as three-fourths of their annual budget, compared to the late 1970s.

State and local governments as well as philanthropic institutions and nonprofit organizations have also contributed resources to this complex system of producing housing. Some for-profit builders have made this activity a major portion of their business, such as HRH Construction Corporation, which developed more than 25,000 units of subsidized housing when it was headed by Richard Ravitch in the 1960s and 1970s, including Waterside, an attractive high-rise apartment complex in Manhattan built in 1974 on a platform overlooking the East River. HRH is now owned by Starrett, another large builder and owner of subsidized housing, most notably its massive Starrett City development in Brooklyn.

Development Movements in Inner-City Neighborhoods

As large-scale urban renewal through clearance and displacement became increasingly controversial and expensive in the 1960s and early 1970s, many community residents and urban policymakers searched for methods to save and improve the existing housing stock, preserving and revitalizing the fabric of neighborhood life for those who already lived there. The idea of neighborhood conservation and housing rehabilitation grew in popularity, with new government programs like Section 312 rehabilitation loans, federally assisted code enforcement, and community development block grants available to assist the process. One of the biggest stumbling blocks was "redlining"—real estate lenders' refusal to lend money on property in older inner-city neighborhoods inhabited by people with modest incomes. Whites were as negatively affected by redlining as nonwhites. Whites normally had an easier time obtaining a mortgage to buy a house in the suburbs, but if they wanted to stay in their old neighborhood, they often could not even get a home improvement loan. For many years, the federal government redlined properties through FHA and VA, but by the late 1960s, various legislative and policy directives had led to reform of the practice—and in some neighborhoods FHA and VA became the only source for housing loans. Private lenders, however, including banks, insurance companies, S&Ls, and mortgage companies, continued the practice. In the 1960s and 1970s, a movement was organized to reverse the tide.

Gale Cincotta, an Italian housewife and PTA leader in the west side Chicago neighborhood of Austin, helped lead a crusade for community stabilization and improvement, starting with the discovery that banks and thrifts were taking millions of dollars in deposits from local residents but refusing to lend even thousands of dollars to those very same customers. Cincotta's neighborhood crusade against redlining and for "greenlining" united people across racial, ethnic, religious, and geographic boundaries—all could agree to help preserve their own communities. Starting with the Organization for a Better Austin, she later helped establish the Chicago Reinvestment Alliance and the National People's Action, leading to city, state, and federal intervention and eventually to a variety of neighborhood lending agreements with banks, thrifts, and insurance companies. These agreements have helped bring needed loan and grant money back into long-ignored communities where existing property owners are anxious to reinvest and upgrade their homes, and where for-profit and nonprofit developers are ready and willing to rebuild both houses and stores. From Cincotta's movement came two key national laws, the Home Mortgage Disclosure Act of 1975 and the Community Reinvestment Act of 1977. Both laws discourage redlining and encourage affirmative lending. A related initiative is the federal government–supported Neighborhood Reinvestment Corporation, which promotes conservation of communities through the successful Neighborhood Housing Services plan pioneered on the north side of Pittsburgh in the mid-1970s. Congress and the federal financial regulatory agencies strengthened the Community Reinvestment Act in 1989, and it will probably play an even larger role in ensuring available capital for neighborhood development in the 1990s.

While residents of inner-city neighborhoods were struggling to pump economic life into and physically improve their immediate surroundings, corporate and civic leaders were engaged in an identical process focused on the area around the CBDs of their respective cities. Most downtowns that had experienced real estate booms during the 1920s had then experienced two or three decades without any significant new development. Urban renewal and the highway programs were designed to jump-start the process of downtown development through the combination of land reassembly, public improvements, and public subsidies, and by the 1960s, results were showing. The growth of the service economy and the white-collar labor force helped stimulate the construction of new offices, and the rising incomes and changing lifestyles of both young and old led to new investment in retail development and, in some cities, housing downtown.

In 1985, the Urban Land Institute published a survey conducted by the Real Estate Research Corporation that documented the long hiatus in office construction in 24 of the country's biggest cities from the 1920s to the 1950s and consequent massive growth from the late 1960s to the mid-1980s.[9] The survey documented the completion of new privately owned large office buildings (100,000 square feet or more) located in central business districts and found the following gaps in development of these generally tall symbols of progress and prosperity:

Atlanta—before 1961
Baltimore—1929 to 1963
Boston—1930 to 1966
Chicago—1934 to 1957
Cleveland—1928 to 1964
Dallas—1921 to 1943
Denver—before 1957
Detroit—1929 to 1962
Fort Worth—1930 to 1969
Houston—1929 to 1960
Los Angeles—before 1964
Miami—before 1967
Minneapolis—1929 to 1960
New York (downtown)—1933 to 1956
New York (midtown excluding
  Rockefeller Center)—1931 to 1950
Newark—1930 to 1962
Philadelphia—1931 to 1968
Pittsburgh—1933 to 1950
St. Louis—before 1970
St. Paul—1931 to 1973
San Diego—before 1963
San Francisco—before 1955

132

Seattle—1929 to 1969
Tampa—before 1971
Washington D.C.—before 1970.

These cities made up for the long hiatus with varying degrees of a downtown construction boom during the past two decades. From 1970 through 1983, for example, the central business districts of these cities added 627 new, privately owned office buildings of more than 100,000 square feet, for a total of over 340 million square feet of new office space! The most active downtown office markets during this 14-year period were New York, Chicago, San Francisco, Houston, Washington, D.C., Denver, Boston, Los Angeles, Dallas, Philadelphia, Atlanta, and Seattle. Many of these—and other—cities experienced an accelerated volume of office construction after 1983 and for much of the remainder of the 1980s.

Along with the growth of office space and tall office buildings came a gradual revival in the fortunes of retail space, with large department stores being partially eclipsed by new specialty multistore malls. The success in the early 1970s of Chicago's Water Tower Place, an enclosed vertical mall with two department store anchors and 130 other stores on seven levels, led to similar projects in other cities, including Boston's Copley Place, developed by the same firm, Urban Investment and Development Company. A variation is the Hahn Company's Horton Plaza in San Diego, an architecturally distinctive downtown vertical mall that is not fully enclosed, taking advantage of the city's year-round dry and temperate climate.

Even more widely publicized has been the success of the tourism-, entertainment-, and food-oriented "festival marketplaces" that rely exclusively on specialty shops and do not use department store anchors. The leading developer in this field is unquestionably the Rouse Company, headed in the 1970s by its charismatic founder, James Rouse. The first two such marketplaces, both surprisingly successful for a new concept being tried in what were considered unfavorable locations, were Boston's Faneuil Hall, opened in 1976, and Baltimore's Harborplace, opened in 1980. *Time* magazine was so enthusiastic about the impact of these two projects on the

Horton Plaza, 780,000 square feet of gross leasable area, was developed by the Ernest W. Hahn Company and the Centre City Development Corporation of San Diego as a means of reversing the deterioration of the downtown. The open-air design of the vertical mall contains many distinctive architectural treatments.

revitalization of downtowns that it featured James Rouse on its cover in 1981 under the heading, "Cities Are Fun!"[10] By 1990, the Rouse Company was operating 14 such centers in cities around the country, the largest being Pioneer Place in Portland, Oregon, and the most recent being Underground Atlanta. James Rouse's new venture, the Enterprise Development Company, which he established to earn income to help finance low-income housing through his Enterprise Foundation, has also developed and operates several festival marketplaces. Interestingly, many of these projects, including Horton Plaza and the various downtown retail and mixed-use centers of the Rouse Company and the Enterprise Development Company, were urban redevelopment projects whose initial costs were heavily subsidized by their city governments.

James Rouse was also heavily identified with another key trend of the 1960s

Photo courtesy of the Rouse Company

Faneuil Hall consists of 160 stores and 219,000 square feet of gross leasable retail area housed in three 536-foot-long converted industrial and public market buildings, all of which predate 1826.

and 1970s: the attempt to create new large-scale, mixed-use communities as an alternative to urban decay and to suburban sprawl. Beginning in the early 1960s, a Rouse Company subsidiary, Community Research and Development, secretly purchased more than 16,000 acres of mostly contiguous farmland in Howard County, Maryland, halfway between Baltimore and Washington, D.C., and began planning and building the new community of Columbia, Maryland. Rouse convinced his main lender, the Connecticut General Life Insurance Company (CIGNA), to provide financial backing for the massive community development project, beginning with the cloak-and-dagger operation of land acquisition that involved several hundred transactions.

Rouse assembled a team of distinguished city planners and social scientists to advise him on how to produce a better design for urban living, and they came up with such innovations as a prepaid community health plan, a minibus system, shared multipurpose community facilities for worship, recreation, and other uses, and a focus on quality education and active participation. While Columbia endured financial hard times with the collapse of its homebuilding program during the recession of 1973 to 1975, it survived to become a thriving community of 73,000 people. Built around residential villages and man-made lakes, Columbia has a "downtown" featuring a regional shopping mall (owned and operated by the Rouse Company), office centers, entertainment and cultural facilities, and branches of five colleges and universities. The community was intended to be balanced between residence and employment and includes various industrial and office parks employing nearly 50,000 people—not all residents of Columbia. Housing is mixed and covers a wide range of incomes, including subsidized, moderate-income rental units. Racial integration, one of Rouse's explicit goals, has been achieved through a policy of nondiscrimination: nearly one-fourth of Columbia's population is African-American. The Rouse Company also helped to launch a successful new homebuilding firm, Ryland Homes, which now operates nationally but started in and is still headquartered in Columbia.

The Wave of New Communities

Columbia was just one of a wave of new private communities developed beginning in the 1960s and 1970s. Most of these efforts were concentrated in Sunbelt climates: the most common locations were California, Texas, and Florida, though many other states were also represented. Some of the developments were associated with resource-based corporations that already owned large amounts of land, such as the oil companies—Reston, Virginia, previously owned by Gulf Oil and now by Mobil, and Friendswood, Texas, owned by Exxon, for example. Others were large agricultural and cattle ranches, such as Las Colinas, Texas, and a great number of developments in California where the legacy of the Spanish land grants of massive, contiguous, undeveloped acreage under single ownership survived into modern times.

California ranches that have become new urban centers in the past few decades include Thousand Oaks, Valencia, Laguna Niguel, Mission Viejo, Rancho Santa Margarita, and the biggest of them all, the Irvine Ranch. Owned by the Irvine Company, this ranch consisted of more than 100,000 acres, nearly one-fifth of the land in Orange County. By the early 1960s, the construction of two interstate freeways and postwar suburbanization brought metropolitan growth to the northern boundaries of the Irvine Ranch, and the Irvine Company hired architect William Pereira to devise a master plan for a new city, Irvine, to be built centered around a new campus of the University of California. Irvine is still rapidly growing today, home to 102,000 people and 145,000 jobs. In addition to the city of Irvine, land that was part of the Irvine Ranch has also been developed for urban uses in Newport Beach, Laguna Beach, Costa Mesa, Tustin, and several other communities in central Orange County.

Other variants of new communities have included retiree- or adult-oriented centers, such as Leisure World in Florida and California, recreation-oriented subdivisions and second-home communities in many areas of the country, and urban "new-town-in-town" mixed-use residential complexes in some big cities. One lesson learned from these types of developments is that they require strong, long-term financial backing to succeed, because the initial costs of land acquisition, planning, improving infrastructure, and development are high and take many years to recoup through sales and leasing of land and buildings. Eventually, prices appreciate substantially when enough of the actual community is in place, but it takes time and patient investors. The federal government's New Communities Program, managed by HUD in the 1970s, sponsored developers who for the most part were too thinly capitalized and received woefully inadequate operating support from HUD. Consequently, all of these community development projects went bankrupt except one: The Woodlands, near Houston, Texas, owned by the Mitchell Energy and Development Corporation, was able to draw from the corporate resources of its parent firm during a time of high profits and from the substantial personal commitment of George Mitchell to build the town of his dreams.

Certainly the single most catalytic development was the entry of the Disney Corporation into central Florida. In 1965, Disney purchased 27,000 acres of undeveloped swampland near Orlando and began to develop Walt Disney World, including the Magic Kingdom and EPCOT Center. Two years later, Florida's legislature created for Disney its own private government, the Reedy Creek Improvement District, with full powers of taxation, borrowing, servicing, regulation, and development. Disney's intention was to control the pace and type of development surrounding the main facilities, something the company had been unable to do with its 250-acre Disneyland in Anaheim, California. Despite these careful plans, the response to the East Coast theme park was so overwhelming that it set off a wave of speculation, growth in population and employment, and real estate development in the greater Orlando metropolitan area that has not subsided two decades later. On opening day in December 1971, cars were backed up for 15 miles on I-4 to enter the Magic Kingdom. Today, Disney continues to expand, building a motion picture and television theme park and studios (together with MGM), architecturally distinctive hotels, a shopping center, office buildings,

Photo courtesy of Mitchell Energy and Development Corporation

The Woodlands, which opened in 1974, is a planned new community on 25,000 acres of heavily forested land 27 miles north of downtown Houston. Pictured here is The Woodlands country club, with industrial buildings in the background.

recreational facilities, and housing, including a planned community called Lake Buena Vista. For a time, Disney was heavily involved in residential development throughout Florida, acquiring the Arvida Company, a major land development and homebuilding firm now owned by JMB Realty. Disney is concentrating its current development plans for Florida entirely on the greater Orlando area. The result of Walt Disney's choice of this sleepy spot on a map is that today Orlando has 61,000 hotel rooms, more than any metropolitan area in the United States except Los Angeles and New York, and one of America's busiest airports. Metropolitan Orlando's population increased by 50 percent during the 1980s.

The heavy investment in new communities and large-scale development on the periphery of big, established central cities led to a new phenomenon in the 1970s and 1980s—the growth of "urban villages," "suburban megacenters," and "growth corridors." Concentrations of super regional shopping malls, office and industrial parks with enormous quantities of space, major highway interchanges, and low- to medium-density housing, they are often located in more than one government jurisdiction and create a prime activity area away from the traditional urban downtown. Some have grown around a large suburban shopping center, such as Tysons Corner, Virginia, or Woodfield Mall in Schaumburg, Illinois. In other cases, a highway has been the focal point, such as Route 1 in the vicinity of Princeton, New Jersey, or I-285 north of Atlanta. The image of these centers ranges from the corporate office complexes headquartered in Fairfield County, Connecticut, to the research and industrial parks of the Silicon Valley in Santa Clara County, California. Nearly every major metropolitan area now has multiple CBDs that compete with and often surpass the older downtowns.

Developers have often played major roles in the planning and creation of these alternative centers, from J.C. Nichols's Country Club Plaza in Kansas City to William Zeckendorf's Roosevelt Field on Long Island and Century City in Los Angeles. One of the best-known, more recent projects is Gerald Hines's development of the Post Oak–Westheimer area as Houston's main high-end retail center and a thriving location for office space and hotels. In 1969, Hines opened the Galleria Shopping Center, a mixed-use facility that now contains 1.8 million square feet of retail space and five department store anchors. The project also includes a 450-room luxury hotel and the 25-story Post Oak office building, completed in 1973, which at the time was one of only two Houston office buildings with more than 500,000 square feet of space located outside the CBD. In 1983, Hines built the 64-story, 1.6 million-square-foot Transco Tower in the Post Oak area. Transco, designed by the New York architects Philip Johnson and John Burgee, was and still is the tallest office building ever built in an essentially suburban environment. Gerald Hines Interests has been among the biggest commercial developers in the United States during the past two decades, with major office buildings, shopping centers, and hotels in Houston and many other cities. The Galleria–Post Oak center continues to be his trademark project, and it has had a major national impact on retail and mixed-use development.

THE 1970s TO THE 1990s

Real estate development has always been a cyclical industry. Since the 1930s, economists like Homer Hoyt, Roy

A nighttime view of Gerald Hines Interests's suburban Houston development. To the left is the 64-story Transco Tower; in the foreground is the Galleria, with close to 2 million square feet of retail space.

137

Wenzlick, Clarence Long, Leo Grebler, and Manuel Gottlieb have been collecting data and analyzing historical patterns of the ever-changing rise and fall in the volume of real estate activity and the value of property.[11] Downturns may be caused by general economic recessions or depressions, by changes in money markets that restrict the supply or drive up the cost of money, and by overbuilding that leads to too many buildings competing for too few tenants or buyers. Upturns may be caused by a significant increase in demand as a result of growth in population, employment, and income, by changes in money markets that lead to a plentiful supply of relatively low-cost financing, and by speculative responses to rapidly increasing rents, prices, returns, and perceived values.

The past two decades have seen a great deal of cyclical fluctuation precipitated by a wide variety of factors. A boom in the late 1960s and early 1970s fueled by strong growth, military spending, and modest inflation was followed by a bust from 1973 to 1975 induced by the shock of quadrupled oil prices, double-digit inflation, and a severe economic recession. A boom in the late 1970s stimulated by the entry of a large portion of the baby boom generation into housing and job markets was followed by a crash in the early 1980s caused by extremely high interest rates and a contraction in financing combined with severe unemployment and an economic recession. And in the mid-1980s, money flowed freely again, job growth was strong, and real estate development took off on a speculative binge that by 1990 was ending in very high vacancies, low occupancies, large unsold inventories, falling prices, rents, and yields, and the most defaults, foreclosures, and bankruptcies since the Great Depression.

Inside this broad pattern existed, as always, much variation. Within a metropolitan area or a multistate region, some neighborhoods and communities flourish while others languish. In the early 1980s, Dallas continued to thrive while Houston was declining—and by the late 1980s, their fortunes began to reverse. Throughout the decade and all across the country, shiny new office towers and shopping centers coexisted with abandoned housing and the homeless. Cycles also varied between regions. Beginning in the mid-1970s, the Southwest boomed while the Northeast stagnated, both affected by the dramatic rise in energy prices. In the 1980s, energy prices fell substantially, and the Southwest sank while the Northeast rose again. In addition to the prime factor of geographic location, the relative fortunes of real estate differ cyclically by type of product. During the late 1980s, when office buildings and hotels were generally overbuilt in most markets, developers and investors turned to residential apartment buildings and industrial warehouses.

The massive population influx of the postwar baby boomers who reached adulthood and formed separate households, the shift in population growth from the Frostbelt states to the Sunbelt states, the substantial increase in single and divorced households, and the rise in the numbers, income, and wealth of senior citizens all had a major impact on housing development. The housing industry responded by building and rehabilitating a record volume of units in the 1970s and maintaining high production through much of the 1980s. Condominiums as a new form of owning an individual apartment burst onto the scene in the early 1970s, accounting for a significant portion of new and converted multifamily units.

Prices, especially of single-family houses, rose rapidly in many markets as demand outran supply, with the costs of new and existing housing and developable land all outpacing the increase in median household income during the past two decades. The gap in wealth between homeowners and renters widened, and both longstanding tenants and newly formed households strained their resources to rush into homeownership before prices rose higher and to take advantage of anticipated appreciation in equity and tax benefits. Mostly on the West and East Coasts at various times from the mid-1970s to the late 1980s, sales and prices of housing rose and fell in successive waves of speculative frenzy followed by recessionary panic. Construction of multifamily housing was boosted substantially in the early and mid-1980s by the use of syndications, accelerated depreciation, passive loss, and other income tax benefits created under the Economic Recovery Tax Act of 1981. The reduction of these benefits under the 1986 tax reform law immediately set off a significant reduction in new investment and development and a rapid decline of the syndication industry.

Contributing to the instability and wide cyclical swings during the last two decades was the impact of a greater degree of general price inflation than most U.S. citizens had ever seen combined with revolutionary changes in capital markets and real estate finance. The easy availability of relatively low-cost, fixed-interest, long-term residential mortgages at a time of rapidly rising interest rates in the late 1970s, for example, helped to finance and encourage the boom in homeownership. It also led to the near insolvency of the S&Ls, when their liabilities were deregulated and they began in 1979 to 1981 to compete for funds by paying higher interest on deposits than the interest they received on much of their mortgage loan portfolios. This disaster of deregulation was followed in 1981 by permitting the S&Ls to move away from home mortgage lending and toward commercial real estate markets, to engage in equity deals, to purchase "junk bonds," and to get involved in many high-risk ventures while bearing no risk of failure to depositors, because all their deposit accounts were federally insured up to $100,000 each. A combination of corruption in some cases, bad judgment in others, and bad luck from cyclical downturns, especially the massive real estate depression of the late 1980s in the energy-producing states, led to widespread bankruptcy among S&Ls and the government's taking over much of the thrift industry, beginning in 1989. The federal Resolution Trust Corporation, created to handle the S&L debacle, entered the 1990s owning many billions of dollars in real property, a potential major force in the future fortunes of the real estate industry.

The collapse of many thrifts, difficulties in a significant number of commercial banks, and tighter federal regulations on real estate lending meant that, in the early 1990s, developers were having a much harder time financing new projects. This pattern is a complete reversal of the dominant trend in the 1980s, when highly leveraged nonrecourse debt from financial institutions was plentiful and many developers rushed to construct new space, often without sufficient demand for occupancy at the projected rents or sale prices.

While the decline of the thrifts has left a temporary vacuum for financing development, it has had little impact on financing homebuyers because of the dramatic growth in securitization, mortgage banking, and the secondary market during the past two decades. Through the medium of large government-backed agencies like Fannie Mae, Freddie Mac, and Ginnie Mae and a host of private securities firms, mortgage companies have been able to draw capital from a wide range of individual institutional investors. Insurance companies, pension funds, depository institutions, and global investors all now participate in the secondary mortgage market. These new sources of capital provide ample funds for primary lenders and borrowers, though often at much higher real interest rates than existed before deregulation, when funds for housing loans were partially sheltered from competition on the capital market.

Pension funds and other institutional investors have also begun playing a much bigger role as lenders, purchasers, and joint venture partners, both for new development and for acquisition, refinancing, and redevelopment of existing properties. The growth of real estate investment funds has generated a new industry since the 1970s, in which financial advisers are more prominent in development and management and real estate is becoming increasingly professionalized. New trade associations like the Pension Real Estate Association and the National Council of Real Estate Investment Fiduciaries are all signs of the financial and organizational changes the real estate industry has recently experienced.

A related change is the increasing involvement of large corporations in real estate. Most industrial and commercial firms have traditionally ignored the profit potential of the real property they own and use. Beginning in the 1960s, however, many resource-based companies that owned surplus land, such as the railroad, forestry, oil, mining, and agricultural giants, entered the development business with everything from rural recreational subdivisions to urban mixed-use complexes. The federal government also encouraged the corporate entry into high-volume production of housing through HUD's Operation Breakthrough. Many of these early efforts failed, and corporations withdrew to safer and more familiar territory. But the threat of hostile takeovers and leveraged buyouts financed by undervalued real estate and the cost-conscious era of international competition in the 1980s led to renewed interest on the part of many major companies to use their real estate assets more intensively and productively, to manage them more effectively, and to sell to or enter joint ventures with developers more frequently. (Both the pension funds and the corporate perspective are covered in Chapter 18.)

The greater presence of large institutions in real estate was matched by the growing size of many development firms. As early as the 1960s, large national developers emerged in the homebuilding field, including Kaufman and Broad, Centex, Ryan Homes, National Homes, and U.S. Home. Similarly, shopping center developers like Edward DeBartolo, Melvin Simon, Alfred Taubman, Ernest Hahn, and James Rouse went national. In the 1970s and 1980s, they were joined by nationwide office developers like Trammell Crow, Gerald Hines, John Galbreath, Lincoln Property, the Urban Investment and Development Company, and Tishman Speyer, along with big life insurance companies like Prudential, Metropolitan, and Equitable and several large Canadian development firms, including Olympia & York, Cadillac Fairview, and Trizec. Many of the largest developers built office, retail, hotel, industrial, apartment, and mixed-use projects. The entry of the Canadians into the U.S. development market also signaled a trend toward international development, as many of the major North American developers looked to Europe for new projects and prospects in the 1990s. Tishman Speyer, Kajima, and Citicorp are constructing a 70-story office tower in Frankfurt that will be the tallest office building in all of Europe. Olympia & York is developing Canary Wharf on London's docklands, a mixed-use "megaproject" to rival its massive Battery Park City in New York.

One profound change that began with the movement for neighborhood par-

Rector Place at Battery Park City, one of the new residential neighborhoods planned for the southern tip of Manhattan Island. The Battery Park City esplanade will eventually extend more than a mile along the riverside, linking the North Park to the South Park.

ticipation in the 1960s and accelerated after Earth Day in April 1970 was a growing concern for the effects of real estate development on the natural, physical, and human environment in metropolitan and nonmetropolitan areas. The 1969 National Environmental Policy Act and its various state equivalents led to public regulators' and legislators' use of environmental impact reviews to decide whether or not proposed development projects should be approved. The 1966 National Historic Preservation Act helped to focus attention on conserving existing structures rather than permitting their demolition to make way for entirely new developments. These and many other new federal, state, and local laws and practices—growth controls, sewer moratoriums, impact fees, linkage payments—all served to slow the process and add to the costs of public and private real estate development in many communities.

In the 1970s and 1980s, California, which in the 1950s and 1960s was considered a developers' paradise for obtaining public infrastructure and services and fast and favorable regulations, became an embattled and difficult state in which to build new projects, with active protests by citizens, strict and time-consuming regulatory processes, and extensive and costly exactions. This change in the political sea helped to cut down on overbuilding, especially residential development, and greatly contributed to the rapid escalation of housing prices because supply could no longer keep pace with demand. The California syndrome was repeated in the Northeast during the housing boom of the mid-1980s. In some cases, developers joined with activists in civil rights and affordable housing to attack exclusionary zoning and other related practices. The New Jersey State Supreme Court's *Mount Laurel* ruling mandated regional fair housing, and Massachusetts's statewide "antisnob" zoning law attempted to deal with the exclusionary practices of many communities. NAHB, HUD, ULI, and other private and public organizations have attempted to search for solutions by lowering housing costs through regulatory reforms.

Part of the problem is that all levels of government have cut back their expenditures for roads, bridges, and a vast array of other needed infrastructure and services. The tax revolt of the 1970s has in many cases led to reduced maintenance and the neglect of vitally needed replacements and expansion of key facilities. In the context of overburdened infrastructure, new private development often appears to add to traffic congestion, air and water pollution, crowded schools, and other undesirable environmental impacts without bringing enough additional tax revenues to improve the overall situation. Developers find themselves increasingly involved in public relations campaigns and public policy initiatives, working with local residents, business and civic groups, community leaders, and government officials to have projects approved by agreeing to pay a greater share for public facilities and amenities and

finding new ways to address neighborhood concerns and mitigate the perceived negative effects of proposed development. This form of cooperation and negotiation will lead in the 1990s to a renewed search for cooperative physical and financial solutions that meet society's needs for adequate and affordable housing, attractive and livable environments, and dynamic and efficient urban economic development.

SUMMARY

This chapter has described and analyzed the growth of a mature, modern, and professional real estate development industry with more complex sources of financing and greater sophistication in relating to government and to the public. During the last four and one-half decades after World War II, developers have increasingly specialized in different types of products—offices, shopping centers, industrial parks, and hotels. They have built larger and more efficient organizations, and they have faced the two crises of inflation and recession. Sensitivity to racial and environmental issues has become much more important. The global economy will bring future changes in real estate development probably even greater than present ones.

NOTES

1. "Housing: Up from the Potato Fields," *Time*, July 3, 1950, p. 67.

2. John Keats, *The Crack in the Picture Window* (Boston: Houghton Mifflin, 1957); and William H. Whyte, Jr., *The Organization Man* (New York: Simon & Schuster, 1956).

3. Robert A. Caro, *The Power Broker: Robert Moses and the Fall of New York* (New York: Random House, 1975), pp. 850-94.

4. "Northland: A New Yardstick for Shopping Center Planning," *Architectural Forum*, June 1954, pp. 102-19. The article begins with the statement, "This is a classic in shopping center planning, in the sense that Rockefeller Center is a classic in urban skyscraper-group planning, or Radburn, N.J., in suburban residential planning." On Northland and Victor Gruen, see also Howard Gillette, Jr., "The Evolution of the Planned Shopping Center in Suburb and City," *Journal of the American Planning Association*, Autumn 1985, pp. 449-60.

5. Kenneth T. Jackson, *Crabgrass Frontier: The Suburbanization of the United States* (New York: Oxford Univ. Press, 1985), p. 254.

6. Daniel Seligman, "The Enduring Slums," in The Editors of *Fortune, The Exploding Metropolis* (Garden City, N.Y.: Doubleday, 1957), p. 132.

7. Catherine Bauer, "The Dreary Deadlock of Public Housing," *Architectural Forum*, May 1957, p. 140.

8. Ibid.

9. Real Estate Research Corporation, *Tall Office Buildings in the United States* (Washington, D.C.: ULI–the Urban Land Institute, 1985).

10. "He Digs Downtown—For Master Planner James Rouse, Urban Life Is a Festival," *Time*, August 24, 1981, pp. 42-53.

11. See, for example, Clarence D. Long, Jr., *Building Cycles and the Theory of Investment* (Princeton, N.J.: Princeton Univ. Press, 1940); Homer Hoyt, *The Urban Real Estate Cycle—Performances and Prospects*, Technical Bulletin No. 38 (Washington, D.C.: ULI–the Urban Land Institute, 1950); Roy Wenzlick, *The Coming Boom in Real Estate* (New York: Simon & Schuster, 1936); Leo Grebler, David M. Blank, and Louis Winnick, *Capital Formation in Residential Real Estate* (Princeton, N.J.: Princeton Univ. Press, 1956); Manuel Gottlieb, *Long Swings in Urban Development* (New York: National Bureau of Economic Research, 1976).

Bibliography

Part II. The History of Real Estate Development In the United States

THE COLONIAL PERIOD TO THE LATE 1800s

Abrams, Charles. *Revolution in Land*. New York: Harper, 1939.

Akin, Edward N. *Flagler: Rockefeller Partner and Florida Baron*. Kent, Ohio: Kent State Univ. Press, 1988.

Blackmar, Elizabeth. *Manhattan for Rent, 1785–1850*. Ithaca, N.Y.: Cornell Univ. Press, 1989.

Cates, Paul W. *History of Public Land Law Development*. Washington, D.C.: U.S. Government Printing Office, 1968.

Dumke, Glenn S. *The Boom of the Eighties in Southern California*. San Marino, Cal.: Huntington Library, 1944.

Ely, Richard T., and George S. Wehrwein. *Land Economics*. New York: Macmillan, 1940.

Fogelson, Robert M. *The Fragmented Metropolis: Los Angeles, 1880–1930*. Cambridge, Mass.: Harvard Univ. Press, 1967.

Friedricks, William B. "A Metropolitan Entrepreneur Par Excellence: Henry E. Huntington and the Growth of Southern California, 1898-1927." *Business History Review* 63 (2), Summer 1989, p. 354.

Hartog, Hendrik. *Public Property and Private Law: The Corporation of the City of New York in American Law, 1730–1870*. Chapel Hill: Univ. of North Carolina Press, 1983.

Hoyt, Homer. *One Hundred Years of Land Values in Chicago: The Relationship of the Growth of Chicago to the Rise in Its Land Values, 1830–1933*. Chicago: Univ. of Chicago Press, 1933.

Keating, Ann Durkin. *Building Chicago: Suburban Developers and the Creating of a Divided Metropolis*. Columbus: Ohio State Univ. Press, 1988.

Lubove, Roy. *The Progressives and the Slums: Tenement House Reform in New York City, 1890–1917*. Pittsburgh: Univ. of Pittsburgh Press, 1962.

Moehring, Eugene P. *Public Works and the Patterns of Urban Real Estate Growth in Manhattan, 1835–1894*. New York: Arno Press, 1981.

Platt, Harold L. *City Building in the New South: The Growth of Public Services in Houston, Texas, 1830–1910*. Philadelphia: Temple Univ. Press, 1983.

Real Estate Record Association. *A History of Real Estate, Building, and Architecture in New York City*. New York: Real Estate Record and Guide, 1898.

Reps, John W. *The Making of Urban America: A History of City Planning in the United States*. Princeton, N.J.: Princeton Univ. Press, 1965.

Riis, Jacob. *How the Other Half Lives: Studies among the Tenements of New York*. New York: Scribner, 1890.

Robbins, Roy M. *Our Landed Heritage: The Public Domain, 1776–1936*. 2d ed. Lincoln: Univ. of Nebraska Press, 1976.

Robinson, W.W. *Land in California: The Story of Mission Lands, Ranchos, Squatters, Mining Claims, Railroad Grants, Land Scrip, Homesteads*. Berkeley: Univ. of California Press, 1948.

Rosen, Christine Meisner. *The Limits of Power: Great Fires and the Process of City Growth in America*. New York: Cambridge Univ. Press, 1986.

Sakolski, A.M. *The Great American Land Bubble: The Amazing Story of Land-Grabbing, Speculations, and Booms from Colonial Days to the Present Time*. New York: Harper, 1932.

Smith, Arthur D. Howden. *John Jacob Astor: Landlord of New York*. Philadelphia: Lippincott, 1929.

Taylor, George R. *The Transportation Revolution, 1815–1860*. New York: Harper, 1968.

Thomas, Dana L. *Lords of the Land: The Triumphs and Scandals of America's Real Estate Barons from Early Times to the Present*. New York: Putnam's, 1977.

Vanderblue, Homer B. "The Florida Land Boom." *Journal of Land and Public Utility Economics* 3 (2), May 1927, pp. 113-31; and 3 (3), August 1927, pp. 252-69.

Warner, Sam Bass, Jr. *Streetcar Suburbs: The Process of Growth in Boston, 1870–1900*. Cambridge, Mass.: Harvard Univ. Press, 1962.

Weiss, Marc A. "Real Estate History: An Overview and Research Agenda." *Business History Review* 63 (2), Summer 1989, pp. 241-82.

——. *The Rise of the Community Builders: The American Real Estate Industry and Urban Land Planning*. New York: Columbia Univ. Press, 1987.

Wolf, Peter. *Land in America: Its Value, Use, and Control*. New York: Pantheon, 1981.

Wright, Carroll D. *The Slums of Baltimore, Chicago, New York, and Philadelphia*. Seventh Special Report of the Commissioner of Labor. Washington, D.C.: U.S. Government Printing Office, 1894.

Wyckoff, William. *The Developer's Frontier: The Making of the Western New York Landscape*. New Haven, Conn.: Yale Univ. Press, 1988.

THE LATE 1800s TO WORLD WAR II

Bishir, Catherine W., Charlotte V. Brown, Carl R. Lounsbury, and Ernest H. Wood, III. *Architects and Builders in North Carolina: A History of the Practice of Building*. Chapel Hill: Univ. of North Carolina Press, 1990.

Caro, Robert A. *The Power Broker: Robert Moses and the Fall of New York*. New York: Random House, 1974.

Colean, Miles L. *American Housing: Problems and Prospects*. New York: Twentieth Century Fund, 1944.

Community Builders Council. *Community Builders Handbook*. Washington, D.C.: ULI–the Urban Land Institute, 1947.

Cranz, Galen. *The Politics of Park Design: A History of Urban Parks in America*. Cambridge, Mass.: MIT Press, 1982.

Cromley, Elizabeth Collins. *Alone Together: A History of New York's Early Apartments*. Ithaca, N.Y.: Cornell Univ. Press, 1990.

Davies, Pearl Janet. *Real Estate in American History*. Washington, D.C.: Public Affairs Press, 1958.

Eskew, Garnett Laidlaw. *Of Land and Men: The Birth and Growth of an Idea*. Washington, D.C.: ULI–the Urban Land Institute, 1959.

Ewalt, Josephine Hedges. *A Business Reborn: The Savings and Loan Story, 1930–1960*. Chicago: American Savings and Loan Institute, 1962.

Fisher, Ernest M. *Urban Real Estate Markets: Characteristics and Financing*. New York: National Bureau of Economic Research, 1951.

Foster, Mark S. *Henry J. Kaiser: Builder in the Modern American West*. Austin: Univ. of Texas Press, 1989.

Gibbs, Kenneth Turney. *Business Architectural Imagery in America, 1870–1930*. Ann Arbor, Mich.: UMI Research Press, 1984.

Goldberger, Paul. *The Skyscraper*. New York: Alfred A. Knopf, 1981.

Golden Book of Wanamaker Stores. Philadelphia: John Wanamaker, 1911.

Grebler, Leo, David M. Blank, and Louis Winnick. *Capital Formation in Residential Real Estate: Trends and Prospects*. Princeton, N.J.: Princeton Univ. Press, 1956.

Howard, Ebenezer. *Garden Cities of Tomorrow*. London: Faber & Faber, 1945.

Hoyt, Homer. *The Structure and Growth of Residential Neighborhoods in American Cities*. Washington, D.C.: Federal Housing Administration, 1939.

Hubbard, Theodora Kimball, and Henry Vincent Hubbard. *Our Cities Today and Tomorrow*. Cambridge, Mass.: Harvard Univ. Press, 1929.

Hurd, Richard M. *Principles of City Land Values*. New York: Real Estate Record and Guide, 1903.

Jackson, Kenneth T. *Crabgrass Frontier: The Suburbanization of the United States*. New York: Oxford Univ. Press, 1985.

James, Marquis. *The Metropolitan Life: A Study in Business Growth*. New York: Viking, 1947.

Kahn, Judd. *Imperial San Francisco: Politics and Planning in an American City, 1897–1906*. Lincoln: Univ. of Nebraska Press, 1979.

Klaman, Saul B. *The Postwar Rise of Mortgage Companies*. New York: National Bureau of Economic Research, 1959.

Krinsky, Carol Herselle. *Rockefeller Center*. New York: Oxford Univ. Press, 1978.

Mayer, Harold M., and Richard C. Wade. *Chicago: Growth of a Metropolis*. Chicago: Univ. of Chicago Press, 1969.

Morton, J.E. *Urban Mortgage Lending: Comparative Markets and Experience*. Princeton, N.J.: Princeton Univ. Press, 1956.

Rabinowitz, Alan. *The Real Estate Gamble: Lessons from 50 Years of Boom and Bust*. New York: AMACOM, 1980.

Schaffer, Daniel. *Garden Cities for America: The Radburn Experience*. Philadelphia: Temple Univ. Press, 1982.

Scott, Mel. *American City Planning since 1890*. Berkeley: Univ. of California Press, 1969.

Shultz, Earle, and Walter Simmons. *Offices in the Sky*. Indianapolis: Bobbs-Merrill, 1959.

Starrett, William A. *Skyscrapers and the Men Who Build Them*. New York: Scribner's, 1928.

Stein, Clarence S. *Toward New Towns for America*. New York: Reinhold, 1957.

Stern, Robert A.M., Gregory Gilmartin, and Thomas Mellins. *New York 1930: Architecture and Urbanism between the Two World Wars*. New York: Rizzoli, 1987.

Straus, Nathan. *The Seven Myths of Housing*. New York: Alfred A. Knopf, 1944.

Taylor, Waverly, Hugh Potter, and W.P. Atkinson. *History of the National Association of Home Builders of the United States*. Washington, D.C.: National Association of Home Builders, 1958.

Teaford, Jon C. *The Unheralded Triumph: City Government in America, 1870–1900*. Baltimore: Johns Hopkins Univ. Press, 1984.

Thompson-Starrett Company. "A Census of Skyscrapers." *The American City* 41, September 1929, p. 130.

Walker, Robert A. *The Planning Function in Urban Government*. Chicago: Univ. of Chicago Press, 1950.

Weber, Adna Ferrin. *The Growth of Cities in the Nineteenth Century: A Study in Statistics*. New York: Macmillan, 1899.

Weiss, Marc A. *The Rise of the Community Builders: The American Real Estate Industry and Urban Land Planning*. New York: Columbia Univ. Press, 1987.

Willis, Carol. *Form Follows Finance: The Empire State Building and the Forces that Shaped It*. New York: Social Science Research Council, Committee on New York City, 1990.

Wood, Edith Elmer. *The Housing of the Unskilled Wage Earner*. New York: Macmillan, 1919.

——. *Recent Trends in American Housing*. New York: Macmillan, 1931.

——. *Slums and Blighted Areas in the United States*. Public Works Administration, Housing Division Bulletin No. 1. Washington, D.C.: U.S. Government Printing Office, 1935.

Woodbury, Coleman. *The Trend of Multifamily Housing in Cities in the United States*. Chicago: Institute for Economic Research, 1931.

Worley, William S. *J.C. Nichols and the Shaping of Kansas City: Innovation in*

Planned Residential Communities. Columbia: Univ. of Missouri Press, 1990.

POST–WORLD WAR II TO THE PRESENT

Abrams, Charles. *The City Is the Frontier.* New York: Harper & Row, 1965.

Alterman, Rachelle, ed. *Private Supply of Public Services: Evaluation of Real Estate Exactions, Linkage, and Alternative Land Policies.* New York: New York Univ. Press, 1988.

Beauregard, Robert A., ed. *Atop the Urban Hierarchy.* Totowa, N.J.: Rowman & Littlefield, 1989.

Boyte, Harry C. *The Backyard Revolution: Understanding the New Citizen Movement.* Philadelphia: Temple Univ. Press, 1980.

Bratt, Rachel G. *Rebuilding a Low-Income Housing Policy.* Philadelphia: Temple Univ. Press, 1989.

Breckenfeld, Gurney. *Columbia and the New Cities.* New York: Ives Washburn, 1971.

Caro, Robert A. *The Power Broker: Robert Moses and the Fall of New York.* New York: Random House, 1974.

Checkoway, Barry. *The Politics of Postwar Suburban Development.* Berkeley: Univ. of California Childhood and Government Project, 1977.

Downs, Anthony. *The Revolution in Real Estate Finance.* Washington, D.C.: Brookings Institution, 1985.

Edel, Matthew, Elliott D. Sclar, and Daniel Luria. *Shaky Palaces: Homeownership and Social Mobility in Boston's Suburbanization.* New York: Columbia Univ. Press, 1984.

Eichler, Ned. *The Merchant Builders.* Cambridge, Mass.: MIT Press, 1982.

——. *The Thrift Debacle.* Berkeley: Univ. of California Press, 1989.

Feagin, Joe R., and Robert Parker. *Building American Cities: The Urban Real Estate Game.* Englewood Cliffs, N.J.: Prentice-Hall, 1990.

Fisher, Ernest M. *Urban Real Estate Markets: Characteristics and Financing.* New York: National Bureau of Economic Research, 1951.

Frieden, Bernard J., and Lynne B. Sagalyn. *Downtown, Inc.: How America Re-*builds Cities. Cambridge, Mass.: MIT Press, 1989.

Friedman, Lawrence M. *Government and Slum Housing: A Century of Frustration.* Chicago: Rand McNally, 1968.

Gelfand, Mark I. *A Nation of Cities: The Federal Government and Urban America, 1933–1965.* New York: Oxford Univ. Press, 1975.

Goldberger, Paul. *The Skyscraper.* New York: Alfred A. Knopf, 1981.

Goldenberg, Susan. *Men of Property: The Canadian Developers Who Are Buying America.* Toronto: Personal Library, 1981.

Goodkin, Lewis M. *When Real Estate and Homebuilding Become Big Business: Mergers, Acquisitions, and Joint Ventures.* Boston: Cahners Books, 1974.

Gottlieb, Manuel. *Long Swings in Urban Development.* New York: National Bureau of Economic Research, 1976.

Grebler, Leo. *Large-Scale Housing and Real Estate Firms: Analysis of a New Business Enterprise.* New York: Praeger, 1973.

Grebler, Leo, David M. Blank, and Louis Winnick. *Capital Formation in Residential Real Estate: Trends and Prospects.* Princeton, N.J.: Princeton Univ. Press, 1956.

Griffin, Nathaniel M. *Irvine: Genesis of a New Community.* Washington, D.C.: ULI-the Urban Land Institute, 1974.

Haar, Charles M., and Jerold S. Kayden. *Zoning and the American Dream: Promises Still to Keep.* Chicago: Planners Press, 1989.

Hayden, Dolores. *Redesigning the American Dream: The Future of Housing, Work, and Family Life.* New York: Norton, 1984.

Hays, R. Allen. *The Federal Government and Urban Housing: Ideology and Change in Public Policy.* Albany: State Univ. of New York Press, 1985.

Hays, Samuel P. *Beauty, Health, and Permanence: Environmental Politics in the United States, 1955–1985.* New York: Cambridge Univ. Press, 1987.

Helper, Rose. *Racial Policies and Practices of Real Estate Brokers.* Minneapolis: Univ. of Minnesota Press, 1969.

Hoyt, Homer. *The Urban Real Estate Cycle: Performances and Prospects.* Technical

Bulletin No. 38. Washington, D.C.: ULI–the Urban Land Institute, 1950.

Jackson, Kenneth T. *Crabgrass Frontier: The Suburbanization of the United States*. New York: Oxford Univ. Press, 1985.

Keats, John. *The Crack in the Picture Window*. Boston: Houghton Mifflin, 1957.

Lachman, M. Leanne. *Decade to Decade: U.S. Real Estate Adapts to Revolution in Finance and Demographic Evolution*. New York: Schroder Real Estate Associates, 1988.

Laventhol & Horwath. *Hotel/Motel Development*. Washington, D.C.: ULI–the Urban Land Institute, 1984.

Lo, Clarence Y.H. *Small Property versus Big Government: Social Origins of the Property Tax Revolt*. Berkeley: Univ. of California Press, 1990.

Long, Clarence D., Jr. *Building Cycles and the Theory of Investment*. Princeton, N.J.: Princeton Univ. Press, 1940.

McMahan, John. *Property Development*. 2d ed. New York: McGraw-Hill, 1989.

Mayer, Martin. *The Builders: Houses, People, Neighborhoods, Governments, Money*. New York: Norton, 1978.

Mollenkopf, John H. *The Contested City*. Princeton, N.J.: Princeton Univ. Press, 1983.

Morgan, George T., Jr., and John O. King. *The Woodlands: New Community Development, 1964–1983*. College Station: Texas A&M Univ. Press, 1987.

Plunz, Richard. *A History of Housing in New York City: Dwelling Type and Social Change in the American Metropolis*. New York: Columbia Univ. Press, 1990.

Portman, John C., and Jonathan Barnett. *The Architect as Developer*. New York: McGraw-Hill, 1976.

Real Estate Research Corporation. *Tall Office Buildings in the United States*. Washington, D.C.: ULI–the Urban Land Institute, 1985.

Sabbagh, Karl. *Skyscraper: The Making of a Building*. New York: Viking Penguin, 1990.

Seligman, Daniel. "The Enduring Slums." In *The Exploding Metropolis*, by the editors of *Fortune*. Garden City, N.Y.: Doubleday, 1957.

Sigafoos, Robert A. *Corporate Real Estate Development*. Lexington, Mass.: Lexington Books, 1976.

Sobel, Robert. *Trammell Crow, Master Builder: The Story of America's Largest Real Estate Empire*. New York: John Wiley & Sons, 1989.

Teaford, Jon C. *The Rough Road to Renaissance: Urban Revitalization in America, 1940–1985*. Baltimore: Johns Hopkins Univ. Press, 1990.

Trump, Donald J., with Tony Schwartz. *Trump: The Art of the Deal*. New York: Random House, 1987.

Walsh, Annmarie Hauck. *The Public's Business: The Politics and Practices of Government Corporations*. Cambridge, Mass.: MIT Press, 1978.

Weaver, Robert C. *The Urban Complex: Human Values in Urban Life*. Garden City, N.Y.: Doubleday, 1964.

Weiss, Marc A., and John T. Metzger. *Neighborhood Lending Agreements: Negotiating and Financing Community Development*. Cambridge, Mass.: Lincoln Institute of Land Policy, 1988.

Weiss, Marc A., and John W. Watts. "Community Builders and Community Associations: The Role of Real Estate Developers in Private Residential Governance." In *Residential Community Associations: Private Governments in the Intergovernmental System*. Washington, D.C.: U.S. Advisory Commission on Intergovernmental Relations, 1989.

Wenzlick, Roy. *The Coming Boom in Real Estate*. New York: Simon & Schuster, 1936.

Whyte, William H., Jr. *The Organization Man*. New York: Simon & Schuster, 1956.

Zeckendorf, William, with Edward McCreary. *The Autobiography of William Zeckendorf*. New York: Holt, Rinehart & Winston, 1970.

PART III
IDEAS

Chapter 7

Stage One: Inception of an Idea Through Experience And Awareness

With the historical evolution of the public/private partnership clearly in mind, we are ready to move forward with stage one of the development process—inception of an idea.

Of all the activities that constitute real estate development, generating successful prospective ideas for projects should be the least mechanical and the most creative. The excitement of identifying an unfilled human need and creating a product (and a marketing campaign) to fill it at a profit is the stimulus that drives development—even if the product is as unglamorous as self-storage units or pads for time-share mobile homes. The best ideas result in products that serve the user well and add value to the community—something that most often distinguishes good development from bad.

Where do developers get their ideas? How do they know which ideas deserve further analysis and which do not? And when do developers decide to act on ideas? No magic formula exists for generating good development ideas because everyone processes information differently. The spark comes from the way different pieces of information are put together to solve a problem—not from the information itself or from the techniques used to manipulate it.

One thing that *is* certain is that developers generally need background information to make the most of good ideas, which, along with experience, results in what is often called "a feel for the market."

While generating ideas might be thought of as always unpredictable and intuitive, in development it is just as often methodical and calculated. Developers need to *plan* future projects to keep their firms in business. Tight, overbuilt markets require sound business judgments based on supported assumptions if a project is to have a chance to succeed. Thorough market research has become as important as a developer's drive to complete the project.

Very little human experience and observation go to waste when players try to understand real estate markets. Developers, members of the development team, investors, regulators, and policymakers can be most effective and successful in looking at all knowledge (history, current reality, and forecasts) as potentially useful in making decisions. In a sense, people *unconsciously* do market research in almost all their waking moments as they read, drive, eat, play, meditate, or interact with other people—as well as *consciously* when they analyze the regional economy and local population growth, employment figures, zoning, traffic counts, occupancy rates, and preferences. Curiosity, interest, and observation increase the resources for generating ideas.

This text focuses on the importance of good market research and marketing: in fact, the importance of marketing cannot be emphasized too strongly. Marketing begins long before the actual selling or leasing of space. Good real estate marketing begins, even before an idea is born, with developers' curiosity about the ways people use space and with their sensitivity to the changes in markets over time. This chapter emphasizes a developer's need to understand the total marketing concept: 1) finding out what the customer wants, 2) producing it, and 3) convincing the customer, using market research to generate ideas for a concept that will fill demand. Basic marketing definitions, techniques, and sources of information are presented in this chapter, which can be applied throughout the eight-stage model of the development process to bridge the gap between thought and action.

Although marketing and market research underlie every stage of the development process, in this text these concepts are highlighted at four points in the development process (see Figure 7-1). As a beginning, this chapter covers the following topics:

- The different motivations behind ideas;
- Strategic decision making and generating ideas;
- Techniques for generating ideas;
- Words of warning and signposts; and
- Risk control during stage one of the real estate development process.

MOTIVATIONS BEHIND THE IDEAS

While the inception of an idea is often the most difficult stage in real estate development, it can also be the most fun. A developer can spend 20 to 30 percent of the time required for a project in this stage, taking many moments every day. Every new idea serves as a catalyst, which when brewed with the background already in the developer's mind, generates new ideas. With this background, the developer moves into stage one of the development process.

This text characterizes developers as people informally brainstorming, searching their background and current experience for an idea with potential. But during the development process, ideas are generated in many different ways. For example, developers often come upon *a site looking for a use*. For one reason or another, the owners of a particular parcel, whether public or private, want the site to be developed, creating possibilities for the developer. Alternatively, developers might find

FIGURE 7-1
MARKET PRINCIPLES AND MARKET RESEARCH PERVADE THE DEVELOPMENT PROCESS

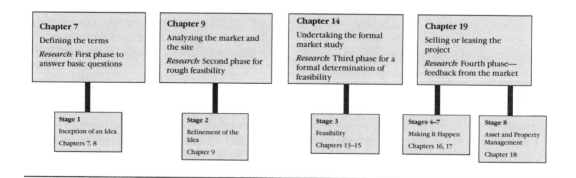

152

a use looking for a site, frequently the case when corporations want to expand, introduce a new product, or restructure their operations, creating a need for constructed space. Finally, powerful capital market forces might be at work, so that *capital is looking for a development opportunity*. This case has occurred in the past two decades, with pension funds seeking to diversify into real estate and foreign investors looking for opportunities in the United States.

Whatever the situation, the developer takes the lead role, prepared to act if the idea appears worthwhile. And regardless of motivation, the developer still must transform the general idea into bricks and mortar. In all three cases, the developer must have the background—relevant experience in development and familiarity with the latest changes in the industry—to be able to respond to the stimulus. Successful developers also have extensive contacts that provide a sounding board for new ideas and suggest potential members of the development team to be assembled if the idea proves sound. Background is the soil where the seed of motivation is sown.

While the developer is the driving force during subsequent stages of development, landowners, space users, or sources of capital can also pursue opportunities for development. For example, organizations like railroads and paper companies that own vast tracts of land have created development subsidiaries to plan and develop selected sites. Many large corporations have established real estate units or subsidiaries to develop space as well as to manage their leased space. Some have gone so far as to spin off a separate company to develop and manage their extensive real estate holdings.

It is also possible for an idea to spring from the developer's own imagination—a purely entrepreneurial idea. Often, however, a combination of motivations occurs. John Portman, for example, generated the idea for a new form of development in his initial Hyatt hotel project from his belief that interior space could be designed to serve people better and that the existing hotel market could be expanded if space served people. He combined this idea with urban renewal sites (see Chapter 11) in Atlanta and San Francisco to create a new use appropriate to the sites.

While the initial idea may be rough, to prove worthwhile the type of project must fit the location, which fits the tenant, which fits the financing. Ultimately, this fit is more important than the source of the idea.

The Back-of-the-Envelope Pro Forma

Stage one of the development process ends when the developer tests the new idea with a "back-of-the-envelope pro forma"—a simple comparison of value to cost. At this stage, ideas are not refined enough to be subjected to detailed numerical analysis of discounted cash flow. And because most ideas generated at this stage are never carried out, the developer cannot justify spending a great deal of time analyzing each idea's preliminary feasibility.

To prepare a quick pro forma, developers typically use their concept of the tenant to project the tenant's willingness to pay for a particular type of space with appropriate services in a particular location. This projection consists of a rough estimate of income per square foot and operating expenses per square foot without great detail as to the level of tenant improvements, cost escalations, length of lease, and the many other factors that become important at later stages during development. The next step is to multiply leasable square feet in the project by estimated income per square foot less projected operating expenses and then multiply by 10 (the inverse of a 10 percent cap rate). The rough estimate of *value* thus inelegantly generated is then compared to a rough estimate of *cost*, which at this point typically is projected from estimates of what the land might sell for plus site development costs plus construction costs per square foot of building. If value exceeds cost, at least based on the numbers, the idea is still alive. If cost exceeds value, it is back to the drawing board.

Like all research-based projects, the vast majority of ideas do not pass muster. Thus, most of the time, this stage ends with the best possible device to control risk: the decision to stop. That prospect is simply a fact of life and a natural part of the development process. But the compensation for nine ideas that die on the back of the envelope is one good idea worth refining in stage two.

Strategic Planning and Generation of an Idea

The rise of large development companies and of corporate real estate departments has accelerated the use of strategic planning for decisions involving real property. This trend is interesting, given the image the public often associates with developers as freewheelers unfettered by bureaucracy. Although the specifics of strategic planning are beyond the scope of this text, all members of the development team should appreciate the basics.

Strategic planning consists of formulating ends and means and determining courses of action. The choice of a project affects the development company undertaking it, and before deciding on projects, developers should think about how large an organization they want to control, the extent of vertical or horizontal integration they want (the amount of structure they can live with), and the talent, ambition, and money available to the organization. Any idea chosen for development becomes de facto part of an organizational *strategy*; in fact, developers can identify specific projects and locations and consider those choices part of the organizational strategy they want to pursue. Ideally, developers should think beforehand about how a particular project might fit into a strategy for their organization. In other words, to use marketing research effectively for a project, developers should have a clear idea of why they want to do the project and how much of their money, people, and reputation they can afford to devote to it.

STRATEGIC DECISION MAKING, GENERATING IDEAS, AND MARKET RESEARCH

Ideas end in choices—developers hope to make the right ones from the beginning—and it is useful to look at market research as a tool for strategic decision making. Real estate developers must recognize the importance of planning and control, particularly in competitive, highly regulated environments. Seat-of-the-pants decision making works in some forgiving markets, but many developers today do not have the luxury of operating so loosely.

Developers' decisions can be classified as strategic planning, management planning, or management control, which together constitute the union of planning and control. *Strategic planning* is pure planning, *management control* is pure control, and *management planning* is both planning and control. In strategic planning, developers outline desired ends, legitimate means, and general courses of action. In management planning, developers consider the best way to accomplish the strategic plan with specific actions, given desired ends and available means. Most rational decision making is an exercise in management planning. Using management control, developers achieve specific ends with the chosen courses of action and means provided. Figure 7-2 explains formal planning and control in more detail.

Although distinctions between planning and control are relevant to decision making throughout the development process, they are particularly important in marketing decisions. The total marketing concept in any industry begins with researching market opportunities, selecting target markets, and formulating competitive strategies; they constitute *strategic planning*. Next, marketing requires a marketing plan and marketing systems, which constitute *management planning*. Finally, implementation and control of the plan are based on *management control* decisions. Market research contributes to all three functions; in fact, it can be used throughout the eight stages of real estate development (see Figure 7-3).

In real estate development, developers engage in strategic planning during the inception of an idea, when they consider the big picture. Searching for opportunities, they study real estate markets defined by location and by product type and broadly consider market segments, the competition, and a possible marketing mix. During refinement of the idea and analysis of feasibility, the developer and development team pursue management planning by analyzing specific market segments in

154

FIGURE 7-3
MARKET RESEARCH IN THE REAL ESTATE DEVELOPMENT PROCESS

Stage	Research Provides
1 Inception of an Idea	Background for brainstorming, initial information for a back-of-the-envelope pro forma
2 Refinement of the Idea	Input for refining the rough idea
3 Feasibility	Input for rigorous market analysis
4 Contract Negotiation	Information to sell all participants in the development process on the project
5 Formal Commitment	Background material for lawyers to work from
6 Construction	The basis for planning marketing tactics, relating changing market conditions to construction
7 Completion and Formal Opening	Input for implementing and controlling marketing
8 Asset and Property Management	Input for eventually repositioning the project, using marketing-oriented property management

the various formal techniques, brainstorming, the nominal group process, the Delphi method, and environmental scanning (or a combination of them) are used most frequently to generate and test ideas for a project. These techniques are sufficiently systematic and precise to help generate good ideas without making exorbitant demands on limited time and money.[1]

Brainstorming is a group (or individual) exercise devoted to producing the largest possible number of creative ideas during a period of time. To encourage an atmosphere of creativity, the group or individual initially accepts *every* idea, no matter how unusual. Whether done in a group or individually, several rules for brainstorming should be followed: write down every idea, defer judgment on the value of ideas, list as many ideas as possible, and, most important, look for combinations of listed ideas. After a brainstorming session is completed, the development team can study the lists more closely and select the most promising ideas for projects.

The *nominal group process* is a technique for establishing priority among ideas

identified by a group. It can be used to analyze in more detail ideas generated through brainstorming, and it is particularly useful when a development team is responsible for arriving at a consensus about ends and means for choosing among alternatives. The facilitator lists, clarifies, and screens opinions, based on the group's preferences, and members submit a written, confidential vote on alternatives. Preferred projects emerge out of the process. The usefulness of this technique depends upon the developer's willingness to work with a group—the development organization or development team—to set priorities among project ideas.

The *Delphi method*, first used to analyze military strategies and the impacts and implications of new technologies, is a formal way to bring expert opinion to bear on a research question. Developers can use the technique to gather the informed opinions of real estate experts about a complex question. One obvious application is forecasting the real estate market. The developer prepares a set of questions, aiming to find a consistent set of answers. After exam-

Photo courtesy of the Beacon Companies

Some ideas result in grand, unusual projects with a lot of visibility, such as this unusual mixed-use project. Rowe's Wharf on the Boston harbor brought contextual design and quality public spaces, including waterfront promenades, to Boston's financial district.

ining the experts' independent forecasts, the developer can prepare more structured and close-ended questions and then ask the experts to compare their views to others and to consider revising their opinions. The process may require several rounds of review. If the process is successful, the developer can elicit a single, coherent picture of the environment under study.

Developers might find the Delphi method attractive when the questions are complex, the experts are dispersed and few in number, or antipathy exists within the development team. On the negative side of the method, maintaining anonymity among experts and structuring a specific set of questions may reduce the quality of responses.

Environmental scanning is a systematic way for developers or a development team to monitor the local, regional, national, and global environments and to predict the possible implications of environmental events. For example, developers engaged in a large-scale project with a lengthy period for completion might consider the implications of a recession on the project's feasibility. Scanning can be simplified by identifying a few readily available, easily interpreted indicators to monitor environmental events, for example, the prime interest rate or quarterly changes in the GNP. The developer or team specifies the events and the actions they would trigger, often writing scenarios to play out these implications and the results of alternative courses of action in concrete terms. Although environmental scanning is widely used and highly recommended for strategic organizational planning, it is a very time-consuming way to generate project ideas.[2]

WORDS OF WARNING AND SIGNPOSTS

A few caveats are in order before the next great idea appears.

Macroeconomic Trends

Rarely if ever can information on macro trends be used directly to arrive at ideas for a project, even if the Delphi method is used to refine the experts' opinion. First, macroeconomic trends are by far too general and aggregated. Developers must reduce trends to the local level to arrive at useful ideas. Second, macroeconomic projections and related forecasts are unavoidably risky and uncertain. Even if developers have great foresight and at the same time practice risk control, the econometric projections will probably always miss the wild cards like an oil crisis or a stock market crash. Third, macroeconomic information is very complex, making it virtually impossible to examine *all* the interactions and implications of different trends. Thus, after all is said and done, creative insights and problem solving are still necessary to cut through the complexity and to combine macro information in new ways applicable to the local level.

Test Marketing a New Idea

One traditional form of market research—test marketing a new product—generally does not work in real estate development, for real estate products are expensive, large, physically fixed to a location, and long-lasting. Thus, developers cannot simply test a new concept in hotels by building one and inviting a sample group of guests to try it. Once a large project is built, the developer is committed, at least to the part that has already been built.

Consequently, developers kick a lot of tires and show friends a lot of pictures. And sometimes they build projects in what appears to be uneconomically small phases, allowing market response to shape the later phases. But because the product is so expensive, good market research is particularly important. Trial and error is almost never a viable method of proving the market.

Limitations of Research

Winning developers have been able to cope with too little information, too much information, inaccurate information, and rapidly changing information, somehow managing to synthesize successful new ideas. Sometimes the idea is a small change in familiar elements—perhaps developing a fairly standard 300-unit apartment complex with a slightly larger master bath in a new city. Sometimes the idea is a startling new combination of elements, like Trump Tower. But behind almost all these ideas lies some form of market research.

The American Marketing Association has defined marketing research as the "systematic gathering, recording, and analyzing of data about problems relating to the marketing of goods and services."[3] This broad definition would include routine information collection (formal and organized research activities) by marketing or sales staff. Marketing research deals with a marketing problem, designs a research strategy for analyzing the problem, collects and organizes information related to the problem, analyzes the information, and draws conclusions based on that analysis. Furthermore, good research must be systematic and objective. Systematic marketing research tests all plausible responses to the problem, not just one or two. Objective marketing research requires a research design that is not tainted by the analyst's biases or preconceived answers. Marketing researchers aim at precise and accurate answers to questions, not convenient or popular answers.

Marketing research is organized in a variety of ways. In small firms, one person in the organization might be responsible for research, but constraints on resources usually severely limit the scope of such efforts. In larger firms, the marketing research function appears on the organizational chart. Often the research department reports to the executive in charge of marketing or sales and marketing. In some cases, research may be part of the firm's overall strategic planning function and be part of the staff that reports directly to the chief executive.

Within the marketing research unit, activities can be organized in a variety of

Some development ideas have special features that are less visible. This video conference at Harbor Bay Business Park in Alameda, California, is one feature that fuses real estate development and telecommunications technology and distinguishes this community. Harbor Bay also features a satellite teleport.

ways. According to Gilbert Churchill, organization of research can be:

1. By area of application, such as by product line, by brand, by market segment, or by geographic area;
2. By marketing function performed, such as field sales analysis, advertising research, or product planning;
3. By research technique or approach, such as sales analysis, mathematical and/or statistical analysis, field interviewing, or questionnaire design. Many firms with very large marketing research departments still further combine these "pure" organizational structures into a hybrid approach.[4]

The firm's organizational structure—particularly whether centralized or decentralized—also affects the organization of the marketing research function.

RISK CONTROL DURING STAGE ONE

Pragmatic developers can take several steps to reduce risk in stage one of the development process:

- Know yourself. Developers who carefully evaluate their own capabilities (financial and intellectual) will be in a better position to deal with the pressures of development. Having the right friends in financial institutions, in groups of prospective tenants, and in construction companies can be very helpful. A large bank account is also usually helpful. Ideas feasible for one developer may be less feasible for another; know your limitations. If your net worth is in the low seven figures and you have no construction experience beyond garden apartments, do not try to develop $50 million high-rise residential towers in the most overbuilt markets.

- Know your image. Often the public perception of a developer is as a gunslinger (without a white hat). Successful developers are often quite averse to risk and function much like movie producers, packaging ideas and producing a product from many individuals' talents, all to satisfy society's needs for space. Aspiring developers should understand both what a developer does (the movie producer's role) and how the public views the profession (the image of gunslinger). Self-perception and public perception are both useful background for self-preservation.

- Developers must determine the quality of all other possible participants in the development process at an early date. During stage one, as developers decide on a general type of project, a general location, and a general type of tenant, they at the same time think of players who might be brought into the team to make the development possible. People with great track records, financial strength, and capabilities will reduce long-term risk. They probably will also increase the cost.

- From the beginning, developers must coordinate the individuals involved in the process. This task is critical in later stages when they switch to a more managerial role, but even at the beginning, developers must *talk* to contractors, subcontractors, potential tenants, and city managers, not just read about them.

- The more current developers' backgrounds, the more likely they are not to move beyond stage one poorly informed. The various elements change over time: key factors in the national economy, supply conditions, political conditions, tax laws. The more current developers stay on both local and national issues, the safer they are.

- Personal relationships and ethics are important parts of the development process, and it is often difficult to rely on the courts for a solution when problems arise. The stronger the personal relationships and business ethics of all those involved, the safer the investment in the development.

Developers increase their risk when they enter a new market where they have little or no experience. To partially control risk, developers must assess their position in the marketplace and their goals.

Fraser Morrow Daniels, as a new entrant in the Research Triangle Park market,[5] relied heavily on formal inquiry, as Whit Morrow describes in the continuing case study. The company's market research and definition of a target market reflect the steps outlined in this chapter, but the steps are not clearly defined. As Fraser Morrow Daniels learned more about emerging trends in the market, it synthesized the information, moving back and forth between market research and planning tactics, to revise the initial concept.

EUROPA CENTER

WHIT MORROW EXPLAINS THE GENESIS OF AN IDEA

Analyzing Market Opportunities

Why did we form a new company to undertake new ventures in a new area, and what made us choose the Research Triangle? What did we consider in picking our products, and how did we structure our company in that environment? The area as a whole was attractive to us; it was an area where we would personally want to live and work.

We looked at several factors: growth and diversity in employment, demographics, infrastructure, government regulations, prices, product supply, availability of financing, politics (different from the regulatory environment, it is the attitude in the area, what people are thinking, what will happen when the bulldozer starts), labor supply, and quality of the natural environment.

With all those factors in mind, we started looking at the whole Research Tri-

angle area. It was a new business environment, unlike Atlanta, for example, which is a big city with a beltway and all the traditional factors that go along with working in a fairly steady, predictable business environment. In the Research Triangle, four small cities make up the metropolitan area.

We tried to develop an overall business strategy for the 1980s and the 1990s. We looked not just at population growth but also at changing segments. Census data showed that the area was growing at a higher rate than the national average. We took what was happening in the national economy and national population statistics and compared it with local data.

Researching and Selecting Target Markets

Then we looked at Raleigh/Durham to see how the trend was playing out there. Who was moving there? Which market segments, defined by age group, were being built for shopping opportunities, for housing? What effect did those trends have on the homebuilding market and other segments?

We found that local job growth and diversification were probably the best mix of any area we looked at in the country. The factors driving the local economy were universities, state government, and growth in Research Triangle Park, where high-tech businesses were growing rather than being overbuilt or dying out. What those factors told us was that that marketplace was the place to be if we wanted to be in the development business for the next 15 to 20 years.

Developing a Marketing Strategy

Next question. What do we do and where do we do it? The first factor we started looking at was who else was doing what in the marketplace. Who were the major players? Who had been around for a long time building office buildings and shopping centers? Where were they located? We wanted to put things on a map

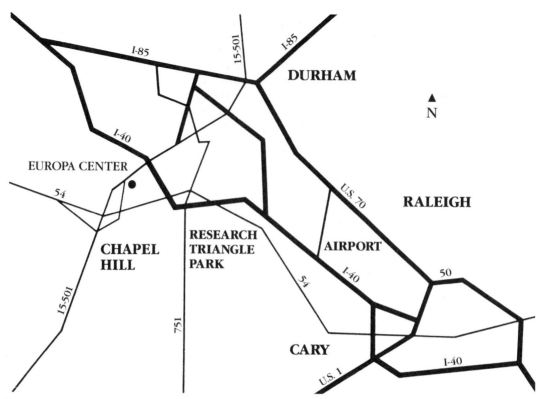

Europa Center is strategically located on the U.S. 15-501 corridor, 1½ miles west of I-40.

and decide where the opportunities were. We wanted to combine that information with our analysis of infrastructure.

I went to the local map store and asked for a map of the Research Triangle area and was shocked to find that none were available anywhere. I went to the Council of Governments for the six-county area. All it had were county road maps pieced together—without even the cities on it—a map of the water supply, and a map that had schools on it but basically nothing else. No one had put together all the nitty-gritty details that are necessary for the area as a whole, making it such a peculiar opportunity for real estate development.

The Research Triangle area was also different because it had 750,000 people spread over three or four cities, which together have all the activity equivalent to one major city that attracts businesses. Individually, however, the cities are small towns. The competitors we found in this

marketplace were people like the Yorks, who had started the Cameron Village shopping center 40 years earlier in Raleigh. The Davidson and Jones Company construction company had been building buildings for the universities and the state government. And some big companies, like IBM, had built their own campuses as well as leased space in other buildings.

This was a key finding. No active, competitive, national speculative office building developer was operating in the area. Nobody had gone out on a limb and built a building and hoped to fill it because of office population growth. There had been only companies doing it for themselves and local builders building for existing committed demand. As of 1983, the supply was 100,000 square feet and absorption was 100,000 square feet—totally unlike any other place in the country with a population of 750,000.

Our next stop was the local chambers of commerce to talk to the people who

162

were promoting business activity and pushing development. Raleigh's chamber had all the statistics on Raleigh and knew all about Raleigh's beltway, how long it would take to get the outer beltway built, and some other statistics as well. Durham's chamber had all their statistics, although it still had somewhat of an inferiority complex because Durham had been just a tobacco town and isn't beautiful. In Chapel Hill, the chamber of commerce represented about 2 percent of the community's population. The university represented one part, retirees another part, and residents who commuted to jobs in other parts of the Triangle the rest of the community. So Chapel Hill's chamber was basically of no help. And people there didn't even want to talk about development.

So we were, in a sense, real pioneers (along with many other people as it turned out) in a new business environment ripe for plucking from the outside. The people there had all their assumptions about the way it was: "Nobody's going to live in Durham. Nobody's going to move to Durham." They told us about the last developer that tried to build houses on the south side of Durham in 1972, on Highway 54 near Research Triangle Park. That developer went bankrupt. Total failure.

Well, some other newcomers realized that it was not possible to buy a nice house next to a swimming pool and tennis court, despite the high rate of growth. They took a chance and bought 750 acres at dirt-cheap prices south of Durham in the same location that had failed 10 years before near Research Triangle Park. Boom! Woodcroft was born, selling 2,000 housing units over a two-year period. That's how rapidly this business environment was changing.

The individual chambers of commerce had no concept of a unified MSA. They were individual communities, fighting among themselves for recognition. So we took the U.S. Geological Survey maps and pieced them together to make a big map. It was the only detailed topographic map available of the whole area, and it was 10 feet long. Standing back from it,

anyone could see that a very strong link would develop between the east and west sides of the community (Raleigh to Chapel Hill) with the completion of I-40 as well as a great deal of opportunity in the middle that did not exist before because of cars backed up on two-lane Highway 54. Simple things became apparent: the Research Triangle Park had no restaurants, it shuts down at 5:00 at night, there's only one hotel, and nightlife is as boring as it can be.

These ideas are very simple. The infrastructure changed: the airport built a real runway and the number of flights quadrupled. American Airlines put a hub there. The Park accelerated from a very steady 4 to 5 percent increase over the 20 years from 1960 to 1980 to 20 percent increases every year for the next five or six years. And in the middle of this abundant land, the federal government and the state were spending oodles of money on the highway systems, and the airport was reaching huge capacity.

At the Raleigh chamber of commerce, the chief concern was developing Raleigh's outer fringe—trying to force development to the east side of Raleigh, exactly the opposite direction from Research Triangle Park. In Durham, most of the power brokers live north of town, also opposite from the Park, and the north side of Durham was being developed. Even some bright, forward-thinking people said that the solution was a replication of Research Triangle Park in that area and proposed Treyburn, a mixed-use project on 5,500 acres northeast of Durham. But the natives still thought of Durham and Raleigh and Chapel Hill as separate cities— even though a multimillion dollar interstate highway runs right through the area between Durham and Chapel Hill within eight minutes of the heart of the Park.

Thus, we had an obvious strategy: buy 100 to 200 acres to build office buildings. With the growth we saw and the communities' coming together, we foresaw the need for a large amount of office space. The old absorption rate of 100,000 square feet per year would change. In fact, we noticed that in 1983, 500,000 square *feet of office space had been used (with some businesses building their own space on top of that). Population growth, demographics, and infrastructure combined to tell us that someone could take advantage of a big opportunity. We did just that, buying 100 acres of land to develop office space. As it turned out, we were not alone in our astute observations.*

SUMMARY

The inception of an idea is the first stage in the development process. Ideas come from several different motivations, but regardless of source, the ideas can be quickly tested with a back-of-the-envelope pro forma. Ideally, the generation of ideas is integrated with the development company's strategic planning, tying market research into a rigorous process of planning and control. Numerous techniques are available for generating ideas: brainstorming, the nominal group process, the Delphi method, and environmental scanning. Regardless of the level of rigor or the techniques employed, several potential pitfalls should be avoided in the application of market research to the generation of ideas. Consequently, risk control is necessary during the first stage of the development process.

NOTES

1. The references at the end of this section provide excellent descriptions of basic techniques for generating ideas (although not in the context of real estate development).

2. Environmental scanning and contingency planning ordered by Alan Greenspan before the October 1987 crash of the U.S. stock market apparently enabled the Federal Reserve to maintain liquidity in the severely strained capital markets. *The Wall Street Journal* reported (November 25, 1987) that Greenspan organized a crisis management team in his early days as the Fed's new director and requested analyses of projected potential crises in the stock market, the value of the dollar, and the U.S. banking system. When the actual crisis occurred very soon thereafter, the Federal Reserve was prepared. It is hard to imagine a better reminder that planning pays off.

3. Gilbert A. Churchill, Jr., *Marketing Research: Methodological Foundations* (Chicago: Dryden Press, 1987), p. 11.

4. Ibid., p. 14.

5. The Research Triangle of North Carolina includes Raleigh (the state capital), Durham, Chapel Hill (where Europa Center is located), Cary, Research Triangle Park, the University of North Carolina at Chapel Hill, North Carolina State University (in Raleigh), and Duke University (in Durham).

Chapter 8

Market Research:
A Tool for
Generating Ideas

Because market research is fundamental to the generation of ideas—the starting point for all development—it is useful to look in depth at how market research fits with the total concept of marketing taught in basic marketing courses. This chapter thus adds structure to the material developed in the preceding chapter.

Before starting any project, developers should understand the market—market being defined both as users of a type of property (e.g., light industrial buildings) and as buyers and tenants located in a geographic area. A good market does not necessarily equate to a good development opportunity, nor does a bad market mean that no good ideas can be done. In other words, a good market from the perspective of demand may be oversupplied, and a good idea may win even in low-growth markets by relocating existing tenants. (Conversely, poor implementation can ruin the most attractive opportunities in any market.) Still, understanding the market is a necessary part of generating ideas, stage one of the development process.

This chapter discusses the elements involved in looking at a market, focusing on several areas:

- The basics: marketing and market research;

- What marketers (and developers using marketing) do; and
- Market research and development ideas.

THE BASICS: MARKETING AND MARKET RESEARCH

Developers who have succeeded in the past might assume that their next project will be successful just because they are building it; that is, that "their" supply will create its own demand. This assumption sometimes holds for hot recording stars and clothing designers but is rarely true in real estate. As one developer said when asked at what point in his career he finally felt safe being on his own: "You're never safe."

Real estate developers, like all business people, need to pay close attention to their customers. Peter Drucker, the grand master of management consultants, underscores this point by defining marketing as taking the customer's perspective on the business. In the same vein, marketing specialist Philip Kotler argues that marketing should not be construed narrowly as the process of selling products but more broadly as satisfying human wants and needs. Developers who pay careful attention to markets fare far better than those

165

Historically, markets were places where buyers and sellers met, typically in the town center. Today, if a city is interested in opening such a market, an extensive market study delineating potential groups of customers must be done to justify its development.

who do not in today's highly competitive real estate industry.

Although deals driven by the marketplace tend to be the most successful, many examples exist of deals done for reasons other than the market. Until 1984 and 1986, when tax reform removed several provisions favorable to real estate, incentives in the federal tax code prompted a number of otherwise uneconomic developments. Where financing was readily available, many dubious projects were developed because some participant in the process benefited even if the project was not successful. And some projects were developed to realize the dream of a particular developer with scant attention to the market.

Developers may have many nonpecuniary reasons for undertaking a project, including satisfaction of ego. Usually the nonpecuniary motivations behind development are legitimate, but such projects should still be realistic and based on an accurate understanding of the market.

When developers can persuasively demonstrate that they have found customers with unfilled wants and needs, they can use that market information to garner public support and financial backing for a project. When the project is not justified by the market, as in the case of housing for the very poor described in Chapter 12, they should know the extent of the subsidy required.

Competitive developers should use principles of marketing not only to sell a particular project but also to position their organization over the long term. Principles of marketing and management science are valuable to developers as executive officers of a development organization. This textbook focuses on *project* planning and management; therefore, it discusses market research and marketing in terms of project development. Developers looking for future success, however, need to use marketing as a tool to promote their organizations as well as to sell specific projects. (Appendix B contains an article on strate-

166

gic positioning for real estate development companies.)

The following overview of marketing principles draws heavily on Philip Kotler's well-known marketing textbook.[1] It lists five key marketing concepts:

- Marketing is social: it takes at least two people to make a transaction.
- Marketing occurs because humans have needs and wants, some of which can be satisfied by acquiring products.
- If people have a choice among products, their choice will usually be guided by their notion of value and their expectation of satisfaction.
- Although products can be obtained in several ways—producing it ourselves, begging, stealing, or exchange, for example—most of us acquire goods by exchange. Therefore, most of us become specialists in producing particular products, which we trade for other things we need.
- A market is simply a group of people who share a similar need, for instance, a hotel room in Seattle. The size of that market depends upon how many people share the need *and* have the purchasing power to satisfy it.

The term "market" can be used in a variety of ways. Historically, markets were places where buyers and sellers met—the town center or the farmer's market. Business people usually use the term to refer to different ways of grouping customers, including geographic location (the Pacific Northwest, the Midwest), demographic profiles (yuppies, empty nesters), and product types (those who use personal computers). The concept also includes groups like labor markets or donor markets not comprised of customers. Economists refer to both buyers and sellers when describing markets in terms of supply and demand, while marketing professionals (the people who try to convince us to buy a Chrysler instead of a Ford) consider the sellers as the industry and the buyers as the market. Industry and market, sellers and buyers, are linked in four ways. Sellers send 1) goods or services and 2) communications to the market; in return, they receive from the market 3) money and 4) information.

In essence, marketing is the activity that turns the crank: possible transactions become actual transactions when people are stimulated to exchange money (or something else of value) for something they want or need. People—employees—create and manage marketing campaigns to achieve the company's objectives—no less in real estate development companies than at Procter & Gamble or General Foods. In theory, objectives for marketing ought to be part of most management functions like, for example, manufacturing. In practice, however, finding and keeping customers at times are left to the marketing staff alone—which, in real estate development, means leasing or salespeople. As in any company, projects are more successful when people marketing the product understand how it is produced and financed and when they communicate what they learn from dealing directly with the customer to those producing and managing the project.

Marketing as a Concept

"Putting the customer first" became a business cliché of the 1980s as U.S. companies sought ways to regain customers lost to our international trading partners, notably the Japanese. One phrase that characterizes "putting the customer first" is "marketing concept";[2] that is, a company starts from the needs and wants of its target customers and then tries to satisfy their needs better than its competitors. This approach should be the foundation of a business. In fact, surprisingly often, and for their own reasons, companies put other interests ahead of the customer. These narrower interests, in contrast to the "marketing concept," can be characterized as the "production concept," "product concept," or "selling concept."

The production concept supports sales by keeping prices down through efficient *production* and wide distribution. The product concept emphasizes continual improvements in the *product's* quality. And the selling concept focuses on sales and *promotional* efforts to stimulate consumers' latent demand. They are all potentially worthy objectives but should serve, not supplant, the company's primary purpose—identifying customers and satisfying their needs competitively. Efficiently produced, well-advertised sites for single-family houses do not make a profit and do not improve a community unless they satisfy customers' needs for such sites.

Illustrations of the marketing concept include these widely heard slogans:

> "Find wants and fill them."
> "Make what you can sell instead of trying to sell what you can make."
> "We have to stop marketing makable products and learn to make marketable products."
> "Have it your way." (*Burger King*)
> "You're the boss." (*United Airlines*)
> "To do all in our power to pack the customer's dollar full of value, quality, and satisfaction." (*J.C. Penney*)[3]

The real estate development industry's increasing reliance on the marketing concept can be seen in developers' responses to growing corporate demand for human services. To address these demands, developers have dedicated marketing efforts to respond to workers (not just to industrial concerns). The accompanying profile describes developer Willard Rouse and Rouse & Associates's Great Valley project. To improve the quality of the workplace, Great Valley offers amenities, including daycare for children and elderly parents. Great Valley was not always a success. Originally conceived as a warehouse distribution park, it changed as Rouse's sensitivity to the market and the emerging demands of workers guided the development of a new use for vacant warehouse space. According to Rouse, corporations now view people as a greater asset than before, requiring buildings more sensitive to human needs.

The *societal* marketing concept extends the idea of marketing beyond a company's profits and consumers' satisfaction to collective or societal satisfaction. By definition, real estate is a long-lived asset in a fixed location. Meeting only space users' needs is not enough. Developers should satisfy at least some of the needs of neighbors and regulators and should consider government their partner. When a project is developed, if it does not serve the community, then the community will ultimately alter the rules to the detriment of the project's owner.

Photo courtesy of Rouse & Associates

Great Valley, an office and industrial park near Malvern, Pennsylvania, developed by Rouse & Associates, prides itself on the extra attention to design details and tenant services.

PROFILE: **WILLARD G. ROUSE, III**

Partner, Rouse & Associates
Malvern, Pennsylvania

According to *The Wall Street Journal*, Willard G. Rouse, III, founder of Rouse & Associates, made himself famous in Philadelphia for heading the bicentennial celebration of the U.S. Constitution and infamous (in some circles) for building Philadelphia's first skyscraper. About his role in planning and raising money for the bicentennial, Rouse told the *Journal*, "I see it as one of the few events in my lifetime that can positively change a lot of attitudes in this city. The city needs a psychological boost of doing something successful."

In his private role as a developer, Rouse has known success himself. Rouse & Associates had under way in 1987 development worth $500 million (at project cost), roughly broken down into 60 percent office space, 20 percent industrial space, and 20 percent service/flex buildings (light industrial/office). Rouse's Great Valley project, begun in 1974 near Malvern, Pennsylvania, and still under way in 1987, exemplifies several concepts mentioned in this text:

1. **Sensitivity to the market and to surroundings.** The Great Valley project was originally conceived as a warehouse distribution park on 210 acres because of its good road access to markets. When acquired, Great Valley's site was the only piece of industrially zoned land with utilities on Highway 202 south of King of Prussia, Pennsylvania. Rouse bought a distinctive site, then defended it with additional purchases. (Great Valley now includes 600 acres.) When Great Valley began, the developers put a little extra on the first building by giving it a stone facing of local Delaware Valley origin (familiar to many from the paintings of Andrew Wyeth). In another break with convention, a 30-foot-high stainless steel sculpture marks the entrance to the park, providing, in Rouse's words, "a little sizzle." The park changed direction in 1978 when Rouse converted a new, vacant, U-shaped warehouse with truck doors to high-tech office space by filling in the truck doors with glass and partitioning the interior. Creating a new use for the project worked, and Rouse filled the space. Above-average appearance added to its appeal and helped make subsequent industrial and high-tech office use possible. Detriments—a quarry and a sanitary landfill surrounding Great Valley on three sides—are not visible from the ground, and, Rouse says, "We do not show the property by air."

2. **Quality of life.** Rouse says that managing the culture at work is like managing a residential complex: "We tried to create an environment where the same kind of pride about one's home would exist in the workplace." From the beginning, a softball league of eight teams, now expanded to 55, served the employees in the park (12,000 in 1987). Rouse gradually added on-site daycare (for both workers' children and elderly parents), converted a barn to a restaurant with seated service, a cafeteria, and a bar/disco, started a business development training center (with a consortium of 33 local colleges), commingled insurance and health care for smaller companies, added a health club, and in the near future plans a hotel. Rouse puts on an annual picnic for everyone at Great Valley.

3. **Cooperation with local government and neighbors.** Rouse's company routinely meets with the township government before purchasing property, "because we don't want to get into zoning battles and no-growth battles." The company approaches its neighbors, asking, "What would you like to see on a piece of property?" Then, Rouse notes, the company describes its view of the property. The two parties quickly learn "whether you're going to get along or not."

Managing Demand

Good marketers do more than beat the bushes for customers: they not only stimulate demand but also *manage* demand—the level, timing, and composition—to achieve the company's objectives. In developing office buildings, the notion of what constitutes Class A space often changes suddenly when every large legal, accounting, and financial firm wants to upgrade space at once. Quality developers strive to manage such lumpy demand by matching the timing of construction to expiring leases.

WHAT MARKETERS (AND DEVELOPERS USING MARKETING) DO

Those who market a product first *analyze market opportunities,* paying careful attention to the market at micro and macro levels. The macro level includes the major forces influencing society and institutions: technology, tastes, demographics, sociocultural developments, political attitudes, legal structures, and economic trends. The *micro* (or industry) level includes both current and potential suppliers, customers, and competitors and the public that regulates or influences the market.[4] Good marketers analyze potential opportunities mindful of the limitations on macro analysis discussed in Chapter 7.

Marketers then *research and select target markets* with, at a minimum, good information on customers who have purchased or leased a similar real estate product in the past. Developers also collect market intelligence on potential consumers and on competitors. They can go farther, pursuing one or more forms of research described in the next section of this chapter—research on market conditions and trends of past, present, and future users.

Developers seek to identify market segments, whether socially, spatially, or behaviorally defined. Historically, real estate development has been a spatially segmented industry: most developers worked in only a few locations and constructed only one or two product types. Since the 1950s, however, developers' geographic scope and product mix have increased with the size of their companies. Now, in addition to serving a variety of geographically and functionally segmented markets, developers search for important socioeconomic and behavioral distinctions among potential customers. Research into these different factors identifies target market segments that usually consist of a distinctive combination of people, lifestyles, purchasing power, and place. In the accompanying profile, developer Stephen Drogin describes an example of one such market segment. At the Orchard, the Drogin Company offers low-income rental housing to the healthy elderly of San Diego. In a competitive environment, Drogin has achieved 100 percent occupancy by tailoring management services, product design, and financing to match the demands of customers within this sharply defined market niche.

As part of their research, developers must also recognize the competition, because they must position their own product competitively to reach the target market. Price, quality, and location are obvious attributes of competing real estate products. Reputation, expertise, financial depth, and market share are attributes of competing development companies.

Those involved in marketing must *develop a dynamic marketing strategy*—one that continues to evolve. One key aspect is recognizing that planning never stops; it must be continuous because products, markets, the development organization, the competition, and the environment continue to change. Markets are moving targets. Partially successful strategies ought to be flexible enough to be revised for better results, and even wildly successful strategies should be watched for signs of diminishing effectiveness.

A marketing strategy is a detailed plan for meeting marketing objectives; it includes a clear statement of the target market, measurable objectives for that market, a marketing budget (a critical part of the project's overall feasibility), and the marketing mix. In classic marketing terms, the marketing mix includes the four P's: product, place, price, and promotion.

In real estate, *product* refers to property type—apartments, offices, warehouses, and so on. Quality, features, op-

PROFILE: **STEPHEN B. DROGIN**

President, The Drogin Company
San Diego, California

Specialty: Low-income rental housing for the healthy elderly. Develops properties for his own account and manages projects owned by others.

Background: Attended Whittier College. A second-generation real estate professional, Drogin went to work for his father at age 22 and was fired by his father at age 25 for "differences of opinion." At the start of his independent real estate career, his capital consisted of "a very good name and an aggressive attitude."

Main project: The Orchard, San Diego, California—563 units at 55 dwelling units per acre, built in two phases on land leased from the city of San Diego. Average rent (as of 1987)—about $300 per month.

Strategy: Drogin occupies a very sharply defined niche: developing and managing low-income rental housing for the healthy elderly—a niche not comparable (in his view) to congregate care for the elderly. Land planning, product design, financing, and management are all tailored to the consumers. At The Orchard, 70 percent of the residents are women, 70 percent receive social security, and 20 percent have Section 8 certificates. (The entire city has only 1,380 Section 8 certificates, of which 114, or 8.3 percent, go to residents of The Orchard.)

Because most of The Orchard's residents cannot afford cars, Drogin was able to get a variance from the city for the first phase, allowing him to provide only one parking space for every four units. As a result, the 55 units per acre do not seem as dense as they would otherwise. This design works because of its location in a major city with public transportation and infrastructure already in place.

Buildings at The Orchard are two stories because the residents are healthy. Second-story units rent for the same amount as ground-floor apartments and rent as quickly. Apartments are either studios or one-bedroom units. They are small—435 and 465 square feet. Landscaping includes curved walks and dense vegetation (with fruit trees for which The Orchard is named). It has a central recreation room but no expensive amenities. Two full-time activities coordinators schedule free lectures, workshops, and other activities offered by city, county, state, and federal agencies. The meeting room is also a polling place, and politicians visit frequently to court elderly voters.

Management: Drogin says that real estate owners have learned the importance of good management over the last 10 years. In managing his projects, Drogin tries to make repairs within 24 hours. He refers to renters as "residents," not tenants. He appears three times a year at "town meetings" and, as owner, talks directly with residents about rent, maintenance, activities, and whatever else is on their minds. He believes that concern for residents is part of good management but that very few owners ever attempt to meet their residents face to face. Occupancy at The Orchard is 100 percent.

Future for real estate players: Real estate activities—from market analysis to lending—will be conducted on a more professional level as young people enter the field, having taken real estate courses at college. To succeed, new developers will have to find niches.

tions, and style relate to the project's architecture, construction, layout, and finishes. Brand names may be equivalent to the developer's reputation. Packaging a real estate product refers to the physical features, functions, and benefits added to the given type of property to make it appeal to particular customers—extra electrical outlets or extensive landscaping, for example. Services are the developer's commitment to property management, providing security and janitorial service, for example.

Place is the project's location. (In classical marketing, "place" refers to channels of distribution, coverage, locations, inventory, and transport.) In marketing real property, many people still believe the three key factors are location, location, and location. This whole book is about providing space with appropriate services *at a fixed location*.

Price includes special allowances for tenants to outfit space (for example, $30 per square yard for carpet or mahogany paneling in the senior partner's office), free rent, renewal options, expense pass-throughs, and comparable other terms. Payment period and credit terms are particularly important, because real property is an expensive, long-lived asset.

Promotion refers to elements of advertising and selling readily identified with real estate marketing (covered in detail in Chapter 19), but they should not obscure the importance of the other three P's in setting strategy.

A winning strategy is consistent across all four P's. Part of implementing a strategy is *planning tactics*, which requires a finer analysis of elements in the marketing mix, particularly the time and costs of each. In smaller developments, strategy and tactics tend to blend together. In larger projects, the distinction is clearer, with the overall development team setting strategy and the marketing staff working out the tactics.

Finally, the developer must *implement and control* the marketing strategy. Skillful management is required to staff, monitor, and control implementation of the marketing plan.

Appendix B worries about controlling, without stifling, both creative planning and active selling that are critical to successful implementation. Planning can-

not change the product too frequently (construction costs jump disproportionately with even small changes), and salespeople motivated by commissions cannot promise too much future service (for example, extra security) or postdevelopment operations will not be profitable.

Research provides the input for analyzing marketing opportunities and selecting target markets. Ideally, the development team never stops gathering market intelligence, continually using new information to reposition the project as change occurs.

MARKET RESEARCH AND DEVELOPMENT IDEAS

Good ideas flow from specific sources with specific knowledge of the industry and its markets. Developers need to understand themselves, the company, the competition, the other players who help build and finance projects, the regulatory and socioeconomic environment, and, most important, potential clients. Where does this knowledge come from? Practical experience, reading, and formal inquiry to answer specific questions are all important sources of knowledge.

When entering a new market where they have little or no experience, developers increase their risk. To partially control risk, developers must assess their position in the marketplace and the realism of their goals and objectives. As the case study of the Europa Center continues, Whit Morrow describes Fraser Morrow Daniels's search for a site and the impact of detailed market research on the company's initial strategy.

EUROPA CENTER

WHIT MORROW ON COMPETITION AND RISK

People who were buying land in the Research Triangle area started doing it based more on politics than on the economics of the area. And they started speculating on land prices a little bit, so that the situation got to be very competitive, with the obvious strategy to buy 100 to 200 acres in and around the Research

Triangle Park to build 10 or 12 buildings over 15 years. We were just hell-bent-for-leather to develop there. We had bids in on four or five pieces of land, but the politics of the area made us uncomfortable, so we got setbacks, we got height amendments.

Within a year, while we were trying to buy the land, at least 15 or 20 other people with more money, more staff, more power, and more connections than we had dived right into the marketplace. Every time we identified 100 acres to buy, three other people were bidding on it, trying to buy it.

So we stopped, looked at our company, and looked at our capacity. We didn't have 500 banks trying to give us money or 2,000 employees. We were a tiny company—five or six people. So what could we do in that highly competitive business environment?

We totally shifted our strategy from "let's be a big organization and do 15 office buildings and a big office park and make our first profits on the fifth building" to "let's be a little organization." Let's acknowledge who we are and what the real competitive market is. We decided instead to buy 10 acres and build one or two buildings. We made our profit projections based on that and not based on what we were going to do over a 10-year period.

We focused on the I-40 extension corridor from Research Triangle Park to the U.S. 15-501/I-40 intersection just east of Chapel Hill, where we looked at the major intersections closest to the population centers. There were really just two centers, Durham and Chapel Hill. And we weren't alone. We identified 23 different projects that came on line or were about to come on line during the three-year period that it takes to get something started.

In 1984 when we moved our company to the area, we really wanted to recognize it as the Research Triangle area, so we did not want our office in Raleigh, Durham, or Chapel Hill. We wanted to be in the Research Triangle Park or on the edge of the Park. We tried to lease office space, but no good space was available. We got into about 4,000 square feet of crummy space at $14.50 a square foot. In 1989 if I had wanted to rent office space around the Park, at least 500,000 square feet was available at a net effective rent of about $12 per square foot for Class A space.

In 1986, a lot of money was available to build office buildings in Research Triangle Park. Many banks would put up exactly what you needed, build the building, and the day it opened finance all the tenant improvements. And there was no shortage of potential tenants. Looking ahead, we saw the competitive environment in three years to be different. We asked five or six banks for an extra million dollars or more to carry the finished building through the leasing period. We held out for the extra financing for a long lease-up period that lasted two years.

My partner, Charles Fraser, was unwilling to sign a guarantee where he was the sole source of that extra million dollars, and we knew the banks would not lend it to us. So Charles decided to give up half his projected profit to get a financial partner and let him share the risk with us.

The important thing for a company entering this kind of environment is to ask what its staying power is, what its risk profile is, and how much of a chance it is willing to take. How much do you really believe your projections? We decided to get a financial partner for this office venture to put up money to buy the land and guarantee an extra million if we needed it.

Any time you have a great idea that takes several years to implement, you won't be the only one there, even if you're first. Furthermore, the other companies have different risk profiles. Our risk profile was such that we could not stand the heat if it came to a competitive environment with 17 projects all aimed at the same tenants. It was a matter of survival for us.

In a three-year cycle, your potential tenants have to recognize you. The site with only one building on it has to be attractive. You can't sell somebody a 100-acre parcel with a future lake and trails; it has to be right today. So the difference between us and some of the other players *was that when we switched from 100-acre purchases at $50,000 an acre to 10-acre tracts at five times that amount per acre for land, the economics changed a little bit, too. You do not have to carry all that land, but you do have to pay more for the one piece that's available now. So our strategy changed from finding a good site that we could market over 10 years and draw people to to one of finding a site that they stumble over every hour today—and we were willing to pay a lot for that.*

Watching experienced developers work leaves the impression that real estate development is much more an art than a science. But formal research requires patient and systematic investigation to discover facts and principles pertinent to the subject of inquiry. What could such a time-consuming process have to do with generating good development ideas?

Consider the creativity of jazz musicians whose improvisations prompt critical acclaim. Their music appears spontaneous; they create it as they go. In fact, the apparent freedom and ease of play stem from years of study and practice. Through practice, they have mastered the techniques of the instrument and of jazz forms. Through study, they have come to understand the principles. By reading about them or by listening to the interpretations of great jazz players, they have refined knowledge. Thus, freedom and discipline, improvisation and technique, interact when they play. In general, creativity and logic work together, just as the brain's right and left sides form an organic whole.

Structured research provides the discipline, feeds the logic, helps set the criteria, and to some extent even prompts the intuition by which people respond creatively to events occurring around them. Most successful real estate developers have engaged in careful, systematic study of specific markets and types of property over time. In addition, they have tested ideas for projects by planning, building, and selling space. Thus, even in cases where the inception of an idea appears to be a flash of brilliance—something very original—the idea can often be traced to the interplay of past study and analysis of widely known facts and basic principles. The new idea is usually a new combination of known elements. More typically, good development ideas replicate to a great extent previously tried ideas tailored to a particular niche.

Structured Market Research And Successful Generation Of Ideas

The condition of the market is generally described in terms of the supply of and demand for space. Developers and real estate professionals must read market forecasts and talk to people who know the national and local economies to keep in touch with short- and long-run aspects of the market. Knowledge about both demand and supply is necessary background for the generation of ideas, stage one of the development process. Knowledge should begin with a very broad, national picture, because financing is national (and increasingly international), some tenants are national, and some contractors are national. Knowledge should also include a regional and a local, even neighborhood, picture. At that level, developers ask themselves how comparable properties are doing and what the trends are.

Looking first at demand, developers should be familiar with forecasts of the general direction of the U.S. economy, for economic opportunity translates to growth in the number of jobs. Based on a forecast of job growth, the total number of people in any location can be projected, including demographic estimates of age, sex, and income. These characteristics are useful for segmenting markets to project emerging requirements for types of space. Macro forecasts are available from several sources (detailed in Chapters 14 and 15) and can be used to develop accurate forecasts of local supply and demand. The developer then translates these forecasts into an absorption schedule relevant for the proposed project (see Chapter 14 for details).

Paralleling the very broad national look at demand are a variety of supply-side considerations. First, developers gather aggregates of the existing national supply of types of space, distinguished by use as well as by size, location, function, style, and overall quality, noting vacancy rates in the existing stock. Figures across the nation are available from large brokerage firms, such as Coldwell Banker, Grubb & Ellis, and Cushman & Wakefield, while regional financial institutions and local brokerage firms often supply additional details on specific markets.

Developers should be aware that vacancy everywhere is difficult to measure. Some space is unoccupied but committed under signed leases with occupancy to start at a later date, some space is rented but not fully occupied, and several other variations are possible. And, alas, owners of buildings with large vacancies do not always truthfully report vacancies to people who gather such data. The key question is what percentage of this space is actually being *used* by tenants, not what part is being paid for, because in slow markets, some tenants lease more space than they need so as to provide for their own expected future expansion. If these tenants are already holding excess space, they are less likely to lease new space as the economy rebounds.

Data on the amount of space currently under construction and the expected completion date are also critical to analyzing supply in any market. "Announced" space may or may not be built, but space already under construction will probably be completed and should certainly be included in the estimate of supply.

Beyond knowing the current local supply, the vacancy in that existing supply, the space under construction, and announcements of space to be built, developers also need a feel for the local legal and political situation. How easy is it to initiate a new building? Local zoning ordinances put legal constraints on the volume and location of new space. The easier it is to build and the shorter the political lead time, the faster the market will respond to tight conditions.

Another factor dealing with local supply is physical. How much "unbuilt" capacity does the market have? The concern in this case is not to measure the "unbuilt square feet inside the city limits" but rather a question of how much land (or air rights) is available for a particular type of use. Only certain locations fit certain needs. Drainage, topography, and soil conditions prohibit development in certain areas. Infra-

structure is an increasingly important constraint (see Chapter 10).

In sum, knowledge of supply begins with knowledge of existing space, current vacancies in that space, and space already in the pipeline. It includes the legal and political dimension (not only current zoning but also potential changes in zoning). Physical constraints—mountains, lakes, and the like—give developers a perspective on the supply that exists today and on the potential to increase that supply over time. Development is a forward-looking endeavor. Developers who stop their analyses with only the first dimension, current supply, are likely to come up short.

Successful development responds to the needs of space users and, to a lesser extent, to the requirements of government and citizens/neighbors. The successful projects highlighted in the profiles of Willard Rouse and Stephen Drogin earlier in this chapter show how these developers effectively used information about the market to satisfy diverse interests. Products, places, people, and capital add up to many useful areas of inquiry.

Where does the information on national and regional determinants of supply and demand come from? The amount of available information is almost too great. Developers rarely perform sophisticated national forecasts because such projections are readily available from government agencies, universities, trade groups, and consulting firms. Most developers use existing national and regional forecasts as a basis for making rough local projections. Census data provide a wealth of statistical information useful for market studies. The list of monthly newsletters now available to provide updates would fill an entire chapter, and industry and university research centers also supply data (see Chapters 14 and 15).

Market Segments

Identifying new markets or niches within established markets is the most critical application of marketing research in real estate development during an era of overbuilding. In 1985, John Benton, a creative young developer in Phoenix, matched the housing preferences of urban migrants

FIGURE 8-1
A HIGH RISE IN CACTUS COUNTRY

A 39-year-old developer has taken an unconventional path by building a high-density condominium project, catering to people who want an urban way of life, in a region of suburban sprawl.

The developer, John Benton, started the project in 1985, a time of overbuilding and record vacancy rates. But instead of suburban Phoenix, Benton built in downtown Tempe, a city of 140,000 adjacent to Phoenix.

He incorporated plans for a 118-unit complex in his $25 million Hayden Square mixed-use project, which also has retail and office space and a small park. The plan was to build the condominiums above a parking deck, an unusual procedure there. A block of four model condominiums was built on the ground first, so that it could be picked up and moved later. "We had a hard time securing financing," says Benton. "We did it virtually out of our own pockets, so that we could prove to local lenders that we would be able to sell condos in this location."

After construction, financing was obtained on the basis of presales, the two-and-one-half-acre parking deck was begun, and the models were moved atop the deck by crane. The project has achieved sales of 92 percent on the first 80 condominiums. One- and two-bedroom condominiums are priced at $65,000 to $115,000.

The architectural firm Knoell & Quidort designed the project, putting wood-frame houses at a density of 40

Public activities are an important part of the mixed-use Hayden Square project in Tempe, Arizona.

units to the acre above the concrete parking deck. "The deck allowed us to build at a high density, but it also allowed us to build houses on a scale that is more appropriate to life in the Southwest," Benton says.

"A certain segment of people have moved to Phoenix from New York, Boston, or Chicago, who are here for the weather and the other benefits of the community but don't necessarily fancy themselves living on an acre in the desert with cactus," says Benton. "They want an urban lifestyle, and Hayden Square is filling that demand."

Source: New York Times, September 13, 1987.

with an unusual product (see Figure 8-1). In a seemingly overbuilt condominium market, he found a successful market niche. Like the other developers interviewed for this book, he had studied potential market segments to design a particular project. The underpinnings of this research of market segments includes sociology and urban history, demonstrating again the interdisciplinary nature of real estate development.

SUMMARY

The importance of marketing principles and market research to real estate developers, particularly in highly competitive markets, cannot be emphasized enough. Marketing begins long before the selling of space—and even before design of the product; it begins with the marketing concept, the idea that any business should start with the needs and wants of customers and satisfy those needs and wants competitively.

Market research is the investigation into needs and wants (demand) and into products and competitors that might satisfy them (supply). It is usually thought of as formal, focused, and systematic; however, market research for generating ideas for development has a very large informal component made up of experience, observation, reading, conversation, and analysis. Both types of inquiry are useful, and wise developers equip themselves to do both. The generation of ideas, marketing, and market research have both intuitive and rational elements. Successful developers are able to maximize both the intuitive and the rational. Formal knowledge of marketing principles and market research enhances the use of both faculties.

This chapter has taken a very broad view of marketing and market research, as befits the earliest of the eight stages in the development process. In Chapter 9, refinement of the idea and market research, the process narrows and the market research therefore becomes more focused. Chapters 14 and 15 show how focused market research results in a formal market study, one component of feasibility analysis. If commitments to the idea are made—stage five—then the market study becomes a building block in the marketing plan that drives sales or leasing in stage eight (Chapters 18 and 19).

Market research supports real estate development through all its stages. Useful research can be both very broad (including global, national, and regional economies) and very focused (for example, checking the traffic counts along a main artery servicing the site). Very little of a developer's total experience and knowledge go to waste when looking for new ideas.

NOTES

1. Philip Kotler, *Marketing Management: Analysis, Planning, and Control,* 5th ed. (Englewood Cliffs, N.J.: Prentice-Hall, 1984).

2. Ibid., p. 22.

3. Ibid.

4. Required reading for anyone attempting to understand the structure of an industry is Michael Porter's *Competitive Strategy: Techniques for Analyzing Industries and Competitors* (New York: Free Press, 1980).

Chapter 9

Stage Two: Refinement of the Idea And More Involved Market Research

T he Fraser Morrow Daniels development company, because it wanted to enter a new geographical area and to develop products outside its previous expertise, undertook an extraordinary amount of market research when it moved into the Research Triangle area of North Carolina to answer the basic questions from Chapter 7: where do we work and what do we develop? For Fraser Morrow Daniels, stage one of the development process concluded by deciding that the company would work in the Research Triangle and that it would develop several property types, including an office park.

As noted earlier, most ideas never make it out of stage one; they die for qualitative reasons (like image) or they die in red ink on the back-of-the-envelope pro forma. But occasionally the developer's back-of-the-envelope figures are positive, and the idea still holds interest. When that happens, the process moves to stage two, refinement of the idea.

Refining the idea is a deceptively simple phrase, considering the complexity of what actually happens in stage two and how it is done. The outcome, though, is clear: the developer's idea becomes a par-

ticular project design attached to a specific piece of land. Although an idea remains just an idea until the developer finds a site and designs the project, the abstraction is on its way to becoming a physical reality. Finding and acquiring a site and making an initial determination of physical feasibility are therefore two objectives in stage two. When they are met, the other objective is specifying the project, that is, going from the idea of building office space to a preliminary design for a 100,000-square-foot, four-story office building with specific functions, features, and benefits.

Three key concepts underlying site selection must first be understood.

First, finding the right site is crucial, partly because of the potential operating leverage a developer has in land development. A development incurs many costs, the largest being the land itself, site development, construction, and marketing. Land might represent anywhere from 10 to 30 percent of the project's total cost. The cost of residential lots in certain markets represents up to 72 percent (San Diego) of the median price for new and existing houses.[1] While many sites might be available where a structure *could* be constructed, that is, many legally and physically feasible sites, one site will be preferable in the eyes of a typical tenant. Location (situs) is the key to realizable rent: a better site might generate 10 percent, 20 percent, or even 50 percent more rent, depending on the particular components of value. The point is that, because it costs roughly the same amount to construct a given building on any of the possible sites, the increase in rent falls on the value of the land. With other costs relatively fixed, the premium from location is attributable to land.

Capturing profit from the land is, in fact, why people develop land, why they fit it to the needs of prospective users. By finding the most appropriate location and creating on it a better product through innovative design and/or better packaging and management, the developer hopes to achieve a higher realizable rent. If that is possible, the entrepreneurial enhancement of value falls to the land.

Second, a developer's profit motive often conflicts with the desire to control risk during site selection, leading to a Catch-22: the developer must tie up a site early, before demonstrating its feasibility, to capture the maximum profit on the land, yet to do so he must spend money, increasing financial exposure. Minimizing outlays of cash in the early stages is a prime method of controlling risk, but if the developer waits to tie up the land until physical, legal, political, and design feasibility is proven, the landowner may charge more (and others may be willing to pay more). If the developer ties up the land and the idea proves infeasible, he sacrifices some of the money spent on the altar of dead ideas as the site is resold.

Third, the public sector is the developer's partner in site selection: public sector officials enforce the rules while the body politic determines how rules will change in the future (the developer could

Another San Francisco ordinance, Proposition K, known as the sunlight ordinance, virtually mandates year-round, all-day access to sunlight for approximately 70 open spaces and parks within the jurisdiction of the city's recreation and parks commission. As a result, the building at 343 Sansome Street had to be redesigned to comply with these rules.

influence change, for example, by lobbying for rezoning). Zoning regulations reflect the public partner's acceptance of the type of development. Today, zoning in most jurisdictions gives a developer the right to present a proposed site plan; it does not necessarily allow the developer to *develop* retail or office space. Jurisdictions vary. In Florida, for example, before a plan is approved, statutes require that the municipality prove the existence of adequate infrastructure, while in downtown San Francisco, where an initiative of the voters (Proposition M) sets limits on the overall amount of development, the developer must offer the "best use" of the space compared with other ideas for the site (more detail on such issues is found in Chapter 11). The time required to have projects approved today often lengthens the development period so much that developers either must risk more of their own money (if it is available) or must find the equivalent of venture capital to fund the project during planning and approval.

In the process of finding a site and specifying the proposed project, developers undertake many tasks simultaneously:

- Scanning the environment for significant forces—possible competitors, government jurisdictions, political power bases;
- Analyzing the market, that is, the areas or neighborhoods within the market that might contain an appropriate site;
- Setting market, physical, legal, and political criteria for site selection;
- Analyzing possible sites and choosing a site that best fits the criteria;
- Negotiating for the chosen site and structuring a contract (usually one that constitutes an option) to secure the site;
- Conducting discussions with elected and appointed officials and city planners to ascertain their interests and any possible constraints on the project;
- Analyzing the competition—competing development companies and competing projects—to learn more about the market and supply;
- Discussing a project design that fits the market with engineers, architects, land planners, contractors, and/or financial sources to test the design's preliminary feasibility;

- Periodically retesting the numbers on the back of the envelope for financial feasibility and beginning to project cash flow over the development period;
- Deciding whether to advance with the idea to stage three (formal feasibility), to rework the idea, or to quit.

Refining the idea is complex not only because so many activities are involved in putting the right use on the right site, but also because those activities are simultaneous and interactive. (Figure 9-1 captures this complexity in two dimensions.) The answer to the big question—is this idea feasible in this area?—is conditioned on the answers to many other questions being asked at about the same time but not always being answered quickly, completely, or at all. Therefore, refining the idea is not usually a neat process. Developers must tolerate some messiness, uncertainty, and risk as they try to bring an idea to physical reality—and each development will be done slightly differently. Still, at some point, land must be acquired, contact made with other players, and a specific project designed; typically, those activities occur at this stage of the development process. And very often penalties are incurred that increase risk or decrease reward when activities are accomplished too far out of the logical sequence of the development process.

This chapter elaborates on these points:
- Scanning the environment;
- Choosing the site;
- Deciding what can be built on the site and determining initial design feasibility;
- Discussing the project with other players;
- Segmenting the market and differentiating the product as the next step in market research; and
- Controlling risk during stage two.

It concludes with a discussion of weighing the factors involved in deciding to go ahead with the Europa Center.

SCANNING THE ENVIRONMENT: COMPETITORS AND GOVERNMENTS

Home-grown developers know the projects, financial depth, and political clout of competitors in the local market, but newcomers have to figure out who the compe-

FIGURE 9-1
ACTIVITIES INVOLVED IN REFINEMENT OF THE IDEA

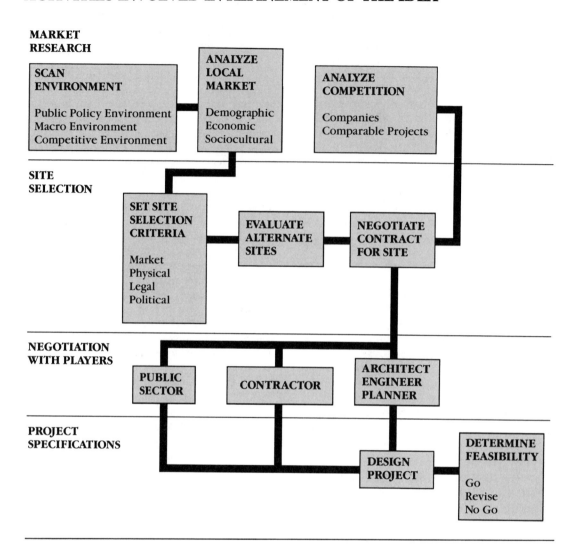

MARKET
RESEARCH

SCAN ENVIRONMENT

Public Policy Environment
Macro Environment
Competitive Environment

ANALYZE LOCAL MARKET

Demographic
Economic
Sociocultural

ANALYZE COMPETITION

Companies
Comparable Projects

SITE
SELECTION

SET SITE SELECTION CRITERIA

Market
Physical
Legal
Political

EVALUATE ALTERNATE SITES

NEGOTIATE CONTRACT FOR SITE

NEGOTIATION
WITH PLAYERS

PUBLIC SECTOR

CONTRACTOR

ARCHITECT ENGINEER PLANNER

PROJECT
SPECIFICATIONS

DESIGN PROJECT

DETERMINE FEASIBILITY

Go
Revise
No Go

tition is. And developers have to understand the ways in which local politics and regulations will affect the viability of their projects—which means knowing city officials, politicians, and the public. Understanding the human and organizational sides of a market is as important to formulating successful development ideas as is understanding the physical patterns of infrastructure, interactive land uses, and urban growth.

Recall that Fraser Morrow Daniels perceived an excellent opportunity to build speculative office space in the Research Triangle in the early 1980s because almost all space in the area was "build-to-suit" by local developers. The opportunity, however, also brought a flock of much larger out-of-town developers to the market. Thus, the competitive situation changed rapidly in the mid-1980s, and Fraser Morrow Daniels had to reassess its ability to compete with other newcomers. After assessing the competition, Fraser Morrow Daniels abandoned plans to build an office park and looked for a niche to fill with one or two office buildings on a smaller site, realizing its own risk profile was not the same as other, larger players.

Similarly, Fraser Morrow Daniels recognized the different climates for development in the different political jurisdictions within the Research Triangle market. The city where it finally chose a site happened to be the most difficult of the four major Triangle cities for developers wanting to work quickly. Its accurate perception of the city's regulatory climate guided the company's site selection: any site would have to have appropriate zoning already in place to avoid delay.

Learning about competitors, governments, and politics is an ongoing process for developers, for in a dynamic real estate market, competition, regulation, and politics are all changing. A developer might believe that apartments could be developed profitably in one submarket, but an established apartment developer might already be located in that area with solid political connections and a good public image. Unless the new entrant can clearly distinguish its project from those of the prominent developer, it might be well advised to find another submarket.

Alternatively, a developer might find an opportunity in the private market, only to confront rigid opposition from the public sector. The market for apartments might exist only because residents successfully opposed previous projects. Or the local council or planning board might want to severely restrict this type of land use to avoid adverse fiscal impacts. In other instances, constraints on building could be more subtle. Project review might be too long to allow the developer to retain site control at an affordable price. Infrastructure might appear to be adequate, but other planned projects coming on line before the developer's proposed project could use up available capacity and lead to moratoriums on new development. And impact fees (see Chapter 10) could undermine the project or at least reduce its profitability.

Developers have to choose not only the economic submarket to work in but also the jurisdiction and the competition. They should all be informed, conscious choices, the product of developers' realistic self-analysis and an equally real-istic analysis of the competitive and political environments.

Searching the City for a Site: Patterns of Urban Growth

A bit harder to explain than transportation, technology, immigration, and economic opportunity in shaping U.S. cities is culture—the "personality" of a city and how that personality influences what gets built in the urban landscape.

An important lesson for developers is the role of entrepreneurship in urban growth. Certainly New York City's leading role in this country can be explained in large part by physical advantages. It was in the middle of the 13 colonies, it had a nearly perfect harbor, and it was closest to the immigrants from Western Europe. *The* success story of the last several decades, however—success that in fact began in 1880—is Los Angeles. Los Angeles, other than a benign climate, has very few natural advantages. In 1880, it was on its way to nowhere: its ports were inferior to those of San Francisco and other western cities, and, most important, it had no water. Urban historians like Roger Lotchin, who have studied the evolution of Los Angeles, often attribute its remarkable growth to an entrepreneurial attitude among its leaders, the people who organized Cal Tech and the people who originally brought water in 1900 with the first 250-mile aqueduct, right on down the line to the Colorado River Compact in 1928 and eventually the Hoover (now Boulder) Dam.[2] Los Angeles exists because people, including Asian and Hispanic immigrants, made it happen. In today's urban environment, developers can still make it happen, and a sense of history can enhance one's appreciation of entrepreneurial opportunities awaiting discovery in today's cities.

Models of urban growth give developers, particularly newcomers, a useful way of understanding a city's current patterns of land use and indicate to some extent the future direction of change. These theoretical urban models assume that the local economy is growing, focusing on *where* growth takes place and how different land uses interrelate. People and firms cluster in spaces rather than spreading uniformly over the territory for a number of reasons, one of which is to minimize the "friction of distance." Because resources are needed to move people, goods, and information, agglomerations can reduce the costs of moving and handling goods, fostering economies of scale. Because cities are agglomerations of people and activities, all cities reduce some of these transfer costs, but the largest cities have grown around nodes where transportation lines met (often a *break* or transfer between modes of transportation, such as water to rail), either physical or commercial.

People congregate to pursue economic opportunities that are much less available at low social and physical densities. The modern city has taken on economic functions that overshadow the historically important reasons of defense, religion, government, and local trade. The new telecommunications infrastructure often locates at existing transportation hubs (large cities) to profit from existing large markets, thereby strengthening existing urban centers.

Urban Economic Theories

In searching for a site, developers should consider three theories of urban economics together: concentric zone theory, axial theory, and sector theory. Concentric zone theory says that, assuming no variations in topography or transport corridors or limits on land supply, cities would grow in concentric rings, with more competitive land uses replacing less competitive ones moving out from the center over time. Generally, land values decline the farther land is from the central intensive uses.

Axial theory accounts for development along transportation corridors, which typically radiate outward in several directions from the city center. Changes in transportation systems and improvements in transport technology have, over time, changed patterns of access in many cities and, consequently, land values. Transportation routes usually form paths along which development locates as new areas are made accessible.

Sector theory says that because geographic features and differential access exist in the real world, waves of develop-

ment tend to move out from the center, forming wedge-shaped sectors following the path of least resistance and lower costs (like a pie cut into wedge-shaped pieces).

Careful analysis of the development of particular cities over many years often reveals a sectoral pattern of growth, possibly overlain by more recent circumferential highways that create new suburban nodes with high potential for development. In fact, Homer Hoyt (the originator of the sector theory) based his general model of urban sectors on such an analysis of the evolution of U.S. cities during the late 19th and early 20th centuries.

Atlanta is a good example of a city with no major geographic restrictions preventing concentric spread. In fact, the railroad line and terminus, representing an important break in transportation, established the original city center, which still serves as the CBD. Strong north-south corridors developed, influenced by the rail lines. The first upper-income residential area expanded to the north of downtown on physically attractive land. Over many years, the higher-income residential areas continued to be developed northward, forming a wedge-shaped sector moving outward to the northeast and northwest. The major industrial zone moved outward in the opposite direction, south of downtown, and today also includes Hartsfield International Airport and the Fulton County stadium. The lower, flatter industrial zone also happens to be downwind of the northern residential areas. In fact, many cities with prevailing winds from northwest to southeast have evolved with higher-income residences in the northwest sector and industrial uses in the southeast.

As the perimeter highway in Atlanta developed, new nodes of development of office and retail uses sprang up. Primarily north of downtown, these nodes formed the base point of new sectors that pushed Atlanta's urban fringe farther out and formed a multicentered pattern.

The developer who is well grounded in models of urban growth can have a competitive advantage in finding appropriate sites. The usefulness of these models for site selection is obvious. They are also useful for understanding transitions that result in the replacement of one land use

A site looking for a use. This site ultimately became Bishop Ranch Business Park in San Ramon, California, developed by Sunset Development.

with another. In Atlanta, for example, developers have purchased entire residential subdivisions to redevelop the land more intensively for nonresidential uses. Redevelopment of parts of existing sectors is another useful insight provided by the combination of these three theories.

By using these theories of urban growth, developers should have a better grasp of the long-term potential for development of any site they are considering. Whit Morrow, unlike many competitors, viewed the cities making up the Research Triangle as a converging market area, assuming that office growth would spread beyond Research Triangle Park (the center of the triangle formed originally by three cities) along the transportation corridors, especially I-40. He also anticipated the coming oversupply of office space earlier than most competitors, because he had compiled a list of planned office buildings for the entire Triangle market rather than only any one of the individual cities (Raleigh, Durham, Chapel Hill, and Cary) whose spatial distinctions were weakening.

CHOOSING THE SITE

Developers find sites in a variety of ways. One obvious way is by keeping up with real estate listed for sale. Often developers do considerably more work, by finding likely parcels on zoning and tax maps and by examining deeds and then approaching owners of property not listed for sale. The grapevine is yet another source: an attorney might happen to mention over lunch that a competitor is strapped for cash, and it occurs to the developer that the competitor might like to let go of some real estate to gain liquidity.

The fact is that developers love real estate, are fascinated by it, and think about it a lot of the time. They go to professional meetings to get new ideas and more background, but they often take time wherever they are visiting to kick the tires. While looking for a site in their own market, they also drive around kicking tires. They get out, talk to people, and see sites, creating their own data base in their heads. To developers, kicking tires is actually a lot of fun.

185

Professional data bases are another source of information about real estate. Soon developers will use Geographic Information Systems (GIS) to look at a city on a computer screen, first calling up a map of the nation and the state, then the region, then the city, and then zooming in on a particular point. The file will contain all the property tax records, all the Multiple Listing Service records, all the census records, all the water and sewer records, all the transportation records, and possibly even satellite photography so that viewers can go back and forth in time to see how development around the site has changed. Parts of GIS exist in many cities today; by 2000, it will be nearly everywhere.

Even as advanced real estate models evolve, however, technology will not replace old-fashioned tire kicking, because developers work in an uncertain world. To anticipate emerging trends, developers will continue to rely on personal contacts—with people and the site. More important, developers recognize the advantages of im-

perfect information and will not give up any advantage by transferring all their insights and information to publicly available data bases.

From the chosen sources, developers begin to narrow their search to several specific sites. How do they look at them? Typically, developers look first at a site's physical and legal dimensions. An approach to analyzing sites is to look for binding constraints—reasons for excluding a site. For example, when Fraser Morrow Daniels began looking at possible office sites in Chapel Hill, one binding constraint was zoning. Any site for consideration had to have the right zoning already in place, because rezoning in that particular municipality would have been too difficult and taken too much time to obtain profitably. The site for the Europa Center met that requirement, but Fraser Morrow Daniels found it only after stepping back, rescanning the environment, and revising its criteria for site selection. In the continuation of the case study, Fraser Morrow Daniels narrows

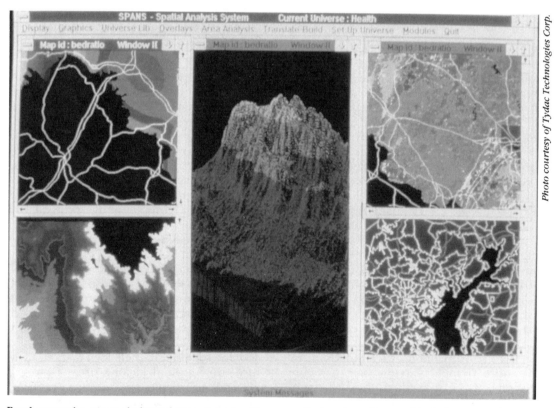

Photo courtesy of Tydac Technologies Corp.

Road networks, zip code boundaries, and elevations are displayed on Geographic Information Systems software applications for microcomputers.

its search for a site, accepting the one for the Europa Center because it removed uncertainties about zoning and quickened the development process. In this decision, the company weighed the competitive edge against the risk of the large financial commitment required by the outright purchase of an expensive site.

EUROPA CENTER

BACK TO THE DRAWING BOARD

We wanted to build west of Research Triangle Park and somewhere strategically close to the I-40 extension. We studied every single intersection in the area of I-40 and all the land around it. We got tax maps, called the landowners, and asked whether they wanted to sell their land. We talked to all the brokers and went after pieces of land that weren't for sale, because everything that was for sale was priced too high or was poorly located.

As part of that process, we discovered the site of the Europa Center, owned by the developers of the Hotel Europa. At first when the owners offered us the land for $250,000 an acre, we said it was three times more than we wanted to pay and what anybody else was paying. But they assured us it was a site with great potential and that they wanted to sell it to someone who would develop an attractive building. They had already turned down K Mart, which was willing to pay the price, but the city did not want a discount store there. The site had been for sale several times for different purposes. The owners tried to convince us that with I-40 going through, it was worth $250,000 an acre, but we still said no.

Instead, we went back to our criteria for site selection, looking at the overall market and what was already built on Durham–Chapel Hill Boulevard toward Chapel Hill. We looked at other factors like the demographics and the office/business neighborhood. No other office buildings existed there except for Eastowne (11 two-story office buildings), but Blue Cross was just up the street from the Hotel Europa.

We conceded it might fit as an office/business environment. We talked to some potential tenants who were interested in moving into a nice building near their present location (Eastowne Park). Some potential tenants said they would like a place that was in between Durham and Chapel Hill so they could combine offices. That kind of feedback pointed us toward the intersection of I-40 and Durham–Chapel Hill Boulevard (U.S. 15-501).

We were committed to building an office building somewhere between Durham and Chapel Hill close to that intersection, and things kept coming back to this site. We justified the high price by saying it would mean only $.80 a square foot more in rent.

But what about the politics in Chapel Hill? We had heard dozens of horror stories.

We decided we would go ahead with the project only if we didn't have to ask for any approvals. The site was already zoned for office buildings, and the planning board had already approved some proposed office buildings for construction. We thought the Europa site would be easy because the planning board had already blessed it, the city council had already blessed it, and we didn't have to do anything to get a site plan approved. We decided to pursue the site.

Then we started looking at the competition and the marketing significance of that competition. North Raleigh had a lot of activity and a lot of land. Downtown Raleigh had a lot of space. Downtown Durham was trying to give away land for office buildings. But in Chapel Hill, a fight broke out at every turn for anybody who wanted to develop commercial or office buildings. Every other piece of land that had been zoned for offices was already built on. Eastowne, across from Blue Cross–Blue Shield on Durham–Chapel Hill Boulevard, had two small tracts of land left, about an acre and a half each, for office buildings. So we figured we would be the only game in town for the foreseeable future. The possibility that competitors could enter the market and attract the same tenants was relatively small.

At that time, a McDonald's fast-food restaurant was proposed in front of the site on U.S. 15-501. It would be an upscale building, however, with an inconspicuous sign. And the Hotel Europa was one of the nicer buildings in town. The building we had in mind would be a very nice building. The product fit our self-image as a company. Based on thorough analysis, we could justify the cost of the site. The Europa site became, in all of our analyses, the best site available: it fit all of our criteria for our company profile, the market profile, and the competitive environment.

The only real unknown was the political environment. We could not purchase the land contingent on certain conditions. The seller would not allow it in this case. We had to buy it with the existing zoning.

The planning board and city council said informally that our idea looked good, to have the project designed and they would decide. So we decided to buy the land and paid $5.00 per square foot for it (in late 1985). Several people around town chuckled. The Hotel Europa was in deep financial trouble at that time, needed the money very badly, and, we found out later, probably would have sold it to us for $3.50 a square foot. But we had justified the price in our minds and paid the asking price.

Other binding constraints face developers: traffic (too much or too little), access, infrastructure, and parking, for example. A summary of major factors to consider in site selection is presented in Figure 9-2.

FIGURE 9-2
FACTORS IN SITE SELECTION

- *Zoning*
  Legal use of the site
  Restrictions on density and layout
  Contiguous land uses
- *Physical Features*
  Size
  Soils
  Topography
  Hydrology (floodplains, subsurface water)
- *Utilities*
  Sewage (usually most constraining factor)
  Water (important constraints in certain parts of the United States, particularly the Southeast and Southwest)
  Computer lines, cable, telephone, gas, oil, electricity; usually readily available except in large-scale projects
- *Transportation* (all modes)
  Especially important in determining access and in evaluating ingress, egress, and visibility of alternative sites
- *Parking*
  Usually needed on site and therefore competes with the building for land
- *Environmental Impact*
  Adverse impacts on air, water, and noise levels

Other areas of concern, including historic districts, parks, open space, trees
- *Government services*
  Police and fire service
  Garbage collection
  Schools, health facilities, and other government services
  Impact fees, property taxes, and permit fees
- *Local Attitudes*
  Defensive (How powerful are anti-development forces?
  Neutral (What social costs does the project impose? What are the benefits to the locality? Is the project in the public interest?)
  Offensive (What are local attitudes and how can they be used to help shape, refine, and specify the project to be built?)
- *Price of the Land*

Source: G. Vincent Barrett and John P. Blair, *How to Conduct and Analyze Real Estate Market and Feasibility Studies* (New York: Van Nostrand Reinhold, 1982). Used with permission.

The Site's Physical Characteristics

The important factor is not simply the number of acres but the number of *buildable* acres with the appropriate configuration. Thus, 100 acres may be more usable than 400 acres if part of the 400 acres is in a floodplain or if a portion of the 400 acres is one long, narrow strip along the side of a mountain. This fact may seem obvious, but corporate owners of large tracts do not always invest in land planning as readily as they invest in a qualified architect to design a building and prepare its specifications.

Soils help determine a site's potential for development; they must have adequate load-bearing capacity for the structures the developer has in mind. In many areas, soils are not a problem, but would-be developers should not take them for granted. First, even where soils are generally good, special conditions like old landfills may create problems that even long-time residents have forgotten. Second, newcomers in town should talk to more than one knowledgeable local (broker, builder, banker, geologist, soils engineer) about local soils. Avoid finding out after the deal is finalized that its poor bearing qualities, well known to local builders, will cost extra dollars in excavation and foundation work.

Two other considerations are hazardous wastes and requirements for an archaeological survey. It is the purchaser's responsibility to remove hazardous wastes *to a safe place* (much more in Chapter 16), and the expense could be ruinous. Environmental scientists usually conduct hazardous waste studies, though not for free. Many cases warrant elaborate studies, but in stage two the developer must hold down major cash outlays; stage two, again, is a period of many trade-offs.

Some governmental units require an archaeological survey, and if artifacts are found during the survey, archaeologists may then have to excavate the area by hand, possibly holding up development for months. This possibility is not as high in urban and suburban areas as that of hazardous wastes, but developers should be aware of it.

Developers should also consider a site's ties to surrounding infrastructure. How far is it from water and sewer? Where is road access possible? Increasingly, developers need more than *access* to water and roads; they need to ascertain whether the local municipality can and will *provide* sufficient water and sewer infrastructure and roads. In more intensely used areas, a city may properly deny access from certain directions to any given site. And such denial can turn a feasible site into an infeasible one, even with ideal topography, configuration, and soils.

Fifteen years ago, developers who had access to these municipal services could expect the city to deliver them. No longer. More and more, developers absorb some or all of the costs of constructing adequate infrastructure (see Chapter 10). In the case of Europa Center, for example, traffic and traffic control were major concerns of the planning board and the town staff. To allay the city's concerns and solve the traffic problem, Fraser Morrow Daniels volunteered to realign the affected intersection. Developers must be concerned today with whether a municipality can provide essential services and whether they can afford the related fees.[3]

EUROPA CENTER

ANTICIPATING EXACTIONS

During our negotiations with the town of Chapel Hill, many questions arose about traffic and traffic control, a major concern of the planning board and the town staff. We knew some improvements were needed in the intersection of U.S. 15-501 and Europa Drive, primarily because of all the recent residential development nearby on Erwin Road and increased traffic between Durham and Chapel Hill. For our project to work well, we needed some traffic control signals and some adjustments in turning lanes, and we volunteered to perform the entire amount of work for $50,000. That's not a normal anticipated cost of development.

Most cities in the past have done that work themselves because they wanted economic growth. In Chapel Hill, the situation was different. We volunteered to do the work, knowing that otherwise, it would not get done. We needed to allay the town's fears, and we needed to solve an anticipated traffic problem.

The North Carolina Department of Transportation did the work, and we paid for it. It realigned the whole intersection, not just a turning lane into our project. And we managed to find a way to do it that didn't cost as much as some of the other alternatives.

Another legal consideration is the intensity of use. Thus, a site may be zoned for multifamily housing but at such a low number of units per acre that the idea is infeasible, given the costs. Today, developers must look at *current* zoning for both the tract under consideration and surrounding parcels as well as the flexibility of current zoning and the possibility of major changes. The way developers work with the city within the rules or to change the rules and the way developers of competing sites influence the legal/political process are important considerations. The political climate of a town or a neighborhood can be a potent force to contend with. Politics can create opportunities just as easily as obstacles.

Beyond zoning, subdivision regulations are usually in place not only in metropolitan areas but also in the "extraterritorial jurisdiction," that is, areas that the city may in the future choose to annex. (Some states have subdivision regulations for all areas.) Subdivision regulations generally specify the quality of the infrastructure, and those requirements must be met if the developer expects to dedicate that infrastructure to the city and have it take over maintenance. And in most cases, developers want to dedicate infrastructure to avoid the costs of ongoing maintenance.

Besides subdivision regulations, building codes can slow development if building inspectors are not used to evaluating innovative designs and technologies. The ideal building code is one that specifies a particular standard, not a particular material. In some cities, suppliers of materials have occasionally managed to write their particular products into the building code, which can be an especially difficult issue for manufactured housing, because its construction takes place far from the installation site. Highly rigid building codes clearly restrict a developer's creativity in fitting product to location to satisfy tenants.

Contracting for the Site

At this point, the developer faces a Catch-22. While the site meets the criteria and is probably feasible physically, legally, politically, and in terms of design, a complete feasibility study has not yet been conducted. Because the developer wants to keep down initial investment, he does not want to buy the land. On the other hand, the more the idea for development is made public and the more the idea takes shape and becomes believable, the more money the current landowner is likely to ask for the land. Thus, the developer's objective is to obtain the right to buy the land at "today's price," should the refined idea and subsequent feasibility study prove positive, without committing a great deal of money.

The most obvious solution to this problem is an option. Ideally, the developer would like to pay $1.00 for the right to buy the land at any time over the next five years for today's stated price. Regrettably, however, owners are not enthusiastic about tying up their land for a long time for no remuneration. Thus, depending on the landowner's objectives and on how hot the site is, negotiations will lead to a trade-off between the developer's desire to pay as little as possible for the option with as long a lead time as possible and the owner's desire to receive a large payment for a short option period.

An option agreement is a complex document. Even in the most straightforward transaction, the option, if exercised, will become a contract of sale and legally drive the entire process of purchasing land, through closing. Thus, the option must specify all necessary requirements for the transfer of title from the seller to the buyer, including details about any financing by the seller, such as release clauses and subordination agreements that facilitate subsequent financing.[4] Most important, the buyer will want the opportunity to examine the quality of the seller's title, the buyer will want time to arrange financing, permits, and possibly zoning, and the agreement must specify the price and any warranties in the deed (and any possible deed restrictions) and include escape clauses based on the results of environmental or engineering tests. The option is a forward-looking agreement that, if exercised, will drive the entire transaction. Like many aspects of the development process, it should be as complete as possible, anticipating actions and reactions that are yet to come. If the developer, for example, needs rezoning to allow the proposed project on the chosen site, the option agreement might contain a clause specifying that the developer had 120 days to propose the change to the town council and that the option would run until 90 days after the council's decision or one year, whichever comes first.

The possible economic content of the option agreement, like all real estate contracts, is theoretically very flexible, with the developer limited only by the extent of his or her imagination. In fact, the agreement might not, strictly speaking, be an option. For example, in a low-down-payment, nonrecourse purchase, the developer actually buys the property but with 95+ percent financing by the seller, and the seller's only recourse is to the property. In economic terms, it is not that different from paying 5 percent of the asking price for an option.

At times, it could be useful to include landowners in the development process. Sometimes the landowner wants a long-term equity position in the developed structure. At other times, the landowner's surrounding parcels could cause him to offer attractive incentives to encourage the developer of his choice in his neighborhood. Developers should use their imagination to create an appropriate vehicle for the particular development, given the financial resources and desires of investors, the city's requirements, the position and needs of the landowner, and, always foremost, the needs of prospective tenants.

DECIDING WHAT CAN BE BUILT ON THE SITE: INITIAL DESIGN FEASIBILITY

In some instances, developers might choose not to option property until more information is available. In larger developments, or in smaller developments on diffi-

cult sites, it has become customary for developers to determine feasibility of the layout before committing large sums to site acquisition. To do so requires engineering and architectural information and may include soils tests, exact grade measurements, a look at setbacks combined with various projected land and building configurations, and projections of space for parking and other requirements.

The problem with major design issues, including the feasibility of the layout, is that for the first time, developers must pay outside consultants, often a design professional, an architect, and possibly engineers, to survey the specific site to determine whether it satisfies the developer's objectives. This investigation begins with the ground. In many areas, a soils engineer is needed to determine the soil's load-bearing capacity and to handle problems with groundwater and stormwater. Changing the direction of water can be very expensive, and ignoring drainage can be disastrous. Soils and mechanical engineers, working as part of the development team (for a fee), can often go beyond a simple determination of physical viability to suggest better ways to handle problems. The soils engineer, the architect, and sometimes the grading subcontractor can advise the developer on solving problems with the grade of a site—from designs that use grade to create an image to engineering solutions that permit development on difficult grades to finding better ways to cut, adjust, and bank the land.

Going beyond the developer's initial idea of building configuration, the architect lays out an initial building footprint on the site and determines, given intended access points, whether the building and parking can be placed on the site. The layout must honor all setbacks in the code without damaging the image the developer hopes to create; at the same time, it must make the tenant happy about living in the final product.

In some cases, assistance from architects, engineers, land planners, and/or subcontractors can be obtained without upfront payment. Large developers who generate a great deal of business can call on professionals they have used in the past and expect some services at deferred costs.

FIGURE 9-3
RELATING TO AN ARCHITECT

What to Expect from The Architect

1. Quality design satisfying the owner's program.
2. Timely answers to the owner's requests and suggestions.
3. Alternative suggestions and schemes during the early phases of the project, for an architectural problem never has only one solution.
4. Sensitivity to and understanding of zoning and building codes, environmental issues, and other governmental restrictions.
5. An understanding of construction costs relating to particular types and uses of buildings.
6. Ability to interact (not fight) with government agencies and understand the positions of groups opposing the project.
7. Ability to be a team player, joining with owners, consultants, and others who contribute to the project and meeting with them frequently.
8. Suitable graphic presentations to portray the project in its best light to governmental agencies and local interest groups. An open mind to requests for modifications of the project when necessary.
9. Good (not perfect) construction documents, well coordinated with other consultants.
10. Architectural observation throughout the construction of the project, with field reports on each site visit, for it is easier to respond to a contractor's questions on the job than to make serious corrections later.
11. Timely and accurate processing of all paperwork—change orders, bulletins, pay requests, and final certifications as required by lenders (with the wording not in conflict with what an architect is allowed to sign under professional liability insurance).

What Not to Expect

1. Cut-rate fees, free services, or work "on spec." Quality service with the proper amount of time spent by experienced professional personnel requires proper remuneration. If a

---

While astute developers minimize costs and use past relationships appropriately, successful developers also know when to spend additional dollars. The developer's role is to decide which items require additional investment to control risk.

In most cases, the primary design contract is with an architect—and it is a relationship that usually is maintained throughout the project. Figure 9-3 provides suggestions about what to expect from an architect, what not to expect, and how to select an architect.

During the process of selecting the site and defining the physical product to fit the client to the site,[5] it is wise to remember that urban land value relies more on the land's proximity to customers and services and on visibility than on its inherent productivity (the soil's fertility, coal reserves, or timber stands, for example). Thus, when developers evaluate alternative sites, they carefully consider access to residences, businesses, or pedestrian and vehicular traffic flow and the proximity of amenities off site that make it more or less attractive to customers.

Sites also have links to supply. Physical and legal characteristics of the site limit how much space can be built. Surrounding land uses might include competing projects that limit how long the developer can expect to enjoy spatial monopoly at the site. Thus, developers must screen competing sites while considering the proper scale for a project.

FIGURE 9-3 (continued)

large payment up front is a problem for the developer, perhaps deferred payments can be negotiated.

2. The ability to design *anything*. Special consultants with proper training and experience should be used for traffic, parking, interiors, graphics, landscaping, and so on.

3. A guarantee of the contractor's work. Architects cannot guarantee to lenders work that they do not control or have not seen put in place.

4. Work on a fixed fee before the program and final scope of the project are determined.

5. Changes by the owner without affecting the architect's fees, construction costs, and schedule.

6. Detailed, highly accurate cost estimates unless a professional cost estimator is on staff or has been retained to do this work.

How to Select an Architect

1. Do not retain an architect because you have seen a project that pleases you aesthetically. The most attractive project can be totally unsuccessful in terms of financial performance, profitability, and quality of construction.

2. Make sure your architect or the key person on staff who will manage your project is very experienced in the specific type of project.

3. Do not retain an architect based on an extensive portfolio of renderings of unbuilt projects.

4. Talk to the owners and/or users of other projects the architect has designed to determine the project's success and the architect's responsiveness throughout the project.

5. Be sure you can relate to and respect the individual assigned to your project.

6. Make sure the architect's current workload allows the required attention to your project and the project's completion on schedule.

Source: Charles Kober, The Kober Group, Santa Ana, California.

DISCUSSING THE PROJECT WITH OTHER PLAYERS

Developers do not work in isolation. They talk to other building professionals and people who might be affected by the proposed development, thereby refining the idea and planning its implementation.

Contractors

In the project's early stages, developers need to determine how many people in the area have the expertise to construct the project. Some general contractors take on all types of projects; others specialize in one type or another. In a hot market, developers must also determine how many of the general contractors have the time to take on another project. The business cycle also affects the quality of available building tradespeople. Construction workers tend to move up the line so that in a boom period, when ample work is available, the rough carpenter becomes a finish carpenter, the finish carpenter becomes a superintendent, and the superintendent becomes an independent general contractor. As the business cycle peaks, construction costs more. It might also be more difficult for developers to hire people when they want them, and only less skilled people might be available for several jobs. During slower times, developers can hire better people when they want them, at a lower price.

From the perspective of marketing, contractors can help developers by outlining the typical functions and features and quality of materials and finishes of comparable buildings in the market area. They might also estimate the cost of construction.

Tenants

During this stage, developers begin discussions with possible tenants to determine users' specific requirements, refining the general idea developed during stage one. As the idea becomes more refined and tied to a particular site, developers must begin discussions with real prospective tenants, for they may find that targeted users do not want what is proposed. Designing a project with desired features is much cheaper than adding them to a completed structure. Conversely, developers can eliminate other items tenants do not need and will not pay for.

The focus on marketing in this stage is on tailoring the product to make sure it serves customers' needs. Refining an idea and then formally determining its feasibility are the critical links between a good idea and fully occupied space. During this stage, the developer moves from a general use to a specific project design and develops a marketing strategy that the sales and leasing staff can execute.

Property Managers

Early in the process, the developer should begin working with a qualified property manager, particularly when developing facilities that will involve extensive, ongoing services. Property managers who have specialized in a particular type of operation can be very valuable in helping plan features of the design that will make the building easier to manage. They may also help avoid a costly design mistake.

Keeping tenants happy requires good management, and good management requires a building realistically designed to accommodate real people. Experienced managers can advise the developer about floor plans, layout, and equipment or features that make managing the building easier and more efficient. As money for development becomes less and less available and

overbuilt markets give tenants more bargaining power, wise developers give management a key role in the process.

Lenders

Because most developments require some type of outside financing, developers must contact potential lenders and investors at an early stage. A typical sequence begins with discussions with permanent lenders—institutions that might want to finance the project for the long term and are willing to take the long-term market risk or at least some portion of it—and/or other long-term equity investors.[6] Lenders have preferences, some financing only certain types of projects and others financing projects only in certain ways. To obtain the most advantageous and compatible source of financing, developers might rely on their knowledge of financial markets or obtain mortgage banking assistance. Hiring a mortgage broker is an additional expense and does not relieve the developer of the responsibility of making decisions. Developers must still choose the appropriate source of financing and the appropriate structure for the deal.

Developers also need a lender to finance construction. The construction lender assumes the risk that the project will not be completed on time and within budget, but not the long-term market risk (the permanent lender assumes this risk). So long as the project is built according to plans and specifications, the construction lender has a "takeout" in the form of a permanent loan commitment. At this early stage, developers seek merely an understanding of lenders' interests in the area, in the type of project, and, most important, in any specific guidelines like parking requirements that exceed city minimums or sprinkler systems. By knowing their interests at this stage, developers can often refine a project so that the number of potential lenders is increased, their interest heightened, and, it is hoped, the cost of financing lowered.

In addition to facilitating the financing, mortgage brokers and lenders can help developers understand the market. Local lenders may understand local tenants' needs and preferences, and they often have rules of thumb that bear on a project's feasibility.

Investors

Developers might also want to discuss the project with long-term equity investors, those who take the greater risks over time. As real estate capital markets have evolved, pension funds, life insurance companies, S&Ls, corporations, wealthy individuals, syndications of less wealthy individuals, and many other long-term investors are now involved. By anticipating some of the equity investors' needs, particularly tax-oriented needs, at an early stage, developers can refine their ideas more effectively.

An important issue is whether to bring in equity investors at the beginning or at the end of the development process. Early equity investors typically pay less because they assume more risk. On the other hand, involving equity investors early reduces the risk to permanent and construction lenders, thereby lowering the cost of debt financing. Depending on developers' financial position and the nature of the project, however, they must, at least by stage three, decide when to involve outside equity investors. Typically, the longer developers can wait, the higher their potential profits. And just as developers can use a mortgage broker to help in determining debt financing, they can also seek outside counsel on equity investments. For larger projects, it might be an investment banker, for medium projects, a regional investment banker, and for smaller projects, a local syndicator. While specialized assistance may increase the developer's awareness of options, it does not replace the developer's responsibility for making decisions.

Venture Capitalists

Because the development process now takes longer than it used to, many projects today now involve a period requiring venture capital and investors distinct from traditionally equity investors. Developers therefore must have start-up capital or be able to get it. The hardest kind of money to raise, venture capital, is also the most expensive, because traditionally venture capitalists have not financed real estate

development. Those that do, however, are a relatively few wealthy individuals. Because venture capital is so costly, developers want to take as little as possible as late as possible—another reason for keeping early cash investment to a minimum.

The Public

Possibly the most important player developers must talk to at this stage is the general public, as represented by government, neighborhood associations, and other advocacy groups. The public sector is always the developer's partner in a long-lived investment requiring substantial infrastructure. The project must be promoted to both elected and appointed public officials and to affected groups of citizens, and the developer hopes, by the end of stage two, that the public will have a positive impression of the project.

Public officials can offer input that enhances the value of the finished project and, often more important, speeds approval time. Just as lenders and investors have different preferences and concerns, so do government officials and agencies. Developers should investigate their desires and how the project might satisfy public needs in various jurisdictions. Sources of information on local policy and politics include newspapers, the municipality's master plan, elected and appointed officials, developers of projects in the local market, political consultants specializing in the local market, and public meetings where developers present their proposals.

Public sector officials, either as regulators or as codevelopers (see Chapter 11), protect the public interest. The public (the neighbors of the site and the public at large) is an important aspect of market research from the standpoint of impact and consumption. While tenants rent space or units with services, the public is exposed to the physical asset the developer creates as part of the long-lived built environment. Savvy developers want to satisfy these citizens, or they might not let them serve their intended customers. This public market is concerned primarily about the project's appearance, its fit to the land, its compatibility with surrounding land uses, its impact on the community in terms of on-site and off-site costs, and its benefits, such as taxes paid, jobs created, and new amenities and services offered.

SEGMENTING THE MARKET AND DIFFERENTIATING THE PRODUCT

After introducing the project to others involved and assessing their responses, developers are close to deciding whether the project is worth taking to stage three, a formal determination of feasibility, where the emotional and financial stakes go up. Before then, however, the developer initiates some more detailed market research. (Figure 9-4 distinguishes between market research during stage two and stage three.) The more thorough the research, the better the developer can define his niche in the market.

While talking with other players, developers continually think about who will use the proposed space and how the public will react to the project. As the choice of sites narrows, developers are able to define roughly the relevant market areas for the project. At some point, they can explicitly focus on the market (the demand) in relation to existing and proposed supply. They need to move from the broader idea of building apartments in Kansas City, for example, to the narrower plan of building 225 one- and two-bedroom units of three-story garden apartments on the northwest corner of 1st Avenue and 18th Street targeted to single persons and couples earning over $30,000. How do developers accomplish this task?

Generally, they begin by examining supply—specific projects suspected as competition. Next, they consider demand—not only for the features, functions, and benefits presently available from the competition but also for their own project. In searching for the winning strategy that will capture the market, developers move back and forth between considerations of supply and demand. During this process, they segment demand and differentiate their own product from the competing supply. In fact, when placed in terms of market research, refining the idea can be viewed as

The developers of Second Street Studios in Santa Fe, New Mexico, took advantage of Santa Fe's popularity among artists and aimed successfully for that specific market niche. They constructed live/work loft space with workspace on the first floor and a small studio apartment on the second level. The units were 100 percent leased on opening day.

the interactive process of segmenting the market and differentiating the product.

Typically, developers still do their own research in stage two to keep costs down. The discussions with other professionals that make up this research are only one component; other unavoidable parts are making phone calls to see who has vacant space, driving around to look at competing projects, delving through public records, and checking the newspaper for announcements of new projects. All of this information goes into the developer's data base to get a handle on demand, characteristics of space users, and unmet needs (potential demand). For Fraser Morrow Daniels, researching the converging segments of the Triangle market required two years of analysis to break out segments of the market and to define demand and supply. Location emerged as a key feature in developing Europa Center in the Triangle office market.

FIGURE 9-4
OFFICE MARKET SEGMENTATION

Stage Two Refinement of the Idea	Stage Three Feasibility
Analyze competing projects and developers to determine what is selling or leasing.	Forecast demand and supply to gauge overall market conditions in the metropolitan area.
Consider trends creating more specialized use of office space.	
Consider trends changing locational requirements for office space.	Designate the characteristics for describing products: location, size, physical features, price, quality, age, and amenities.
Define office segments based on users' needs, for example, large floorplates, low rent, central city versus suburban location.	Relate characteristics to differences among space users to define relatively homogeneous segments of space users.
Compare potential supply and development controls across spatial submarkets.	Assess supply and demand in each market segment to forecast rents, inventory, absorption, and vacancies for each segment over the next three to five years.
Remember the goal: to capture a share of the market by differentiating the product from competitors' products and to satisfy the demand for space of a particular group of users (a market segment).	
Understand potential space users to target marketing and promotion.	
Keep an open mind: remember that a differentiated product could lead to the discovery of a new product to serve the changing market.	Identify complementary segments for opportunity based on greatest potential absorption.

Source: David E. Dowall, "Office Market Research: The Case for Segmentation," *Journal of Real Estate Development*, Summer 1988, pp. 34–43.

EUROPA CENTER

SEGMENTING THE MARKET

In selecting a site, we had to seek first-class, gold-plated sites that in a competitive market would win out at even rental rates. Developers who will succeed are those whose sites are good right now, today. Tenants don't want to move to the middle of the wilderness, where customers don't come. Renting office space in an office environment is only 2 to 5 percent of your business budget. People will pay $.75 per square foot more to get an office space if it's the right space for their business. Being a pioneer is not necessarily good.

In deciding which land to buy, we had a choice between some land selling at $1.00 a square foot ($45,000 to $50,000 an acre) and $5.00 a square foot ($250,000 an acre, the Europa site next to the Hotel Europa). The less successful and less visible land was cheaper, but is the Europa land five times more valuable than the other land? Who knows? But what is the bottom line?

The land component per square foot of building area turned out (at $5.00 per square foot) to be $.80 per square foot in the building rental rate—$16.80 instead of $16.00 per square foot to put somebody on a site next to the Hotel Europa rather than three blocks away behind a sewer plant. For $.80 a square foot in the rental rate, can you add that much more value from the tenant's point of view? If you're building only one building, absolutely.

To help us make our decision, we looked at the office buildings in the area to assess how much space was available, what quality it was, how much space was being built, what kind of tenants leased space there, who was likely to move, who was not. We listed every building in every segment of the market on a computer printout. Our list had 500 buildings. A Chapel Hill undergraduate worked for me for four hours a day after school for two years, calling owners, agents, and tenants and asking how many square feet of office space they had. It's this kind of nitty-gritty detective work you have to do for the project coming up three months from now.

Another use of information about demand and supply, particularly in a rapidly changing market, is planning for contingencies. Developers should first consider the impact of substantial shifts in demand and supply. If demand increases dramatically, what will happen? How quickly can competing developers bring new products on line? Can existing space be readily converted in response to increasing demand? Conversely, if demand falls sharply, how far will the competition go to retain tenants or customers? Developers should have a decent estimate of the development cost per square foot of directly competing projects. And they can get a reasonable idea by knowing when a competing project was built and what prevailing development costs were at that time. If those projects were built at substantially lower cost, the developer's own project may be undercut by existing supply in a down market. (Developers might also learn about financial arrangements for competing projects, specifically milestones when balloon payments are due and refinancing is required.)

Second, developers must consider the posture of local government with respect to new supply. In some markets, developers can be relatively certain that constraints on supply imposed by local regulations will protect their market niche for some time. In other instances, constraints on supply are minimal, and competing projects can come on line quickly and at comparable cost.

Strategies for Segmenting The Market

Data on comparable projects, the growth of supply and demand, and characteristics of space users are primary aids in segmenting the market. Developers hope to fill a new market niche with a properly designed project or to enter an established niche by differentiating a project. Existing space is usually (though not always) less expensive than new construction, as it was probably constructed at lower cost. Because the distinction of newness disappears rapidly, developers seek more permanent forms of differentiating a product to sustain monopolistic rents. Using projections of demand, developers specify the features, functions, and benefits of the project that will capture the targeted market segment for both the short term and the long term.

Figure 9-4 presents a strategic approach to segmentation especially useful for refining ideas. The description of a research process for systematically analyzing segments of an office market carries over into stage three of the development process, formal market analysis.

Developers must define and refine market segments in analyzing potential demand; otherwise, they will have to depend upon growth alone to create marginal excess demand sufficient to absorb the space of an undistinguished product. While no criticism is directed at generic projects so long as they meet public standards and sell well, in overbuilt markets, they probably will not sell as well. Segmentation at times gives developers a potential tool for building a successful project despite overbuilding. With a special combination of attributes—asking rents, finishes, layout, amenities, access, location, and marketing—developers can succeed if the selected market segments are large enough and the project serves those segments better than other competing products.

A checklist of the project's attributes can form the basis for differentiating a product in response to segmentation of the market. Major features include location, asking rents that recognize concessions and tenant improvements, size of the floorplate and layout, and on-site amenities like parking and physical appearance. Minor features include flexibility of the layout, finishes in common areas, communications hookups, and the like.

The developer's goal during refinement of the idea is to determine a believable *strategy* for capturing the market. Indeed, to know that some companies are willing to lease warehouse space at so many dollars per square foot does not indicate *which* blend of features, functions, and benefits will attract tenants or *how* developers will successfully lease the finished warehouse space.

The proposed project's competitive characteristics are critical, whether they are defined in relation to market segments or not. How will developers distinguish their products from the competition? Is a market niche convincingly defined? How can the project attract sufficient demand in a fairly static market or in an overbuilt market? By answering these questions in stage two, developers anticipate the formal market analysis of stage three that will be used to convince potential lenders and investors to participate. The results of the market research done in stage two must be believable *to developers themselves*, for moving into stage three, a formal feasibility study by an outside consultant, definitely increases the financial commitment. During stage two, developers strive to minimize costs but spend what is necessary to convince themselves that potential returns justify the risks of moving to stage three—or if they do not, they give up or revise the idea.

Financial Feasibility

An ongoing function during refinement of the idea is to translate all the information collected and analyses completed into a framework that relates potential risks and rewards to the developer's objectives. If the developer seeks pecuniary rewards only, the financial feasibility analysis will be enough to base a decision on about proceeding with the project. As noted in Chapter 1, however, developers rarely build projects for money alone. They need to address explicitly each goal and determine how the project can be modified to meet that goal.

Typically, developers continually revise the initial back-of-the-envelope analysis as they refine the idea, comparing cost versus value, estimating hard and soft costs, and projecting revenues and expenses to arrive at an indication of value. The pro forma does not have to be fancy, notwithstanding the capabilities of modern spreadsheets and commercial real estate analysis programs. During refinement of the idea, the developer should be listening and talking to knowledgeable people and potential tenants, not beating a spreadsheet to death.

During stage two, however, financial feasibility goes a critical step farther: developers begin estimating cash flows during the period of development. Can the developer finance the project through start-up? It does not really matter that the project's value exceeds cost if the developer cannot survive to completion. A key part of the analysis at this stage is figuring out how much start-up capital is needed and where it will come from.

Again, indicating the interactive nature of refining ideas, the financial feasibility analysis brings the developer back to the two central tasks of stage two: selecting the site and designing the specific project. The selected site affects costs: land is one cost, but so are site improvements—difficult to estimate yet intimately related to the site's physical and legal characteristics. The specified project will largely determine construction costs and related soft costs.

The selected site and specified project also determine the amount and timing of revenues. Pro forma revenues are based on the market segments served by the project and the links to demand, given competing supply, that the site makes possible. By looking at revenues and costs together, developers arrive at an estimate of net operating income over the projected holding period. Stage three extends this estimate of net operating income. With an appropriate discount rate, that is, one that includes both risk and the time value of money, developers can look at the project's feasibility. The assessment returns to two key ideas presented at the beginning of this chapter. First, by capitalizing net operating income and comparing value to cost, developers can estimate how much operating leverage is possible from the proposed development on the chosen site. Second, by estimating an appropriate discount rate, developers can explicitly address the trade-off between risk, which can be reduced by spending more in several areas, and reward, which is always reduced by spending more. Each technique to control risk discussed in the following section can be evaluated for the specific project using discounted cash flow.

Developers use intuition through stage two to assure themselves that the expenditures required in stage three are justified. Stage three extends the analysis to a complete, formal feasibility study to convince the other players to join the endeavor.

CONTROLLING RISK DURING REFINEMENT OF THE IDEA

The method of acquisition can itself be a measure to control risk during stage two. Because a developer seeks to limit financial exposure before formally committing resources to the project, controlling the site through an option or a low-down-payment, nonrecourse, seller-financed purchase is one way to minimize exposure in stage two.

Any option and/or purchase agreement should ideally (from the developer's perspective) contain contingency clauses and specify that protective warranties will be included in the deed. Developers want to make sure that the seller has provided all possible guarantees as to the title's quality. Beyond that, the remaining terms of the sale (which should be included in any option) can help limit the developer's risk. One common provision, for example, stipulates that the developer will receive the down payment and/or option amount with no further responsibility if appropriate zoning cannot be obtained.

In most real estate transactions, constructive notice to the general public happens by recording the instrument. The first instrument typically executed is the option agreement to acquire the land. So long as it is in proper form and, in most states, notarized, it can be recorded. Recording this agreement places it in the chain of title and thus gives notice to all others of the developer's right to the land. At times, this step can be particularly helpful in reducing the possibility of a landowner's executing subsequent contracts to use the land for purposes other than what the developer intended.

Release clauses and/or subordination clauses in the option or purchase agreement are also possible techniques for controlling risk. A release clause is common in a seller-financed mortgage; essentially, it allows a borrower or developer to obtain a first lien on a portion of the land by paying a portion of the note. For example, if a developer purchases 100 acres for $10,000 an acre, a release clause might provide that any one of ten 10-acre parcels included in the overall tract could be released from the lien at $150,000. Thus, if the developer wants to begin the development with a 10-acre site and needs a first lien for the construction lender, the original purchase money mortgage could be removed from that 10-acre site for payment of $150,000, as opposed to payment of the entire note for $1 million.

Subordination clauses accomplish a similar objective while providing even more risk coverage for developers. They must also be written into any option agreement so that they will subsequently be included in the seller's financing. An agreement to subordinate by the seller or lender is a promise to move from a first lien to a second lien in specified circumstances. For example, a seller who owns thousands of acres in a particular area and wants to encourage a particular developer to develop one site within that area might agree to subordinate its claim of financing on that one site to the bank's construction financing. Thus, when the purchase closes, the seller will have a first lien. When the developer begins construction and needs to give the construction lender a first lien, the seller then agrees to move to a second lien. Subordination is superior from the developer's perspective because it enhances his ability to borrow money. From the construction lender's perspective, the landowner's subordinated interest looks almost like equity in that it is an investment that is paid after the owner's loan. In effect, if the landowner subordinates its claim, the land serves as collateral for the development, even though the developer has not yet paid for it.

In addition to removing the uncertainties of a site's availability, developers can control risk by helping ensure that a project is acceptable to the community. If developers can show from the beginning that the development plan fits or coordinates well with the city's master plan, fewer time-consuming delays are likely. Astute developers plan a development that fits with the concept and intent of the city's master plan. When a proposed development is consistent in spirit with the master plan, developers can then demonstrate this consistency to the town council, other governing boards, and surrounding residents.

Informally presenting the project to city officials and building inspectors to elicit responses can eliminate potential opposition during this early stage. Not only do such officials become more committed to the project, but they also, like other participants, make suggestions that the developer can incorporate to avoid future problems. Note, however, that elected officials can leave office during the time required for large projects to be approved. Therefore, it behooves developers to seek approvals and opinions in writing. Documentation will not always secure a developer's position against changes in policy and rules during the process, but it helps.

The most important device to control risk is developers' curb on their own egos; they must not let runaway ego and excitement carry them beyond what is rational.

EUROPA CENTER

WEIGHING THE PROS AND CONS

The site of Europa Center appeared to fit the bill: location on the major transportation artery connecting the two cities and adjacent to the highest-quality hotel at that time in Chapel Hill or Durham (see map on p. 162). The land was well configured, nearly rectangular, with a pond that represented an amenity, not a problem. Access was not perfect but was possible.

The fact that the site was nearly ready for development fit with our evaluation of the overall Research Triangle market; while long-term prospects were good, substantial new construction was coming on line soon, and it was thus important to bring the project to fruition as soon as possible. We had already invested heavily in research and building an image in the market and wanted to recapture some of those costs through a series of developments, one of which was Europa Center.

Although we had done an excellent job of overall background research on the Triangle market and had worked hard at producing a positive image in the community, we were still taking a chance with that particular site. While it was ideally situated in the middle of growth and close to major transportation arteries and while it was physically attractive without major constraints on construction or an unusual configuration, the location had not traditionally projected an image of quality in the community. Although located next to the most expensive hotel in the area, the hotel was only four years old and had already been through one foreclosure caused by lower-than-expected average rates and very low occupancy during the summer. Near the site on the east side was a subsidized housing project, farther to the northeast, low-income retirement housing. With McDonald's and new car dealers on the south and west, it was potentially a great site but would require substantial marketing and operating expertise to develop a successful project. We chose particularly high-quality architecture and construction to try to influence the market's perception.

SUMMARY

Stage two in the development process involves what many people call "real" real estate, further refining the idea generated during stage one. Toward the end of stage two, the rough idea has been attached to a specific site that is legally, politically, and physically capable of supporting that idea. Moreover, the developer, through a series of conversations, believes that one or more general contractors will be available, that tenants will be interested, that lenders will want to lend money, and that equity interests and venture capitalists can be attracted to the project.

By this time, the developer has probably decided whether or not the idea is feasible. Because others have not, however, a formal feasibility study is therefore necessary. While 99 out of 100 ideas generated in stage one fail the back-of-the-envelope pro forma test, the pass rate is higher in stage two. Perhaps one in three, maybe two in five, ideas will pass this stage. If the refined idea still seems feasible, the developer takes it to stage three, where financial and emotional commitments are greater.

NOTES

1. "Higher Cost of Land Is Pushing Up Prices," *Washington Post*, August 18, 1990.

2. Roger W. Lotchin, *The Martial Metropolis: U.S. Cities in War and Peace, 1900–1970* (New York: Praeger, 1984). See also Marc A. Weiss, *The Rise of the Community Builders* (New York: Columbia Univ. Press, 1987), Chap. 4.

3. Impact fees can wreck a pro forma and are a large factor influencing site selection. They thus are an extremely hot issue in some states. In Florida and California, for example, impact fees in some cities recently rose 300 to 400 percent in one year. In one extreme case, the impact fee inside the city of Tampa was declared to be several million dollars for a 500-bed hotel; at the same time, no impact fee was levied outside the city. On the other hand, public services must be paid for, and the rule that those receiving the benefits should pay the costs is probably a good one. See Chapter 10 for more detailed information.

4. The many items likely to be specified are covered in most elementary textbooks and more completely in R. Kratovil and R. Werner, *Real Estate Law*, 8th ed. (Englewood Cliffs, N.J.: Prentice-Hall, 1983); or William D. Lusk and Harold F. French, *Law of the Real Estate Business*, 5th ed. (Homewood, Ill.: Richard D. Irwin, 1984).

5. See John Clapp, *Handbook for Real Estate Market Analysis* (Englewood Cliffs, N.J.: Prentice-Hall, 1987), for a useful way of relating site selection to the process of refining the project design to fit the local market.

6. See W. Brueggeman and Leo D. Stone, *Real Estate Finance*, 8th ed. (Homewood, Ill.: Richard D. Irwin, 1989), for an excellent description of these different lenders; C. Wurtzebach and M. Miles, *Modern Real Estate*, 4th ed. (New York: John Wiley & Sons, 1991), for a discussion of real estate finance in general; and publications by Goldman Sachs real estate research and Salomon Brothers real estate research for a more current discussion of the basic terms and innovations attached to some of these loans.

Bibliography
Part III. Ideas

INCEPTION OF AN IDEA

Anthony, Robert N., and Dearden, John. *Management Control Systems: Text and Cases.* 3d ed. Homewood, Ill.: Richard D. Irwin, 1976.

Delbecq, A.L., et al. *Group Techniques for Program Planning.* Glenview, Ill.: Scott Foresman, 1975.

Feig, Barry. "How to Run a Focus Group." *American Demographics* 11, December 1989, pp. 36-37.

Linstone, H.A., and M. Turoff, eds. *The Delphi Method: Techniques and Applications.* Reading, Mass.: Addison-Wesley, 1975.

Malizia, Emil E. *Local Economic Development.* New York: Praeger, 1985.

MARKET RESEARCH

Aaker, David A., and George S. Day. *Marketing Research.* 3d ed. New York: John Wiley & Sons, 1986.

Barrett, G. Vincent, and John P. Blair. *How to Conduct and Analyze Real Estate Market and Feasibility Studies.* 2d ed. New York: Van Nostrand Reinhold, 1988.

Benson, Ann. "Markets, Markets, Markets." *Urban Land* 46, June 1987, pp. 38-39; August 1987, pp. 38-39; and November 1987, p. 39.

———. "Tracking Trends." *Urban Land* 47, February 1988, pp. 38-39.

Born, Waldo L. "On-Line Data Bases." College Station: Texas A&M Univ., Real Estate Center, 1988.

———. "Real Estate Market Research: Data Publications." College Station: Texas A&M Univ., Real Estate Center, 1987.

Churchill, Gilbert A., Jr. *Marketing Research: Methodological Foundations.* 4th ed. Chicago: Dryden Press, 1987.

Graaskamp, James A. *Fundamentals of Real Estate Development.* Washington, D.C.: ULI–the Urban Land Institute, 1981.

———. "Identification and Delineation of Real Estate Market Research." *Real Estate Issues* 10, Spring/Summer 1985, pp. 6-12.

Gruen, Nina, Claude Gruen, and Wallace F. Smith. *Demographic Changes and Their Effects on Real Estate Markets in the 1980s.* Washington, D.C.: ULI–the Urban Land Institute, 1982.

Kotler, Philip. *Marketing Management: Analysis, Planning, and Control.* 5th ed. Englewood Cliffs, N.J.: Prentice-Hall, 1984.

Lachman, M. Leanne, and Dan Martin. "Changing Demographics Shape Tomorrow's Real Estate Markets." *Urban Land* 46, November 1987, pp. 8–11.

Lehmann, Donald R. *Market Research and Analysis*. 2d ed. Homewood, Ill.: Richard D. Irwin, 1985.

Leinberger, Christopher B. "Survival of the Fittest." *Builder* 9, March 1986, pp. 93–97.

O'Hare, William P. "How to Evaluate Population Estimates." *American Demographics* 10, January 1988, pp. 50–52.

Porter, Michael E. *Competitive Strategy: Techniques for Analyzing Industries and Competitors*. New York: Free Press, 1980.

Ratcliff, Richard. *Real Estate Analysis*. New York: McGraw-Hill, 1961.

Raymondo, James C. "How to Estimate Population." *American Demographics* 11, January 1989, pp. 46–49.

Redman, Arnold L., and C.F. Sirmans. "Regional/Local Economic Analysis: A Discussion of Data Sources." In *Readings in Market Research for Real Estate*, edited by James D. Vernor. Chicago: American Institute of Real Estate Appraisers, 1985.

ULI Market Profiles: 1991. Washington, D.C.: ULI–the Urban Land Institute, 1991.

Vernor, James D., ed. *Readings in Market Research for Real Estate*. Chicago: American Institute of Real Estate Appraisers, 1985.

PART IV
PLANNING AND ANALYSIS: THE PUBLIC ROLES

Chapter 10

Zoning, Impact Fees, And Financing Infrastructure

D evelopers increasingly find themselves working closely with government officials to ensure that their projects meet public objectives for development. In almost every local jurisdiction, developers encounter adopted public plans, zoning and subdivision requirements, and other policies and regulations that affect their development. Increasingly, also, state governments are stepping into the land development process to make additional demands on both local governments and developers. Anticipating public needs and desires for private development and meshing the interests of private development with public goals and requirements will be essential for all developers of the future.

Governments in the United States traditionally have relied to an extraordinary extent on spontaneous economic forces (the "free market system" or "free enterprise") to carry out urban development. The right of private individuals to own and use real estate has been a cherished and constitutionally protected tradition. But the public sector always has been a strong force in establishing the rules of the development game: providing the legal framework for landownership and contractual

understandings, supporting development by providing the underlying infrastructure and other incentives, prescribing standards for development, and regulating the character and location of development.

The roles of the public sector as *regulator of private development* and as *provider of needed facilities and services* are constantly evolving. In recent years, many local governments, constrained by limitations on powers of taxation and changing attitudes toward development, have shifted much of the burden of financing infrastructure to the private sector. Communities have responded to voters' wishes for no growth and slow growth by imposing limits on development. Environmentalists and other interest groups have pressed for more rigorous standards and complex requirements. Developers today must work in a complicated climate of changing public/private responsibilities and goals.

This chapter examines these important roles of governments—regulator of private development and provider of needed facilities—as they affect the development

The authors are indebted to Douglas R. Porter, ULI's director of development policy research, for writing this chapter.

207

process and the development industry. The chapter's central theme is that real estate development is a shared process in which the private and public sectors continually interact for their mutual benefit, using examples of codevelopment and projects that were built as a result of true public/private partnerships and focusing on:

- the public sector as regulator; and
- public/private roles in planning and financing infrastructure.

THE PUBLIC SECTOR AS REGULATOR

Developers usually first contact local governments in their role as regulators, first encountering local governments even before acquiring a site. Those contacts increase in frequency and intensity throughout the process that leads to final permits for construction and occupancy. Along the way, developers must deal with public expectations for development framed in comprehensive plans and zoning ordinances and public standards and requirements for development contained in subdivision regulations and building codes.

State and local governments' regulation of land development is based on the police power—the requirement of government to protect the health, safety, and general welfare of citizens. Oddly, the police power is not a constitutional power of the federal government except in cases of interstate commerce, land in federal ownership, and private land subject to major federal public works, such as dams and irrigation systems. Rather, the police power is reserved for the states, which have usually elected to delegate it to local governments through enactment of statutes, called enabling legislation, that specify the powers given to local governments.

In most states, most regulation of the police power was given to counties, cities, and some types of special-purpose districts early in the 20th century. Since then, local officials have become accustomed to thinking of these powers as theirs, believing them to be absolutely essential to maintaining the community's desired character. Developers have also tended to support local control of development, believing that state governments are too removed from

the realities of development in specific areas. Increasingly, however, states are moving to reassert a role in managing the development process.[1] A reminder of state prerogatives in land use control occurred in Fairfax County, Virginia, in 1990, when the state legislature rescinded part of the county's downzoning of industrially zoned land. Although this case is unusual, it serves to illustrate the potential power of states in regulating development.

Exercise of the Police Power

Although the courts recognize the right of local governments to exercise the police power, they also are concerned with safeguarding private property rights. The history of land use law in the United States describes the working out of an uneasy—and continuously evolving—balance between the rights of local governments to protect the public's health, safety, and general welfare and the rights of individuals to enjoyment of private property. In a sense, regulations based on the police power tread the fine line between legitimate uses of the power that impose nominal or no burdens on individual property rights and invalid uses that seriously hamper such rights.

That balance has shifted as the courts have expanded their interpretations of "health," "safety," and "general welfare" to include aesthetic and other concerns. The courts also have tended to allow local governments wide latitude to legislate the police power under the doctrine of "legislative presumption"—the notion that the courts should give great deference to properly enacted regulations. Local governments' use of the police power has therefore grown considerably in scope and application, especially after the courts supported such actions.

Two early court cases, *Welch* v. *Swasey* in 1909 and *Hadacheck* v. *Sebastian* in 1915 established the right of local governments to regulate development. (All references to court cases in this chapter can be found in Figure 10-1.) A major judicial step supporting regulation of the police power occurred in 1926, when the U.S. Supreme Court, in *Euclid* v. *Ambler Realty,* upheld zoning as a valid form of regulation.

FIGURE 10-1
SOME IMPORTANT LAND USE CASES

- *Welch* v. *Swasey,* 214 U.S. 91 (1909). The U.S. Supreme Court upheld Boston's height restrictions within districts.
- *Hadacheck* v. *Sebastian,* 239 U.S. 394 (1915). The U.S. Supreme Court upheld a city ordinance prohibiting the continuance of brick manufacturing within designated areas as a nuisance to nearby residents as a proper exercise of the police power.
- *Pennsylvania Coal Company* v. *Mahon,* 260 U.S. 393 (1922). The U.S. Supreme Court ruled that a state law forbidding coal mining under private property so as to cause subsidence "went too far" and therefore could constitute a taking of property without due compensation. In 1987, however, in *Keystone Bituminous Coal Association* v. *De Benedictis,* 480 U.S. 470 (1987), the Court upheld a similar Pennsylvania statute because it was deemed to protect the public interest in preventing an environmental harm.
- *Village of Euclid, Ohio* v. *Ambler Realty Co.,* 272 U.S. 365 (1926). This case was the first U.S. Supreme Court case to uphold zoning as a valid form of regulation of the police power.
- *Berman* v. *Parker,* 348 U.S. 26 (1954). The U.S. Supreme Court upheld the use of the police power and eminent domain for the District of Columbia to carry out redevelopment for general public purposes rather than only for a public use.
- *Golden* v. *Planning Board of Town of Ramapo,* 285 N.W.2d 291 (N.Y. 1972). This case is one of the first and most important cases upholding regulations for timing, phasing, and quotas in development generally and in Ramapo specifically, making development permits contingent on the availability of adequate public facilities.
- *Village of Belle Terre* v. *Boraas,* 416 U.S. 1 (1974). The U.S. Supreme Court upheld zoning restrictions against group student housing in districts containing single-family houses.
- *Southern Burlington County NAACP* v. *Mt. Laurel Township,* 336 A.2d 713 (N.J. 1975) and 456 A.2d 390 (N.J. 1983). These two cases involve Mt. Laurel Township and other New Jersey municipalities, which the state court ruled must provide for development of a fair share of lower-cost hous-

Through countless court decisions since then, the courts have consistently upheld the right of local governments to regulate land use and development so long as they establish a legitimate public interest and follow due process. Under the police power, private property owners' rights to use of their property may be severely limited. In appropriate circumstances, governments may legally prohibit development to preserve floodplains, wetlands, sand dunes, and habitats of endangered species, and may restrict the amount or height of development to protect erodible hillsides, mountain views, access to beaches, solar access, and other public interests.

Rights to the police power are muted, however, by court-established limits and by self-imposed limits on local governmental power. The question of just how restrictive regulations can be has continued to vex developers and public officials. Two famous U.S. Supreme Court decisions in 1987 sounded warning notes about overly expansive use of the police power. In *Nollan* v. *California Coastal Commission,* the Court ruled that the Commission had not established an appropriate connection between a requirement for property owner Patrick Nollan to allow public access along his beach frontage and the cited public objective of providing public views of the ocean. The Court indicated that, in cases of this type, it would more closely scrutinize governmental actions to ensure that regulations were properly related to public

FIGURE 10-1 (continued)

ing and then imposed court oversight of the process.

- *Avco Community Builders, Inc.* v. *South Coastal Regional Commission,* 132 Cal. Rptr. 386, 553 P.2d 546 (1976). The California Supreme Court's decision that Avco did not have vested rights despite local approvals and expenditures of over $2 million led directly to the state development agreements act.
- *Penn Central Transportation Co.* v. *New York City,* 438 U.S. 104 (1978). The U.S. Supreme Court upheld New York City's imposition of landmark status on Grand Central Station, thus preventing construction of an office building over the station, as a justifiable regulation that required no compensation.
- *Kaiser Aetna* v. *United States,* 444 U.S. 164 (1979). The U.S. Supreme Court upheld the owners of a private lagoon in their claim that a taking had occurred when they were forced to allow public use of the lagoon.
- *Agins* v. *City of Tiburon,* 447 U.S. 255 (1980). This case was one of a series in which the U.S. Supreme Court held

that the cases were not "ripe" for a decision, usually meaning that the plaintiffs had not exhausted the administrative procedures that might have resolved their complaint before going to court. Other similar cases were *San Diego Gas and Electric* v. *City of San Diego,* 450 U.S. 621 (1981), *Williamson County Regional Planning Commission* v. *Hamilton Bank of Johnson City,* 473 U.S. 172 (1985), and *McDonald, Sommer & Frates* v. *Yolo County,* 477 U.S. 340 (1986).

- *Nollan* v. *California Coastal Commission,* 483 U.S. 825 (1987). The U.S. Supreme Court ruled that the California Coastal Commission had not established an appropriate connection between a requirement for an exaction and the cited public objective for the exaction.
- *First English Evangelical Lutheran Church of Glendale* v. *the County of Los Angeles,* 482 U.S. 304 (1987). This decision was the first by the U.S. Supreme Court that a regulatory taking of property can require compensation to the owner, even if the regulation has only a temporary effect.

purposes. Then, in *First English Evangelical Lutheran Church of Glendale* v. *the County of Los Angeles,* the Court ruled that if regulations are found to take property, the public authority may be required to compensate the owner. (In this case, however, later state court actions determined that regulations preventing rebuilding of structures destroyed by a flood effected no taking.)

The weight of these cases suggests that governments' regulation of development must follow strict rules, with due caution for rights of private property.

The other, perhaps more pervasive, brake on governments' use of the police power is public opinion, expressed politically. Many U.S. citizens own property and

place great store on their rights to its use. It is not surprising, therefore, that public officials, when deciding to regulate land use and development, usually attempt to allow property owners a reasonably economic use of their property. Attitudes of public officials on this question, however, vary considerably from state to state, so that what might be considered typical regulation in California is anathema in Virginia.

Thus, local governments have a great deal of latitude in determining how to regulate development. State enabling legislation provides a starting point and court decisions erect a legal framework, but final decisions often depend on the political position of the public officials making them.

FIGURE 10-2
PROCEDURES FOR SITE PLAN REVIEW

CHARTER TOWNSHIP OF BATH (MICHIGAN) ZONING ORDINANCE[a]
DECEMBER 9, 1982

ARTICLE XX—SITE PLAN REVIEW

Sec. 20.01 Purpose

It is the purpose of this section to require Site Plan Review approval for certain buildings, structures, and uses that can be expected to have a significant impact on natural resources, traffic patterns, adjacent parcels, and the character of future development. The regulations contained herein are intended to provide and promote the orderly development of the township; safe and convenient traffic movement, both within a site and in relation to access streets; the stability of land values and development by the erection of structures or additions or alterations thereto, without proper attention to setting or to unsightly or undesirable appearance; harmonious relationships of buildings, other structures, and uses, both within a site and/or adjacent sites; and the conservation of natural amenities and resources.

Sec. 20.02 Approval Required

Site Plan Review approval is required as follows:
a. For those uses requiring Special Use Permit review, as specified.
b. All land uses, *excepting* single-family detached dwellings, two-family dwellings, and nonresidential uses requiring fewer than five parking spaces.

Sec. 20.03 Procedures for Site Plan Review

a. *Application*: Application for Site Plan Review shall be submitted through the Township Clerk to the Planning Commission on a special application form for that purpose; each application shall be accompanied by the payment of a fee in accordance with the duly adopted "Schedule of Fees" to cover the costs of processing the application. No part of any fee shall be refundable.

b. *Data Required in Application*: Every application shall be accompanied by the following information and data:
   (1) Application form supplied by the Township Clerk filled out in full by the applicant.
   (2) Fifteen copies of a site plan, plot plan, or development plan, drawn to a readable scale showing:
      (a) Property dimensions.
      (b) Size, shape, and location of existing and proposed buildings and structures.

The Local Regulatory Process

Cities, counties, and other local governments undertake planning, zoning, and additional forms of development regulation according to state enabling statutes and, in some cases, through home rule charters granted by the state. Local governments are allowed (and sometimes required) to prepare and adopt comprehensive plans for the future development of the community.

Local governments also may adopt zoning ordinances, subdivision regulations, and other regulations that set standards, requirements, and procedures for securing permits to develop. (Figures 10-2 through 10-4 present examples of the types of regulations and regulatory procedures found in most communities.)

Based on these adopted policies and regulations, local governments establish procedures that require property owners

FIGURE 10-2 (continued)

(c) The location of parking areas, all parking spaces, and driveways.

(d) Existing public rights-of-way and/or private easements.

(e) Water courses and water bodies, including surface drainage ways.

(f) Existing significant vegetation.

(g) A landscaping plan indicating locations of proposed planting and screening, fencing, signs, and advertising features.

(h) Zoning classification of abutting properties.

c. *Planning Commission Review*

(1) Upon receipt of an application for Site Plan Review, including all data required in Sec. 20.03(b), the Township Clerk shall transmit one copy of the site plan to each of the following agencies considered to be impacted or affected by the request (e.g., county drains—Clinton County Drain Commission; curb cut access—Clinton County Road Commission, etc.)—

(a) Clinton County Road Commission,

(b) Mid-Michigan District Health Department,

(c) Clinton County Drain Commission,

(d) Clinton County Department of Development Control,

(e) School District—Superintendent of Schools (Bath, Laingsburg, or Haslett),

(f) Fire chief,

(g) Police chief—

for their review and comment. The Clerk shall transmit the remaining copies of the site plan to the Planning Commission.

(2) The Planning Commission, upon receiving the comments of the above affected agencies, shall proceed with review of the site plan to determine compliance with permitted land use, density of development, general traffic and pedestrian circulation, and other provisions of this Ordinance.

The Planning Commission shall respond to the applicant within 45 days of filing as to the approval, denial, or approval with modifications of the site plan. If denied, the Commission shall cite reasons for denial, and if approved, a Certificate of Site Plan Approval shall be issued to the applicant by the Zoning Administrator.

[a]Compare these procedures to Figure 10-3, which contains review procedures for a small city in California.

to obtain zoning, building, and occupancy permits. Developers submit applications for these permits, usually with supporting documentation. If the type of development is allowed "by right," according to zoning for the property, only administrative action is required. If the proposed development is allowed only under certain conditions or requires a change in zoning, special hearings and other procedures are required, some of which can be quite lengthy.

As indicated in Figures 10-5 through 10-7, many varieties are in use today, and more are being formulated every day. They extend from more precise standards for development to actual restrictions on the amount of development that may take place. In San Diego County, California, for example, two-thirds of the municipalities have imposed some type of limit on growth; in the Boston area, almost two dozen towns have adopted moratoriums on

Executive villas and a hotel/office complex of the Bayport Plaza project in Tampa, Florida, with a view of restored wetlands. Before development, the site was a weed-infested area littered with junk cars, mattresses, bathtubs, and other debris. The developer, working with four main permitting agencies, was able to restore the wetlands as necessitated by regulations and use them as a selling point for office tenants and hotel guests.

one or more forms of development. In San Francisco, an initiative of citizens (Proposition M) succeeded in capping the amount of development that may occur each year in the downtown area.

Another emerging regulatory technique that goes beyond traditional planning and zoning is the use of requirements for "adequate public facilities." These regulations make development contingent on the existence of adequate capacity in local infrastructure that will serve the development. Developers encountering such requirements could find their proposals grinding to a halt unless they step forward to assist in upgrading roads, schools, or other public facilities.

As development regulations become more complicated and convoluted, developers are faced with many decisions about making their way through the permitting process. Frequently, to develop a marketable product or to maximize their investment, developers opt to request changes in adopted plans or zoning or to use special procedures that allow alternative uses or a more flexible design. This decision usually exposes their project to closer scrutiny by public officials and the general public and often also creates opportunities for public officials to require additional amenities or contributions to infrastructure. Depending on the circumstances, however, developers may find the results worth the effort, especially if their projects become well known in the process. In fact, more than one developer has been able to use "required" amenities as major marketing tools. One project in Florida required to retain a habitat for eagles made it the centerpiece of the project, featured in its marketing materials. Many developers have learned to

FIGURE 10-3

AN APPLICANT'S GUIDE TO SUBMITTAL REQUIREMENTS: TENTATIVE MAP

CITY OF WALNUT CREEK, CALIFORNIA
COMMUNITY DEVELOPMENT DEPARTMENT

I. *Application forms* completed and signed.

II. *$___ deposit*. (The actual fee is based on the amount of time spent by staff reviewing the application, using a standard charge rate. If the fee is less than the deposit, the remainder will be refunded; if more, the balance must be paid before building permits will be issued.) Make checks payable to the City of Walnut Creek.

III. *Site photos* (Polaroid OK) showing topography, vegetation, existing and adjacent structures, views of and from the site.

IV. *Preliminary Map* (optional) for review by the Design Review Commission. Actual Map (Step 5) may be used if preferred.
Plans: 10 copies required (folded to approximately 9" × 11"). Required data:
   A. Existing boundary lines, trees, waterways, structures, contours, streets, and easements.
   B. Proposed grading, street layout, lot lines, open space, and recreation and building sites.
   C. North arrow, scale, and contour interval.
   D. Vicinity map, showing nearby cross streets.

V. *Tentative Map* (must be prepared by a Registered Civil Engineer).
Plans: 35 copies (25, if Preliminary Map was submitted), folded to approximately 9" × 11". (All but five copies may be reduced to 11" × 17" if permitted by staff.) The map must be legibly drawn on one sheet of paper containing the following:
   A. A title containing the subdivision number, subdivision name, and type of subdivision.
   B. Name and address of legal owner, subdivider, and person preparing the map (including registration number).
   C. Sufficient legal description to define the boundary of the proposed subdivision.
   D. Date, north arrow, scale, and contour interval.
   E. Existing and proposed land use.
   F. A vicinity map showing roads, adjoining subdivisions, towns, creeks, railroads, and other data sufficient to locate the proposed subdivision and show its relation to the community.
   G. Existing topography of the proposed site and at least 100 feet beyond its boundary, including:
      1. Existing contours at two-foot intervals if the existing ground slope is less than 10 percent and at not less than five-foot intervals for existing ground slopes greater than or equal to 10 percent. Contour intervals should not be spread more than 150 feet apart. Existing contours should be represented by dashed lines or by screened lines.
      2. Type, location, and dripline of existing trees over 28 inches in circumference. Any trees proposed to be removed should be so indicated.
      3. The approximate location and outline of existing structures, identified by type.
      4. The approximate location of all areas subject to inundation or stormwater overflow and the location, width, and direction of flow of each water course.
      5. The location, pavement, and right-of-way width, grade, and

214

FIGURE 10-3 (continued)

name of existing streets or highways.

6. The widths, locations, and identity of all existing easements.

7. The location and size of existing sanitary sewers, water mains, and storm drains. The approximate slope of existing sewers and storm drains should be indicated.

8. The approximate location of the 60, 65, and 70 CNEL (Community Noise Equivalent Level) contours, if any.

H. Proposed improvements, including:

1. The location, grade, centerline radius, and arc length of curves, pavement, and right-of-way width, and names of all streets. Typical sections of all streets must be shown.

2. The location and radius of all curb returns and culs-de-sac.

3. The location, width, and purpose of all easements.

4. The angle of intersecting streets if such angle deviates from a right angle by more than four degrees.

5. The approximate lot layout and the approximate dimensions of each lot and of each building site. Engineering data must show the approximate finished grading of each lot, the preliminary design of all grading, the elevation of proposed building pads, the top and toe of cut-and-fill slopes to scale, and the number of each lot.

6. Proposed contours at two-foot intervals must be shown if the existing ground slope is less than 10 percent and not at less than five-foot intervals for existing ground slopes greater than or equal to 10 percent. A separate grading plan may be submitted.

7. Proposed recreation sites, trails, and parks for private or public use.

8. Proposed common areas and areas to be dedicated to public open space.

9. The location and size of sanitary sewers, water mains, and storm drains. Proposed slopes and approximate elevations of sanitary sewers and storm drains must be indicated.

I. The name or names of any geologist or soils engineer whose services were required in the preparation of the Tentative Map.

J. The source and date of existing contours.

K. All lettering must be 1/8" minimum.

L. Certificates for execution by the Secretary of the Planning Commission indicating the approval by the City Council if the map was reviewed by the City Council.

M. If it is planned to develop the site as shown on the Tentative Map in units, then the proposed units and their proposed sequence of construction should be shown on the Tentative Map.

VI. *Accompanying Data and Reports.* The Tentative Map must be accompanied by the following data or reports:

A. *Soils Report.* A preliminary soils report prepared in accordance with the City's Grading Ordinance must be submitted. If the preliminary soils report indicates the presence of critically expansive soils or other soil problems that, if not corrected, would lead to structural defects, the soils report accompanying the Final Map must contain an investigation of each lot within the subdivision.

B. *Title Report.* A preliminary title report, prepared within three months before filing the Tentative Map.

FIGURE 10-3 (continued)

C. *Engineering, Geology, and/or Seismic Safety Report.* If the subdivision lies within a "medium-risk" or "high-risk" geologic hazard area, as shown on the maps on file in the Community Development Department, a preliminary engineering, geology, and/or seismic safety report, prepared in accordance with guidelines established by the Community Development Department. If the preliminary engineering, geology, and/or seismic safety report must accompany the final map, it shall contain an investigation of each lot within the subdivision.

D. *School Site.* The subdivider must obtain from the school districts involved their intentions, in writing, concerning the necessity for a school site, if any, within the subdivision and must present this information to the Community Development Director before consideration of the Tentative Map by the Planning Commission.

E. *Utility Certification.* Certification in writing from all utilities that the proposed subdivision can be adequately served.

F. *Other Reports.* Any other data or reports deemed necessary by the Community Development Director.

Source: Albert Solnit, *Project Approval: A Developer's Guide to Successful Local Government Review* (Belmont, Cal.: Wadsworth, 1983), pp. 30–32.

use required retention ponds and other stormwater drainage facilities as attractive natural features. Developers who must safeguard stands of trees usually find that lots near the trees substantially increase in value.

The use of these special "discretionary" procedures has grown in recent years. In part it has occurred because public officials have discovered that they can control the size and quality of development more directly by case-by-case reviews than through written regulations. But special interest groups and citizens' groups have also discovered the opportunities for intervening in decisions through such procedures (see Figure 10-8 for an example). More and more developers have found that they must spend almost as much time dealing with neighborhood or special interest groups as with public officials charged with approving projects. In many instances, developers must employ consultants and prepare special studies to respond to questions and demands from such groups. Developers in many communities have had to become public relations experts to have their projects approved.[2]

A time may come, however, when the local regulatory process clearly needs to be rethought and reorganized. Communities have frequently formed task groups, comprised of both public and private interests, to review existing regulations and procedures and recommend ways to "streamline" them. Complex or overlapping requirements and lengthy, bureaucratic procedures can be simplified to reduce wear and tear on both the public and private sectors in the permitting process. At the same time, design and construction standards can be reviewed to make certain that they are geared to the community's objectives, particularly if affordable housing is a concern.[3]

State Regulatory Actions

Although state governments delegate most regulation of land use and development to local governments, states have always exercised some control over development through their powers of taxation and spending. States typically build most of the major highways and roads upon which so

FIGURE 10-4

TYPICAL PROCEDURES FOR DEVELOPMENT APPROVAL

This figure indicates a "generic" process that might be used for subdivision plan review, rezoning, or plan amendments.

Concept Phase	Developer:	• Identifies site, defines preliminary development concept. • Evaluates feasibility of concept with consultants. • May test ideas with citizen groups.
Preapplication Phase	Developer:	• Prepares basic descriptions of proposed project, including location, types of uses, general densities, public facilities. • Meets with public staff to discuss concept, define initial issues, determine appropriate approval procedure.
	Public Staff:	• May test preliminary concept with other agency staff.
Application Phase	Developer:	• Prepares reports, drawings, plans for application.
	Public Staff:	• Routes application to other agencies. • Meets with developer to resolve questions, problems. • Initiates official notice of upcoming hearing(s) to public, adjacent owners.
	Developer:	• Prepares final plans.
	Public Staff:	• Prepares final report and recommendations.
Public Decision Phase	Public Officials:	• Conduct one or more hearings at which developer presents plans (perhaps before multiple agencies).
	Public Officials, Staff, and Developer:	• Propose modifications or conditions necessary for approval.
	Public Officials:	• Approve, approve with conditions, or deny application.

FIGURE 10-5
MAJOR LAND USE CONTROLS

Zoning ordinance. Regulates the uses of buildings and land; restricts the height and size of buildings and percentage of lot occupied by buildings; sets minimum sizes of lots, yards, and open spaces. Often contains other regulations for signs and parking, for example. Ordinance contains these provisions for each type of zoning district (e.g., "low-density residential") and map indicates districts' boundaries.

Subdivision regulation. Requires recording of approved subdivision plat (or plan) before any lots may be sold. Regulates width, depth, and size of lots. Provides standards for design and construction of streets, drainage, water and sewer lines, utilities, and often recreational facilities. May also restrict development in sensitive environments.

Comprehensive plan. An official document that describes how a community should develop over 10 to 20 years. Usually consists of written policies, supplemented with maps, to guide the quality, location, and amount of development, and may contain plans for specific elements of development (such as housing) and for infrastructure systems. May be adopted as law or merely advisory to public officials. Zoning may or may not be required to be consistent with the plan.

Growth management program. Builds on traditional planning and zoning to emphasize more direct means of influencing the amount, type, timing, location, and quality of future development. (Figure 10-7 discusses specific techniques for managing growth.)

Capital improvement program. A list of planned capital improvements, in order of priority and indicating expected sources of funds. Usually adopted each year for a six-year period. If paired with a thorough analysis of revenues and expenditures and a plan, can be very useful in managing growth.

---

much development depends, for example, and preserve large amounts of open space in parks and conservation areas. Most states, in addition, regulate municipal and individual water supply and sewage treatment systems and have enacted various environmental laws that affect where and how urban development will take place. A number of states, for example, have adopted environmental protection acts similar to the federal act that requires major projects to undergo environmental analysis.

In general, these state actions were not directed in any coordinated sense to guiding urban growth. In the past 10 to 15 years, however, a number of states have taken more specific action to control urban development, in the form of growth management laws. The first wave of such laws occurred in the early 1970s as an outgrowth of the environmental movement.

Legislatures in Vermont, Oregon, California, Florida, Colorado, Rhode Island, North Carolina, and Hawaii enacted laws that were intended to curb the excesses of urban growth and protect natural resources. Ten years later, most of those laws were found wanting, either because they had failed to achieve their objectives or because they had stirred up unproductive controversies.

A second wave of state acts to manage growth began with Florida's enactment, in 1985, of a sweeping new law to strengthen previous requirements for local planning and to require state-level planning. Florida's law was quickly followed by actions in Vermont, Maine, Rhode Island, and New Jersey. All the acts focused on setting state goals for development and requiring local plans, state agency plans, and regional plans, in some cases, to be consistent with these goals. These requirements for consistency mean, in essence, that public plans for future development must meet certain minimum standards described in the state goals. In addition, most state acts require the formulation of follow-up programs to implement the plans.

Once a community has received approval of its plan and adjusted its zoning and other regulations to the new plan, development approval proceeds in a traditional manner. The differences, for developers, are that the state requires every community to plan, instead of rezoning

---

FIGURE 10-6
SELECTED ZONING INNOVATIONS

Planned unit development. An optional procedure for project design, usually applied to a fairly large site, that allows more flexible site design than ordinary zoning would allow by relaxing or waiving some requirements and substituting individual plan reviews. Frequently permits a variety of housing types and sometimes several uses. Usually includes an overall general plan that is implemented through specific subdivision plans.

Cluster zoning. Allows groups of dwellings on small lots on one part of the site to preserve open space and/or natural features on the remainder of the site. Minimum lot and yard sizes are reduced. Like PUDs, site designs are subjected to more detailed reviews.

Overlay zoning. A zoning district, applied over one or more other districts, that contains additional provisions for special features or conditions, such as historic buildings, wetlands, steep slopes, and downtown residential uses.

Floating zones. Zoning districts and provisions for which locations are not identified until enacted for a specific project. Used to anticipate certain uses, such as regional shopping centers, for which locations will not be designated on the zoning map until developers apply for zoning. Usually requires special review procedures.

Incentive zoning. Zoning provisions that encourage but do not require developers to provide certain amenities or qualities in their projects in return for identified benefits, such as an increase in density or rapid processing of applications. Often used in downtown areas to gain open space, special building features, or public art.

Flexible zoning. Zoning regulations that establish performance standards and other criteria for determining appropriate uses and requirements for site design rather than prescribe specific uses and building standards. Rarely applied to all zoning districts but often used for selective locations or types of uses (e.g., PUDs).

Inclusionary zoning. Zoning that requires or encourages construction of lower-income housing as a condition of a project's approval. May provide density or other bonuses in return for commitments to such housing. May require housing on site or allow location at another site.

Transferable (or transfer of) development rights (TDRs). A procedure that permits owners of property restricted from development to recoup some lost value by selling development rights to developers for transfer to another location where increased densities are allowed. Often used to preserve buildings of historic or architectural importance and sometimes to preserve open space or farmland.

219

FIGURE 10-7
MAJOR TECHNIQUES FOR MANAGING GROWTH

Urban growth boundary/urban service limit. Boundaries established around a community within which the local government plans for provision of public services and facilities and beyond which urban development is discouraged or prohibited. Boundaries usually set to enclose growth over 10 to 20 years. Intended to provide more efficient services and to protect rural land and natural resources. Used extensively in Oregon, Florida, Colorado, Maryland, and California.

Designated development area. Similar to urban growth boundary in that certain areas within a community are designated as urbanized, urbanizing, future urban, and/or rural, within which different policies for future development apply. Used to encourage development in an urbanizing area or redevelopment in an urbanized area.

Adequate facilities ordinance. Requirement that approvals for projects are contingent upon evidence that public facilities have adequate capacity for the proposed development. When facilities are found inadequate, development is postponed or developers may contribute funds to improve facilities.

Extraterritorial jurisdiction. In some states, local governments' powers to plan and control urban development outside their boundaries until annexation can take place. May also be effected through intergovernmental agreements, such as between a city and a county.

Affordable housing allocation. Requirement in some states that local governments plan to incorporate a fair share of all housing types geared to regional housing needs. These targets can then be met through various programs to encourage or mandate lower-income housing (see "inclusionary zoning" in Figure 10-6).

Growth limit. Establishment of an annual limit on the amount of development allowed. Usually applied to the number of building permits issued, and most often applied to residential development. Requires some method for allocation of permits, such as a point system (see below). Can be either interim or permanent measure.

Growth moratorium. Temporary prohibition of development, based on immediate need to forestall a problem with the public health, safety, or welfare, such as lack of sewage treatment capacity or major traffic congestion. May apply to one or more types of development and be communitywide or specific to an affected area. Typically in effect for one to three years to allow time for the problem to be solved, but may last for many years.

Point system. A technique for rating the quality of proposed developments by awarding points according to the degree to which projects will meet stated standards and criteria. Typically, the various factors are weighted to reflect public policies. Used in flexible zoning and techniques to limit growth.

project by project, and that the state expects local governments to back up plans with solid implementation programs, such as for capital improvements. It is difficult to determine just how these acts will affect development in those states and how many

other states will follow suit. On the negative side, the resulting multiple layers of plans and bureaucracies may breed a sluggish and somewhat inflexible approval process. On the positive side, local governments are required to meet basic standards

FIGURE 10-8
THE (SOMETIMES CIRCUITOUS) ROAD TO PROJECT APPROVAL

COLORADO PLACE
SANTA MONICA, CALIFORNIA

The Becket Group, a well-known 50-year-old California firm engaged in architecture and engineering (Welton Becket Associates) and real estate development, assembled a 15-acre property in Santa Monica, California, with the intent of building a new headquarters building and a first-rate, mixed-use development, including its own offices, to be called Colorado Place. The ambitious project was planned to contain about 1.2 million square feet of usable space plus 600,000 square feet of parking, including 800,000 square feet of office space; a 400-room hotel; some 60,000 square feet of food, beverage, and restaurant operations; and a 45,000-square-foot health club. A central plaza, designed to accommodate public events, would have 3,500 parking spaces below grade. This major mixed-use project, the culmination of Becket's years of experience and interest in urban design, was scheduled to be developed in two phases.

Becket planned the Colorado Place project entirely within existing regulations and Santa Monica's adopted general plan. The firm spent about a year and a half in discussions with city officials and in the planning and design process to bring the project to the point of financing, with signed leases for 85 percent of the office space.

Construction began on April 1, 1981. On April 22, the newly elected city council met for the first time and imposed a building moratorium that stopped all construction. Becket then discovered that the firm's "vested rights" under California law did not protect it beyond the ability to complete the footings for which a permit had been issued before April 22.

After enactment of the moratorium, the city adopted a procedure for requesting exemption from the moratorium based on California's vested rights law and "hardship," as determined by an apparently subjective decision of the city council. The council could also allow the project to proceed if it were deemed sufficiently meritorious, notwithstanding the moratorium. The Becket Group applied for exemption as quickly as possible, but the city denied the firm's application for exemption, thereby placing Becket in an untenable position. The firm was unable to perform under multimillion-dollar construction contracts, and because of the threatened loss of a favorable lending commitment in a period of increasing interest rates, the project's financing was imperiled.

Becket proposed that the city resolve the impasse by establishing a development agreement pursuant to California law. Naturally, because of the highly adverse economic pressure on Becket, the company's bargaining position was limited. The city was well aware of its superior position but also recognized the massive project's substantial benefits in terms of employment, property taxes,

for workable and reasonable plans that promise some predictability in development.

Florida's 1985 law requiring all local governments to plan (see Figure 10-9) demonstrates some of the pros and cons of state involvement in land use regulation. Local governments have had to meet standards for responsible planning for development, making the development process more predictable. The state law, however,

FIGURE 10-8 (continued)

user fees, and favorable redevelopment in a somewhat blighted area of the city. Two of the city's specific aims were to include a commitment to low- and moderate-income housing in any deal and, if possible, to downscale the project in response to comments from the apartment dwellers immediately surrounding the development.

Ultimately, the parties reached a development agreement restricting development to 900,000 square feet of "usable space" above grade (meaning the street-level plaza, as all parking is below grade) and producing about 1.2 million square feet of gross building area. Restrictions on Phase I also included a 45-foot limitation on height, lower than existing zoning, but Phase II development was permitted a height of 65 feet for the office structures and 95 feet for the hotel, both greater than permitted under the existing zoning.

The agreement reached after considerable negotiation between the city council and the developer called for Becket to build or furnish the following:

- 50 units of low- and moderate-income housing, in each of two phases;
- A 3.5-acre public park in Phase II;
- A 2,000-square-foot daycare center with an outdoor play area (and a $5,000 fund for equipment) in Phase I for lease to an operator for $1 per year;
- A hotel with a minimum of 250 rooms (a reversal of the city's previous veto of a hotel, based on expected tax revenues);
- An art and social services fee of 1.5 percent of the cost of land and development (amortized over 20 years and offset by operating expenses for the public space);
- Affirmative action and job training programs for neighborhood residents;
- Energy-saving systems;
- A traffic and emission abatement program; and
- Other improvements, such as wider streets.

Phase I was completed in January 1984.

According to the original agreement, Phase II was to include two office buildings, additional restaurants and shops, a luxury hotel, and a 3.5-acre park, totaling $120 million, plus the remaining 50 units of low-income housing. The city made zoning concessions to allow the higher buildings and permitted a reduction in the number of parking spaces to reflect the more efficient parking achieved by mixing uses.

The latter change in particular fueled neighbors' fears about the project's impacts on its surroundings. Neighborhood residents formed an organization called Mid-City Neighbors to demand a part in formulating the revised agreement. After heated debates involving the neighborhood group, Becket, the planning commission, and the city council, the city allowed the reduction in parking, subject to the developer's provision of prepaid parking for employees and validated parking for visitors, which would encourage employees and visitors to park at the project and not on nearby streets. Similar trade-offs occurred throughout the development process.

Then financing became a critical issue as Becket found itself $10 million short of the funds needed for Phase II, the result primarily of cost overruns on Phase I induced by the moratorium and a month-long carpenter's strike. Becket asked the city to apply for a $10 million federal urban development action grant in which the city would lend the grant funds to Becket to complete the project and Becket would repay the loan with interest. In addition, the city was to obtain $5 million more from a share in the hotel and office income. HUD, however, denied the application for block grant funds.

In June 1984, Becket announced indefinite postponement of Phase II because of rising interest rates, the lead lender's financial instability, and a lack of commitments for office leases. Thus, it came as no surprise when, in January

FIGURE 10-8 (continued)

1985, Colorado Place was sold to Southmark Pacific, a subsidiary of Dallas-based Southmark Corporation.

Southmark Pacific immediately obtained a year's extension of Phase II's initiation date to August 1986 to permit reconsideration of the current plan. Five months later, the company announced its intention to seek substantial changes in the agreement inherited from Becket. At that point, the city flatly refused to consider a change in height, the developer sued the city for failing to fulfill its obligations under the agreement, and Mid-City Neighbors broke off talks with the developer, claiming that the newest proposal indicated that the developer did not take neighbors' concerns seriously. The project reached an impasse, and construction of Phase II was seriously in doubt.

After repeated attempts at renegotiation, however, the city and the developer reached a tentative out-of-court settlement in May 1986. For a year afterward, Southmark continued to negotiate revisions to the agreement as new problems and new demands arose. In addition, the soft leasing market caused the developer to delay construction of Phase II. Approval of the new plan, Phase III, appeared imminent until it was threatened by a citywide no-growth movement. Charging that the city council was allowing uncontrolled development that aggravated traffic problems, activists demanded suspension of all major construction projects in Santa Monica, including Colorado Place.

Despite opposition, Phase III of Colorado Place was narrowly approved in September 1987, when the mayor (one of the initial antidevelopment council members) cast the deciding vote in favor of the project. Approval came only after Southmark agreed to pay an additional $5 million in fees for traffic improvements and to build a sewage treatment plant on site. Three months later, after activists failed to collect the 6,000 signatures necessary to force a public referendum, the amended agreement for Phase III was finally approved. The provisions of the final agreements are as follows:

Phase II
- A five-story office building on the site where the hotel was previously planned;
- A 3.5-acre neighborhood park on site;
- A 1,500-seat motion picture theater with four screens (the original eight-screen complex was scaled down in response to the community's protests over traffic congestion).

Phase III (to be completed within 12 years)
- A nine-story, 250-room hotel built on a site adjacent to Colorado Place;
- A 60,000-square-foot health club;
- 620,500 square feet of office space;
- 20,000 square feet of banks;
- 10,000 square feet of retail space;
- 25,000 square feet of restaurants.

In exchange for the approval for Phases II and III, Southmark agreed to contribute more than $8.8 million for community projects:
- $5 million to the city for future traffic improvements (to mitigate the effects of congestion and pollution of large public developments);
- $2.6 million in cash to substitute for the earlier requirement of building the remaining 50 units of low-income housing;
- $1 million for a community park;
- $250,000 for city art projects and events;
- A community meeting room open to the public free of charge.

Sources: David O'Malley and Richard F. Davis, "Development Agreements: Colorado Place, Santa Monica, California," in Douglas R. Porter, Patrick L. Phillips, and Colleen Grogan Moore, *Working with the Community: A Developer's Guide* (Washington, D.C.: ULI–the Urban Land Institute, 1985); and Rita Fitzgerald and Richard Peiser, "Development (Dis)agreements at Colorado Place," *Urban Land,* July 1988, pp. 2–5.

FIGURE 10-9

SUMMARY OF REQUIREMENTS IN FLORIDA'S LOCAL GOVERNMENT COMPREHENSIVE PLANNING AND LAND DEVELOPMENT REGULATION ACT

(Adopted in 1985, amending the 1975 act)

- Each county and municipality must conform its comprehensive plan to state goals and requirements of the act within a specified time period, or the plan will be prepared by the regional planning body.
- All plans shall include a capital improvements element, and no development permits shall be issued unless public facilities are adequate to serve the proposed development.

- The coastal zone element of each plan must meet new and tougher requirements.
- The state Department of Community Affairs must review and approve local plans according to rules drafted by the department and approved by the legislature.
- All plans must be reviewed every five years.
- Land development regulations must be adopted to implement the plan within a specified time period after the plan is approved.

also imposed a requirement that no developments be approved until public facilities were concurrently adequate or programmed to serve them (the "concurrency requirement"). Because the state failed to back this law with new funds to improve highways, however, development has halted in many parts of Florida. With time this issue probably will be resolved, but other issues are sure to surface that will affect development.

State and local regulation of development promises to become more, not less, complex and more restrictive in general. Developers, in addition to their knowledge of the physical, financial, and economic factors of development, will also have to become more skillful at working with public officials and the general public to conclude their projects successfully.

PUBLIC/PRIVATE ROLES IN PLANNING AND FINANCING INFRASTRUCTURE

One primary function of governments has always been the financing and construction of capital facilities that provide essential services for the general public. It

is seen as a governmental function for several reasons. First, it involves construction of communitywide systems, such as roads and water and sewer lines, that serve large areas and many people. Second, it is recognized that some public facilities and services, such as schools, should be made available even to people who cannot afford to pay their direct costs. Third, governments at all levels have provided infrastructure to stimulate economic growth.

While such capital facilities have been seen primarily as a public responsibility, the private sector has often been called upon to provide the facilities, either in association with private development or as a profitable enterprise. Thus, developers of new sections of communities often finance and build the roads and other basic facilities necessary to market the property. For over two centuries, private companies built canals, railroads, and toll roads, expecting to pay for their construction from tolls and fares. In many communities, some even today, private companies supply water, and private utilities supplying natural gas, electric power, and telephone service are common.

Planning and financing infrastructure therefore have been carried out sometimes by public entities, sometimes by private entities, and sometimes by organizations bridging the two sectors. And it is not surprising that developers will encounter varied allocations of responsibilities for construction of capital facilities, depending on the state and locale involved, the type of infrastructure, and the size and nature of the project.

More and more of the burden of constructing capital facilities is being shifted to the private sector. Overall public expenditures for capital facilities have not kept pace with increases in economic activity or in population. Federal and state capital expenditures have fallen steadily since 1977, leaving local governments to take up the slack. They, in turn, have been beset with rising costs for social services and taxpayers' revolts against increasing taxes. The result is that local governments have turned to the private sector to "make development pay for itself"—a favorite phrase in rapidly growing communities. Public officials and developers are experimenting with many forms of public/private planning and financing of infrastructure (see Figure 10-10).

Sources of Public Capital Funds

Local governments find capital for improvements to infrastructure from within their annual budgets, from issuance of

---

FIGURE 10-10

PUBLIC/PRIVATE TECHNIQUES FOR FINANCING INFRASTRUCTURE

Special taxing district. District within which revenues are raised by taxes, fees, or assessments to fund one or more types of public facilities and services. May be organized as independent units of local government or dependent on local governments. Districts usually issue bonds to finance construction and depend on user fees for day-to-day operation of facilities.

Tax increment financing (TIF) district. Special taxing district that essentially depends on earmarked tax revenues raised only from new development, net of the existing revenue base in the district, for construction of public facilities. Widely used for redevelopment but also sometimes for newly developing areas.

Subdivision improvement. Requirement for dedication of land, construction of facilities, or payment of fees for the purpose of providing basic infrastructure within subdivisions, usually including roads, water and sewer lines, drainage, parks and recreational facilities, and sometimes sites for schools and other public facilities.

Exaction. In general, any contribution to public facilities by private developers, but usually applies to extraordinary on-site improvements (such as sewage pumping stations) or off-site improvements (such as improved intersections) that benefit more than users of the site. May include bordering, nearby, or remote improvements and land dedication, facility construction, or payment of fees (see "impact fee").

Impact fee. Payment required of developers to defray costs of public facilities necessitated by new development, most often off site. Usually imposed when building permit is issued for one or more types of improvements.

Privatization. Financing, construction, and operation of public facilities by private entities. Used primarily when public resources are inadequate to provide needed facilities. Depends on user fees to cover all costs. Used occasionally for water companies and toll roads and infrequently for other purposes.

225

bonds, and from state and federal funding programs. Construction (or reconstruction) of local streets, for example, is frequently financed from annual budgets, but revenues earmarked for those purposes flow from fuel, motor vehicle, and other taxes and from state and federal grants that originate in some of the same sources. Improvements in municipal water supply systems often are drawn from general revenues or from issuance of general obligation bonds although more often from user fees and revenue bonds.

Most communities depend for most of their capital expenditures on funds derived from general obligation bonds or revenue bonds, and most employ consultants to advise them on issuing and marketing bonds. Many states, in addition, provide packaging and marketing services for small local governments. Interest rates for both types are lower than market rates, because the bondholder's interest income is generally tax free. General obligation bonds are backed by the full faith and credit of the municipality and so have a fairly low interest rate. Revenue bonds are repaid from specified sources of revenue, usually fees and charges for services, and carry a somewhat higher interest rate. Within these two broad categories of debt instruments, the bond market has invented a large variety of special types of bonds to suit various needs of the community or conditions of the bond market.

One category of revenue bonds that enjoyed wide popularity for a time was tax-exempt industrial development (or industrial revenue) bonds, known as IDBs and IRBs. These bonds were issued to assist in financing economic development projects, often involving land and building development, but the 1986 Tax Reform Act severely limited their use.

Bonds are repaid from a variety of sources. For many years, the basic source was property taxes, but by the mid-1980s, property taxes had dropped to less than half (47 percent) of all revenues from local sources. In their stead, sales and income taxes and various fees and charges have increased in importance. User fees and charges, in particular, are much-favored sources of revenue for many capital facilities, because they are paid by the facility's

users for services rendered. Water and sewer systems, for example, typically charge user fees to fund construction and operation of the systems.

Special Taxing Districts

Special districts formed to finance construction and/or manage the operation of infrastructure systems levy many fees and charges. Such districts may be formed by local governments (assessment districts, public improvement districts) to permit levying a special tax on property owners who will benefit from the improved infrastructure. Although they might be governed by special boards or commissions, their budgets and actions usually are subject to local government's review and approval. Developers and property owners who wish to establish a mechanism of financing for capital facilities required for new development might also initiate special districts. In this case, local governments or the state often must approve the districts, but otherwise the districts function as independent authorities.

All special districts are established according to state legislation that sets out the requirements for initiating, financing, and operating districts. Special taxing districts are allowed in all states, but they are particularly numerous in some states, including Illinois, Texas, California, Florida, and Pennsylvania. A great variety of districts exists, including districts for single purposes, such as constructing roads or junior colleges, and soil conservation. In a number of states, districts can be formed to supply almost all the facilities and services required to serve new development.

Special taxing districts are especially useful to developers because they avoid taxing existing residents for facilities required for new development and because they spread the costs of improvements over a targeted group of consumers and over a repayment period of 15 to 20 years. They are also invaluable in developing areas where local governments have little incentive, administrative capacity, or financial resources to fund infrastructure.

Organizing special districts, however, requires a considerable amount of time and talent. The district must be initiated accord-

The developer of this business park is also responsible for putting in new infrastructure in the area. Here construction workers are installing curbs and gutters.

ing to specific state rules relating to voting powers, the managing board, and the district's powers. Securing financing involves the services of bond counsels, underwriters, rating agencies, and insurers. Undertaking construction and managing the district demand still other specialties. Once formed and operating, of course, districts are subject to the same political controversies that any local governing entity attracts. Still, special taxing districts offer a useful alternative to local government's financing infrastructure (see Figure 10-11).

Exactions and Fees

Another alternative to local government funding of capital improvements is the imposition of exactions and fees to be contributed directly by developers. Variously termed "exactions," "extractions," "contributions," "proffers," and other names, these contributions may consist of dedication of land, construction of facilities, or payment of fees. Their importance has increased, especially over the past decade, as more local governments turn to the private sector for improvement of public facilities.

Subdivision regulations commonly require developers to fund, build, and dedicate for public use the basic facilities required for residents and tenants of developments: local streets, sewer and water lines, drainage facilities, and parks and recreational facilities. Many jurisdictions also require selected improvements to bordering major streets and intersections and reservation of sites for schools. Usually such requirements are specified in ordinances, which also provide standards to determine the size and character of the facilities.

Impact fees are a fairly new form of exaction. More and more communities impose such fees because they help to pay for facilities outside development projects that may be affected by those projects. For years, developers have paid "hook-up" or "tap-in" fees to connect their projects to water and sewer systems; such fees are

227

FIGURE 10-11
SPECIAL DISTRICTS IN COLORADO

As a western high-growth state, Colorado has used special districts widely to provide services and facilities in support of new development. In the Denver area in particular, metropolitan districts have proliferated throughout the region's towns, cities, townships, and counties. In the state as a whole, the 1982 Census of Governments reported 1,031 special districts, of which 112 provide water, 152 sewage service, and 126 both water and sewage service. Colorado ranks sixteenth among the states in the number of special districts, fifth in district expenditures for water service, and eleventh in expenditures for sewage services.

Metropolitan districts. Created by state legislation in 1981 (Title 32, Special District Act), metropolitan districts function much like special districts elsewhere, except that metropolitan districts can provide a range of services, including water and sewage service, road improvements, parks, and other public facilities. Developers or landowners who wish to provide a special source of funding for public improvements initiate the creation of metropolitan districts. Local county commissioners, the district court, and a vote of residents must approve the formation of such districts. Once approved, districts are recognized as distinct government entities with the power to issue tax-exempt bonds to finance public improvements.

Metropolitan districts enjoy many of the same powers as municipalities, including the authority to issue bonds, set tax rates, and acquire property. State law also grants districts the special authority to exercise the power of eminent domain, to levy and collect ad valorem taxes, to issue negotiable coupon bonds and tax-exempt revenue bonds, and to provide public transportation. The districts have primary responsibility for developing adequate support systems internal to their own boundaries. For important regional facilities, however, districts can pool their financial resources.

Public improvement districts and building authorities. Interjurisdictional problems in some communities have arisen in coordinating the activities of many districts, and some districts have been organized with dubious financial support. Given these problems, some communities have resisted the formation of independent districts, opting instead for the formation of improvement districts—essentially assessment districts dependent on the governing body of the local jurisdiction. When a dependent district is combined with a nonprofit, public building authority, an entity blending the attributes of dependent and independent districts is created.

used to make major capital improvements in trunk lines, pumping stations, treatment plants, and the like. Now, however, impact fees are also charged to pay for large parks and recreational areas that residents of many developments will use, major highways and interchanges, drainage systems, schools, and many other types of facilities. Ordinances imposing such fees normally spell out methods for calculating them.

Impact fees can range from a few hundred dollars to many thousands of dollars. A survey of 33 jurisdictions by the Center for Governmental Responsibility at the University of Florida found impact fees in 1990 to average $3,001 for single-family houses, $968 per 1,000 square feet of industrial space, $2,165 per 1,000 square feet of general office space, and $3,321 per 1,000 square feet of retail space (see Figure 10-12). Not surprisingly, fees had increased substantially since a previous survey in 1988—up 38.8 percent for single-family houses, for example.

A few communities have adopted special types of fees, often called "linkage fees," intended to contribute to housing programs and other community needs. The

FIGURE 10-11 (continued)

A few Colorado developers are currently experimenting with such districts to avoid the problems associated with metropolitan districts in some jurisdictions.

A majority of registered voters in the jurisdiction who own real or personal property in the district initiate the district. These voters must also obtain the consent of property owners who are not voters who, together with the voter-owners, must own property constituting at least one-half of the total assessed value of property in the district.

After a public hearing, the governing body of the jurisdiction must determine that a proposed improvement will confer a general benefit on the district and that the costs of improvements are appropriate when compared with the value of property in the district. Once the district is established by ordinance, the presiding officer, clerk, and treasurer of the municipality perform ex officio in the same capacity as the board of directors of the district.

Improvement districts have the power to borrow money and incur debt, to acquire, construct, install, and operate public improvements, to manage the business of the district, and to levy charges and ad valorem taxes to finance district facilities and operations. Bond issues must be approved in an election but do not constitute an obligation of the jurisdiction where the district is located.

While no specific legislation authorizes building authorities, a building authority is simply a nonprofit corporation formed in accordance with the Colorado Nonprofit Corporation Code. Past rulings of the U.S. Internal Revenue Service have held bonds issued by such nonprofit organizations to be tax exempt. Essentially, the rulings mean that bond obligations of corporations organized under the general nonprofit corporation law of a state are considered obligations of a state or its political subdivisions.

Developers interested in funding the provision of utility services to their property through bond issues, then, may organize public building authorities. The local government, however, must approve the tax-exempt status of the bond issues. Once issued, bonds are repaid through assessments levied against the land upon transfer of the land. In other words, as developers sell land for building, a portion of the proceeds of sale retires the bonds. Whether the buyer or the seller assumes that cost is negotiated in the sale agreement.

Source: Douglas R. Porter, Ben C. Lin, and Richard B. Peiser, *Special Districts: A Useful Technique for Financing Infrastructure* (Washington, D.C.: ULI–the Urban Land Institute, 1987), pp. 30–32.

best known and most stringent is San Francisco's Office Housing Production Program, which requires all developers of downtown office buildings of over 50,000 square feet of floor space to pay a variety of fees for improvements to transit, housing, public art, child care, and public open space. Jersey City, New Jersey, requires all developers to contribute to affordable housing.

Although exactions and fees can be imposed through written provisions in ordinances, many jurisdictions also exact other contributions that are determined through negotiations. Such exactions become possible when developers request rezoning or use special procedures, such as PUDs, that require approval by a board or legislative body. Many public officials (and neighborhood groups) find such procedures an opportune time to request additional contributions from developers. Legally, developers are obligated only to offer facilities and improvements that benefit primarily their developments, but developers pressed to move forward with a project often agree to other contributions as well, sometimes including such offerings as

FIGURE 10-12
NATIONAL AVERAGES FOR IMPACT FEES BY TYPE, 1990

Type of Impact Fee	Single-Family House (Per Unit)	General Industrial Space (Per 1,000 Square Feet)	General Office (Per 1,000 Square Feet)	General Retail Space (Per 1,000 Square Feet)
Road	$1,547	$800	$1,840	$2,881
Parks	526	NF	NF	NF
Public Facilities	95	37	87	115
Police Protection	53	55	89	103
Fire Protection	135	76	149	222
Library	86	NF	NF	NF
Schools	559	NF	NF	NF
TOTAL	$3,001	$968	$2,165	$3,321

NF = No fee is charged.
Source: James C. Nicholas and Kellie Ruscher, "Impact Fees on the Rise," *Growth Management Studies Newsletter* (Center for Governmental Responsibility, Univ. of Florida, College of Law), June 1990, p. 2.

scholarships for neighborhood youths and relandscaping neighborhood parks.

These requirements for facilities contributed by developers are specified as conditions in rezoning actions or, in the case of subdivision approvals, in the final plats and engineering drawings that receive official approval. In the later case, the subdivision drawing would indicate the standards of construction for each type of facility. Before proceeding with construction, developers usually must post a bond to ensure the satisfactory completion of the facilities, and during construction, public inspections are made to determine that standards are being maintained. Usually the completed facilities are then dedicated to the local government for public use, although increasingly they instead become the responsibility of a community or homeowners' association organized to manage the common facilities.

The written and unwritten rules for determining exactions and fees raise three major issues that deserve consideration: legal constraints, equity, and administrative concerns.

Legal Constraints

The questions of the extent to which local governments can demand contributions from developers and for what pur-

poses have been sources of continuous litigation in state and federal courts. Three constitutional provisions—taking property without just compensation (eminent domain), equal protection, and due process—limit local governments' powers to require exactions. Exactions must be necessary under the police power of protecting health, safety, and public welfare, they must be applied equally to all types of development, they should not have an exclusionary effect, and the specific exaction must be clearly related to a public purpose.

The general test, applicable in virtually all states, is that exactions should bear a "rational nexus" to a development's impacts on local public facilities. That is, a local government may, for example, require a developer to improve a certain intersection if the developer's project will generate enough traffic to warrant the improvement. The local government cannot, however, legitimately require developers to pay for improvements to intersections many miles away that traffic from their projects will seldom use.

The legal foundation for development or impact fees presents more problems than other forms of exactions. First, it must be established that fees are allowable under the police powers granted to the local government by the state rather than defined as a form of tax for which specific state authorization is usually required. Then, assuming that the state deems impact fees allowable, their calculation and administration must meet stiffer criteria than tax revenues. The amounts of fees should take into account regular taxes that property owners will pay for public improvements (to avoid double taxation) and must not include funds needed to correct existing deficiencies (for which existing residents are responsible). Fees must be administered to ensure that fees collected from specific developments are expended within a reasonable time for facilities that will benefit those developments.

If exactions and fees are imposed and administered reasonably and backed by solid planning and a detailed implementation program for funding public facilities, the courts will nearly always uphold them.

Equity

Exactions raise some issues about who should pay for improvements to infrastructure. At one time, it was assumed that the general community should be responsible for funding major infrastructure systems, while developers should be responsible primarily for facilities on their sites. But that simple division of financial responsibility is breaking down. Communities, urged by taxpayers, are increasingly concerned with defining the precise impacts of new development on public facilities and making sure that developers compensate them for those impacts. In the process, developers complain that many citizens besides those in their projects benefit from improvements they pay for, especially when capital expenditures benefit future generations of users.

Another issue concerns governmental services that are financed on the basis of ability to pay: that is, people who earn more pay more. Elementary and secondary education, for example, is normally considered important enough to society as a whole that it is financed largely by property tax revenues that reflect levels of personal income. Which capital facilities should be financed in this way and which should be targeted to users is a continuing issue. The question becomes more complex when one realizes that much infrastructure confers value on property it does not directly serve: a good

park system, for example, improves everyone's property values in addition to offering direct benefits to the parks' users.

Administrative Concerns

Exactions and fees pose two administrative concerns: the general lack of administrative guidelines or rules for determining exactions and the difficulties inherent in the use of impact fees. As noted earlier, many exactions of land or improvements, especially those located off the development site, are negotiated during project approval procedures. Seldom do guidelines exist to determine the appropriate types or amounts of exactions, to suggest how financial responsibilities should be shared among public and private interests, or to guide negotiations. As a result, developers often complain of extortionary exactions unrelated to the impacts of their projects, and public officials frequently believe that developers are not being required to do enough.

These problems supposedly are solved in large part by the use of impact fees that provide predictable measures and payments of impact. Legally sound and politically stable fee programs, however, take a considerable amount of time to adopt. Once enacted, such programs require administrative time to determine correct fees for each project, collect and account for them, and make expenditures for facilities that benefit the payers. Fees also should be reviewed and updated every year or two. Cities, such as San Diego, that use impact fees as a major mechanism of financing employ full-time staffs to administer their programs.

Exactions and fees provide a method for obtaining private contributions of needed public facilities, but they should not be viewed as a panacea because such contributions rarely cover all the costs of required infrastructure. Exactions and fees should be employed only within an overall public program of financing capital facilities as one of several sources of revenue. In this context, however, they may provide the essential funds to permit development to proceed.

Furthermore, although developers and builders usually decry exactions and fees, they often find that the resulting facilities add market value to their projects. Public requirements for open space or drainage, for example, usually enhance building sites. Environmental features preserved from development often become valuable amenities for the site's residents and tenants. Other benefits relate to management of the development process. Developers who have paid impact fees have greater assurance that needed public facilities will be built. Developers who construct facilities have a significant amount of control over the timing and quality of those facilities, for they can make certain that facilities are there when they need them. For these reasons, exactions and fees may prove beneficial rather than harmful to developments.

Privatization

In recent years, a number of local governments have experimented with the idea of having private companies build and operate public facilities. It is not a new idea: private water companies, private solid waste disposal facilities, and private transit companies are not uncommon. Semiprivate authorities manage many toll roads and bridges. Special taxing districts that provide sewer and water service are often managed by private companies under contract to districts. And in many small- and large-scale developments, community associations own and manage recreational and other facilities.

Proponents of such ventures assert that private companies provide superior service at lower cost (partly because of more efficient management but also because of lower wage scales). Public officials, however, often worry that private companies may make unreasonable profits or fail to provide equal service to all residents. Certainly no great rush has occurred to convert public to private facilities, and at this point, privatization is the exception rather than the rule.

SUMMARY

Developers must expect to interact closely with public officials and administrators in accomplishing their objectives. Developers not only must adhere to regulations and rules in choosing sites, designing projects, and carrying out construction, but also frequently may pursue options offered in regulations that give special opportunities for types of projects or designs. Thus, developers should acquire a keen knowledge of local regulations affecting development, either personally or through trusted consultants.

This principle also holds for the provision of needed infrastructure to support proposed developments. Especially as more communities attempt to shift the costs of infrastructure to developers, it behooves developers to keep up to date on requirements and options that will have an important effect on a project's bottom line.

In both cases, developers will find it good business practice to know local public officials and administrators and to participate in community decision making regarding future development. Developers can lend their special understanding of the practical aspects of development to discussions about new comprehensive plans, rezoning, annual capital improvement programs, and other public actions that directly affect the climate for development in their communities. At bottom, successful development requires that private and public objectives match.

NOTES

1. See Douglas R. Porter, "The States Are Coming, The States Are Coming," *Urban Land*, September 1989, pp. 16–20.

2. See Douglas R. Porter, Patrick L. Phillips, and Colleen Grogan Moore, *Working with the Community: A Developer's Guide* (Washington, D.C.: ULI–the Urban Land Institute, 1985).

3. Two publications by the American Planning Association provide helpful advice on streamlining techniques and review of standards: John Vranicar, Welford Sanders, and David Mosena, *Streamlining Land Use Regulations* (Chicago: APA Press, 1980); and Welford Sanders, Judith Getzels, David Mosena, and JoAnn Butler, *Affordable Single-Family Housing: A Review of Development Standards*, Planning Advisory Service Report No. 385 (Chicago: APA Press, 1984).

Chapter 11

Meshing Public and Private Roles in the Development Process

Development in the United States has traditionally occurred through a conventional process in which the public and private sectors perform independent functions and therefore tend to remain at arm's length. As a general rule, simple projects in strong markets used conventional modes of development, and any mix of function between the public and private sectors was seen as a conflict of interest on the part of the local government. The public sector was expected to perform the functions of regulation and broad planning, providing the needed services—schools, roads, fire and police protection—to support new development, while the private developer originated projects based on information about the market and formulated a specific plan for a project with public policy in mind but without a direct public role in stages one and two of the process. Consequently, the public sector did not have to assume any risks or costs that were typically borne by the private sector.[1]

As seen earlier, the general exclusion of nonmarket forces in conventional development is no longer true. Developers must now deal with a host of political pressures and community interests when developing conventional projects.

While governments have used a variety of financing tools to provide infrastructure, which has traditionally been a public responsibility, reduced sources of public funding, however, have put the onus of providing infrastructure on the private sector, particularly in growing areas of the country. This redefinition of roles has forced developers to provide various public services and improvements that were previously paid for out of general tax revenues, thus mixing the roles of the public and private sectors.

This chapter takes a close look at how those roles have been joined, examining:
- The advent of public/private development; and
- The process involved in formulating public/private partnerships.

The authors are indebted to Rachelle L. Levitt, ULI's staff vice president for education, for writing this chapter.

THE ADVENT OF PUBLIC/
PRIVATE DEVELOPMENT

Each decade since the 1940s has seen federal, state, and local public policies aimed at stimulating development for the benefit of the public (see "The Historical Basis for Federal Intervention" later in this chapter). A majority of these efforts have been directed toward the urban cores and distressed neighborhoods of the nation's cities, although in recent years suburban areas have used the process as well. In Fairfax County, Virginia, for example, the county arranged to swap land with a private developer to develop an $83.4 million gov-

Coldspring, a new town, was developed on this site, the last sizable vacant tract within the city limits of Baltimore.

ernment center. This public/private venture combines the Charles E. Smith Company and the Artery Organization Partnership to build the county government center on 100 acres in exchange for 116 acres of adjoining land, $24.6 million in cash, and $16.6 million in other forms of compensation. The county bought 183 of those acres for $4.1 million in 1979, and the 116 acres involved in the exchange of land have been valued at $42 million.[2] Public intervention significantly alters the conventional development process and introduces the public sector as a viable partner in the process (see Figure 11-1 for an outline of the codevelopment process).

Public/private development became a growing trend to stimulate the development of projects that would otherwise not occur. Distressed communities needing economic and community development provided incentives to the private sector to entice development, often becoming partners in the process. Intervention in the market has been used successfully to stimulate urban revitalization in downtowns and inner-city neighborhoods, developing mixed-use projects, festival marketplaces, commercial buildings, and the like.

A number of cities are well known for their joint public/private efforts—Baltimore, San Antonio, Milwaukee, Philadelphia, Indianapolis, and others. Each city has developed its own method of harnessing private investment to stimulate revitalization of that city's economy. Some entrepreneurial local governments have—through their own initiative and their willingness to take risks—become joint venture partners with private developers on some projects.

In Baltimore, for instance, the city has undertaken several joint venture agreements, both in the revitalization of its well-known Inner Harbor and in other development projects. Coldspring is an in-town planned community developed at the instigation of the city of Baltimore's Department of Housing and Community Development (HCD). In addition to complete master planning and overall coordination, HCD provided land, infrastructure, parks, public facilities, and financing in an agreement with the F.D. Rich Housing Corporation in 1978. In meeting its goals for the site, which was the last large undeveloped

FIGURE 11-1
THE CODEVELOPMENT PROCESS

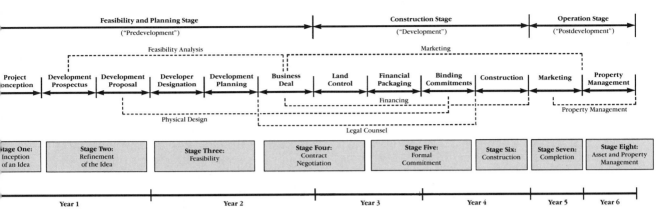

Note: This sequence is substantially simplified, as individual steps (denoted by solid lines) may occur in a somewhat different order and often merge and overlap in time. Moreover, certain activities, such as feasibility analysis and physical design (denoted by dotted lines), continue through several steps in codevelopment. Finally, the time required for codevelopment is highly variable and depends upon a project's complexity, public review procedures, and other factors.

tract in the city, HCD specified the exact form of development to occur, limiting the developer's profit to 10 percent. Assuming a role as "senior partner" in this particular project, HCD succeeded in meeting goals for affordable housing and other aims for the site. Risk and reward for the developer were considerably lower than in conventional private developments.[3]

The Philadelphia Redevelopment Authority entered into a joint venture with the Rouse Company to develop The Gallery, a downtown retail/office project incorporating many of the attractive features of suburban shopping malls. Private developers were not interested in the site because of the perceived risk in revitalizing the Market Street area and the large number of funding sources involved. Acting as both joint developer and general contractor, the Redevelopment Authority provided $18 million toward two-thirds of the costs of the shell. The Rouse Company provided $20 million of equity for the project, covering one-third of the costs of the shell in a 99-year ground lease arrangement in which Rouse also finishes space and sublets it. The city has been criticized for failing to capture a significant portion of the project's financial rewards, which flow mainly to the developer and the retailers.[4]

In 1974, the city of Indianapolis initiated development of a superblock mixed-use project by assembling 26 downtown parcels adjacent to the state capitol and Monument Circle. In addition to acquiring the land, the city cleared the site and financed the project through a bond issue,

The Gallery at Market East, in Philadelphia, was one of the first contemporary shopping malls to be developed in the old downtown of a major U.S. city. The Gallery opened in August 1977 and continues to enjoy successful retail operations.

235

executing an annual ground lease of $360,000 with the developer, PRT Joint Venture. Winning the city-sponsored design competition, PRT's Merchant's Plaza includes 1.4 million square feet total, at a price tag of $48 million.[5]

Public/private efforts in San Antonio led to the successful redevelopment of a deteriorated historic structure in the Alamo Plaza historic district. The San Antonio Local Development Commission (LDC) worked with the developer to couple special financing (an Urban Development Action Grant [UDAG] with matching funds from the LDC) with local tax incentives (a five-year reprieve on property taxes offered to renovated historic structures) to make development of a hotel on the site of a former medical building feasible. The terra cotta facade of the Gothic revival structure was preserved, and the new use—the Emily Morgan Hotel—capitalized on the burgeoning tourist trade in San Antonio.[6]

The individual characteristics and history of each city determine which methods are most appropriate for such deals. Generally speaking, public entrepreneurship is necessary in weak markets with fairly com-plex projects, as a city capitalizes on its resources and uses incentives to make a real estate project feasible for both public and private participants.

THE PROCESS INVOLVED IN FORMULATING PUBLIC/ PRIVATE PARTNERSHIPS

The traditional roles of the public and private sectors are dramatically redefined in public/private partnerships. In such situations, a joint effort is needed between the public and private sectors to develop a project in which each partner shares risks and benefits. Such joint efforts involve many steps similar to conventional development, but they differ in several ways:

• The use of relatively limited public resources to attract larger amounts of private investment for community and economic development (leveraging);

• Deals between business and government and much earlier involvement of the private sector than is traditionally the case, even under conventional urban renewal;

• Public financing and therefore a concern with public accountability, income to the public sector, and requirements for private investment;

• The active cooperation of public, private, and community sectors and hence broader public/private partnerships; and

• Consideration of public objectives (for example, community goals, design criteria, affirmative action) in addition to private objectives.[7]

Public/private partnerships have many advantages. Developers anticipate a more cooperative regulatory environment when a governmental agency is their partner.[8] The perception is that governmental entities are more apt to approve and often to accelerate the approval process for those projects in which they have an investment. Such partnerships give the public sector more control over projects throughout the development process and enable cities to achieve social objectives, for example, affirmative action, use of minority contractors, and jobs for low-income residents. The involvement of the public sector often means substantial delays for the developer,

San Antonio's Emily Morgan Hotel, a significant historic rehabilitation involving public/private efforts.

236

however, because of increased public review and comment, contracting requirements, and political concerns.

Figure 11-2 shows how three levels of government encouraged private development in St. Louis in a concerted and comprehensive effort to bring back the city's downtown and inner-city residential districts through public/private initiatives. The public sector fostered an economic and social environment within which the private sector was willing to take the necessary risks. Particularly unusual was Missouri's Urban Redevelopment Corporations Law (Chapter 353), which allows establishment of a private, for-profit corpora-

FIGURE 11-2
THE ST. LOUIS STORY: BRINGING BACK A DOWNTOWN

One of the more visible examples of downtown and inner-city residential redevelopment using public and private resources is in St. Louis. After St. Louis's downtown bottomed out in the 1970s, a concerted effort began to take advantage of the huge inventory of underused and abandoned downtown buildings. Despite some dour predictions, St. Louis was able to use many components of the

Photo courtesy of St. Louis Union Station Merchants Association, Inc.

Once the largest and busiest passenger rail terminal in the world, St. Louis Union Station, first opened in 1894, was dramatically restored in 1985 and redeveloped as a festival marketplace.

FIGURE 11-2 (continued)

public sector to encourage development: the Community Development Block Grant (CDBG) program, the UDAG program, the state of Missouri, including its Chapter 353 Urban Redevelopment Corporations Law, federal historic preservation tax codes, and local officials.

St. Louis's effort included the complete renovation of Union Station, one of the grandest train stations of the 1800s, which, developed by Oppenheimer Properties, is now the site for a two-level specialty shopping and dining mall, a private rail-car facility, a one-acre lake, a beer garden, a parking lot, and a 550-room Omni Hotel. Laclede's Landing, the last French settlement in North America, was revitalized when a group of businessmen, property owners, and government officials formed a corporation under Chapter 353. The plan for the redevelopment area includes the rehabilitation of 45 buildings containing 1 million square feet and new construction of another 1 million square feet. The project contains a mix of office, residential, entertainment, retail, and hotel uses. And St. Louis Centre, another example of a downtown mixed-use development, contains more than 1.5 million square feet of retail space, a 412,000-square-foot office building, and a parking garage accommodating 1,450 cars. Earlier construction had brought a 36-story bank building, retail and office buildings, and a major hotel to that same area.

St. Louis was more successful than many other cities in incorporating downtown residential redevelopment into the complete effort. Nationally recognized for its successful approach, the Housing Implementation Program (HIP) assisted in the rehabilitation and production of rental units in transitional neighborhoods benefiting many low- and moderate-income families. Begun in 1978, HIP provides low-interest or no-interest, subordinated loans for housing developments. It provides a one-time subsidy of the developer's costs. Occasionally, the city takes a modified equity position in return for funding by HIP. Returns are channeled back into other development projects. The city also liberally used investment tax credits (ITCs) that were part of the Economic Recovery Tax Act of 1976.

The sweeping revitalization included residential areas like Lafayette Square, Tower Grove East, Fox Park (led by the DeSales Community Housing Corporation, originally sponsored by St. Francis DeSales Catholic Church), and the Washington University Medical Center (steered by the Washington University Medical Center Redevelopment Corporation).

The city's creative use of financing to "customize" public/private partnerships formed to enhance city neighborhoods has resulted in the beginning of a major improvement effort downtown, which has brought new life to a city that was decaying 20 years ago. Many established groups, like St. Francis Church and the Washington University Medical Center, as well as respected city officials were successfully brought into the process.

---

tion in economically disadvantaged areas. Such corporations have the power to condemn land, attach property taxes, and use bonds to finance the project.

Public officials usually apply the following steps to determine whether significant levels of public assistance for development and financing will be required:

- Determine the total costs by project component.
- Determine the level of private financing available.
- Capitalize net operating income.
- Establish loan value.
- Determine available equity financing.
- Calculate total private funding capacity.

- Identify a gap between project costs and project affordability.
- Attempt to close financing gaps and gain "reasonable" project returns.[9]

When deciding the least costly and least risky measure to apply in helping developers close financing gaps, public entities must define and measure public risk and rewards for their actions.

The Historical Basis for Federal Intervention

The first major federal grant program for private developers to revitalize urban areas in the United States was the urban renewal program, adopted as part of the 1949 Housing Act. Experience in Pennsylvania and earlier public housing programs provided the basis for the urban renewal program. The philosophy behind the program depended on clearing slums as a means of commercial, residential, and industrial redevelopment. The idea was to revitalize the declining areas of U.S. cities through large-scale land acquisition and clearance. The act specified that local agencies were to assemble, clear, and prepare sites for sale and lease for uses specified in the community's redevelopment plan. Federal capital grants would pay two-thirds of the subsidy to private redevelopers through the discounted sale of land and the cost of public improvements by local agencies on such projects.

Under conventional urban renewal, the public sector concentrated on planning and land assembly, the private sector on project-related activities. With hindsight, the development industry has learned that clearing land alone does not provide the stimulus for development. Although some urban renewal projects were successful, experience has shown that many such projects were not designed to meet market conditions and other projects were so delayed that market conditions changed. Although urban renewal resulted in numerous vacant lots throughout the downtowns of the United States, it taught many lessons regarding how joint public/private efforts could be more effectively implemented.

Under the rubric of urban renewal, cities acquired and cleared sites for private redevelopment without the promise of private investment, except in New York, Chicago, the District of Columbia, and a few other cities. Public development agencies often overestimated the potential for private redevelopment. As a result, existing businesses were displaced, neighborhoods and commercial areas disrupted, and scarce public dollars spent without achieving the hoped-for redevelopment. In response to the problems encountered in traditional urban renewal, an approach was designed that in effect tied public investment to private investment. The concept of such public/private partnerships became the basis for the UDAG program, initiated in 1976 and administered by the U.S. Department of Housing and Urban Development. UDAGs enabled local governments to work closely with developers to design projects. Cities could use UDAGs to entice developers to invest in areas that they would not otherwise have been interested in. Many downtown projects developed in the late 1970s and early 1980s used UDAGs. Although funds were initially invested in capital facilities, cities used the majority of UDAG funds to provide low-cost debt financing. Paybacks from these projects will continue to fund future development in those communities. In 1989, the UDAG program was eliminated, but like the urban renewal program, the program left a legacy of lessons. Its contribution was the creation of a favorable environment for an array of public/private partnerships and a degree of innovation in public incentive tools before unknown.

Types of Public/Private Projects

The nature of public involvement in projects has included such capital improvements as provision of infrastructure, parking garages, transit systems and stations, public amenities (outdoor plazas, pedestrian malls, other open space), and convention facilities. Capital improvements provide amenities and/or an improved environment in which a project is more likely to succeed. Indirect or "softer" measures to save costs could be passed on to developers in the form of density bonuses, government agencies' commitments or guarantees to leave space in a new development, development rights transfers, land

and/or building exchanges, air rights transfers, regulatory relief from zoning and building codes, reduced processing time for project approvals, private use of eminent domain (in some states only), coordinated design of projects in an area, the government's preparation of environmental impact statements or reports, arbitration of any disputes that might arise, and work with or organization of neighborhood and business groups. These public actions do not entail an outlay of public money but provide the developer with savings in time and money, reduced risk, or increased opportunities for development.

Financial incentives (see Figure 11-3) include direct loans, tax abatements, second mortgages (perhaps using repaid

FIGURE 11-3
PUBLIC FINANCING INCENTIVES

Sources of Assistance	Stages One to Three Predevelopment (1)		Stages Four to Six Development (2)					Stages Seven and Eight Postdevelopment (3)	
	Plan Development	Feasibility Study	Land/ Building Acquisition	Clearance and Relocation	New Construction	Building Rehabilitation	Infrastructure	Business Equipment and Machinery	Property Management/ Working Capital
Federal									
Housing and Urban Development									
CDBG	X	X	X	X	XO	XO	X		
Economic Development Administration									
Planning and Technical Assistance	X	X							
Public Works			X	X	X	X	X		
Economic Adjustment									
Grant	X	X	X	X	X	X	X		
Grant for Loan			O		O	O		O	O
Business Loan Guarantee			O		O	O		O	O
Local									
Eminent Domain			XO						
Tax Increment Financing	.		X	X		X			
Tax Abatement	.								O
Land Lease			O						
Cost Sharing		X							
Second Mortgage			O		O	O			O
Dedicated Property Tax									O
Land Cost Writedown			O						
Industrial Revenue Bond			O		O	O		O	O
Revolving Loan Fund			O		O	O		O	O
General Revenue	X	X	X	X	X	X	X		
Special Assessment District							O		
Capital Improvements					X	X	X		
Site Assembly			X	X					
Enterprise Zones					O	O	O	O	O
Equity Participation			X	X	X	X			

Key:
X–Direct public investments for complementary investments or portion of development.
O–Direct financing to private developer or pass-through from city to private developer.
Source: Gary E. Stout and Joseph E. Vitt, *Public Incentives and Financing Techniquest for Codevelopment* (Washington, D.C.: ULI–the Urban Land Institute, 1982), p. 11. Updated 1990.

UDAGs), writedowns of interest rates, site assembly and clearance (sometimes including land banking), enterprise zones (see Figure 11-4), writedowns of land costs, land leases, funding of predevelopment activities, and others. The public sector can take a more direct financial stake in projects to secure a specified percent of a project's cash flow (an equity interest) through such mechanisms as loan paybacks, participatory leases, and equity participation.[10] In these situations, public entities often resemble the entrepreneurs they are negotiating with rather than protectors of the public interest. The extent of public involvement allowed is controlled by each state's laws.

The city of Orlando's negotiations with Lincoln Property Company for the development of a new 245,000-square-foot city hall, a public park and plaza, 1 million square feet of commercial office space, an-

---

FIGURE 11-4

ENTERPRISE ZONES: A TOOL FOR ECONOMIC DEVELOPMENT

It has been argued that enterprise zones stimulate development without direct financial support from the government. A number of states have endorsed the idea and adopted state enterprise zone programs. Under such state programs, a distressed area within a city is designated an enterprise zone, and within those zones, businesses are eligible for tax incentives to create jobs.

The structure of enterprise zones varies substantially. According to HUD, "Some state programs are oriented toward heavy industry, some to light industry or warehousing, others to retail[ing]. Some states provide a specific residential component; some do not."[a]

The 38 states that have enterprise zones also offer a variety of incentives—from tax credits for new employees to low-interest venture capital and small business loans to exemption from sales and use taxes for the purchase of construction materials, equipment, and machinery.[b]

Support has grown in the Bush administration for greater federal initiatives in the establishment of enterprise zones. HUD Secretary Jack Kemp, a long-time advocate of enterprise zones, would like to add federal tax incentives to the program. The Bush administration has proposed such incentives as exemption from capital gains taxes for at least two years before realization of the gain, a refundable wage credit for low-income employees in a zone, and deductions of investments by corporate investors with fewer than $5 million in assets.

Evidence about the usefulness of enterprise zones is conflicting, however. The Congressional Research Service has concluded that residents of enterprise zones do not benefit from jobs created in the zones. A study by the Center for Regional Business Analysis at Pennsylvania State University, however, has examined 17 states with the longest-established programs and found that improvements have occurred in many zones.[c] More than 25 percent of the studied zones achieved gross employment growth rates above the national job growth rate during the same time periods. The most significant findings are that residents of zones hold a majority of the jobs gained and that unemployed and low-income workers receive a considerable share of available positions. The verdict is therefore still out on the usefulness of enterprise zones, but with few federal initiatives on the horizon, hopes for economic development are pinned to this idea.

---

a. Diana R. Savastano, "Enterprise Zones Cook Up Soup-to-Nuts Incentives Menu," *Plants Sites & Parks,* May/June 1989, pp. 1, 89.

b. Ibid.

c. Rodney Erickson and Susan Friedman, *Enterprise Zones: An Evaluation of State Government Policies* (Washington, D.C.: U.S. Department of Commerce, 1989).

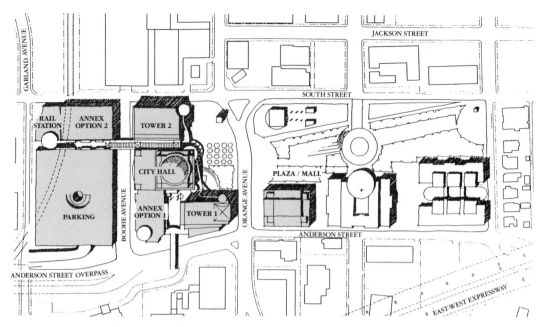

Orlando's planned City Commons features a common plaza at the bend in Orange Avenue, Orlando's main downtown street. The sites determined to be best for private use were reserved for the two towers.

cillary retail space, and associated parking provide an example of how effective joint ventures between the public and private sectors can speed the process significantly (see Figure 11-5). This project will be part of the 30-acre master-planned Southern Gateway redevelopment district on the south side of downtown Orlando.

Profit-sharing agreements have not, however, produced substantial returns to many cities. In a recent study of 16 cities with projects with profit-sharing arrangements, only three, as of 1988, were generating any cash return for the city.[11] Boston officials, for example, waited 17 years before realizing any profit from the Faneuil Hall festival marketplace, in which the city acts as a limited development partner, sharing a percentage of the center's net cash flow in lieu of property taxes and conventional lease terms. It is possible that the perception of such a return to the public body legitimizes the transaction for the public, but the motivations for these kinds of joint venture arrangements are complex and do not necessarily relate to immediate return. A city receives many other economic benefits in return: increased sales and sometimes increased property taxes,

spin-off developments, an improved image for an area, strengthened market potential, increased employment, increased tourism, among others.

Organizations and the Public/Private Process

The involvement of state and local organizations has grown in innovative ways. Various forms of governmental structures have been organized to handle public/private development, including an array of quasi-public governmental bodies, development corporations, and new city departments with expanded functions. Development organizations are frequently organized as quasi-public organizations because they are less bound to the severe restrictions a city must adhere to when involved in development. Though partially publicly funded, a quasi-public development organization can conduct negotiations in private—particularly useful as developers are reluctant to negotiate when their financial dealings are made public. Examples of quasi-public organizations are the Centre City Development Corporation in San Diego, California, the Pennsylvania Av-

242

FIGURE 11-5
ORLANDO'S CITY COMMONS

Orlando's government outgrew its 1950s-vintage city hall, and its operations were scattered among a number of buildings, producing inefficient service to the public. The city also faced escalating rental costs in privately owned buildings. Although Orlando could finance a new city hall without resorting to immediate tax increases or bond referenda, the mayor and the city council wanted an alternative scheme of funding.

To achieve that objective, the city chose to lease its land to a private developer to develop a large project designed to include significant commercial elements. The ground rents from the private development would partially offset the costs of constructing the city hall, and the developer could be persuaded to subsidize the costs of certain amenities on the site. Capitalizing on a strong market and the prime location, the city negotiated simultaneously with three finalists over six months during which competition included even the final details of the development and lease documents. Despite the extra time and effort required, city officials believe that the benefits to the city, which also holds a reversionary interest in the project, were greatly enhanced. The important points of the final agreement with the developer, Lincoln Property Company, are as follows:

- The city retains fee simple title to approximately 2.5 acres of land (of the total seven-acre site), where the new city hall and a park/plaza will be constructed. The city will own the building outright in the conventional manner. (The city would also have been willing under certain circumstances to rent the city hall from a developer to facilitate financing of the private portion of the project.)
- Lincoln Property Company is paid a negotiated development fee on performance of a guaranteed fixed-price contract to demolish the old and construct the new city hall and park/plaza. This arrangement was mutually satisfactory because it gave Lincoln the opportunity to achieve some economies of scale in constructing a larger project. Lincoln is known for its cost-effective construction management, giving the city confidence in its ability to complete the project satisfactorily.
- Lincoln and the city will jointly plan and design the project. Lincoln pays the planning costs and manages the process, assuming that the overall project will conform to development practices of the private sector.
- Lincoln agrees to rent the remainder of the seven-acre site from the city in two phases—one beginning in 1992 and the other in 1996. The term for each parcel of land is 75 years. The city conservatively estimated and developed projected ground rents and equity participation to equal the city's bond service for the new city hall and the park/plaza within 10 to 12 years.
- Upon execution of the ground leases for the private phases, Lincoln will reimburse the city for the entire cost of a planned $1.8 million park/plaza and two-thirds of the cost of demolishing the existing city hall.

This project underscores the complexity of joint public/private development. The developer not only has to handle the complexities of any large-scale project but also must meet the government's many requirements: extensive public interaction, review and input from the community, the need to respond to the many government constituencies, the necessity for meeting statutory provisions regulating the selection and use of consultants, contractors, and other services. All these requirements mean that, for a project to succeed, it must have true potential for development.

Source: Lewis Oliver and Eric Smart, "Orlando's City Commons: A Model Public/Private Venture," *Urban Land*, January 1990, pp. 21–25.

enue Development Corporation (see Figure 11-6), and the Milwaukee Redevelopment Corporation (see Figure 11-7).

The Centre City Development Corporation was created in 1975 in connection with the increasingly complex redevelopment of the Horton Plaza project, San Diego's first post–World War II investment in a badly deteriorated downtown. As the city's sole representative in such activities as condemnation, relocation, land acquisition, and negotiations with private developers, CCDC played an aggressive role in an extensive planning process involving 13 contract revisions with the developer, Ernest W. Hahn, Inc.[12]

Conflict of Interest

As the public sector has become more involved in making deals, concerns have been raised about its objectivity in regulating development. At a ULI policy forum in 1988, leading experts in the field of pub-

---

FIGURE 11-6
PENNSYLVANIA AVENUE DEVELOPMENT CORPORATION

Charged with the revitalization of Pennsylvania Avenue in downtown Washington, D.C., the Pennsylvania Avenue Development Corporation (PADC) was established by an act of Congress in 1972. The PADC plan called for extensive public improvements to be made to America's Main Street, carried out by the corporation, and new commercial development financed by private investors, assisted by PADC's acquiring land where necessary. To support the plan, Congress vested PADC with the power of eminent domain (unusual for this form of organization) and broad authority to regulate both private and public development, providing expertise in planning, facilitating private development, building public improvements, and serving as a partner and developer of last resort where required.

PADC has encouraged private sector initiatives and avoids commitments to land assembly where the same job can be done by private development. Although the evolution of PADC's organization is unusual, that is, establishment of the organization by an act of Congress and federal funding, the experience derived from the development and implementation of the plan is applicable to other municipalities.

The evolution of PADC can be traced to June 1, 1962, when President Kennedy established the President's Council on Pennsylvania Avenue to develop a plan that would provide a mixture of public and private construction emphasizing the role of the Capitol as the center of Washington, D.C. In 1972, Congress enacted the Pennsylvania Avenue Development Corporation Act, determining that the national interest required the area adjacent to Pennsylvania Avenue between the Capitol and the White House be developed and used in a manner suitable to both the legislative and executive branches of the federal government and the needs of the community and the nation.

The powers of PADC are essentially those of a private, nonprofit corporation with two important exceptions—the power of eminent domain and the power to regulate the activities of other federal agencies. In other cities, the city government exercises these powers, and the development entity can call on the city when such powers are needed.

Development organizations like PADC can provide a point of focus to attract private investment by providing reasonable assurances to private investors that:
• Essential public services will be provided.
• Transportation and parking requirements will be expedited.
• Complementary and coordinated development will take place around the project in question.

---

lic/private development discussed whether public/private development leads to a conflict of interest for the public sector. Participants noted that the dual role of the public sector creates a "two-hat" dilemma, that is, the potential conflict of interest inherent in the public sector's acting as land seller and as land regulator. At its simplest, the conflict arises because a city's goals in selling versus regulating land are potentially at odds, and the city's role as seller might improperly influence the regulatory role (see Figure 11-8).[13] Several questions should be considered in examining whether such a conflict exists:

- Is the city overlooking longer-range public interest goals?
- Can cities make good deals, especially when bargaining with sophisticated private parties?
- Are regulatory concessions given away too cheaply?
- Are planners as deal makers focusing on short-term real estate development

---

FIGURE 11-6 (continued)

- Sufficiently large levels of new development will occur to create a critical mass and enhanced levels of activity in the area.

PADC's projects have included:
- The Willard Hotel and Willard Office Building. PADC acquired the vacant hotel and adjacent properties in 1978 and conducted a national competition for the redevelopment of the hotel. The Oliver Carr Company, the Inter-Continental Hotels Corporation, and

Photo courtesy of Carol M. Highsmith, The Willard Complex

The Willard Hotel and Office Building, a cornerstone rehabilitation project of the Pennsylvania Avenue Development Corporation.

Stuart Golding, with a contribution from PADC to the historic preservation, completed renovation of the hotel and the surrounding mixed-use complex. The complex includes 24,300 square feet of retail space and 218,600 square feet of office space.
- National Place, including the Shops, the J.W. Marriott Hotel, and National Theatre.
- A number of office buildings and mixed-use projects, including the first residential buildings along Pennsylvania Avenue.
- The Pavilion at the Old Post Office.
- The Evening Star Building, including the preservation of its beaux arts facade.
- Market Square, a mixed-use project featuring classical architecture that, along with other projects now in various stages, will make up Pennsylvania Quarter, a new residential neighborhood.
- The Washington Hotel, a complete renovation of the 1918 structure with its ornamental frieze using the rare Italian sgraffito technique.

Source: W. Anderson Barnes, *Downtown Development: Plan and Implementation* (Washington, D.C.: ULI–the Urban Land Institute, 1982).

FIGURE 11-7
MILWAUKEE REDEVELOPMENT CORPORATION

The Milwaukee Redevelopment Corporation (MRC) is a private, nonprofit corporation working with city government to revitalize downtown. Though it is a private organization with a board of directors comprised of chief executive officers of major area corporations, MRC works closely with the city.

MRC began in 1973 as a limited-profit development company. It raised $3 million in seed money by selling stock to over 40 Milwaukee-based firms. Though shareholders were told not to expect a quick or market rate of return on their investment, MRC reorganized as a nonprofit corporation in 1983 to reflect its actual performance. Operating funds now come from membership dues rather than from the sale of stock.

In its first two years of operation, MRC met with business and government leaders to identify priorities and to establish an agenda for the revitalization of downtown. Priority districts were targeted, with the first being the central retail area west of the Milwaukee River. A three-pronged strategy involved the development of a hotel, a regional retail center, and an office building.

To develop the hotel, MRC made a cash equity investment in the project while the city participated in landscaping and in the construction of a skywalk. For the office building, MRC optioned much of the land at risk to ensure the building's location between the retail center and the hotel. The city also assembled a portion of the land. For the retail center, MRC forged the coalition with the city and the Rouse Company, its developer, and developed the entire $70 million project. It provided more than $16 million of the equity, purchased two of the buildings used in the redevelopment, acquired other land in the project area, and executed a lease of the retail space with the Rouse Company.

Since the completion of its first three projects, MRC has continued its work downtown. It became a joint venture partner in the development of 354-unit Yankee Hill, the first major housing development in downtown Milwaukee in 20 years. Completed in 1988, Yankee Hill is a market-rate rental project. MRC is also working with Trammell Crow Residential Company to develop a 20-acre project on the edge of downtown that will include more than 700 units of housing and 20,000 square feet of commercial space. In another partnership with the Crow organization, MRC participated in the redevelopment of a historic building as the new home of the Milwaukee Repertory Theatre. As part of the project, the city restored the historic Pabst Theater, while Trammell Crow developed an adjoining hotel and office complex.

As compensation for its involvement in projects, MRC negotiates a percentage of the cash flow from the project as well as a percentage of the residual sales proceeds. A negotiated fee is also sometimes part of its share in the deal.

MRC has used both informal and formal processes in initiating deals. The theater project exemplifies the informal process. With the project still in the conceptual stage, Jon Wellhoefer, executive vice president of MRC, contacted Trammell Crow to see whether he had any interest in the project. A similarly informal process had been used to work with the Rouse Company on The Grand Avenue.

A more formal process involving a request for proposals has been used on the 20-acre residential project. Letters to more than 60 local and national developers resulted in "something of a beauty contest" in which finalists submitted plans for the project in a competitive selection process. Both processes have worked well for Milwaukee.

Source: ULI–the Urban Land Institute, *Downtown Development Handbook,* 2d ed. (Washington, D.C.: Author, forthcoming 1991).

FIGURE 11-8
THE COLUMBUS CIRCLE PROJECT

The Columbus Circle project, a 4.5-acre development on the site of the old Coliseum on the southwest corner of Central Park is an example of a court's characterization of a development transaction as a cash sale for a zoning bonus, reflecting the trial judge's fundamental unease with New York City's dual role. In 1985, Boston Properties won a city-sponsored competition to develop the site. The design would have produced one of the biggest private buildings in the world, a 925-foot-high structure with 2 million square feet of office space, street-level shops, cinemas, several hundred luxury condominiums, and a 300-room hotel. The deal between the city and Boston Properties exchanged the city-owned site and permission to exceed the zoning by 20 percent for a payment by Boston Properties of $455.1 million and a commitment of up to $40 million for improvements to the nearby Columbus Center subway station. With the bonus, the allowable floor/area ratio increased from 15 to 18, allowing 2.7 million square feet to be built. The city would have realized about $100 million in taxes each year.

The Municipal Arts Society, watchdog over the city's physical environment, filed suit, along with the metropolitan chapter of the American Planning Association and the New York Parks Council, asserting that the city's financial stake in the sale tainted the approval process and that environmental analysis of traffic and light and air quality was not adequate. The judge found that the city had exchanged density bonuses for money. The pivotal issue was the contractual clause allowing Boston Properties to cut its payment by $57 million should the city withhold the bonus of 448,500 square feet. Donning the hat of entrepreneur, the city attempted to generate the highest income from a sale of public land while simultaneously approving the use of a discretionary density bonus as part of its regulatory function. Some unease also seemed to be apparent with the city's new role as intervenor in the market rather than conservator and with the city's acting in league with the developer, raising the fear that cities, in their eagerness to cut attractive deals, might do so at the expense of the public good.

Source: Richard F. Babcock, "The City as Entrepreneur: Fiscal Wisdom or Regulatory Folly?" in *City Deal Making*, edited by Terry Jill Lassar (Washington, D.C.: ULI–the Urban Land Institute, 1990), pp. 23–29.

rather than on long-range comprehensive planning?

- Can traditional notions of due process be fulfilled when deals are hammered out behind closed doors?

Although intellectually reasonable, the question of conflict of interest has been raised infrequently, particularly given the large number of public/private projects. In addition to the Columbus Circle project, another such conflict arose with the Government Center project in Fairfax County, Virginia (described in Chapter 10). The conflict arose because the county was accused of selling the land at too low a price to get its new building. Critics said it should have held onto the land (which rose substantially in value after the trade) and sold bonds to finance the government center. The issue to consider is a question of equity. Does gaining income for the city through the disposition of city-owned land further the public interest?[14]

SUMMARY

The evolution of the relationship between the public and private sectors has clouded the division of functions. It is unlikely that the security of years ago, when the functions of each actor in the development process were clear, will return. Today, one finds innovative and complex arrangements developed to solve individual problems. Anyone entering the development field from either the public or the private side should therefore be keenly aware of these roles in the development process. The private and public sectors alone cannot accomplish all that is necessary to build the city of today. A true partnership is a necessity. The challenge is for developers and the public sector to formulate their roles so as to be mutually beneficial.

NOTES

1. Robert Witherspoon, *Codevelopment: City Rebuilding by Business and Government* (Washington, D.C.: ULI–the Urban Land Institute, 1982).

2. Richard F. Babcock, "The City as Entrepreneur: Fiscal Wisdom or Regulatory Folly?" in *City Deal Making*, edited by Terry Jill Lassar (Washington, D.C.: ULI–the Urban Land Institute, 1990), pp. 9–43.

3. *Project Reference File*, vol. 9, no. 9 (Washington, D.C.: ULI–the Urban Land Institute, April–June 1979).

4. *Project Reference File*, vol. 8, no. 4 (Washington, D.C.: ULI–the Urban Land Institute, January–March 1978).

5. *Project Reference File*, vol. 7, no. 15 (Washington, D.C.: ULI–the Urban Land Institute, July–September 1977).

6. *Project Reference File,* vol. 16, no. 20 (Washington, D.C.: ULI–the Urban Land Institute, October–December 1986).

7. Witherspoon, *Codevelopment,* pp. 8–9.

8. Babcock, "The City as Entrepreneur," p. 14.

9. ULI–the Urban Land Institute, *Downtown Development Handbook,* 2d ed. (Washington, D.C.: Author, forthcoming 1991).

10. Lassar, *City Deal Making*, p. 3.

11. Bernard Frieden and Lynne Sagalyn, *Downtown, Inc.* (Cambridge, Mass.: MIT Press, 1989).

12. See Jacques Gordon, *Horton Plaza, San Diego: A Case Study of Public/Private Development*, Working Paper No. 2 (Cambridge, Mass.: MIT Center for Real Estate Development, 1985).

13. Lassar, *City Deal Making*, p. 3.

14. Ibid.

Chapter 12

Affordable Housing

For most U.S. citizens, housing is not an important issue. Most are well housed, and the problems confronting those who are not—except in the case of the homeless—are not highly visible. Some critics, however, say that the United States is rapidly becoming a nation of housing haves and have-nots. The number of homeless is escalating beyond any city's ability to care for them, and young married couples who in the past could always plan on buying a small starter house must now defer that dream because of the skyrocketing costs of housing and financing.

This chapter introduces and defines the concept of affordable housing as one very important example of the public sector's role in development. It discusses the nature and extent of the problem of affordability, arrays some of the current activities and policy considerations involved, and discusses current public and/or private efforts to increase the supply of affordable housing. It looks in depth at the following topics:

- A definition of affordable housing;
- Low-income housing; and
- Affordable ownership housing.

A DEFINITION OF AFFORDABLE HOUSING

The term "affordable housing," because it is so broad, might mean different things to different people. Some define affordable housing as a general term that refers to housing that has not risen rapidly in price over the last several years. Others think in terms of houses that young people entering the housing market for the first time can buy. Some might equate affordability with rental, rather than for-sale, housing, and still others consider affordable housing as synonymous with government-subsidized housing or even with public housing. In fact, the term encompasses a wide spectrum of housing types, housing prices, and housing occupants.

As a general rule, housing can be considered affordable for a given household if that household can purchase (own or rent) that housing unit for an amount up to 30 percent of its household income.[1] A prob-

The authors are indebted to Diane Suchman, ULI's director of housing and community development research, for writing this chapter.

The Boston Housing Partnership facilitates the production of low-income housing units, such as the Washington Street project shown here before and after rehabilitation, through financing, seed money, property transfer, technical, and other assistance.

lem occurs when there is a gap between what housing costs and what those in need of housing can afford to pay.

The definition of affordable housing based on 30 percent of income has certain limitations:

1. Higher-income households might be able to pay much more than 30 percent of their incomes for housing and still have enough left over to cover basic needs—food, clothing, medical care, and so on—whereas low-income households paying 30 percent of income may find that they have so little left over that they must do without other necessities.

2. This standard ignores variations in the size of families. An individual with an income of $15,000 per year might be able to find adequate market-rate housing for his or her own needs for 30 percent of that income, while a family of eight with the same income could not.

In addition, in using this definition to determine whether a given geographic area contains an adequate supply of affordable housing, the analysis must involve more than comparisons of numbers of households at various levels of income and numbers of housing units at various prices or rents. Access to housing also implies a certain amount of choice in housing types and locations so that various needs, particularly the commute to work, can be accommodated.

Although by this definition the term "affordable housing" can apply to any in-come group, in discussions of public policy it usually refers to either 1) low-income rental housing—housing that requires subsidies for production or for occupants or both to make it affordable to low- and very-low-income households, or 2) affordable ownership housing—market-rate, unsubsidized housing for moderate-income households, particularly those buying a house for the first time.

Though provision of all types of affordable housing is a creative search for reduced costs at every step of the process, to increase the supply of low-income subsidized housing, governments and developers generally seek below-market financing and subsidies for occupants to achieve affordability, whereas to produce affordable ownership housing, the general approach is to try to minimize the direct costs of development: land, land development, and construction. These differences are explored throughout this chapter.

One serious issue contributing to affordability experienced by many households at all income levels that is not explored in this chapter is racial discrimination, whether overt (and blatantly illegal) or covert (and difficult to document in court). Discrimination, or "steering," by homesellers, real estate agents and brokers, leasing agents, or lenders can limit the effective supply of housing available to certain households. More subtly, affluent communities might fight the development of nearby lower-cost housing based on a wide variety of socially and legally acceptable concerns, while the underlying force behind their arguments could in fact be veiled racial discrimination.

The Changing Role of the Federal Government

Since 1980, the federal government has systematically dismantled its housing production programs and has withdrawn from its role as leader and its funding support for affordable housing, primarily low-income housing. In the early part of this century, production of housing at all levels was considered an activity of the private sector. The federal government's role was limited to expediting mortgage lending associated with homeownership. From the Great Depression through 1980, the history of the federal government's involvement in housing—through financial assistance to producers and occupants, direct production, tax incentives, insurance and credit programs, specialized thrift institutions, and neighborhood revitalization programs—was one of expanding responsibility. Especially during the 1970s, federal housing programs supported massive production of low-income housing.

Housing policy shifted dramatically in the 1980s as the federal government withdrew its commitment to housing by eliminating or substantially reducing funding for a broad cross section of programs. Federal authorizations for housing dropped 80 percent between 1980 and 1988 (see Figure 12-1). According to the 1987 American Housing Survey, only about one-third of the households with income at or below the poverty threshold received housing assistance in 1987.[2]

Because of the size of the federal deficit, little money will likely be available for new or expanded federal housing programs during the 1990s. This likelihood is significant because it means that the burden of ensuring an adequate supply of low-income housing must come from states, local governments, or private sources, which is often more difficult politically. The federal government has a distinct ability to redistribute resources effectively. States and localities can draw only from within their own boundaries, and, as An-

FIGURE 12-1
FEDERAL SPENDING FOR HOUSING, 1976 TO 1989 (Billions of Dollars)

Year	Appropriations	Outlays
1976	$19.5	$ 3.2
1977	28.6	3.0
1978	32.3	3.7
1979	24.8	4.4
1980	27.9	5.6
1981	26.9	7.8
1982	14.6	8.7
1983	10.5	10.0
1984	12.7	11.3
1985	26.9	25.3
1986	11.6	12.9
1987	9.9	12.7
1988	9.7	13.9
1989 (estimate)	10.0	15.3

Note: Actual outlays were not reduced during the 1980s despite the reduction in appropriations, as funds appropriated each year are spent over five- to 20-year periods. The number of five-year housing vouchers actually increased, while the number of long-term vouchers decreased, in the 1980s. *Source:* Paul A. Leonard, Cushing N. Dolbeare, and Edward B. Lazere, *A Place to Call Home: The Crisis in Housing for the Poor* (Washington, D.C.: Center on Budget and Policy Priorities and the Low-Income Housing Information Service, 1989), p. 32.

thony Downs of the Brookings Institution observed, "If local jurisdictions tax the rich to serve the poor, the rich can—and often do—move elsewhere."

Some states and local governments have proved willing and at least partially able to accept responsibility for meeting the challenge of providing low-income housing, but others have not.

The Shrinking Supply

After 40 years of steadily increasing rates of homeownership, the proportion of households that own their own homes has been dropping since 1980, placing greater pressure on the stock of low-cost rental housing. At the same time that fewer families can afford to purchase houses, fewer new affordable rental housing units are being built, despite increasing demand. The Tax Reform Act of 1986 eliminated or reduced many of the tax incentives for private for-profit developers to produce market-rate multifamily rental housing. Tax reform provided for lowered marginal tax rates, longer depreciable lives for real estate assets, the repeal of accelerated depreciation, limitations on passive losses associated with real estate, and increased tax rates on capital gains.[3] As a result, the rental housing that was produced during the 1980s was targeted to more affluent markets. Certain local regulatory measures, notably rent controls, also constrain the supply of lower-cost, market-rate rental housing and "reduce the long-run accessibility of the limited stock of rental housing to low-income households."[4] As a result, consumers are bidding up the price of existing rental units.

In addition, vacancy rates for public housing are at an all-time low (3 percent, compared to 15 percent 20 years ago), and many public housing projects are in poor physical condition and need repairs that could cost a combined total of $21.5 billion.[5]

Preservation of the existing stock of low-income housing is also an issue. The federal government's commitments to provide rental subsidies (Section 8 certificates or housing vouchers) for nearly 1 million units under existing programs will expire between 1990 and 1995—unless those contracts are renewed or continued in some form. Under other programs,[6] private developers of housing built with federal mortgage subsidies may prepay the mortgages after 20 years and convert the units to market-rate residences or other uses. The 20-year period will expire for 243,000 units beginning in the early 1990s. Unless some action is taken, many of these units may drop out of the low-income housing stock, and their occupants will find themselves competing with the swelling ranks of the poor for scarce market-rate affordable shelter.[7]

Existing low-cost housing is deteriorating rapidly in many neighborhoods. As competition for developable land increases, property owners are demolishing existing low-income housing projects or converting them to other uses. According to the 1988 report of the National Housing Task Force, demolition and conversion removed approx-imately 4.5 million units from the housing stock between 1973 and 1983.[8]

Increasing Demand

At the same time that the size of the low-income housing stock has declined, the number of poor households needing such housing is substantial, particularly among the young and among single-parent families. These lower-income households are caught in a squeeze, unable to purchase houses yet paying an increasingly large share of their incomes for rent.

Reports on the extent of the problem vary, but all point to the growing inability of poor renters to find affordable shelter. According to a 1989 report based on 1985 American Housing Survey data, 45 percent of all poor renter households—a total of over 3 million households—paid at least 70 percent of their income for rent and utilities in 1985, and two-thirds of all poor renter households paid at least 50 percent of their income for shelter. Five out of six paid more than 30 percent of their income for housing.[9]

Other aspects of the problem are evident in overcrowding and occupancy of substandard housing. The most dramatic and visible manifestation of this problem, however, is the growing number of homeless individuals and families lining the streets of every major U.S. city.

Public Policy Issues

Several key policy issues must be addressed in formulating a response to the extensive, complex, and difficult problems associated with affordable housing. Most of them envision cooperation with or a response from private sector developers.

Achieving a Consensus for Action

The first issue is how to achieve consensus regarding the nature of the problem and the means of approaching it. As mentioned, the majority of well-housed U.S. citizens generally do not perceive housing as a serious issue. To begin, the problem must be recognized and its key components and priority needs agreed to. And the questions of whether and to what extent the public has a responsibility to provide

San Diego's Sara Francis Hometel is one of several new single-room occupancy (SRO) hotels encouraged by the city as a result of the loss of SRO housing stock brought about by downtown redevelopment. A private, for-profit development by the Reichbart Family, the project benefited from revised codes and regulations enacted by the city to make construction of SRO housing feasible.

housing for those who cannot compete in the marketplace must be answered. Housing has never been considered an entitlement—a good or service that one automatically receives if eligible—and resources are always limited. These problems are not unique. "No country—advanced or developing, capitalist or socialist—is without housing dilemmas. Shelter resources are rationed either by price or by queue and, if the latter, are usually regulated by a thick web of administrative rules. Housing dissatisfactions are nearly universal and severe hardships are pervasive."[10]

Allocating Scarce Resources

Given that resources are scarce and will always be inadequate to "solve" this problem, decisions must be made on how available funds should be allocated to provide assistance. Who should receive assistance, how much, and in what form? What are reasonable goals? Should few households be provided with sufficient resources, or should the same dollar amount be stretched or leveraged to reach a greater number of households with smaller subsidies?

Once direction has been established, mechanisms must be chosen that could be used to achieve the stated goals: subsidies for new construction, rehabilitation, or occupancy; rental programs or homeownership programs; direct assistance, tax incentives, or credit enhancements. Each has certain advantages and disadvantages, and policy makers must choose the mix of mechanisms that best fulfills their objectives.

Roles and Responsibilities

What are the appropriate roles for the federal, state, local, and private sector actors? How and to what extent should the poor be empowered to decide for themselves how their needs should best be met? Who represents the interests of "the poor"? Within these broad categories of actors, who should be involved, and how can that participation be encouraged, sustained, and coordinated?

Related Issues

In addition to the components of the problem outlined above, several related issues must be addressed in developing a housing policy:

- *Maximization of financial resources.* We must identify, generate, and/or tap additional sources of funding and find ways to leverage available funds. We must find the means to streamline and simplify the financing of low-income housing so that an efficient and replicable delivery system can be established. In this context, funding must be more predictable to enable long-range planning.
- *Supporting physical and social services.* In impoverished neighborhoods without supportive services and programs for revitalization, physical shelter deteriorates rapidly and does little to improve the lives

of the poor. Related issues, such as inadequate income, education, job training, drug counseling, security, and medical and social services, must be addressed if goals for housing are to succeed.

- *Populations with special needs.* Certain population groups—the elderly, the disabled, single-parent households, rural households, the homeless—have special needs that cannot be adequately met by policies and programs designed for more typical populations.

- *Preservation of low-income housing.* Once constructed and operating, how can low-income housing be preserved to ensure its long-term affordability and to avoid the pattern of rapid deterioration and decay? Where will funds for operation and maintenance come from? How can commitments to long-term affordability best be ensured?

- *Responsiveness versus efficiency.* How can the tension between the need for local solutions and responsiveness to social goals and the need for systemization and efficient production be resolved?

- *Subsidies for middle- and upper-income* owners. As many advocates of low-income housing point out, the groups receiving the largest federal subsidy are middle- and upper-income homeowners—through the income tax deduction for home mortgages. Whether this benefit is in fact a "subsidy" and whether or to what extent it should be continued will likely be part of the housing policy debate in the 1990s.

State and Local Government Activities[11]

While not all states and localities have yet risen to the challenge of devising or identifying resources for housing needs, the range of responses to date demonstrates determination, creativity, and success in tapping into existing resources and/or creating new ones. Some states, such as California and Florida, require local governments to include provisions for affordable housing in the housing elements of their comprehensive plans. Massachusetts has an "antisnob" zoning law that enables the state to override local zoning to

This large Victorian house in Gaithersburg, Maryland, outside Washington, D.C., was renovated and restored in a cooperative public/private effort. The Wells-Robertson House now functions as a 14-bed transitional shelter for homeless individuals who are recovering from alcohol and substance abuse.

254

ensure that affordable housing projects are not arbitrarily denied development approvals. Localities in New Jersey are required to take positive action to assume their responsibility for providing a "fair share" of affordable housing.

State housing finance agencies have long been active in a variety of mortgage finance and housing programs, particularly through the issuance of tax-exempt bonds (see Figure 12-2). Because the 1986 tax act curtailed tax incentives for real estate in-

---

FIGURE 12-2
TAX-EXEMPT BOND FINANCING

Tax-exempt bonds issued by state or local governments have helped finance the development of low-income housing directly or indirectly. Issuers sell bonds to investors whose income from such investments is exempt from federal income taxes. Consequently, issuers can market the bonds at lower-than-conventional interest rates. Issuers usually seek a bond rating from one of the rating agencies (Standard & Poor's or Moody's, for example), thereby enabling them to pay the lowest possible interest. They might also use some form of credit enhancement to keep interest rates low. For example, the bond issue could be secured by either a letter of credit or bond insurance. A letter of credit gives the bonds the same rating as the bank issuing the letter.

The Tax Reform Act of 1986 restricts the range of private uses eligible for tax-exempt funding and reduces the annual volume of bonds that may be issued for the remaining permitted uses. Most private-purpose bonds, including bonds for ownership and rental housing, are subject to uniform state-by-state volume ceilings equal to the greater of $50 per resident or $150 million.

Projects financed with tax-exempt bonds that use low-income housing tax credits are not subject to the cap on volume for tax credits. Instead, tax-exempt financing is subject to its own cap—the "private activity bond volume cap." Thus, a 4 percent tax credit is available for qualified expenditures on low-income units financed with tax-exempt bonds.

Under the Tax Reform Act of 1986, public agencies can issue a new class

Atlanta's Urban Residential Finance Authority provided tax-exempt bond issue mortgage funds to condominium buyers, helping make Siena at Renaissance Park more affordable than comparable in-town apartments.

of tax-exempt bond if a Section 501(c)(3) tax-exempt entity uses the proceeds for its exempt purposes and complies with other restrictions. Such an organization can use the proceeds of the bonds to develop housing that it will own. The bonds are not subject to the cap on volume applicable to most multifamily bonds. Each Section 501(c)(3) organization can use up to $150 million issued on its behalf. The bonds tend to sell at an interest rate that is about 25 basis points lower than other tax-exempt bonds, as interest on the bonds is not subject to the alternate minimum tax. One potential disadvantage of these bonds, however, is that the nonprofit entity cannot form a limited partnership to syndicate the project and sell low-income housing tax credits to investors. Syndication would violate the rule that requires the benefiting project to be owned by a Section 501(c)(3) organization.

Source: Diane R. Suchman et al., *Public/Private Housing Partnerships* (Washington, D.C.: ULI–the Urban Land Institute, 1990), p. 15.

vestments and restricted tax-exempt bond financing for private purposes, states have started to experiment with a variety of programs and techniques:

- Off-budget funding vehicles, such as housing trust funds, for the production of housing and to assist occupants (see Figure 12-3);
- Creative financing techniques;
- State tax credit programs, such as California's and Connecticut's programs that piggyback on the federal tax credit;
- Programs to rehabilitate and retain existing housing;
- Programs to help first-time buyers purchase houses;
- Revised building codes and housing standards to reduce costs and to facilitate production;
- Programs targeted to special groups;
- Simplified procedures, requirements, and delivery systems for the production of subsidized housing;
- Incentives and programs to encourage the private production of low- and

moderate-income rental and for-sale housing. Massachusetts has a program (SHARP), for example, that allows participants to write down interest on Massachusetts Housing Finance Agency mortgages to 5 percent for mixed-income rental housing.

LOW-INCOME HOUSING

The Definition of Low Income

"Low income" is generally defined according to criteria used in determining whether a household is eligible for government housing assistance. In most cases, according to the U.S. Department of Housing and Urban Development:

- A four-person household with an income no more than 50 percent of the local area median household income is considered "very low income";
- A four-person household with an income from 50 percent to 80 percent of the local

---

FIGURE 12-3
HOUSING TRUST FUNDS

Trust funds are characterized by a permanent endowment dedicated to the investment of capital assets in housing. A trust fund's endowment may be capitalized by one-time contributions or by annually renewable sources of revenue. Revenue sources may come from a wide range of both publicly and privately controlled funds. Publicly controlled funds, for example, include surplus bond reserve funds, mortgage recordation or real estate conveyance fees, revenues from the extraction of natural resources (severance taxes), appropriations, tax increments, and so on. Privately controlled funds include interest earned on real estate escrow deposits, security deposits from tenants, mortgage escrow deposits, and private sector contributions to trust fund endowments. Trust funds established by one-time allocations of funds provide for loans from their endowments or grants from the

endowments' investment earnings. Those capitalized by annually renewable revenues can afford to grant or lend funds from the trust's principal.

Trust funds for housing provide several valuable functions for states and cities. First, they represent sources of scarce dollars for subsidies, the critical element in capital investment in low-income housing. Second, they enable all parties in the development enterprise—lenders, developers, states, and cities—to enjoy long-term financial commitments. Such commitments remain insulated from the vagaries of annual budget battles, are predictable, and represent the long-term commitments necessary for housing development.

Source: Diane R. Suchman et al., *Public/Private Housing Partnerships* (Washington, D.C.: ULI– the Urban Land Institute, 1990), p. 15.

area median family income is considered "low income"; and

- A four-person household with an income 80 percent to 120 percent of the local area median income is considered "moderate income."

(The percentages vary somewhat along with variations in family size.) Because the local area median income is the standard for comparison, a household with a fixed income could fall within different defined categories of income in different areas of the country. And using a standard of "relative deprivation" ensures that a certain proportion of households will always, by definition, fall into each of the designated categories. Generally speaking, however, low-income and very-low-income households cannot compete effectively for market-rate housing, and in many locations in the Northeast, on the West Coast, and in Hawaii, it is true also for moderate-income households.

HUD's definition of low income is not generally as low as another common measure of economic deprivation—the "poverty line" as defined by the Census Bureau, based on a household's ability to purchase a hypothetical "market basket" of goods and services. The income ceiling for HUD's very-low-income household averages about two-thirds higher than the poverty line. (The poverty line is used to determine eligibility for certain kinds of government assistance other than housing.)

These measures do not, however, take into consideration two other aspects of a household's financial situation: 1) ownership of assets and equity in one's home (which may be significant in some groups, such as the elderly); and 2) government assistance, such as food stamps, medicare, and housing assistance (although Aid to Families with Dependent Children is taken into account when calculating income).

The Nature and Extent Of the Problem[12]

Over time, housing has become much more expensive relative to other goods. Since the 1890s, the costs to produce and maintain a housing unit have risen more than twice as fast as the cost of other consumer goods and services. Rising housing costs have also outpaced increases in incomes in general and disposable incomes in particular. That trend is at the crux of what has come to be known as "the affordability problem," which has replaced physical deficiencies as the leading indicator of unmet housing needs.[13]

Though housing supply and demand are influenced by many factors and vary from location to location, the national pattern—and especially in growing metropolitan areas—is that lower-cost housing has become increasingly scarce. Various circumstances affecting both the supply and demand sides of the equation have converged to create a serious shortage of low-income housing in particular. On the supply side, poor households seeking housing today face an ever-tightening squeeze caused by high purchase prices, increasing competition for affordable rental housing, and a diminishing supply of subsidized housing.

Current Efforts to Assist Low-Income Households Obtain Affordable Housing

Federal Government Activities

The federal government has played a variety of roles in encouraging and supporting low-income housing in the past. Though some federal programs that assist the production and operation of low-income housing have lapsed, several are still somewhat active. The most significant federal activities in support of housing are:

- Subsidies for occupants, primarily housing vouchers, to enable the poor to pay for subsidized and/or market-rate housing;
- Locally allocated Community Development Block Grants;[14]
- Low-income housing tax credits to encourage private investment in low-income housing, which was authorized in the Tax Reform Act of 1986 (see Figure 12-4);
- The Historic Properties/Older Buildings Tax Credit, which, though amended by the Tax Reform Act of 1986, still exists and may be used in producing low-income housing;
- Supportive housing finance programs and institutions, such as the Federal National Mortgage Association (Fannie

---

FIGURE 12-4

LOW-INCOME HOUSING TAX CREDITS

To encourage production of low-income housing, Congress, in the Tax Reform Act of 1986, authorized a credit for investments in mixed- or low-income rental housing. The low-income housing tax credit replaces earlier federal tax incentives for low-income housing that provided accelerated depreciation rates, shorter useful lives, five-year amortization of expenses for rehabilitation, and a full write-off of interest and taxes during the construction period. The tax credit offers investors one of two levels of benefit. It returns, over a 10-year period, either 70 percent or 30 percent of the costs (present value) of the investments in qualifying units. The size of the credit is fixed at the time the property is placed in service and is based on an average of federal interest rates. For properties placed in service in 1987, the percentages of the credit were fixed at 9 percent and 4 percent, respectively. A project using the 9 percent credit will receive a tax credit equal to 9 percent of the cost of developing qualified low-income units. Investors receive credits annually for 10 years. In terms of present value, the credit would equal about 70 percent of such costs. Use of the credit is generally limited to properties placed in service after 1986 and before 1991.

The regulations governing use of the credit are complex and discouraged early experimentation with its application. It has, however, proved an incentive for corporate investment in low-income housing that would not have occurred otherwise.

According to the National Council of State Housing Agencies, approximately 124,500 units of low-income housing and an overall total of 133,840 units of housing were developed in 1989 using the low-income housing tax credit. Since the credit's enactment in 1986, about 235,900 low-income rental units have been developed, rehabilitated, or acquired by applying the incentive.

The tax credit was scheduled to expire at the end of 1989 amid growing debate over the consequences of lost taxes as a result of its use but was extended through 1990 with nine months of credit authority. As of this writing, another extension of the tax credit has been proposed but not yet subjected to a vote.

Source: Diane R. Suchman et al., *Public/Private Housing Partnerships* (Washington, D.C.: ULI–the Urban Land Institute, 1990), p. 14.

Mae), the Federal Home Loan Mortgage Corporation (Freddie Mac), and the Government National Mortgage Association (Ginnie Mae) secondary mortgage markets; the Federal Housing Administration (FHA) and Veterans Administration (VA) mortgage insurance programs; and Farmers' Home Administration (FmHA) subsidies for rural housing programs; and
- Public housing.

State and Local Activities

State administration of federal programs has enabled state agencies to develop a sound base of experience. In fact,

many state programs are modeled after now-unfunded federal initiatives, such as Massachusetts's Community Development Action Grant (CDAG) program, modeled after the now-unfunded federal UDAG program. CDAG helps finance site improvements in distressed areas, thereby making housing and economic development projects feasible.[15]

Local governments have been experimenting with many other creative approaches tailored to community resources and opportunities:
- Using real estate taxes and new sources of revenue (such as fees on new developments and community loan funds) as well

258

as tax-exempt or taxable bond financing to support low-income housing;

- Donating or otherwise making available surplus publicly owned land at low cost or through land lease arrangements;
- Using linkage programs or regulations that require contributions for the development of low-income housing to obtain approvals for other types of development (see Figure 12-5);
- Using inclusionary zoning or requirements to include a set percentage of housing units for low-income households in new market-rate communities, often with the "sweetener" of a density bonus;
- Providing credit enhancements like mortgage insurance, letters of credit, or funding reserves that reduce risks and make investment in low-income housing more secure for private developers or investors and often make possible lower interest rates;
- Using local housing vouchers, as in Pennsylvania and Maryland;
- Employing land use concessions and flexible zoning provisions, subdivision ordinances, density allowances, building code requirements, and waivers or reductions of fees—thereby adding value to a project;
- Fast-tracking the approval process, saving developers time and money;
- Using funds creatively, such as San Francisco's use of linkage payments to fund loan origination fees;
- Forgiving or abating taxes;
- Allocating funds repaid for UDAGs to low-income housing.[16]

The types and levels of financial resources available locally vary tremendously from one jurisdiction to another for reasons that include the extent of local experience in the production of low-income housing, state and local statutes limiting the amount of capital that governments can raise, the depth of the existing tax base, and the relationship of the city or county to quasi-public authorities like housing finance agencies, local housing authorities, and school districts.

Private Sector Participants

Private sector participants include various actors—nonprofit and for-profit developers, banks and other lending institutions or organizations (such as trade unions, insurance companies, and pension funds), intermediary organizations, foundations, and other philanthropic groups. The anticipated users of low-income housing are also participants in the process, though to what extent varies from place to place and often from project to project.

Private development entities typically produce and often manage low-income housing. In some cases, for-profit private developers develop low-income housing, either exclusively or in conjunction with other, market-rate developments through linkage programs or in fulfillment of requirements for inclusionary zoning. Because of their entrepreneurial approach, for-profit developers are generally efficient and capable housing producers, but they require incentives sufficient to enable them to remain in business and to make at least a minimal profit. In today's environment, incentives for for-profit developers are not often available, and some housing markets are not strong enough for linkage or inclusionary zoning programs to operate effectively. For this reason, as well as for the current preference for grass-roots, "bottom-up" decision making and implementation, governments and private funders are increasingly looking to nonprofit developers to produce low-income housing.

Nonprofit community-based developers typically know and understand firsthand their communities' needs and resources, and they generally have a strong local political base and the community's support. They tend to be accountable to the community and show a long-term commitment to low-income housing. According to Neil Mayer of Berkeley, California's, Office of Economic Development, neighborhood-based organizations "need not be cajoled into choosing troubled neighborhoods in which to pursue their efforts." They are less likely to displace current residents, and they are more likely to involve neighborhood people in their work.[17] They also have an advantage in seeking certain charitable and public funds. Such groups, however, often have small, overworked staffs with limited experience or technical capability, especially in the areas of financial feasibility analysis and financial packaging.

259

FIGURE 12-5
HOUSING LINKAGE PROGRAMS

Linkage programs are designed to offset the impact that employment has on the need for housing within a community. Some communities that have constrained the housing market have found it necessary to require new industrial, commercial, and office development to aid in the development of housing. In a mandatory linkage program, a nonresidential project's approval is conditioned on the applicant's directly providing market-rate and/or affordable housing or paying in-lieu fees for housing. Development standards can also be part of a linkage program. Linkage programs with land use incentives, such as density bonuses and allowances for shared and reduced parking, can encourage residential development. Cities experiencing large-scale employment growth can use linkage programs to mitigate the impact of new jobs on the local housing market of the community as a whole. This mitigation is especially significant in communities where housing prices are unaffordable or unattainable to most workers in the proposed development. And providing residential housing on site with employment can reduce traffic.

Linkage as a concept has certain political attractions, calling as it does for taking from the apparently rich and giving to the patently poor. Economic realities, however, have raised obstacles in several communities where linkage programs have been considered. The chief complaint against linkage is its potential dampening effect on downtown economies in cities otherwise committed to revitalizing their business districts—which may explain why an idea that had considerable sizzle just a few years ago may fizzle in most communities.

EXAMPLES OF HOUSING LINKAGE PROGRAMS
(Excluding inclusionary housing requirements for residential buildings)

City	Date Adopted	Area and Uses Where Applicable	Fee Requirement (or Equivalent Production Commitment)	Results in 1988
Palo Alto, California	1979	All buildings over 20,000 square feet	$2.69 per square foot over 20,000 square feet (mandatory)	Payments of $2.4 million, which have assisted production of 200 units
San Francisco, California	1980	Downtown office buildings over 25,000 square feet	$5.69 per square foot over 25,000 square feet (mandatory)	Commitments of $29.7 million, which have assisted production of 4,026 new units and 1,664 rehabilitated units
Boston, Massachusetts	1983	Office, retail, institutional buildings over 100,000 square feet anywhere in the city	$5.00 per square foot over 100,000 square feet paid over seven years if in downtown, 12 years if in neighborhood (mandatory)	Commitments of $45 million, which have assisted production of over 2,000 units
Jersey City, New Jersey	1985	All commercial buildings	About one unit for each 2,595 square feet (based on formula) (mandatory)	Commitments of $9 million and direct development of 704 units

FIGURE 12-5 (continued)

City	Date Adopted	Area and Uses Where Applicable	Fee Requirement (or Equivalent Production Commitment)	Results in 1988
Santa Monica, California	1986	All office buildings over 15,000 square feet	$2.25 per square foot up to 15,000 square feet and $5.00 per square foot over 15,000 square feet (mandatory)	Commitments of $400,000 plus production of about 150 units negotiated before present program
Menlo Park, California	1988	All commercial buildings over 10,000 square feet	$1.33 per square foot over 10,000 square feet or (for lower-intensity uses) $.53 per square foot (mandatory)	None
Cambridge, Massachusetts	1988	All buildings developed under special permits in three defined districts	$2.00 per square foot over 30,000 square feet (mandatory)	None
Miami, Florida	1983	Office buildings in defined downtown districts	Optional zoning density bonus: $4.00 per bonus square foot	Contributions of $700,000, unexpended
Seattle, Washington	1984	Downtown office buildings	Optional zoning density bonus; $15.30 per bonus square foot in core, $10.00 in expansion district	Production of 274 units
Hartford, Connecticut	1984	Downtown commercial buildings	Optional zoning density bonus; $15.00 per bonus square foot	Commitments of $400,000 and direct development of 90 units

Sources: Local Housing Element Assistance Project, *Blueprint for Bay Area Housing* (San Francisco: Association of Bay Area Governments and Bay Area Council, 1989), p. 51; and Douglas R. Porter and Terry Jill Lassar, "The Latest on Linkage," *Urban Land*, December 1988, p. 9.

The other private sector participants, spurred in part by the requirements of the Community Reinvestment Act,[18] are primarily involved in financing low-income housing. Banks, insurance companies, and pension funds (see Figure 12-6) may provide for the development of low-income housing. In addition, some private organizations have created special programs that set aside funds for low-income housing projects, while several insurance companies have initiated social investment programs that provide limited amounts of specially targeted funds for low-income housing.

Some banks, following the lead of Chicago's South Shore Bank, aggregate and hold funds from individuals, government agencies, and foundations in low- and no-interest accounts. These "linked deposits" are earmarked for investment in community development projects. Because the South Shore Bank is federally chartered, depositors assume no risk, and the federal government insures deposits up to $100,000.

Intermediaries are organizations that exist to raise and distribute funds and to provide various kinds of technical support for (usually nonprofit) developers of low-income housing. Intermediaries can include public/private housing partnerships, such as the Boston Housing Partnership or the Cleveland Housing Network, that operate locally to support nonprofit community-

---

FIGURE 12-6
CONSORTIA OF LENDERS

Lending consortia are separate lending entities established and controlled by a group of banks or other lending organizations with the intent and ability to make loans specifically for low-income housing. They allow participating lenders to finance a greater volume of such housing more efficiently than would be possible if each entity were to act individually. Lending consortia offer several advantages over the participation of individual lenders in the production of low-income housing.

- They simplify, facilitate, and coordinate the lending process for individual participants. Because their only business is to finance low-income housing, staffs are knowledgeable and efficient in managing the distinctive aspects of the projects and programs involved—without taking time and resources from the lenders' usual business.
- They provide a focal point through which participating lenders can work with government to establish and use programs that coordinate with private lenders to enable production of low-income housing.
- They enable participants to share risks.

To be credible with both public officials and borrowers, a lending consortium must have the ability and capital to make loans in its own name. The individuals representing the participating lenders must be of sufficient stature to make decisions, approve loans, and commit funds. To be effective, a consortium must operate where a local consensus for and commitment to encouraging the production of low-income housing exist.

A consortium typically limits the types and locations of projects it will support, at least until its procedures and credibility are well established. In making loans for low-income housing, lending consortia need not as a rule offer below-market loans or relax underwriting criteria, such as loan-to-value coverage. According to the Community Preservation Corporation in New York City, "Affordable housing cannot be seen as a charity endeavor. In most lending regions, hundreds of millions of mortgage dollars are needed to produce enough low-income housing. Exceptional treatment will never generate [it]. The resources—public and private—that produce it must be structured to make it a normal business transaction."

The value of a lending consortium lies in its ability to identify weaknesses in the economics of producing low-income housing in a given locality. It can advise governments on the types of programs or assistance that could help remedy those weaknesses and make projects financially feasible. Government actions might include relaxing rent restrictions on subsidized housing, allocating or providing rental subsidies and programs that offer below-market interest rates for a portion of the development costs, or providing mortgage insurance.

If successful, lending consortia have the potential to help produce significant amounts of low-income housing and to encourage other lenders, by example, to invest in such projects as well. The Community Preservation Corporation, for example, furnished over $450 million in mortgages for more than 22,500 units between 1974 and 1990 with virtually no defaults. It is the model for similar efforts in Chicago, San Francisco, and other cities.

Source: John McCarthy, "Lender Consortia for Affordable Housing," *Real Estate Finance Journal,* Spring 1989, pp. 61–68.

Intermediaries like the Cleveland Housing Network assist in the production of low-income housing, such as these renovated structures targeted to households earning $10,000 per year or less.

based developers. They might also include private national organizations, such as the Local Initiatives Support Corporation—a national nonprofit corporation created in 1980 by the Ford Foundation—or the Enterprise Foundation—established by developer James Rouse in 1982 (see Figure 12-7).

A third national intermediary of note is the Neighborhood Reinvestment Corporation (NRC), a congressionally chartered public nonprofit corporation formed in 1978 to revitalize deteriorating urban neighborhoods and promote affordable housing. NRC's Neighborhood Housing Services (NHS) program—which involves local residents, business leaders, and governments—and 239 other local partnerships together form the NeighborWorks system and receive small grants of seed money from NRC. One of NHS's most important

contributions to spurring the production of low-income housing was the creation of its Local Government Secondary Market. Designed to recycle local government loans that private lenders consider "unbankable" mortgages, the Local Government Secondary Market enables the provision of loans to low-income borrowers who cannot satisfy standard underwriting criteria.[19]

Corporations assist the development of low-income housing by investing in equity funds. They also make direct contributions to developers or housing partnerships specializing in low-income housing, indirect contributions to intermediary organizations, and in-kind donations of goods, property, and expert time. Corporations and other large employers might also have special programs designed to assist their employees in obtaining housing in expensive localities. These "employer-assisted housing programs," designed to enable employees to live near their jobs, could take the form of assistance with the down payment, low-interest mortgages, equity sharing, rent subsidies, or contributions to

---

FIGURE 12-7

THE ENTERPRISE FOUNDATION

The Enterprise Foundation, a non-profit, publicly supported charitable foundation created in 1982, facilitates the development of low-income housing in the United States through a variety of initiatives, programs, and activities carried out on its own and with its subsidiaries. In particular, it creates and supports public/private housing partnerships.

The foundation's activities are funded by its own for-profit subsidiary, the Enterprise Development Company, as well as by public and private contributions. More than 100 local nonprofit housing groups are part of the Enterprise Network. Together, the groups secured financial commitments for over 8,000 new or rehabilitated units between 1982 and 1989, all of which are either completed or under construction.

The Enterprise Social Investment Corporation (ESIC), a wholly owned for-profit subsidiary of the foundation, provides financial assistance to local community development organizations. Created in 1984, ESIC identifies and develops new sources of financing for low-income housing. It structures financing for projects that are typically managed and controlled by a nonprofit general partner and arranges complex financing packages that include corporate contributions, equity participation, foundation funds, federal subsidies, and money from local lenders, often resulting in the successful financing of high-risk projects that would otherwise remain unrealized. Since its inception, ESIC has helped to produce over 5,000 units of low-income housing and has packaged over $118 million in tax credits or equity financing of low-income housing. ESIC also acts as a developer of low-income housing through its subsidiary, the Enterprise Construction Corporation. ESIC's Enterprise Loan Fund has raised over

$6 million at 3 percent interest from over 400 lenders.

The Enterprise Foundation's Rehab Work Group encourages "selective rehabilitation"—cost-conscious redevelopment that calls for repair rather than replacement and methods and materials at least cost. The group has undertaken demonstration projects throughout the United States and, in some cases, has reduced costs of rehabilitation by as much as 30 percent when compared to similar, locally sponsored projects. The Rehab Work Group has also advised HUD on the application of cost-cutting measures to the rehabilitation of public housing and has published a manual on cutting costs for general distribution.

In recognizing that other approaches like job training are needed to break the cycle of poverty, the Enterprise Foundation expanded its mission in 1984 with the Enterprise Job Placement Network, which now consists of 18 job placement centers in 14 cities. The central office of Enterprise Jobs provides ongoing training and technical assistance to its national network, which is responsible for over 3,500 placements per year. The network has placed people in over 16,500 jobs since its inception. Its sources of funding include the Allstate Foundation and other private sources as well as local and federal government funds.

The Enterprise Foundation also advises local, state, and federal governments on the creation of finance and tax programs for new housing to encourage the development of low-income housing. The foundation played a major role in drafting provisions for low-income housing tax credits in the 1986 tax reform bill.

Source: The Enterprise Foundation, *1989 Annual Report* (Columbia, Md.: Author, 1990).

The historic rehabilitation of this Renaissance Revival–style building—the Paddock Kensington in Beatrice, Nebraska—was financed through the use of historic and low-income tax credits. To qualify for the credits, low-income housing must be maintained for 15 years. This senior-care facility was developed by the Westin Financial Group.

local communities' efforts to develop affordable housing.

Foundations invest in low-income housing developments through such vehicles as program-related investments (PRIs).[20] They have also been the chief supporters of intermediary organizations, including many local housing partnerships. Finally, foundations provide grant money directly to nonprofit, community-based housing developers or to housing partnerships.

Limitations on Financing

The essence of the problem of financing low-income housing is the need to fill the "affordability gap"—the difference between what shelter costs and what a family can afford to pay (see Figure 12-8). The size of the gap and thus the magnitude of the problem vary with the locality.

Financing low-income housing is complicated by the fact that no single source of subsidies is available that can

on its own make a project financially feasible. Resources available for financing low-income projects are fragmented and vary according to different types of projects and locations. Projects typically require funds from many sources, and it is not unusual to have seven or eight sources of funds supporting a single project. Funds from one source become the basis for securing commitments for others.

In addition, because each provider of funding has its own social agenda and underwriting criteria, financing arrangements must be flexible enough to respond to the various requirements. The resulting financing packages are time-consuming and expensive to structure and require sophisticated financial expertise. And, because they are tailored to a particular project, time, and place and involve local resources, the financing arrangements are typically unique to the projects they support and therefore not replicable from place to place or even from project to project within the same city.

FIGURE 12-8

UNDERSTANDING THE AFFORDABILITY GAP:
THE ECONOMICS OF A PROTOTYPICAL PROJECT

This information describes the economics of a prototypical 100-unit multifamily rental development containing a mix of very-low-, low-, and moderate-income units. The numbers are for illustration only; in actual cases, costs and incomes may be higher or lower than suggested here.

Assumptions Underlying the Prototype

Number of Units:	100
Median Income in Area (4-person household):	$36,000
Income Mix:	20% at 50% of median
	20% at 80% of median
	60% at 120% of median
Annual Operating Expenses (including taxes but excluding debt service):	$2,200 per unit
Total Development Cost:	$7,500,000 (including land) or $75,000 per unit
Loan Terms:	30-year term at 10% fixed interest

Tenants' Ability to Pay Rent:

Percent of Median	Annual Income	Monthly Income	25 Percent of Monthly Income	Allowance for Utilities	Monthly Income Available for Rent
120	$43,200	$3,600	$900	$75	$825
100	36,000	3,000	750	75	675
80	28,800	2,400	600	75	525
50	18,000	1,500	375	75	300
25	9,000	750	188	75	113

Amount of Loan Supportable with Rents from Project

Rental Payments	Per Month	Per Year
20 units @ 50% of median = 20 × $300	$ 6,000	$ 72,000
20 units @ 80% of median = 20 × $525	10,500	126,000
60 units @ 120% of median = 60 × $825	49,500	594,000
Gross Income Available for Rent	$66,000	$792,000
Less 5% Vacancy		39,600
Less Annual Operating Expenses, Including Taxes		220,000
Net Annual Rent Available for Debt Service		$532,400

The net rent of $532,400 supports a loan of $5,097,748, which is 68 percent of the cost to develop the project. The financing gap—before allowing for debt service coverage—is $2,402,252 for the entire project, or about $24,000 per unit.

Source: Goldfarb & Lipman, *Redevelopment and Affordable Housing: New Requirements and Opportunities* (San Francisco: Author, 1989), pp. 40–45.

AFFORDABLE OWNERSHIP HOUSING

The second aspect of what is commonly termed "the affordability problem" is the increasing inability of households of moderate means—especially young households—to purchase houses. The problem has crept steadily up the income ladder. In addition, the 1980s were a time of rapidly escalating land values in growing metropolitan areas and a time when household incomes began to polarize: the proportion of households with higher incomes and the proportion of households with lower incomes increased, while the proportion in the middle declined.

The Definition of Affordable Ownership Housing

The precise parameters of affordability differ according to conditions in the local housing market, but for purposes of this discussion, "affordable ownership housing" refers to housing units that moderate-income households can purchase, which can be said to occur in a housing market where households in the median income range can afford housing in the median price range. The problem varies by location (see Figure 12-9).

Factors Affecting Prices for Land and Housing

To understand why housing prices are higher relative to incomes, it is useful to consider the kinds of costs that are involved in producing a house and what variables influence those costs. Although local housing markets, with their many different influences, are notoriously difficult to explain or predict, certain factors commonly affect all housing prices:

- The nature, amount, and price of developable residential land;

Below-market-rate apartment condominiums are one component of Clarewood, a 125-unit development in Westchester County, New York. To illustrate the demand for moderately priced housing, the 40 units in this converted school building sold in one weekend!

267

FIGURE 12-9
AFFORDABILITY OF HOUSING IN SELECTED METROPOLITAN AREAS

How to Read This Chart: The affordability index for Boston, for example, shows that in the fourth quarter of 1989, a family earning the median family income of $45,664 had 74.7 percent of the income needed to qualify for a conventional loan covering 80 percent of the median price of $183,000 for an existing single-family house.

Selected Metropolitan Areas by Major Components: Fourth Quarter 1989 (revised)

Metropolitan Area[a]	Median-Priced Existing Single-Family House	Mortgage Rate[b]	Median Family Income	Qualifying Income[c]	Composite Affordability Index
Baltimore	$ 97,600	9.97%	$38,684	$ 32,807	117.9
Boston	183,000	10.09	45,664	61,118	74.7
Chicago	109,300	10.06	36,681	37,019	99.1
Cleveland	74,200	9.96	36,548	24,920	146.7
Dallas	92,200	10.12	43,172	31,385	137.6
Denver	86,800	9.97	40,985	29,177	140.5
Detroit	73,600	10.11	38,775	25,032	154.9
Houston	62,600	9.90	44,033	20,918	210.5
Indianapolis	72,200	10.08	41,055	24,495	167.6
Kansas City	70,900	10.01	36,920	23,913	154.4
Los Angeles	217,000	9.98	35,075	73,003	48.0
Miami/Hialeah	89,000	10.20	30,571	30,498	100.2
Milwaukee	79,700	10.06	38,182	26,994	141.4
Minneapolis/St. Paul	88,300	9.67	44,687	28,933	154.5
New York/Northern New Jersey/Long Island	179,300	10.07	31,127	60,778	51.2
Philadelphia	110,600	9.88	38,627	36,895	104.7
Phoenix	77,500	10.13	36,028	26,403	136.5
Pittsburgh	66,900	10.17	30,436	22,868	133.1
St. Louis	76,900	10.31	38,096	26,914	143.4
San Diego	178,700	9.80	34,620	59,208	58.5
San Francisco Bay Area	260,600	9.84	44,315	86,638	51.1
Washington, D.C.	145,600	9.74	54,463	47,995	113.5

[a]All areas are metropolitan statistical areas as defined by the U.S. Office of Management and Budget. They include the named central city and surrounding areas.

[b]Effective rate on loans closed on existing houses, according to the Office of Thrift Supervision.

[c]Based on current lending requirements of the Federal National Mortgage Association using a 20 percent down payment.

Note: The California Association of Realtors publishes a housing affordability index for areas within the state that differs significantly from these values because it measures the proportion of households that could theoretically afford to purchase the median-priced house rather than the ability of a median-income family to carry the mortgage. Data for Los Angeles, San Diego, and San Francisco are provided for comparison only and are not to replace the currently available measures. The indices are roughly consistent.

Source: National Association of Realtors, *Home Sales* (Washington, D.C.: Author, March 1990), p. 17.

- The nature and volume of current and projected demand for housing;
- Characteristics of individual houses—structural considerations, the physical and social environment where they are located, their location and accessibility, and so on;
- The availability and cost of financing for production (including carrying time, perceived risks, and availability of credit enhancements);
- The availability and cost of financing for purchase (including requirements for down payments, fees, and mortgage terms);
- Costs associated with land development, including preparation of the land, on-site and off-site infrastructure, procedural delays and a complex permitting process, required dedication of some of the land and extra amenities, and fees (impact fees, utility hook-up charges, permit fees, and so on);
- Costs of constructing housing units (labor and materials);
- Marketing costs; and
- Overhead and profit.

Of these factors, the costs associated with the purchase and development of land have risen most rapidly in recent years. They are also the cost components most influenced by local government's policies and regulations.

The Nature of the Problem

In many areas of the country—the Chicago metropolitan area, the New York/New Jersey/Connecticut suburbs, the Boston metropolitan area, and in much of California, for example—the price of an average house has escalated well beyond the means of households with median incomes for the area, resulting in a decline in the rate of homeownership since 1980—the first decline in 40 years. Young households—those aged 25 to 34, historically the age of first-time homebuyers—have been most strongly affected (see Figure 12-10).

The incidence of the problem is uneven, varying considerably among housing markets. While it is therefore difficult to generalize about the nature and extent of the problem, where it exists, three reasons are foremost.

The first reason has to do with *demand*. During the 1980s, the maturing of the baby boomers created a surge in demand for entry-level houses, and decentralization of employment to suburban locations focused increased competition for workers' housing in suburban areas. In addition, the number of households as a proportion of the population increased dramatically during the 1970s and 1980s, as more people remained single well into their adult lives. More households means

FIGURE 12-10
HOMEOWNERSHIP RATES BY AGE OF HOUSEHOLD HEAD
(Percent)

Age	1973	1976	1980	1983	1988
Under 25	23.4	21.0	21.3	19.3	15.5
25–29	43.6	43.2	43.3	38.2	36.2
30–34	60.2	62.4	61.1	55.7	52.6
35–39	68.5	69.0	70.8	65.8	63.2
40–44	72.9	73.9	74.2	74.2	71.4
45–54	76.1	77.4	77.7	77.1	76.0
55–64	75.7	77.2	79.3	80.5	79.6
65–74	71.3	72.7	75.2	76.9	78.2
75 and Over	67.1	67.2	67.8	71.6	70.4
Total	64.4	64.8	65.6	64.9	63.9

Source: William C. Apgar, Jr., Denise DePasquale, Jean Cummings, and Nancy McArdle, *The State of the Nation's Housing: 1990* (Cambridge, Mass.: Joint Center for Housing Studies of MIT and Harvard Univ., 1990), p. 12.

that more housing units are required for a given level of population. Some observers believe that as the baby boomers age and create continuing strong demand for move-up housing, the entry-level housing they vacate will create affordable housing for the next generation of first-time buyers.

The second reason relates to *financing* (including sustained higher real interest rates for all phases of residential development and for home mortgages and requirements for higher down payments). With the enactment of the Financial Institutions Reform, Recovery, and Enforcement Act (FIRREA) in 1989, residential developers face additional concerns, specifically regarding restrictions on the amount of loans that can be obtained for land acquisition and, more generally, on sources of capital for development.

And third, *higher land and land development costs* have affected affordability. Costs have risen as a result of competition among prospective purchasers because of increased demand, speculation, and, particularly, increasing regulatory interventions that add to the costs and risks associated with developing land:

- Rationing building or sewer, water, and utility connection permits;
- Limiting the amount or location of developable land through boundaries on urban limits and by zoning insufficient vacant land for residential use;
- "Exclusionary zoning," or allowing only very-low-density development on residential land;
- Excessive subdivision regulations, such as unnecessarily high standards for grading and drainage, street spacing or width, thickness of the pavement, design of curbs and sidewalks, lighting, utility mains, or other physical improvements to the site;
- Requirements for developers to construct or to pay fees for construction of infrastructure beyond what is required for the specific project;
- Imposition of development fees or exactions in excess of actual costs associated with the new development;
- Complex and time-consuming permitting procedures that increase developers' holding costs and exposure to risk;

- Regulations to protect the environment, such as measures to control air pollution, protection of water supplies, limitations on the demand for water, protection of wetlands and endangered species, and management and removal of toxic wastes.[21]

Increased construction costs are also a factor in the rising cost of homeownership. Practices that can contribute to increased construction costs include restrictions on building design or materials used in construction through building codes or zoning ordinances. Individual dwellings are affected by specifications of limits on height, setbacks, and coverage of a site, and specifications for construction materials or standards that are unnecessarily restrictive when other, less expensive alternatives would suffice. In addition, requirements to use union labor may also add to the cost of dwelling units.

Issues

All of these regulations are enacted to serve legitimate public purposes, such as protecting health and safety, and the regulatory environment typically reflects a community's values and preferences. The number, type, complexity, and cost of regulations, however, have greatly expanded in recent years as requirements for construction have become more stringent, knowledge of environmental dangers has increased, and energy conservation has become more important.

"Excessive" regulations may have side effects that are undesirable to the communities they exist to serve. One undesirable, though possibly not unintentional, side effect may be exclusion of lower-income households. In addition, restrictive regulations can discourage cost-cutting technological innovations. Overregulation of residential development may encourage lower-density development that creates inefficient land use and transportation. Where low-density development is widespread, dwelling costs tend to be higher and individuals' dependence on automobiles for transportation more common. The results can include high costs for infrastructure, traffic congestion, high levels of energy use, increased air pollution, and shortages of certain categories of (lower-wage) labor.

One of the most pervasive and difficult issues confronted by communities seeking to encourage production and purchase of affordable houses is the lack of political will among leaders and the resistance of affluent neighborhoods to the inclusion of lower-cost housing in their communities. Even though no reductions in property values resulting from inclusion of moderately priced dwellings within expensive neighborhoods have been documented, housing is usually the largest single expenditure for any household, and homeowners are highly motivated to protect and enhance that investment. And people apparently prefer to live among others of similar or higher incomes. Furthermore, especially where housing prices (and property taxes) have risen rapidly, a marked and understandable resistance to higher taxes and a general preference for shifting all the costs associated with new development to the new "users" are apparent. Such politics push up the price of housing.

Encouraging the Production of Affordable Housing

Affording homeownership involves two primary difficulties: making the down payment and meeting the monthly payments. Efforts to increase access to homeownership can focus on one or the other or both by seeking to lower the price of housing.

In addition, various types of credit enhancements—particularly mortgage insurance—affect the lender's exposure to risk and therefore requirements for down payments and mortgage interest rates. Nontraditional mortgage instruments, such as adjustable-rate mortgages (ARMs) or graduated-payment mortgages (GPMs) may make possible lower monthly payments than fixed-rate mortgages would require.

Two federal programs that have been used to facilitate homeownership are mortgage revenue bonds (MRBs) and mortgage credit certificates (MCCs). Both are under review at this writing. MRBs are bonds issued by state and local housing agencies to fund mortgage lending for the purchase of moderately priced houses, typically by households within stated income limits. Mortgage rates to eligible borrowers average two points lower than those on conventional loans. State and local housing finance agencies can elect to use part of their authorization for MRBs to issue MCCs, which enable participating homebuyers to obtain federal tax credits for part of their mortgage costs.

One of the most effective ways to reduce the cost of housing is to reduce the cost of land per unit by allowing higher densities than has been customary. New concepts of lotting have made it possible to develop single-family houses of 1,000 to 2,000 square feet at densities of seven to 10 units per acre. With proper siting, unit design, and landscaping, such houses can be attractive, private, and less expensive than houses on larger lots (see Figure 12-11).

Attached houses—townhouses, duplexes, quadruplexes, and stacked flats—have achieved strong market acceptance in expensive areas and offer a multitude of interesting and attractive designs. Attached houses realize savings by using common walls and common utility lines and in their lower land costs per unit.

Various groups have demonstrated that reductions in the cost of producing housing can be achieved through regulatory reform. Through the Joint Venture for Affordable Housing, HUD and the National Association of Home Builders demonstrated the cost savings that could be realized by updating or eliminating certain regulations affecting residential land development and construction (see Figure 12-12). Working with builders constructing houses ranging from $30,000 to $60,000 in 18 communities nationwide, HUD and NAHB documented cost savings of $855 to $15,647 per unit resulting from regulatory reform. Among the 18 communities, cost savings averaged about 15 percent.

The kinds of regulatory reforms suggested by the Joint Venture for Affordable Housing include:
- Zoning for higher densities;
- Encouraging PUD zoning and clustering of housing units;
- Allowing zero-lot-line zoning;
- Basing subdivision ordinances and requirements for infrastructure on anticipated needs rather than set standards;

FIGURE 12-11
SINGLE-FAMILY HOUSES ON SMALL LOTS

PALOMINO HILL
LAKEWOOD, COLORADO

Palomino Hill is a development of single-family houses on small lots undertaken in the soft Denver housing market of 1986. The development strategy for Palomino Hill was simple: offer well-designed and quality houses that would be larger in size and lower in price than competing products. The anticipated market segment for Palomino Hill was entry-level and move-up buyers seeking affordable housing in the greater Denver metropolitan area.

Site and Approvals

The site of Palomino Hill is located in Lakewood, a suburban community west of Denver. The 8.78-acre infill parcel is served by a major arterial street and is surrounded by an irrigation canal and a city park. Neighboring development includes a grade school, single-family housing, and a townhouse project.

The major constraint in planning was that the density needed for the proj-

The density necessary to build affordable housing presented design challenges at Palomino Hill. Planners and architects created an interesting streetscape by varying lot dimensions, curving streets, staggering setbacks, and varying house designs in this planned unit development.

- Streamlining the entitlement/permitting process;
- Modifying the building code to allow the use of less expensive building materials and more flexible construction standards where possible;

- Waiving fees.

Communities can also enable production of lower-cost housing by promoting alternative building types, such as manufactured housing. Modular housing units have been used successfully, especially on infill

FIGURE 12-11 (continued)

ect to be affordable was six-plus units per acre, which required smaller lots than customary for single-family housing in the area.

Thus, the project was subject to approval as a PUD. The Lakewood Planning Commission, other city officials, and neighboring residents viewed the proposed basic lot size of 50 feet by 90 feet as too small and frowned on the project as a whole. They feared the project would create a streetscape consisting of rows of garage doors. Because the solution was specifically tailored to alleviate this condition, community concerns were successfully addressed, and the small lots were approved.

Planning

The principal goal of planning for the site was to achieve a varied and pleasing streetscape within requirements for density. Although the architect adhered to the average lot dimensions of 50 feet by 90 feet for most of the houses, these dimensions are varied on occasion to achieve maximum flexibility in planning. For example, lots adjacent to public streets were made wider and shallower to allow changes in orientation. Dimensions were also varied so that a maximum number of lots on corners and culs-de-sac could be included in the plan. Curvilinear streets and slightly staggered setbacks were incorporated to further enliven the streetscape.

Architecture

In addition to the maximum yield on density, a project's affordability often relies on a high degree of repetitive de-

sign, which can be aesthetically unappealing in a subdivision with small lots. To counteract this possibility, the architect incorporated a variety of designs with the proposed plans.

So that all plans offered by Palomino Hill could respond to the various lot sizes and orientations, each house is designed for two different front elevations: the first specifies a 50-foot frontage, and an alternate side elevation serving as the front can be used when houses are placed on wider lots, or on lots where orientation is modified, such as those on Garrison Street. Side elevations that face the street are upgraded with additional brick treatment and dormer or recessed windows. Without substantially affecting engineering or construction costs, these minor variations help to animate the streetscape and increase architectural appeal.

Materials and straightforward exterior forms are consistent with the prevalent style of the region, both because affordability demands simplicity and because the developer adhered to the design norms of a highly traditional marketplace. Lively colors differentiate the project from other residential projects in the area, however.

Interiors were designed to appeal to move-up buyers. The 1,109- to 1,959-square-foot houses emphasize baths, master suites, and kitchens with breakfast nooks. Principal living areas are designed with high ceilings, and fireplaces are standard.

Marketing

Price ranges were reasonable for both entry-level and move-up buyers,

sites, to construct inexpensive housing quickly and efficiently. Much of the cost savings comes from standardization, efficient land use and construction, and savings in time, which translates into savings in carrying costs. Building trades generally

oppose modular housing because it requires less on-site labor to construct, and building inspectors may find modular housing complicated to inspect.

Modular housing units are generally 90 percent to 95 percent complete when

FIGURE 12-11 (continued)

and financing was an added inducement. Because the developer owned his own finance company, all buyers were offered financing that was not only more conveniently obtainable but also somewhat less costly than generally available from Denver financial institutions. Palomino Hill enjoyed immediate success: all houses were sold within a year of its opening.

PROJECT DATA

Land Use Information:

Site Area: 8.78 acres
Total Units: 55
Density: 6.27 units per acre
Average Lot Size: 4,500 square feet

Land Use Plan:	Acres	Percent of Space
Open Space	4.83	55%
Buildings	2.20	25
Roads/Parking Area	1.75	20

Unit Information:	Square Feet	Sale Price
2-BR/1-bath/optional master bath/ranch style	1,109	$ 79,250
2-BR/1-bath/optional master bath/optional 3rd BR/3 levels	1,404	$ 88,450
3-BR/2½-bath	1,638–1,644	$ 94,950
3-BR/loft or 4th BR/2½-bath	1,959	$105,450

Economic Information:

Site Value: $385,000 ($7,000 per unit)
Site Improvement Costs: $880,000 ($16,000 per unit)
Construction Costs: $32 per square foot

Developer:

Michael A. Kell
Carmel Homes
950 South Cherry, Suite 1100
Denver, Colorado 80222

Architect:

Michael A. Kephart
Kephart Architects
850 Lincoln
Denver, Colorado 80203

Source: James W. Wentling and Lloyd W. Bookout, eds., *Density by Design* (Washington, D.C.: ULI–the Urban Land Institute, 1988).

delivered to the site. The building foundation is prepared, and sections—modules 12 to 14 feet wide and up to 60 feet long—are connected to the foundation and to one another. Constructed in compliance with state and local codes, modular housing can be constructed as single-family houses, apartments, or stacked flats.

Localities can assist private developers' efforts to produce affordable,

FIGURE 12-12
SUMMARY OF SAVINGS IN JOINT VENTURE FOR AFFORDABLE HOUSING DEMONSTRATION PROJECTS

Place	Total Unit Savings	Administrative and Process Savings	Land Development Savings[a]	Direct Construction Savings	Price Range	Savings Based on Average Price
Blaine, MN	$4,963	$283	$2,680	$2,000	$44,900/48,900	10.6%
Birmingham, AL	4,278	86	4,191	–	51,900/58,900	7.7
Boise, ID	2,119	–	2,119	–	65,000/95,000	2.6
Christian County, KY	8,886	(400)	3,279	6,007	28,000/37,400	27.2
Crittenden County, AR	6,294	–	4,789	1,505	26,885/35,040	20.3
Elkhart County, IN	855	–	855	–	37,500/54,920	1.8
Everett, WA	9,984	1,477	7,089	1,418	64,500/76,500	14.3
Knox County, TN	2,545	443	1,487	615	43,500/55,000	5.2
Lacey, WA	7,396	2,052	3,083	2,261	39,000/62,000	14.6
Lincoln, NE	7,044	1,116	4,953	975	38,450/46,000	16.7
Mesa County, CO	5,257	770	3,174	1,313	39,000/47,500	13.1
Oklahoma City, OK	5,477	181	5,296	–	39,000/57,500	11.4
Phoenix, AZ	8,037	2,198	3,674	2,165	45,000/63,000	14.9
Portland, OR	15,647	2,047	12,387	1,213	50,000/55,000	30.0
Santa Fe, NM	9,140	2,992	3,845	2,303	49,950/61,950	16.3
Sioux Falls, SD	1,640	–	1,640	–	55,000/70,000	2.6
Tulsa, OK	12,469	–	10,390	2,079	47,000/63,000	25.4
Valdosta, GA	9,685	300	7,650	1,735	42,500/46,500	21.8

[a]Including savings from higher density.

Source: U.S. Department of Housing and Urban Development, *Affordable Housing: Challenge and Response*, Vol. 1, Affordable Residential Land Development: A Guide for Local Government and Developers (Upper Marlboro, Md.: NAHB National Research Center, 1987).

market-rate housing in other ways. The following incentives could be offered in exchange for provision of affordable housing:
- Exempting the project from growth control regulations, such as limits on the number of units that can be built;
- Using surplus public land for affordable housing;
- Encouraging high-density mixed-use and infill housing;
- Experimenting with techniques like air rights, transferable development rights, and landbanking;
- Expediting the processing of development approvals for affordable housing

projects: to the extent possible within the requirements of public trust and responsibility, minimizing the length of time required to process approvals, the number of permits, the number of agencies requiring permits, and the depth and breadth of information required;
- Reducing requirements for infrastructure, subdivision regulations, and the construction code through development agreements specifying that cost savings must be passed on to homebuyers (which may require the state's authorization);
- Allowing density bonuses for affordable housing projects or for specially targeted

affordable housing projects (for the elderly, the disabled, and so forth);
• Judiciously using tax incentives, abatements, or forgiveness.

SUMMARY

The need for affordable housing for moderate-income and low-income households is great and will continue to increase. In the early 1990s, developers looking for successful new projects will find opportunities for filling the unmet demand for affordable housing attractive, given the market and financial constraints on most other segments of the real estate market. Many communities, confronted with the desire to attract and retain economic development, especially during a period when labor is in short supply, will seek to encourage housing that is affordable to workers within commuting distance of employment centers. This public push, coupled with unmet demand, will create opportunities for development. Low-income housing's dependence on state and local initiatives will require community involvement and developers who are able to work closely with the public sector. Innovative financing vehicles will be a large part of the solution to the lack of lower-income housing. Much innovation is already occurring in this area, and although the need is great and increasing, the public's need can be met if the development community responds to the challenge.

NOTES

1. Thirty percent was selected because the U.S. Department of Housing and Urban Development uses this standard in its determinations of affordability. (Until 1981, HUD's standard of affordability was 25 percent of income.)

2. William C. Apgar, Jr., Denise DePasquale, Jean Cummings, and Nancy McArdle, *The State of the Nation's Housing: 1990* (Cambridge, Mass.: Joint Center for Housing Studies of MIT and Harvard Univ., 1990), p. 22.

3. Michael A. Stegman and J. David Holden, *Nonfederal Housing Programs: How States and Localities Are Responding to Federal Cutbacks in Low-Income Housing* (Washington, D.C.: ULI-the Urban Land Institute, 1987), p. 75.

4. Anthony Downs, *Residential Rent Controls: An Evaluation* (Washington, D.C.: ULI-the Urban Land Institute, 1988), p. 6.

5. Nora R. Greer, "Housing: Deepening Crisis and Stirrings of Response," *Architecture*, July 1988, p. 58.

6. The 221(d)3 Below-Market Interest Rate program and the Section 236 program.

7. Paul A. Leonard, Cushing N. Dolbeare, and Edward B. Lazere, *A Place to Call Home: The Crisis in Housing for the Poor* (Washington, D.C.: Center on Budget and Policy Priorities and the Low-Income Housing Information Service, 1989), p. xviii.

8. National Housing Task Force, *A Decent Place to Live* (Washington, D.C.: Author, 1988), p. 6.

9. Leonard, Dolbeare, and Lazere, *A Place to Call Home*, p. xi.

10. Ford Foundation, "Affordable Housing: The Years Ahead," A Program Paper (New York: Author, 1989), p. 2.

11. For detailed information on the range of state and local activities, see Stegman and Holden, *Nonfederal Housing Programs*; Mary K. Nenno and George S. Colyer, *New Money and New Methods: A Catalog of State and Local Initiatives in Housing and Community Development*, 2d ed. (Washington, D.C.: National Association of Housing and Redevelopment Officials, 1988); and John Sidor, *State Housing Initiatives: The 1988 Compendium* (Washington, D.C.: Council of State Community Affairs Agencies, 1988).

12. The information in this section and in parts of the rest of the chapter was originally published in Diane R. Suchman et al., *Public/Private Housing Partnerships* (Washington, D.C.: ULI-the Urban Land Institute, 1990).

13. Ford Foundation, "Affordable Housing," p. 7.

14. CDBG funds have, since their enactment in 1974, provided a flexible source of funding for community and economic development. HUD gives CDBGs to qualified cities and counties on the basis of entitlement; smaller cities and towns receive project-specific funds through state governments on a competitive basis. Money may be used for projects in which 60 percent of the beneficiaries receive low and moderate incomes, to eliminate slums and blight, and to serve "urgent community needs."

15. Stegman and Holden, *Nonfederal Housing Programs*, p. 35.

16. UDAGs are grants from the federal government to cities for economic development; the cities then lend the money to private developers. As the loans are repaid, the city can use the accu-

mulated funds in different ways. In Cleveland, for example, according to ULI member David Goss, repaid UDAGs are used in much the same way as CDBG funds.

17. Neil S. Mayer, *Neighborhood Organizations and Community Development: Making Revitalization Work* (Washington, D.C.: Urban Institute Press, 1984), p. 3.

18. Congress passed the Community Reinvestment Act (CRA) in 1977 to encourage banks to invest in their local communities. The CRA affects state-chartered banks, bank holding companies, federal S&Ls, federal banks, state-chartered savings institutions, savings and loan holding companies, and national banks. It requires the four federal financial regulatory agencies (the Board of Governors of the Federal Reserve System, the Federal Deposit Insurance Corporation, the Office of the Comptroller of the Currency, and the Office of Thrift Supervision) to examine these financial institutions and rate them on their records for meeting the credit needs of their entire communities, including low- and moderate-income neighborhoods. The CRA requires that institutions prepare a statement of their investment in the community at least once a year, which must outline the types of credit offered by the institution to the community. The regulatory agencies examine the institutions' records of reinvestment in the community and may use examination reports during any application process. Increasing public pressure on the regulatory agencies to be more stringent in their evaluations has driven banks to look for economically feasible ways to issue credit to low- and moderate-income households.

19. Neighborhood Reinvestment Corporation, "New Local Government Secondary Market to Aid Low-Income Residents; Cincinnati Proposes First Sale," news release, June 9, 1988; and Nenno and Colyer, *New Money and New Methods*, pp. 62–63.

20. The Ford Foundation instituted PRIs in 1968. PRIs are not grants but investments made by a foundation from its endowment or annual earnings. Investments can take the form of loans, loan guarantees, or equity investments. Detailed information on foundations' activities in housing and community development is available from the Foundation Center in New York, Washington, D.C., Cleveland, and San Francisco.

21. These categories of regulation were developed by Ira S. Lowry in conjunction with ULI-sponsored research conducted in May 1990 on the relationship between the restrictiveness of regulatory environments and housing costs.

Bibliography

Part IV. Planning and Analysis: The Public Roles

PUBLIC/PRIVATE PARTNERSHIPS

Advisory Commission on Intergovernmental Relations. *Improving Urban America: A Challenge to Federalism*. Washington, D.C.: U.S. Government Printing Office, 1976.

Alterman, Rachelle, ed. *Private Supply of Public Services: Evaluation of Real Estate Exactions, Linkage, and Alternative Land Policies*. New York: New York Univ. Press, 1988.

Anton, Thomas J. *American Federalism and Public Policy: How the System Works*. Philadelphia: Temple Univ. Press, 1989.

Babcock, Richard. *The Zoning Game*. Madison: Univ. of Wisconsin Press, 1966.

Babcock, Richard, and Charles L. Siemon. *The Zoning Game Revisited*. Boston: Lincoln Institute of Land Policy, 1985.

Barrett, Susan, and Patsy Healy. *Land Policy: Problems and Alternatives*. London and Brookfield, Vt.: Gower Publishing, 1985.

Barrows, Richard L. *The Roles of Federal, State, and Local Governments in Land Use Planning*. Washington, D.C.: National Planning Association, 1982.

Bender, Lewis G., and James A. Stever. *Administering the New Federalism*. Boulder, Colo.: Westview Press, 1986.

Bollens, John C. *Special Purpose District Government in the United States*. Berkeley and Los Angeles: Univ. of California Press, 1957.

Bosselman, Fred, Duane A. Feurer, and Charles L. Siemon. *The Permit Explosion: Coordination of the Proliferation*. Washington, D.C.: ULI–the Urban Land Institute, 1976.

Bowman, Ann, and Richard C. Kearney. *The Resurgence of the States*. Englewood Cliffs, N.J.: Prentice-Hall, 1986.

Brower, David J., David R. Godschalk, and Douglas R. Porter, eds. *Understanding Growth Management*. Washington, D.C.: ULI–the Urban Land Institute, 1989.

Colman, William G. *State and Local Government and Public-Private Partnerships*. New York: Greenwood Press, 1989.

de Neufville, Judith I., ed. *The Land Use Policy Debate in the United States*. New York: Plenum Press, 1981.

Fisk, Donald, Herbert Kiesling, and Thomas Muller. *Private Provision of Public Services: An Overview*. Washington, D.C.: Urban Institute, 1978.

Frank, James E. *The Costs of Alternative Development Patterns*. Washington, D.C.: ULI–the Urban Land Institute, 1989.

Frieden, Bernard, and Lynne B. Sagalyn. *Downtown, Inc.* Cambridge, Mass.: MIT Press, 1989.

Griner, John M., et al. *Productivity and Motivation: A Review of State and Local Government Initiatives*. Washington, D.C.: Urban Institute, 1981.

Haar, Charles. *Land Use Planning: A Casebook in the Use, Misuse, and Re-Use of Urban Land*. 3d ed. Boston: Little, Brown & Co., 1977.

Haar, Charles M., and Jerold S. Kayden. *Landmark Justice: The Influence of William J. Brennan on America's Communities*. Washington, D.C.: Preservation Press, 1989.

Hagman, Donald G., and Julian Conrad Juergensmeyer. *Urban Planning and Land Development Control Law*. 2d ed. St. Paul, Minn.: West Publishing Co., 1986.

Hagman, Donald, and Dean Misczynksi, eds. *Windfalls for Wipeouts: Land Value Capture and Compensation*. Chicago: Planners Press, American Planning Association, 1978.

Haveman, Robert H. *The Economics of the Public Sector*. New York: John Wiley & Sons, 1976.

Jackson, Richard H. *Land Use in America*. New York: Halsted Press, 1981.

Klaasan, Leo H., ed. *The City: Engine behind Economic Recovery*. Brookfield, Vt.: Avebury, 1989.

Lassar, Terry Jill. *Carrots & Sticks: New Zoning Downtown*. Washington, D.C.: ULI–the Urban Land Institute, 1989.

———. *City Deal Making*. Washington, D.C.: ULI–the Urban Land Institute, 1990.

Levitt, Rachelle L., ed. *Cities Reborn*. Washington, D.C.: ULI–the Urban Land Institute, 1987.

Levitt, Rachelle L., and John J. Kirlin., eds. *Managing Development through Public/Private Negotiations*. Washington, D.C.: ULI–the Urban Land Institute, 1985.

Lineberry, Robert L. *Equality and Urban Policy: The Distribution of Urban Services*. Beverly Hills, Cal.: Sage Publications, 1977.

Marlin, John Tepper. *Contracting Municipal Services: A Guide for Purchase from the Private Sector*. New York: Ronald Press, 1984.

Merritt, Richard L., and Anna J. Merritt, eds. *Innovation in the Public Sector*. Beverly Hills, Cal.: Sage Publications, 1985.

Moffitt, Leonard C. *Strategic Management: Public Planning at the Local Level*. Greenwich, Conn., and London: JAI Press, 1984.

Moore, Barbara H., ed. *The Entrepreneur in Local Government*. Washington, D.C.: International City Management Association, 1983.

Musgrave, Richard A., and Peggy B. Musgrave. *Public Finance in Theory and Practice*. 3d ed. New York: McGraw-Hill, 1980.

Nelson, Richard R., and Douglas Yates, eds. *Innovation and Implementation in Public Organizations*. Lexington, Mass.: Lexington Books, 1978.

Palumbo, Dennis J. *Public Policy in America: Government in Action*. New York: Harcourt Brace Jovanovich, 1988.

Paumier, Cyril B., et al. *Designing the Successful Downtown*. Washington, D.C.: ULI–the Urban Land Institute, 1988.

Picard, Louis A., and Raphael Zariski, eds. *Subnational Politics in the 1980s: Organization, Reorganization, and Economic Development*. New York: Praeger, 1987.

Porter, Douglas R. *Flexible Zoning: How It Works*. Washington, D.C.: ULI–the Urban Land Institute, 1988.

———, ed. *Downtown Linkages*. Washington, D.C.: ULI–the Urban Land Institute, 1985.

———, ed. *Growth Management: Keeping on Target*. Washington, D.C.: ULI–the Urban Land Institute, 1986.

Porter, Douglas R., Ben C. Lin, and Richard Peiser. *Special Districts: A Useful Technique for Financing Infrastructure*. Washington, D.C.: ULI–the Urban Land Institute, 1987.

Porter, Douglas R., and Lindell L. Marsh. *Development Agreements: Practice, Policy, and Prospects*. Washington, D.C.: ULI–the Urban Land Institute, 1989.

Porter, Douglas R., et al. *Covenants and Zoning for Research/Business Parks*. Washington, D.C.: ULI–the Urban Land Institute, 1986.

Porter, Douglas R., et al. *Working with the Community*. Washington, D.C.: ULI–the Urban Land Institute, 1985.

Reilly, William K., ed. *The Use of Land: A Citizens' Policy Guide to Urban Growth*. New York: Thomas Y. Crowell Co., 1973.

Roddewig, Richard J., and Christopher J. Duerksen. *Responding to the Takings Challenge: A Guide for Local Officials and Planners*. Chicago: American Planning Association, 1989.

Rutter, Lawrence. *The Essential Community: Local Government in the Year 2000*. Washington, D.C.: International City Management Association, 1980.

Schultze, William A. *State and Local Politics: A Political Economy Approach*. St. Paul, Minn.: West Publishing Co., 1988.

Scott, Randall W., David J. Brower, and Dallas D. Millner, eds. *Management and Control of Growth: Issues, Techniques, Problems, and Trends*. 5 vols. Washington, D.C.: ULI-the Urban Land Institute, 1975.

Simko, Patricia, et al. *Subdivisions and the Law*. Promised Lands, vol. 3. New York: Inform Books, 1989.

Snyder, Thomas P., and Michael A. Stegman. *Paying for Growth*. Washington, D.C.: ULI-the Urban Land Institute, 1986.

Sonenblum, Sidney, John J. Kirlin, and John C. Ries. *How Cities Provide Services: An Evaluation of Alternative Delivery Structures*. Cambridge, Mass.: Ballinger Publishing, 1977.

Squiros, Gregory D., ed. *Unequal Partnerships: The Political Economy of Urban Redevelopment in Postwar America*. New Brunswick, N.J.: Rutgers Univ., Center for Urban Policy Research, 1989.

Starling, Jay D. *Municipal Coping Strategies: As Soon As the Dust Settles*. Beverly Hills, Cal.: Sage Publications, 1986.

Stever, James A. *Project Approval: A Developer's Guide to Successful Local Government Review*. Belmont, Cal.: Wadsworth Publishing, 1980.

Stone, Clarence N., and Heywood T. Sanders, eds. *The Politics of Urban Development*. Lawrence: Univ. of Kansas Press, 1987.

Stout, Gary E., and Joseph E. Vitt. *Public Incentives and Financing Techniques for Codevelopment*. Washington, D.C.: ULI-the Urban Land Institute, 1982.

Sutherland, John, ed. *Management Handbook for Public Administrators*. New York: Van Nostrand Reinhold, 1978.

Williams, Norman, Jr., and John M. Taylor. *Land Use and the Police Power*. American Planning Law, vol. 1. Rev. ed. Deerfield, Ill.: Callaghan & Co., 1988.

Witherspoon, Robert. *Codevelopment*. Washington, D.C.: ULI-the Urban Land Institute, 1982.

Zeckhauser, Richard J., and Derek Leebaert, eds. *What Role for Government: Lessons from Policy Research*. Durham, N.C.: Duke Press Policy Studies, 1983.

AFFORDABLE HOUSING

Brodke, Mary E. *Developing Housing Trust Funds*. Washington, D.C.: Center for Community Change, 1988.

Council of State Community Affairs Agencies. *State Housing Initiatives: The 1988 Compendium*. Washington, D.C.: Author, 1988.

Dolbeare, Cushing N. *Out of Reach: Why Everyday People Can't Find Affordable Housing*. Washington, D.C.: Low-Income Housing Information Center, 1989.

Downs, Anthony. *Residential Rent Controls*. Washington, D.C.: ULI-the Urban Land Institute, 1988.

Ford Foundation. *Affordable Housing: The Years Ahead*. New York: Author, 1989.

Friedrichs, Juergen. *Affordable Housing for the Homeless*. New York: Walter de Gruyter, 1988.

Hughes, James W., and George Sternlieb. *The Dynamics of America's Housing*. New Brunswick, N.J.: Rutgers Univ., Center for Urban Policy Research, 1987.

Joint Center for Housing Studies. *The State of the Nation's Housing, 1990*. Cambridge, Mass.: Harvard Univ., 1990.

Kelly, Christine, Donald C. Kelly, and Ed Marciniak. *Nonprofits with Hard Hats: Building Affordable Housing*. Washington, D.C.: National Center for Ethnic Affairs, 1988.

Leonard, Paul A., Cushing N. Dolbeare, and Edward B. Lazere. *A Place to Call Home: A Crisis in Housing for the Poor*. Washington, D.C.: Center on Budget and Policy Priorities/National Low-Income Housing Information Service, 1989.

National Association of Home Builders. *Affordable Housing: Challenge and Re-*

sponse. 2 vols. Upper Marlboro, Md.: NAHB National Research Center, 1987.

National Association of Housing Redevelopment Officials. *Housing and Community Development: A Fifty-Year Perspective*. Washington, D.C.: Author, 1986.

National Housing Task Force. *A Decent Place to Live*. Washington, D.C.: Author, 1988.

Nenno, Mary K., and Paul C. Brophy. *Housing and Local Government*. Washington, D.C.: International City Management Association, 1982.

Pickman, James, et al. *Producing Lower-Income Housing: Local Initiatives*. Washington, D.C.: Bureau of National Affairs, 1986.

Rosen, David Paul. *Public Capital*. Washington, D.C.: National Center for Policy Alternatives, 1988.

Rosen, Kenneth T. *Affordable Housing: New Policies for the Housing and Mortgage Markets*. Cambridge, Mass.: Ballinger Publishing, 1984.

Salins, Peter D., ed. *Housing America's Poor*. Chapel Hill: Univ. of North Carolina Press, 1987.

Sanford, Welford, Judith Getzels, David Mosena, and Joann Butler. *Affordable Single-Family Housing: A Review of Development Standards*. Chicago: American Planning Association, 1984.

Schwartz, David C., Richard C. Ferlauto, and Daniel N. Hoffman. *A New Housing Policy for America: Recapturing the American Dream*. Philadelphia: Temple Univ. Press, 1988.

Stegman, Michael A., ed. *Housing and Economics: The American Dilemma*. Cambridge, Mass.: MIT Press, 1970.

Stegman, Michael A., and J. David Holden. *Nonfederal Housing Programs: How States and Localities are Responding to Federal Cutbacks in Low-Income Housing*. Washington, D.C.: ULI–the Urban Land Institute, 1987.

Suchman, Diane R., et al. *Public/Private Housing Partnerships*. Washington, D.C.: ULI–the Urban Land Institute, 1990.

U.S. Conference of Mayors. *Partnerships for Affordable Housing: An Annotated Listing of City Programs*. Washington, D.C.: Author, 1989.

Welfeld, Irving. *Where We Live: A Social History of American Housing*. New York: Simon & Schuster, 1988.

The following organizations can provide information about affordable housing.

American Institute of Architects
1735 New York Avenue, N.W.
Washington, D.C. 20006
(212) 626-7300

American Planning Association
1313 East 60th Street
Chicago, Illinois 60637
(312) 955-9100

Association of Local Housing Finance Agencies
1101 Connecticut Avenue, N.W., Suite 700
Washington, D.C. 20036
(202) 857-1197

Center for Community Change
1000 Wisconsin Avenue, N.W.
Washington, D.C. 20007
(202) 342-0567

Community Information Exchange
1029 Vermont Avenue, N.W., Suite 710
Washington, D.C 20005
(202) 628-2981

Council of Large Public Housing Agencies
7 Marshall Street
Boston, Massachusetts 02002
(617) 742-3720

Council of State Community Affairs Agencies
444 North Capitol Street, N.W., Suite 251
Washington, D.C. 20001
(202) 393-6435

The Enterprise Foundation
505 American City Building
Columbia, Maryland 21044
(301) 964-1230

Fannie Mae
3900 Wisconsin Avenue, N.W.
Washington, D.C. 20016
(202) 752-6030

Farmers Home Administration
Multifamily Housing Division
14th and Independence, S.W.
Washington, D.C. 20250
(202) 382-1615

Ford Foundation
300 East Third Street
New York, New York 10017
(212) 573-5000

Freddie Mac
Government Affairs Division
1776 G Street, N.W.
P.O. Box 37347
Washington, D.C. 20013
(202) 789-4750

Habitat for Humanity
811 Lee Street
Americus, Georgia 31709
(912) 924-6935

Housing Assistance Council
1025 Vermont Avenue, N.W.
Washington, D.C. 20005
(202) 842-8600

Local Initiatives Support Corporation
666 Third Avenue
New York, New York 10017
(212) 949-8560

Mortgage Bankers Association
1125 15th Street, N.W.
Washington, D.C. 20005
(202) 861-6500

National Association of Counties
440 First Street, N.W., 8th Floor
Washington, D.C. 20001
(202) 393-6226

National Association of Home Builders
15th and M Streets, N.W.
Washington, D.C. 20005
(202) 822-0200

National Association of Housing and
Redevelopment Officials
1320 18th Street, N.W.
Washington, D.C. 20036
(202) 429-2960

National Association of Realtors
430 North Michigan Avenue
Chicago, Illinois 60611
(312) 329-8200

National Coalition for the Homeless
105 East 22nd Street
New York, New York 10010
(212) 460-8110

National Community Development
Association
522 21st Street, N.W.
Washington, D.C. 20006
(202) 293-7587

National Congress for Community
Economic Development
1612 K Street, N.W.
Washington, D.C. 20006
(202) 659-8411

National Corporation for Housing Partnerships
1225 I Street, N.W.
Washington, D.C. 20005
(202) 347-6247

National Council of State Housing Agencies
444 North Capitol Street, N.W.
Washington, D.C. 20001
(202) 624-7710

National Housing Conference, Inc.
1126 16th Street, N.W.
Washington, D.C. 20036
(202) 223-4844

National Housing Trust
1074 Thomas Jefferson Street, N.W.
Washington, D.C. 20007
(202) 333-8931

National League of Cities
1301 Pennsylvania Avenue, N.W.
Washington, D.C. 20004
(202) 626-3000

National Low-Income Housing Coalition
1012 14th Street, N.W.
Washington, D.C. 20005
(202) 662-1530

National Multi Housing Council
1250 Connecticut Avenue, N.W., Suite 620
Washington, D.C. 20036
(202) 659-3381

National Trust for Historic Preservation
1785 Massachusetts Avenue, N.W.
Washington, D.C. 20036
(202) 673-4000

Neighborhood Housing Services of America
1970 Broadway, Suite 470
Oakland, California 94612
(415) 832-5542

Neighborhood Reinvestment Corporation
1325 G Street N.W., Suite 800
Washington, D.C. 20005
(202) 376-2400

U.S. Conference of Mayors
1620 I Street, N.W.
Washington, D.C. 20006
(202) 293-7330

U.S. Department of Housing and Urban
Development
Office of the Secretary
451 Seventh Street, S.W.
Washington, D.C. 20410
(202) 755-6417

United Way
701 North Fairfax
Alexandria, Virginia 22314
(703) 549-4447

Urban Institute
2100 M Street, N.W.
Washinton, D.C.
(202) 833-7200

ULI–the Urban Land Institute
625 Indiana Avenue, N.W.
Washington, D.C. 20004
(202) 625-7000

PART V
PLANNING AND ANALYSIS: THE MARKET PERSPECTIVE

Chapter 13

Stage Three: The Feasibility Study

Although developers might have a strong intuitive feel for a project based on activities during stage two, typically they must still formally demonstrate the project's viability to other participants. Demonstrating viability is stage three—formal feasibility. If the project survives refinement of the idea in the developer's mind, then it very likely will be a viable project. This assessment is important, because during stage three, developers commit more dollars to the project to do more detailed analyses along several dimensions. In fact, at the end of stage three, developers can still decide not to do a project—but at a higher cost than at the end of stage two. If developers enter stage three too many times without moving to the next stage as a result of a "go" signal from the formal feasibility analysis, they will certainly bankrupt themselves.

Development is more than a series of numbers gleaned from the marketplace; it involves entrepreneurial energy and creativity as well. Still, even the most creative, intuitive developers who bring to the marketplace new concepts of space with associated services benefit from running all the numbers and touching all the bases. The feasibility study, in addition to being a mar-keting tool, is also a very important way to control risk.

This chapter begins with a comprehensive definition of feasibility and then moves to the initiation of the feasibility study and an overview of the market study. The market study is so critical that Chapters 14 and 15 are devoted to it. The chapter then discusses other traditional elements of the feasibility study, newer topics under the broad heading "the concept of enterprise and the notion of venture capital," and techniques to control risk during stage three. It covers the following major topics:

- The definition of feasibility;
- Initiating the feasibility study;
- The market study;
- Preliminary drawings;
- Initial construction cost estimates;
- Lenders and investors;
- Building permits and other government considerations;
- The value statement and formal estimate of feasibility;
- The enterprise concept and the notion of venture capital;
- Techniques to control risk during stage three; and
- Moving toward the determination of feasibility.

The feasibility study might not always be clearly delineated as the third stage of the development process. It might start during refinement of the idea and spill over into the fourth stage. The stages delineated serve more as a convenient and logical format within which to explore the many interactive aspects of real estate development.

FEASIBILITY DEFINED

The best definition of feasibility remains the one that renowned real estate educator James A. Graaskamp stated in his classic article, "A Rational Approach to Feasibility Analysis": "A real estate project is 'feasible' when the real estate analyst determines that there is a reasonable likelihood of satisfying explicit objectives when a selected course of action is tested for fit to a context of specific constraints and limited resources."[1]

Each phrase of this long sentence is important. First, feasibility never demonstrates a certainty. A project is feasible when it is reasonably *likely* to meet its goals, so that even favorable results of the feasibility study will not guarantee the project's success. Second, feasibility is determined by satisfying *explicit objectives*, which must be defined *before* initiating the feasibility study. It is not just a matter of satisfying the developer's explicit objectives, though they may be the initial driving force. All of the players have objectives that must be met, the most important being the objectives of the public sector partner and the final user.

Third, the definition talks about a *selected course of action* and its test for fit. In other words, logistics, particularly timing, matter. It is not simply whether the idea might work, but whether a *particular* plan for turning the idea into bricks and mortar is likely to work within a specific time frame. Fourth, the selected course of action is tested for *fit in a context of specific constraints*, which include the legal and physical limitations enumerated in stage two of the development process. In

Photo courtesy of Joseph Molinaro

Seaside, in Walton County, Florida, is a new town on 80 acres with 2,800 feet of beach frontage. Detailed initial planning revealed to the developer and planners that authenticity required multiple architects and designers, hence a much more complicated process for developing this small resort community.

addition to the obvious constraints of the public sector's involvement and the land itself, people and capital are limited. For a project to be feasible, it must be feasible given those constraints and given the amount of capital and number of people to be dedicated to the project, according to a specific course of action at a particular time.

This broad definition of feasibility goes far beyond the simple idea of value's exceeding cost. If the word "constraints" is pushed into the ethical dimension that Graaskamp himself suggests, then both personal and social ethics as well as formal legal and physical constraints must also be satisfied.

INITIATING THE FEASIBILITY STUDY

The feasibility study is the formal study to determine whether a proposed project is viable. A typical feasibility study includes an executive summary, a market study, preliminary drawings, cost estimates, information about lenders and investors, governmental considerations, and the estimate of value.

Depending on the size and complexity of the development, the feasibility study can vary dramatically in length, scope, and cost. At one extreme, if the project is a duplex in an area already developed with other duplexes, using a previously built plan and the same contractor and lender, then the feasibility analysis is a very simple study involving the new market information described in Chapters 7 to 9 applied to a proven course of action. In other words, new market data are used to project rent and absorption, with most other factors refined modestly from preceding developments. For such a simple case, developers would probably choose to do the feasibility study with in-house staff at minor cost.

This situation contrasts with a planned 5,000-acre new town and industrial park. Such a planned community includes several types of developed real estate and requires extensive infrastructure as well as above-ground construction. Because the project is likely to take many years to complete, recognizing long-term trends will be more important—even for designing the first stage of the project. An idea for a complex, expensive, long-term project often results in a complex, expensive feasibility study that involves at least one and possibly more land planners, soils engineers, hazardous waste experts, and other design professionals. More than one architect might be used to specify designs for key facilities and architectural constraints for projects to be constructed by outside builders.

Because the relationship between developers and city governments is more dynamic and complex than it used to be, it will probably require substantial interaction with and involvement of the local government from the beginning. In some jurisdictions, developers use political consultants, who function like pollsters, testing the local political waters. Likewise, the market analysis and relations with tenants are more complex because of the possibility that people will move to the location not simply from within the city, but also from around the country and possibly from around the world, depending on existing and future economic growth. Thus, marketing is more involved for a larger project. The developer must coordinate all the professionals, being certain that they are all talking about the same project and that collectively they can determine its feasibility.

Many companies and professional organizations perform or coordinate complex feasibility studies, should the developer choose to use an outside specialist. Locally owned and operated appraisal firms or national firms with local or regional offices can be commissioned. Likewise, most large accounting firms and major business consultants offer this service.

Because the federal government regulates lenders who bear a portion of the risk in major developments, financial institutions often have requirements for commissioned feasibility studies. The most recent evidence of the government's interest in feasibility studies is Rule R 41c ("Appraisal Policies and Practices of Insured Institutions and Service Corporations"), which forces appraisers of development projects to do more than simply collect a few comparable facts illustrating today's situation. Introduced in 1987 and updated in 1989, the bill requires appraisers to estimate formally the "highest and best use" and project a schedule of absorption over time. Further, as a measure to control risk, appraisals of proposed developments must now include the value of the project as is as well as its projected value upon completion. The government hopes, through this continuing federal regulatory initiative, to end the unsubstantiated assertions of feasibility and value that have led to several recent financial disasters. While theory never suggested such an approach, low fees often forced appraisers to do less than a full feasibility study. Today, if developers want financing, they must usually have a formal estimate of the highest and best use and an explicit schedule for absorption.

THE MARKET STUDY

The market study is the most critical item in a feasibility analysis. It highlights all the long-term global, national, regional, and local trends that were gathered to refine the idea in stage two and are now formally brought to bear on the existing local situation, as the analyst projects a schedule for absorption for the project. This task is so important that real estate market studies for various types of property are outlined in Chapters 14 and 15.

The market study begins with national economic conditions (including international influences) and projected long-term trends, then progressively focuses on characteristics of the region, locality, neighborhood, and site. Long-term national trends are important to the site. It has been well documented, for example, that, nationally, types of jobs available and types of job seekers in central cities are mismatched.[2] The United States has moved progressively away from the strong back (manufacturing) and toward the strong mind (information processing) in numbers of jobs available. At the same time, an increasing number of people in inner cities are not completing high school. Entry-level jobs for dropouts that used to be available in manufacturing have declined drastically in inner cities; jobs involving information processing have increased in number but are out of reach for dropouts.[3]

This national trend is particularly apparent in certain regions and is very relevant to development in many central cities. Developers of office space in central cities may find that prospective tenants worry about their ability at that location to attract needed high-level secretarial help. At the same time, suburban retail developments might have difficulty finding individuals willing to take lower-paying positions at fast-food restaurants and retail shops. In both cases, the lack of available workers may decrease the value that prospective tenants put on the space. Market analysts should not lose sight of such important national trends as they move to a projection of operating numbers for the specific site; at the same time, they must remember that even small projects have two- to five-year time horizons for planning, construction, and sales and leasing, increasing the importance of good forecasting.

Most real estate markets are local markets, sometimes even neighborhood markets. Global, national, and regional trends clearly affect local markets, but, for many projects, local trends tend to be the best, most immediate predictors of future success.

Second, market analysts investigate comparable properties to determine what features, functions, and benefits of those properties are important. Because market analysis is expensive, it is important that the proposed development benefit from the analyst's insights gained from studying comparable projects. Knowing the value that space users place on particular functions and features should help developers specify the key features of the proposed development. If the best leasing in the area has been achieved by an office building that has no health club but more parking than the competition, then extra parking is more important than a health club and the subject property should be designed accordingly.

Third, the market study always concludes with projected schedules of absorption for the market segment and for the specific property. How many units at what price over what time period will the target market be likely to absorb? It is necessary first to segment the market carefully, defining all the features, functions, and benefits of comparable projects to be able to predict the *overall absorption rate for the market segment*. The developer can then attach

Photo courtesy of Norman McGrath

Fitting the project to the site, at Riverwoods in Chappaqua, New York, involved clustering houses on ridges to preserve trees and wetlands and to take advantage of river views. A network of footpaths and bridges traverses the natural terrain, which includes streams, the river, wooded hills, and the ruins of a pre–Civil War homesite.

value to the distinctive features of the subject property and compare the subject to the market to estimate the proposed development's capture rate and its expected rents and occupancy rate.

PRELIMINARY DRAWINGS

Once an idea's viability becomes apparent, developers in stage three commit dollars to preliminary drawings. Preliminary drawings show exterior elevations and specify rentable square feet or salable units, parking, type of heating, ventilating, and air-conditioning (HVAC) systems, and the like.

The formal feasibility study requires drawings much closer to final design plans than were needed in stage two. Although different architects and engineers can be used for the initial architectural layout and for final construction drawings, it is usually more efficient to use the same architect and engineer throughout the process. This consistency reduces the learning curve involved in bringing in new players and prompts their commitment to and understanding of the development team's objectives.

Tough calls for developers involve the quality (read "out-of-pocket costs") of these two professionals and the amount of their time to use. The more complex and innovative the job, the more important it is to hire competent architects and engineers. On the other hand, for simpler projects that are very much like other projects and on sites that are very much like other sites, it is probably not cost-efficient to bring in Phillip Johnson or I.M. Pei or a full team of supporting engineers. The developer decides the quality of talent to use and how much of it.

Overall, quality design is becoming much more important, as more communities are implementing design standards. Quality design can go a long way toward successfully leasing and managing the finished project. Landscaping is also increasing in popularity and importance. A good landscape architect can enhance and beautify an already striking project and, when necessary, cover up previous errors in design.

Although the selection of architectural support often reflects a project's distinctiveness or complexity, it can also be

291

made to complement the developer's experience or reputation. In selecting architects for the Europa Center, Fraser Morrow Daniels balanced the high cost of a well-established firm against its own lack of development experience in the local office market.

EUROPA CENTER

A KEY HIRING DECISION

The next step after justifying the cost of the land was to decide which architects and construction companies to use—major decisions for our company. Usually people in the business of building offices have long working relationships with architects and ask for five or six bids. Our company had no history of building major office buildings, but all our lenders told us that building office buildings was quite simple compared to the complicated resort development we had done earlier and that it ought to be relatively easy for us.

What I wanted to do, even if it cost more money, was to hire the best, most experienced architect that I knew we could trust and the best construction company with a record of getting the job done—even if their prices weren't the best going. Our choice was Cooper-Cary Architects from Atlanta, who have built hundreds of office buildings.

As the Europa Center case study reveals, outside professionals can bring valuable experience to the development team and can reduce risk when a development company lacks experience in a certain type of project. As specialists, architects play a crucial role in the development process, but they cannot design the project unless they are aware of other players' activities and objectives. To be successful, the final product must be *marketable, manageable,* and *cost-effective.* Communication and feedback among the members of the development team are critical from the beginning, because preliminary drawings must compare and trade off three basic items: marketing appeal (the project's eye

appeal to prospective tenants), the project's physical cost, and the ease of ongoing management. A beautiful building that costs too much and is hard to manage is not a successful development. On the other hand, a low-budget project could be both visually unappealing and hard to manage and therefore even less successful. Optimal results occur when property management (described in Chapter 18) is combined with the factors discussed in this chapter and the concepts of marketing discussed throughout the text. The development team's clear conveyance to the architect of marketing information stimulates the design of manageable space that is attractive to prospective tenants.

A balance among marketing appeal, cost, and ease of management cannot be achieved without fitting the project to a specific site, for the primary distinguishing characteristic of real estate is its specific, unchangeable location. Often a project that fits one site well is far less successful when replicated on a second site. Fitting the project to the site takes creativity and is often a time-consuming process, but it is an invaluable device for controlling risk. Early refinements in the design can prevent the development of structures that cannot be managed or leased. Changes can also reduce or eliminate opposition from the public sector. During the development of preliminary drawings for Europa Center, the building's design underwent many changes to satisfy the requirements of Chapel Hill's city council and the developers.

EUROPA CENTER

WORKING WITH THE ARCHITECT

Designing the project was another delicate process because we did not have a lot of money. The architects designed the whole building for $250,000 cost for a chance to participate in the project, even though they would not be paid until after we got a loan funded. They had to prepare fairly complete working drawings of the whole building so that we could put it out for bids to contractors and get a firm guaranteed maximum price. The archi-

tects did all that work before we got our construction loan.

We gave the architects general parameters: design something distinctive, relatively conservative, and reflecting the architecture and style of the Hotel Europa. It should be heavy on landscaping, should not remove any of the existing trees (we knew in Chapel Hill that saving the seven or eight remaining trees on the site was critical), and should not fill in the small pond (a landmark that people valued). We wanted to concentrate the building on the back of the site.

We asked the architects, based on the 50 buildings they had designed before, what the best, most compatible design for this site would be. The architects came back with about five plans and told us the only way we could get a cost-effective amount of square footage for the $5.00 per square foot we had paid for land would be to fill in the pond, cover it over with asphalt, and build a building there. They recommended a seven-story building.

We went back to the planning board and the town council informally and asked whether the architects' proposed plan could work. They said it wouldn't and told us to have the architects redesign the building to take into consideration the trees, the pond, and the general aesthetics of the site.

Again we had to justify cost. Either we had to build a smaller building, build surface parking, and keep the pond, or we had to build the amount of square footage that it took to justify $5.00 per square foot for the land and build structured parking. Economically, structured parking is borderline unless you've paid about $6.00 or $7.00 per square foot for land. Based on just one building analysis, we would have been better off to build one building on this site, make less money, and buy another piece of land somewhere else for a second building, because the cost of the land for the second building would be cheaper than the incremental cost of building the parking deck. But we could not identify another site that was as good as this one for a second building. The logical solution would be to put the parking somewhere else, not under ground.

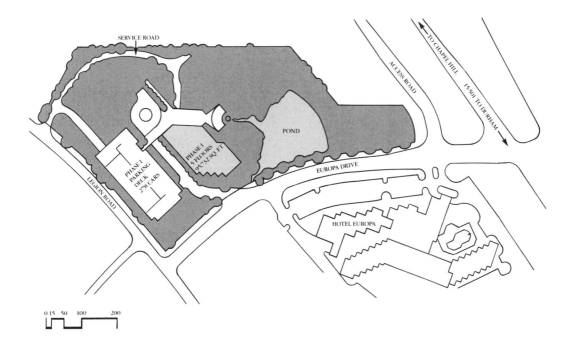

Phase One of the Europa Center contains 95,732 square feet of space (89,499 square feet of rentable office space) and 278 parking spaces in a parking deck with covered access. Landscape amenities include an abundance of trees and a pond.

We decided, however, that we would be better off paying the extra price, building a five-story building, adding another $.70 a square foot to the rental rate, building structured parking, and getting 200,000 square feet of building on the site.

So we gave the architects some very tight boundaries to work within, all based on economics. They came up with a building, described in the accompanying floor plans and specifications, that fit the shape of the site, reflected the architecture of the Hotel Europa, and preserved the pond and landscaping nearest the major frontage road. It took about an extra three months in the process.

The relationship with the city was complex, simply because the town council and planning board staunchly supported Chapel Hill's no-growth climate. The planning board, concerned about the building's height, wanted to see what the site would look like after construction and asked us to put up balloons that would delineate the building's top floor. The day the board was to visit the project, the wind was blowing at 20 miles an hour. We brought four high-rise cranes to the site, one for each corner, and had ribbons stretched across the tops of the cranes to outline the top of the proposed five-story building. It worked, although balloons clearly would have been cheaper. The cost of delay and rescheduling the council's site visit, however, would have been greater than the cranes.

BUILDING SPECIFICATIONS

Location:
U.S. 15-501 and Europa Drive

Building Size:
Total Gross Square Feet, Phase One: 94,517
Total Rentable Square Feet, Phase One: 92,407

Suite Sizes:
Approximately 1,000 square feet to full floor (approximately 18,860 square feet). Capability of expansion in Phase Two to a contiguous floor area of approximately 40,000 square feet.

Parking:
258 spaces in an open-air parking structure consisting of one on-grade parking level and two elevated levels.

Elevator:
Two custom hydraulic elevators in the entrance lobby. Interiors of cabs finished with raised-fabric wall panels with polished stainless steel accents, carpeted floors, and polished stainless steel 9'6" ceiling with recessed downlighting.

STANDARDS

Partitioning:
All partitions to be drywall construction using 1/2-inch gypsum wallboard over 2 1/2-inch metal studs. Tenant allowance to be 1 linear foot of partitioning per 10 square feet of usable area. Of this linear footage, 20 percent will be soundproofed.

Wall Finishes:
Interior walls will be finished with standard vinyl covering. Tenants to have choice of colors. Upgraded finishes available.

Ceiling:
Suspended 5/8-inch acoustical fireguard tile with recessed edge in exposed 2-foot by 2-foot grid.

Electrical:
A. **Lights**: 2-foot by 4-foot, three-lamp, lay-in fluorescent energy-saving lamp and ballast fixture with parabolic louver diffuser. One per 83 square feet of usable area.
B. **Power Outlets**: One duplex wall outlet per 100 square feet of usable area.
C. **Light Switches**: One double-pole switch per 300 square feet of usable area.
D. **Telephone Outlets**: One outlet per 150 square feet of usable area, wall mounted in interior partitions.

Floor Covering:
Standard carpet is 30-ounce tufted cut-pile nylon commercial carpet installed by direct gluedown. Colors to be selected by

tenant, with upgraded carpet available. Vinyl asbestos tile 12 inches by 12 inches by ⅛ inch available for kitchen and storage areas. Four-inch vinyl cove base is also standard.

Entry Door:
One single, full-height, 3-foot-wide, solid-core door in an aluminum frame. Hardware to include lockset, wall stop, and automatic closer. One set of double-entry doors will be provided for leased premises over 3,000 usable square feet.

Interior Doors:
One single, full-height, 3-foot-wide, solid-core door in an aluminum frame with passage set hardware, one per 225 square feet of usable area (including entrance door).

Window Covering:
1-inch blinds with Top-Lok feature or equal to be provided at all fixed exterior windows.

Heating and Air Conditioning:
Multiple-zone variable–air volume system using heat reclaim with thermostatically controlled zones. Distribution for each zone will be with ceiling diffusers. One supply per 150 usable square feet; one return per 200 usable square feet.

Space Planning:
Layout and design services to provide blueprints for construction will be furnished at no cost by the landlord.

Graphics:
One tenant identification and suite number sign to be provided by landlord at entry door. One listing on building directory to be provided by landlord on interior building directory. All graphics to be standard throughout the building.

Floor Loading:
70 pounds per square foot, including wall partitions.

Space is created for people, not vice versa. Moreover, space that appeals to people can generate a new market for the future beyond the demand indicated in the market study. Today, heightened interest in the functionality and aesthetics of con-structed space leads to research into the value created by outstanding architecture that specifically addresses the question of whether buildings that are clearly design landmarks (or are particularly beautiful) bring a higher return to the developer and investor.[4] Whether or not the research will eventually prove that greater returns accrue to "great" architecture, certainly developers are willing to hire well-known architects when their lenders and investors want to be associated with "big names."

Besides how a building fits its site and its intended tenants, developers ought also think about how a building blends into the urban setting. Pittsburgh, for example, has been said to have one of the most beautiful skylines of any major city, with its several corporate headquarters buildings, three rivers, and mountains. In contrast, other writers have characterized Dallas as "a bunch of buildings screaming at each other." Dallas's cityscape seems less to bring together a harmonious group of different buildings than to show different buildings competing with each other. The lesson is that an individual building may appear attractive in isolation, but once built, it will have to interact with surrounding structures. Contextualism is the key.

Truly great architecture overwhelms visually by synthesizing the elements of context and design. Size and scale, massing and setbacks, landscaping, circulation in the parking area, lighting, stylistic details, relationships, image, range of difference, and forms and materials are all important within the context of the building. Foreshadowing and the entry, contrast and consistency, form and space relationships, volume, ordering systems, edges in transition, activity areas, levels, circulation in movement, the building's footprint, human scale, surfaces and materials, varied elements, ornamentation and color, and landscaping are relevant in design.

For a nonarchitect, this list may sound like an expensive group of intangible combinations. The ideal way for most individuals to learn about architecture is to visit great buildings to study how their architecture fits with the city and how it functions for those who inhabit it—probably one of the most enjoyable parts of kicking tires in the real estate business.

Seascape, near San Diego, is an innovative residential project along the Pacific Coast that fits the project to the site. It includes subterranean parking and a number of design elements responsive to the natural terrain.

INITIAL CONSTRUCTION COST ESTIMATES

The estimate of the cost to construct the project should include the land, usually contracted for in stage two, the infrastructure, and improvements to the land. In large, complex developments, both of the latter requirements can be very expensive. Off-site costs of infrastructure, whether assumed voluntarily or imposed on the developer by regulation, must be combined with on-site costs for water, sewers, streets, and the like to obtain an estimate of the total cost of land improvements. The basic development costs are the land and the physical improvements necessary to bring it to a condition that is ready for above-ground construction to begin. In Japan, where a hectare of land in Tokyo can sell for more than a small ranch in Montana, land is usually the costliest item; in this country, the greatest cost is usually for construction of the building—the bricks, the mortar, and the labor necessary to build the space.

It is easy to list categories of costs. The hard part is estimating the dollars associated with those costs. The cost for the land will probably be known after stage two, but with some variability for more complex options, lease fees, subordination agreements, and the like. Probably the most difficult cost to estimate accurately is infrastructure. Without extensive borings, it is difficult to know that the place for laying pipe is not through rock. And even with the advice of the best soils engineer, it sometimes becomes more expensive to handle water than expected. Every developer can offer war stories about problems encountered during construction, and underestimating the cost of infrastructure usually heads the list.

Above ground, readily accessible guides are available to estimate construction costs, which break down cost elements, adjusted monthly and for the geographic location of the proposed development.[5] The breakdown between materials and labor or at least components is on the basis of square feet or linear feet. Besides construction of the building, other above-ground improvements are often lumped under landscape architecture: parking lots, trees, lights, and signs.

Developers should use these standard industry costs to compile in-house cost projections to compare with local general contractors' estimates. In-house cost projections should provide an estimate that is very close to the general contractor's own cost estimate. When a difference occurs, the developer needs to recheck the figures and discuss them in more detail with the general contractor. If differences remain, they must at least be explainable.

At times, this process involves meeting with individual subcontractors. For example, if an unusual amount and type of glass is being used in a particular project, it might be important to discuss with the glass subcontractor the specifics underlying the cost estimates used in the feasibility study. Lessons learned from talking to contractors and subcontractors should be used to redefine parts of the project so that it becomes more attractive or more cost-effective overall. During the initial solicitation for construction bids, Fraser Morrow Daniels used the suggestions of three contractors to revise the architect's preliminary drawings. The accompanying section of the case study reveals the motivation for selecting a contractor for the Europa Center. While the architect's selection was based on reputation, cost entered more heavily into the selection of the contractor.

EUROPA CENTER

THE TRADE-OFFS IN CHOOSING PLAYERS

We put the design out to bid to three different contractors. We reviewed the project in detail with each one, incorporating some of their suggestions for saving money, got a final price, and then chose the construction company based on price as well as its reputation for finishing jobs. In this case, we violated one of our own rules. To save $200,000 on the cost of construction, we picked the company that had a less solid reputation than the others (although all three companies were good ones). In this way, we reached the base construction price; then we had to later negotiate the parking deck, which wasn't designed yet.

The changes prompted by the contractors' suggestions rippled through to the cost estimates. The feasibility study should not be a static document, but one that is continually refined to reflect changes in both the project and market conditions at any point in the development process.

Beyond the costs of land with improvements and above-ground construction, a project involves substantial costs in marketing, financing, taxes, and insurance. Depending on the type of project, marketing could start months, or even years, before completion. Market research should start even earlier. Postconstruction costs for leasing during initial periods of low occupancy are part of the total marketing cost. Advertisements, commissions, and special concessions to tenants during the initial leasing period make up the major portion of the costs of marketing the development.

Lenders charge fees. Long-term lenders charge a commitment fee for the promise to replace the construction lender. Construction lenders will probably charge origination fees (points) and certainly will charge interest over the period of a loan. Additional points may be payable on the permanent loan when it is closed.

Insurance should cover fire and extended coverage in addition to various forms of liability coverage. Accounting costs and a variety of overhead costs should also be included in the overall cost estimate. When both overhead and a development fee over and above overhead costs are included, it means the developer is planning to draw some profit during the construction period. Traditionally, even in such cases, the developer's major profit was a function of the excess of value over cost. With the increase in merchant builders during the difficult period of the early 1990s, however, development fees are becoming a major item of profit, with more of the value created accruing to investors.

PROFILE: **PRESTON BUTCHER**

President, Lincoln Property Company
Foster City, California

Background: With a degree in electrical engineering, Butcher worked first in electrical contracting, then for Texas Instruments, before he joined Lincoln Property Company in 1967. Today, he develops industrial space and rental apartments for Lincoln.

Product: Standard 200-unit apartment projects remain a successful product; Lincoln currently builds about 10 such projects a year. Innovations in each project tend to be cosmetic (ceiling fans and miniblinds) rather than structural; the really big changes have taken place not in the product but in sources of financing and in regional and local economies.

Market analysis: A start-to-finish market study is not always necessary when building a standard product in a familiar market. Butcher looks at nonagricultural employment figures and net in-migration (a function of employment). He says it is possible, however, to overanalyze markets and that in difficult times developers would never proceed if they looked hard at five-year projections: "Deals rarely make sense from a risk-reward analysis on paper." Based on 20 years of experience, Butcher might decide to build a project, even with a projected slow leasing period, particularly to secure an exceptional site in a market whose prospects are good for the long term. In other overbuilt markets, he does not build until demand warrants it. For Lincoln, the key to feasibility in some markets is a long holding period: "Our time frame is 10 years. Good assets in good locations over time will pay."

On developers: "It takes three to five years to become accomplished at building any type of property, and it takes more than one deal to be a developer—three or four transactions at least. And the same holds true if you start over in a new type of property."

Most costs of marketing, borrowing, taxes, and insurance can be estimated based on prior experience and a projection of future trends. It is possible, for example, to know what common commissions for marketing consultants are, to estimate how much media time is needed and the cost of that time, and, based on trends in the marketplace, to project leasing periods—and thus to estimate accurately the cost of initial periods of low occupancy. Likewise, financing costs can be estimated based on a combination of projected construction time and projected interest rates.

Overall, past experience and intuition can be very helpful in estimating costs for a standard product in a familiar location. Looking at the history of recent comparable developments can provide updated information, allowing a developer to adjust for the special characteristics of the site, changes in tax law and public policy, and evolving market conditions. Preston Butcher, president of Lincoln Property Company, relies on such intuition and experience when developing standard apartment complexes in a familiar market (see the accompanying profile).

Finally, costs for contingencies should be estimated for every project. In an uncertain world, where feasibility is only "reasonably likely" and not guaranteed, it is important to set aside funds for unexpected costs and cost overruns. Because the total cost estimate is based on a number of other estimates, some of which can, at the same time, come out much higher than originally estimated, it is important to provide contingency funds commensurate with the project's risk. In a standard development, 5 percent might be adequate; in complex mixed-use developments, 10 percent may not be enough.

LENDERS AND INVESTORS

The preliminary discussions with lenders and investors begun in stage two now become much more formal. Based on initial reactions, the developer is close to finding the most appropriate permanent lender, construction lender, and, possibly, investor and/or joint venture partner. In stage three, developers present more specific information about logistics, design, and costs to lenders and investors. At this point, the project's estimated value is used to encourage participation. Lenders look for returns with low risk, that is, a high projected debt-service-coverage ratio, a low loan-to-value ratio, and the project's ability to maintain value through long-term appeal in a particular market. Construction lenders usually prefer a simple project designed and built by highly skilled individuals. If developers always follow lenders' guidelines, however, profit (value minus cost) may be slim indeed. Investors want both low risk (often interpreted as "it's been done before") and a high expected return. Investors seldom get both, and lenders will deviate from their preferences—but only for logical reasons and usually only if those reasons are supported by the feasibility study.

As discussions with lenders and investors become more serious and more spe-

Photo courtesy of Barry K. Humphries

An aggressive marketing campaign was used to sell congregate-care units at 10 Wilmington Place in Dayton, Ohio. Tactics included direct mail, telephone marketing, and newspaper, radio, and television advertising.

cific, the developer must know their particular needs, their histories, their self-images, and their current preferred mix for their portfolios to find the appropriate financiers for the development. By doing so, developers minimize both the costs of financing and the financial hassles involved in the development process.

How does a particular investment fit one lender better than another or one investor better than another? On the surface, the answer is fairly straightforward. Larger life insurance companies typically finance larger projects developed by national firms. Regional life insurance companies and S&Ls are more likely to finance smaller, more local projects. Commercial banks, because of their predominantly short-term sources of funding, are more typically construction lenders on safer projects. S&Ls, who could take equity positions more easily than commercial banks, were once more likely to make higher-risk construction loans requiring equity participation. That situation has changed substantially, however, and the remaining solvent S&Ls have become very cautious lenders indeed.[6]

The critical concept is matching the right lender to the particular development. With recent consolidation in the financial markets, financial supermarkets, from Citicorp to NCNB (North Carolina National Bank), now typically engage in a variety of real estate loans through subsidiaries and affiliates, if not directly. Again, a mortgage broker might help developers deal with the financial community. Just like the selection of an architect and an engineer, the more complex and the more critical the financing, the more skilled the developer or agent must be to deal with the financial community.

The developer's ability to match lenders and investors to specific projects requires even more sophisticated skills of negotiation as new sources of financing become available. Barry Humphries, a developer of congregate-care housing, equates this emerging market to running a hotel with health-related services. Humphries foresees two major categories of investors in congregate-care housing: existing service providers like hotel and health-care chains and established nonprofit organizations with credibility and bonding capacity. The complexity involved in arranging financing from diverse players is exemplified in his profile.

BUILDING PERMITS AND OTHER GOVERNMENT CONSIDERATIONS

During stage three, it is important not to forget the number one partner—the government—which is responsible for issuing the necessary building permits for the project. In some areas, obtaining permits is a very political process, and developers who misjudge the local political environment or suggest a project that does not fit the community's long-term interests can have difficulty even if they technically meet the letter of the law.

Some individuals working for the local government need to be involved in the determination of feasibility. If the regulators understand all the pressures on the development and how they relate to joint public/private objectives, they will more likely be supportive and less likely delay the process. Quite often, municipal staff are technically well trained and will accept the development concept so long as it fits with the city's master plan. If the public sector is brought in early and is fully committed to the concept, it is less likely to throw up time-consuming roadblocks as the process continues.

Successful developers must not forget the political side of government. Elected officials representing the public at large and individuals representing particular interest groups may present a challenge, and the political environment has in many areas become a nightmare for developers. Projects that elected officials may have endorsed earlier suddenly become unpopular as officials respond to an unexpected public outcry (see Figure 10-8). Developers are learning to work with citizens and local governments to address citizens' concerns, such as unwanted traffic, and to make some concessions.

Turnover in public offices poses problems for developers when projects conflict with the platforms of newly elected officials. When administrations change, prior approval does not always guarantee that the newly elected officials will be good

---

PROFILE: BARRY HUMPHRIES

President, Renaissance Group, Inc.
Columbus, Ohio

Background: With a graduate degree in city management from North Texas State University, Humphries worked briefly in city management in the late 1960s. From 1970 to 1976, he headed downtown redevelopment in Beaumont, Texas, then moved to Batelle Memorial Institute in Columbus, Ohio, as head of Batelle's real estate subsidiary. In Columbus, he worked on the Renaissance project, a redevelopment of a 125-acre neighborhood of Victorian houses, which won a national award for excellence. In 1982, Humphries left to start his own company, the Renaissance Group.

Congregate care: The Renaissance Group's first project was a for-profit congregate-care housing project in Dayton, Ohio. Humphries bought an old 330,000-square-foot state mental hospital and converted it to 223 apartments, a 300-seat restaurant, and 50,000 square feet of commercial space. Although his market in Dayton could be defined as everyone over 62 (with sufficient assets), the main segment for congregate care is people 74 and older. To be salable, congregate-care units need associated services in place (dining room, security, janitorial services), which means heavy front-end costs.

Financing came from HUD-insured state bonds, an additional state bond issue, cash from investors seeking an investment tax credit under the old tax law, insurance money following a fire that damaged the old building, and additional cash contributions from the limited partners when the project came in slightly over budget. The project was extremely complex from day one because of the public and private financing required, the age of the buildings (dating from 1855), their inclusion in the National Register of Historic Places, their ownership by a labor union originally seeking to build Section 202 housing (subsidized private apartments for senior citizens), and—above all—the unknown market. Pioneering this relatively new product in Dayton, Humphries learned how to market it trying everything he could think of: preleasing during construction by an in-house sales staff, direct mail, open houses, and "secondary marketing," that is, "counseling" by prominent members of the community.

Lessons: Superior negotiating skills are essential; Humphries characterizes his project as 70 percent politics and only 30 percent real estate. Likewise, real estate is a small portion of the final product; buyers perceive the product as lifestyle—security and companionship. In essence, it is a hotel with health-related services. Marketing is a slow process—up to six months from finding a prospect to closing the sale. An outside factor instrumental to the sale is the strength of house sales in the community, for buyers of congregate-care housing must usually sell their old houses first.

---

partners. For Europa Center, an election in Chapel Hill had considerable impact on Fraser Morrow Daniels's project. At that point in the process, the company was in a vulnerable position, because (well into stage three) it had committed a great deal of time and money to specify a project and obtain approval, but construction was not yet under way.

EUROPA CENTER

POLITICS AND CHANGING THE RULES IN MIDSTREAM

After we chose a contractor and spent a great deal of money to design the building, one political uncertainty in the

301

process jumped up and bit us. An election in Chapel Hill in November 1985 saw new players in the game. The people who were elected vowed that no more tall buildings would be built in town and that they would lower the density of everything. We thought that wouldn't matter because our project had already been approved and we had bought the land. But we found out otherwise. If the new officials' proposals went through, the amount of time that it would take to put the new limits and restrictions in place would have been about three months. So we had three months to begin construction, for we found out that if the project was not under construction, all of the approvals were dead. There we were with a set of financial calculations based on 200,000 square feet of building and a parking deck, already having been through planning review and site planning and in the final stages of bidding with the contractors, with only three months to begin building without any financing. We really had to scramble. About the middle of February, the town fathers decreed that any project not under construction on April 15 probably would be under the new rules instead of the old ones.

THE VALUE STATEMENT AND FORMAL ESTIMATE OF FEASIBILITY

The result of the market study is an estimated schedule of leasing or sales for the proposed development that projects rent, occupancy, and a stabilized net operating income over the leasing (or sales) period. During the feasibility study, developers must ensure that the marketing staff are planning to sell the same product that the builders are planning to construct, which in turn is the same project that the public sector is expecting to review.

It is also critical that projected rents or sales be based on truly comparable figures. A good feasibility analysis always includes a comparison grid from the market study. Whether the project is for sale or for lease, the attributes of value of the comparable projects are explicitly laid out on the

grid and specific adjustments shown that indicate the project's rent or selling price. The comparison must be sufficiently rigorous to give readers confidence in the estimate of how the subject property's features and functions will benefit the market. The larger the adjustments the analyst makes to the comparable rents or sales, the more likely some error has been or will be made and the greater the need for a larger budget for contingencies and/or a higher premium for risk in the discount rate.

The grid showing comparable factors should be used interactively with the proposed project to modify the project according to the features, functions, and benefits that are justified by cost in relation to current supply and demand in the particular market. Once the project's final amenities have been chosen, expected prices (or rents) and the sales (or leasing) schedule are derived from the grid and the projected cash flow generated. As seen from the pro forma for the Europa Center (Figures 13-1–13-3), the process is quite straightforward: potential revenues minus those lost to vacant space equals gross revenues minus operating expenses equals net operating income. The hard part is making reasonable assumptions.

Since the change in tax laws in 1986, it has become more common to base the value side of the feasibility analysis on pretax cash flows. In such a situation, the net operating income plus an estimate of residual value is discounted to a present value. The discount rate is taken from the marketplace. If it is a major national project, the rate can be derived from published property indices.[7] For smaller projects, local appraisers and financial institutions keep a record of comparable project returns. Feasibility is a forward-looking concept, and historic returns are only a guide to what investors will require for a current project. Hence, in preparing the feasibility study, the analyst looks at historical numbers, then adjusts them for future differences in the expected inflation rate as well as any other projected changes in market conditions that may affect the relative risk of the subject property. Once a discount rate has been determined in this manner, the analyst should confirm it by questioning investors who are currently actively seeking this type of project. If they are looking for a return consistent with historical returns (adjusted as noted), then the analyst should feel comfortable with the estimated discount rate.

Using this discount rate, projected operating flows are reduced to a current value, incorporating everything that can be known about the project. In other words, all the information about the market, the quality of the space relative to the competition, future trends, and the risks associated with those projections are all brought back to one value at one point in time. This value is then compared to the total cost estimated earlier (see Figure 13-4).

A project satisfies Graaskamp's definition of feasibility if the value, adjusted for risk as stated, exceeds the cost, where the cost includes all the logistics as well as all the items necessary to satisfy the legal, physical, and ethical rules, and where the developer has the resources to finance those costs and the people necessary to make it happen. Thus, the developer uses appropriately defined value and completely specified costs together to determine formal feasibility.

After estimating the value based on net operating income, an after-financing and after-tax scenario is necessary to show

FIGURE 13-1
EXPECTED CARE ANALYSIS FOR CHAPEL HILL OFFICE BUILDING

	Year 2	Year 3	Year 4	Year 5	Year 6	Year 7	Year 8	Year 9	Year 10	Year 11
Assumptions										
Rentable Square Feet	92,700	92,700	92,700	92,700	92,700	92,700	92,700	92,700	92,700	92,700
Rent per Square Foot	$17.50	$18.03	$18.57	$20.24	$20.84	$21.89	$22.98	$24.13	$25.34	$26.60
Escalation (percent)	0.00	0.03	0.03	0.09	0.03	0.05	0.05	0.05	0.05	0.05
Vacancy (percent)	0.05	0.05	0.05	0.05	0.05	0.05	0.05	0.05	0.05	0.05
Operating Costs per Square Foot										
Utilities	$1.35	$1.42	$1.49	$1.56	$1.64	$1.72	$1.81	$1.90	$1.99	$2.09
Janitor	0.70	0.74	0.77	0.81	0.85	0.89	0.94	0.98	1.03	1.09
Maintenance	0.50	0.53	0.55	0.58	0.61	0.64	0.67	0.70	0.74	0.78
Security	0.25	0.26	0.28	0.29	0.30	0.32	0.34	0.35	0.37	0.39
Professional Fees	0.48	0.50	0.53	0.56	0.58	0.61	0.64	0.68	0.71	0.74
General Escalation (percent)	0.00	0.00	0.00	0.00	0.00	0.00	0.00	0.00	0.00	0.00
Utilities	0.00	0.05	0.05	0.05	0.05	0.05	0.05	0.05	0.05	0.05
Janitor	0.00	0.05	0.05	0.05	0.05	0.05	0.05	0.05	0.05	0.05
Maintenance	0.00	0.05	0.05	0.05	0.05	0.05	0.05	0.05	0.05	0.05
Security	0.00	0.05	0.05	0.05	0.05	0.05	0.05	0.05	0.05	0.05
Professional Fees	0.00	0.05	0.05	0.05	0.05	0.05	0.05	0.05	0.05	0.05
General	0.00	0.05	0.05	0.05	0.05	0.05	0.05	0.05	0.05	0.05
Fixed Costs per Square Foot										
Property Taxes	$0.51	$0.54	$0.56	$0.59	$0.62	$0.65	$0.68	$0.72	$0.75	$0.79
Insurance Escalation (percent)	0.09	0.09	0.10	0.10	0.11	0.11	0.12	0.13	0.13	0.14
Property Taxes	0.00	0.05	0.05	0.05	0.05	0.05	0.05	0.05	0.05	0.05
Insurance	0.00	0.05	0.05	0.05	0.05	0.05	0.05	0.05	0.05	0.05
Management Fee (percent)	0.02	0.02	0.02	0.02	0.02	0.02	0.02	0.02	0.02	0.02
Leasing Fee (percent)	0.00	0.00	0.00	0.00	0.00	0.00	0.00	0.00	0.00	0.00
Cost of New Tenants										
Percent of Space Turned Over	0.00	0.00	0.00	0.10	0.10	0.10	0.00	0.00	0.00	0.00
Square Foot Turnover	0.00	0.00	0.00	9,270	9,270	9,270	0.00	0.00	0.00	0.00
Allow per Square Foot	$10.00	$10.00	$10.00	$10.00	$10.00	$10.00	$10.00	$10.00	$10.00	$10.00
Cost (in thousands)	0.00	0.00	0.00	$93.00	$93.00	$93.00	0.00	0.00	0.00	0.00
Rent for First Month	$0.00	$0.00	$0.00	$17.00	$17.00	$18.00	$0.00	$0.00	$0.00	$0.00

303

FIGURE 13-2
EUROPA CENTER PRO FORMA 12/18/86 (000)

	Year 2	Year 3	Year 4	Year 5	Year 6	Year 7	Year 8	Year 9	Year 10	Year 11
Revenues										
Gross Potential Rent	$1,622	$1,671	$1,721	$1,876	$1,932	$2,029	$2,130	$2,237	$2,349	$2,466
Less Allowance for Vacancies	81	84	86	94	97	101	107	112	117	123
Effective Gross Rent	$1,541	$1,587	$1,635	$1,782	$1,835	$1,928	$2,023	$2,125	$2,232	$2,343
Cash Expenses										
Operating Costs										
Utilities	$125	$131	$138	$145	$152	$160	$168	$176	$185	$194
Janitor	65	68	72	75	79	83	87	91	96	101
Maintenance	46	49	51	54	56	59	62	65	68	72
Security	23	24	26	27	28	30	31	33	34	36
Professional Fees	44	47	49	52	54	57	60	63	66	69
Field Costs										
Property Taxes	47	50	52	55	57	60	63	67	70	73
Insurance	8	9	9	10	10	11	11	12	12	13
Leasing and Management	31	32	33	35	36	38	40	43	45	47
Cost of New Tenants	0	0	0	110	110	111	0	0	0	0
Total Cash Expenses	$389	$410	$430	$563	$582	$609	$522	$550	$576	$605
Cash Income before Depreciation	$1,152	$1,177	$1,205	$1,219	$1,253	$1,319	$1,501	$1,575	$1,656	$1,738
Debt Service @ 9.5%	996	996	996	996	996	996	996	996	996	996
New Income	$156	$181	$209	$223	$257	$323	$505	$579	$660	$742

FIGURE 13-3
EUROPA CENTER CASE STUDY

	Total	Q1	Q2	Q3	Q4	Q5	Q6	Q7	Q8	Q9	Q10	Q11	Q12
Percent Leased by Quarter—Occupied		0	0	0	0	25	15	15	10	10	10	5	5
Percent Leased by Quarter—Full Rent		0	0	0	0	0	15	15	20	20	15	5	5
Capitalized Expenses (000)													
Land Purchase and Startup	$1,000	$1,000											
Maximum Construction Cost Including Site Development	4,985	1,246	$1,246	$1,246	$1,247								
Hard Cost Contingency	200				200								
Financing Fees (2%)	190	145						$45					
Construction Interest (11.5%)	379	11	40	75	113	$140							
Leasing Deficit	457					120	$100	80	$60	$45	$30	$15	$7
Design and Engineering (5%)	275	138	69	68									
Tenant Finishes ($12)	1,112	0	0	0	0	278	167	167	111	111	111	86	81
Leasing (5%)	308	0	0	0	0	77	46	46	31	31	31	23	23
Management (4%)	253	45	45	45	45	45	28						
Legal and Inspection Fees	20	10	5	5									
Soft Cost Contingency	160	40	40	40	40								
Total Capitalization	$9,339	$2,635	$1,445	$1,479	$1,645	$660	$341	$338	$202	$187	$172	$124	$111

how all of the participants fit into the project. Ideally, the sum of the parts will be greater than the whole. In other words, if tax benefits occur, the appropriate investor will take them. For example, cash flow and appreciation in equity can go to a pension fund, which is tax exempt, the tax shelter to a wealthy individual. After the 1986 changes in the tax law, fewer and less valuable shelters were available, but some are still there. An after-tax analysis should also be done as part of the formal feasibility analysis.[8]

Once the entire cost and all the value statements have been determined, the developer may want to run a sensitivity analysis to see whether some feature or aspect of the project can be improved. For example, a slight increase in operating costs may be justified because it lowers the project's total cost substantially. If the cost and income statements are set up on a simple computer spreadsheet, it is easy to check the trade-off between operating costs and visual appeal, between construction costs and management costs, and so on. Using sensitivity analyses, a feasibility study moves beyond a static accounting system and becomes a dynamic planning tool.

One important caveat is necessary. Computer spreadsheet models are often used to force feasibility: it is very easy to change a number here or a number there to produce a value that exceeds costs by an appropriate amount. The computer and the software for spreadsheets make sensitivity analysis very easy, but the same tools also make cheating easier. Fudging the numbers will surely come back to haunt a developer during the very stressful stage six of the process and/or during the long life of stage eight.

THE ENTERPRISE CONCEPT AND THE NOTION OF VENTURE CAPITAL

Development more and more frequently involves the combination of an operating business with the construction of physical space. In today's overbuilt markets, it is ever more important that the space specifically fit the user's needs—and continue to do so over its life—meaning simply that some of the things that were always important in running a hotel are becoming even more important in running a warehouse. Is a merchandise mart, for example, a real estate project or an operating business? Is Trammell Crow's Infomart in Dallas a business or a real estate project? Both projects involve constructed space that can satisfy a range of users, and all of the standard questions about real estate development apply. The constructed space is specially oriented toward the functioning of one particular business, however, and if that business fails, the next best use will produce a far smaller value for the constructed space. Consequently, traditional real estate feasibility analysis is interwoven with traditional business planning. Management is becoming more important in all phases of real estate—and is critical when one moves from a simple speculative office building to the more complex combination of real estate development with the formulation of business.

The concept of enterprise is a view of the development process as a living, breathing organism with ongoing problems of cash management, just like an operating business. For a proper feasibility study, it is necessary to decide how much of the ongoing business risk is "developmental" and how much will be passed on to tenants. The part that is passed on to tenants generally reduces the developer's risk so long as the lease agreement *and* the tenant's credit are strong. The more a building is necessar-

---

FIGURE 13-4

COST ESTIMATES FOR EUROPA CENTER

Land (Phase One)	$1,000,000
Building (Phase One)	4,985,000
Hard Cost Contingency	200,000
Financing Fees (2%)	190,000
Construction Interest (11.5%)	379,000
Leasing Deficit (net 36 months)	457,000
Design and Engineering	275,000
Tenant Finishes	1,112,000
Leasing (5%)	308,000
Management (4%)	253,000
Legal and Inspection Fees	20,000
Soft Cost Contingency	160,000
Total Cost	$9,339,000

ily combined with significant management operations, such as a hotel, where food and beverage and other service items are critical to realizing the rent, the more complex the feasibility study. Two issues are involved: 1) how much difference does the operating management make to the project's long-term success, and 2) is the developer or the tenant responsible? A hotel exemplifies the enterprise concept, but if the net lease is with Hyatt for 99 years, then the investor will receive bond-like returns.

Likewise, the more small, short-term tenants involved, the more the development must be seen as an operating business. The active marketing required in such circumstances puts a focus on the ongoing "business aspects" of the project. As players involved in the development process have realized the importance of enterprise, feasibility studies have changed significantly. Some feasibility studies look more like formal business plans than simply explanations of the value and cost of constructed space.

Another aspect growing in complexity is the increasing likelihood of the need for venture capital. For a 5,000-acre combined residential and industrial development, for example, it might be two to six years between the time the developer moves from stage two to the actual beginning of construction. During that time, when the formal feasibility study is undertaken, extensive government relations worked out, and long-term tenant relations negotiated, the source of money becomes a very important consideration. Because developers are usually at great pains to minimize the amount of their own money involved before commitment, substantial front-end dollars from other sources are needed.

In such a situation, it is probably more appropriate to judge this interim period—the period between the end of stage two and the beginning of stage six (construction)—as a "venture capital period" than as a real estate development period. The dollars invested are substantial, and a great deal of risk is associated with it because it is uncertain whether the project, whose size and value are unknown, will ever be undertaken. Consequently, investors during this period look for extraordinarily high

returns, not unlike traditional venture capitalists. Venture capital changes the investor's, the lender's, and even the developer's traditional roles. All of the traditional players are still important, but venture capital brings an additional level of complexity. The astute developer uses as much of the less expensive financing (e.g., commercial banks) as possible and as little of the expensive financing (e.g., venture capital) as possible.

The development company is a business, and the collection of development projects must be structured so that the development company as a company is viable. Thus, at times the developer may trade longer-term profits (the percentage of the difference between value and cost) for higher immediate development fees to keep the development company solvent.

During the Europa Center's development, Fraser Morrow Daniels was also attempting to get approval for a condominium hotel, also in the Research Triangle. Close to a state university, most of the hotel's business was projected to be for events associated with the school. Furthermore, the project was to be located in a historic section of town, complicating political issues, traffic, and even physical construction. Fraser Morrow Daniels, a relatively small developer working in a relatively small town, had over $2 million invested in the project before the city finally approved it. Think about how much more money would be involved in a complex project in Manhattan! And think about how the providers of the capital felt when the project proved infeasible and the developer chose not to move to stage four, leaving the investor with $2 million worth of plans for a project that would not happen.

TECHNIQUES TO CONTROL RISK DURING STAGE THREE

Certain techniques are available to control risk during stage three:
1. Feasibility analysis is a technique to control risk. The more time and effort put into estimating all of the costs and values for the final decision about feasibility, the more likely that the decision will be correct. In almost all cases, the better the forecast, the less risk involved. On

the other hand, the feasibility study for a large project is expensive and time-consuming. Overdoing the feasibility analysis is a waste of money that can seriously extend, to the developer's detriment, the length of the development process. How much is enough but not too much? That is where the developer's judgment comes into play.

2. The financing arranged during this stage critically affects how the project's risks are shared. Different lenders and the equity investor have different preferences. The construction lender wants a floating-rate loan with very strict procedures for dispensing funds, early equity contributions, and both the developer's and any investors' personal liability. On the other hand, the developer would like a cap on the interest rate, no personal liability, easy procedures for requesting payments, and the right to contribute his own cash after the bank puts up its cash. How these desires are traded off depends on the quality of the project, the lender, and the developer, and general conditions in the money market. In a lender's market, the developer may have to toe the line. When financing is readily available from many sources, however, lenders are more likely to accommodate developers' desires.

Permanent lenders likewise have certain interests that must be considered in the trade-off between risks and returns. Adjusting the principal balance for inflation (and/or an equity participation) moves some of the risk centered around inflation out of the lender's portfolio. The higher the debt-service-coverage ratio and the lower the loan-to-value ratio, the more likely the lender is to get paid and, in the event of default, to collect the total loan balance. Again, the positions of the permanent lender and the developer are almost mirror images. Investors have their own perspective. They would like to make their cash contributions late and be assured that in the event of an additional need for cash, it would be made up by the developer or the lenders. Certainly they do not want to be personally liable, and they do want to maximize their after-tax returns.

3. The review of the architect's design plan by operating, marketing, and construction people and public officials is a critical item in controlling risk. A formal review by *all* players is important.

4. The developer must check to ensure that utilities and other infrastructure are available. Even though a project is legally feasible and publicly desirable, the city might be unable to provide sewer, water, or other infrastructure. The developer must begin discussions early, document comments made, and formally pursue available public facilities and services.

5. When considering all of the costs of infrastructure for a project, developers must go beyond negotiations for "permissions" and ask the city for concessions when they are providing the city something of value. A joint venture with other private sector users or the general public who benefit from the development might be appropriate. A new or very positive development for an area might result in shared costs with others who will benefit. Sometimes when sharing costs is not possible, it is feasible to acquire some of the surrounding land and capture some of the increased value.

The idea is to not forget the concept of situs—interactions of a project with surrounding sites and the impact of those surrounding uses on the subject property.[9] This principle is basic real estate. No site operates in isolation. In a competitive world, it is useful to share costs and, at times, to capture some of the benefits that the development will have on surrounding developments. It is not always possible, but it is useful to consider the possibility.

A graphic example of the impact of situs is the difference between the development of Disney Land in Anaheim, California, and Disney World in Orlando, Florida. At Anaheim, all the peripheral "action" accrued to others, whereas, because of the recognition of this loss of profitable opportunities, the huge site acquired for the Magic Kingdom has allowed Disney to reap most of the benefits of additional development that feeds on the central theme park's facilities.

6. The developer must check to make sure that a building permit has actually been issued to the chosen contractor, and in some cities, it is important to make sure that subcontractors have obtained the appropriate permits. At times in their haste to get a job, contractors overlook certain rules or promise something that has not been done or the company cannot do. Checking details is a good way to control risk.

7. It is often useful to provide structural warranties in the architect's contract. (Some people even consider insuring the contract if the architectural firm is small.) After the windows fell out of the John Hancock Building in Boston, it became obvious to many developers that they personally were not adequately prepared to undertake a final review of all the technical aspects of construction. Warranties from the architect, suppliers, and builders and a guarantee that those involved have sufficient financial worth to make a lawsuit worthwhile mean the developer has a remedy if such a disaster happens. While it is seldom a good idea to stop development for a lawsuit, the potential for a successful lawsuit often encourages players to perform up to the commitment they have made. The more concrete the legal documentation of responsibilities, the easier it will be to convince individual players that serious problems will result if they fail to perform. Thus, structural warranties and, more important, clearly drawn contracts can be tools for negotiating from strength.

MOVING TOWARD THE DETERMINATION OF FEASIBILITY

In the development of Europa Center, no sudden movement, but a gradual slide, occurred from stage two into stage three. The architect, from an independent firm, was involved in both stages, because architecture was not an in-house skill of Fraser Morrow Daniels. Because the firm was new at office development, it chose the best architect to minimize risk and to establish credibility. The developer focused on fit-

ting the building to its site and surroundings (a political as well as design decision). By acquiring a very buildable piece of land and using the highest-quality architect, the developer hoped that savings would be realized from avoiding both construction cost overruns and delays in permitting.

The case study focuses on the trade-off among costs, rents, and operating efficiency. In this development, the emphasis was on the market for this type of space without any need to create something particularly special—a quality development, but not a unique development.

The developer worked closely with the city, because city fathers were known to be particularly difficult. The relationship was a dynamic one, because the political side dominates the regulatory side. In this case, the developer came close to fast-tracking construction simply to avoid losing building permits.

SUMMARY

The definition of feasibility presented in this chapter is very broad. It begins with a formal definition of the development's objectives, which may involve money, ego, civic enhancement, or other related items. The defined objectives are then tested for fit in a context of specific market, legal, physical, and ethical constraints and limited financial and human resources. A project is feasible when it is reasonably likely (almost never certain) that the objectives can be accomplished in a particular situation. The primary task in the feasibility analysis is to produce a sound market analysis, one that culminates in a schedule of pricing and use that is then used to project net operating income over the subject property's time frame. The developer takes these numbers and estimates value for the project, using discounted cash flow analysis. A project is said to be feasible when that value exceeds *all* of the projected costs of development.

The feasibility analysis is only one technique for controlling risk during stage three of the development process. Once completed, the formal feasibility study is the sales tool used to bring together all the different players to accomplish the objectives for development.

Feasibility studies typically contain an executive summary and a market study, moving progressively from the big picture to the specific site. Numerous maps and photographs illustrate the analyses. Their focus, however, is on the statements of value and cost, both of which must be complete in every detail.

NOTES

1. James A. Graaskamp, "A Rational Approach to Feasibility Analysis," *Appraisal Journal*, October 1972, p. 515.

2. See, e.g., John Kasarda, "America's Changing Commercial Real Estate Markets: Population, Jobs, and Investment Performance to the Year 2000," in *Real Estate Investment Strategy: A Year 2000 Perspective* (New York: The Prudential Realty Group and Univ. of North Carolina, 1989).

3. Ibid.

4. See, e.g., Kerry Vandell, "Will Good Design Pay? The Economics of Architecture and Urban Design," in *Real Estate Investment Strategy: A Year 2000 Perspective* (New York: The Prudential Realty Group and Univ. of North Carolina, 1989).

5. Information is available from, for example, Marshall and Swift, the Dodge Building Cost Calculator, found at all major appraisal firms and some public libraries.

6. Charles H. Wurtzebach and Mike E. Miles, *Modern Real Estate*, 4th ed. (New York: John Wiley & Sons, 1991); and William Brueggeman and Leo D. Stone, *Real Estate Finance*, 8th ed. (Homewood, Ill.: Richard D. Irwin, 1989) describe all the lenders (and their analytical techniques) in considerable detail. Goldman Sachs and Salomon publications describe the more current bells and whistles that attract certain larger lenders to certain deals.

7. For example, the *FRC Property Index*, published quarterly by the National Council of Real Estate Investment Fiduciaries and the Frank Russell Company, Tacoma, Washington.

8. See Wurtzebach and Miles, *Modern Real Estate*, for an in-depth illustration of calculations.

9. Richard Andrews, *Urban Land Economics and Public Policy* (New York: Free Press, 1971).

Chapter 14

Analysis of the
Real Estate Market

*C*hapter 13 noted that market analysis is the key ingredient in the feasibility study. A market analysis attempts to identify the share of the demand the subject site is expected to capture expressed as x square feet (or units) to be leased (or sold) at y dollars during each period for the duration of the leasing (or sales) period.

Often, the feasibility study and the market analysis are tools the developer uses to gain the support of investors, lenders, and city officials, who usually require an outsider's unbiased analysis of the market. For small-scale, uncomplicated development proposals, they might be satisfied with the developer's own market analysis. Developers themselves may look to an outsider's analysis for aid in making decisions when the project is complex, innovative, or expensive, for example, a mixed-use development with hotel, retail, and office space, or a land development where lots will be sold for houses in several different price ranges over a period of years. Regardless of the size of the project or who does the market study, however, this analysis should be systematic and rigorous, forcing the developer to check assumptions against findings about the market. Ideally, the market analysis and the complete feasibility study will prevent the developer

from committing more time and money unless the project is highly likely to realize his objectives. Equally important, the market analysis should indicate adjustments to the project (features and functions) that will enhance both its probability of success and its profitability.

This chapter outlines market analysis so that its major parts can be adapted to different situations as well as what issues developers must analyze to lessen their risks. Specifically, this chapter looks at the following topics:
• Market analysis versus economic studies;
• A general outline of market analysis;
• Identifying demand;
• Forecasts;
• Market areas;
• Prices;
• Characteristics of supply;
• Competing projects;
• Absorption;[1] and
• Problems, pitfalls, and limitations of market analysis.

MARKET ANALYSIS VERSUS ECONOMIC STUDIES

A key difference between market analysts and developers is that analysts are supposed to be objective and dispassion-

311

FIGURE 14-1
MARKET AND ECONOMIC STUDIES

Type of Study	Question to Be Answered	User	Provider	Focus	Development Preexisting or Assumed	Estimation of Value (or Return on Investment)
Appraisal	What is the value of this improved or un-improved site?	Property owner Investor Lender	Appraiser	Subject property (improved or unimproved site)	Maybe	Yes
Cost/ Benefit Analysis	What is the net value of this project to the public?	Government agency	Economist	Public invest-ment in the project	Yes	Yes
Analysis of Economic Base	What is the outlook for near-term growth for this city/metro-politan area?	Planning agency	Urban analyst[a]	Economy of the city or metropolitan area	No	No
Analysis of Economic Impact	What is the economic impact of this development on the surrounding area?	Government agency	Urban analyst	City or market area	Yes	No
Study of Highest and Best Use	What is the optimal use of this site?	Investor Property owner Lender	Appraiser Market analyst	Subject parcel of land	No	Yes
Land Use Study	What is the pattern of land use in this geographic area?	Planning agency	Planner	All parcels of land in the jurisdiction	No	No
Market Study	What is the demand for and supply of this type of property in this market area?	Developer	Market analyst	Market area that inludes the subject project	Maybe	No
Market-ability Study	What prices, sizes, functions, and fea-tures are required to capture a market share?	Developer	Market analyst	Subject property compared to all competing projects	Yes	No
Financial Feasibility Analysis	What financial return is attainable for this project, given con-straints on develop-ment?	Developer Investor Lender	Real estate invest-ment analyst	Private investment in the project	Yes	Yes

[a]Urban analysts include regional scientists, economic geographers, or city planners.
[b]If market prices are used, the study of highest and best use becomes an elaborate feasibility analysis that considers alternative projects. If social values are used, the study of highest and best use becomes a cost/benefit analysis in which the user has the same objective function as society as a whole.
Note: Market and feasibility studies may contain an economic base study, a market study, a marketability study, and a financial feasibility analysis. Market and marketability studies are often combined.
Source: Based on original classifications in Anthony Downs, "Characteristics of Various Economic Studies," *Appraisal Journal*, July 1966, pp. 329–38.

FIGURE 14-1 (continued)

Type of Study	Sources of Value Estimates	Estimates of Absorption	Estimates of Market Capture	Estimates of Project's Timing	Description of Conditions For Success	Stage in Development Process
Appraisal	Market prices Replacement cost Future worth (DCF)	Yes	Maybe	No	No	4 or 8
Cost/ Benefit Analysis	Social values (DCF)	Yes	Yes	Yes	No	1 or 2
Analysis of Economic Base	N/A	No	No	No	No	3
Analysis of Economic Impact	N/A	No	No	Yes	No	3
Study of Highest and Best Use	Market prices or social values[b] (DCF)	Yes	Yes	No	No	3 or 8
Land Use Study	N/A	No	No	No	No	1 or 2
Market Study	N/A	Yes	Maybe	Maybe	No	3
Market-ability Study	N/A	Maybe	Yes	Yes	Yes	3
Financial Feasibility Analysis	Market prices Future worth (DCF)	No	No	Maybe	Yes	3

ate, whereas developers typically are enthusiastic about an idea they think will work. Entrepreneurs tend to believe they can succeed. The analyst's role is to undertake systematic research after the developer has initially tested and refined the idea, making sure the developer's assumptions are realistic.

Market analyses differ from one another and from other types of economic

313

studies, and the variety of terms used can confuse even people with considerable experience in real estate. The types of studies are summarized in Figure 14-1.[2] The first six types listed in the figure contribute to the developer's understanding of the local market. The last three are the ones that help the developer decide whether to move ahead to stage four of the development process (contract negotiation). What is called "market analysis" brackets the questions and focus of both market and marketability studies. These studies provide the "top-line" revenue estimates used in financial feasibility analysis and should help developers substantiate estimates of stabilized net operating income (NOI). The better ones also indicate the degree of confidence that the estimates deserve and therefore help developers set an appropriate premium for risk in the discount rate. Stage three (feasibility) considers the full range of legal, physical, market, and financial dimensions. The market study and the marketability study evaluate the subject project in relation to the market. And the financial feasibility analysis estimates risks and rewards for developers, investors, or lenders.

As Figure 14-1 shows, market research is conducted for the benefit of different players at different stages of the development process. It is helpful to know who performs the analysis at each stage of development and what their objectives are. In stages one and two, for example, developers have the lead role in analyzing the market, albeit informally. In stage three, developers often ask a market analyst to evaluate formally the subject project, then use the market study, marketability study, and financial feasibility analysis to make the final decision on feasibility. They might also commission and present results of an economic impact analysis to garner public support for the project.

In stage four, developers negotiate the contracts needed to build a project that appears feasible. At this point, the other participants must reach their final decisions about whether the market will support the project as proposed and whether they are likely to achieve their objectives. Lenders are required to underwrite loans to determine the project's expected market value, following "accepted professional standards." Large investors often commission appraisals as part of the "due diligence" process. These players decide whether estimated value justifies their financial participation. Major tenants and even local governments may want assessments of the project from their particular perspectives before committing their support. Major tenants often have in-house market analysts or hire firms to assess competing sites.

Finally, the public sector is being called upon in many areas to sponsor market studies to help rationalize markets, especially as they are overbuilt. Although in-house capability or resources to hire market analysts are often scarce, the public sector has a legitimate role in providing good information about expected demand and the anticipated response to supply. Good market analysis can improve planning and zoning, guide the provision of development incentives, and reduce the social costs of overbuilding by accommodating growth while protecting the environment and quality of life.

A GENERAL OUTLINE OF MARKET ANALYSIS

This section on demand, supply, market areas, and other components of market analysis may be easier to follow by first looking at the contents of a market analysis presented in Figure 14-2, then returning to the text. The outline in the figure includes both a market study and a marketability study, as defined in Figure 14-1. Figure 14-2 offers one detailed outline of real estate market analysis, representing a snapshot of the final report. The text discusses the process of assessing the market, explaining how to estimate the components of market and marketability studies.

The market analyst usually begins with the developer's preliminary project design at a specific site. The methodology should be logical, defensible, systematic, and reasonably detailed, leading to an overall opinion of the project's market feasibility. The analyst should also identify risks that could fatally harm the project. In the overview, the analyst should review the international, national, and regional economic outlook as they could affect the site

314

FIGURE 14-2

OUTLINE OF MARKET ANALYSIS FOR AN ENTREPRENEURIAL PROJECT

(A general outline to be adapted for specific situations)

I. Executive Summary
   A. Goals and objectives
   B. Methods of analysis, key assumptions, risk factors
   C. Recommendations—go/no go/postpone/improve project

II. Overview
   A. National (or global) economy and key growth areas
   Discuss relevant demographic, economic, and financial factors and "megatrends," such as an aging population or declining household size. Give prima facie evidence and examples that the project has merit as an entrepreneurial enterprise. To minimize errors in forecasting and arrive at a reasonable forecast, carefully and objectively assess the economic environment; document findings and key assumptions.
     1. Justify property type—the targets of opportunity
     2. Make timing relative to the business cycle
   B. Regional economic outlook
   Include as appropriate: Shift-share analysis or other techniques to compare area's growth by industry against national or regional norms, employment forecasts by federal agencies or private groups, original research on the region to determine the economic outlook.

C. Local economy
Include economic base study to forecast short-term outlook or to step down regional/metropolitan area forecasts to the locality under study. Relate potential for development in the smaller market area to growth trends in the larger urban area and region.
     1. Employment trends in metropolitan area compared to regional and national employment trends
     2. Short-term forecasts of metropolitan area employment
     3. Identification and outlook for primary industries, companies, and products

D. Market delineation and site analysis
Define the relevant local or non-local market area for the project at a specific site. Local market area may be contiguous, such as a retail trade area, or diffuse, such as demand for housing.
     1. Geographic identification of market area and description by census tract, incorporated area, or county. Land area, major topographic features, barriers.
     2. Site description
     Suitability for proposed use: visibility, topography, barriers, ingress, and egress. Zoning, property taxes, municipal ser-

as well as the market outlook for the subject type of property. Trends in macroeconomics, demographics, and lifestyle are of immediate interest to developers; from these trends, developers continually search for viable ideas. The market analyst's job is to check the reasonableness of the idea compared to neighborhood, local, and regional trends and to national and global dimensions.

IDENTIFYING DEMAND

The demand for space, as estimated by the market analyst, is both derived and driven by the market. Market-driven demand means that the local economy must remain competitive to support sustained demand for space. The role of the local or regional economy within the national or

FIGURE 14-2 (continued)

vices, and other development regulations and impact fees.

3. Site access
Capacity, condition and types of transportation facilities, traffic counts, commuting times. Links to major land uses (for example, employment centers).

4. Market area dynamics
Compatibility of proposed use with surrounding land uses. Neighborhood growth trends. Location of competitive sites/ degree of spatial monopoly.

III. Analysis of Demand
A. Projected overall demand
Analyze in detail employment, population, households, and/or income in the market area to forecast market demand for the subject property type.

1. Employment
Current estimates, past trends, disaggregation to relevant sectors and/or groups of occupations. Employment forecasts, including assumptions on participation in the labor force for total employment and relevant subgroups.

2. Population and households
Current estimates, past trends, disaggregation to relevant age cohorts. Forecasts, including estimates of migration, natural increase, and population per household. Total and relevant subgroup

population or total households and relevant household groups.

3. Income
Current estimates and trends in personal income. Forecasts of total, per capita personal income and household income.

B. Analysis of absorption
Forecast demand for each relevant market segment to estimate absorption for ranges of price and quality

1. Absorption and vacancy trends: adjust demand estimates relative to historic and recent absorption.

2. Project the market absorption schedule: demand for each year over the relevant time period.

IV. Analysis of Supply
A. Survey existing stock, past trends, and future supply.

1. Inventory for relevant property type: number of units or square footage existing, under construction, planned starts, permits, conversions, and demolitions.

2. Estimate attrition of planned starts and permitted projects.

3. Estimate new supply. Short-term response to supply includes projects in the pipeline; response to supply in three to five years is very difficult to gauge.

B. Analyze existing zoning and possible changes. Zoning, subdivi-

global economy must also be examined. Similarly, within a town or city, nodes of employment, commercial centers, or residential areas must be accessible, garnering a sufficient share of the metropolitan market to thrive. The ebb and flow of metropolitan economies and areas within them are continuous; they represent that combination of interdependence and competi-

tion that generates change and affects long-term survival. Thus, both competition and cooperation among people and firms affect a place's economic viability. And spatial arrangements within an area are important in influencing firms' profitability and local residents' well-being.

Demand for space is said to be derived because space users locate in a market area

FIGURE 14-2 (continued)

sion ordinances, and building codes are not static. Properties may be converted to respond to changes in demand. Review land use, transportation, and capital investment plans.

C. Consider business cycle and building cycle to compare projections of demand and supply. Make initial estimates of demand minus supply over the relevant future time period for the market area.

V. Analysis of Competition

A. List functions and features of the project in relation to the competition. Price, quality, and draw will depend on the specific design of the project, its functionality, and its package of amenities.

1. Describe existing competitive projects
Price, quantity (units or square feet), age, vacancy, competitive features.

2. Describe proposed competitive projects: price, quantity, competitive features, and probability and timing of construction.

B. Analysis of market segmentation Review analysis of demand. Identify key attributes of space users targeted for the proposed project.

1. Attributes can refer to status (age, sex, occupation, income), behavior (lifestyle, expectations, spending patterns), or geography (location and mobility of demand).

2. Consider expected wants and needs of space users in each market segment.

3. Compare demand by segment to the functions and features of competitive projects and identify ways to differentiate the product.

VI. Analysis of Capture Rate

A. Based on analysis of the competition, estimate total absorption and absorption schedule by market segment and the project's market share to account for the distinct features and competitive advantages that should attract customers and tenants.

1. Estimate project's capture rate.

2. Justify capture rate for the market, given features, functions, and benefits of subject project.

3. Outline key marketing features (relevant to stage seven's marketing plan and budget).

B. Develop final estimate of market capture rate. Project leases or sales per period. Specify price. Specify total time to complete leases or sales.

1. Number of units or square footage leased or sold over time at $x.

2. Suggest improvements in the project that might increase the amount or pace of market capture.

to provide goods or services for the area's residents as well as for nonresidents and companies. Users of residential space typically locate in an area because their jobs are within reasonable commuting range. Most commercial space users are in the market to gain access to local customers. Commercial and industrial space users serving nonlocal customers locate for access to local resources, supplies, and transport facilities adequate to reach their regional, national, or global customers.

The analyst considers demand to depend on one or more of the following factors: employment, population, income, the relative price of space versus all other commodities, and, importantly, space users' expectations about the future. Demand is also influenced by the tax structure, interest rates, and financing requirements to the extent that these factors affect space users' available resources. In the project's market area, the market analyst considers employment, population, or income primarily as the direct influences on demand, using knowledge of the big picture and megatrends to examine and possibly challenge the assumptions that support local socioeconomic forecasts.

To make informed judgments about the future, market analysts must examine trends. Forecasts of population, income, or employment form the basis for forecasts of space absorption in a market area; the key is recognizing patterns and how they could change. For example, a trend in the late 1980s was for an increasing number of single adults to live with their parents rather than to form new households. If it continues, this trend will affect the residential market, whether first-time homebuyers or apartment dwellers. Studying historical trends to understand how absorption has changed relative to indicators of demand for space leads to better-informed forecasts of demand.

FORECASTS

Market analysts make their own projections of population, jobs, and income, using analyses prepared by government agencies, universities, and other private institutions. Rather than making original forecasts for cities or metropolitan areas, analysts are better off checking and refining *existing* forecasts, which are available free from local, regional, state, and federal agencies or at a modest fee from for-profit sources. Part of being a good market analyst is knowing the appropriate sources of information.[3] Savvy analysts collect and compare estimates from several sources, but the analyst's *real* job is to make reasonable estimates for subareas or market segments for which no projections exist.

As a general rule, analysts should compare all local estimates to regional or national averages. For example, analysts frequently use location quotients, which take the percentages employed in each major industry group in the locality and divide them by the percentage employed in the industry group nationally. Thus, a location quotient of 1.0 shows that a local industry is represented as it is nationally. Industries with location quotients of less than 1.0 are underrepresented. Those with location quotients of well above 1.0 account for the locality's economic specialization. In local economic analysis, learning how a market is different from the region or nation is as important as knowing the absolute values. Comparisons to reference areas either in the same locale or in other parts of the country can help the analyst understand the macro forces and megatrends that are at work behind observed outcomes.

In the comparison of forecasts, an outlier forecast is often as interesting as a consensus forecast because it challenges the analyst to figure out why the deviation exists. Variability among forecasts may indicate greater market risk and may warrant an increase in the premium for risk. Equally important is the time frame or forecast period. A market analyst who provides the developer with a good three-year forecast is not providing sufficient information when the developer needs to estimate sales, rents, or NOI for the next 10 years. At minimum, analysts should be explicit about the assumptions made in providing forecasts for too short a period. For example, the developer may need forecasts of office rent for the subject project over the next 15 years, but the market analyst offers a five-year projection over which time the building is expected to be leased to the target occupancy. For market information to be adequate for the financial feasibility analysis, the market analyst assumes that all tenants have signed 10- to 15-year leases with substantial prepayment penalties and that all tenants will remain viable and creditworthy over the terms of their leases or that existing tenants' five-year leases will expire at the same rates. For most speculative office projects built in the mid-1980s, both assumptions were very optimistic, if not heroic.

Population

In forecasting population, births and deaths are relatively easy to estimate. Estimates of migration, on the other hand, can be difficult. It is also difficult to aggregate population properly into consuming units, as required in residential or retail studies. City or county planning departments should have forecasts of population. Local chambers of commerce may also have forecasts, although such estimates often tend to be overly optimistic.

Most states have an office of management and budget that makes projections for counties to estimate long-term revenue for the state; usually the budget agencies are a good source of accurate information. Many use in-house econometric models for forecasts or subscribe to outside econometric services for the information they need. Regional planning agencies often provide demographic and economic information, which is also available from the U.S. Census Bureau. Subscription services collect, analyze, and sell this information.

Market analysts are limited in knowing which forecasts will prove the most accurate. But in evaluating forecasts, they should know how accurate the base-line information is. Even the most careful projections can be wrong because the underlying assumptions about behavior no longer hold or because very recent market behavior has not been incorporated in the projection. For example, market analysts could miss the fact that households in an area are buying houses with an extra bedroom that can be used as an office. Or behavior may be changing where people want to spend more or less income on housing. Frequently, current information is the most difficult to find, and analysts must "forecast" present conditions.

The basic idea is that projections are a point of departure for market analysts rather than something to take as authoritative gospel. Good market analysts try to determine whether projections make sense. For example, are the forecasts of income supported by emerging changes in the local economy? Are forecasted rates of in-migration sustainable, given the availability of properly zoned and serviced land?

Good analysts check the details. They might, for example, look at recent utility hook-ups and telephone installations as a way of estimating whether migration is slowing down or speeding up. Usually such data are quite good. In some areas, where use of cable TV is heavy, installations can also be used to gauge recent migration. National moving companies are a source of current information on interstate moves. At one time, for example, it was impossible to rent a moving van in Louisiana, because the outward migration was so heavy that moving companies could not keep enough vans and trucks on hand to satisfy the demand.

The best available, most comprehensive information on population is usually the most recent decennial census; those figures are used as benchmarks because the census is the sole source of specific socioeconomic estimates for individuals or households by small geographic areas—census tracts in metropolitan areas or minor civil divisions elsewhere. Census information is available in major libraries and in most city or county planning departments. Market analysts update the last census, indicating the increment of population or employment that has either come into or gone out of the community. Estimates of migration are the primary source of information about change in population and the labor force. The local office of the State Employment Security Commission keeps track of current employment, at least those workers covered by unemployment insurance.

Income and Employment

Sound analysis for residential and retail market studies requires looking at patterns of income for subareas of the community, such as census tracts, as well as patterns of population. A correlation exists between income and residential location. The information on average income and average value of housing by census tract from 1990 is highly correlated, and new information on specific areas of population growth and housing obtained from local planning agencies can be used to understand how the composition of the community's income is changing.

The same sources that provide information on population and income also provide information on employment. Most of the published figures ultimately depend on estimates by the U.S. Departments of Commerce and Labor. For example, the Bureau of Labor Statistics (BLS) publishes employment statistics for metropolitan areas monthly in *Employment and Earning*. For nonmetropolitan areas, the Economic Research Service (ERS) in the Department of Agriculture has numerous county-level studies available free or at a nominal cost.

BLS uses a disaggregated input-output model to forecast employment nationally. Based on estimates of final demand for goods and services and estimates of productivity, BLS generates industry-specific estimates of employment. Using BLS estimates as control totals, the Bureau of Economic Analysis (BEA) in the U.S. Department of Commerce steps them down to states and metropolitan areas with a combination of location quotient, shift-share, and economic base analysis, plus some well-informed judgments. The National Planning Association (NPA) also publishes proprietary estimates for counties, metropolitan areas, and states based on BEA and BLS figures. BEA does more comprehensive analysis but publishes forecasts only every five years. NPA revises forecasts biennially but less extensively. Many other groups estimate employment as part of their macroeconomic forecasting, but little consistency exists among models used by these groups. A number of proprietary models provide short-term forecasts for states and, in some cases, for counties and metropolitan areas. Annual subscriptions range from $10,000 to $20,000.

A method of checking for consistency between population and employment estimates is to compute an employment-to-population ratio and examine how that ratio has changed over time in the locality.[4] Using decennial or annual estimates, analysts can determine whether the ratio is constant, trending up, or trending down. With the ratio and the trend, analysts can then compare projections of population with projections of employment. Although the two factors are interdependent, job growth tends to lead population growth. If the ratio for future projections is way out of line with the past, it is worth taking the time to figure out how to adjust one or both projections. For example, it might be reasonable to assume that participation in the labor force in a city will gradually decrease and that the average age of the city's population will gradually increase. If so, the employment-to-population ratio will decline over time. If independent projections of employment and population yield ratios that change *erratically* over time, the projections may need to be revised; at the least, the assumptions must be carefully checked.

Although it is difficult to come up with reliable forecasts of employment, public sources—city or regional planning agencies and state government—are usually as good as any. Local economic development authorities may offer useful insights, although they tend to be a bit bullish on their area. Local people can add good information about an area's economic opportunities and problems that will never be picked up in any of the top-down models. It is therefore wise to complement top-down projections of employment with bottom-up assessments by experts. Market analysts can interview major employers, executives of local banks, university researchers, economic developers, and others to collect expert opinion.

Another use of the bottom-up approach is to examine the details of the employment base: age of facilities in the area, the credit ratings of major employers, and the product mix generated by employers in the community. Some communities produce products on the leading edge in a particular industry. Some products face stiff local or foreign competition, while others sell in less competitive markets. For market studies that emphasize forecasts of employment, such as office or industrial studies, analysts should look within an area's major industries to understand the mix of goods or services they produce. Being good at market analysis is like being good at development: experience, a feel for the market, and knowing when to keep researching and when to stop are all important. In market analysis, there is no substitute for a thirst for details, for local knowledge, and for intelligence.

Why put so much work into forecasting population, income, and employment for a metropolitan area? Market analysts use local and regional forecasts to establish the baseline and benchmark figures for the demand for space. Thus, they must comprehend the future direction of the regional economy. Having a grasp of the next few years and some sound understanding of the relevant changes likely to occur in five to 10 years is necessary, because developers should be interested in feasibility over the next five, 10, or more years. Because the demand for space is derived and driven by the market, sound metropolitan economies will generate more sustained demand for space. In stagnant or declining areas, the demand for space will either decline or come from subgroups of people or firms in the area. In any case, declining, stagnant, or unstable economies increase the risk for any proposed project. Frequently used methods for forecasting overall local demand are summarized in Appendix C.

MARKET AREAS

With forecasts of population, income, and employment for the relevant larger area in hand, market analysts can focus on the area around the subject site. Each type of property has a market area from which demand is drawn. This market, trade, or service area depends on the location of potential buyers, their travel patterns, and their link to the site. Depending on the type of property, market analysts must generate specific forecasts of employment, population, or income for the relevant market area. Usually, analysts have to approximate market areas by using the boundaries of census tracts or counties. In general, however, knowledge of the nodes of activity and patterns of movement is more important than political or administrative boundary lines.

The market area, then, is defined by identifying who will demand the goods, services, or benefits offered by the project, where those potential consumers are located, whether reasonable access exists, and how consumers and producers will overcome the "friction of distance." Other suppliers of space operating in the market area represent the project's competition—usually for customers but possibly also for the scarce inputs explained below.

Residential development establishes locations from which the local population has access to jobs and local goods and services. The metropolitan area or labor market area therefore represents the overall housing market area. Market analysts, how-

Residential development market studies must evaluate location and market demand for different types of housing, as well as the community's attitudes. The Venice Renaissance project in Venice, California, includes 66 market-rate condominiums, 26,000 square feet of retail space, and, as a result of a neighborhood assessment that revealed community concern about losing low-cost housing for Venice's elderly residents, 23 efficiency apartments for the elderly. It is the first major project to be approved in Venice since the 1970s.

ever, devote most attention to submarkets that are distinguished by the specific nature of demand or by differences among housing units, such as age, structure, or neighborhood characteristics (the supply factor). On the demand side, tenure, location, and amenities distinguish the major market segments. Preferences for tenure allocate demand to owners or renters. Adding preferences for locations and amenities leads to finer-grained segments for which data might not be available. For the marketability study, the market area where the subject project is located receives most attention, but competitive supply almost always exists in other locations. As a result, residential market areas are often noncontiguous areas within the same labor market or metropolitan area. Residential developments in different sections of the metropolitan area often compete to attract the same in-migrants or homebuyers and renters who are moving up.[5]

Retail trade areas are the most obvious examples of market areas: consumers living or working near the retail location travel there to purchase goods. Retail trade areas are typically broken down into three levels—primary, secondary, and tertiary—based on driving time and the category of good to be purchased (see Chapter 15).

Office market areas assume two forms. Services like routine medical or dental care have market areas similar to retail trade areas because of their orientation to local residents; local consumers visit those service sites to receive treatment. In contrast, regional or export services have large, noncontiguous service areas. Customers do not visit the service sites. Rather, information flows to and from the sites, and service providers (for example, accountants, architects, engineers) usually travel to deliver services to customers at their locations. Access to qualified labor, needed business or governmental services, and key modes of transport helps define export-service markets.

Industrial trade areas are also noncontiguous, as most manufacturers export products to regional, national, or international markets. Unlike retailers, who compete for the same customers from within their overlapping trade areas, industrial tenants generally sell to different customers in

An architecturally unique outdoor sunning and swimming complex at the Hyatt Regency in Scottsdale, Arizona, gives the hotel a distinctive element that can be used to market the project.

PROFILE: **JOHN M. KEELING**

Former Partner, Laventhol & Horwath
Houston, Texas

Background: Keeling graduated from UCLA, earned an MBA in hotel administration at Michigan State, and worked in operations with Marriott before joining Laventhol & Horwath as a consultant to the hotel industry.

Market segments: Finding a niche is critical in the mature hotel industry, and recognizing market segments and measuring occupancy by segment are therefore crucial to doing a competent market study. It is a mistake to measure overall occupancy for all the hotels in a market, for segments include frequent business travelers, professional groups, transient tourists, and specialized segments, such as airline, medical, or military personnel.

Seasons: Making the right distinctions is one key to good market research. The hotel business is not only segmented but also seasonal. In urban markets, weekdays and weekends are two different seasons, with different rates, guests, and approaches to marketing. For example, weekday occupancy can be 100 percent, weekend occupancy only 20 percent. Consequently, in urban markets good market research does not stop with average weekly occupancy; it breaks out weekend and weekday rates.

Qualitative information: This factor is extremely important but often overlooked. Primary demand interviews with users can reveal opportunities, trends, and mistakes to avoid and can be used as a check on the data base on competitors. Interviews with users tell who is using the product, when, how, why, and whether the user is satisfied. Finding the person who books rooms for corporations is important. Laventhol & Horwath did a minimum of 20 primary demand interviews and as many as 50 to understand the market; it also conducted some demand interviews for every project.

Output—the quantified result: A good hotel market study quantifies current supply and demand by segment and season; "turnaway demand," that is, the number of requests for rooms that could not be filled because occupancy was 100 percent; and projected future supply and demand. Future supply is easy to project in highly regulated cities like San Diego but more difficult to project in cities with less regulation, like Houston. In places like Houston, analysts must talk to people to find out what the future competition is. Future demand is more difficult to predict, particularly for longer periods, but skilled analysts will be able to tell a convincing story based on long-term trends in the market.

---

dispersed locations. They might well compete for local inputs, however—infrastructure, labor, intermediate goods or services, and properly zoned industrial land.

Hotels serve their market differently from retail centers in that most guests reside somewhere outside the locality rather than near the accommodations. The large majority of guests therefore are passing through rather than residing in the area permanently. Like retail centers and offices, hotels compete for sites at highly accessible nodes of transportation or key destinations. The accompanying profile of hotel analyst John Keeling touches on critical factors necessary to analyze the mature, cyclical hotel industry.

Geographic information systems (GIS) help analysts understand market areas. Their use has grown rapidly as microcomputers and remote sensing have become widely available in the development industry, and new software is making GIS accessible even to small development firms in small to medium markets. Newer applications of GIS can now define market areas using drive times instead of just distance, population, or income.[6]

PRICES

Once analysts have a good sense of the fundamental economics of the metropolitan area, the patterns and trends in the market area, and the spatial links and accessibility of the site, they next focus on prices relative to the proposed use at the selected site, using estimates of development and operating costs to project the minimum price and therefore the affordability of the proposed project to different market segments. Operations and maintenance costs also are used to arrive at estimates of stabilized NOI for income-producing projects. For property serving households, market analysts must know income levels and expenditure patterns of households in the market area to estimate effective demand. For example, knowing expected mortgage rates and qualification standards for a proposed residential project that will offer houses ranging from $150,000 to $200,000, analysts can calculate the number of households with sufficient income to afford the houses. Within households grouped by income, analysts can target the segment most likely to buy in the projected price range.

At times, market analysts conduct their own surveys of the market. At other times, they find that enough published information is available. Often, they use both published information and private survey data in combination. Primary information based on sample surveys or focus groups can allow analysts to sharpen estimates of the quality of housing desired by different social groups. In some areas, keeping up with the Joneses may be important, with households willing to spend a disproportionately large share of wealth and income on housing. Yet mortgage lenders' qualifying standards are nearly uniform across the country as a result of widespread use of

secondary mortgage markets in the 1980s. The basic objective is to examine residential preferences and households' willingness to pay for various housing features.

For office or industrial property, market analysts use employment figures by place of work to indicate demand in the metropolitan market area. It is helpful to disaggregate employment forecasts by industry and occupation group to gain an understanding of the mix of industries and product types in the metropolitan area. Disaggregated employment forecasts suggest stronger or weaker demand relative to area-wide economic trends. Analysts can estimate the average prices of goods and services to be sold by potential tenants from the subject location and their anticipated expenditures for space and then see how realistic prices for the space are by using standards and survey-based information on future space use and asking rents. Of course, these estimates of demand establish a price range that cannot be refined further without including supply in the analysis.

Good market analysts recognize that it is important but difficult to predict how technology and tastes will change users' behavior and relative prices of space. New technology creates new ways to use space, while changes in prices affect the amount and quality of space demanded. No rules can be easily applied to incorporate these influences, and market analysts must guard against mechanically applying quantities, ratios, and other parameters to arrive at demand for the schedule of absorption.

One way to partially incorporate technology and tastes in estimates of demand is to recognize substitution, as well as growth, as a source of demand. Space users often consume more space when rents relative to other costs decline and less space when relative rents increase. In other words, if the relative price of the proposed space is moving up as a result of excess demand, prospective space users tend to buy less. If prices are moving down as a result of excess supply, prospective users might consume more. Based on a comparison of employment trends among office users and trends of office absorption in several large metropolitan areas, tenants appear to lease more space per worker as overbuilding increases. Thus, as markets tighten and effective rents rise, certain tenants may be able to add employees without leasing more space in the short term.[7]

CHARACTERISTICS OF SUPPLY

Market analysts forecast supply of the subject type of property to compare it with forecasted demand. If forecasted demand exceeds forecasted supply, demand is excess. If the difference is zero or negative, analysts usually expect no absorption from expected growth and therefore a more difficult market for the project.

The supply side is analyzed by examining the given stock and planned increases (starts and permitted projects). With these figures, market analysts can forecast the inventory in units or square footage over the next several years. It can be somewhat difficult, however, to get a handle on the longer-term response to supply than on longer-term demand. Are other developers examining the feasibility of this type of property? How many of them will enter the market over the relevant time period? How will the public sector react?

One approach to the longer-term response to supply is to make some assumptions about the market's behavior and governmental responses to the market. In some areas, development companies continue to build in an overbuilt market when allowed to do so. Domestic or foreign investors may be awash in funds for real estate, resulting in too much money chasing too few deals. With overactive developers and plenty of financing, the market may fail to regulate supply adequately. Local governments have planning, zoning, and other regulatory tools that enable them to restrict supply; they may choose to increase development restrictions rather than to let overbuilding continue. Under these assumptions, market analysts should predict long-term supply primarily by estimating the degree of governmental restrictiveness in the subject market area. Obviously, it is not easy.

Another approach is to recognize that longer-term supply is sensitive to business and construction cycles. Although forecasts of cycles are often unreliable, one need only analyze the past to comprehend that new supply does not increase on a straight line or at some constant rate of change. It is worthwhile to consider cyclical conditions during the forecast period, especially for periods when project sales or leasing is expected to be high.

Analysts collect information on existing supply and planned projects from local planning agencies, and they do surveys to see which projects are being built. They should identify space that will probably be eliminated or converted because of its age or because of its economic obsolescence. While it is fairly easy to measure existing supply, more effort is required to collect information on building permits and approved projects. Still more effort is required to estimate the age and economic obsolescence of structures to forecast reductions in stock. Analyses can be brief or detailed, depending on the size of the market and the extent to which competing projects exist there. The more narrowly focused the specific demand for the project, the smaller the relevant supply. Looking at recently completed projects is the best way to determine the type of product being offered in the marketplace. Analysts can use this market intelligence to help developers evaluate the market niche for the proposed project.

All of these factors boil down to an accounting equation for supply: anticipated supply = existing stock + (space under construction, expected starts, planned new projects, and conversions of space) - (demolitions, removals of stock, and abandoned projects). But filling in the values for future projects, conversions, and removals is the part that separates skillful market analysts from the rest of us.

COMPETING PROJECTS

While studying supply, market analysts begin to examine the competition, looking for:
- Features of the product (number, size, density);
- Product mix (different types of space in the project);
- Levels and ranges of prices or rents;
- Time on market and price changes if any (including discounts);
- Actual occupancy by type of tenant;
- Special amenities of the space or site;

- Functionality, including access and visibility;
- The quality of management and the original developer.[8]

Market analysts get only limited information by driving past projects. They must talk to people who are using and selling the space. Brokers are potentially helpful, and current space users might be willing to talk about the space they occupy. Do they have problems with functions, features, services, layout, or other factors? Talking with space users brings market analysts back to the demand side, where they can assess the accuracy of the developer's perception of demand in the relevant market segments. Market analysts will want to disaggregate forecasted demand in the market area, having thoroughly studied targeted market segments. At the end of this process, forecasted demand for the subject project must logically fall into one or more segments that the analyst can defend. One of the most common pitfalls of market analysis is inconsistency between a careful analysis of demand and supply in general for the type of property (for example, apartments) and the sloppy or incomplete estimates of demand and supply for targeted space users (for example, elderly couples with moderate-to-high retirement incomes). In other words, the market study is sound, but the marketability study is weak.

The market analyst's task of examining potential customers by identifying competitive projects is similar to that of an appraiser who is searching for comparable projects. Both are trying to identify potential or existing space users who are willing to pay x dollars for the subject space. Both collect information on a sufficient number of potential customers or comparable projects to arrive at reliable estimates. Market analysts seek estimates of the quantity of demand within a given price range. Appraisers want to gauge the value (price) of space, given the existing amount of space used. In either case, the results indicate whether analysts have defined the market segments consistently and logically. Otherwise, they have overestimated potential absorption, and the project is exposed to greater risk in the market. Market analysts might suggest longer leasing or sales periods, greater expenditures for marketing, or

even postponement of the project when uncertainty is considerable. Appraisers might increase the premium for risk or examine value under different future scenarios in analyzing discounted cash flow.

ABSORPTION

Market analysts are concerned about absorption at three levels: the overall market for the type of product, the relevant market segments, and the subject project. For the overall market, expected future demand, expressed in units of space, yields the forecast of market absorption.

Thorough market research can often uncover market absorption in excess of projected supply, even in areas with no overall population growth or with stagnant employment. Opportunities could exist in such markets when the quality of space demanded is changing because of changing tastes or composition. For example, with zero migration, the composition of the population could be changing from younger people with less income to older people with more income. Likewise, a trend toward smaller households can also generate greater demand for housing without overall growth in population.

Systematic market research requires consideration of the specific market segments targeted by the developer and the projects likely to be attractive to space users. Market analysts zero in on that portion of overall market demand sought by the subject project and compare the amount of space demanded by each target market segment to the amount of competitive supply. At this juncture, skillful market analysts can create value far in excess of their fee by identifying flaws in the preliminary project design and suggesting more appropriate functions and features.

From the forecasted schedule of absorption for the proper market segments, market analysts can estimate the *project's* capture rate and schedule of absorption (see Figure 14-3). The project's capture rate and its eventual profitability will actually depend on how well the developer understands demand and what the competition is doing, beyond cursory market or marketability studies containing only numbers, tables, and graphs. Market analysts can learn

FIGURE 14-3
ESTIMATING A PROJECT'S CAPTURE RATE

	Rankings		Units Leased		
	Location	Amenities	Time 1	Time 2	Total
Subject	3	3	25	75	100
Project 1	4	1	75	75	150
Project 2	1	2	100	0	100
Project 3	2	4	50	100	150
			250	250	500

much about consumers' behavior and provide useful feedback to developers by interviewing customers to understand how space is being used and how use might be changing. Furthermore, they can anticipate supply from studying the competition and investigating which developers will continue with one type of product and which are more flexible and responsive to changes in demand. Extensive marketing research is needed to refine a product that truly fits the marketplace, and market analysts serve their developer-clients well by conducting detailed, primary research as required.

Although market capture rates are subjective and more than one rate is often used, analysts must justify the range of selected rates by explicitly identifying the key marketing factors. Developers can use this justification (see Chapter 19) to improve the marketing plan by studying the competition vis-à-vis the project and determining what to do differently to be successful, linking marketing research to merchandising.

No single pat method exists for allocating absorption to the subject project. Some market studies proceed on the implicit assumption that the subject project will get its fair (proportionate) share of demand. In such studies, market penetration rates are based on the size of the subject project relative to total competitive supply. Most sophisticated market analysts, however, use a variation of the appraiser's grid in which the appraiser relates specific features of comparable projects to the subject project to arrive at an estimate of value (market price). Market analysts use the grid for a different purpose, that is, to allocate space within a given price range to the subject project.

The analyst's survey of existing competitive projects is used to create the grid for evaluating features of several comparable projects and relating them to the existing market share of those projects. Analysts then add planned projects and the proposed subject project and project the market share for each, based on the strength of their features. For example, in some cities all apartments within walking distance of the primary employer (a hospital center, for example) fill completely, so their market share is the number of units divided by the number of units in the market. Less well-located apartment units compete for the remaining demand, with market share based largely on price, amenities, square footage, kitchen design, or other features important to the targeted tenants.

If the grid contains all relevant projects, total demand for the market segment should be allocated to the subject plus the comparable projects. If the grid excludes the supply expected to handle current demand, then subject plus comparable projects equals the new supply expected to absorb forecasted demand. In either case, analysts estimate the subject's market share at the *end* of the absorption period. Next, they must forecast *project* absorption by showing how estimated capture will occur *during* the marketing period in units per week, per month, or per year to correspond to dynamics of the market. When completed projects are fully sold or leased, they can be removed from the matrix, and as new projects come on line, they are added to the grid. If vacancies are above normal, that amount of space is recognized as unoccupied space in existing, competitive projects and is included in the grid. The grid, in fact, is an accounting system that analysts use to assign expected absorption to available space over time.

As a simple illustration, a subject apartment complex is expected to lease over two time periods. Three competing projects offer apartment units at comparable rent levels but with varying access and amenities. Total absorption for this market segment is related to product supply, including required vacancies. Absorption is assumed to be constant for the two time periods, and all units are expected to be absorbed by the end of the second time period. In the example, capture is a function of location and amenities, which are given priority in the grid. Using an explicit comparison grid adds rigor to the analysis. At the same time, the analyst should not be deluded by the neatness of columns and rows into thinking that projected outcomes will surely come true. Not even the best analysts can remove all of life's uncertainty.[9]

As noted in Chapters 18 and 19 on marketing and management, the absorption of a well-designed, well-timed project ultimately depends on the quality of the marketing team selling or leasing the space and the quality of property management after operations begin. Forecasting capture rates and project absorption can help identify the key elements upon which success depends, but it is up to the developer's team to shape those elements into a realistic marketing plan and to make it a reality.

For some projects, when they plan to put a product on the market and sell it quickly to users or investors or to lease it to quality tenants for a long term, developers might be satisfied with near-term projections only. But in most markets, such expectations are often not realized. Increasingly, developers and investors are finding it necessary to project income and expenses for 10- to 15-year periods at minimum. Many work with longer planning horizons, and market analysts must be prepared to make projections for these time frames.

Simulation is a useful way to supplement near-term forecasts with longer-term projections.[10] The basic approach, shown

below in the first equation, relates population to demand for speculative office space by multiplying population by several ratios: workers to population, white-collar workers to total workers, speculative office workers to total white-collar workers, and speculative office space to workers in speculative office space. Instead of four (average) ratios, a probability distribution is established for each. This approach simply requires using these probabilities to select numerical values for each ratio. By using the probabilities to select values and running the numbers repeatedly, analysts can get a range of total and annualized forecasts of absorption. This approach is quite feasible as an application of spreadsheet programs.[11]

Demand for Speculative Office Space =

$$Population \times \frac{Total\ Workers}{Population} \times$$

$$\frac{White\text{-}Collar\ Workers\ (WCW)}{Total\ Workers} \times$$

$$\frac{WCW\ in\ Speculative\ Buildings}{WCW} \times$$

$$\frac{Rentable\ Square\ Footage}{WCW\ in\ Speculative\ Buildings}$$

This model can be extended to incorporate supply. As shown in the second equation below, total supply is estimated by adding the required vacancy to the occupied inventory, which sets an appropriate cushion for vacancies, adding a factor for new supply for the estimated rate of completions and subtracting a factor for adjusting stock for estimated reductions caused by aging and conversions. Market analysts can assign a subjective probability distribution for each of the three supply-side factors, using values based upon an understanding of current market conditions, possibilities for new development, and the local government's propensity to regulate the development process. These factors will influence rent levels and therefore space use.

Supply of Speculative Office Space =
Occupied Inventory + Required Vacancies +
New Projected Supply – Reductions in Inventory

This risk simulation approach is actually a comprehensive form of sensitivity analysis in which the market analyst scrutinizes key assumptions numerically as well as logically. The empirical analysis involves using a range of figures and comparing the results. Standards like square footage of space per worker or expected vacancy rates are prime candidates for sensitivity analysis. Sensitivity analysis becomes increasingly complex as the analyst tries to account for changes in technology, preferences, and spatial patterns over time.

PROBLEMS, PITFALLS, AND LIMITATIONS

While this chapter's viewpoint is that of a market analyst conducting market research for a developer, developers should also be aware of some problems, pitfalls, and limitations of market analysis. This awareness provides the developer with another tool to control risk and limit exposure as well as a means of evaluating the competence of market and marketability studies commissioned.

Market studies may lack *reliability* and *validity*. Reliability depends on precise measures and accurate quantitative information. Because much real estate information is derived from nonrandom surveys and expert opinion, it may not be reliable. And at times respondents may be less than completely candid, although ambiguous questions more often lead to imprecise answers. Office vacancies are measured differently for different data bases. The absence of uniform definitions is at the heart of inconsistent reported rates. (Low reliability may translate into a higher risk premium in the discount rate.)

Researchers define validity as the extent to which market studies actually measure what they are supposed to measure. Clearly, the measures of market supply and demand used in real estate market research are only crude surrogates for the market conditions and economic behaviors they are supposed to reflect. For example, employment growth is the best available measure of new demand for space. Yet standards like space used per worker change continually, sometimes in unexpected ways, affecting the validity of the correspondence between employment and space. Gains in manufacturing productivity are expected to continue. Do slower rates of employment growth in manufacturing mean less demand for industrial facilities? Automated facilities responsible in part for increases in labor productivity may require more space overall than before a factory was automated. Market analysts should therefore continually reexamine the meaning of each key measure to keep current in the field and project trends accurately.

Statistical validity refers to the accuracy of information when a partial census is taken from which conclusions are inferred about all things in that category. Constraints on time and cost almost always limit market analysts to collecting partial information. Occasionally, analysts can draw on random samples and thereby calculate inherent error in sampling. More frequently, however, samples are biased and the sampling error is unknown. The best approach is to define the subject and comparable projects as carefully as possible so that the elements in the sample are meaningfully similar and representative of the entire category. An alternative is to take an inventory of the entire category population, which may be feasible in smaller markets.

More fundamental than statistical validity is the research methodology. The question is whether the market analyst has designed the research properly in the first place to answer the questions accurately. The outline shown in Figure 14-2 offers a general framework for designing the market analysis properly; the analyst must avoid certain pitfalls of retail market studies that fail to pay attention to key issues of research—overestimating the trade area or making unreasonable assumptions about capture, for example, but also more subtle problems, such as ignoring retail business failures in the area or ignoring the limitations of data sources, which could lead to overestimated demand or underestimated supply.[12]

Another important aspect of validity is one that gives market researchers the ability to generalize from one analysis to others. Certainly, market research firms with excellent reputations in the industry are assumed to use experience, institutionalized knowledge, and well-maintained data bases to draw sound conclusions about the subject project. The most careful work involves continual reevaluation, because assumptions held in the past may well change in the future.

Standards and Sensitivity Analysis

The standards discussed earlier in this chapter represent the ratio of two averages. Market analysts should be aware of the errors of estimation inherent in using such ratios. First, any ratio may be plotted as a linear function that passes through the origin, that is, $y = bx$, where b represents the standard ratio. For example, if y represents space demand in square feet, x is employees using office space and b is square feet of space per employee. By using this ratio, market analysts automatically assume a linear relationship taking this particular form.

Second, standard ratios come from previously completed empirical analysis. They may have been good rules of thumb in the past but may not hold up well in the future. Third, the ratio may be viewed as a crude approximation of a statistically estimated equation, for example, the least-squares regression line. If the actual equation has a negative or positive intercept term instead of a zero value as assumed, the ratio, in this example space per employee, either overestimates or underestimates change.[13] Furthermore, the confidence interval around the assumed equation is at a minimum at the intersection of means and increases moving in either direction. Therefore, the larger the deviation in x (employment) from the average, the less reliable the estimate of y (space demand). Although no market analyst can consistently decide when slopes will change or turning points will be reached, good analysts ask how reasonable the assumption is that the relationship will not change. The probabilistic approach mitigates this problem to some extent by permitting use of a range of values, but the underlying points remain valid.

Too often, market studies contain estimates for revenues, costs, and vacancies that are predicted in the near term and subsequently assumed to change at constant rates. Although it is reasonable for developers to make such assumptions dur-

ing refinement of the idea (stage two), market analysts must go farther in stage three by forecasting over the relevant period and pursuing sensitivity analysis of results. By increasing revenues and expenses at constant rates, the rate of increase in NOI is constant, but the amount of NOI increases in absolute amount. Any 10-year pro forma can be reviewed making this assumption to confirm the result. A seemingly harmless shortcut can make projections look better than warranted. Furthermore, the estimates of NOI at the end of 10 years, when compared to the projected sales price, could yield a cap rate that is different from cap rates currently existing in the market place. Market analysts using the approach of a constant increase are obliged to explain why the capitalization rate suggested in the final year of the pro forma financial analysis is justifiable. Market analysts should try to estimate a realistic revenue stream by period based on realities of the market, not one that can be generated by pushing a few buttons on the computer.[14]

Another pitfall involves using a standard vacancy rate. First, in the overbuilt markets of the late 1980s, standards changed and benchmark vacancy rates lost their meaning. Market analysts should build up a vacancy rate like a composite capture rate by considering a plausible tenant mix and estimating a reasonable revenue stream based on specific tenants. Obviously, leasing commissions, tenant finishes, and concessions must be recognized in forecasting effective rental income.[15]

A final and all-too-common pitfall refers to the correspondence between the proposed project and the project that is actually constructed. Ideally, market analysts should allocate demand from relevant market segments to the grid containing the subject project and other comparable ones. The problem arises when the project actually built is different from the proposed project the market analyst studied. Just as developers should use the same pro forma in stage three in seeking commitments from other players, market analysts should examine the project that will actually be built. It is very easy to become inconsistent here as the design of the project moves from preliminary form to final design with drawings. Developers try to make their proj-

More and more, developers are paying attention to design as a means of distinguishing projects from the competition. The Crescent, a dramatic urban mixed-used development next to downtown Dallas, is instantly recognizable because of the crescent shape of the building and its "Texas classic" style, incorporating French architectural influences of the late 19th century.

ects distinctive to gain a competitive advantage. Market analysts, who should almost never consider a project unique, search for comparable projects among existing or planned projects. Clearly, estimates of market capture depend on the proposed project's location, functions, and features in relation to those of the competition. When functions and features later change, the grounding for the expected capture disappears.

In relating this outcome to demand, market analysts break down overall market demand to find segments with different status, behavior, or location that can be matched to differentiated products (supply). Changing the project creates a mismatch between this supply and the targeted market segments; therefore, the sales

and leasing staff will be prospecting in the wrong segments unless more marketing research is commissioned to eliminate the mismatch.

Limitations

Market analysts should realize the limits of good market research. Although the market study can be an effective technique to control risk, it does not answer all relevant questions with perfect certainty. First, market analysts must rely on their sources, and local sources of primary information, as well as secondary sources, may prove unreliable over the long term. Scientific sampling increases the accuracy of information, but it cannot improve the precision of estimates.

Second, research does not necessarily indicate the subject property's highest and best use, as the market study thoroughly examines only one alternative for development. In contrast, the study of highest and best use compares all alternatives for development that meet the site's physical constraints, the legal constraints on use, the economic objective of maximizing profit, and realities of the market. The property owner, in identifying the highest asking price, is usually the person most interested in highest and best use and may hire an appraiser to conduct such a study.[16] The classic version is applied to raw land, but the study can be applied to improved sites as long as alternatives for redevelopment are considered.

The market study does not determine the optimum site for the proposed project design that is given along with the proposed use. Analysts involved in site selection begin with a known specific use, such as a J.C. Penney store or a Burger King, and analyze location and accessibility systematically to arrive at attractive sites. Furthermore, market analysts do not calculate optimum project scale. The developer usually gives the analyst the project's scale in units or square feet based on analysis in the second stage. The analyst then uses that quantity of space in the market study. Yet a developer may not always rigorously analyze the project to find the optimum scale. Often the preliminary design maximizes scale, given legal and physical constraints. The developer should carefully compare marginal revenues to marginal costs, possibly using cash flow analysis or break-even analysis, to determine the scale of the proposed project.

Third, market analysts cannot gauge the long-term response to supply with great accuracy. In microeconomic terms, analysts focus on short-term changes in supply, not the long-term supply schedule. Although real estate markets are inefficient to some degree, analysts lack the tools to predict the length of time a property can enjoy monopoly rents. Even with knowledge of the other developers in the market and their financial backing and likely behavior, market analysts cannot predict the number or timing of new entries in the market. As major development companies continue to expand their geographic scope, local markets will probably become more open and more efficient. Obviously, overbuilt markets, extended leasing periods, and shorter-term leases make accurate revenue forecasts ever more difficult and fundamentals of the metropolitan area and location in the area even more important.

With more than one developer hiring different market analysts to study an idea, it cannot be guaranteed that several developers will not come to the same conclusion and break ground at about the same time—a "prisoners' dilemma" in which two developers, acting individually, create a situation unfavorable to both of them. The public sector can avoid this dilemma but only by reducing competition. Local governments are often unable to provide objective market intelligence or are unwilling to turn down redundant projects.

At one extreme, the public can tightly regulate supply. At the other, the public can minimize restraints on development and let developers overbuild if they choose to do so. A middle position is to restrict development at specific locations to avoid damaging the environment and to zone enough land elsewhere to accommodate anticipated growth. In this instance, the public sector informs developers about how much land is zoned in each use and what requirements for development exist. The public sector thereby influences the private sector to make more rational decisions.

Fourth, market analysts can seldom predict the behavior of owners of the existing supply or of existing tenants. Tenants leasing space now may not continue to occupy that space. Analysts consider the space absorbed, but it later becomes vacant. Tenants may sublet space with or without the landlord's permission, usually discounting rents in the process. As a result, analysts can overestimate absorption in the specific rental range. The demand for space is sensitive to prices. Tenants might lease more space than needed in a buyers' market and then reduce space use per employee as rents increase. Analysts might overestimate the absorption of new space when existing leased space can accommodate more employees.

Existing owners could respond in ways that cut into forecasted excess demand. Because they are in the market at lower capital costs, they might be willing to cut rents to attract tenants in soft markets. They might be able to expand or convert facilities to create competition that market analysts cannot anticipate.

Thus, the techniques of analyzing demand and supply, while representing the best practice of market studies, can only approximate human behavior. The future cannot be predicted accurately, for the volitional actions of developers, investors, regulators, and, most important, space users drive real estate markets. Observed real estate conditions and trends result from those actions, but if this reality were not positive, development would not be so engaging, creative, and exciting.

Finally, the discussion of limitations is not complete without considering the limited resources for market analysis. Developers are often unwilling to pay market analysts enough to conduct systematic and rigorous research. It is not uncommon to commission $30,000 market studies for $30 million projects. Because market analysts are part of a competitive industry, resources for market analyses of proposed projects are not likely to increase appreciably. Furthermore, market analysts often work under pressing deadlines that make corroboration of all key numbers or assumptions difficult, if not impossible. Limited time and dollars—as well as the basic competence of the market analyst—affect the quality of the resulting product. Therefore, market studies cannot be fairly judged without knowing why they were commissioned, how long they were under preparation, and how much they cost.

SUMMARY

To conduct detailed, systematic market analyses, market analysts forecast demand by moving quickly from global, national, regional, and local information to estimates of demand appropriate for the type of property specific to the delineated market area that includes the site selected by the developer in stage two. The analysis of supply derives estimates of current inventory, additions from renovations or new construction, and deletions from conversions or demolitions to forecast expected supply. Near-term forecasts can be quite accurate, while forecasts for three to five years in the future could be highly uncertain.

Market analysts study the competition carefully to sharpen the definition of competing supply, to verify price (rental) ranges, and to understand demand more thoroughly. The competitive analysis helps refine the appropriate market segments—customers, tenants, or space users—willing to pay for the proposed space. Armed with this information, analysts estimate a schedule of absorption for the appropriate market segments. From that schedule and an understanding of the special features of the subject project relative to the competition, analysts estimate the project's capture rate and schedule of absorption and, in justifying these estimates, help the developer refine the marketing strategy for the project.

Thus, the market and marketability study done in stage three should contain analyses of the overall market, the specific market segment, and the key marketing features needed to complete a reliable estimate of a project's feasibility.

NOTES

1. In this chapter, absorption is the amount of space occupied during a period of time. It may be measured as the difference between increases and decreases in occupancy gauged at several times. Because the measure is a difference, it is sometimes called "net absorption." The following terminology, used in this chapter, is clearer: *leasing activity*—the total amount of space leased during the time period; *terminations*—the total amount of space abandoned during the time period; *absorption*—the total amount of space occupied during the time period, measured as leasing activity minus terminations. Ideally, absorption would exclude leased but unoccupied space but include sublet space.

2. Anthony Downs, "Characteristics of Various Economic Studies," *Appraisal Journal,* July 1966, pp. 329–38.

3. Sources of information are listed in G. Vincent Barrett and John P. Blair, *How to Conduct and Analyze Real Estate Market and Feasibility Studies* (New York: Van Nostrand Reinhold, 1988); John Clapp, *Handbook for Real Estate Market Analysis* (Englewood Cliffs, N.J.: Prentice-Hall, 1987); and Neil Carn, Joseph Rabianski, Ronald Racster, and Maury Seldin, *Real Estate Market Analysis: Techniques and Applications* (Englewood Cliffs, N.J.: Prentice-Hall, 1988).

4. Barrett and Blair, *How to Conduct and Analyze Real Estate Market and Feasibility Studies.*

5. More detailed discussion is found in Carn et al., *Real Estate Market Analysis.*

6. See David R. Godschalk, Scott A. Bollens, John S. Hekman, and Mike E. Miles, *Land Supply Monitoring: A Guide for Improving Public and Private Urban Development Decisions* (Boston: Lincoln Institute for Land Policy, 1986), for more details about GIS.

7. Although gathering the information is difficult, analysts need to measure effective rent, which is contract (or asking) rent minus rent concessions and unusual tenant finishes. See Robert P. Tunis, "The Negotiation Differential," *Real Estate Review,* Winter 1989, pp. 49–55. Effective rents should be cited on a comparable basis.

8. Barrett and Blair, *How to Conduct and Analyze Real Estate Market and Feasibility Studies.*

9. The survey of the competition forms the basis of the analyst's grid. For elaboration, see Carn et al., *Real Estate Market Analysis,* pp. 89–94.

10. Joseph J. Del Casino, "A Risk Simulation Approach to Long-Range Office Demand Forecasting," *Real Estate Review,* Summer 1985, pp. 82–87.

11. Ibid.

12. Glen Weisbrod and Karl Rador, "The Seven Deadly Sins of Retail Market Studies," *Urban Land,* February 1988, pp. 21–25.

13. To illustrate the point, draw x and y axes and a straight line out from the origin in the first quadrant representing $y = bx$. Assume some point on the line represents the intersection of the aver-

age values of x and y $(\bar{x}, \bar{y})$. Now add two lines passing through that point, one with a positive intercept A and one with a negative intercept D. Starting from the intersection of the means, compare estimates of y given changes in x, using the original line to estimates using either dotted line.

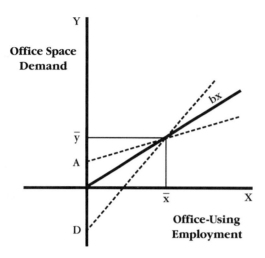

14. Vernon Martin, III, "Nine Abuses Common in Pro Forma Cash Flow Projections," *Real Estate Review,* Fall 1988, pp. 20–25.

15. Tunis, "The Negotiation Differential," pp. 49–55.

16. As noted in Chapter 9, investors also hire appraisers. In fact, institutional investors often require MAI appraisals for deals over some specified threshold, say $10 million. The appraisal is used in acquisition or underwriting as part of the process of due diligence.

Chapter 15

Real Estate Market Studies

T his chapter uses the fundamentals of market studies from the preceding chapter as a foundation for the discussion of developing actual market studies. Theory is consistent across the four principal types of property, but the mechanics and what is most important can vary substantially. The chapter focuses on four types of market studies:

- Residential market studies;
- Retail market studies;
- Office market studies; and
- Industrial market studies.

RESIDENTIAL MARKET STUDIES

A good point of departure for residential market studies is shown in Figure 15-1. This approach is used frequently to examine an area's entire housing market and the amount of new space that can be absorbed over a period of time, in this case 10 years. Key information includes a projection of population, the conversion from population to housing (assuming in this example that each household has three people), and a vacancy factor, which are then combined to estimate total housing required. Estimated supply equals existing stock plus planned stock.

This approach has both strengths and weaknesses. On the positive side, the method is simple, it uses reliable, available data, and it requires minimal commitments of time and money. On the negative side, the key parameters assumed to be constant—for example, average household size or required vacancies—might change. Further, permitted units ("planned stock") might or might not be constructed. And the approach does not recognize the influence of the business cycle on timing; it simply projects excess demand for the entire 10-year period. It is better therefore to project supply and demand annually, recognizing cyclical and secular trends for the local economy and the construction industry. Figure 15-2 lists some of the possible government publications that provide relevant data about employment and population.

Market analysts continually face the trade-off between ideal market research and the time and resources available to complete the analysis. In their competitive business, margins are usually thin and clients' expectations high. It is therefore incumbent for would-be market analysts to identify the strengths and weaknesses of each type of study and determine how to improve the research methodology by ex-

FIGURE 15-1
HOUSING MARKET ANALYSIS: SUPPLY AND DEMAND EQUILIBRIUM[a]

Item

1. Population Projection, Adjusted, to 1985		314,000
2. Estimated Required Housing, 314,000 ÷ 3 =		104,666
3. Plus 5% Vacancy Factor		5,233
4. Total Estimated Housing Required by 1985		109,898
5. Minus Units Presently Constructed	66,808	
6. Minus Units Permitted but Not Constructed	8,016	
TOTAL EXISTING HOUSING STOCK		74,824
7. Additional Housing Required by 1985		35,074
8. Required per Year to 1985, 35,074 ÷ 10		3,507
9. Estimate of Present Population		200,000
10. Estimate of Present Housing Requirement, 200,000 ÷ 3		66,666
11. Plus 5% Vacancy Factor		3,334
12. Estimate of Total Present Housing Requirement		70,000
13. Minus Housing Stock Existing under Construction (items 5 and 6)	74,824	
14. Existing Supply Condition (oversupply)		4,824
15. Estimated Time to Deplete Existing and Planned Stock, $\frac{4,824}{3,507}$ =		Approximately 1.4 Years

[a]Conversions in are assumed to equal conversions out, and persons living in group quarters are not considered significant in numbers.

Source: G. Vincent Barrett and John P. Blair, *How to Conduct and Analyze Real Estate Market and Feasibility Studies*, 2d ed. (New York: Van Nostrand Reinhold, 1988), p. 61.

---

pending more effort to achieve greater detail and determining under which circumstances it would be cost-effective to do so.

For residential market studies, an overall analysis of demand is not adequate. Because many markets have important submarkets, the market analyst must define market segments and allocate overall demand to them. In housing, a segment is determined primarily by residents' income and tenure, although in some areas other important characteristics—ethnicity or age or lifestyle—might play a role. Residential market segments are usually not contiguous. The developer's objective could be to serve an income group or an age group currently residing in more than one location in the community or expected to migrate to the community.

Analysts first describe features of the target income group that help relate their preferences for housing to price, because they want to get a sense of the trade-offs between amenities and price. In the analysis of competition, they study the way existing and planned projects are meeting or missing those preferences. Such research helps identify particular niches or particular amenities or particular cost-saving devices that the developer can exploit. It also points to the competitive characteristics of the proposed project in terms of scale, layout, site amenities, price ranges, size of units, interior features, and so on. This type of research represents a systematic check on the initial residential design the developer completed during refinement of the idea.

Absorption for the relevant residential market segment must be related to the price, quality, and scale of the proposed project for analysts to justify the project's estimated capture rate and absorption schedule. Analysts create a grid for comparing the subject project to competitive projects point by point in terms of price, scale, and other relevant attributes. By estimating the absorption of all such projects in the market area, they make an initial estimate of capture for the subject project. Although the estimate is subjective, analysts must

---

FIGURE 15-2

SOURCES OF GOVERNMENT PUBLICATIONS

Data	Source	What?	How Often?	Coverage
Employment	County Business Patterns, U.S. Census Bureau	Total employment, total establishments	Annual, one- to two-year lag	Every county, most industries
	Labor and Earnings Report, Bureau of Labor Statistics	Employment, unemployment rates	Quarterly	Every state, largest MSAs, employment by sector
	Five-Year Industry Census, U.S. Census Bureau	Employment, sales, establishments	Every five years: 19x2, 19x7	Manufacturing, selected services, retail trade, transportation
	State Departments of Planning, Finance, Economic Development, Employment Security	Employment, unemployment rates	Annual	Usually by county and sector
	Metropolitan Planning Agencies	Employment	Varies	Varies
Population; Households and Housing	Decennial census, U.S. Census Bureau	Population and housing counts, characteristics	Every 10 years	All states, counties, and incorporated places
	City and County Databook, U.S. Census Bureau	Selected population, housing characteristics	Every three years	Cities, counties, and metropolitan areas
	P-26 reports: Local population estimates	County population estimates	Yearly	County
	C-40 reports: Building permits authorized	Building permits by type	Monthly	State and county
	C-21 reports: New residential construction (Department of Commerce, U.S. Census Bureau)	New residential construction	Quarterly	40 largest MSAs
	State Departments of Planning	Population, housing counts	Varies	Usually by county
	Metropolitan Planning Agencies	Population, housing counts	Varies	Varies

specify why the selected capture rate makes sense. Again, the analysis of comparable projects gives analysts an understanding of the factors on which capture depends.

The checklist in Figure 15-3 is useful for any residential project. Use of the checklist depends on the collection of primary data. As noted earlier, a market study based strictly on data from published sources is not usually adequate. Analysts need to know with certainty what is being built in the market and which key features, functions, and benefits are selling. Analysts often can improve published data with their own observations and thereby provide an advantage over competitors who do not study the market carefully. (See Appendix D for a more complete look at potential problems in residential market studies.)

Dowell Myers has developed another, more extensive method for doing residential market studies. He begins with existing and projected population broken down by age and sex and then estimates their propensity to form households and to own or rent space.[1] Households are assigned to types of housing in the initial year and over the entire period of the forecast. Household formation is influenced both by new entrants and by the aging of existing households. Thus, this method not only focuses on the formation of new households but also accounts for demographic change. Its adjustment for vacancies goes beyond simply adding units to meet an expected vacancy rate, instead assuming an "equilibrium vacancy rate" for the market area and projecting the positive or negative amount of housing required as each submarket trends toward balance over the period of the projection. On the supply side, it accounts for demolitions and the need to replace the existing, aging stock, as well as for conversions and rehabilitation, which create new supply. Estimated absorption is phased over time in the submarket. Required construction meets the demand created by the net households formed, vacancies needed for the market's adjustment, and net additions resulting from changes in stock (replacement of losses resulting from demolitions and conversions to nonresidential uses minus rehabilitations and conversions to residential uses).

RETAIL MARKET STUDIES

Retail sales depend upon the disposable income of potential customers and their patterns of expenditure. Customers either live in the trade area and make shopping trips to retail sites or visit the trade area during trips generated for some other purpose, such as commuting to and from work or taking children to school.

Retail market analysts take estimates of income and expenditure that have been made for subareas of the community, usually census tracts, and combine the subareas to define the trade or market area. To define a trade area, analysts must make assumptions about the scale and character of the proposed retail development that influence its draw, access, visibility, physical barriers, and competition, often using the following rules of thumb.

Shopping centers come in several sizes: neighborhood, community, regional, and super regional. Roughly speaking, a neighborhood center contains up to 100,000 square feet, a community center from 100,000 to 300,000 square feet, a regional center from 300,000 to 1 million square feet, and a super regional center from 1 million to 2 million square feet.

A neighborhood center has an undifferentiated trade area, a community center a primary trade area and a secondary trade area, and regional centers primary, secondary, and tertiary areas. Boundaries of the trade areas are stated in terms of driving time from the proposed site: five minutes for the primary area, five to 10 minutes for the secondary area, and 10 to 30 minutes for the tertiary area. Different capture rates are expected for each area.[2] For example, a neighborhood center is expected to capture about 90 percent of the market from within its trade area within a five- to 10-minute drive from a proposed site along arterials, a community center within 10 to 15 minutes, a regional center within 15 to 30 minutes, and a super regional center within something over 30 minutes.[3]

For each subarea in or overlapping the trade area, the market analyst estimates demand and supply. Estimates of demand for retail space are derived from information on population, income, and retail expenditures. The three primary sources of readily

FIGURE 15-3
PRELIMINARY MARKET RESEARCH CHECKLIST

City
Date
By

Population Characteristics

City
County
MSA
Target Area
Age Group (percent)
Households (number)
Average Income
Percent Renters
Average Home Value
Occupation
City Location
In-Migration (every five years)
Out-Migration (every five years)
Net Migration (every five years)
Why?

Sources of information: Census maps, chambers of commerce, newspaper research

Growth and Neighborhood Patterns

Location
  New Construction
  Building Range
  Existing Use
City/County Utilities (areas serviced)
  Sanitary Sewer
  Water Line
  Storm Sewer

Sources of information: Utility company's planning commission, Board of Realtors, lenders, city engineer, home-builders' association

Major Employers—Commercial

Employers
  Location

Employees
  Salaried (income)
  Clerical (income)
  Hourly (income)
  Expansion, Influx, Transfer
  Desired Housing, Residential Areas
Unemployment
  Figures by Month and Year
  City/County Average
  National Average
  Projected Unemployment

Shopping Centers

Builder-Owner
Location
Size
Neighborhood
Community
Regional
Key Tenants

Transportation Facilities

Highways
  Limited Access
    Service
    Interchanges
    Timing
  Proposed
  Primary State Routes
    Downtown Access
    Key Intersections
Airport
  Location
  Access
Bus
  Area Serviced

Sources of information: Industrial development groups, personnel departments, chambers of commerce, state employment service

FIGURE 15-3 (continued)

Housing Characteristics

Housing Starts
Single-Family Building Permits
Multifamily Building Permits
Apartment Vacancies
Homeowners (percentage)
Renters (percentage)

Sources of information: Local building departments, census, Board of Realtors, lenders, management companies

Apartment Supply

Area
Units
One-, Two-, Three-bedroom
Sales versus Rental
High Rise versus Garden
Status
Opened
Vacancies
Overbuilt
Underbuilt

Competition Checklist

Project Name
Location
  Acreage
Builder or Owner
Management Company
Units Completed
  Buildings under Construction
  Buildings Planned
Rental Opened
  Rented
  Vacancy
  Miscellaneous Plans
Unit Type
  Efficiency
  One-bedroom
  Two-bedroom
  Three-bedroom
  Four-bedroom
  Other
  Living Levels
  Townhouse

Rental Range
  Efficiency
  One-bedroom
  Two-bedroom
  Three-bedroom
  Four-bedroom
Square Feet
  Efficiency
  One-bedroom
  Two-bedroom
  Three-bedroom
  Four-bedroom
Exterior Style
Parking
Carports
Access and Neighborhood
Apartment Units
Living Room
  Walls
  Floor
  Other
Kitchen
  Walls
  Floor
  Range
  Refrigerator
  Disposal
  Dishwasher
  Laundry Facilities
  Eat-in
  Other
Bedroom
  Walls
  Floor
  Closets
  Other
Dining Area
  Walls
  Floor
  Formal
  Counter/Bar
  Other
Foyer, Hallway, Entrance, and
  Interior Storage
Miscellaneous

Source: J. Ross McKeever, *Apartment Development: A Strategy for Successful Decision Making* (Washington, D.C.: ULI–the Urban Land Institute, 1974).

340

Recommending the appropriate tenant mix and estimated rents is an important part of retail market studies.

available published information are the Census of Retail Trade, the Bureau of Labor Statistics (which provides information on expenditures by different income or family groups), and *Survey of Buying Power,* published by *Sales and Marketing Management*. Given overall buying power, for example (population times demand per capita from *Sales and Marketing Management*), the next step is to estimate what portion existing retail activities currently absorb.

Dollars & Cents of Shopping Centers[4] can be used to estimate retail sales by category, such as boots and shoes, women's clothing, automotive goods, and food, generally found in a retail center of the proposed size. Within the primary trade area, the analyst locates the competing shopping centers, estimates sales for individual stores in them by multiplying the actual square footage of the store (supplied by the center's leasing agents) by the average sales per square foot for that type of store as listed in *Dollars & Cents of Shopping Centers*, and then repeats the estimates for other shopping centers with trade areas significantly overlapping the subject's primary trade area. Subtracting expected new supply (under construction) leaves excess demand in the primary area by type of tenant.[5]

Additional Sources of Retail Information

Market analysts collect primary information in the field on important categories of retailers, such as supermarkets, drug stores, branch banks, and restaurants. For less important information, they can use secondary data from *Dollars & Cents*. Another good source of information is state sales tax receipts for specific retail categories by county. Although analysts might have to adjust estimates from fiscal year to calendar year, receipts can be used to compile monthly figures for retail sales that provide a check on the total figures derived from other sources. The point is to focus limited time and resources to ensure that key information is as accurate as possible. The best approach is to use a variety of sources to make several estimates of critical items—for retail studies, sales forecasts for proposed tenants and users of out-parcels.

Using these field-based and secondary sources, analysts can then forecast supply and demand in dollars and in gross leasable area by type of store over the projection period, say 10 years. The project's estimated absorption is the square footage of total retail space needed and not expected to be served by the competition in the trade area.[6]

For most analyses of demand, market analysts distinguish "convenience goods" from "shoppers' goods." Customers seek convenience goods almost exclusively at the most accessible locations. For shoppers' goods, which include durable goods representing more expensive purchases, they travel farther and usually are willing to make several shopping trips to compare items before purchasing one. Although analysts usually define a single primary or secondary trade area, it is more accurate to picture a series of *nested* trade areas, each relating to different categories of goods.

Market analysts must pay close attention to existing and projected traffic flow, taking into account construction of new highways.[7] Furthermore, analysts must handle information about residential demand and traffic volume in the market area carefully to avoid double counting. They must be aware that residents make retail expenditures within the market area and outside it. Mail order sales, which are growing in volume, are part of external sales. Pedestrian and vehicular traffic flowing through the market area generates local sales in proportion to visitation rates, and in high-density areas, pedestrian traffic may be more important than vehicular traffic. Analysts can estimate sales per square foot from information on visitation rates and expenditures per visit at existing retailers.

Area residents are among those visitors, and their purchases are already accounted for. Nonresident visitors represent new demand. Most are tourists or residents of the metropolitan area on their way to or from work.

Estimating Rents and Deciding The Final Tenant Mix

After generating sales figures and expected absorption for each retail category, market analysts estimate rent per square foot, beginning by surveying the marketplace and asking what space rents for. What people ask and what existing tenants actually pay usually differ, because leases were negotiated earlier. Consequently, estimates of what prospective tenants are willing to pay should be adjusted accordingly. Estimated rentals should establish a reasonable range, and if they are not reasonable, analysts must rethink the process. Maybe the market is out of balance and an opportunity can be exploited, or maybe some key assumption is wrong (for example, an improperly delineated market area).[8] Furthermore, studies of shopping centers should distinguish anchors from other tenants in quoting average rent or vacancy levels, for anchors typically pay lower rents. This factor is increasingly important, as the quality and definition of anchors change over time.

For some retail studies, market analysts recommend a mix of tenants, but more typically developers try to attract anchor tenants to their site during refinement of the idea. In effect, developers ask potential anchors to evaluate sales per square foot at the site. If the anchor's market analysis suggests profitable operations at the developer's site, the anchor might make a commitment.[9]

Retail market studies are one application of location theory in which analysts examine the possibility of providing a range of retail goods and services at one space—the center's site—and serving consumers located in or traveling through surrounding areas. City planners use a similar approach to locate public facilities like schools or fire stations. Finance/insurance/real estate and other service firms use these techniques to gauge their local market, such as where to locate branch banks.[10]

OFFICE MARKET STUDIES

Office use is the most dense, concentrated use of land, and the services located in office zones serve larger trade areas than most retail services. Over the last several decades, prime office locations have shifted from central cities to suburban areas, especially near highway intersections and in transportation corridors. The office market comprises different segments, and filtering often occurs when segments change location.[11] Except in communities with only one office cluster or one type of space, the developer and the market analyst must define spatial submarkets to understand the office market and to test the feasibility of the subject project. While office market studies are done for speculative office space, office space increasingly is being built to tenants' specifications.

The demand for office space comes from overall economic growth and from employment growth in those specific categories that use office space (versus retail space, for example). Demand also comes from the replacement of older obsolete office space. One typical technique to estimate demand focuses on employers that use office space. The two major categories are services (professional, business, or government) and finance/insurance/real estate. Analysts estimate future employment in those two sectors, then estimate space needed per employee. BEA, NPA, and other organizations project employment for metropolitan areas and counties, and BOMA and ULI generate information on square footage per employee. The analyst then converts industry-specific projections of employment to a projection of space required. The analyst can use a standard of 200 to 250 square feet per employee initially and then refine it by talking with prospective tenants and Realtors.[12] In the 1970s, many analysts assumed that the electronic cottage and other changes in efficiency would reduce space per employee. In fact, the standard has moved in the opposite direction to accommodate larger work stations and office computers.

An analyst usually estimates total space demand for a metropolitan market area by looking at employment trends and by adding a vacancy factor as in the residential study. Raymond Torto and William Wheaton argue in Coldwell Banker's "Office Outlook" that normal vacancy is not an absolute but varies across office markets,[13] and different rates have been used to project excess demand for about 50 large metropolitan markets. Analysts should discuss trends in both absorption and vacancy rates in the locality with informed commercial leasing agents to come up with reasonable estimates. When the office market is overbuilt, analysts should assume that vacancy rates will decline over the period of projection.

Analysts must be aware of the relationship between net leasable space and gross building area, which is called the "efficiency ratio." Because it is sensitive to a project's scale, the efficiency ratio is usually higher in bigger office buildings. BOMA compiles information for buildings that distinguishes occupied space, common areas, and residual space for utilities, maintenance, and so on. For example, an efficiency ratio of 0.85 indicates that for every 100 feet of gross space built, 85 square feet can be leased. BOMA also provides a standard for net leasable space that most office market analysts follow to measure the demand for or supply of office space. Local tenants, architects, and brokers can provide primary information on space use, floor plates,[14] and efficiency in specific office submarkets.

After estimating absorption over the relevant time period, analysts account for existing and planned supply in the relevant submarket. Office supply can be differentiated by type and quality of tenants, geographic location, floor plate, architectural quality, amenities, and rental range. After allocating absorption in the metropolitan area to the submarket and identifying existing and planned competitors, analysts estimate the project's capture rate by comparing the subject project's attributes to those of the competition and assigning the subject a reasonable market share based on its relative strengths. For this part of the analysis, analysts follow the same approach to competitive analysis outlined for residential and retail studies.

Figure 15-4 contains an outline of a market study for a multitenant office building, but Hugh F. Kelly offers a more sophisticated approach to office market analysis,

FIGURE 15-4

OUTLINE FOR A MARKET STUDY OF A SPECULATIVE OFFICE COMPLEX

I. Introduction
 A. Overview of the Market Study
 B. Review of Data Sources
 C. Major Market Risk Factors
 D. Summary of Findings and
  Recommendations
II. Description and Overview of
 Community
 A. Location
 B. Transportation
 C. Education
 D. Medical Services
 E. Recreational and Cultural
  Activities
 F. Communications
 G. Government
III. Identification of Market Area
 A. Primary Area
 B. Secondary Area
 C. Labor Force and Employment
 D. Major Employers
 E. Occupational Structure
 F. Unemployment
 G. Population Trends and
  Characteristics
IV. Site Analysis
 A. Location
 B. Area Development

C. Zoning and Physical
 Characteristics
D. Supply and Comparable Projects
 1. Location
 2. Age
 3. Size
 4. Amenities
 5. Average and Range of Rents
 6. Absorption
 7. Vacancy
 8. Size Range of Units
 9. Tenant Mix
E. Inventory of Office Development
 by Year and Subarea
V. Projections of Demand and Supply
 A. Employment
 B. Demand for Office Space
 C. Supply of Office Space
 1. Existing
 2. Planned Additions
 D. Historic Absorption for Target
 Rent Range by Subarea
 E. Projected Market Absorption
VI. Capture Rates by Major Market
 Segment
 A. Project Capture Rate
 B. Sensitivity Analysis of Different
 Project Capture Rates

first noting the difference between forecasting demand and supply.[15] Supply is embodied in a tangible physical product, while demand is abstract and difficult to pin down. Even in retrospect, only space users who are able to locate and occupy space in the market are counted. To track demand in a market area, market analysts should compile statistics over the past several construction cycles and analyze the level of supply and vacancies and changes in them. Thus, market analysts must examine the history of the local office market.

For office space in downtown and midtown Manhattan, this approach examines existing stock, new construction, and vacancies over time to estimate demand indirectly. The change in the stock of space (which is the new supply marketed during the year minus the change in the amount of vacant space available for lease during the year) is the amount of space absorbed in that year. Absorption is not the total amount of space leased during the period but is equal to leasing minus lease terminations and other withdrawals of tenants from the market.[16] With figures on vacant space, absorption, and new supply estimated over several previous construction cycles, market analysts have a basis for making near-term forecasts of demand, remembering that trends are expected to follow cycles in real estate and are not straight-line extrapolations from the past.

Kelly challenges market analysts to try to understand the factors causing the observed variation in absorption. For example, employment figures from 1969 to 1980 for Manhattan, totals and annual changes disaggregated by seven industrial sectors, give a more detailed picture, using employment by place of work as the most relevant surrogate for demand for office space. Population, income, or employment by place of residence are inferior measures, as the markets driving demand for Manhattan office space are economic and global. Manhattan's economic base evolved during the 1970s to provide more employment in finance/insurance/real estate services relative to manufacturing and wholesale and retail trades. Overall, Manhattan lost over 300,000 jobs during the decade, even as demand for office space grew.

To learn more about market dynamics and the demand for office space, Kelly estimates the number of office workers in Manhattan and relates office employment to changes in absorption from 1969 to 1980. Knowledgeable market analysts have the ability to make important decisions about the subject office market. Manhattan is designated as a market area with two submarkets—downtown and midtown. Geography provides some rationale for this delineation, but market segments are more critical; assessing the characteristics of tenants in particular is a means of segmenting demand between these two submarkets and other New York City markets. For example, established corporate organizations that can afford to pay relatively high rents occupy Manhattan office space, while investment houses and nonbank financial companies are clustered downtown, banks and other corporate headquarters in midtown.

Market analysts should piece together detailed employment data by industry and occupation to make reasonable near-term forecasts of white-collar employment in each industry, examining four categories of information: employment by detailed industries, occupational employment by industry, spatial location of industry employment, and changes in employment over time. (Analyzing changes over time encourages analysts to consider nonlinear change and avoid straight-line extensions of current trends into the future.) Two-digit, major industry groups from the Standard Industrial Classification (SIC) or more re-

The development program for the LL&E tower in New Orleans was based on detailed market analysis and the developer's considerable experience. The classical form and hierarchical massing of this 36-story office building is reinforced by alternating bands of mahogany-colored, flame-finished granite and bronze-tinted glass.

fined industrial detail should be used, depending on available data.[17] The ratio of employment in Manhattan in each industry, divided by citywide or areawide industry employment calculated annually indicates which industries are concentrating, dispersing, or staying in about the same locations. Kelly has analyzed these data from 1970 to 1981 to forecast employment for 1982 through 1985, experimenting with three-year and five-year moving averages and annual change to make different near-term projections. He forecasts employment by industry, percentage of white-collar workers, and the dispersion index to find Manhattan office jobs for each industry considered. Total white-collar employment is the product of these employment and ratio estimates summed over all relevant industries.

Market analysts must decide how best to define relevant industries for office studies. Employment in business services, finance/insurance/real estate, and government may be appropriate for most estimates of office space used. In other instances, the office market should be defined more narrowly, requiring the analysis of a more detailed set of industries. The relevant market segments depend in part on where the potential site is located, what tenant profile the developer seeks, expected asking rents, levels of tenant finishes, and so on. Some service industries seek central locations and higher densities. Others are more amenable to business parks. In general, more refined market segments refer to more detailed categories of employment.

One additional refinement may further improve forecasts of space demand. Analysts should know whether estimates of supply include or exclude owner-occupied space. Most published reports consider only leased space, but inconsistent definitions abound. If supply refers to leased space only, then analysts should survey the local market to make industry-specific estimates of tenancy. Financial institutions and government agencies often own the space they occupy. Depending on the market, the insurance industry also tends to own space. Analysts must know the market well enough to make such estimates and, if not, should acquire the knowledge by interviewing brokers and leasing agents and by visiting representative buildings.

The key to sound office market analyses hinges on understanding the relevant market segment(s) that mesh with the developer's profile of projected tenants. Analysts can use profiles of tenants to estimate minimum square footage to be leased, quality of space (that is, Class A versus Class B space), probable effective rents, space consumed per employee, and other factors to describe the relevant market segment in more detail. These categories vary from city to city and change over time. For example, Class A space in one market area may not qualify as Class A space in another (usually larger) market. As newer and better space is built, formerly Class A space is often filtered down. Analysis of segments is essential in overbuilt markets. If supply exceeds demand for all Class A office space, perhaps a stronger demand exists for a particular type of Class A space.

Market analysts must be careful to define market segments for which effective demand exists and not just more specific categories of space. They should avoid considering any speculative project as completely unique; substitute space almost always exists. If the developer has done a good job in refining the idea, the proposed project should fill some legitimate niche in the market. Market analysts can extend this work and provide further insights about design, phasing, and leasing. In some cases, analysts will find that no effective demand exists and must recommend that the project be scrapped or postponed. The formal market and marketability study is a technique to control risk to help the developer avoid the costly error of pursuing an unmarketable project. With industry-specific forecasts of employment adjusted for occupation, dispersion, tenancy, space use, and related factors, market analysts are well on the way to sound forecasts of expected absorption and capture.

INDUSTRIAL MARKET STUDIES

Industrial market studies consider tenants that use manufacturing facilities, flexible office space ("flex space"), or research and development (R&D) space. The special features of such studies are anticipated, primarily nonlocal, demand and the potential supply of industrial land, which is often very large. Usually, outside businesses must be attracted to an area to buy or lease industrial space.

Industrial development usually proceeds in two ways: building industrial parks, a form of speculative land development where companies usually construct and own facilities on their own sites, or building speculative industrial space to attract particular clients not currently represented in the local market or to capture small local firms with the potential for growth.

Market analysts can follow one of two strategies to estimate nonlocal demand to develop a methodology for industrial mar-

Photo courtesy of NAIOP

Accessibility is an important ingredient in the success of office and industrial parks. This aerial photo of an office park in Richardson, Texas, shows the network of nearby freeways and the neighboring pattern of low-rise development.

ket studies,[18] but differences exist between these approaches and conventional market analyses. One strategy is to analyze industries the locality could attract, given its existing competitive advantage. Local economic development agencies should be able to identify feasible and desirable industries that could be the basis for industrial recruitment.

Another strategy is to study comparable facilities located in areas that have already experienced the growth that could reasonably be anticipated for the subject area over, say, the next 10 years. If the area is in fact growing at the same pace and has a similar mix of industries, local industrial space should be absorbed in the future at a similar rate. The experience of developers of comparable industrial land in cities that were developed earlier could suggest future prospects for the subject project. Focusing on comparable experiences of other areas is often a reasonable way to estimate

local absorption for industrial space or industrial land.

In areas with excess industrial land, infrastructure is usually the binding constraint. Infrastructure has become less available as federal construction programs fund fewer and fewer projects. Examining local land use plans and capital improvement programs can help analysts estimate the effective supply of industrial land.

Flex space or R&D space combines room for sales, production, and storage; it looks like high-end industrial space or low-rise office space. Depending on the specific project, the analyst approaches this use as an industrial market study, an office market study, or a combination of the two. Distribution warehouse space housing an area's wholesale trade functions could be analyzed like an office market study, with employment in wholesaling the key indicator of demand for space, particularly in areas like Chicago, Dallas, or Atlanta. In small

347

FIGURE 15-5
REUSING INDUSTRIAL FACILITIES

LEE COUNTY, FLORIDA

When the commercial airport in Lee County, Florida, was relocated to a more suitable site near I-75, the county, as owner of the facility, wanted to know whether it should retain the general aviation facility or redevelop the site. The original downtown area was about three miles from the county's highest-volume intersection, which bordered the site. The mall across from the site contained about 1 million square feet and charged the highest rents in the county.

The panel studying the question suggested relocating the general aviation facilities, because general aviation was not an appropriate use at that specific location; it proposed instead a 200-acre mixed-use development to include a business park, a hotel, and specialty retail space. Based on market studies for the area, it would take about 70 years to absorb the amount of office space typical in the small metropolitan market that could be built on 200 acres, but the panel proposed a type of office space not currently available in the area. Local economic development agencies noted that no available space was appropriate for the kind of national tenant the area was beginning to attract. The panel suggested that a development such as it proposed would create a new market of space users and attract demand that was in no one's calculations.

The panel's proposal was predicated on the idea that the region would start to change qualitatively as well as quantitatively as it grew beyond 250,000 in population. When the county reached that size, major national companies would begin to look seriously at the area as a location for distribution operations or regional offices, for Tampa and Miami are within 150 miles of Lee County.

The site's other 400 acres offered an even greater opportunity. The panel recommended holding the land for the future to attract a campus of the University of Florida system or a major health park housing the Mayo Clinic, which had recently located in Jacksonville. Few places offer 400 acres 10 minutes from an interstate highway, 10 minutes from downtown, and 15 minutes from an airport and beaches on the Gulf Coast. The centrally located site, the panel noted, could provide a decisive competitive advantage for attracting economic activity.

Source: ULI–the Urban Land Institute, *Page Field, Lee County, Florida*, Panel Report (Washington, D.C.: Author, 1987).

---

cities, a retail market study is more reasonable, because wholesalers sell almost exclusively to local retailers, whose buying potential and location are relevant for estimates of market demand.

Recent trends in production and distribution are blurring many distinctions among product types. The trends for corporations to reduce the size of certain facilities and use sources from outside, for example, have stimulated the growth of independent production and service firms that serve large corporate clients. Many such firms demand a combination of relatively small-scale office, fabrication, and storage space. Others need highly adaptable space. "Just-in-time inventory systems" have shifted the burden of timely deliveries and storage to suppliers, which affects manufacturers' needs for space and location. As competition grows, the need for flexibility in the application of all productive factors, including land and space, will increase.

Large-scale projects are usually phased over time. In addition to a market analysis during the first phase, market research must be conducted continuously from stage to stage. Feedback from the marketing staff selling or leasing space is used to refine subsequent phases. Marketing always affects the timing of the later stages and may even affect design.

Other large-scale projects can have a great effect because the project brings some new type of space user into the local market or creates the potential for a new market. Figure 15-5, for example, describes the reuse of a general aviation facility in Lee County, Florida, to a proposed large mixed-use project. In such cases, market analysts need not look at existing relationships between supply and demand or the growth trends and development history of the market area. Instead, they must address the behavior expected from new and different mixes of space users.

The market study for a distressed property requires special talents, because the market analyst must examine an existing product at a specific location with an operating history and faces two problems in research. One is to study the project's history to figure out why it was unable to meet debt service payments—perhaps an inferior property manager, a bad location, poor market intelligence, a dishonest developer who failed to build the project as proposed, cost overruns during construction or when it was operating, or a decline in the area's economy. Once the first question is answered, the analyst can move to the second task—a straightforward market study focusing on alternatives for redevelopment for the site. The market study becomes a marketing tool used like a business plan to find a buyer for the property.

SUMMARY

The information gathered for a market study and the important analytical points change, depending on the type of property studied. Each type entails specific items that must be carefully calculated and analyzed, but the general outline presented in Chapter 14 is a good starting point for understanding the details that should be contained in residential, retail, office, and industrial market studies. Appendix D discusses the problems encountered in preparing one residential market study.

NOTES

1. Dowell Myers, "Extended Forecasts of Housing Demand in Metropolitan Areas," *Appraisal Journal*, April 1987, pp. 266–78.

2. See Neil Carn, Joseph Rabianski, Ronald Racster, and Maury Seldin, *Real Estate Market Analysis: Techniques and Applications* (Englewood Cliffs, N.J.: Prentice-Hall, 1988), pp. 187–97 and 207–13, for an excellent discussion of techniques for delineating retail trade areas.

3. See, for example, John McMahan, *Property Development* (New York: McGraw-Hill, 1989), pp. 157–62.

4. Published triennially by the Urban Land Institute, Washington, D.C. Latest edition is 1990.

5. For individual stores outside shopping centers, average sales and average square footage listed in *Dollars & Cents* for the type of store could be used. See John M. Clapp, *Handbook for Real Estate Market Analysis* (Englewood Cliffs, N.J.: Prentice-Hall, 1987), pp. 144–56, for another approach using regression analysis.

6. First-cut market capture rates of 60 to 80 percent of the square footage in the primary trade area and 20 to 30 percent of the square footage in the secondary area are applied to the estimates of absorption. The analyst's estimates of market share depend on the project's advantages relative to the competition's. Key features include access (site location), amenities, and cost (rent per square foot).

7. They should also know whether local commercial lenders use rules of thumb with reference to traffic counts and what minimum level is generally acceptable for underwriting shopping centers and other retail projects.

8. Three commonly used techniques for estimating retail sales and rents are customer surveys, the vacuum technique, and microanalysis (see McMahan, *Property Development*, pp. 162–92). Customer surveys can be expensive, but, if samples are properly drawn, they are most accurate as well. They are especially useful when a shopping center owner wants to reposition an existing center. In that case, existing customers can be surveyed to find out where they live, their demographics, and why they shop at the existing center. For new centers, analysts have to survey shoppers at competing centers in or near the trade area, which can be expensive and take time. For larger centers (regional or super regional) or specialty retail centers without an anchor, developers should pay analysts to do consumer surveys at competing retail locations and/or assemble focus groups of prospective consumers.

The vacuum technique is so called because it assumes that new retail space will "suck up" its fair share of estimated demand roughly in proportion to its size relative to the total amount of space, existing and planned, serving the market area. Market analysts calculate buying power, compute sales of existing and planned facilities, and examine the difference. Usually the amount of residents' expenditures going elsewhere ("leakage") is significant. A new retail facility might both reduce leakage and attract its proportionate share of the market because it is more accessible to that market. Although it is an application of Reilly's law of retail gravitation (which relates attraction of customers directly to the size of the center and inversely to the time or cost of travel to the center; see David L. Huff, "Defining and Estimating a Trade Area," *Journal of Marketing*, July 1964, pp. 34–38), this assumption is reasonable only to the extent that locational factors are important. The technique is based on the notions that shopping trips are allocated in proportion to the size of competing centers and are generated only from the place of residence, which is clearly not the case. Leakage may be 30 percent or higher because residents work in other trade areas and go shopping in those areas while commuting. A center's amenities, customers' loyalty, and a host of other factors skew the pattern of trade from what would be predicted on the basis of location and accessibility alone.

Geographers often suggest using microanalysis, the third technique, by establishing a spatial grid encompassing areas smaller than census tracts and allocating demand, namely retail expenditures, to each cell. Computer-based spatial data are increasingly available in geographic information systems, and if one is available, information can be allocated to cells fairly easily. Without GIS, allocations must be based on actual customer surveys, which, as noted earlier, take time and are expensive. In most metropolitan areas, transportation plans contain estimates of trips that could provide useful information on residence-based shopping trips. Demand is usually estimated by using a gravity model that assumes an exponential decline in sales as one moves away from the center, either in distance or time. (See Clapp, *Handbook for Real Estate Market Analysis*, especially pp. 62–74, for an extensive introductory discussion of the gravity model's applications to real estate market studies. In addition to estimating retail demand, Clapp shows how to use the model for defining trade areas, measuring excess demand, and estimating market capture.)

9. Anchor tenants are critical to most retail projects. Anchors do most of the advertising, generate the most traffic, and pay lower rents per square foot than nonanchors. They are the most creditworthy tenants, use the greatest amount of space, lower unit costs for construction and tenant finishes, and offer economies in management and maintenance. Lenders look primarily at the strength of the anchors in underwriting shopping centers and other retail projects.

10. Besides Carn et al., Clapp, and McMahan, other references in the bibliography deal with concepts and methods of retail market analysis. Case studies can be found in G. Vincent Barrett and John P. Blair, *How to Conduct and Analyze Real Estate Market and Feasibility Studies*, 2d ed. (New York: Van Nostrand Reinhold, 1988); Stephen D. Messner et al., *Analyzing Real Estate Opportunities: Market Feasibility Studies* (Chicago: Realtors National Marketing Institute, 1977); and Robert Mier and Wim Wiewel, *Analyzing Neighborhood Retail Opportunities: A Guide for Carrying Out a Preliminary Market Study*, Planning Advisory Service No. 358 (Chicago: American Planning Association, 1981).

11. Filtering is the process whereby space users change as the quality of space changes. Usually, space filters downward; for example, Class A office space becomes Class B or Class C as it ages and as new types of office products come on the market. As a result, relative rents decline, and new tenants seeking such rent levels come to occupy the space.

12. The General Accounting Office's "official" standard is 128 square feet per office employee, but Salomon Brothers uses 200 square feet per office employee. See, for example, "Economic Diversification in Real Estate Portfolios" (November 1988).

13. See Raymond Torto and William Wheaton, "Office Outlook" (New York: Coldwell Banker, Spring/Summer 1987).

14. The floor plate is a simplified floor plan equivalent to a building footprint, only for a multistory building.

15. Hugh F. Kelly, "Forecasting Office Space Demand in Urban Areas," *Real Estate Review*, Fall 1983, pp. 87–94.

16. Kelly actually calls absorption "net new absorption," the meaning used in this chapter. Total or gross absorption is referred to as "leasing activity" or total space leased during the period. New absorption is distinguished from existing absorption with reference to time. New absorption is the amount of space occupied during a time period. Existing absorption equals the amount of occupied space at any point. Thus, existing absorption is a stock variable, such as the amount of vacant space or total space inventory. New absorption is a

flow variable estimated by changes in supply and vacancies.

17. The SIC system, a classification scheme applied to all types of economic activity, is managed by the U.S. Department of Commerce. The one-digit, or division, level identifies groups of economic activities as agriculture, mining, construction, manufacturing, transportation, wholesale trade, retail trade, finance/insurance/real estate, and services. The two-digit, or major group, level is most commonly used in market studies; it breaks down total employment into about 100 sectors called "major industry groups." For example, SIC 54 is food stores, 63 is insurance carriers, and 81 is legal services. Three-digit industry groups or four-digit industries are used to make the more specific industry estimates discussed here. For example, within real estate (SIC 65), real estate agents and managers (SIC 653) are distinguished from land subdividers and developers (SIC 655). Operators of nonresidential buildings (SIC 6512) are classified separately from operators of apartment buildings (SIC 6513). Detailed information on employment and earnings from the Bureau of Labor Statistics, for example, can be helpful to make better-informed judgments about which employment categories to include in an office market study.

18. See Michael D. Beyard, *Business and Industrial Park Development Handbook* (Washington, D.C.: ULI–the Urban Land Institute, 1988).

Bibliography

Part V. Planning and Analysis: The Market Perspective

FEASIBILITY STUDIES

Barrett, G. Vincent, and John P. Blair. *How to Conduct and Analyze Real Estate Market and Feasibility Studies*. 2d ed. New York: Van Nostrand Reinhold Company, 1988.

Campbell, Burnham O. *Population Change and Building Cycles*. Urbana: Univ. of Illinois, Bureau of Business and Economic Research, 1966.

Carn, Neil, Joseph Rabianski, Ronald Racster, and Maury Seldin. *Real Estate Market Analysis: Techniques and Applications*. Englewood Cliffs, N.J.: Prentice-Hall, 1988.

Clapp, John M. *Handbook for Real Estate Market Analysis*. Englewood Cliffs, N.J.: Prentice-Hall, 1987.

Clapp, John M., and Stephen D. Messner, eds. *Real Estate Market Analysis: Methods and Applications*. New York: Praeger, 1988.

Downs, Anthony. "Characteristics of Various Economic Studies." *Appraisal Journal* 34, July 1966, pp. 329-38.

Fanning, Stephen, and Jody Winslow. "Guidelines for Defining the Scope of Market Analysis in Appraisal Assignments." *Appraisal Journal* 56, October 1988, pp. 466-76.

Featherston, J.B. "Approaching Market Analysis in a New Economic Environment." *Journal of Real Estate Development* 2, Spring 1986, pp. 5-10.

George, Vernon. "Market Feasibility." In *Financing Income-Producing Real Estate*, edited by Eric Stevenson. Washington, D.C.: Mortgage Bankers Association, 1988.

Haddow, David F. "Making the City Overview Meaningful." *Appraisal Journal* 52, January 1984, pp. 48-52.

Hartzell, David, and Emil Malizia. "Market Analysis for Investors: A Special Breed of Real Estate Market Research." *Urban Land* 48, January 1989, pp. 6-8.

Huff, David L. "Defining and Estimating a Trade Area." *Journal of Marketing* 28, July 1964, pp. 34-38.

Johnson, L.M. "Feasibility Study." *Real Estate Today* 12, August 1979, pp. 10-13.

Martin, Vernon, III, "Nine Abuses Common in Pro Forma Cash Flow Projections." *Real Estate Review* 19, Fall 1988, pp. 20-25.

Messner, Stephen D., et al. *Analyzing Real Estate Opportunities: Market Feasibility Studies*. Chicago: Realtors National Marketing Institute, 1977.

353

Perkins, B. "Why Real Estate Feasibility Analyses Have Not Worked." *Real Estate Review* 9, Fall 1979, pp. 33–37.

Peterson, K. "Snapshot Feasibility Analysis." *Real Estate Review* 9, Fall 1979, pp. 88–89.

Shenkel, William M. "Refining Valuation Estimates with Census Data." *Real Estate Appraiser* 39, September/October 1973, pp. 11–20.

Siegel, Richard A. "Market Structures and Market Studies." *Journal of Real Estate Development* 2, Winter 1986, pp. 30–34.

Vandell, Kerry D. "Market Analysis: Can We Do Better?" *Appraisal Journal* 56, July 1988, pp. 344–50.

Weiss, J.M. "Deductibility of Marketing and Feasibility Studies." *Management Accounting* 63, April 1982, p. 60.

Young, G.I.M. "Feasibility Studies." *Appraisal Journal* 38, July 1970, pp. 376–83.

REAL ESTATE MARKET STUDIES

Applebaum, William. "Methods for Determining Store Trade Areas, Market Penetration, and Potential Sales." *Journal of Marketing Research* 3, May 1966, pp. 127–41.

Beyard, Michael D. *Business and Industrial Park Development Handbook.* Community Builders Handbook Series. Washington, D.C.: ULI–the Urban Land Institute, 1988.

Birnkrant, Michael. "Shopping Center Feasibility Study: Its Methods and Techniques." *Journal of Property Management* 35, November/December 1970, pp. 272–79.

Coldwell Banker Commercial/Torto Wheaton Services. *Office Outlook.* Boston: Author, Spring/Summer 1987 and twice yearly thereafter.

Del Casino, Joseph J. "A Risk Simulation Approach to Long-Range Office Demand Forecasting." *Real Estate Review* 15, Summer 1985, pp. 82–87.

Dilmore, Gene. *Quantitative Techniques in Real Estate Counseling.* Lexington, Mass.: Lexington Books, 1981.

Dowall, David E. "Office Market Research: The Case for Segmentation." *Journal of Real Estate Development* 4, Summer 1988, pp. 34–43.

Ellis, David G., and Greg Brown. "Nominal and Real Vacancy Rates in Office Market Analysis." *Real Estate Review* 19, Fall 1989, pp. 67–71.

Goldsteen, Joel B. "What Fills an Office Building? Its Neighborhood or Its Design?" *Urban Land* 48, April 1989, pp. 2–5.

Goldstucker, Jac L., et al. *New Developments in Retail Area Trade Analysis and Site Selection.* Atlanta: Georgia State Univ., 1978.

Goodman, John L., Jr., and Stuart A. Gabriel. "Why Housing Forecasts Go Awry." *Real Estate Review* 17, Fall 1987, pp. 64–71.

Hand, H.H. "Economic Feasibility Analysis for Retail Locations." *Journal of Small Business Management* 17, July 1979, pp. 28–35.

Imus, Harold. "Projecting Sales Potentials for Department Stores in Regional Shopping Centers." *Economic Geography* 46, January 1961, pp. 33–41.

Kelly, Hugh F. "Forecasting Office Space Demand in Urban Areas." *Real Estate Review* 13, Fall 1983, pp. 87–94.

Kenney, Michael D. "Market Studies for Real Estate Projects." *NAIOP News* 17, December 1985, pp. 28–32.

Kimball, J.R., and Barbara Bloomberg. "Office Space Demand Analysis." *Appraisal Journal* 55, October 1987, pp. 567–77.

Mier, Robert, and Wim Wiewel. *Analyzing Neighborhood Retail Opportunities: A Guide for Carrying Out a Preliminary Market Study.* Planning Advisory Service No. 358. Chicago: American Planning Association, 1981.

Myers, Dowell. "Demographic Waves and Retail Development." *Urban Land* 46, May 1987, pp. 2–5.

———. "Extended Forecasts of Housing Demand in Metropolitan Areas." *Appraisal Journal* 55, April 1987, pp. 266–78.

———. "Housing Market Research: Time for a Change." *Urban Land* 47, October 1988, pp. 16–19.

Roca, Rueben. "Market Research for Shopping Centers." In *Basic Research Procedures*, edited by William J. McCollum. Washington, D.C.: International Council of Shopping Centers, 1987.

Scott, J.F. "Importance of Feasibility Studies in Site Selection and Disposition of Industrial Properties." *Journal of Prop-*

erty Management 45, January 1980, pp. 39–40.

Singer, Bruce Sheldon. "A Systematic Approach to Housing Market Analysis." In *Readings in Market Research for Real Estate*, edited by James Vernor. Chicago: American Institute of Real Estate Appraisers, 1985.

Sumichrast, Michael. "Housing Market Analysis." In *Readings in Market Research for Real Estate*, edited by James Vernor. Chicago: American Institute of Real Estate Appraisers, 1985.

Tunis, Robert T. "The Negotiation Differential: A New Approach to Office Market Analysis." *Real Estate Review* 18, Winter 1989, pp. 49–55.

Urban Land Institute. *Community Builders Handbook Series*. 7 vols. Washington, D.C.: ULI–the Urban Land Institute, various.

Weisbrod, Glen, and Karl Radov. "The Seven Deadly Sins of Retail Market Studies." *Urban Land* 47, February 1988, pp. 21–25.

Wofford, Larry E. "Significant Trends Affecting Office and Industrial Real Estate: A 21st Century Perspective." *Appraisal Journal* 55, January 1987, pp. 94–107.

PART VI
MAKING IT HAPPEN

Chapter 16

Stages Four and Five: Contract Negotiation and Formal Commitment

Stage three of the development process, the formal feasibility study, brings research and projections together, concluding with statements of value and cost. The project's estimated value should exceed costs, broadly defined. With a statement indicating that the project is feasible, the developer has the necessary information to pull together the development team. Thus, the feasibility analysis serves as a sales and a negotiating tool and as a coordinating device to set up stage four: contract negotiation. During stage four, contracts are arranged to implement the decision to proceed with the project; during stage five, the contracts are executed.

A detailed agreement must be negotiated with each member of the team. The developer must ensure that all the different aspects of the project have been included in the individual contracts and that the various relationships among players are clearly defined. Because many of the contracts are contingent on one another, stage five represents the joint execution of the contracts negotiated in stage four.

Contracts are another method of controlling risk. They set the rules for the phys-

ical, financial, marketing, and operating activities that will occur during construction, formal opening, and operation (stages six, seven, and eight). If all contracts are properly drawn and consistent with each other and the rules of the game correctly defined, then the collective risk of all members of the development team should be reduced. It does not mean, however, that a naive participant will necessarily benefit from tightly drawn contracts that might favor others. Developers can shift some of the risk to others.

A major transition occurs in development as it moves from stage three to stage six; stages four and five are thus the last opportunity to back out before major construction costs are incurred. During stage four, negotiations make sure that the idea is still feasible when all the details are settled in formal contracts that make the details explicit and free of ambiguities. Once the documents are executed in stage five, most of the players no longer retain the option to walk out of the deal. In reality, of course, it is still possible to leave, but the pain is quite intense after contracts have been executed. During the earlier stages, developers are primarily idea generators and promoters. As the process moves toward construction, the developer's role becomes *primary negotiator* to bring all the members of the team together. And in stage six, the role shifts again to *manager of the development team*.

This chapter covers the issues involved in contract negotiation and formal commitment:

- Arranging financing;
- Environmental issues affecting real estate;
- Decisions about design and contractors;
- Decisions about major tenants;
- Decisions about equity;
- The government as partner; and
- Commitment, signing contracts, and initiating construction.

STAGE FOUR: CONTRACT NEGOTIATION

Like other stages of the development process, everything interacts. The players do not negotiate financing without considering the impact of the timing of financing on construction, for example. This discussion begins with permanent and construction financing and some recent innovations in financing, then moves to the handling of hazardous materials and other environmental concerns (probably the hottest topic in real estate today), consideration of the contract and contractors, marketing contracts with tenants, equity contracts with joint venture partners and equity investors, and contracts covering enterprise and venture capital.

Arranging Financing

The market study and the investment analysis contained in the feasibility study can be included in the loan application. Traditionally, developers begin arranging financing by seeking a permanent lender and obtaining a commitment, then finding a construction lender.

The Permanent Lender

The permanent lender provides long-term capital and thus takes on some of the project's long-term market risks—concern with how the space will meet society's needs for the next 20 to 30 years, for example. While permanent lenders typically receive a commitment fee and possibly an origination fee, the majority of their return is spread over the life of the loan, often as long as 20 to 30 years.[1] For that reason, permanent lenders have probably the longest view of any of the participants (except possibly the community itself). Thus, the critical part of the feasibility study for long-term lenders is the market analysis.

Most long-term lenders begin by looking at the feasibility study submitted by the developer and then adjust it according to their own perceptions of the market. Sophisticated permanent lenders maintain a substantial data base on the markets where they lend money. Most employ underwriters, who determine how well a particular project should meet the community's special needs. Because various markets have different demands, permanent lenders examine market potential and how well the location, design, construction plan, and operating plan submitted fit together to create a space that will serve the local market's projected needs.

Permanent lenders are also concerned with other space that might compete in the niche defined for the project—existing competition, comparable projects under construction, and sites that, while not under construction, offer the potential for long-term competition. Sophisticated lenders have learned that looking only at existing competitors is very naive and that they would do better to consider potential competition. Thus, in analyzing long-term prospects for a particular development, lenders look to see whether cash flows can be protected over the long term. While lenders rely on the developer and local market consultants for the initial feasibility study, they must render their own judgment about the project.

The developer's ability to provide the services that accompany the project is also critically important. The customer's heightened awareness in all forms of real estate development and management translates into more skilled management of the delivery of services. Long-term lenders increasingly look at the developer's capacity to provide ongoing management, either with in-house staff or through some type of joint relationship.

If the permanent lender feels that the project is feasible after adjusting the submittal as necessary and if the project fits into the lender's portfolio,[2] the lender executes an agreement. From the developer's perspective, the agreement is a commitment for the permanent loan. It is a contract and its flexibility thus limited only by the creativity of the humans involved. Basically, the document provides that the lender will make the loan within a certain time, say 12 to 18 months in the future. The contract also stipulates the amount and terms of the loan; it is conditioned on the project's completion in accordance with the specifications outlined in the feasibility study.

Depending on the developer's and the lender's relative bargaining strength, either party may have the upper hand. A lender in control might write provisions into the loan protecting it from future uncertainties, for example, adjusting the interest rate as market interest rates change or allowing the lender to withdraw from the permanent loan commitment if market conditions or preleasing is not favorable at the end of construction. A developer in control could obtain fixed commitments on the interest rate, maturity, and provisions for default, as well as the promise to make the loan regardless of any change in market conditions between the date of commitment and the actual closing of the loan.

Often, however, the final terms are somewhere in between these extremes. The lender might agree to fund up to a certain base amount, say $8 million, regardless of market conditions, and an additional amount, say $2 million, assuming the developer meets the quota specified for leasing. Thus, the developer would have a firm commitment for $8 million and a commitment for as much as $10 million if leasing is as stated in the pro forma.

For smaller development projects, developers seek permanent financing from local sources or through their own contacts, because life insurance companies and pension funds would not usually be interested (the costs of completing the transaction are too high relative to the loan's prin-

cipal value). In these cases, local investors may contribute debt capital as well as equity.

The Construction Lender

With permanent commitment in hand, developers traditionally proceed to a construction lender to provide financing for the period of construction. Construction lending involves different risks when a commitment for the permanent loan has been received. With the takeout commitment in hand, construction lenders know that their loan should be paid off at a certain time and that they have to assume no market or other long-term risk. Rather, construction lenders take the risk that the project will not be completed on time and within budget. Thus, construction lenders are much more concerned with the developer's ability to construct the project as planned.

Construction lenders tend to focus instead on a developer's experience and reputation, the quality of the architect, the quality of the general contractor, the difficulty of the project, and other immediate risks specific to the project. The more complex the project and the more inexperienced the developer and other participants in the process, the greater the risks to the construction lender.

Construction lenders attempt to obtain a variable interest rate, with the developer hoping for at least a cap on increases in the rate. Developers would like to have maximum flexibility with regard to the ability to draw down funds, whereas lenders want maximum control and oversight of the construction process.

Short-term lenders tend to have shorter-term liabilities in their portfolios, making commercial banks the leading construction lenders. With 14,000 commercial banks in the country, they are also more likely to be located close to any given project—high on the list of priorities because they want to supervise construction to reduce risk.

Recent Trends in Financial Markets

In the distant past, S&Ls and mutual savings banks were primarily permanent lenders, usually for residential projects. With deregulation in 1980 and 1982, however, traditional lending changed significantly. Deregulation allowed traditional long-term residential lenders *and* diversified financial service firms to provide both construction loans and permanent loans. And as institutions expanded boundaries, they became more creative with the provisions attached to both types of loans.

The miniperm loan, now fairly common, is a combination of short- and long-term financing, lenders providing construction financing as well as financing for the first few years of operation. This extension is a positive feature when developers need a large permanent loan but cannot prove sufficient operational viability to justify one. A miniperm loan buys time for the project in the marketplace, particularly if it has stiff competition. From the lender's standpoint, the benefit is often multiple fees but underwriting only once.

In the mid-1980s, with foreign money available and pension funds seeking to diversify into real estate, an abundance of funding was available. Developers definitely had the clout in negotiations—one of the main reasons for the overbuilt markets of the late 1980s. The collapse of the S&Ls and the nearly incalculable amount of real estate now owned by the federal government have completely turned around the financing mechanisms available. More cautious lenders are now financing fewer and fewer projects. Foreign investors are also more cautious—and they now have new opportunities in Eastern Europe—thereby severely limiting available financing.

As in any market, when competition increases on the supply side, sellers (lenders) have offered lower rates to close development deals. Interestingly, lenders in a weaker bargaining position (as in the mid-1980s) have traded off on *risks* and *returns*. Lenders taking a fixed fee have fairly limited flexibility in prices; thus, lenders find it difficult to compete solely on price. Lenders obviously would prefer to compete on service, but when money is easily available, they are often forced to compete on other levels as well. With only a certain range in which to compete on price, risk becomes a primary trading chip in the competition. Thus, lenders might be able to obtain customers (make loans) by providing a higher loan-to-value ratio or simply by providing a higher estimate of value. Further, lenders could buy business by eliminating the developer's personal liability and/or allowing the developer to take major fees while development is under way or even at the beginning of the development process.

The very poor financial condition of many S&Ls in the 1990s clearly shows that some institutions did not adequately consider risk in the mid-1980s. With deregulation, S&LS began to make loans on commercial projects as well as single-family houses. They sometimes let income from fees override considerations of risk in their involvement in both the construction and the permanent loan for commercial and residential projects. While the failures of many large S&Ls can be attributed to general overbuilding in real estate and to particularly bad economic conditions in the oil and farm states, a certain portion of the failures has to be attributed to bad underwriting. Whether problems posed for commercial banks by these same conditions will be as severe as the S&Ls' problems remains to be seen. But, like the S&Ls, certain deficiencies in underwriting among commercial banks have become clear. From the perspective of development, it can be expected that long-term lenders as a group will learn from this experience and be less likely to make some of the same mistakes in the future. Even lenders with solid financial positions can be expected to tighten their lending policies as a reaction to the problems in the industry.

This discussion has covered primarily for-lease projects that the developer-investor will own at the close of the development period. Permanent loan commitments simply do not apply to for-sale projects, because customers obtain their own financing. Thus, builders of single-family houses have traditionally operated without permanent commitments. More sophisticated residential developers often obtain "blocks" of permanent loan commitments for their buyers, but doing so is quite different from the construction lender's standpoint. While it indicates that funding will be available for buyers, it does not guarantee that buyers will be there. If market conditions change over the development period and no buyers are found, the construction lender is still left with the risk.[3]

FINANCING AND A QUICK MOVE TO CONTRACT NEGOTIATION

Fraser Morrow Daniels had no financing for the Europa Center and was under pressure to begin construction before the town's new rules restricting a building's height and density became effective. We beat the April 15 deadline by starting construction before the completion of financial negotiations. But we traded one kind of risk for another.

It takes a long time to execute documents and to get the contractor and the architect to agree on all the final details—how they will proceed, order materials, get the bulldozer subcontractor to come out and start bulldozing. The financial negotiations were not quite finished on April 15, but we had our site plan approved and we started clearing ground on April 14.

We called the town fathers and told them they wouldn't see a lot of building soon but that we were starting. We just didn't want to get caught technically because of the political environment. If we had missed the deadline, this building would have become a three-story building instead of a five-story building and 120,000 square feet in two phases instead of 200,000 square feet. We would have lost money on the day we started under those circumstances.

To get funding for the Europa Center, we needed a financial partner—on this project the Centennial Group, a group partially comprised of former Sea Pines people who manage a fund that they've invested. It's a publicly held stock company that has invested in various projects around the country. They put $2 million into the Europa project. For that, they got 50 percent of the deal. Financing was arranged through Investor S&L out of Richmond, which had a working relationship with the Centennial Group. The Centennial Group as a financial partner brought more to the table than just money; it also brought a reputation and a working relationship with a lender. We funded the

research, planning, purchase negotiations, staff, and so on before the joint venture and were partially reimbursed in the joint venture agreement. So we had a small initial dollar risk: $50,000 to $100,000, partially reimbursed. We invest time and money on many ideas that never come to fruition. For every project we end up working on, we may have spent time and money on 10 other ones that didn't happen. We usually wouldn't get to the stage of having invested $50,000 or $100,000 on a project that wasn't going to go anywhere. But we may spend $10,000 to $15,000 or $20,000 many times before we ever get to a project that works.

The financial models we used included a little section called "capitalized expenses"—the capital cost of building a project. It's a list covering the relative cost of doing things in a project like this. The land purchase is half of the $2 million land price, because this model is for one building (the first phase of two). Centennial holds land for the second phase for the Park Forty project and for Europa, accruing interest on it. When we use it, it will be a separate calculation. But as far as the bank is concerned, it's $1 million for land, and Centennial and our group together have another million dollars invested in another piece of land.

Our financial partners ended up bearing the risk of that million in addition to the other million for the second phase. The lender agreed to fund everything else on the list, so instead of $9,339,000, the lender loaned us $8,339,000. We negotiated the construction price, $4,985,000, with the construction company building the building. It included an allocation for the parking deck. The parking deck was not yet fully designed, so we estimated the cost and had some money allocated for it.

To attract a lender, we had to pay fees up front—in this case, 1.5 percent in the beginning and another 0.5 percent for an extension of the amount they're lending, which is about $200,000. We budgeted for interest on the construction loan at 11.5 percent during construction; fortu-

nately, during the process, the interest rate went down.

The next item was a deficit in leasing over the 36 months of funding for the project. That amounted to $457,000 that we had to fund for operating the building while no rent was being paid and to pay the interest on the empty space. The budget also included normal design and engineering costs, the cost of finishing space for tenants at $12.00 a square foot, leasing commissions for the leasing agent, salaries for the developer's staff, and some other soft costs, for a total capitalization of about $9,339,000.

The management fee in the budget is the 4 percent development fee. The construction company handles construction management. We got $250,000 in fees during the construction period and the leasing period—$15,000 a month over about 17 months. After it ran out, that was all we got until we made some profit on the building.

The S&L made us an open-ended construction loan with an extension period. There was no takeout on the deal. The S&L also agreed to fund the deficit during leasing, which doesn't normally happen. The agreement stated that we would lease the office building in Chapel Hill gradually over two years after the building was finished; that's 100,000 square feet over two years with the first tenant moving in the first day the building is completed and then not filling it for two years afterward.

We projected that we would lease 25 percent of the building to rent-paying tenants during the first quarter after construction, then 5 percent a month, then about 3 percent a month. That meant getting four or five tenants to move in when the building was completed and then one or two small tenants requiring 3,000 to 5,000 square feet a month for the remaining year and a half.

Thirty-six months of the leasing period includes the 12 months of construction, so the deficit item in the loan is really funding for the 24 months after construction is complete. That seemed pretty reasonable to us, and we didn't see any major

competition for our project. The extension to I-40 from Research Triangle Park to U.S. 15-501 was scheduled to open about the same time our building was scheduled to be complete.

But what happens if that amount is not enough? What happens if we have to come up with another million dollars? We decided that it was a good insurance policy for us to have that extra million dollars lined up before we executed the agreement on the loan. We said the two 50/50 partners jointly should be willing to give up 30 percent of the project, leaving each with 35 percent. All the third party had to do was guarantee with a letter of credit or something else that it would have the money available to lend if we didn't meet the schedule for leasing and construction costs and other things.

Instead of having to get a third party to come in as an investor, Centennial decided it would do it. The agreement was as follows: the million dollars that Centennial had put up to purchase the land was not funded by the bank. So instead of $9,339,000, the bank funded $8,339,000, and the million dollars was left in the deal. We ended up with a 65/35 deal, with Fraser Morrow Daniels receiving 35 percent and Centennial 65 percent of the project's profits.

When you calculate how much it costs to operate the building versus how much rent you're getting, the occupancy figure drives the cost of operating the building. And the number of rent-paying tenants drives the revenue side. Our revised model gave us the $9,339,000 capital cost over three years from when we started—a building 95 percent occupied at $17.00 per square foot, two years out. If you rent the office space today and you get six months of free rent, then start paying at $16.00 per square foot, your rent escalates after a year by 5 percent and after another year by another 5 percent and you're paying about $17.50 by the time we would sell or refinance the building.

What it cost to get from a raw piece of land to a fully occupied, income-producing building two years after con-

struction, including all the interest carrying costs, was $9,339,000, total. The construction cost was $5 million, the land was $1 million, and tenant finishes, interest, marketing, and commissions were $3.3 million. With conventional financing, owning an office building that leases at these rates provides a relatively marginal return to the building owner.

The capital cost is what we have to pay back when we sell the building. The selling price is a function of net rental income after operating costs and before debt service. When you build an office building, basically it's always for sale. Our expected profit was $2.2 million, and we expected to get 35 percent of that $2.2 million at the end.

Environmental Issues Affecting Real Estate

Awareness of the environment increased dramatically in the 1970s as the courts took a very active role in protecting the nation's environment, and today developers should not buy land without first asking whether the property is contaminated and whether it is defined as a wetland. Two federal environmental laws have profoundly affected real estate development: Superfund and the Clean Water Act. Lenders, developers, buyers, and sellers have all been touched by these far-reaching laws.

Hazardous Wastes: Now Everyone's Concern

In 1980, Congress enacted the Comprehensive Environmental Response, Cleanup, and Liability Act (CERCLA), commonly referred to as "Superfund," to fund the cleanup of the nation's worst toxic-waste sites. Under Superfund, and now the Superfund Amendments and Reauthorization Act of 1986 (SARA), past and present owners of land contaminated with hazardous substances can be liable for the entire cost of a cleanup, even if the material was dumped legally by someone else three or four decades ago and even if the owner did not know about the contamination. Mere ownership is enough to establish liability.

Superfund's all-inclusive liability caught many developers and lenders off guard. In 1985, for instance, Shore Realty

Asbestos removal requires workers to wear special protective gear to prevent risks to workers' health.

Corporation was held responsible for cleaning up hazardous wastes on land it had recently purchased, even though it had neither owned the property at the time the wastes were dumped nor caused the release to occur (see *New York* v. *Shore Realty Corporation*, 759 F.2d 1032). The developer knew of the contamination, however, before buying the property. Shore Realty paid $435,000 in 1983 for the 3.2-acre site; the cleanup is estimated to cost over $4 million. In another case, a bank was responsible for cleanup costs after foreclosing on property that was contaminated. As a result, most lenders will not issue a loan for commercial or industrial property unless the property receives a clean bill of health.

SARA created a defense for so-called "innocent landowners," that is, landowners who "did not know and had no reason to know" that the property they purchased was contaminated. To qualify as an innocent landowner, purchasers must be able to prove that they made all appropriate inquiries into previous uses of the property to uncover any possible evidence of contamination—known as the "due diligence test." Unfortunately, neither Congress nor the Environmental Protection Agency (EPA) established standards on exactly what constitutes due diligence, thus leaving members of the real estate community in a quandary: they must take steps to meet the vague standards of due diligence with no guarantee that they will be absolved from liability should contamination later be uncovered. A number of bills have been introduced in Congress to clarify and standardize the test of due diligence, but as of March 1990, none had been enacted.

In the absence of federal standards, most real estate lenders have developed their own standards, which generally require purchasers to conduct a Phase I environmental audit that includes, for example, a background check on previous uses and owners of the property, a visual inspection of the site, and, if available, a review of aerial photographs of the property.

Many states have enacted laws to clean up hazardous waste sites within their borders. California has adopted its version of Superfund. New Jersey, with over 100 Superfund sites, enacted perhaps the toughest hazardous waste law in the country; its Environmental Cleanup Responsibility Act requires industrial property owners to certify that their properties are free from contamination before they can be sold. Owners must devise an acceptable cleanup plan for contaminated property, and if a seller declares a property clean and a buyer later discovers contamination, the state or the buyer can void the sale. Massachusetts may clean up a site and charge the responsible party or parties treble damages and place a lien on the property to recover its costs. A handful of states have adopted so-called "superlien" laws that give the state priority over all other liens.

Asbestos

Asbestos was used extensively during the 1950s and 1960s to insulate, fireproof, and soundproof commercial and industrial buildings. In fact, many building codes required that asbestos be used for those purposes. In 1973, however, following mounting evidence that asbestos posed significant health risks (particularly lung cancer), EPA banned most uses of asbestos in buildings. The agency estimates that over 500,000 office buildings and over 200,000 apartment buildings contain asbestos. Depending on the condition and treatment of the asbestos, those who own those buildings may be sitting on a toxic time bomb.

Asbestos is a natural, fibrous material mined primarily in Canada, South Africa, and the Soviet Union. Its mere presence in buildings does not pose a hazard; only when airborne does it become dangerous. Asbestos can become dry and brittle and when disturbed release dust-like fibers into the air. When inhaled, those tiny but durable fibers can lodge in the lungs, leading to asbestosis and lung cancer. Most of the estimated 100,000 deaths linked to asbestos occurred among those who worked in asbestos mining or manufacturing plants. But many fear that those who live or work in buildings containing asbestos may also be at risk. This fear has made bankers and investors wary of lending money for buildings containing asbestos. Indeed, a 1989 survey by the Real Estate Research Corporation found that over half of institutional investors said they would walk away from a prospective venture if asbestos were discovered in the building. Many other lenders and investors would buy buildings containing asbestos only if they were offered at bargain-basement prices.

In 1986, Congress enacted the Asbestos Hazard Emergency Response Act (AHERA) to address the problem posed by asbestos in public schools. Commercial building owners, however, are not required by federal law to do anything to buildings containing asbestos with the exception that, under the Clean Air Act, asbestos must be removed before a building is demolished. Building owners and managers may, however, face common law and workman's compensation liability as a result of claims by employees who were exposed to asbestos.

In 1987, Congress considered extending AHERA-like regulations to commercial buildings but deferred any action to the early 1990s, pending resolution of a number of problems and concerns raised by the building industry. Building owners feared, for example, that fly-by-night asbestos removal contractors would proliferate if Congress suddenly required asbestos to be removed from commercial buildings.

A few states have adopted regulations governing buildings containing asbestos. In California, for instance, owners and lessees of buildings containing asbestos must inform their employees of the location and condition of asbestos in the building, the results of any studies to monitor the air, and any potential health risk stemming from exposure to asbestos in the building.

In response to investors' jitters, many owners of such ill-fated buildings have spent considerable sums of money removing asbestos—anywhere from $20 to $40 per square foot. Widespread removal of asbestos from buildings, however, may not only be exceedingly expensive; it might actually worsen the problem by increasing the level of airborne fibers and the associated health risks.

Wetlands

Not too long ago, bogs, swamps, and marshes—commonly known as wetlands—were considered nuisances. Developers and farmers alike were encouraged to convert those "worthless" areas into productive uses. Until 1985, the federal government actually subsidized farmers for draining, plowing, and planting wetlands. Today, however, the situation has changed. After centuries of mistreatment, wetlands are now valued for their enormous environmental and economic importance.

Wetlands are one of the Earth's most productive natural ecosystems and can outproduce even the most groomed and pampered Iowa cornfields. They have an extraordinary ability to shelter fish and wildlife, cleanse polluted and silt-laden water, and protect against floods. Over half of North American ducks nest in wetlands of the north central United States and southern Canada. And about two-thirds of U.S. shellfish and commercial sports fisheries rely on coastal marshes for spawning and nursery grounds.

As our understanding and appreciation of wetlands expand, so do the number and scope of federal and state laws to protect them. Under Section 404 of the Clean Water Act, for instance, developers must first get a permit from the U.S. Army Corps of Engineers (the Corps) before building in wetlands. The Corps usually issues a permit on the condition that the developer mitigate any adverse impacts on a wetland stemming from the development. In addition, a growing number of states have adopted laws to protect wetlands that are more stringent than federal laws. Ten years ago, only a few states had laws protecting wetlands; now over half the states do, and the list is growing.

Before receiving a permit to develop in wetlands, developers must first demonstrate that, for so-called non-water-dependent uses like a mall or a housing development, no practicable, nonwetland sites exist. (Water-dependent uses include, for example, marinas and ports.) Furthermore, both the Corps and state regulators generally require developers to minimize adverse effects on a wetland and to compensate for any wetland lost by restoring or creating a wetland nearby. This process is generally referred to as "wetland mitigation."

Wetland mitigation, particularly creating a wetland, has become very controversial. Wetlands are complex, dynamic ecosystems, and attempts to create them have

Wetlands were considered nuisances not long ago but are now protected areas because of their enormous environmental and economic importance. Developers must be prepared to deal with new, stringent regulations for developing in or near wetlands.

yielded mixed results. Environmentalists argue that man-made wetlands can scarcely be considered adequate substitutes for natural wetlands. Developers counter that creating a wetland allows development to occur in wetlands, particularly where fill is unavoidable, while improving the quality and quantity of wetlands overall. Each side of what has become an impassioned debate can point to failures and successes to support its argument, and no easy answers are available. It appears that some wetlands, such as tidal marshes, can successfully be created but that others, such as bogs and bottomland hardwood forests, are more problematic. Given the uncertainties, regulatory agencies have grown increasingly reluctant to allow developers to exchange man-made wetlands for natural ones. As a result, developers are beginning to shy away from development in wetlands.

Our Environmental Future

In April 1990, the world celebrated the 20th anniversary of Earth Day. As one communist government after another fell in Eastern Europe, the world became aware of a harsh reality that had only been suspected for quite some time: pollution in Eastern Europe far surpassed the wildest expectations. Cesspools of toxic chemicals forced whole towns to move; factories spewed such amounts of toxins that little children had to wear masks because of the extreme danger of cancer. With these revelations and the catastrophe at Chernobyl, we have realized finally that the environment is a global issue, not just a national, state, local, or neighborhood issue.

Real estate development no longer occurs in a vacuum, away from environmental realities. Savvy developers foresaw that the new involvement of communities would lead to more and more interest by citizens in environmental concerns and began to publicize their efforts to save trees and ponds and other natural amenities on new developments. Businesses and developers began to work with governments to find acceptable compromises.

One case in Kenosha County, Wisconsin, illustrates how a business and a conservation group collaborated with the state to further ecologically sound development. The Des Plaines River originates in the farming country of southeastern Wisconsin and winds its way south before entering the Chicago metropolitan area. WISPARK, a subsidiary of the Wisconsin Energy Corporation, is developing a corporate park in Kenosha County, to include a 1,200-acre business park, a 150-acre office park, and a 600-acre conservation area on the Des Plaines River floodplain. In addition, a 100-acre lake, formerly a gravel pit, lies immediately northwest of the business park.

The site was ideally located—midway between Chicago and Milwaukee, one mile north of the Illinois border, and only 1.5 miles from I-94—but it had one drawback: the river prevented direct access to the interstate. County Highway Q ran part way through the parcel but stopped short of the river. The missing link was completed in 1988 when the state of Wisconsin, Kenosha County, and WISPARK built a bridge and two miles of highway. Construction involved filling several acres of wetlands and floodplain. In exchange, the company created over 30 acres of wetlands and several acres of floodplain, and donated over 400 acres of wetlands and floodplain to The Nature Conservancy, one of the largest conservation groups in the United States.

Developers and businesses can no longer afford not to anticipate potential community responses to environmental issues; they must work with government agencies to mitigate possible unpleasant effects.

Decisions about Design And Contractors

Entering stage four, developers will have at least preliminary drawings, and it is necessary to finalize the arrangement with the architect and other design professionals, including engineers. Before the architect draws final plans, a contract must be drawn establishing the formal relationship between the developer and the architect.

Most architects prefer to use the American Institute of Architects's (AIA) standard contract (A111) (see Figure 16-1).

The contract was redesigned in 1987, and developers must be very careful not to execute it blindly. Like all contracts in stage four, it must be negotiated and executed so that all parties agree to produce the appropriate product with risks and responsibilities clearly defined. The standard contract is frequently modified to add items not covered, for example, responsibility for errors and omissions. In fact, lenders might require many changes to the contract. What is *not* in the standard contract is as important as what is there.

It is often necessary to have an architect clearly responsible for all design, for developers have difficulty closing a loan unless someone is professionally responsible for the quality of all work. Thus, the contract with the architect drives related contracts with other design professionals.

Because the contract was drafted by the AIA, it might be expected that it protects the architect in certain ways. Developers might want to negotiate and change the standard AIA contract.

1. All budgeting (estimating costs) is listed as "additional services" that must be paid for in addition to the basic price of architectural design. Indeed, the current version of the AIA contract specifies almost everything as "additional services"; public hearings, interior layouts, and several other items are specifically excluded from the basic contract price. If developers want any of these additional services, they need to be very clear about whether they will pay extra for them.

   Architects also have the right to notify developers that they need certain additional services. If the developer does not respond promptly, the architect has the right to do the work and bill the developer for the services.

2. Insurance for errors and omissions is not included in the form at all. It varies in cost with the amount of dollars involved and the time covered. Developers should note these facts and determine the proper amount for the insurance and the proper carrier, and who—developer or architect—is responsible for obtaining it. In any case, a source of funds must be available should a claim be made.

3. In the current version of the AIA contract, the architect is arbitrator of everything and responsible for very little. In fact, if any member of the development team—contractor, marketing person, developer—alleges a problem with design, the first reviewer or arbitrator is the architect itself.

4. The construction contract (the contract with the general contractor) usually follows the architect's contract fairly directly. Thus, it is important to

---

FIGURE 16-1
AIA DOCUMENT A111

STANDARD FORM OF AGREEMENT BETWEEN OWNER AND CONTRACTOR
where the basis of payment is the COST OF THE WORK PLUS A FEE, with or without a guaranteed maximum price

1987 EDITION

THIS DOCUMENT HAS IMPORTANT LEGAL CONSEQUENCES; CONSULTATION WITH AN ATTORNEY IS ENCOURAGED WITH RESPECT TO ITS COMPLETION OR MODIFICATION.

The 1987 edition of AIA Document A201, General Conditions of the Contract for Construction, is adopted in this document by reference. Do not use with other general conditions unless this document is modified.

This document has been approved and endorsed by the Associated General Contractors of America.

ARTICLE 1
The Contract Documents

ARTICLE 2
The Work of This Contract

ARTICLE 3
Relationship of the Parties

ARTICLE 4
Date of Commencement and
Substantial Completion

ARTICLE 5
Contract Sum

ARTICLE 6
Changes in the Work

ARTICLE 7
Costs to Be Reimbursed

ARTICLE 8
Costs Not to Be Reimbursed

ARTICLE 9
Discounts, Rebates, and Refunds

ARTICLE 10
Subcontracts and Other
Agreements

ARTICLE 11
Accounting Records

ARTICLE 12
Progress Payments

ARTICLE 13
Final Payment

ARTICLE 14
Miscellaneous Provisions

ARTICLE 15
Termination or Suspension

ARTICLE 16
Enumeration of Contract Documents

370

determine at this stage whether disputes are to be handled by arbitration or litigation. It may be that architects prefer arbitration, while developers often enjoy using at least the threat of litigation as a negotiating point.

5. The AIA contract requires the owner to hire a geotechnical engineer. While doing so is often appropriate, particularly given the possibility of liability for hazardous wastes, developers may not want to do so on every job; if not, they must remove this provision from the contract.

6. The contract does not specify the exact form on which the architect is to certify the quality of the work if certification is needed when the loan is closed. Thus, the developer must specify the form in the contract so that no problems will arise at closing.

7. The standard contract specifies that the plans drawn belong to the architect, not the developer, even though the developer has paid for them. This provision could well be changed.

8. A provision in the contract prohibits assignment of the contract to any other developer. The lender should clearly require that this provision be deleted, for if the original developer cannot perform, the lender might want another developer to step in and finish the project, salvaging the lender's position. This provision, if not eliminated, could seriously affect financing of the project.

9. The provision to retain a portion of the money due the contractor based on work completed but withheld to ensure final completion must be coordinated with the construction contract and with the loan agreement. The developer must be able to draw down the amount of money owed on the construction contract.

10. Developers are well advised to watch for "allowances" as opposed to fixed prices in the construction contract. Allowances, such as $20,000 for carpeting, rather than a fixed price can lead to serious problems in stage six. With allowances, a set amount can be drawn from the construction lender. If costs, which are determined later, exceed this amount, serious financial pressures can result.

Drafting the design contract typically requires advance thought about the construction contract. Developers can choose to have all the building done by in-house staff; those who come from a general contracting background often take this approach. Most developers, however, use outside construction contractors for the majority of their work. Like all aspects of the development process, many variations are possible, depending on the developer's in-house skills.

Bidding versus Negotiations

The developer and general contractor can reach agreement on a construction contract in several ways. The two ends of the spectrum are bidding and negotiation of a "cost-plus" contract. If bidding is chosen, the developer puts out plans and specifications to all the builders in the area considered qualified, asking them to supply one set price or a base price with additions per unit for certain items that cannot be planned totally in advance. For example, an office building might require a price for the building plus a certain amount per linear foot for interior walls. Not until leasing is completed will the developer know how many linear feet of walls are needed. In the bid itself, however, the contractor promises to do the job according to plans and specifications for one cost plus a certain amount per foot.

At the other end of the spectrum is the cost-plus arrangement, in which the developer typically negotiates with one general contractor, agreeing that the general contractor will do the work and bill the developer for its cost plus a certain profit margin.

Clearly, developers would prefer a fixed price, while contractors would prefer a cost-plus agreement. Consequently, many jobs are in between. It is common for developers to negotiate with only one contractor and to obtain a price based on the developer's estimate of cost plus a reasonable profit margin. The two then might agree that if costs exceed the agreement, they will share them equally and that if costs are below the plan, they will share the savings, possibly on some other basis.

Fraser Morrow Daniels negotiated a similar agreement with the contractor for the Europa Center.

EUROPA CENTER

CONSTRUCTION COSTS

The contractor gave us a guaranteed maximum price, and the agreement stated that if actual costs came in under that price, they could keep half of what they saved us. We were so tight in negotiations that I was certain it would not occur.

During construction, the contractor builds the project exactly as it is drawn. If you change anything, a step or a rail or a nail, it's extra—in some cases, much extra. We have learned over the years that even though a project can be improved by changing it during the process, it costs about four times as much as improving it before building starts. So you live with it the way it is bid except for critical omissions or safety features. We added a $200,000 contingency to cover just such possibilities.

In reality, most developments involve a great deal of the unknown, even after the formal feasibility study. Quite often, marketing feedback during construction will require change orders. Thus, the developer is to some extent exposed to renegotiation, no matter how tight the original contract. On jobs that tend to have few change orders and where public scrutiny is more intense, bidding is most common—in projects involving the federal, state, or local government, for example, where the plans are set firmly in advance and no formal marketing occurs. Further, the bid process satisfies the public's need to know that the price paid is fair.

Formulating a bid requires the contractor to spend considerable time motivating subcontractors to submit their bids, consolidate them, and submit the complete bid to the developer. When contractors have some clout—for example, when they have plenty of work—they might refuse to bid on smaller jobs. At other times, they might bid high on the theory that they do not need the work but if they are awarded the contract at that price, so much the better. In such situations, developers who

A site at the beginning of construction. In a few months, this site will be covered with an industrial office park.

372

have developed long-term relationships with quality contractors might find it better to negotiate directly with one contractor.

Typically, the developer and the general contractor sign one contract, and the general contractor and various subcontractors sign another set of contracts. The developer negotiating a contract with the general contractor might also be concerned with the quality of subcontractors, however. Depending on the job's complexity, certain subcontractors might play key roles in construction. In such situations, developers might specify in a bid or during negotiations for a cost-plus contract that particular subcontractors be used.

Developers can negotiate directly with key subcontractors with whom they have a good relationship. In such situations, the developer might negotiate a price with that subcontractor and then approach the various possible general contractors and ask for a bid, assuming that a particular subcontracted job will be done by a certain subcontractor. The general contractor is then relieved of the difficulty of finding a subcontractor to do the job and the difficulty of getting the subcontractor to take bidding seriously. Consequently, general contractors might be more willing to submit a bid, assuming that they respect the particular subcontractor's work. As with many aspects of the process, no hard and fast rules exist, and because there are no rules, developers must devise the process that best serves their needs.

Fast-track Construction

In markets where interest rates are very high or the project must be completed early to satisfy a tenant or the government, it could be beneficial to engage in fast-track construction. The idea is to have as many steps under way at the same time as possible. One possibility is to start excavation as soon as the architect has completed the general layout and to start building the structure before interior design has been completed. Fast-track construction involves the developer in negotiation for a cost-plus contract. Fast-track construction can be beneficial when it works, because the developer can beat competitors to the marketplace and reduce interest costs.

When coordination is lost on such a schedule, however, the results can be disastrous.

A classic illustration of fast-track construction out of control is a development south of Mexico City. With high interest rates in Mexico, fast-track construction there is common. Volcanic subsurface soils can make construction very tricky, however. In this case, with the project half finished, the architect decided that it would be very difficult to complete the part that had already been built according to plans within budget. The foundation work the architect had specified had been constructed before all the building plans were completed; it happened that the foundation would not support the structure and the architect was not sure how to fix the problem. While the developer may have had the basis of a lawsuit against the architect, lawsuits are usually a poor remedy for problems encountered under the pressure of constructing a building on time. With the high interest costs in Mexico, speeding the opening was critical. Thus, regardless of long-term legal alternatives, the developer had to knock out that portion of the foundation that did not fit the new architect's plan. The additional cost put considerable stress on construction financing.

Bonding

Bonding is a guarantee, either of completion or of performance. The city might require the developer to provide a bond to prove that the developer has the capacity to complete the infrastructure. The developer might ask the general contractor to provide a bond to prove that the general contractor has the wherewithal to complete the job. Insurance companies typically issue bonds to examine the credibility of individuals or institutions being bonded. The assessment covers both their capacity to do the work and their financial substance. Bonds are the most common approach, although alternatives can be used, such as a letter of credit or depositing assets in escrow. Bonds enable the developer or general contractor to ask an insurance company to stand behind them in a lawsuit.

During stage four, developers might want general contractors to be bonded if they fear the contractor might not be able to perform or have the financial backing to pay a judgment in the event of a lawsuit. Federal, state, and local government contracts often require the general contractor to be bonded. In public construction projects, government agencies often do not have the personnel to monitor construction and want to ensure that taxpayers' dollars will not be lost.

Bonding has several different connotations. Completion bonds and performance bonds, for example, are quite different. For a completion bond, the insurance company guarantees that the project will be completed according to plans at a certain cost. Insurance companies almost never guarantee completion on time, and without it, developers can easily lose key tenants and pay more interest. A performance bond, on the other hand, means that the insurance company stands behind the contractor. In the event of a lawsuit in which the developer successfully gets a judgment against the general contractor, the insurance company is liable for that judgment. In this situation, the insurance company can use all the defenses open to the general contractor. If the developer has caused part of the problem, he might not be able to collect.

Most developers believe that when they are forced to call upon a bonding agent, they will certainly lose some money for time lost and higher interest rates. Thus, bonding provides some protection, albeit not complete protection.

During stage four, all the necessary contracts must be executed. Because the contracts are interactive, it is often appropriate to have a checklist of clauses to be included (see Figure 16-2). The contracts must stipulate how the design and construction will be handled, how all the parties will be compensated, how risks will be shared, and who is responsible for approving the quality of construction along the way.

Decisions about Major Tenants

Since stage one of the process, the developer has had an idea of the main tenant and/or the tenant mix anticipated for the project. In the case of a for-sale project, the developer has had some idea of who the end customer will be. That idea is refined in stage two and further formalized in stage three. At this point, the developer must make the final decision. Possibly using sensitivity analysis on the pro forma numbers from the feasibility study, the developer decides how much space to allocate to major tenants and when to sign them.

The first question pertains to major tenants. Large tenants—ranging from anchors in a regional mall (the major department stores) to tenants occupying a full floor in an office building to industrial tenants occupying 50,000 square feet—know their power and drive a hard bargain. Thus, the more major users of space (particularly those with prominent names) the developer signs, the less the net rent (rent after consideration of concessions for tenants, impact of unusual expense stops, and the like). On the other hand, large tenants draw other tenants. A regional mall is not usually possible without several department stores as anchors. From the developer's standpoint, the more space the major tenants take, the lower the average rent per square foot. Signing those anchors is usually the key to drawing smaller tenants, however, as well as the key to convincing lenders of the project's long-term viability.

In regional malls, developers might actually give away space to the anchor tenants and make all their return on smaller tenants. The practice is not unfair, as it is the advertising and name recognition of the major tenants that draw customers to the mall and thus provide the livelihood for the smaller tenants. The critical decision is what percentage of the space, if any, goes to a major tenant. On the one hand, it is usually safer to have more space for major tenants. On the other hand, it is more lucrative to have a large share of smaller tenants if they "stay and pay."

In addition to deciding what percentage of space to allocate to major tenants (and all gradations between major and minor tenants), developers must decide *when* to sign tenants. Tenants signed early in the process are committing to something they cannot see physically and to an uncertain future date. To induce tenants to make such a commitment, developers must offer something—a concession in price or a choice location.

Mission Viejo Commerce Center includes the usual mix of dry cleaners, restaurants, and video stores. The remaining two-thirds of its building space, however, is designed for and occupied by car care tenants. Auto service and care in the United States are worth over $100 billion annually. This center went after that niche by providing an attractive environment for an activity that is normally confined to unsightly buildings.

From the developer's perspective, signing a tenant early has certain advantages. The more tenants signed early, the smaller the vacancy rate if the market looks less robust or the project less inviting after it is built. While early leasing is a way to reduce risk, however, a cost is also involved—concessions to tenants.

After making decisions about signing tenants in advance and the number of major tenants, developers must specify the general conditions desired in other leases. What is involved is not just rent per square foot, which varies depending on where the tenant locates, the amount of space, and so forth. Developers must also decide who pays what portion of which operating costs, the amount of the tenant improvement allowance, and who provides what services. Who pays for carpeting and other interior features? If the developer pays, typically the rent is higher. Often developers give the tenant a certain allowance; the tenant then pays whatever additional amount is necessary for upgraded fixtures beyond the amount specified in the lease. From a lender's perspective, tenant allowances are attractive, as money spent on permanent interior improvements creates additional collateral for the first lien on the project.

Because the developer typically negotiates the first lien, it is often easier to include in those negotiations a certain tenant allowance and pass it along to tenants. The alternative is for tenants to borrow the money. Smaller tenants will find it difficult to finance improvements because their lenders do not get the improvements as collateral.

The ongoing operating guidelines are also important. What services will the landlord provide? How often will the bathrooms be cleaned? How fast will the elevators travel? What kind of security will be provided? In many projects, tenants also have obligations, particularly in shopping centers. What are the minimum hours of operation? How much cooperation is necessary for joint promotions? All of these items must be worked out before leases are executed to ensure that the *total* marketing effort matches the expectations laid out in the feasibility study.

Most of these decisions are driven by the market. The landlord would like higher rents with more expenses passed on to tenants and fewer allowances for tenants. The market may not allow it, however. No one may be willing to sign before seeing more of the project, particularly if the market is overbuilt, the developer inexperi-

FIGURE 16-2
CHECKLIST FOR CONSTRUCTION CONTRACTS

	Owner	Architect	Contractor
1.0 Program Development			
1.1 Project requirements, including design objectives, constraints and criteria, space requirements and relationships, flexibility and expandability, special equipment, and systems and site requirements			
1.2 Legal description and a certified survey; complete, as required			
1.3 Soils engineering; complete, as required			
1.4 Materials testing, inspections, and reports; complete, as required			
1.5 Legal, accounting (including auditing), and insurance counseling, as required			
1.6 Program review			
1.7 Financial feasibility			
1.8 Planning surveys, site evaluations, environmental studies, or comparative studies of prospective sites			
1.9 Verification of existing conditions or facilities			
2.0 Construction Cost			
2.1 Budget and funds			
2.2 Estimate of probable costs			
2.3 Detailed estimates of construction cost			
2.4 Control of design to meet fixed limit of construction cost			
3.0 Design			
3.1 Schematic			
3.2 Design development			
3.3 Consultants: structural, mechanical, electrical, special			
4.0 Construction Documents			
4.1 Final drawings and specifications			
4.2 Bidding information, bid forms, conditions of contract, and form of agreement between owner and contractor			

FIGURE 16-2 (continued)

	Owner	Architect	Contractor
4.3 Filing for governmental approvals			
4.4 For use in construction			
4.5 On-site maintenance of drawings, specifications, addenda, change orders, shop drawings, product data, and samples			
5.0 Bidding			
5.1 Obtaining bids or negotiated proposals			
5.2 Awarding and preparing contracts			
5.3 Documents for alternate, separate, or sequential bids; extra services in connection with bidding, negotiation, or construction before completion of construction documents			
6.0 Administration of Construction Contract			
6.1 General			
6.1.1 Owner's representative			
6.1.2 Periodic visits to the site			
6.1.3 Construction methods, techniques, sequences, procedures, safety precautions, and programs			
6.1.4 Contractor's applications for payments			
6.1.5 Certificates for payment			
6.1.6 Document interpretation/artistic effect			
6.1.7 Rejection of work; special inspections or testing			
6.1.8 Shop drawings, product data, and samples			
6.1.8.1 Submittals			
6.1.8.2 Review and action			
6.1.9 Change orders			
6.1.9.1 Preparation			
6.1.9.2 Approval			
6.1.10 Close-out			
6.1.10.1 Date of substantial completion			

FIGURE 16-2 (continued)

	Owner	Architect	Contractor
6.1.10.2 Date of final completion			
6.1.10.3 Written warranties			
6.1.10.4 Certificate for final payment			
6.1.11 Coordination of work of separate contractors or by owner's forces			
6.1.12 Services of construction manager			
6.1.13 As-built drawings			
7.0 Schedule			
7.1 Design schedule			
7.1.1 Development			
7.1.2 Maintenance			
7.2 Construction schedule			
7.2.1 Development			
7.2.2 Maintenance			
8.0 Payment			
8.1 Basic design services			
8.1.1 Accounting records			
8.2 Construction (the work)			
8.2.1 Progress payments			
8.2.2 Final payment			
8.3 Evidence of ability to pay			
8.4 Secure and pay for necessary approvals, easements, assessments, and changes for construction, use, or occupancy			
9.0 Construction			
9.1 General			
9.2 Labor, materials, and equipment			
9.3 Correlation of local conditions to requirements of the contract documents			
9.4 Division of work among subcontractors			
9.5 Right to stop work			
9.6 Owner's right to carry out work			

FIGURE 16-2 (continued)

	Owner	Architect	Contractor
9.7 Review of contract documents for errors, inconsistencies, or omissions			
9.8 Supervision and direction of the work			
9.9 Responsibility to owner for errors and omissions in the work			
9.10 Obligation to perform the work in accordance with contract documents			
9.11 Provide and pay for all labor, materials, equipment, tools, machinery, utilities, transportation, and other facilities and services for the proper execution and completion of the work			
9.12 Enforce discipline and good order among those employed on the work			
9.13 Warranty for all materials and equipment			
9.14 Sales, consumer, and use taxes			
9.15 Secure and pay for all permits, fees, licenses, and inspections			
9.16 Compliance with all laws, ordinances, regulations, and lawful orders			
9.17 Employment of superintendent			
9.18 Cutting and patching			
9.19 Cleaning up			
9.20 Communications			
9.21 Payments of all royalties and license fees; defense against suits and claims			
9.22 Indemnification; hold harmless			
9.23 Award of subcontracts			
9.24 Owner's right to perform work and award separate contracts			
9.24.1 Award			
9.24.2 Mutual responsibility			
9.24.3 Cleanup dispute			
10.0 **Miscellaneous**			
10.1 Performance bond, labor, and material payment bond			
10.2 Tests			

FIGURE 16-2 (continued)

	Owner	Architect	Contractor
10.3 Protection of persons and property			
11.0 Insurance			
11.1 Contractor's liability insurance			
11.2 Owner's liability insurance			
11.3 Property insurance			
12.0 Changes in the Work			
13.0 Uncovering and Correction of Work			

Source: Niles Bolton, Architect, Atlanta, Georgia.

enced, the project distinctive, or the location dubious. Further, while the landlord may hope to pass escalations in operating expenses through to tenants, the market may not permit it.

The developer is accountable for certain numbers in the feasibility study. If the developer concludes that the numbers in the feasibility study cannot be met, this is the last chance to get off the wagon. At this point, developers also decide whether leasing is to be handled by in-house staff or by consultants. For some types of projects and some locations, it is preferable to use outside leasing agents, at least partially. In other cases, sales of retirement housing, for example, the product is so unusual and complex that developers often do well to have that talent on staff where they can monitor it more closely.

Decisions about Equity

The difference between what a project costs and what can be financed is the required equity. The ideal project is one whose value is so far above cost that the developer can go to a very conservative (low-cost) permanent lender and obtain a 70 percent loan-to-value mortgage that will be sufficient to cover all costs (a hefty development fee, major reserves for the leasing period, and a large reserve for contin-gencies). Few "standard" projects today allow the developer such luxury.

When developers cannot finance the entire project and in the process pay themselves for becoming an owner, they must find additional sources of capital. Three basic alternatives are possible: developers provide the necessary equity from their own funds or the firm's funds, developers bring in an outside investor, or developers establish a joint venture with a lender. These three approaches have numerous variations, all of them compensating investors according to the risk associated with their contribution to equity.

In its deal for the Europa Center, Fraser Morrow Daniels ended up with a 65/35 split with Centennial. A small development company, Fraser Morrow Daniels traded off a share of ownership and potential monetary rewards to reduce the risk inherent in leasing a new product—Class A office space in a new location.

When developers lack the resources for equity or choose to allocate their funds differently, they consider outside investors and joint venture partnerships. Before the changes in the tax law in 1986, long-term real estate investment provided substantial benefits, essentially because losses induced by depreciation could be offset against ordinary income. In such a world, it made sense for wealthy individuals to invest in real estate projects. With the revision of the tax law in 1986, fewer tax shelters are available, and more developers are thus moving toward a joint venture that involves the permanent lender's receiving not only the stated amount for interest but also a "participation."

The participation can be 20 percent of gross revenues over a certain amount, 50 percent of net operating profit, or any other variation. Typically, permanent lenders receive not only a periodic additional payment but also some percentage of the proceeds from final sale or any intervening refinancing.

In structuring the deal, developers extend the cash flow forecast from the feasibility study to include taxes and debt service. Potential trade-offs can be quite complex. Often, the amount of the developer's fees and exposure to risk change materially, depending on the source of permanent financing. It takes experience—and the discounted cash flow analysis—for the developer to decide on the optimal structure for any required equity. The developer performs sensitivity analyses on revised cash flows, using alternative forecasts of future events to determine the impact that each scenario might have on cash flows. Experience comes into play in specifying likely scenarios. Just how likely is the combination of interest rates 10 percent lower, an increase in local demand with the relocation of a major employer to the area, and a steady competitive supply as a competing property owner chooses not to expand? It takes experience and "feel" to estimate the likelihood of alternative scenarios.

Developers must decide when and whether to bring in outside investors. If the prospective investors are looking for tax advantages, as was often the case in the early 1980s, it is usually better for developers to build the project with their own funds and then sell it upon completion. At that time, the investor, seeing less risk because the development process is over, should be willing to pay a higher price. On the other hand, doing so requires developers to put substantially more cash into the development during construction.

Before tax reform in 1976, 1981, and 1986, the development period offered sub- stantial tax advantages through the deduction of construction interest, property taxes, and operating and marketing expenses before opening. As tax benefits have been taken away, it has become more difficult to entice investors to invest early.

With a joint venture, participation from the outset is more common. Long-term lenders or investors are often willing to invest money before the project is built, thereby reducing the amount of cash the developer needs. Sophisticated long-term lenders know the value of this commitment and are likely to negotiate a more advantageous split of the rewards for the additional risk assumed. The more developers can guarantee in terms of construction costs, completion dates, and leasing, the higher the percentage participation they will enjoy in the rewards from development.

The Government as Partner

Astute developers keep their public partner fully informed throughout the early stages of development. In stage four, just as they contract with other members of the development team, developers would like to contract with the city. In some situations, it is no problem. The city's issuing the building permit is like signing a contract with private sector members of the development team.

The relationship with the city and, equally important, with the public, is not always one that can be managed with one contract executed at one time, however. In California, for example, a referendum can override an accepted development agreement. Unless the developer's interests are vested, a vote by the general public can cancel the development agreement, even though the city and the developer executed and signed it in good faith.

Rules for contracting with the public sector vary by location. In Massachusetts, for example, the developer's interests are vested if a building permit has been issued *and* construction starts within six months. Unlike California, local governments in Massachusetts honor all signed agreements so long as initiation of construction is not delayed more than six months. Also in Massachusetts, as long as a plat for a new sub-division is filed before a rezoning hearing, zoning is frozen for a period of eight years (because subdivision is considered an administrative act in Massachusetts). Downzoning is therefore not an immediate problem once the plat is filed.

In formalizing the relationships among parties, developers should not lose sight of the changing face of the urban landscape. Projects that began as industrial distribution centers have become high-tech office parks and in the process made their owners very wealthy.

Evolving land uses are usually stimulated by growth in surrounding areas, public restrictions on the development of other land, and other forces prompting change. While the stimulation might come from the outside, however, developers can create the *possibility*. Developers who realize the inevitability of change and provide as much flexibility as possible in design, selection of tenants, and financing are the ones most likely to enjoy the benefits of "second-order effects."

The fine print in the contracts negotiated during stage four greatly affects the possibilities for change. Astute developers do not ignore the seemingly small details that lawyers want to put in contracts to maximize their clients' flexibility—in the process often minimizing the developer's. And developers must ensure future flexibility with various contractors when drawing up agreements. It is not sufficient for tenants to allow the developer to do something if the lender will not. And it is not useful to have flexibility for tenants in year five and flexibility for the lender in year ten. To provide for change, developers need to coordinate these details so that their flexibility is consistent with that of different contractors and over time.

STAGE FIVE: COMMITMENT, SIGNING CONTRACTS, AND INITIATING CONSTRUCTION

Several of the contracts negotiated during stage four can be contingent on other contracts. It is quite common for the permanent lender to be unwilling to make a commitment until certain major tenants have signed a commitment. The construction lender's agreement is often contingent on a permanent loan takeout. Developers do not want to make a commitment to a contractor until they have the funds available to pay for construction, and major tenants do not want to sign a contract until they are sure the developer has sufficient money and people to complete the project.

Hence, many of the parties examine contracts in which they are not direct participants but that are necessary for them to realize their objectives. It is often necessary to have different contracts executed simultaneously. Regardless of whether the contracts are executed sequentially or simultaneously, however, most must be fairly firmly in hand before any are signed. And a certain series of events must happen as they are signed.

In stage five of the process, the contracts negotiated in stage four are executed. If outside investors are involved, a limited partnership agreement typically must be signed. In larger projects, a public offering registered with the Securities and Exchange Commission could be involved. To complete financial arrangements, the permanent loan commitment must be signed and the fee paid and the construction loan agreement signed and that origination fee paid. The contract with the general contractor is signed, and the general contractor signs a series of contracts with subcontractors.

The local jurisdiction is also involved. If possible, permits are obtained in stage three or at least early in stage four, but negotiations in stage four often cause changes that require renegotiation with the city. In larger projects (and increasingly with smaller projects), local governments require impact fees and/or major off-site improvements before approving a development. These agreements must also be signed in stage five.

As for marketing, any preleased space needs a formally executed lease, and most of the leases will be recorded. If an outside leasing agent or sales agent is used, a listing agreement may be necessary or at least a memorandum of understanding. A memorandum describes the type of space to be leased or sold and the conditions under which it is to be done.

To close the construction loan, the developer probably will have to close on the option to buy the land and/or pay off any land loan in the event the land has already been purchased, which is necessary to ensure the first lien commercial banks typically require. On the administrative side, insurance during the construction period must be put in force—liability, fire, and extended coverage, an update on title insurance, and the like—at the same time the developer switches to a more formal accounting system. Up to this point, the developer has probably simply aggregated all the costs associated with the project, but now a formal budget and cash controls are necessary. The budget came from the feasibility analysis (as amended by negotiations in stage four), was blessed by the bank, and will be part of the procedure to draw down funds as construction proceeds. It is also the basis of the contract with the general contractor and probably the arrangement with prospective tenants.

Cash controls require looking at the budget to compare funds expended and funds committed with original plans, while keeping a careful eye on remaining funds. Likewise, the bank will use a similar procedure to keep track of the draws by the developer to fund construction.

Most important, the developer must install some sort of control mechanism for the development itself, either instructing the architect to do a certain amount of supervision or employing an on-site construction manager. The general contractor must also use some sort of formalized process for control, the most common being the program evaluation and review technique (PERT) and the critical path method (CPM), which are available for use on personal computers. Appendix E contains an illustration of CPM applied to scheduling in a small project.

EUROPA CENTER

INITIATING CONSTRUCTION

*We formalized the relationship that had been negotiated with the S&L. Final negotiations were tough because both the S&L and Centennial were initially unwilling to expand the loan to cover the exten-*sive leasing period we sought. When things started to get tight, it became obvious that different members of the team had different goals. The firm's senior partner did not want to lose his established net worth, while the younger members did not want to lose an opportunity. All the members of the team realized their respective positions, however, and held firm in their negotiations with the lender/financier, eventually obtaining the desired $1 million reserve for the leasing period.*

We negotiated the price of construction, dealing seriously with three potential general contractors and finally obtaining a contract that did not need to be bonded because of the general contractor's quality. The architect's judgment had been key throughout, but we did not turn over the final decisions involving rent, costs, and operating efficiency to the architect. And because quality construction was very important to us and because local builders did not have much experience with Class A office buildings, we added a partner to the team to supervise construction for a salary plus a small percentage of the profits.

SUMMARY

Once the project is formally deemed feasible in stage three, the development team can move toward formalizing all the relationships necessary to implement the plan. During stage four, detailed relationships are negotiated, quite possibly with some changes in the plan necessitated by negotiations. And in stage five, the contracts negotiated in stage four are executed.

During stages four and five, it is still quite possible for the developer to determine that the project is not feasible. It is far more expensive to decide to stop during stage four or stage five, however, than it was earlier. Developers who frequently arrive at stage four and decide to stop find that they are building up a tremendous amount of uncovered overhead. Failure to stop when the signals indicate it in stages four and five, however, can cause tragedy in stages six, seven, and eight.

NOTES

1. Often the stated maturity for amortization purposes and for measuring the debt-service-coverage ratio is a lengthy period, but a "bullet" provision calls for a "balloon payment" (maturity) in a shorter period (say 10 years) to protect the lender from longer exposure.

2. As noted in Chapter 13, typical permanent lenders have liabilities with a long duration and seek maturities matched with their liabilities. Consequently, pension funds, life insurance companies, and foundations are the traditional long-term lenders.

3. The interested student should use the material in this chapter and the financial logic developed in Chapter 3 as bases for exploring the professional real estate journals (e.g., *Real Estate Review* and *National Real Estate Investor*) for new ideas that can be modified to fit a proposed development.

Chapter 17

Stages Six and Seven: Construction, Completion, And Formal Opening

Stage six, construction, differs from all other stages covered so far in one key way: time becomes even more critical. At stage six, the developer is exposed to many more uncertainties, all of them potentially expensive. Unlike earlier stages of development, where an option keeps the developer's cash contributions to a minimum, major amounts of cash and human effort are now committed. Even when developers have nonrecourse financing and receive substantial fees up front, their reputations—and usually a lot more—are on the line.

During the earlier stages, particularly contract negotiation and formal commitment, the specific rules governing the relationships among the parties were formalized and their obligations defined. Once the agreements are signed, developers become managers more than before. They need to ensure that all players do their jobs on time and within budget.

This chapter examines two major stages in real estate development: construction of the project and its completion or formal opening, specifically:

- The continuing interaction among major players;
- Building the structure;

- Drawing the construction loan;
- Leasing space and building interior space;
- Landscaping and exterior construction;
- Long-term land development;
- Potential problems that might arise during stage six;
- Completion and formal opening; and
- Techniques to control risk during stages six and seven.

STAGE SIX: CONSTRUCTION

In stage six, the developer (along with the other players formally committed to the project) takes a financial leap, beginning the expensive process of construction. And developers must be able to manage construction in an environment characterized by a high degree of uncertainty.

The Continuing Interaction Among Major Players

Managing the Construction Process

A developer's role as manager does not end when a general contractor is hired to oversee construction. Developers must still manage the general contractor and the rest of the development team. By carefully selecting players whose objectives are compatible and establishing formal relationships during stages four and five, developers can coordinate the working relationship among the construction, marketing, financial, operations, and public sector players. Coordinating players through the construction process is especially important in complex multiphase developments that can involve several builders, many different users, and many chances for the general public to express its opinion. The developer, however, makes the final call when a tough judgment is needed.

James DeFrancia, the land developer of Countryside, a planned community in Loudoun County, Virginia, recognized from the outset the problems with coordination that could impede development and consume time (see the accompanying profile). By clearly delineating each builder's responsibilities, negotiating compromises with local officials, and periodically using a market analyst to fine-tune plans, DeFrancia smoothed the project's entry into the community.

DeFrancia assembled a development team that he felt would work well in the long run. If things cease to work well, however, developers must be prepared to make changes in the team. During the early stages of construction, Fraser Morrow Daniels encountered problems because of poor on-site supervision. To correct the problem, Fraser Morrow Daniels brought in its own person, one who had construction management experience in the Research Triangle market. He was made construction manager and a partner in the project. Certainly he cost more than his predecessor, but the predecessor was not getting the job done.

Developers can provide on-site management in several ways. One is to have the architect who designed the project examine the work at various stages and certify that the work has been done according to plans and specifications. Another is to hire a construction manager in house, typically an engineer of some type, to stay on the site and monitor the general contractor's performance throughout the process.

Fifteen years ago, architectural supervision was most common. Today, with more complex jobs, periodic supervision by the architect is often not enough. On larger jobs, most developers have someone on the payroll who is on site all the time and who acts as their agent in dealing with the general contractor. The more complex the job, the more unusual the items that will likely arise. And as problems occur, somebody must be available to make decisions quickly. Either the developer himself or some member of the staff must be there to work with the general contractor.

Construction lenders are very interested in how supervision will be handled. Periodic sign-offs by the architect or construction manager will be needed as part of the process when the developer asks for a draw on the construction loan. Construction lenders also inspect work, but they are intended to reinforce, not replace, technical reviews.

Construction Manager

The construction manager, whether an architect supervising the general contractor, an in-house general contractor, or an engineer managing the relationship with the general contractor, oversees construction and ideally should have experience in the type of project being built. Without such experience, the construction manager could miss opportunities to reduce the inevitable conflicts that arise as the builder attempts to minimize costs, the operating people clamor for changes to make the structure more functional, and the architect tries to hold on to a certain aesthetic concept. Although all of these issues have been negotiated since stage three, changes often are necessitated by the changing market or by unanticipated construction problems during stage six. Without direct experience, construction managers certainly have less personal clout to convince the parties that they have made the right decision.

Marketing Manager

Unless all plans and specifications are known at the beginning and all space is preleased (the case of the construction of a public hospital, for example), marketing goes on continuously. During construction in particular, a marketing strategy must be implemented in full force. Advertising must be professionally done and well timed. The biggest sales tool is the sales force that meets with prospects and sells the space.

The sales and leasing manager is responsible for giving feedback acquired from potential customers to the rest of the

---

PROFILE: JAMES M. DeFRANCIA

President, Lowe-Weston Enterprises
Sterling, Virginia

Jim DeFrancia develops planned residential communities on both coasts. He is also a contract developer for financial institutions working out troubled residential properties.

Background: U.S. Naval Academy, degree in engineering. After seven years in the Navy, DeFrancia worked for a development company building high-volume, low-cost housing in Venezuela; he later worked for ITT's Levitt and Sons. In 1977, he started his own firm.

Taking the long view: In 1977, DeFrancia bought 1,200 acres in Loudoun County, Virginia, 27 miles from downtown Washington, D.C. In a joint venture with the Hartford Insurance Company, he created a planned community called Countryside, which contains 2,500 townhouses and single-family dwellings selling for $75,000 to $250,000 (in 1987). DeFrancia was the land developer; he carefully picked local builders (ultimately there were eight) and gave each one an exclusive segment, for example, townhouses ranging from $74,000 to $105,000, to prevent head-to-head competition in any segment.

Factors in success:
1. By reducing competition among builders, DeFrancia got good bids from them.
2. DeFrancia used an outside market analyst for homebuyers, whose recommendations proved very accurate. In year three, DeFrancia called him in again to fine-tune the plan. They identified an image for the community and price as the key selling point. DeFrancia says, "You are in the *housing* business, even though you develop the land, not build the houses. You can't rely on builders to tell you what kind of lots people want. The community, not the builder, suffers when homeowners get mad."
3. The pieces of land DeFrancia bought had been in litigation over permitted density for eight years. DeFrancia approached county officials, offering to *reduce* density if the county would work with him to end litigation. Not only did he offer cooperation; he also worked with local officials *himself*, along with the land planner he hired, rather than let lawyers handle the situation.
4. The developer provided organizational support for homeowners and some financial subsidy in the very beginning for the homeowners' association, with the goal of building a sense of community and creating trust.

Advice:
1. In a zoning dispute, put yourself in the other person's shoes. Take the government's problems to heart and try to blend opposing needs into an ideal situation.
2. Momentum is critical. Don't be greedy up front.
3. In a housing community, promote a sense of place, a sense of arrival.
4. Land planning is critical. Choose people with both the right technical skills *and* the right style, because your people have to work well with local officials.

development team. As space is leased or sold, it usually becomes clear that certain designs fare better in the marketplace than others. Ideally, the original overall design has enough built-in flexibility that, during the development process, interior configurations, color schemes, and other features can be changed to suit the market as tenants' preferences are specified (and as they change over time). The design for the Europa Center stressed appeal to tenants and future flexibility. In each decision, Fraser Morrow Daniels considered the trade-off between immediate cost benefits and longer-term impacts.

EUROPA CENTER

THE BUILDING ITSELF

The Europa Center has a high ratio of usable space compared to the core utility and common areas, 85 percent, and we maximized the amount of window space for tenants. Everyone likes windows and extra corners. It costs a little bit more for construction, but I don't think it affects utility costs very much.

Almost all of the mechanical systems in a well-designed multitenant building have a lot of flexibility for different heating and cooling in different zones. We used high-efficiency glass. We used the very best elevators so that we could move people more efficiently, because in a five-story building with 20,000-square-foot floors, a lot of people would need to move up and down in the building. The building has two separate sets of stairs; a freight elevator is planned in the second building.

We also had to choose how much telecommunications and electronics capability to put in the building. Initially in looking at office building development, we thought we should build a state-of-the-art building with built-in computer systems, but we learned in talking with others that 80 or 90 percent of tenants won't pay for that extra cost: they don't know how to use it yet and don't want it. The best thing to do is build flexible conduit space and wiring into the building so that

you can add those systems as they become economically feasible for tenants. We got clearance for a satellite dish on the roof. Such decisions gave us flexibility about how to use the building in the future.

We also did some special on-site landscaping, changing the land plan to increase some landscaped areas. We sank the parking deck into the ground at significant cost so that it would have a low profile and be hidden by berms and trees. That probably cost us an extra $50,000 to $100,000. We'll landscape it so that some marginal leasing benefit might be possible. We liked that from the standpoint of design, but it was more expensive. We would have to increase rent to pay for the added costs, but which pocket could we take it out of? In a very competitive market, we probably would not recover the extra rent.

Later, the building will be more valuable because of that decision. The building is more valuable because of the parking deck. Period. The alternative to a parking deck to serve a fairly large building like the Europa Center would have been to cover the entire site with asphalt.

Financial Officer

The financial officer on the development team manages the relationship with the lender and investors, obtaining the money to pay the construction workers as the structure is built. Whenever feedback from the marketing staff suggests changes, the construction manager must figure the cost of the suggested alternative, and the financial officer must determine whether the increment in value justifies any additional cost and whether the lender or the equity investor can be convinced to increase its financial commitments to the project to cover additional costs.

Property Manager

The property manager should also be involved during construction. As the marketing representative suggests changes and the construction manager responds with alternatives, the property manager should ensure that the proposed changes do not

388

complicate the building's long-term manageability. Particularly when financing becomes tight, short-term decisions to solve financing problems can cause long-term trouble. The property manager is responsible for ensuring that it does not happen without due consideration of all aspects of asset management (see Chapter 18).

Building the Structure

As described earlier, the general contractor typically uses a variety of subcontractors to install electrical, plumbing, HVAC, and other systems. A residential project, for example, might require subcontractors for excavation, the foundation and pouring concrete, framing, drywall, roofing, HVAC, plumbing, and electrical systems, trim, painting, and any other specialties needed for a particular design. In high-rise construction, the structural components are more difficult and the mechanical systems more complex, but the same principle applies. While the general contractor controls the subcontractors, the construction manager represents the developer's interest with the general contractor, and the developer makes sure that construction is coordinated with the ongoing marketing. The developer also makes sure that construction and marketing occur within the financial resources available and with long-term management in mind.

Subcontractors vary dramatically in the size and organizational sophistication of their companies. Some subcontractors for mechanical systems are large regional, even national, firms with sophisticated management procedures and accounting controls. On the other hand, the masonry subcontractor could be one man and his nephew with a few tools in the back of an old pick-up truck. The general contractor must choose the appropriate subcontractor for the job at hand, remembering that it is expensive to hire someone more skilled than necessary and dangerous to hire someone less skilled than necessary. The appropriate subcontractor must have the time to

Photo courtesy of Jim Sink, Artech, Inc.

The parking deck for Phase One of the Europa Center just after construction. Designed to hold close to 300 cars, the parking deck was eventually tastefully cloaked by landscaping.

do the job when needed and should have the general contractor's trust based on reputation, past relations, and the possibility of future business. In some cases, the developer will monitor individual subcontractors' actions, depending on the relationship between the developer and the general contractor and the developer's in-house construction expertise.

The general contractor's most difficult task is probably scheduling the different subcontractors. While everyone knows the difficulty involved in putting a roof on before the walls are up, it is also difficult to know exactly how long it will take to put the walls up when the weather could go bad. Because most construction is done outdoors and weather conditions are uncertain, even the most reliable subcontractors can fall behind schedule. If one task falls behind, the next subcontractor may be committed to another job when the previous subcontractor has finally completed its task. Thus, four days of rain can throw a schedule far more than four days behind. The general contractor must be flexible enough and forceful enough to make certain that subcontractors adjust their other schedules when necessary.

Drawing the Construction Loan

Lenders, being far from naive, are reluctant to make their entire share of the cost of a development available up front. In fact, they typically pay only as progress has been made. Similarly, the developer does not want to pay the general contractor before the work is actually done. In most states, a statutory amount, often 10 percent of the amount of construction, must be retained until the end of the job. Thus, for a $100,000 construction job with the job 20 percent complete and a $20,000 payment due the general contractor, the developer by statute would have to pay only $18,000, keeping $2,000 to make sure that the completed job fully meets all plans and specifications. Only then does the contractor get the balance due. Thus, *retainage* is a major device for controlling risk, carefully specified in the architect's contract.

The paperwork involved in withdrawing funds from the lender typically follows a path. Periodically, often every two weeks or every month, the subcontractor submits an invoice for work completed. The general contractor then compiles invoices from all the subcontractors and examines their work to ensure that the specified percentage of the work has actually been completed according to the plans and specifications. If problems arise, the general contractor works them out with the subcontractor and eventually sends an invoice to the developer for the combined total of all subcontractors' *draw requests* so that the individual subcontractors can be paid by the end of the month for the work completed minus the amount for retainage.

The developer's representative working with the general contractor, whether architect or project manager, verifies to the developer that the total invoice submitted by the general contractor agrees with the contract between the general contractor and the developer, that the work has actually been completed, and that it meets plans and specifications.

At this point, the approved invoices are sent to the developer's financial officer. The financial officer combines the invoice for construction costs (the hard costs) with various other "soft costs" associated with the development—insurance, property taxes, interest on the construction loan, marketing costs, and general administrative overhead, for example—and then sends a total figure to the construction lender.

The loan agreement with the construction lender stipulates that the lender will provide funding as needed to cover the costs, so long as costs are within budget. Thus, the financial officer begins with the budget originally defined in the feasibility study and refined during stage four to produce a monthly draw request showing the original budget, cost to date, amount for the relevant period, and the remaining balance, typically for each item in the cost budget. (During stage four, the developer argued for as few categories as possible to achieve more flexibility in moving funds around, while the lender favored more categories to increase control.)

The construction lender first ensures that the request from the developer is in accordance with the loan agreement, then checks to be sure that all participants (the architect or construction manager, the general contractor, and the financial officer) have initialed the request. The lender could choose to inspect construction to ensure that the project is proceeding as the draw request indicates. Finally, the construction lender wants to ensure that the development appears to be on time and within budget for both hard and soft costs.

Assuming that all requirements are satisfied, the construction lender deposits funds in the developer's account for the total amount of the draw. The financial officer writes a check to the general contractor, who then pays the subcontractors.

One device for controlling risk that lenders often use is to disburse funds only through title companies. In such cases, subcontractors trade lien waivers for their appropriate draw checks. The title company thus ensures that all the subcontractors have acknowledged payment before funds are disbursed so that the lender will be protected from mechanics' liens filed by unpaid subcontractors.[1]

One factor almost always true in the procedure for requesting a draw is the time pressure involved. To make sure that the retainage is an adequate safeguard for all the players takes time. If the books were closed on the 25th of the month, the total process must be accomplished by the end of the month so that paychecks will be ready for construction workers then. Smaller subcontractors live from paycheck to paycheck; if a check is not delivered Friday at 4:30, they may not be able to buy groceries that weekend. Construction workers usually cannot understand technical or administrative difficulties in the draw. And if they are not paid, they will put pressure on the general contractor, the developer, and anyone else involved.

Leasing Space and Building Interior Space

Unleased space at the initiation of construction is marketed during construction. Ideally, someone will be paying rent on every square foot of the building on the day it opens. One cost item in the pro forma, however, is an operating deficit for the period immediately after construction unless the building is sufficiently leased to cover debt service.

A major goal of most developers is to capture this leasing reserve. If total costs include the cost of funding a deficit and the deficit does not occur because the building is fully leased when it opens, then the budget item falls from the cost column directly into profits. Fraser Morrow Daniels, for example, planned to give up 15 percent of its share in the Europa Center's profits to obtain a leasing reserve of $1 million, and Whit Morrow hoped the company would never need that reserve. As it happened, however, the firm could not lease the building during construction because prospective tenants were unfamiliar with the benefits of the proposed Class A office space. Compounding this problem was the disappearance of the planned leasing reserve.

EUROPA CENTER

LEASING DURING CONSTRUCTION

We anticipated signing some leases immediately after the building was completed—mostly small professional firms and service firms—but that it would take two full years to fill the building. And because of rent concessions that had emerged as standard in the marketplace, we were not sure when those tenants would actually pay money. Whether we use free rent or extra tenant improvements is always a consideration. The cost of tenant improvements adds to the building's value; free rent doesn't do anything except induce tenants to move in.

And we ended with no convenient million dollars to draw on if necessary. Investors S&L bought Centennial and required that million dollar cushion in equity. Despite a valid loan contract, the bank negotiated a more secure position as part of the acquisition and absorbed the real million. We then expected to require some additional prorated contribution of capital from the partners, with a possible renegotiation of partnership shares, which was not anticipated going into the project. But if you examine almost any real estate development deal today, the amount of profits that actually ends up with the person who had the original idea

391

for a project is usually a lot less than anticipated at the beginning. [Authors' note: In this case, a failure to anticipate all the project-level implications of the acquisition put the project in jeopardy.]

What would I do differently if I had it to do over again? Bargain for another million. Be more explicit about the long-term contingencies for which money would be used. And continue to reexamine it during negotiations for financing. The feeling that we would be more cooperative, I think, put less pressure on us to spell out every contingency and every detail in a 200-page agreement.

In addition to a leasing reserve, the lending agreement might provide restrictions tied to marketing—for example, the total amount of the loan will be only x dollars until y percent of the building is leased, at which time the remaining amount will be funded. Such a situation puts pressure on the developer. If marketing does not proceed according to schedule, the developer at some point will have drawn down the full *floor* amount of the loan, which can cause problems. As construction rolls on, it is difficult to tell everyone to stop and wait a month until a suite is leased. Construction must continue as scheduled, or costs will surely escalate. Meanwhile, money might not be available to pay workers on Friday, who do not care whether the marketing staff have met the leasing standard. The lender will not fund an amount above the floor, and the pressure mounts.

Astute developers plan in advance for such situations through a line item for contingencies in the loan or, less satisfactory, some arrangement with the construction lender specifying that additional funds will be advanced if the developer pays a penalty. Alternatively, developers can cover cost overruns themselves or induce outside investors to cover them. Once the project is in trouble, it is much harder to get additional money than to plan for contingencies in advance.

The lease for office space in a major downtown building will provide for long-term financial and operating concerns as well as for physical details like the location of interior walls, the number of electrical outlets and plumbing fixtures, and the style of carpeting. Thus, the leasing agent's negotiations directly influence the construction crew's work and what must be financed.

When the market is overbuilt, as it was in the late 1980s, most developers claim to be driven by their customers' demands: if the customer wants it, they will find a way to provide it. Responding to such demands is not a simple task, however, for the requests must be incorporated in the development process in the proper sequence and they must be financed. If the lender will not fund interior physical improvements after the fact, the pressure mounts a little more.

Landscaping and Exterior Construction

The initial feasibility study included at least one item in the budget for landscaping, which is becoming increasingly important in marketing a project. In the past, if the building's design was not appealing, creative landscaping would cover or detract from major flaws. Today, however, landscaping has assumed a different role.

Landscaping is now used to entice tenants because it helps to create an environment that will appeal to future employees, particularly in markets where labor is in short supply. Noteworthy landscaping distinguishes projects from their drab competitors and therefore can accelerate leasing. Marketing specific, visible environmental features can go a long way toward attracting clients and making a project acceptable to neighbors.

Many developers of large commercial projects are now nearly as careful about selecting a landscape architect as they are about selecting a building architect. Office and industrial parks in particular are exploiting some of the most innovative trends in landscape design to gain quicker acceptance in the market.

Landscaping typically occurs late in the process for a variety of reasons. It can reflect a more upscale mix of tenants than originally envisioned, requiring developers

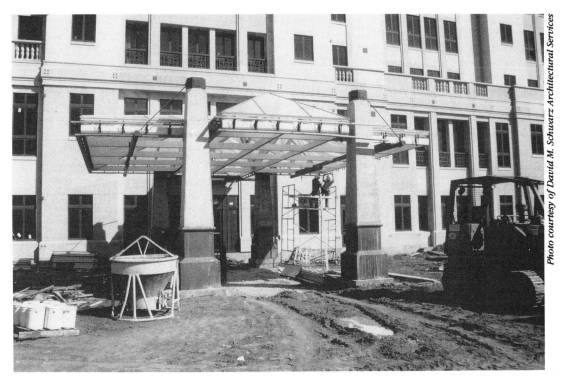

Photo courtesy of David M. Schwarz Architectural Services

While exterior construction is under way, landscaping is not yet put in place, because heavy machinery and construction materials are moved about the site constantly.

to be flexible in this area as well. Once in place, landscaping must be cared for. If installed too early in the process, chances are good that it will be destroyed by construction vehicles still on site and that the appropriate maintenance personnel will not yet be on staff.

Landscaping covers a wide range of additions to the environment. In a development of less expensive single-family houses, it might involve only spreading topsoil, seeding it, and planting a few bushes. A major downtown mixed-use project might involve porches, decks, walkways, benches, lighting, signs, intensively planted areas, and even some works of art. (Art, both inside and outside, has become more than a novelty.)

When finalizing costs for landscaping in the budget, developers must not overlook the intensity and cost of long-term maintenance. Different species of plants and landscape features require different levels of maintenance. Developers must take into consideration the amount of labor

that will be needed to maintain the appearance the landscape architect sought to achieve. Without a proper maintenance program, developers throw away their money and destroy the design's integrity. Ill-kept grounds do not sell well to prospective tenants.

Long-Term Land Development

For a large development, construction is likely to proceed on several buildings at the same time, with two very different activities in progress at once, perhaps infrastructure on one large tract and construction of individual buildings somewhere else.

While such large-scale development has several economic, social, and aesthetic benefits, development could take 10 to 20 years to complete and the construction period itself 20 years. During that period, hundreds of projects could be built, each with its own development process.

393

Thus, land developers move from stage five to stage six after all the members of the team are coordinated and then typically construct the project in phases as the market warrants it. Perhaps an entranceway is installed at the beginning, then roads and amenities as needed as the market calls for them.

For a development of single-family houses, the builder/developer acquires lots from the land developer, puts all members of the team together, and then moves to stage six, which could last 90 to 180 days for one house. Or the developer could build several houses at the same time to keep subcontractors working efficiently for six months to two years.

Potential Problems

Because of unforeseen problems, Fraser Morrow Daniels lost about three months at the beginning of the Europa Center's development and a few more at the end. The construction company was partially responsible for several of the delays in the beginning. For instance, when the lobby was being constructed, some of the granite pieces and some of the special marble from Italy came in the wrong size. Cutting and fitting those pieces on site took time. Fabric panels for the lobby walls were missing, and some of the outside signs were late. Developers cannot foresee all the impediments to construction, but they should assume that *some* will occur and, if they do, they will be able to manage despite them.

The circumstances described in the following illustration probably never all happened on the same project, but they are likely to happen to the same developer at several points throughout a career. Imagine that you are developing a tennis village, designed to be one of the premier tennis facilities in the world, on a 200-acre resort. It is designed in phases, the first phase containing the main clubhouse, courts, a small hotel, and 50 townhouses. In subsequent phases, another 300 townhouses and more tennis courts will be added.

Financing negotiated for the project allows the developer, who is putting up $500,000, to borrow up to $24.5 million at any point as needed. The $25 million thus available will cover the initial cost of the central courts, the 70-room hotel and clubhouse, and the first 50 townhouses.

Under the arrangement, the developer will pay back the $24.5 million when he sells the first 50 townhouses. Assuming the units sell for $250,000 each, as projected in the feasibility study, 50 units will generate $12.5 million. This money is then available for the developer to draw again to continue building townhouses. Thus, the project involves a certain amount of financing on the courts/hotel/clubhouse (which will eventually be repaid from a permanent loan and transfer of the amenities to the property owners) and a revolving amount that allows the developer to continue building townhouses, so long as the first units sell. So long as the developer stays within budget, everything is fine. If marketing slips or if construction is delayed, a problem could arise with financing.

As the developer, you are six months from completion of the clubhouse, the hotel, and the first 50 townhouses. The marketing people tell you that the two-bedroom units are sold out but that the one-bedroom units, which are essentially the same size but with a nice balcony, are not selling at all. The first 50 units were planned to include 25 two-bedroom units and 25 one-bedroom units, but they want you to change the 25 one-bedroom units to two-bedroom units. Your construction manager tells you that the additional walls and minimal additional electrical service needed for the change will require at this point (because the units are almost complete) $450,000 total, or $18,000 per unit. You agree to the change, remembering $625,000 in the budget for contingencies.

Then it rains—every day for two weeks. Because of subcontractors' other commitments, the project is now *four* weeks behind schedule as a result of two weeks of rain. And the rescheduling will cost some money. The subcontractors want an incentive to come back that fast, and the interest meter will now run for a full additional month. The additional expense will likely be $325,000. What to do?

The solution to this second problem is to approach the lender and claim, in a fairly humble manner, that this act of God has wiped out the amount set aside for contingencies (the original $625,000 minus $450,000 for 25 conversions to two-bedroom units having left only $175,000). Any lender who is your partner in the development process should understand that occasional events beyond your control require a little more cash.

If the lender goes along with this request, however, he also puts himself in a difficult position. The original financing provides a permanent takeout loan on the clubhouse and hotel for $12 million (predicated on completion of construction according to plans and specifications). If the cost overrun is allocated there, then the construction lender has loaned more than $12 million for that facility. What is the source of payment for the additional funding? But if the construction lender allocates the excess amount to the townhouses, he must believe that the sale price will be sufficient to cover the loan. In other words, he must take a little more risk or believe that the price can be higher than anticipated in the original feasibility study. He decides, based on your charm, to allocate the excess to the townhouse units, assuming they can be sold at a somewhat higher price than budgeted in the feasibility study.

Two weeks later, the marketing people return, highly upset. Architectural costs for this particular job were kept to a minimum, and an in-house construction manager finalized site plans and managed the process. As the job began, the general contractor noted a large amount of rock at one end of the site, where the first phase of townhouses would go. Working with the construction manager, he determined that if the units were moved slightly closer to the tennis courts they surrounded, far less rock would have to be moved and costs could be kept to a minimum. The construction manager okayed moving the units closer to the courts, and everyone was happy because a potential problem had been solved expeditiously with only a slight shift in design.

Regrettably, when the units were moved closer, the end units with the beautiful bay windows ceased to look out toward the mountains and looked instead into another bedroom window 12 feet away. The end units, according to the marketing people, cannot be sold for any amount close to the projected price and must be rented instead. And you cannot cut the price 10 percent on a luxury item if the item has a flaw that is obvious to even the most unsophisticated consumer. If the end units, eight of them in this first phase, are kept as rental units and not sold and the $12.5 million construction loan for the townhouses is not fully paid back as planned, you will be short of cash as development continues. You might have to produce smaller phases (fewer townhouses in each), which would be inefficient and raise your construction costs.

But the troubles don't stop here. Two weeks before the scheduled grand opening, another deluge of rain falls, and a second flaw in the redesign is discovered. With the units closer to the tennis courts, the runoff cannot be fully absorbed by the original arrangement for drainage, and the units on one side of the court are flooded. The flood ruins the drywall and carpeting in 10 units that had been scheduled to close in two weeks.

In addition to the costs of replacing the drywall and the carpeting, you must find a solution to the drainage problem. Working with your in-house engineer and the general contractor, you find a solution that will cost $90,000. With $70,000 for new materials and other miscellaneous repairs, you're $160,000 short. Unlike the money involved in the no-view, no-sale units, this $160,000 is needed *now*. The end of the construction period is near, and not much room is left to move expenditures between budget categories, even if the lender would allow it. You've already asked nicely at the bank and received more money for the time it was an act of God and not your fault. What do you do?

Assuming you solve that problem, the project moves to the week before the scheduled grand opening. It is August in the Southwest, and the beautiful landscaping is brown. Apparently the landscaper assumed the property manager would take over maintenance. Somehow the property manager did not get the signal, and $100,000 worth of plants are dead. Your high-end buyers will not go to closing with dead shrubs as landscaping, and if you back off the grand opening, you could lose existing presales on other units; that is, people might decide they do not want to buy a unit in your development. How do you solve this problem?

STAGE SEVEN: COMPLETION AND FORMAL OPENING

Beginning operations on site, training the operations staff, final marketing, connecting utilities, opening, tenants' moving in, a transition in financing from construction to permanent loan—all constitute stage seven, completion and formal opening.

Operating personnel are brought to the site before the grand opening, with the amount of time they spend there depending on their functions and the project's size and type. Their job is to make sure that customers get the space with the services promised in the lease agreement and the promotional material. In a convention hotel, for example, some of the marketing people may join the staff two years early.

Marketing people, working with operations people, handle activity before the opening—advertising, promotion, VIP parties, and the like. It is often good business to throw a party to thank the people who have helped you, in the process generating some long-term good will in the community and inviting potential customers. Before the party, however, the utilities must be connected, which means all obligations to the city must have been met. Building inspectors must ensure that final items were installed according to code. Do not assume that city inspections will be only an annoying technicality.

Suppose in the final stages of construction, a pipe on the 25th floor bursts and water seeps into the electrical fire alarm system. A fire inspection is scheduled in two days and tenants are moving in two days after that, but now the alarm system must be rewired—a process that will take longer than two days. Rescheduling the inspection will force a delay of at least two weeks. What do you tell tenants who plan to move in next week?

During the construction phase, all the interior finish work specified by tenants must be completed, and the marketing staff must coordinate work with the tenants so that tenants can move and be ready to operate in the new space. At about the

Photo courtesy of David M. Schwarz Architectural Services

Grand opening party for the Cook–Fort Worth Children's Medical Center, with comic actors, balloons, and games for the children.

same time, the permanent loan is closed and the construction lender repaid. A shift from the developer as the controlling interest to a new investor as controlling interest may occur. The new investor might have in-house management personnel or rely on outside property management companies—or hire the developer as manager. In fact, the developer in many cases stays on as a partner with the new investor. But risk shifts from the developer, who has now completed development, to the long-term investor.

EUROPA CENTER

LEASING AND OPENING THE PROJECT

By December 1987, things were going much more smoothly for us. The Europa Center was complete and had opened in November with a well-attended party. A third of the building was committed, and we expected the building to be 50 percent leased by the end of January 1988.

The market was better. We had been pushing sales hard and pricing space competitively. Our base rate was $15.00 to $15.50 instead of the $17.00 projected—about 12 percent under original projections. We used a combination of free rent and tenant improvements, so it will take us a little longer to reach the amount on the pro forma—two years. We expected to be fully leased by summer 1988 and for everyone to be paying rent by 1989.

We committed 13,000 square feet to an executive business center for very small but high-profile tenants. Basically, it offers space plus services for a one-person office: a 200- to 300-square-foot office, a common reception area and secretarial, phone answering, and copy services provided. Tenants can even rent office furniture. It's ideal for companies with just one person in the region. Costs to tenants are about twice the base rate for space alone, and the arrangement has been very profitable for us.

One thing we found in this extremely competitive market is that almost nobody would lease space before the building was complete. Another thing we learned is that a lot of prospective tenants didn't know what "Class A" meant. We had to attract them to the VIP party to make them aware of our project. Our opening party in November was attended by 450 people. We started planning two months ahead in conjunction with the chamber of commerce's Business After Hours program. With all that lead time, we were able to convince the chamber to hold graduation for its leadership training class there. It makes sense to hold this type of function for an office building expected to be a major part of the business community.

We wanted to get two points across about the building: it's exciting and it's elegant. So we hired party consultants instead of planning it ourselves. They put a baby grand piano and a pianist in the lobby and a huge stream of silver balloons from the first to the third levels of the atrium. We served shrimp and beverages and had a steady stream of people from 4:30 to 9:00 P.M. All kinds of people came—including some town planners and some local political figures.

TECHNIQUES TO CONTROL RISK DURING STAGES SIX AND SEVEN

Under pressure to keep construction and marketing on schedule and costs within budget, developers, more than ever, are at risk and seek to control those risks.

1. Retainage, discussed earlier, and performance bonds are useful methods of controlling risk. An insurance company that will guarantee completion or at least stand behind a general contractor's performance reduces the developer's risk. Likewise, a bonded developer reduces the city's risk when infrastructure is involved. Retainage lets the developer hold back cash to ensure the contractor's completing the work.

2. Union relations are an important consideration. Sensitivity to the unions and to construction workers in general can

only be to the developer's advantage. On a high-rise project in Manhattan, the entire construction process can be stopped by one person—the man who runs the construction elevator. If that person belongs to a different union from any of the other workers and he decides to strike, nobody else can get to their jobs, even if they are willing to cross the one-person picket line.

3. Architectural supervision and/or construction management are techniques whose importance in controlling risk cannot be understated. In addition to supervising the general contractor, however, developers can require warranties from builders in their contracts. Besides requiring these promises of structural integrity, which can be the basis of subsequent lawsuits, developers should also check that subcontractors have the necessary licenses to do the work and that they are being paid a reasonable amount for what the developer expects them to do. Unless the developer is one step ahead of a potential problem, the subcontractor with a problem could become the developer's problem.

4. Liability, fire, and extended insurance coverage are basic to controlling risks. For insurance to work, developers must be covered for what might happen, and the insurance must be in force at the right time. Developers must review their insurance coverage regularly.

5. PERT and CPM are useful techniques for managing time and thus controlling risk by focusing on critical events.

6. Preleasing and presales reduce the risk of initial high vacancies. Careful attention to tenant mix also helps reduce risk. If tenants "fit" together or if one tenant draws others, fewer problems with long-term vacancies are likely.

7. For small tenants, insurance covering lease guarantees or some form of letter of credit is another possible technique. Depending on the strength of the market, it might be possible to obtain high rent from a small tenant and some sort of outside guarantee that the tenant will be able to pay the rent later. While this type of insurance is relatively uncommon, some form of guarantee for a smaller and newer tenant's performance is common. The guarantee can range from the tenant's having a cosigner to doing some of its own finish work, thereby enhancing commitment to the space.

8. Net leases, expense stops, and escalations are all important devices to control risk for long-term investors, and developers, as long-term investors, should structure leases with these possibilities in mind. When market conditions permit, developers want to make sure that they are not the first to absorb all the pain in the event of rapid inflation.

9. The operating agreement negotiated with tenants during the leasing process is also a technique to control risk. By controlling how the tenants relate to one another and to the building, developers can help ensure both long-term operating viability and a minimum of maintenance problems.

10. From an administrative perspective, good internal controls, particularly the accounting system, are critical during the development process.

11. Having operations staff involved in planning and brought on site early is critical. If they are not, initial operation of the facility could be less efficient— and more expensive—than it should be. Poor service can set an image that will be very expensive to change later.

These techniques cover the six basic ways to reduce risk:

1. Avoid it by stopping in stage one, two, or three before much money is committed.

2. Increase the research and know more about the possibilities by completing a more substantial feasibility study in stage three.

3. Engage in some form of "loss prevention," the most obvious of which is a competent development team assembled in stages four and five.

4. Transfer a potential loss to other players.

5. Combine and diversify to reduce the pain of large losses.

6. Assume risks. Some amount of risk is always involved, but developers are the type of people who can live and work in risky environments.

EUROPA CENTER

AFTER CONSTRUCTION

The physical construction of the Europa Center went reasonably smoothly—which was to be anticipated because we hired a very talented and experienced architect, hired and paid well a construction supervisor, fully explored all regulations with the relevant public officials in advance, and bought a site that presented few physical problems.

While the construction was smooth, marketing was anything but. In 1987 and 1988, the Research Triangle area continued to be highly overbuilt, like many other sections of the country. More important, approximately eight months earlier, an office tower with over 200,000 square feet—huge by the area's standards—was completed only four miles away, on the southeast side of Durham at the other end of U.S. 15-501. The earlier completion of another Class A office building that was also pursuing tenants with business in both Durham and Chapel Hill was a serious problem for us. While we tried to woo tenants already committed to the other building, our late arrival in the market allowed the other developer to presign larger tenants, so that even very attractive rental concessions could not cause them to change their minds. And inducing them to jump after signing would involve buying out existing leases for a substantial amount of remaining time.

The Europa Center officially opened with 15 percent occupancy, and the leasing reserve was therefore critical. To spur activity in the building, we entered a joint venture with another promoter for an executive office suite. That joint venture took another 20 percent of the building but certainly did not reduce our risk, because we were equity partners in the ven-

Interior construction at the Europa Center.

Photo courtesy of Jim Sink, Artech, Inc.

ture. Despite the fact that risks were not reduced, the need for activity in the building made it a logical decision.

The city fathers loved the Europa Center when it opened. It was attractive to anyone thinking of moving to town, because the prices asked became very reasonable for the space available. The public sector partner was happy; the neighbors around it were happy. The question was how much longer the lender would be tolerant.

SUMMARY

Throughout the last stages, it is important to maintain as much flexibility as possible, designing the building for alternative uses and changing markets, minimizing prepayment penalties to be able to adjust to changing market conditions, ensuring fast design and construction for tenants' requirements, and carefully controlling the leasing staff, who make the promises that construction contractors must honor.

The physical structure is built during stage six of the development process, requiring constant interplay among construction, marketing, financial, and operating personnel. The developer's role shifts as the move is completed to stage six—less a promoter and more a manager. Time becomes the critical element of risk. It takes an extremely competent manager to coordinate all of the activities that go on simultaneously during stage six.

Stage seven encompasses the activities associated with completion and a formal opening, and entails considerations involving the public sector, tenants, the physical layout, and financing. Stage seven is the end of the active phase of real estate development and sets the stage for asset and property management.

NOTE

1. Mechanics' liens are liens on the property that come about when workers claim to have been unpaid. Lenders find them troublesome because they often take effect as of the first day the subcontractor furnished labor but appear in the title (the legal recorded history of ownership) only when filed at some subsequent date. To avoid such potential clouds on a title, some lenders use title companies as disbursing agents, particularly in states with very strong statutes covering mechanics' liens.

Bibliography

Part VI. Making It Happen

CONTRACT NEGOTIATION AND FORMAL COMMITMENT

Barstein, Fred, ed. *Bowker's Real Estate Law Locator, 1988*. New York: Bowker, 1988.

Culbertson, Alan N., and Donald E. Kenney. *Contract Administration Manual for the Design Professions: How to Establish, Systematize, and Monitor Construction Contract Controls*. New York: McGraw-Hill, 1983.

Friedman, Milton R. *Contracts and Conveyances of Real Property*. 4th ed. New York: Practising Law Institute, 1984 (with 1988 supplement).

Hagman, Donald G., ed. *Land Use and Environmental Law Review*, 1982. New York: Clark Boardman Co., 1982.

Harris, Richard. *Construction and Development Financing: Law, Practice, Forms*. Vol. 1. Boston: Warren, Gorham & Lamont, 1987.

Holtzschue, Karl B. *Real Estate Contracts*. New York: Practising Law Institute, 1988.

Kratovil, Robert, and Raymond J. Weiner. *Real Estate Law*. 9th ed. Englewood Cliffs, N.J.: Prentice-Hall, 1988.

Living with Environmental Law. Boston: Massachusetts Continuing Legal Education, 1984.

Senn, Mark A. *Negotiating Real Estate Transactions*. New York: John Wiley & Sons, 1988.

CONSTRUCTION, COMPLETION, AND FORMAL OPENING

Alfeld, Louis Edward. *Construction Productivity: On-Site Measurement and Management*. New York: McGraw-Hill, 1988.

Brock, Dan S., and Lystre L. Sutcliffe, eds. *Field Inspection Handbook: An On-the-Job Guide for Construction Inspectors, Contractors, Architects, and Engineers*. New York: McGraw-Hill, 1986.

Burt Hill Kosar Rittelmann Associates. *Small Office Building Handbook: Design for Reducing First Costs and Utility Costs*. New York: Van Nostrand Reinhold, 1985.

Coombs, William E. *Construction Accounting and Financial Management*. 4th ed. New York: McGraw-Hill, 1989.

Cushman, Robert F., and John P. Bigda. *The McGraw-Hill Construction Business Handbook*. 2d ed. New York: McGraw-Hill, 1985.

Cushman, Robert F., and George L. Blick, eds. *Construction Industry Forms*. New York: John Wiley & Sons, 1988.

Deatherage, George E. *Construction Company Organization and Management.* New York: McGraw-Hill, 1964.

Dietrich, Norman L. *Kerr's Cost Data for Landscape Construction: Unit Prices for Site Development.* 10th ed. New York: Van Nostrand Reinhold, 1990.

Dodge Manual for Building Construction, Pricing, and Scheduling. New York: Dodge Building Cost Services, annual.

The GSA System for Construction Management. Washington, D.C.: General Services Administration, 1975.

Green, William R. *The Retail Store: Design and Construction.* New York: Van Nostrand Reinhold, 1986.

Harrison, Henry S. House: The Illustrated Guide to Construction Design and Systems. Chicago: Realtors National Marketing Institute, 1980.

Householder, Jerry, and Leon Rogers. *Basic Construction Management: The Superintendent's Job.* Washington, D.C.: National Association of Home Builders, 1990.

Levitt, Raymond Elliott, and Nancy Morse Samelson. *Construction Safety Management.* New York: McGraw-Hill, 1987.

Levy, Arnold S., and Robert F. Cushman, eds. *The Handbook of Real Estate Development and Construction.* Homewood, Ill.: Dow Jones–Irwin, 1987.

Levy, Sidney M. *Project Management in Construction.* New York: McGraw-Hill, 1987.

McMullen, Randall. *Dictionary of Building.* New York: Nichols, 1988.

McNulty, Alfred P. *Management of Small Construction Projects.* New York: McGraw-Hill, 1982.

More Construction for the Money: Summary Report of the Construction Industry Cost-Effectiveness Project. New York: Business Roundtable, 1983.

O'Brien, James J. *CPM in Construction Management.* New York: McGraw-Hill, 1984.

Smit, Kornelis, ed. *Means Illustrated Construction Dictionary.* Kingston, Mass.: R.S. Means, 1985.

Stokes, McNeill, and Judith L. Finuf. *Construction Law for Owners and Builders.* New York: McGraw-Hill, 1985.

Technology and the Future of the U.S. Construction Industry: Proceedings of the Panel on Technical Change and the U.S. Building Construction Industry. Washington, D.C.: AIA Press, 1986.

Trauner, Theodore J., Jr., and Michael H. Payne. *Bidding and Managing Government Construction.* Kingston, Mass.: R.S. Means, 1988.

Turner, Gregory R. *Construction Economics and Building Design: A Historical Approach.* New York: Van Nostrand Reinhold, 1986.

Watson, Don A. *Construction Materials and Processes.* 3d ed. New York: McGraw-Hill, 1985.

PART VII
CONTINUING TO MAKE IT WORK

Chapter 18

Stage Eight: Asset and Property Management

Managing real estate assets, from acquisition to disposition, could best describe responsibilities for asset management, stage eight of the real estate development process. While asset management often includes functions like managing a portfolio, managing commercial property, and engineering leveraged buyouts or mergers and acquisitions, the interest of real estate developers lies primarily in the real estate they hold—whether acquired as a completed project or developed and kept.

The importance of good asset management cannot be overemphasized. As developers find fewer and fewer new opportunities for development, many have been forced to pay more attention to their assets and make them as productive as possible. Consequently, this chapter discusses the following topics:

- The enterprise concept;
- A definition of asset management;
- Fundamentals of property management and the development process;
- Smart buildings;
- Training for property managers;
- Asset management; and
- The corporate real estate director.

No matter how beautiful a new project, it will not generate profit in the long run unless it is properly managed—which is why fundamental asset management still begins with property management. This chapter reviews the basic functions of property management and reexamines their relationship to the preceding seven stages of the development process. Beginning with a look at the enterprise concept espoused by James A. Graaskamp, pioneering real estate academic, it explores the concept of a building as a dynamic entity, not just bricks and mortar. It also explores the differences in managing a 50-story office building with hundreds of employees and complex mechanical and operating systems and a duplex managed by the owner. Some of the more complex issues involved in managing "smart" buildings and the new demands and areas of discipline involving corporate real estate officers are also discussed.

THE ENTERPRISE CONCEPT

The enterprise concept espoused by James A. Graaskamp views real estate as an enterprise and sets the stage for asset management in the 1990s. Long considered one of the most innovative thinkers among real estate academics, Graaskamp campaigned for years for a change from the concept of real estate as bricks and mortar to the concept of a building as an operating entity, a living, breathing business with a cash flow cycle similar to any other operating business. This concept is particularly important for understanding asset management and is the backdrop for all the following discussions about managing real estate.

Graaskamp suggested that developers should anticipate a world in which buildings are like businesses. Businesses continually need to defend their market positions and to seek new niches in the marketplace. From the standpoint of development, it means not only that marketing will be ongoing but also, in all probability, that the structure itself will have to change to meet different needs in the marketplace.

General Motors, for example, is a different company today from what it was 10 years ago. Apple Computer was barely a company 10 years ago. While it is true that real estate projects have a long life and a fixed location, it is also important to note that the needs they serve vary over time, just like GM and Apple. If developers see that they are creating an ongoing business, not simply bricks and mortar, they will be more likely to incorporate the flexibility in design necessary for long-term marketing and success in a changing environment.

An example of the enterprise concept in action is the Showplace development in the South of Market District of San Francisco. The Showplace is a design mart where interior designers bring their upscale clients for a glass of white wine and the chance to browse through hundreds of thousands of square feet of home furnishings, from furniture to pillows. The development originated in a cluster of abandoned industrial buildings. The initial developer, Henry Adams, saw the opportunity to use that space to satisfy a new need in the market. The current developer, Bill Poland, senses that the critical item for success is seeing the real estate as an operating business. Happy tenants need customers and products. To draw customers and products, the developer promotes trade shows, frequently at a loss. To maximize profits and create a "sense of place," the developer has used the vast facilities for weddings and other social

functions in the evenings and on weekends. It is very much a business and requires extensive management. The real estate is central but not the only element: services and creative interior management make the Showplace a successful business enterprise and hence a successful development.

A DEFINITION OF ASSET MANAGEMENT

Against the backdrop of Graaskamp's enterprise concept, this section attempts to define asset management and its emerging role in real estate development. While property management is at the heart of its functions, it has come to include much more in response to changes in the economy and in society's demands.

Effective management of real estate assets must include a willingness to respond to changing market needs, as well as to accommodate investors' and owners' needs by structuring all operations to maximize the value of investors' real estate portfolios. Because asset management also includes investment management, its broad scope can complicate the basic functions of property management. The evolution of real estate investment trusts (REITs) in the 1970s and more active investment management of pension funds in the 1980s brought about the need to manage a client's *position* as well as its real property assets. Asset managers work with investors to determine objectives for investment and the types of properties that fit into the objectives for the investor's larger investment portfolio.

Developers take on the function of asset management—either in house or by contract with a firm—whenever they own and hold onto their real estate assets. Once property is acquired, the asset manager has the largest controllable influence on operating income. Within the enterprise concept, the asset functions not simply as real estate providing space with appropriate services but also as part of a total business serving a broad set of needs including, but not limited to, space requirements. For example, when Trammell Crow developed the Dallas Infomart, it ran a business catering to computer needs as well as building and leasing space. Finally, asset management includes the management activities of corporate real estate, that is, providing the long-term space requirements for U.S. corporate operations while supporting its objectives for earnings.

All of these aspects—traditional property management (which is still the most

---

PROFILE: JAMES A. GRAASKAMP

Former chair and professor
Department of Real Estate and Urban Land Economics
University of Wisconsin–Madison

Graaskamp considered real estate to consist of interaction among three groups—space users (consumers), space producers (those with site-specific expertise), and public infrastructure (off-site services and facilities)—each representing an enterprise. Each enterprise must remain solvent to survive and create a surplus over time to maintain credibility with others; they must continually make assumptions about future social norms, technologies, and the direction of complex changes in personal, natural, and political conditions.

The degree of error between assumptions and realizations is termed "risk," and in an economy based on enterprise, most parties attempt to shift a disproportionate share of the risk to others while retaining a larger share of the benefits. With each real estate project, society has a new opportunity to negotiate, debate, and reconsider the basic issues of an enterprise economy: who pays, who benefits, who risks, and who has standing to participate in making decisions. The best device for managing risk for space producers, which is usually the group that initiates a project, is thorough research so that the product fits as closely as possible the needs and values of consumers, individually and collectively, and the land use ethic of society.

Graaskamp pushed these concepts and tested the appraisal system against that backdrop, calling for a new way of looking at appraisals.

Background: James A. Graaskamp, known as "Chief," was a rare academic who always evoked a reaction from those who came into contact with him. At the time of his death in April 1988, he was the driving force behind the real estate program at the University of Wisconsin–Madison despite being a quadriplegic, confined to a wheelchair since 1951 after contracting polio.

His handicap, however, did not prevent his earning a Ph.D. in 1964, teaching real estate, encouraging new theories of real estate, and consulting through his Landmark Research company. Well-known for his articulate and spell-binding speeches, he was also often an outspoken critic—with many critics of his own—on national and local land use policies, often taking very unpopular views.

When Graaskamp died in 1988 at the age of 54, he left many admirers and friends. Those who knew him and loved him describe him as "exceptional," "special," "one of a kind." Even his severest critics grudgingly express admiration for his amazing ability to live his life fuller than most people who are not physically disabled.

About being faced with life in a wheelchair, Graaskamp once said, "I never went through any depression or period of searching. My self-image was not tied to physical prowess. It was either give up and do nothing or forget it, make the best of it, and go around once."

Source: James A. Graaskamp, *Fundamentals of Real Estate Development* (Washington, D.C.: ULI–the Urban Land Institute, 1981).

important element of asset management), management of operations to fit an investor's portfolio, the enterprise concept, and corporate real estate—must be accomplished with a heightened awareness of customers' needs, because asset management is primarily a service. Beyond serving clients who pay the owner, the asset manager strives to serve tenants. Over the next decade, more emphasis will be placed on serving the user of space. This move has been coming for a number of reasons and has been heightened recently by the oversupply of space in many markets, making tenant services a key factor in success.

But why include a chapter on asset management in a textbook on the development process? The answer is simple. Developers are charged with planning and constructing space, and if they are done with asset management in mind, the building will be more efficient and its long-term ownership more profitable because the building will continue to serve society's needs. Part of Washington, D.C., developer Oliver Carr's success as a long-term owner of his development projects stems from his feel for the changing marketplace and his willingness to provide services that will fulfill users' demands over the long term.

And why should developers in the early years of a building's useful life be so concerned about long-term profitability if they are not long-term owners? Because the developer's return comes in the form of a fee plus some participation in the value created through the process of development. The creation of value results when the expected future benefits to an investor exceed the costs. And those long-term benefits to the investor exist only when the property functions well over its long expected economic life. Thus, to create value, developers must build something that will efficiently serve society's needs over a long period of time.

FUNDAMENTALS OF PROPERTY MANAGEMENT AND THE DEVELOPMENT PROCESS[1]

Space that will be used for a long period of time by various users typically comes with a certain level of service—more

Photo courtesy of David M. Schwarz Architectural Services

An exquisitely designed concierge desk for the lobby of an office building in Washington, D.C. Concierges in commercial office buildings function similarly to concierges in hotels, providing tenants with theater tickets, drycleaning services, photo reproduction services, and so on.

service in the case of hotels, less in the case of industrial buildings, but service nonetheless. Property management is the provision of those services and the maintenance of the physical structure. It is probably the largest controllable influence on the long-term cash flow of the building once the initial seven stages of the development process end. During the process, developers must be continually aware of responsibilities for property management if they are to create a structure that is efficient to manage and flexible in its use over a long time. Higher ceilings in an office building, for example, add to the area of the exterior skin and hence increase costs. More space between floors, however, can be a critical factor in changing electrical and mechanical service for individual spaces as users' needs change.[2]

The basic functions of property management include establishing a management plan, deriving a budget, re-leasing space, collecting rent, maintaining relations with tenants, keeping the books, repairing and maintaining the building,

408

PROFILE: **OLIVER CARR**

Oliver Carr Company
Washington, D.C.

Background: Carr is a fourth-generation developer in Washington, D.C. Having received his undergraduate degree from the University of Maryland, he pursued graduate work at George Washington University in urban studies.

Carr occupies an unusual niche in real estate development: he develops clusters of mixed uses with associated services in established urban and suburban locations. For example, he redeveloped the historic Willard Hotel in Washington along with offices and shops covering a three-block area. A similar project on G Street is under way, placing an office building over an existing department store and including two nearby office buildings and a hotel. Carr is also a long-term owner of his development projects.

Techniques for reducing risk: On a 15-year project like the Willard Hotel and its surroundings, Carr uses a master planner. Different architects then work on different parts of the project. Developers, their planners, and architects should be sympathetic to their surroundings. The best way to know a neighborhood is to get out and walk—to understand it on the ground. Carr believes that most developers can crunch numbers but that not all of them have a sense of the marketplace.

Carr tries to avoid political problems by knowing his market. By working in mature areas with zoning and infrastructure already in place, he often avoids impact fees or rezoning. On large projects, Carr takes a partner in land ownership. Often he works with the owner of land where an obsolete use is being phased out.

Carr has long-term relationships with a few general contractors; in turn, he can count on them to control costs and provide quality work. He has an in-house leasing staff but works actively with outside brokers. His market research is done in house.

Services: Carr sees offices becoming more like hotels, with the addition of services to make tenants happy. He puts a host in the lobby of his buildings and has a parking company to control the quality of tenants' arrival at and departure from buildings. He has also entered the food service business to provide food where none is available near his buildings. He sees service as something that personalizes an otherwise impersonal type of real estate.

---

conserving energy, providing security, supervising personnel, coordinating insurance, and generally preserving the project's short-term and long-term value.

The Management Plan

From the beginning, the management plan is based on an evaluation of the property's competitive position in the market and the owner's explicit needs. It is important to write down both at the beginning and, based on this combination, to develop a financial plan to achieve objectives within a budget.

From the developer's standpoint, the feasibility study provides the basic analyses necessary to assess the strengths and weaknesses of the particular property serving the targeted set of customers. The feasibility study also provides a detailed analysis of the competition so that the particular property can be evaluated point by point relative to the competition. During the development process, developers should use this comparison to identify cost-efficient changes in the initial development plan. Changes are justifiable if higher rents or lower operating costs make the property more competitive or more efficient to operate and more than offset the incremental development costs.

Property management is in the back of a developer's mind even during stages one and two. Property management is a specific input to the feasibility study during stage three. For example, operating costs are a part of developing an estimate of value that is compared to the cost estimate to determine feasibility.

As contracts are negotiated and executed and construction begins, property management becomes increasingly important. In stages four and five, the various participants' roles in the process are established and formalized in executed contracts. Before contracts are signed, tenants specify the features, functions, and benefits they expect as part of ongoing property management. Contractors specify, as part of the cost of the structure, all of the features necessary for ongoing operations. Property managers must determine that they will be able to provide the level of service expected at the costs specified in the operating pro forma. Certainly the financial arrangements (debt and equity) must fund these structural features for adequate property management. Thus, in stages four and five, all players are concerned about property management.

During construction, stage six, the space is leased, the loan drawn, the structure built, and changes made to accommodate future tenants' needs. Property management is a consideration when any changes are contemplated. Tenants may want a certain feature, but initial cost and ongoing operations must be estimated to show whether the change is logical from the developer's perspective. Developers must consider both prospective tenants' and investors' long-term needs. Before changing the development plans, developers must know that the required services can be provided cost-efficiently.

Consider, for example, the review of a prospective lease between the operator of mini–movie theaters in a mall under development. Normally, such an operation would have its own entrance or be free-standing. In this instance, however, a movie theater was not originally anticipated in the mall, and no separate entrance or remaining parcel not already committed to another tenant is available. The leasing agent does have considerable interior space that must be leased and pushes for the minitheaters inside the mall. The construction manager likes the idea because one tenant with one set of operating systems (lighting and so on) would take a major portion of the remaining space. The architect revises pedestrian flow through the mall that causes other stores to benefit from the theaters' patrons. Does the developer approve the arrangement?

Not necessarily. The property manager reviews the revised leasing plan and points out related problems. Not only will janitorial costs escalate, but security at night will also be a major problem, because the theater will be open well after other stores close. The costs incurred to solve these problems exceed the difference between the rent the theaters would pay and the lower rent expected from the next-highest-paying prospective tenant. Quickly running through the discounted cash flow model contained in the feasibility study, the developer sees that this tenant, at this stage in this project, will not provide long-term benefits to the equity investor. When the developer considers longer-term issues, the highest "present value" development results.

During stage seven of the development process, the property management team moves from an advisory role to an operating role. At that time, the management plan must be formalized so that when the asset management team takes over at the close of stage seven, a plan is available that matches the asset's position in the marketplace to the investor's long-term needs. The developer is responsible for ensuring that this initial management plan is established and implemented.

In establishment of the initial management plan, developers must remember the signal that the physical structure sends initially and over time. Architecture makes a statement for the property in the marketplace. For better or worse, this statement is accomplished by the end of stage seven, and it is a constraint on the development of a management plan. The management plan cannot ignore the initial perception of the structure in the marketplace. New colors and innovative promotions can alter the initial perception, but basic design remains a major factor in what is operationally possible.

In addition to initial perception is the issue of wear and tear. A building designed to standards for residential construction should not be managed like a commercial building. A heavy volume of foot traffic, for example, can quickly wear down a structure that has been built to residential standards, regardless of the intensity of property management. On the other hand, a structure built to more demanding standards allows more flexibility in terms of the volume of foot traffic and the intensity of property management. While design is essentially complete when the management plan is done, it still operates as a constraint on the plan. Building codes and zoning help alleviate the problem—but usually on a broad basis. The specific structure that responds to users' specific needs has very clear limits on management based on the quality and flexibility of the initial design. But to design flexibility into the project usually costs something—either in construction dollars or in operating efficiency.

Fundamental Property Management and Initial Design Decisions

Maintaining good relations with tenants, collecting rent, paying the bills, releasing space, handling maintenance schedules, conserving energy, providing security, supervising personnel, and coordinating insurance are all critically important, and anticipation of these tasks can help create a better development project. Security, for example, is an increasing concern of many tenants, and initial design critically affects security. The proper placement of outside lights and entrances that are clearly visible from the street, for example, make property management easier. Some older residential buildings in deteriorating central cities are nearly impossible to fully secure because of the long complex of hallways, sudden unlighted corners, and other features that could have been designed differently and cost-effectively had

Security is an increasing concern for tenants. At Las Colinas in Dallas, this large-scale multiuse development provides its own security force, complete with specially equipped patrol cars. Similar security precautions, albeit less dramatic ones, are being incorporated in most new developments.

the developer anticipated the need. And decisions made during the development process can seriously affect insurance. Older buildings without modern sprinkler systems pay large premiums for insurance.

The Budget

Once the property's place in the market is matched to the owner's needs, resulting in a management plan, the plan is converted to dollars to create a budget. From the developer's perspective, the budget is identical to the top portion of the pro forma income statement used in the feasibility study. From the property manager's standpoint, the property is expected to provide this cash flow (assuming the budget is met). Thus, projections of net operating income are derived from projected gross revenues, projected vacancies, and projected expenditures for real estate taxes, fire and extended insurance coverage, utilities, maintenance, management, replacements, and other expenses. Adjustments for debt service and income taxes after net operating income are not traditional concerns of property management and so are not always included in the asset manager's operating budget.

Examining the details of the operating budget early in the development process can result in fewer—or no—serious errors. Some highly decorative floors in shopping

411

centers, for example, are visually appealing but very difficult to clean. Likewise, certain types of lighting are attractive but need to be replaced more frequently than other types. During the development process, developers must trade off the marketing appeal of certain design features against long-term operating costs. Industry averages are a good starting point, but what counts in the final analysis is the cost of building and operating a particular property relative to what the market will pay for the features, functions, and benefits it provides them. The developer's role goes beyond the initial trade-off of the direct costs and revenues to more subtle questions related to longer-term property management. And the decision should be based on the present value of all expected revenues and expenses, including long-term management.

The Management Contract

The budget quantifies the management plan and ensures that the owner's interests are expressed consistently. A management contract provides a framework for the relationship between the asset manager and the owner. It specifies which management services will be paid for by the owner and which by the asset management firm. It determines whose payroll the employees will be on, who can authorize certain expenditures, who is responsible for keeping certain records, who is responsible for maintaining insurance coverage, who will handle advertising and promotion, and how much the asset manager will be paid. Just as they must be alert for general contractors' bids that do not include all essential cost items, developers must also eye management plans and budgets critically to ensure they do not promise services that cannot be provided for the fee quoted. Only when the management contract is negotiated and committed to paper can developers be certain that a qualified person is ready to perform all specified services at the price quoted.

Unless a building is designed for a single tenant who will both own and use the facility, normally developers are responsible for hiring the first asset manager. Many developers have subsidiaries that perform the service; others hire independent

asset managers. The length of the management contract varies, depending on the prospective owner's desires and the nature of the project. The more the asset management firm engages in initial marketing and other operations that exceed basic property management, the more likely it is that the contract will cover a long term. A performance contingency in longer-term contracts often allows the owner to replace the manager should the property not perform according to budget or some agreed-upon percent of the budget.

Ongoing Marketing

Ongoing marketing and leasing beyond initial occupancy are typically the responsibility of the asset manager. For a small multifamily project, ongoing marketing might involve little more than showing apartments that become available to prospective tenants. In such cases, ongoing marketing is almost always the responsibility of the asset manager. For larger projects, ongoing marketing can be more complex, and the asset manager might cooperate with outside brokerage firms. In a major office building, for example, asset managers would be responsible for advertising, showing the property, approving all final leases, and possibly doing some of the leasing themselves. Outside brokerage firms might well develop prospects, handle negotiations, show the property, and review prospective leases.

Regardless of the size of the property and who handles the ongoing marketing, rental concessions and tenant allowances (which were so important in the initial construction budget) must be included in the pro forma for long-term investment and the operating budget. Initial valuations of properties often include adjustments to rent for inflation and/or improving marketplaces but do not include tenant allowances and/or the rent concessions necessary to attract tenants during the transition period. Developers are always concerned with making sure that value exceeds cost, and value is a function of projected cash flow. Accurately projected cash flows must include all ongoing costs of marketing the space, including brokerage commissions, rental concessions, and tenant allowances.

In other words, from the feasibility study to the operating budget, the bottom line should be *effective* rents, not the higher "asking" rents.

SMART BUILDINGS

Increasing sophistication in asset management has been partially prompted by the advent of "smart" buildings. Smart buildings "combine two previously separate sets of technologies through an information network: . . . the building management technologies (building automation), [which] control such systems as heating and air conditioning, and the information technologies (office automation), which control communications operations" (see Figure 18-1).[3]

From a developer's perspective, smart buildings offer high-tech features whose costs must be included in the feasibility study. Potential additional revenues come from the automated technologies billed to tenants and reduced operating expenses from the building's technologies. Both of these benefits are achieved at a certain cost, however. For any particular market, developers must decide how smart the building should be, which should be one part of the feasibility analysis. If the increase in revenue or decrease in cost justifies the cost, the building should be smarter.

In the overbuilt markets of the late 1980s, several developers learned that the smartest of all buildings is a fully leased building and that few tenants demand many of the high-tech features. Office buildings

---

FIGURE 18-1
TECHNOLOGIES FOR SMART BUILDINGS

TENANT SYSTEMS	BUILDING SYSTEMS

Technological enhancements for smart buildings can include both tenant and building systems.

TENANT SYSTEMS	BUILDING SYSTEMS
Telephone/PBX	HVAC
Mainframe Computers	Energy Management and Temperature Controls
Microcomputers	Life Safety/Fire Suppression
Word Processors	Security
Wiring Schemes/Local Area Networks	
External Communications Network	

Source: Dean Schwanke, *Smart Buildings and Technology-Enhanced Real Estate*, vol. 1 (Washington, D.C.: ULI–the Urban Land Institute, 1985).

built to a specific tenant's needs have been the most successful smart buildings. It is not critical that certain features be needed in year one, but if they are not needed in the first 20 or 30 years, they should not be included because the user will not pay the costs. For the Europa Center, Fraser Morrow Daniels compromised in favor of maximum flexibility by providing conduits for wiring but not actual high-tech communications systems because tenants would not pay for them. Still, future installation is feasible.

A smart building combines appropriate high-tech features and innovative design. In other words, architects and those who provide technology must work together with market analysts to achieve maximum benefit. The overall impact on the operations of tenants is the key. High-tech features and high-tech design are useful only when they provide benefits that the users of the space will pay for, not simply because they are innovative, creative, or new.

The long-term impetus toward smart buildings is quite clear. As we become an information society and try to maintain global competitiveness, our growing service sector must increase office productivity. Automation often does increase office productivity with word processors, electronic messages, and electronic filing systems. At the same time, most of these devices require some changes in building design and technology—more space, more electrical circuits. The truly smart building facilitates innovations and provides flexibility over the long term.

Offering tenants the opportunity to share such services is a possibility asset managers can consider to reap some profits. If the target market is a variety of smaller users, it could be that jointly provided information services—from telecommunications to internal computer time—can be more efficiently provided for all tenants through a central facility. If so, the building might have an additional profit center—additional profit for the developer who seizes the opportunity.

Even more important in the 1990s than the possibility of a new profit center is the potential savings in costs offered by a smart building. New technologies in automation allow much more efficient monitoring of the HVAC system. With labor ever more expensive, more sophisticated security systems become cost-efficient. Even elevators are a critical item. Old elevators provide slow service, create the wrong image, and make the building less functional for tenants.

Smart buildings, with all their possible technological bells and whistles, have yet to take over the world. Thus far, their most important contribution has been the increased sophistication of HVAC systems. The addition of personal computers and other electronic equipment can cause a building's heat to rise. An automated system could respond to changes in temperature to avoid costly overheating of computer equipment without overcooling other parts of the building. Smarter buildings are coming, but where and how fast are as yet unanswered.

TRAINING FOR PROPERTY MANAGERS

Property managers have long had an erratic professional reputation. Typically they have been engineers managing large commercial buildings and less affluent, less trained individuals managing multifamily housing in exchange for free rent. As developers come to realize the importance of property management, however, more opportunities are available for training, including programs offered by several associations. The most well known is the Institute of Real Estate Management, an affiliate of the National Association of Realtors, which offers a designation as certified property manager. Other designations are available for on-site resident managers, including accredited resident management and certified apartment management.

The Building Owners and Managers Association produces an array of statistics on operating office buildings similar to the analyses of income and expenses produced by the Institute for Real Estate Management. The International Council of Shopping Centers provides its own designations, and the Urban Land Institute publishes operating results for shopping centers. All of these organizations seek to enhance professionalism in the field and to provide data that can be used in feasibility studies and to establish long-term operating budgets.[4]

The various programs aim to familiarize managers with the use of a systematic approach to keeping records, ways to best anticipate and respond to tenants' needs, skills in negotiating leases, legal responsibilities to tenants, and sales/marketing techniques. Because real estate management involves meticulous attention to details, techniques for tracking the many functions of building management are often best learned in professional training courses.

ASSET MANAGEMENT

The prospect of smarter buildings enhances the function of property management during development because all of the potential features must be tested for feasibility in a cost/benefit analysis. More important, at a time when many commercial markets are overbuilt and high vacancy rates abound, the property manager's role is enhanced. And more sophisticated asset management has come of age with institutional ownership of real estate portfolios. When their portfolios are more heavily committed to real estate, institutional owners are willing to invest in asset management—from the start of the investment process through analyzing distressed properties and diagnosing problems.

Asset managers are charged with making sure that all of the basic functions of property management are performed and with positioning the asset in the market and structuring the asset or portfolio to meet a client's specific needs. Thus, in addition to the management plan (which was always a responsibility of the property manager), asset managers have an ongoing responsibility to oversee remodeling, restructuring, and re-leasing. As market conditions evolve, asset managers reposition products to match users' changing demands. For distressed properties, asset managers must determine which features, functions, and benefits of the project are valuable and then effect changes that will alter people's perceptions of the project.

Wynne/Jackson, Inc., performs these services for workouts (negotiations between a lender and a developer to salvage troubled properties) in the overbuilt Texas market. Clyde Jackson, president of the company, says that reimaging requires quality people to represent the product (see the accompanying profile).

Asset management can be a financially rewarding occupation. Why do owners pay for this service? Because they perceive the service to preserve and create value.

Value is produced by a manager who understands national trends and local market conditions. An understanding of major national trends, current market conditions, and market statistics, and an intimate knowledge of the client allow asset managers to devise and implement a plan that will enhance the owner's risk-adjusted return on the portfolio. The plan can vary from a new leasing strategy incorporating annual escalations in the consumer price index when increases in inflation are expected, to massive remodeling or a conversion of use when the manager determines a particular market contains an excessive amount of a certain type of space. Such major decisions were in the past made by owners; with today's heavy institutional ownership, they are more likely to be made by an independent asset manager, usually with the agreement of the investor (see Figure 18-2 for an example of remodeling undertaken by new owners).

A variety of companies manage assets. A few are subsidiaries of development companies; others are independent investment managers or subsidiaries of major financial institutions. The largest group of asset managers is probably pension fund investment managers who are members of the National Council of Real Estate Investment Fiduciaries (NCREIF). In addition to providing advice on managing a portfolio and acquiring and disposing of properties, they also manage assets for their pension-fund clients. This group of asset managers—"who's who" in the business—often hires local property management firms to take care of the traditional functions and keeps for themselves the supervisory role in property management and the other aspects of asset management. Thus, it is their charge to be sure that their clients invest in the right types of properties and in the right markets, and that those properties are managed to achieve the maximum benefit for the client. Achieving maximum benefit means in-

---

PROFILE: CLYDE C. JACKSON, JR.

President, Wynne/Jackson, Inc.
Dallas, Texas

Background: Clyde Jackson was born in Dallas, received business and law degrees from Southern Methodist University, and participated in the development of Plaza of The Americas, a mixed-use project on 5.5 acres in Dallas that includes a 442-room hotel, two 25-story office towers, two levels of shops and restaurants, and an athletic club. As of 1987, Jackson was riding out the real estate recession in the Southwest by winding up his own projects and doing workouts for other owners through his asset management company. His largest workout took two and one-half years: a $100 million–plus resort on the coast of Texas, including a marina with 1,000 slips.

On workouts: Turning a project around is harder than starting from scratch because so many elements are already givens: the land, the infrastructure, and the failure. Erasing the image of failure is the key, and hiring top-quality leasing people, looking for the right niche, developing a new marketing plan, and following it are all steps in getting a sick project back on its feet. Hiring good people to represent a property starts its reimaging by erasing the association with dereliction.

Several factors ensure success for mixed-use developments, according to Jackson:
1. Market research must prove adequate demand for *each* proposed use. Synergy does not occur among uses unless each can stand on its own. A strong use will not rescue a marginal one.
2. The design team and the general contractor for a mixed-use project must all have experience with mixed-use buildings. Their prior experience can save a developer millions of dollars.
3. Marketing mixed-use projects is different, because it serves people's needs in a broad, rather than narrow, way. And managing the asset is different, because such a large mixture of tenants and uses must be coordinated.

On market research: Asked how he uses market research, Jackson replied, "To find sites, to decide whether to proceed with a project, to sell lenders on a project, and to develop a marketing plan."

---

corporating protection from inflation in the lease and renovating the space regularly if feasible because the pension-fund investor is·oriented toward long-term ownership.

THE CORPORATE REAL ESTATE DIRECTOR

Ten years ago, chief executive officers (CEOs) often considered real estate management one of the less important functions in a corporation. Today, they recognize that the major part of their balance sheets is in real estate and that in an often harshly competitive world, management of those fixed assets is critical to a firm's success. Real estate is estimated to account for 25 percent of a corporation's assets, and companies are finally realizing the need to maximize the value of real estate assets by making decisions about location affecting the quality of life for employees, tenants' preferences, and use of space that will make the most, financially, of present and future property assets.

A critical function of corporate real estate directors is to present issues about real estate to the corporation so that decisions about real property enhance shareholders' dividends. The director must be involved in the decisions to increase and

FIGURE 18-2
CENTURY PARK PLAZA: ASSET ENHANCEMENT OF A HIGH-RISE OFFICE BUILDING

JMB Realty purchased the 26-story Century Park Plaza office building from Heitman Properties in late 1985. Both buyer and seller were well aware of a variety of physical problems with the 12-year-old building (completed in 1973) at the time of the purchase. The 356,000-square-foot building, however, did possess some excellent features: spectacular views, a corner location at the gateway to Century City, prestigious major tenants, and a low vacancy rate (5 to 7 percent).

The building had more apparent problems at the time of acquisition:

1. Slow, inefficient elevators (up to seven minutes of waiting time);
2. Outdated common areas, particularly elevator cabs, the ground-floor lobby, and multitenant floor common areas;
3. Outdated, low-impact exterior signs and landscaping;
4. Signs, finishes, and the office in the parking garage needing upgrading;
5. Outdated building improvements for fire, the disabled, and Title 24 codes and requirements.
6. Outdated leases with existing tenants that gave extensive tenant rights, such as protection against increased operating expenses, early lease termination, and overextended guaranteed parking rights.

A JMB Realty investment affiliate, Group Trust III, purchased the Century Park Plaza in January 1986 for $66 million. The Group Trust III fund is made up of pension fund investors for the portfolio of 11 properties, primarily office buildings and regional shopping centers.

The upgraded and redesigned ground-floor lobby for Century Park Plaza.

The final purchase price took into consideration the necessary improvements to maintain competitiveness within the Century City and West Los Angeles markets. At the time, numerous office developments were recently completed, under construction, and planned. Further, a major tenant (occupying 3½ floors) was scheduled to vacate its space at the end of its 10-year lease. Thus, the opportunity existed to add value to the property with new leases at higher rates.

design capacity in the same way the property manager is in a speculative building. Corporate real estate directors often chair site selection committees. They assist in decisions to lease or buy space or in the search for financing. They work with the firm's operating management to create the best organization for continuing management and monitoring of real estate assets. They also work to create a management information system for this purpose. They work to identify surplus or underused real

417

FIGURE 18-2 (continued)

The building's owners undertook an enhancement program at an estimated cost of over $3 million. The planning phase of the program took more than nine months, mainly because of the complex rehabilitation of the elevators, which cost over $1.5 million. Rehabilitation of the elevators included new floor-by-floor operational controls and the installation of new microprocessors for the elevators. That work began in early 1987, concurrently with work in the parking garage and most of the common areas.

The enhancement program resulted in the following changes:

1. The average elevator waiting time of over one minute was reduced to the industry standard of 34 seconds.
2. Earth-tone finishes in the ground-floor lobby were replaced with travertine marble and brass accents to both the floors and walls. Travertine marble was used on the floors of the elevator cabs, and the walls and ceilings were upgraded to low-maintenance glass and multicell lights. Common area floors, walls, and ceilings of the multitenant floors were completely refinished and the restrooms brought up to code to accommodate the disabled.
3. New exterior signs and landscaping were installed.
4. The parking garage was repainted and the parking office relocated to accommodate visitors and V.I.P.s.
5. Floor-to-ceiling windows were re-tinted to comply with Title 24 codes, and the draperies were replaced with vertical blinds.
6. As existing tenants' leases expired, they were replaced with new, more detailed forms.

Leasing increased dramatically during the enhancement program, with over 70,000 square feet of new leases signed in late 1986 and 1987. The percentage of occupied space in the building dropped from 93 percent at the time of acquisition to 78 percent when the major tenant's lease expired and other tenants moved out in 1986. But by early 1988, building occupancy was 96 percent as a result of interest generated by the enhancement program. Rental rates are among the highest in the West Los Angeles office market.

The building's current value is conservatively estimated at $90 million. Considerable costs are associated with operating the building, for example, removing asbestos in the vacant space and complying with the new requirement for sprinklers. Operating expenses as of August 1990 were $6.96 per square foot (real estate taxes were $6.42 per square foot). Removing asbestos cost approximately $15.00 per square foot, installing sprinklers $14.00 to $16.00 per square foot (approximately $5.3 million). While rental rates range from $28.00 to $39.00 per square foot (with an annual average of $33.00), costs associated with removing asbestos and installing sprinklers considerably diminish net effective rents and cash flow.

Source: Russ Parker, Regional Leasing Manager, JMB Properties Company. This material has been prepared for information only and does not constitute a representation or warranty to any individual or organization.

property and seek to find ways to reuse those assets. They negotiate for the company in leasing or purchasing space. They initiate suggestions for alternative ways of owning or leasing real estate, such as the opportunity to create a joint venture if the company does not want to create its own development business but still wants to take advantage of its financial strength and reap the rewards of equity participation.

CEOs also know that the flexibility to react to changing market conditions is often hampered by the ownership of long-term assets in fixed locations. The empty steel mills in Pittsburgh are a prime example. Pittsburgh, with its beautiful downtown skyline, still has large vacant, corporate-owned buildings inside the central city because of the poor market for very old, very large industrial space.

Small wonder that real estate is suddenly receiving far greater attention in both the popular press and in professional organizations like the National Association of Corporate Real Estate Executives, the National Association of Industrial and Office Parks, and the Industrial Research Development Council. Most important, corporations themselves are paying it a lot of attention.[5]

Developers need to understand corporations' requirements for space because corporations are the major users of the product. In particular, developers need to include features important to corporate users in the development plan.

The rate of acquiring knowledge in business generally has increased rapidly, leading to increased unpredictability from a CEO's perspective—in essence, to faster product obsolescence. Multiple markets with more products and globalization have complicated planning. Real estate is fixed, almost indefinitely, but what CEOs now need most is flexibility because they cannot forecast events accurately.

The need for flexibility translates to the need to build general-purpose real estate rather than special-purpose industrial or home office buildings. An interesting parallel is that the major new real estate investor, the pension fund, also wants general-purpose real estate. If the prime tenant ceases to be a tenant, general-purpose real estate is clearly easier to re-lease. From a corporate perspective, a smaller version of a general-purpose building also reduces the break-even point by lowering fixed costs. Corporations need to exercise caution and not build corporate headquarters (which involve fixed overhead) too large to resell.

As the United States moves to a world with fewer middle managers and more subcontractors as partners, space needs naturally change. As the configuration of relationships among the key participants in

U.S. industry evolves, so must the space constructed by the development community. Successful developers in the 1990s will be those who anticipate the change in corporate requirements and build space to fit the new relationships.

SUMMARY

Property management is one of the largest controllable elements once development is complete. The enterprise concept introduces the idea of a building as a business, not just a collection of bricks and mortar. Asset management includes the traditional functions of property management plus restructuring and re-leasing the property to fit evolving market conditions and clients' evolving needs. Smart office buildings raise the level of sophistication required for asset management. Finally, the evolving needs of corporations provide further opportunities for developers to provide flexible space.

Most important, all of the issues involved with asset management should be incorporated in planning development and the development process itself. The best structures can be created only when sources of revenue and techniques to reduce expenses are incorporated in the initial planning.

NOTES

1. This heading covers only property management in relation to the development process. To examine both property management and asset management more extensively, see the many references in the bibliography, as well as the *Journal of Property Management* (published by the Institute of Real Estate Management, 430 North Michigan Avenue, Chicago, Illinois 60611) and *Pensions and Investment Age* (Crain Publications, Property Sector, 740 Rush Street, Chicago, Illinois 60611).

2. See James C. Canestaro, *An Introduction to the Design Analysis of Office Buildings*, Development Component Series (Washington, D.C.: ULI–the Urban Land Institute, 1983), for an excellent illustration of the impact of property management on design of a building. Canestaro, for example, illustrates how a square building can minimize energy costs of an office building in Chicago. Given the size of the space, however, a square building would generate more space that is more than 30 feet from windows and would yield less in rents.

The rent for such space is discounted in the market. The property manager's role is to alert the developer to such situations.

3. Michelle D. Gouin and Thomas B. Cross, *Intelligent Buildings* (Homewood, Ill.: Dow Jones–Irwin, 1986), pp. 2–3.

4. Annual publications are very long and very detailed. With similar figures available from the Institute for Real Estate Management for apartments and condominiums, from the Industrial Development and Research Council for industrial facilities, and from accounting firms for hotels, resorts, and restaurants, property managers seldom lack background statistics or organizational support.

5. An extensive bibliography on corporate real estate is provided in the 1990 special issue of the *Journal of Real Estate Research*. Two of the best papers include "Modeling the Corporate Real Estate Decision" and "Information and Aging Issues in Corporate Real Estate," which are summarized here.

Corporate real estate has traditionally been viewed in the context of capital budgeting. As a result of recent innovations in the capital market, it is now more useful to view this decision from a combined framework of capital budgeting and corporate financing. With the new combined perspective, all corporate real estate decisions should be reviewed regularly. Given this need for frequent review and the large number of variables involved, a formal model is helpful.

The individual techniques needed for a model with this joint perspective are well known, but the interactions between real estate valuation, accrual accounting, and corporate valuation methodologies are quite complex, as the first paper demonstrates. Moreover, the application of the theoretical model to real life is a challenging task, as shown in the analysis of recent corporate restructurings.

The second paper investigates corporate real estate decisions and discusses ways to use real estate to reduce an agency's costs, with the analysis carried out in the context of the valuation model described above.

Both shareholder/bondholders and shareholder/managers are addressed and opportunities for corporate real estate financing discussed as a means of reducing agency costs of the first type. Conditions under which the second type of costs arises are discussed, with implications for compensating management.

Chapter 19

The Challenge of Marketing and Sales

The culmination of the entire team's efforts, the place where all of the resources invested thus far produce their return, is marketing and sales. A person who has bought or sold a single-family house or condominium knows how much attention to detail is required. Imagine the complications in leasing 500,000 square feet of prime office space in Manhattan. Successful marketing staff and salespeople must be grounded firmly in all four of the primary components of business education: finance, marketing, production, and management. They must have a thorough understanding of *finance* so that they can competently advise prospects of alternative financial structures for proposed transactions. The principles of the formulation and implementation of *marketing* strategy must be second nature to people contemplating a successful career in this field. Understanding the product and its *production* (the construction process) is a prerequisite to selling the product successfully. Finally, the ability to empathize with and lead people, which are *management* skills, is crucial to the sales process.

The marketing specialist on the development team is an employee of the developer or an outsider who provides service on contract. But the use of a marketing specialist does not relieve the developer of making decisions; calling the plays is still the developer's responsibility. And in small development companies, developers themselves perform much of the marketing.

The challenge of marketing and selling real estate is the focus of this chapter. For the most part, the term "sales" is used broadly to include both leasing and selling. Getting a lease signed takes much of the same effort as getting a sales contract signed. The overriding purpose of marketing and sales is *finding and convincing prospects*. It is the final component of the total marketing effort that has been stressed throughout the text. If research and product design were well done, then sales and leasing will be easier, but even if research and product design were near perfect, prospects must still be found and convinced of the project's merits.

This chapter examines:
- Coordinated marketing and sales;
- Targeted advertising;
- Public relations;
- On-site promotions;

The authors are particularly indebted to William Webb for his extensive contributions to this chapter.

- Merchandising the product;
- Relations with Realtors;[1]
- Education for the sales staff;
- Sales operations; and
- Accepting the challenge of marketing and sales.

With soft and overbuilt markets in all major U.S. cities, the notion that buildings sell themselves has been sorely tested. Rarely does a project—no matter how well done—generate its own market. Fraser Morrow Daniels, for example, turned to an outside firm to lease the Europa Center.

EUROPA CENTER

LEASING SPACE

There's a major question about who will lease your building for you, especially in the Research Triangle area, where the market is just forming. We chose a national organization, Cushman & Wakefield, which leases only office space, because we anticipated that the competition for tenants would be cutthroat. In a highly competitive environment, the tenants run the show anyway. If the company listing your space leases it, it will cost 4 percent of the value of the lease. If it is cobrokered with another company, you pay 6 percent of the value of the lease, including the cobrokerage fee. We budgeted 5 percent, because we figured we or the leasing company could generate tenants for half of the space and the other half would be cobrokered.

The leasing process works mostly like this. The leasing company identifies tenants—trying to find businesses that are expanding or moving to the area or that could be talked out of a current lease, which still has a year to run. Once the leasing agents have a prospect, they come to us and say, "This is how your building stacks up against other buildings. You're

Photo courtesy of Jim Sink, Artech, Inc.

The lobby of the newly completed Europa Center.

this much nicer, your location is this much better, and your rent is $1.00 higher. The tenant needs a loading dock; here's what it values. What will it take to get that tenant here rather than to one of the other three buildings it could move into?" Then we try to guess what the other buildings have to offer and decide how low we can go to beat them out.

Then the leasing agent says, "To get that tenant, I think we'll have to give them a lower rate and six months of free rent. They can't afford to pay for any extra finishes, but they need an extra $3.00 a square foot for nice surroundings. We should offer an extra $3.00 per square foot that we pay for, and I think we can get them. Or we should offer free electricity on weekends rather than charging extra." Then we say, "We're not comfortable with six months of free rent; give them four." Or we might say, "That's a great tenant. We really want them because we think they'll attract more tenants. Let's give them 18 months of free rent. They're really beneficial to the building. Let's pay something to get them in there."

After the building was 30 percent leased, more people came to us and asked to be in the building, instead of the other way around. Getting started is very tough, but the subsequent leasing is usually easier.

By April 1989, Europa Center was over 80 percent leased. Most of the tenants were local, professional companies that have been in Chapel Hill and Durham for some time. Virtually all the tenants moved from substandard space up to our space. A few companies had expanded and just needed larger space. A couple of companies were start-up companies, and some were controlled and located in other parts of the country but used the Europa Center as their Chapel Hill office.

Asset management and ongoing leasing are strong considerations for building owners. All of the existing tenants had different contracts to occupy their space. Each had different terms, different rates, and different escalation clauses, and when overbuilding and high vacancy rates are common, tenants can

pretty much get what they want by shopping around. Building owners become more and more willing to conform to a tenant's needs, first with lower prices or lower escalations and later with higher tenant allowances and a lot of special things you probably wouldn't want to fool with in a better market.

Once a building is finished and occupied, the building owner or building manager worries about the electricity, the water bill, parking, elevator maintenance, and indoor and outdoor landscaping—all of the things that are essential to keeping the tenants happy and the buildings looking good. Because a lot of different tenants have leases with varying lengths, some leases are always coming up for renewal or people are moving out. Leasing in a building like the Europa Center is a continuous process.

COORDINATED MARKETING AND SALES

The experience of builders and developers has shown that a systematic approach to marketing and sales tends to produce superior results. Just as the construction of a new building requires the coordinated assembly of many components, so does the successful selling or leasing of that building depend upon the combination of marketing and sales activities (see Figure 19-1).

Guided by market research and controlled by a strategic plan and the budget, each individual activity plays an important role in satisfying potential users. Developers must guide and support a coordinated system if the efforts of individual sales and leasing professionals are to produce maximum results. And every member of the team must understand how each activity is designed to contribute to the success of the overall sales program.

Market Research

The whole process begins with market research, the goal of which is to project a rate of absorption for a product based on the supply and demand for similar products

423

FIGURE 19-1
PERFORMANCE SYSTEM FOR SUCCESSFUL
REAL ESTATE MARKETING AND SALES

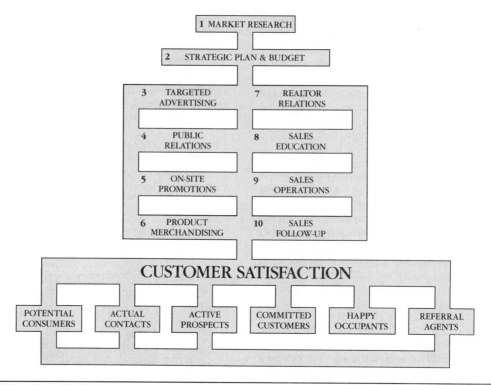

© 1987 William N. Webb.

in a specified market area. Conducted during stage one of the development process, brainstorming may point out an unmet need in the market that the developer could fill. In stage two, market research explores the possibilities of a specific idea at a specific location in sufficient detail to allow rough estimates of a project's feasibility to be generated. If the possibilities look enticing, the developer might commission a formal market study, which should yield details about the target market that the proposed product is intended to attract.

It is also necessary to know as specifically as possible why and how the product the developer intends to create will be appropriate to the exact target market. Developing products driven by the market is critical. Developers should seek the advice of top marketing and sales professionals in design of the product. Sales people are

often the last to be asked what should be built and the first to be fired if they cannot sell it. Ignoring this source of market research is unwise.

Even after a project is designed and construction is under way, members of the marketing and sales team should be consulted frequently. They face potential prospects and measure market conditions every day. Their market intelligence should be evaluated and integrated into decisions continuously if marketing and sales are to be effective.

The Marketing Plan And Budget

Developers like to estimate the cost of marketing and sales in terms of a total dollar amount that will be sufficient to complete leasing or selling the project. This approach is understandable, because the overall costs of so many other components of development are subject to accurate estimates. Coming up with a hard-and-fast number for the expenses of marketing and sales is much more difficult, however. Nobody can forecast very accurately just how much marketing and sales a project will need, but everyone probably *will* agree that the marketing team should at least set out to equal the rate of absorption predicted in the market research. Figuring out what is necessary to reach that goal is the question.

At least two methods of budgeting have proven useful in making projections, and they both start with a marketing plan. As early as possible in the development process, developers and/or the marketing staff should begin formulating a plan to promote the product to the target market. From the beginning, the plan should be written down. Committing it to writing encourages logical thought and thorough analysis.

The plan typically begins with a description of the product and the target market based on earlier market research and includes statements about how the product will be attractive to the target market and how the marketing and sales staff should reach that market. As more detail becomes necessary, a list of specific activities should be included within each category that could be productive. Using a comprehensive checklist of activities appropriate for a wide range of products and markets is an excellent idea, so that nothing promising will be overlooked.

The first step in budgeting involves compiling a reasonable cost estimate for each marketing activity on the list. Spare no expense. Assume no corners will be cut. Encourage brainstorming to develop new ideas. Then total the cost. It should be wildly excessive.

Start paring down the total by going back and squeezing every item. Each activity should justify itself; delete the ones that do not. Presumably, only the strongest ideas will survive, which is the purpose of using this method of budgeting—casting the net as wide as possible, keeping only the best of what is caught.

Some of the items might be one-time investments that will last for the life of the program like building a sales information center. Others will represent consumable items like brochures that may have to be replaced periodically. Still others will recur continually, such as media charges, which will keep mounting as the effort intensifies.

To estimate the grand total, it is necessary to predict how long a presence in the market is needed. Look to market research for a predicted absorption rate. How hard to push (how much to spend per month) to reach that rate is a judgment call. As a result, the second budgeting method could provide a cross check of the estimate.

The second method starts with a question: how many new prospects/contacts will have to be generated to achieve the predicted absorption rate? The answer depends on two factors: the rate of converting new prospects/contacts to completed transactions, which is affected by numerous variables, not the least of which is the effectiveness of the sales staff, and how much space each completed transaction will absorb. In residential marketing, each buyer generally absorbs one dwelling. For commercial properties, the market research predicts square feet per tenant.

How much will each new prospect/contact cost? It depends primarily on how contacts will be made. Commercial real estate marketing relies heavily on active prospecting: members of the sales team try to contact parties directly that they think might be interested. Marketing is intended primarily to support their efforts, generating some leads along the way. In residential marketing, prospecting is very rare, and salespeople depend on advertising to motivate prospects to come to the sales office. The accompanying profile of developer Jim Stuebner shows how heavily his organization, which develops mixed-use projects and industrial parks, relies on aggressive marketing.

Every budget item allocated for marketing and sales carries with it the hope that it will produce positive results beyond its cost. It is critically important that the productivity of marketing and sales activities be measured continuously. Incorporating the list of budget line items directly into the accounting system will prove helpful. In that way, expenditures versus results can be tracked with precision equal to the initial projections. It is important also to use

PROFILE: **JAMES C. STUEBNER**

President, Northland Development Company
Minneapolis, Minnesota

Background: Stuebner grew up in Philadelphia, attended Dartmouth, and served in the Korean War. After he was discharged, he went to work for a chemical company that sent him to Minneapolis to open an office in its plastics division. In 1961, Stuebner helped start a company to manufacture foam-insulated wall panels for large-scale commercial and industrial buildings. During the 1960s, he was a subcontractor on 400 buildings across the United States, working extensively with developers, architects, engineers, and contractors. "In that process," he says, "I discovered that the ultimate challenge was to get involved in the whole process of development—design, engineering, land planning, construction. That's how I evolved into the development business."

Stuebner's beginning as a developer was in late 1969, when he acquired, over a two-year period, several hundred acres in the cornfields outside Minneapolis. "We knew where the freeways would go at some point and hoped that it would really happen. It eventually did, and our marketing approach has always been to develop inventory space. That's how we built the nucleus of our investments. We are really long-term investors in real estate as well as developers. We construct and develop projects for other firms, but most of it is for our own account." In his own park, Stuebner builds both speculative space and build-to-suit space.

Trends in the business: Selecting land for industrial parks remains unchanged. It must be near freeways for good access for trucks, and a good labor supply—both skilled and unskilled workers—must also be available. Stuebner believes in master planning an entire park, whether 200 or 400 acres, because doing so provides flexibility for users as they expand their businesses.

Stuebner believes the biggest innovation of the last decade has been computerized warehouses, ultimately reducing any one company's need for distribution space and stimulating conversion of space all over the country. Obsolescence is the biggest single factor in companies' seeking new industrial space. The second greatest innovation has been the growth of finished office space as a percentage of warehouse space among small users—from 10 to 25 or 30 percent on average over the last decade. As a result, warehouses with a high-tech image, two-story office space, and lots of glass in the building's front have been very successful. And corporate mergers and acquisitions have created demand for operating space as companies move around.

Marketing: Stuebner has a strong in-house marketing staff, which initiates 65 to 70 percent of the leases and build-to-suit contracts. The leasing staff make 100 "cold" calls each per week, collecting data about when leases expire for storage on computer. "Very aggressive marketing has been the key to our success. That's no textbook theory. It's OK to have beautiful buildings, but the key to success is to keep them full." His most recent marketing challenge has been to compete with free rent given by big national developers moving into the Minneapolis market.

On real estate as a long-term investment: "A tremendous amount of taking risks occurs daily, and a lot of patience is required. The hardest thing for young people trained in good business schools to get used to is that real estate is a long-term investment. But then we also have a hard time convincing the most sophisticated financial institutions of that fact."

A logo and a name for a development project are essential for any marketing plan. Both must be carried through consistently on all printed matter—advertising, newsletters, letterhead, announcements, and so on. Pictured here is the stacked stone entrance to the Water's Edge community in Stone Mountain, Georgia.

continuing market research to measure effectiveness. Ask for feedback from the sales team and from prospects. As the team develops a track record, use it to replace the original projections.

TARGETED ADVERTISING

The definition of the target market in the market research should include information about where potential prospects are located geographically. Once the appropriate form of advertising has been chosen (radio or newspaper, for example), advertising should be purchased where the target market is located.

The market research should also suggest the creative content of the advertising message. After all, the product was de-

signed to be especially attractive to a target market. Typically, an outside advertising agency is responsible for writing advertising copy and producing a logo and accompanying graphics for the property. The agency will also purchase media space or time for advertising. It is not advisable, however, to ask the advertising agency to determine the target market or suggest an appropriate marketing budget. These factors are the responsibility of the marketing specialist (or the developer).

Deciding on the best mix of media to use is an important component of targeted advertising. The target market should suggest which media could be most productive. Across the nation, advertising in newspapers is the traditional medium of choice for real estate. If it is judged appropriate for the product and the target market, the next

427

determination is which newspapers to use, based on what the target market is likely to read.

Deciding where in each newspaper the advertising should appear is also critical. A useful basic principle to follow is to place advertising where interested shoppers will look for it. Communicating with an interested audience actively seeking information about a product is much more useful than attempting to capture the attention of someone with no present interest in it. Designing and placing an ad powerful enough to induce an acceptable response is likely to be an expensive undertaking.

Magazines are another medium often used to advertise real estate. In many communities, some magazines survive almost exclusively on advertising oriented toward real estate, particularly for residential developments in rapidly growing communities in the Sunbelt. Local and statewide business magazines are natural choices for developers of almost all types of income-producing properties. And both residential and commercial developers might find opportunities in magazines targeted for newcomers to the area.

Compared to newspapers, magazines have longer cycles and may deliver more highly targeted readers. The print quality of magazines is also much higher, and they frequently include full-color photographs. For particularly attractive developments, these factors can be compelling inducements. Public service publications, such as the local guide to symphony programs, can sometimes make sense when trying to establish a certain tone for a development.

Radio and television offer tremendous impact but generally at commensurate cost. They are especially useful for short-term support of a special event, such as a grand opening. Many metropolitan areas include radio stations targeted to just about any profile of residential buyers imaginable. And the increasing popularity of cable television offers interesting possibilities for business-oriented developments.

Where available, outdoor billboards are a natural for advertising real estate. They can include directions to the project—crucial to a product that depends on location. The trick is to find available boards along roads the target market will use.

Direct mail is the most targeted advertising medium, because recipients of the message can be chosen individually. Wasted exposure, which comes with all other media, is thereby minimized. This efficiency makes multiple exposures feasible, which is why most successful direct-mail campaigns feature repetitive mailings. When the advantage of rapid production is added, direct mail becomes even more attractive.

PUBLIC RELATIONS

In concert with targeted advertising, a coordinated public relations effort is necessary. It might be useful to think of public relations as untargeted promotion aimed at the public at large. But the best generator of positive public relations is the quality of the development itself.

Almost all real estate development today generates some ill will among people who live near the project. They might see the development as damaging the environment, generating excess traffic on local roads, or negatively affecting the value of their own properties because use of the land is "different." And the sensitivity with which such concerns are handled can make or break a project.

Government is always the developer's partner. Because government ultimately responds to the people, any negative concerns must be handled with great care, and developers are usually the best people to respond to them. A message delivered by the developer carries more weight and shows admirable commitment. Thoughtfully receiving feedback from government and the people shows respect for the public interest. Developers also have the most latitude in initiating changes as a result of that feedback. Few actions can be more effective in generating positive public relations than showing such flexibility.

Because government is so important in the development process, a well-conceived public relations program will provide relevant agencies and officials with the comprehensive information they need to discharge their responsibilities efficiently. Taking the initiative to raise and resolve potentially difficult issues when possible can sometimes avert distressingly colorful public confrontations.

Another component of a well-crafted public relations program is generating positive editorial exposure to the development plans. The potential impact of such exposure derives from the power of the implied third-party endorsement. Editorialists can write positive things that a developer should be embarrassed to say about himself and would seem self-serving. The best single generator of prospects' visits to a sales center selling new houses is a feature article with pictures in the real estate section of the local newspaper.

No matter the type of property involved, similar opportunities to benefit from positive editorial exposure are available. The secret of using this tool is simply getting to know the individuals who write the articles or editorials—reporters for the business section of the newspaper and editors of state or local business magazines—getting to know them before their skills are needed and getting to know them as professional friends. An often overlooked fact is that they must meet tough deadlines with interesting copy again and again. The time will come during the life of any real estate development when developers and their professional friends will be able to help one another—but only if developers do their part in advance.

A third component of the public relations program is a newsletter published by the development firm. Newsletters allow developers to tell their own story in their own way, while preserving most of the power of an implied third-party endorsement. It makes relatively little difference whether the newsletter is elaborate or inexpensive; what does make a difference is the frequency with which it is published. Newsletters should be short, newsy, factual, and light, and include photographs of interesting people. No single issue will take over the market; it is more a question of building an overall positive image for the endeavor, one small piece at a time. Newsletters are useful in reaching the target market and in staying close to public officials.

ON-SITE PROMOTIONS

The principle of on-site promotions is to induce members of the target market to visit the site who might not otherwise be expected to come on their own. The idea is to stage an interesting event on the property, hoping that prospects will be attracted to the event.

Perhaps the most obvious on-site promotion is the grand opening. Citizens and government officials the developer met as part of the public relations program should be invited, as well as representatives of the extended development team. Principal prospects or potential prospects should also be included. In many areas, a chamber of commerce function is a worthwhile on-site promotion. Opening the facilities to clubs and hobby groups can also be productive.

Any building should be its own best salesperson, distinctly attractive to the target market. Allowing the market to experience firsthand all of the features and benefits can be a great sales tool. If it were not true, on-site sales presentations would have no validity.

MERCHANDISING THE PRODUCT

Merchandising the product encompasses all the visual impressions prospects receive of the real estate offered other than those clearly stated in advertising or editorials. It includes not only brochures and stationery but also everything prospects might see that supports a sales presentation off site or on the site itself.

When a building's architectural design has been carefully planned, it should be a primary component of merchandising the product. Entrances to most real estate developments are consciously designed to give the impression that the individuals who live, work, or shop in those places are people of substance. An impressive entrance can help sales in at least two ways. First, making a good impression will make the prospect feel better personally. Second, an attractive entrance can impress visitors, whether friends, employees, suppliers, or even competitors.

The same phenomenon holds true for other elements of the site design. Landscaping, layout of streets and parking, and signs all play a part in fostering the idea that this development is worthy of consideration and worth the asking price.

Photo courtesy of Steve Carner

At many larger projects, a number of sales models are constructed early in the process to help sell units to prospects while the rest of the project is being constructed. At Halcyon Del Mar, in San Diego, a completed model unit was featured in the interior of the site.

A sales or leasing information center becomes a major component in merchandising the product. Such a facility should be an artful blend of pleasing aesthetics and efficiency. From the prospect's point of view, approaching, entering, and lingering in this facility should be a pleasant, nonthreatening experience. Fulfilling this requirement is a responsibility best assigned to a competent designer experienced with sales centers.

The efficiency of a successful sales center, however, is best handled by marketing and sales experts. Depending on the specific characteristics of the product, certain displays and graphic sales aids will be required to underscore points being made in the sales presentation. The design of each individual display, the message it conveys, and its placement within the facility should support the presentation being made to the maximum extent possible. Doing so will require cooperation between

the sales staff who know what they want, the graphic artist who knows how to make it, and the interior designer who wants it to look pleasing and to fit within a consistent design theme.

For some products, particularly new houses, furnished models showing a sample of the finished product are effective. Two principal schools of thought concern the effect that should be created. One school says, "No one who comes here will forget where they saw this purple wallpaper!" The other says, "Gee, honey, it looks so comfortable. We could move in here this afternoon."

The final elements to consider in merchandising the product are naming the project and developing a consistent image for it through a logo and a promotional color scheme. Successful names will reinforce the project's attractiveness to the target market. Good names should have the same attributes as well-designed entranceways: they should be impressive and dignified without being intimidating at the same time they are warm and inviting (see Figure 19-2).

With the project's name determined, it is necessary to design a distinctive logo consistent with the impression the developer is trying to create in the target market. Designing logos is a matter for artists specializing in the field. Once the logo is chosen, it should be used consistently, without alteration. The same holds true for the promotional color scheme. Specify colors using a standard system and use only those colors in any promotional pieces produced. Absolutely consistent presentation is the key to building awareness of the product in the market.

RELATIONS WITH REALTORS

Knowing the local Realtors who handle a specific type of property can be beneficial, regardless of whether the developer has an in-house sales staff or employs an outside agency. Successful brokers know about local market conditions and often have advantageous access to prospects.

In residential developments, houses built to serve transferring corporate executives show consistently high ratios of cooperative sales between Realtors, probably because such people need a new house rather quickly. They typically want to avoid interrupting a career or separating the family, and they might receive financial assistance from an employer to facilitate the transaction. The opposite end of cooperation between Realtors is in the sale of houses to first-time buyers. Such sales are most likely made to individuals who are familiar with the local area and have been shopping for a new house for some time. In many markets, such individuals go directly to the sales office at the development and bypass the Realtors.

The influence of local Realtors in commercial sales and leasing is no less powerful. Expanding companies establishing operations in a new area will quite likely view the help of a knowledgeable local agent as essential, whether they seek office, warehouse, or manufacturing space. Even for companies that have operated in an area for some time, the assistance of local agents frees executives to pursue their primary responsibilities.

One of the principal advantages of choosing an agency to handle sales or leasing is the presumption that it has already

---

FIGURE 19-2
THE ELEVATOR MUSIC IS HEAVY ON RUMBAS

When you think of the Chiquita Center, you think bananas. And that can be vexing if you rent an office in the center and you aren't in bananas.

At one time the Chiquita Center, a 29-story building in Cincinnati, was known as Columbia Plaza. Its name changed in 1987, when Cincinnati business tycoon Carl Lindner moved his United Brands Company to Cincinnati from New York, installed the company's headquarters in Columbia Plaza, and rechristened the building after his company's most profitable division, Chiquita Bananas.

Nell Surber, Cincinnati's director of economic development, says that some law, accounting, and other firms were "disgruntled" by suddenly finding themselves tenants not of Columbia Plaza but—click those castanets—Chiquita Center. Indeed, Rod Hickman of LaSalle Partners, which manages the building, says that some tenants "didn't like the idea of putting the Chiquita name on their stationery." And few apparently have.

One tenant, however, a law firm, threw itself into the spirit of things, naming a balcony adjoining its offices the Carmen Miranda Veranda.

Source: William Mathewson, "Shop Talk—The Elevator Music Is Heavy on Rumbas," *Wall Street Journal*, April 21, 1988.

created its own productive Realtor relations program over the years. If the agency is well known and highly respected in the market area, their credibility and charisma can be added to those in the developer's organization and project. More than one successful marketing and sales program has been built upon the credibility of the brokerage agency handling the sales.

On the other hand, if sales and leasing are handled by an in-house staff, the developer might have to work much harder to create a productive Realtor relations program. Brokers are not easily excited by new products unless they are convinced they can sell the property quickly and easily. In the Realtor's world, doing so most often equates to lowering prices, and convincing Realtors that they can make money by introducing prospects to the subject property can be a real challenge.

Publishing a special newsletter for Realtors is one approach to the problem. Even better, the developer can visit offices serving the clientele in person, making presentations designed to sell brokers themselves on the value of the product and getting to know them as individuals. Frequently, the most efficient approach of all is to examine local records to determine which individual agents are the leaders in selling the type of property. Highly personal approaches to these high achievers can sometimes produce extraordinary results.

A Realtor relations program is not likely to go very far until local agents are convinced that the developer's representatives will treat their prospects courteously and professionally. To the extent that the developer can help them build a stronger relationship with *their* clients, local agents will become more enthusiastic about introducing them to the developer.

In some instances, enlisting the aid of brokers outside the local area may make sense. Be cautious, however. Arrangements with faraway brokers designed to overcome a weak local market have been tried for years without much success.

EDUCATION FOR THE SALES STAFF

Sales and leasing agents should be firmly grounded in the four primary components of business education, but what many developers forget is the need for sales and leasing agents to receive continuing professional education. By its very nature, real estate sales is characterized by rejection and failure. Attempted sales far surpass completed sales, and the number of prospects far surpasses the number of buyers. Many more selling days end in defeat than in victory. Keeping salespeople happy and motivated thus becomes a challenge. A traditional way of dealing with this problem has been compensating salespeople with commissions, hoping that the possibility of a substantial carrot will inspire superior effort. A more consistent approach, however, is building salespeoples' professional capability through continuing education. Two benefits occur. First, the salesperson's professional skills are increased. Second, the increase in professional skills almost always brings with it a corresponding increase in self-confidence and motivation (bringing obvious benefits for the developer). A wise developer takes advantage of these benefits by making sure that continuing sales education is an integral part of the marketing and sales system—whether an in-house staff or an outside agency is used.

To sell a product well, an agent must fully understand the product. Recognizing this fact, most developers provide some sort of orientation program for new agents. It would be difficult to go too far in this endeavor, for every detail about the project's design and excellence that can be communicated to salespeople becomes ammunition for their use with prospects.

Most developers also acknowledge that any real estate sale or leasing transaction could well take the prospect into unfamiliar financial territory. For this reason, the agent must be able to act as a financial guide, leading the prospect to a rational and comfortable decision among possibly confusing and conflicting alternatives.

The need to provide education for salespeople about the specific skills of selling is less well understood. The profession of selling is built upon the ability of salespeople to establish clear and compelling communication with prospects. Most often, doing so is helped by establishing as much personal rapport as possible with the prospect as soon as possible. Prospects who feel comfortable with their sales agent and who are convinced that they are sincerely interested in their points of view are prospects much more likely to buy or lease the product.

Building rapport with prospective buyers generally requires breaking down the prospect's emotional defenses against being sold something. Prospects usually perceive themselves to be at risk, believing that such a negotiation could be critically important to them. They want to get as much information as possible from the sales agent without revealing much about themselves, their needs, and their motives. The sales agent's challenge is almost the opposite. Building rapport with the prospect requires the agent to learn as much as possible about the prospect as an individual.

Many training courses incorporate some type of classifying personalities into the sales method. Based on the idea that salespeople can identify a prospect's comfortable manner of behavior, they adapt the presentation to fit the prospect's profile. Reading the prospect's verbal and nonverbal cues in the first few moments allows the agent to place that individual into one of a number of behavioral categories and adapt his own normal style of behavior to the prospect's to lower defensive barriers. The assumption is that different behavioral types are interested in and motivated by distinctly different elements of the product.

A third body of useful knowledge is the technique of negotiation. If the prospect perceives the two parties to be involved in negotiation from the very beginning, then they are. Many of the lessons that have been learned during negotiations, either between nations or between management and labor, are directly applicable to negotiations in real estate sales and leasing. Understanding where power comes from and how to use it can give salespeople a tremendous advantage. Likewise, understanding classic maneuvers and how best to counter them will make some of the toughest situations appear elementary.

All of these techniques apply to the general objective of fostering better communications between the humans involved on either side of a real estate sales presentation, and they are adaptations of techniques that are one foundation of an education in business management. Including them in the education of sales agents can raise the team members' professional capabilities.

Defining the target market and creating a product specifically suited to it are fundamental to successful real estate sales. Market research defines the target market in economic and demographic terms. Understanding the psychographic profile of target markets is a well-established principle in marketing consumer products that is only beginning to affect real estate, yet it represents an extremely powerful component of marketing knowledge that salespeople can use to great effect.

Just as traditional demographic analysis allows salespeople to group customers on the basis of age, sex, income, and family size, psychographic analysis allows them to segment the overall population into groups who share the same general outlook on life. It then becomes possible to design new houses that incorporate the features and functions members of particular psychographic groups desire.

Knowing what customers want as individuals allows sales agents to present the product so that it meets needs customers may not even perceive they have. This principle is the whole basis of psychographic marketing: creating products to meet the strongly felt needs of an identified target market segment and then presenting those products to that target so that their unrealized needs are satisfied just as their explicit needs are.

SALES OPERATIONS

Sales operations is where "the rubber meets the road" in marketing and sales, for it is here that individual prospects and sales representatives convert the space that has been created into revenue. Organizing to accomplish that task is a critical activity itself, and perhaps the developer's most fundamental decision is whether to conduct sales operations with an in-house staff or through an outside agency.

Each has its advantages and disadvantages. Using one's own employees generally provides more control for the developer over the specifics of how the task is accomplished. The developer has the power and the authority to supervise sales

Photo courtesy of David Ferguson

Sometimes an attractively decorated model unit can be the best sales device. This model was used to show condominium units for Vista Montoya, a project for low- and moderate-income households near downtown Los Angeles.

and leasing representatives directly, setting their daily priorities and requiring specific procedures to be followed. On the other hand, these very advantages carry their own costs, both in terms of financial obligations and management.

Perhaps these obligations are the reason so many developers find it advantageous to contract with an outside brokerage agency for sales and leasing. A relatively simple negotiation between developer and broker sets in motion a continuing effort in which the developer may be only superficially involved. The agency is presumed to have special expertise in handling a particular type of product in a particular market and to have a competent and motivated staff. The developer's administrative burden is reduced dramatically, with the agency paid from the proceeds of actual sales.

In sales operations, one of the principal differences between commercial and residential sales is the extent to which active prospecting takes place. In commercial developments, representatives normally identify potential individual members of the target market and contact them directly to initiate the sale.

An enterprising salesperson will spend some time calling on a developer's current clients to see whether they are happy and whether they might be thinking of expanding or relocating their facilities. Lack of attention could send them to a competing project. The developer's existing relationship with them should give him a great advantage if he is not concerned about eroding occupancy in one building to increase it in another. Because the same developer controls both the existing and the prospective lease, timing the move is not so worrisome. It is not uncommon for an asset manager to manage investments for multiple clients, however. In such cases, moving tenants between buildings can create serious conflicts of interest, but keeping up with existing tenants' needs is still a good idea.

The sales staff should also compile a list of firms fitting the profile of the target market and go after them. They need to find out who the targeted firms do business with and note what other businesses are located nearby. They should also call on nearby businesses, because they are already related by location to the primary product to be sold.

If it works, advertising will generate inquiries from additional potential occupants. Their inquiries indicate an existing interest and must be given prompt attention. Calling on interested parties who are responding to advertising is easy. (Calling on current clients is a bit more difficult, because they do not necessarily expect the attention.) But for the remaining potential occupants, "directed prospecting" (also known as "cold calling") must be employed. Calling on current customers and following up on responses to advertising are never enough, however, to cover the target market adequately. Reaching someone new is often the key to extraordinary success in real estate sales.

Successful prospecting requires some advance preparation. The target prospect must be identified, the key person within that organization identified, an appointment with that person made, and the person convinced that he or she is interested in the product. Even then, a considerable amount of time might pass before the contact results in a sale. Patience and positive follow-up are needed and will bear fruit eventually.

Building the Sale

Once an interested prospect has been found, the challenge shifts to making a successful sales presentation. Whether the objective is generating a signed lease or an authorized purchase agreement, a planned sequence for the presentation is always better than improvising, regardless of whether the property is commercial or residential. The agent must identify the prospect's needs and convince him or her that the proffered product will meet them, making sure that the value delivered is at least equal to the price.

Finally, the salesperson must ask for the order. It is this last part that many people find so difficult; it always seems to be too soon to ask. The best salespeople remove this stress from the decision-making process. Following a planned sequence for the presentation guarantees that all the needed information has been presented in a logical order and that ample feedback has been received from the prospect. When the time comes to ask for the order, if the sequence has been followed and the client has received all the necessary information, it will want the agent to ask. If the prospects are not ready to proceed, they would have found some way to terminate the process before this point.

Follow-up

Effective follow-up is essential to any sales transaction. Few sales are closed in the first meeting, and good salespeople work patiently with identified prospects.

In residential sales, following up on presales is intended to encourage return visits to the sales center. The agent should follow a prearranged schedule of written and telephone contacts based on the number of days that have passed since the prospect first visited the sales center. Generally speaking, these contacts should be light and friendly and not oriented toward sales.

For commercial properties, the same general idea holds true with one major exception: the follow-up should increase as the date of the expiration of the prospect's present lease approaches. The initial contact with many excellent prospects could be poorly timed, simply because they are not free to relocate.

Just because an agreement has been reached does not mean that follow-up should cease. One of the most important functions a sales or leasing professional can perform is holding the deal together between signing and moving in. In Florida, for example, the signing of a purchase agreement for a new condominium merely signals the beginning of a 15-day period during which the purchaser can cancel the deal at any time for any reason. This law, reflecting government's continuing role as the developer's partner, merely acknowledges that once people make a decision, they often have second thoughts. It is up to the sales agent to anticipate this event and take steps to prevent it.

After the tenant moves in, follow-up shifts to ascertaining that the space has been delivered in good shape.

It makes no sense to go to the effort and expense of creating a synergistic marketing and sales system if it produces only a one-time contact with a prospect who is never seen or heard from again. It makes no sense to shepherd a prospect to an agreement only to have it fall apart. And it makes no sense to put a prospect into space the team has worked so hard to create only to have him or her become unhappy. The most efficient activity salespeople can undertake to avoid these unfortunate circumstances is to follow up systematically and sensitively.

ACCEPTING THE CHALLENGE OF MARKETING AND SALES

In successful development operations, people come to work early, stay late, work hard, and move fast. Salespeople who are not productive quickly are gone quickly. If salespeople want to avoid failure, they might consider the following suggestions:

1. Learn the product and the customer. Read the feasibility study and the appraisal report for the project. Look at comparable facilities; shop the competitors. Review the plans and specifications for each building under construction. Walk around the property, preferably with someone who can explain its features, functions, and benefits.
2. Know the company's history and its current financial condition. Look for statements of its operating philosophy and plans for the future.
3. Read recent leases and/or purchase agreements. They will show how business is done and with whom. Differences among recent agreements indicate areas of frequent negotiation.
4. Get to know the company's principal suppliers.
5. Estimate where the financial pressures will be in the organization. Compare the current status of the project with the projections included in original plans. Pressure will most assuredly be directed toward operations that are behind schedule, including marketing and sales.
6. Get to know the players on the team. Who controls what in the company? Who is reliable? Where are the territorial lines that should not be crossed?
7. Find out the current status of the relevant local market and apparent market trends. Know how the market is doing and how it is important to potential customers. The local press is a great place to start on both counts.
8. Most important, be professional from the beginning. Work hard. Tell the truth. Never stop learning.
9. And never sell all the lakefront property first.

SUMMARY

This chapter has taken the viewpoint of the marketing specialist and sales or leasing agent. Few people are born salespeople, but many people can learn marketing and *everyone*, whether consumer or supplier of space, should understand what makes space appealing, marketable, and valuable to its users.

NOTE

1. The term "Realtor" is used in its broad sense in this chapter to refer to active members of the real estate sales community.

Chapter 20

A Summary and a Note About the Future

Decisions about the development of real property are critical to the future functioning of our society, because the largest portion of the nation's wealth is invested in real property. The better the development decisions made today, the better tomorrow's built environment. The eight-stage model of the real estate development process discussed throughout this text is a flexible strategic tool that allows developers to make better decisions today—to see the whole while focusing on a particular decision.

The logic behind the model is clearly financial, but the motivation comes from the market. Development involves complex production and many different kinds of interpersonal relationships, yet all of them respond to market segments and the consumers who express their preferences.

A complete understanding of the development process is impossible without historical perspective, for history allows us to understand where we have been and how we have arrived at the present. As such, history is a useful tool in predicting the future, and development is always a forward-looking activity based on knowledge and experience drawn from the past. Because constructed space can be ex-

pected to last several decades, the long-term historical perspective is important in anticipating what society will want over the next several decades (see Figure 20-1).

Decision makers begin with a framework that includes this historical background as well as a set of basic management tools (finance, marketing, production, and organizational behavior). In addition, newspapers, newsletters, and personal contacts keep them up to date on the market where they work. With this background, the process begins with a search for the right idea. What type of space provided over time with associated services will best serve consumers during the long expected life of the real estate? In the second stage of the development process, decision makers refine the initial idea physically, financially, and legally but always keep the total marketing concept in mind. Developers seek to determine, first, what consumers will want, second, how to produce that product, and, finally, how to convince potential consumers that the product satisfies their needs.

The public sector has always been and will continue to be a partner in the development process. The public sector provides the infrastructure necessary for any particular development to function. Because the public sector is responsible for infrastructure and protecting the public interest in development, it becomes involved in the regulation and financing of many aspects of the development process (see Figure 20-2). Because real estate develop-

---

FIGURE 20-1

A HISTORICAL LOOK AT THE FUTURE OF DEVELOPMENT

The long view—from the past and into the future—yields a portrait of recurring patterns as well as entirely new circumstances. For example, the fact that real estate development has slowed from its dizzying pace of the mid-1980s is certainly not a new phenomenon. Real estate is a cyclical business, and it has always experienced the inevitable busts that follow the booms. What is different today is the extent of overbuilding in many markets and among products. Typically, during downturns of the past four decades, the development pendulum would swing back again within two years. This time, however, the supply of available office space, hotel rooms, strip shopping centers, and residential condominiums compared to projected demand is so excessive that it may take the better part of a decade to restore some balance in the market. Nevertheless, while overbuilding was far more extensive in the 1980s than in the 1950s, 1960s, or 1970s, the situation is still much better than it was at the beginning of the 1930s. With the economic impacts of the Great Depression, real estate markets got so far out of line that virtually no new private office buildings were constructed in most urban areas for over 20 years.

One important difference between earlier cycles—all the way back to the 18th century—and the contemporary situation is that the more severe real estate crashes from the 1790s to the 1930s were generally accompanied by a major panic in the financial system. Today, even with federal regulators' recent tightening of credit standards and the crisis of the savings and loan industry, our financial system continues to be relatively stable, as it has been since World War II. Indeed, pension funds' and other institu-

tional investors' new and growing participation in real estate development and ownership has introduced an added element of stability that was missing during the 1930s, when the widespread default of privately insured mortgage bonds led to a long-term withdrawal of private capital from real estate. New financial institutions and global investors will bring many structural changes to real estate development in the 1990s as they did during the 1980s, but they will also help keep the money flowing in ways that are much less volatile than in the past.

Sometimes history repeats itself, with financial instruments of the 1980s like mortgage-backed securities resembling innovations of the 1920s, and new development ideas and practices for the 1990s that include a return to neotraditional street grids in suburban subdivisions and nostalgic main street storefront designs for new shopping malls. Yet at the same time, recent and projected demographic patterns of a rapidly aging population and nontraditional households (such as single-parent families) combined with the challenge of a newly defined set of environmental problems suggest that we may be witnessing the creation of more radically different forms and processes of development than ever before. The prospects for a genuine renaissance in the design and use of space—for a rebirth of the visionary aspects of real estate development—loom large. Further stimulating these prospects is the forthcoming restructuring and increasing professionalization within the real estate industry. Certainly, the growth of graduate school education in real estate development will enhance the physical and institutional innovation and help make the history of the coming decade a great deal more exciting than it may appear at first glance.

FIGURE 20-2
GOVERNMENT POLICIES AND PROGRAMS IN THE 1990s

"Development should pay its own way" is the axiom that guides the move toward new impact fees, more creative exactions, and more complex types of taxing districts. Over the past two decades, federal and state governments have gradually reduced their capital spending on public facilities. Consequently, developers can expect to bear an increasing proportion of the costs of planning, constructing, and even managing improvements to infrastructure to serve their developments.

Local governments, faced with many pressures for increased spending on social programs, have generally not stepped in to make up the shortfall. Instead, they have tended to shift costs to the private sector, either directly through impact fees and exactions or indirectly through greater use of special taxing districts. In some areas, this shift in funding has expanded to agreements for maintenance of completed facilities.

More communities are also enacting regulations that require extensive reviews for concerns like site and building design and environmental impacts or anything that might be deemed unpredictable. While the concerns are legitimate, the quite general standards and criteria in these laws often allow local officials to freely interpret their application to specific projects. Thus, the rule of law formerly provided by zoning by right is giving way to more subjective judgments that can be highly influenced by special interests. Developers may find it necessary to tailor their projects to shifting community attitudes rather than the letter of the local ordinances.

One consequence of the burgeoning growth-management movements is that many local governments have been required to adopt plans consistent with the state's objectives and standards for managing growth, thereby forcing local jurisdictions to clearly provide regulations for development to fit in their plans. Plans will therefore be less susceptible to short-term whims of elected officials and special interest groups, and developers will presumably be able to better predict how local regulations will be applied to their properties.

One final consideration for the future is that the courts appear to be allowing greater latitude in the content of local government regulations but at the same time insist on more responsible linking of regulations to public policies. In recent decades, courts have been more lenient in allowing restrictions on development for a variety of public purposes like environmental and historical preservation, affordable housing, and aesthetic concerns. Recent cases have hinted, however, that courts will be scrutinizing local actions more closely to determine that they are based on well-defined public interests, documented in detailed studies and plans. Developers therefore may be subject to increasingly restrictive regulations but may find courts more receptive to challenges asserting inadequate bases for public actions.

---

ment is such a large portion of the nation's economic activity, it is no small wonder that the public sector partner often takes a proactive role in seeking to foster a higher quality of life. At times, the public sector goes beyond its regulatory and financial roles to motivate new development.

The feasibility study is the primary tool for analysis and risk control in real estate development. It focuses attention on the critical decision during the development period: does the expected value of the project exceed its expected cost? Like all decisions made during development, the answer to this question is driven by the market. The authors expect that the rigor and complexity of due diligence necessary for a feasibility study will increase dramatically over the next decade and that a greater effort will be made to understand risk and return over the life of the investment. That effort will come about because investors are more cautious in overbuilt markets and because public policy is oriented toward avoiding a repeat of the S&L debacle. Both of these pressures will force developers to think more about the future and how the space and services they provide will serve consumers over the long expected life of the real estate asset. As development companies respond to such pressures, development will become a more sophisticated business.

Successful development requires good management throughout the process, especially after construction begins and time pressure becomes intense. As the project's prime mover and coordinator, the developer must carefully control all its aspects, making certain that financing, marketing, and construction are successfully integrated. Real estate is inherently interdisciplinary, and during the construction process, the developer's primary mission is to coordinate the many different people and activities necessary to produce a successful project.

Once the project has been constructed, the property manager is charged with asset management, with ensuring that the desired level of services is provided. Asset management includes traditional functions of property management as well as an awareness that corporate and institutional investors' needs must be continually addressed and their ownership of properties assessed in terms of complete corporate holdings.

Closely linked with ongoing management are continuing sales and leasing. The final aspect of the total marketing concept is convincing consumers that the product does in fact satisfy their needs. In overbuilt markets like those of today, sales and leasing are probably the most critical elements in any development.

All of the activities of the development process, including asset management and sales and leasing, are forward-looking activities. Using the past as a predictor, developers make decisions about the future. No one can know the future with certainty, but one can anticipate what lies ahead by rigorously analyzing the present. Certainly a failure to analyze adequately known facts and clear trends was in large part responsible for the S&L crisis.

While it is not possible to know the future, it *is* possible to extrapolate current trends and to anticipate reactions to those trends and interactions among them. For example, in virtually every region of the United States, the length of the development process is increasing. No one is predicting a reversal of that trend, because the reasons for its protraction have not gone away—changes in financing, a lengthening of the regulatory process, a decrease in the amount of developable land and increase in its cost, more stringent environmental controls, and more involvement by citizens. The ever-increasing amount of regulatory control over the process will affect developers in a number of ways. Due diligence during the development process will focus more and more on a rigorous analysis of future projects so that developments will more likely serve tomorrow's customers. Exactly how today's trends, reactions to those trends, and interactions among the trends point to specific development opportunities is an entrepreneur's job—and successful real property development requires a great deal of entrepreneurship.

Keep in mind, however, that this chapter is not intended to look at specific development trends. Any such attempt will be quickly outdated, and many annual trend reports are available from firms that specialize in forecasting. It is possible within this textbook, though, to identify at least the kinds of trends that developers should keep an eye on.

- **Demographics**. Baby boomers and new patterns of immigration are changing the demographic makeup of this country. As development markets become tighter throughout the United States, developers are realizing the need to direct projects toward much more specific market niches than ever before. And an increasingly sophisticated understanding and use of demographics facilitate it. Housing developments for the elderly are a good example of earlier naivete about demographics. It did not take long for developers and marketers to discover that building housing for the increasingly aging population was not enough. Instead, they had to break the market for such housing into many smaller segments—fully independent living, semi-independent living, semidependent living, and dependent living, for example. This type of segmentation is easier with demographic analyses.

- **Lifestyles.** Understanding where and how people choose to live is essential to successful development. For example, "nonfamily" households outnumber married couples with children in the United States. Thus, the number of households is growing steadily, yet the growth is having a negative effect on homeownership: a larger percentage of married couples own a house than do nonfamily households. Imagine the implications this trend might have for residential development.

- **Environment.** The globalization of world economies has proven, among other things, that environmental issues are no longer local. If, for example, fluorocarbon emissions from refrigerants and aerosols in North America gradually deplete the protective ozone layer over Australia, pollution controls are no longer a local issue. Closer to home, environmental issues, particularly hazardous wastes, can sometimes make or break a project. If property is found to be contaminated, cleanup can be exorbitantly expensive and make development infeasible. These issues will not simply disappear. Keeping abreast of environmental legislation and findings can help developers anticipate possible situations in the future.

- **Technology.** No one needs to be reminded of the role of technology today, for it is easy to identify a handful of technological advances that are now integrated into daily life. Calculators, personal computers, compact disc players, and automobiles all seemed amazingly advanced when first introduced. Now they are all taken for granted. What new creation is on the horizon that will change the way we live? Informed predictions of technological advances may put one developer a step ahead in the future.

- **The development process.** Developing real estate in the 1990s is not like developing real estate in the 1970s. So many other sectors are tied up with development that changes within those sectors often have an immediate and pronounced effect on the development industry (see Figure 20-3). Take financing, for example. The S&L crisis and related credit crunch forced an immediate slowdown in the industry. Keeping up with the development industry and the important issues that affect it is crucial to maintaining a successful development firm.

This list is in no way complete. So many other issues are of prime importance—state and local politics, economic indicators, regional and metropolitan area growth or decline, among others. Thinking and reading about trends of all kinds help developers anticipate how we will live into the next century and therefore what their development plans for that same time period will be. While it is absolutely certain that reflection on these trends is important to successful development, no one knows exactly how they will proceed in the future.

This book is largely about *controllable* factors in development and largely about aspects of the business that can be taught. Whit Morrow, the developer who was profiled throughout the text, shared his real life with readers, reminding them that, first, real estate development is an art, and, second, that it requires some luck. In working out the interactive design and construction of the Europa Center, he was slowed down, allowing his competitor (University Tower, which was eventually foreclosed on by its lender) to fill the same market niche first. At the same time in an overbuilt market, a Class A building had no fallback position; thus, Fraser Morrow Daniels was both unlucky and a step slow in reaching the market.

Today, Whit Morrow is a senior executive with a medical laboratory and is happy in an environment where professionalism counts more than art or luck. Some observers think his moving into salaried management is age-appropriate behavior for a man with four children. Others think he'll be back.

FIGURE 20-3
DEVELOPERS FACE THE 1990s

Development firms are changing their organization for the 1990s, in part because the developers who run the firms have their own hunches about what will happen in the marketplace in the next few years. As they immerse themselves in day-to-day issues, they form opinions about what will happen to developers and the development process over the next decade.

In late 1989, ULI asked nine well-known developers to give their thoughts on what changes could be expected in the process over the next few years. They all agreed that much will change within development firms and with the process of development; they could not, however, agree on what and how things will change. J. Ronald Terwilliger, managing partner for Trammell Crow Residential in Atlanta, predicted that mid-sized developers would not survive the competitive nineties. "The bigger developers who are geographically diversified and better capitalized should be able to survive, if not prosper. At the other end of the spectrum, smaller developers, who carry less overhead and are more flexible, more in tune with local market conditions, should survive."

John Temple, president and CEO of VMS/Temple, Boca Raton, however, holds a different view: "It takes a mix to accomplish the business. The larger firms have as much to worry about because they tend to get cumbersome and musclebound, thus more apt to make mistakes that create failure."

In any case, according to William McCall, chairman and CEO of McCall & Almy, Inc., Boston, "in today's overbuilt markets, development firms, small, medium, and large, are having trouble covering their overhead. I don't think that many development firms are capitalized to cover their daily cash flow needs while the 20 percent vacancy rate that's on the market gets absorbed."

Sensitivity to changes in products will also be increasingly important. While developers used to build 500 of the same kind of unit, they now tend to build 40 or 50. Overall, product types appear to have shorter and shorter lives, and variety must be greater.

All nine developers agreed on the danger of overbuilding and the acknowledged continuing of what Willard Rouse, III, Rouse & Associates, Philadelphia, called the "herd instinct." McCall agreed that continued overbuilding is inevitable, because "so many people are in the business, ready to start building at the first sign of anything good."

"I'm afraid we don't have very long memories," noted Terwilliger. "I'd like to give the lenders and us credit for learning. But any discipline exercised will have to be by the financial community, because I doubt developers in the aggregate are capable of much discipline."

Most developers also agreed that citizens' participation and outside involvement in the development process will continue. "If you're going to develop, you need to be far more attuned than ever to the local scene," said Charlie Shaw, Charles H. Shaw Company, Chicago. "You can't simply go into town and get a local zoning attorney who

EUROPA CENTER

A FINAL WORD

The Europa Center was sold in early 1989 to a Chapel Hill family that has been great benefactors of the overall community. The price was fair at this stage of development, allowing the owner/financial institution to come close to breaking even and giving the investor significant benefits over the long term.

No profits were available for distribution to partners. It was disappointing for us, but when I look at the building, I think I would have done the project any-

FIGURE 20-3 (continued)

knows the system to represent you. It goes far deeper than that and therefore requires more energy, more time, more capital. And you can no longer generalize as easily—that what worked in Washington, D.C., will work in Chicago, or what worked in lower Manhattan will work in upper Manhattan."

This continuing regulation, particularly that in the form of impact fees, will continue to slow development but will also become more consistently applied. Terwilliger believes that "jurisdictions will be pressured to be less arbitrary, and so impact fees will become less uncertain for developers."

The role of foreign investment in the overall real estate picture will continue—and even increase—according to Sheridan Ing, Sheridan Ing Partners Hawaii. "All parts of the United States need capital. We used to be a capital-surplus country; we're now a capital-deficit country. We'll see more people from Singapore, Taiwan, and South Korea, because they have no place else to put their money. They think more of the United States than we do ourselves." At the same time, he believes, foreign investors will work with U.S. companies and workers, fostering business growth in the United States.

Along with the change in who is investing in development will be a change in what is being developed and where. Melvin Simon, Melvin Simon & Associates, Indianapolis, noted that the 1980s saw the resurrection of many CBDs through retail projects. But, unaccompanied by a return of residents to downtowns, retail projects will not halt the downward slide of CBDs for long. Many downtowns, especially smaller ones, do not have the critical mass for the projects being planned and built in them, Simon says. Development that was formerly concentrated in downtown areas will shift to areas now known as suburbs. "I'm not sure I know what a suburban area is," said Wayne Ratkovich of the Ratkovich Company, Los Angeles. "Some areas that we used to think of as suburbs are bigger than our downtowns. You can hardly call such areas suburban anymore, because they're urbanized. We'll have clusters of concentration in a variety of areas as opposed to a single, strongly dominant area."

This realignment of our urban areas is just one type of shift we can expect. Another is one brought about by sky-rocketing housing costs, which many developers believe is reaching crisis proportions. "You will see a lot of industry locating to markets where housing is affordable and infrastructure available," according to Fritz Grupe, Jr., of the Grupe Company, Stockton, California. "More than they have historically, jobs will follow housing costs," in a reversal of the old truism that housing goes where the jobs are.

Source: Matthew Kiell, "Looking to the 1990s: Developers Take a Long View and See Subtle yet Surprising Changes in the 1990s," *Urban Land,* December 1989, pp. 8–14.

way, because it was interesting and exciting. Our final product is gorgeous. It's the best office building in town. Everything about the Europa Center is right.

It is very difficult to have a short-term perspective about real estate and still make money. After we build a project and it's occupied, there is no reason for people to continue to pay us to be involved in it, so we have to move on to different projects. As a small company, we didn't have the equity position for long-term projects. Profits from building management are not significant for a company like ours. It would have been nice to have developed 10 buildings and ended with a continuing

Photo courtesy of Jim Sink, Artech, Inc.

Photo courtesy of Jim Sink, Artech, Inc.

The Europa Center has the advantage of many corner offices, providing much light for occupants.

The completed Europa Center.

source of income from managing all 10, but that's not the situation we were in.

The building's capital structure, financing, and ownership evolved in a way that was not conducive to long-term ownership. We made the decision to sell the building to an investor whose objective was to manage the building over the long term, which was different from our objectives. A company with a different financial structure might value long-term growth more than it values immediate cash. Banks and small development companies like ours are not in a position to take advantage of the long-term benefits of owning a building, even though it might be worth a whole lot more 10 years from now than it is today.

The lender decided that it wanted to sell the building to recover money. A lending institution that owns a property values it differently because of the accounting rules associated with lending. It has to depreciate and write things off and keep reserves against mutual losses, so that owning a building is not as valuable to that institution as it might be to some other kind of institution. Owning the building negatively affected its ability to lend money. The lender knew it could make more in the short term by lending money than it could by managing a building.

I have very mixed emotions about the sale of the Europa Center. While the long-term prospects for ownership are very good, we had evolved to a point where the lending institution had full control and it was more advantageous for it to sell than to hold the property for future marginal gain. Instead of selling the building, we might have restructured the financing so that we remained as owners and just replaced the lender, but a separate question arises about whether or not our small company could have structured itself so that it would be advantageous to stay involved. In my judgment, it worked out better to sell the building outright and not to be in the building management business.

The investor occupied the remaining 20 percent of the first building and imme-

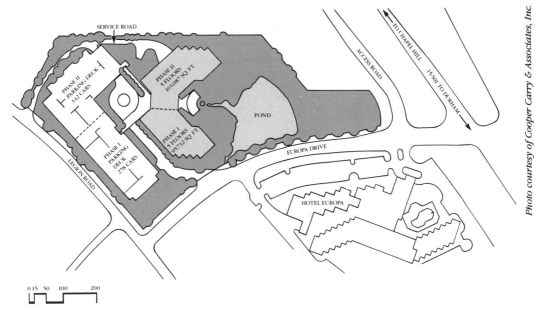

Labels within the image:
SERVICE ROAD

PHASE II
PARKING DECK
342 CARS

PHASE II
5 FLOORS
103,087 SQ. FT.

PHASE I
PARKING
DECK
278 CARS

PHASE I
5 FLOORS
95,742 SQ. FT.

POND

LEGION ROAD

EUROPA DRIVE

ACCESS ROAD

TO CHAPEL HILL

15-501 TO DURHAM

HOTEL EUROPA

0 15 50 100 200

Photo courtesy of Cooper Carry & Associates, Inc.

Site plan showing Phase Two of the Europa Center, being built by the new owners based on original plans developed by Fraser Morrow Daniels. Phase Two will contain an additional 103,000 square feet of office space and accommodate an additional 342 cars.

diately began construction of the approved second phase, a building of 103,000 square feet. The town managers or citizens had no objections; they now regard Europa Center as attractive and beneficial to the community. The local leasing market is better, and Europa Center has no competition from new buildings. With other highly respected occupants in place, prospective tenants now feel very secure that Europa Center is a fine building in a superior location. The completed site is truly spectacular.

SUMMARY

This chapter only touches on what future developers need to consider as they think about upcoming opportunities for development. Even as developers work on one project, they always have to think about the future. If readers come away with only one piece of advice regarding the future, it is to read as much as possible and talk to as many people as possible who are involved in development or will be users of development. Keeping attuned to business cycles and cycles in demand can give developers an edge that could make a difference between a successful development and an unsuccessful one.

While developers might not continually address societal trends and changes in their daily operations, over the long run trends and changes have a tremendous effect on what developers build and where they build. As providers of space, developers respond to the needs and wants of consumers, and sensitivity to underlying shifts in preferred locations, commuting habits, customs and cultural orientations, and household characteristics will be important to effective decision making.

The developer's job is to anticipate what society will want from its built environment—one of the most exciting and challenging tasks of development.

Bibliography

Part VII. Continuing to Make It Work

ASSET AND PROPERTY MANAGEMENT

Bell, Michael. "The Importance of Sound Fixed Asset Management." *Industrial Development* 156, January/February 1987, pp. 11-13.

Briggs, Mary M. "Real Estate Opportunities for Institutional Investors." *Real Estate Finance Journal* 7, Winter 1990, pp. 67-71.

Brown, H. James, and Christopher E. Herbert. "Local Government Real Estate Asset Management: The New England Experience." *Land Lines*, December 1989, pp. 1-2.

Brown, Robert Kevin. "Corporate Asset Management: Hidden Profits in Real Estate." *Valuation Research*, Fall/Winter 1985.

———. *Corporate Real Estate: Executive Strategies for Profit Making.* Homewood, Ill.: Dow Jones–Irwin, 1979.

The Changing Office Workplace. Washington, D.C.: Building Owners and Managers Association/ULI–the Urban Land Institute, 1986.

Collins, Webster A., et al. *Real Estate: A Hidden Corporate Asset.* Chicago: American Society of Real Estate Counselors, 1986.

Cushman, Robert F., and Neal I. Rodin, eds. *Property Management Handbook: A Practical Guide to Real Estate Management.* New York: John Wiley & Sons, 1985.

Downs, James C., Jr. *Principles of Real Estate Management.* 12th ed. Chicago: Institute of Real Estate Management, 1980.

Goodman, Daniel, and Richard Rusdorf. *The Landlord's Handbook: A Complete Guide to Managing Small Residential Properties.* Chicago: Longman Financial Services, 1989.

Gordon, Edward S. *How to Market Space in an Office Building.* Boston: Warren, Gorham & Lamont, 1976.

Hickman, Ron. "Institutional Investors and the Residential Market." *Real Estate Finance Journal* 7, Winter 1990, pp. 72-76.

Irwin, Robert. *Handbook of Property Management.* New York: McGraw-Hill, 1985.

Jaffe, Austin J. *Property Management in Real Estate Investment Decision Making.* Lexington, Mass.: Lexington Books, 1979.

Jussim, Seth E. "The City of Chicago Looks at Its Real Estate." *Urban Land* 48, November 1989, pp. 21-23.

Kyle, Robert C. *Property Management.* 2d ed. Chicago: Real Estate Education Co., 1984.

McMahan, John. *Property Development.* 2d ed. New York: McGraw-Hill, 1989.

Managing the Office Building. Chicago: Institute of Real Estate Management, 1985.

Managing the Shopping Center. Chicago: Institute of Real Estate Management, 1983.

Moody, Frank. "What Institutions Need and Expect from an Asset Manager." *Real Estate Finance Journal* 7, Winter 1990, pp. 90–92.

Nourse, Hugh O. *Managerial Real Estate: Corporate Real Estate Asset Management.* Englewood Cliffs, N.J.: Prentice-Hall, 1989.

——. "Using Real Estate Asset Management to Improve Strategic Performance." *Industrial Development* 155, May/June 1986, pp. 1–7.

Parker, Frank J., ed. *Institutional Real Estate Strategies.* Washington, DC: ULI-the Urban Land Institute, 1988.

Parker, Rosetta E. *Housing for the Elderly: The Handbook for Managers.* Chicago: Institute of Real Estate Management, 1984.

Pederson, Rick. "Establishing a Real Estate Asset Management System." *Management Information Services Report* 21 (4), April 1989.

The Property Manager's Relationship with Developers and Lenders. Chicago: Institute of Real Estate Management, 1986.

Schimpff, Carol R., and Robert M. Fair. "The Emerging Science of Real Estate Asset Management." *Real Estate Finance Journal* 6, Summer 1989, pp. 10–16.

Schwanke, Dean. *Smart Buildings and Technology-Enhanced Real Estate.* 2 vols. Washington, D.C.: ULI-the Urban Land Institute, 1985.

Silverman, Robert A., et al., eds. *Corporate Real Estate Handbook: Strategies for Improving Bottom-Line Performance.* New York: McGraw-Hill, 1987.

Veale, Peter R. *Managing Corporate Real Estate Assets: A Survey of U.S. Real Estate Executives.* Cambridge, Mass.: MIT, Laboratory of Architecture and Planning, 1988.

Walters, William, Jr. *The Practice of Real Estate Management for the Experienced Property Manager.* Chicago: Institute of Real Estate Management, 1979.

Zeckhauser, Sally, and Robert Silverman. "Rediscovering Your Company's Real Estate." *Harvard Business Review* 62, January/February 1983, pp. 111–17.

Organizations

The American Institute of Corporate Asset Management
1150 Century Building
Pittsburgh, Pennsylvania 15222
(412) 391-9726

Institute of Real Estate Management
430 North Michigan Avenue, 7th Floor
Chicago, Illinois 60611
(312) 661-1930

National Association of Corporate Real Estate Executives
440 Columbia Drive, Suite 100
West Palm Beach, Florida 33409
(407) 683-8111

Pension Real Estate Association
1129 20th Street, N.W., Suite 705
Washington, D.C. 20036
(202) 296-4141

Periodicals

Journal of Portfolio Management (quarterly). New York: Institutional Investor.

Journal of Property Management (bimonthly). Chicago: Institute of Real Estate Management of the National Association of Realtors.

National Real Estate Investor (monthly). Regular column on asset management. Atlanta: Communications Channels, Inc.

Real Estate Finance Journal (quarterly). New York: Warren, Gorham & Lamont.

SALES AND MARKETING

Arnold, Alvin L. *Real Estate Syndication Manual: Investment, Tax, and Marketing Strategies.* Boston: Warren, Gorham & Lamont, 1984.

Brown, Donald R., and Wendell G. Matthews. *Real Estate Advertising Handbook.* Chicago: Realtors National Marketing Institute, 1980.

Calero, Henry H., and Bob Oskam. *Negotiate the Deal You Want.* New York: Dodd, Mead & Co., 1983.

Clark Parker Associates. *Marketing New Homes*. Washington, D.C.: National Association of Home Builders, 1989.

——. *Selling New Homes*. Washington, D.C.: National Association of Home Builders, 1989.

Conway, H. McKinley. *Marketing Industrial Buildings and Sites*. Atlanta: Conway Data, 1980.

Hines, Mary Alice. *Marketing Real Estate Internationally*. New York: Quorum Books, 1988.

Karrass, Gary. *Negotiate to Close*. New York: Simon & Schuster, 1985.

Merrill, David, and Roger Reid. *Personal Styles and Effective Performances*. New York: Chilton Book Co., 1981.

Messner, Stephen D. *Marketing Investment Real Estate*. 3d ed. Chicago: Realtors National Marketing Institute, 1985.

Mitchell, Arnold. *Nine American Lifestyles. New York: Warner Books, 1984.*

National Association of Industrial and Office Parks. *Marketing Office and Industrial Parks*. Arlington, Va.: Author, 1983.

Nierenberg, Gerald I. *The Art of Negotiating*. New York: Pocket Books, 1984.

Roberts, Duane F. *Marketing and Leasing of Office Space*. Chicago: Institute of Real Estate Management, 1986.

Scavo, Janet. *The Condominium Home: A Special Marketing Challenge*. Chicago: Realtors National Marketing Institute, 1982.

Senn, Mark A. *Commercial Real Estate Leases: Preparation and Negotiation*. New York: John Wiley & Sons, 1985.

Shenkel, William M. *Marketing Real Estate*. 2d ed. Englewood Cliffs, N.J.: Prentice-Hall, 1985.

Wenner, S. Albert. *Promotion and Marketing for Shopping Centers: A Basic Approach*. New York: International Council of Shopping Centers, 1980.

THE FUTURE

Naisbett, John. *Megatrends*. New York: Warner Books, 1988.

Naisbett, John, and Patricia Aburdene. *Megatrends 2000*. New York: Warner Brothers, 1990.

ULI Development Trends. Washington, D.C.: ULI–the Urban Land Institute, annual.

Periodicals

American Demographics (monthly). Ithaca, N.Y.: American Demographics.

Emerging Trends (monthly). New York: Real Estate Research Corporation and The Equitable.

Future Economic Trends (weekly). Santa Barbara, Cal.: Economic Behavior Institute.

Futurist (bimonthly). Bethesda, Md.: World Future Society.

Omni (monthly). New York: Penthouse International.

APPENDICES
AND
INDEX

Appendix A

Federal Participation In the Secondary Mortgage Market

Creating a secondary market for residential mortgages has been one of the great successes of the public/private partnership in real estate finance. Today, it is almost impossible to imagine the homebuilding and home mortgage industries in the United States without the federal secondary market players. Three federal and quasi-federal agencies guaranteed the overwhelming majority (98 percent) of residential pass-through certificates (publicly offered secondary market instruments) between 1975 and 1987. The aggregate value of pass-through certificates from January 1975 through March 1987 was $580 billion, equal to 34 percent of all loans for single-family houses outstanding.

In the 1930s, Congress tried and failed to get private capital to form national mortgage associations as a secondary market for FHA-insured mortgages. Congress then authorized the Reconstruction Finance Corporation to form a subsidiary called the Federal National Mortgage Association, familiarly known as "Fannie Mae." The underlying purpose of Fannie Mae and its younger siblings, the Government National Mortgage Association (GNMA, or "Ginnie Mae") and the Federal Home Loan Mortgage Corporation (FHLMC, or "Freddie Mac"), was to provide mortgage lenders with fresh infusions of capital by buying their existing mortgages, thereby stimulating them to lend again and to use this new liquidity as a basis for lengthening loan terms (ultimately to 30 years). Longer loan terms

and infusions of capital (along with FHA and private mortgage insurance) helped raise homeownership in the United States from 48 percent in 1930 to 65.6 percent of all households by 1980.

The secondary mortgage market exploded in the 1970s upon Ginnie Mae's introduction of pass-through certificates. Until then, Fannie Mae had bought mortgages and held them in its own portfolio, funding these activities by selling bonds to institutional investors. Ginnie Mae's innovation was to put the federal guarantee on a new security (the pass-through certificate) that entitled the owner to a share of a large pool of mortgages. Ginnie Mae did not hold the pool of mortgages in its own portfolio; rather, the owner of the certificate received payments of interest and principal proportional to its shares from the mortgage originator. The pass-through certificates met with enormous acceptance:

The aggregate amount of mortgage pool certificates has ballooned since 1980. An instrument virtually untried in 1970, these pass-throughs accounted for $92 billion of mortgage debt in 1979 and more than $580 billion of such debt by March 1987—almost 34 percent of the single-family home loans outstanding. Pass-through certificates added more than $260 billion to the mortgage market in 1986. This flow, excluding pass-throughs backed by seasoned loans, totaled almost $200 billion, representing 45 percent of all new mortgage production. In comparison, these agencies had just a 10 percent to 15 percent share of the mortgage market in the late 1970s.[1]

Pass-throughs succeeded so well because they were in small denominations ($25,000) and because a federal agency guaranteed timely payment of principal and interest if the mortgagor defaulted. The importance of the guarantee explains why only the largest private institutions can issue these securities: they must have investors' confidence in their unconditional ability to make up any shortfall in mortgage collections.

Securitization of residential mortgage debt has expanded to new instruments like collateralized mortgage obligations (CMOs) in 1983 and, most recently, real estate mortgage investment conduits (REMICs) in 1987. The principle is the same as that for pass-through certificates: interest and principal make up the payments to the investor, and the instrument is therefore self-liquidating. What differs is the maturity of the instruments and conformity to provisions of the 1986 tax code. In effect, CMOs and REMICs have expanded the range of investment products created from the raw material of individual home mortgages. Their appeal is tremendous: $84 billion of CMOs were issued in 18 months from 1984 to 1985. Freddie Mac issued 25 percent of CMOs in the first year of the product but then was surpassed by private institutions.

Securitization spread to commercial real estate debt in 1984 when $1.2 billion was financed, growing to approximately $6.3 billion in 1986. All players in this market are private institutions. Fannie Mae, Ginnie Mae, and Freddie Mac do not participate because their public function is to promote housing, not real estate

development in general. In fact, securitization has even spread beyond real estate debt to include securities collateralized by car loans—again issued only by private institutions.

Securitization has boomed for several reasons. Obviously, selling mortgages helps mortgage lenders manage the risk inherent in interest rates. For buyers of securities, liquidity, maturity, and the timeliness of payment guarantees are keys. And the federal guarantee has had a huge impact on the success of mortgage-backed securities.

"The increasing federalization of the mortgage market" is evidenced by "more than 50 percent of annual mortgage production securitized by the federal or quasi-federal agencies" and a tripling of "federal involvement in the housing finance system since 1980."[2] Securitization lowers the cost of money, narrows the spread on loans, and therefore helps more efficient lenders at the expense of the less efficient. How federal involvement will affect beleaguered thrift institutions is a policy question that has not been fully solved. Through securitization, the public/private partnership has spawned a booming market—but one in which not every private player benefits equally.[3]

NOTES

1. Ken Rosen, "Securitization and the Real Estate Market" (New York: Salomon Brothers, 1987), p. 3. This discussion of securitization is drawn for the most part from Rosen's article.

2. Ibid., p. 4.

3. See William B. Brueggeman and Leo D. Stone, *Real Estate Finance*, 8th ed. (Homewood, Ill.: Richard D. Irwin, 1989), for a fuller academic treatment of the institutions and programs involved in the secondary market and securitization in general.

Appendix B
Survival of the Fittest

His company's sales had tripled in two years, growing from $20 million to $60 million. But now the company dominated its local market, and the president wondered how he could maintain growth. Entering other nearby markets was an option, but he worried about lack of control in new markets and about eroding margins in his base market. Would he be trading volume for profit? And was the company prepared for recession?

The three partners, sitting face-to-face around a small table, are tired and tense. The 60-hour work weeks have taken their toll, and there's not enough to show for all the hard work. It's been four years since they started the company and cash flow is still a problem, and their personal draws are barely more than what they were promised when it all started. They have a proven product—rental apartments—but obviously they are doing something wrong. The marketing-oriented partner wants to enter other markets and modify the product, while the operations-oriented partner wants to stay put until they become more profitable. The financially oriented partner is playing his customary role of arbitrator.

He felt great. He had put it all on the line and succeeded beyond his wildest expectations. He had left a protected corporate environment, started from a standstill two years ago, and now

his sales stand at $15 million a year with 35 percent gross margins and a net cash flow well into seven figures. His home market is humming, local competition is sleepy, and national builders haven't yet arrived. Yet he knows he can't grow forever without diversifying or expanding, and he needs to build an organization that can stay together in good times and bad.

On the face of it, these three situations may not seem to have much in common, but all are examples of builders wrestling with strategic issues. In each case, they are trying to determine where they want their companies to go and how they're going to get there.

The primary organizational responsibility of the chief executive officer of a homebuilding company is to consider the strategic questions that will affect the direction the company will take over the next three to five years. In other words, CEOs need to develop and implement a strategic plan. And they should realize the plan probably will determine their company's success or failure.

The fact is, almost every homebuilding company has a strategy. But the strategy is not always consciously formulated and understood. Likewise, every top manager of a homebuilding company has a personal strategy, and usually it is well understood by the individual. Sometimes company strategy and individual strategy are in

455

conflict, so one goal of strategic planning must be to reconcile strategies of key people with the strategy of the firm.

General Electric usually is given credit for instituting strategic planning. That was in the 1950s. Management consulting firms, such as McKinsey & Company, Booz-Allen, Arthur D. Little & Company, and Boston Consulting Group, began to develop specialties in strategic planning. By the 1970s, nearly every major corporation either had established strategic planning departments or used management consulting firms to look at new business opportunities and to evaluate the growth potential of existing business.

However, strategic planning is more the exception than the rule in the housing industry. Ask most builders about long-term strategy, and they'll talk about the next piece of property they

---

FIGURE B-1

FIVE KEY COMPONENTS OF A STRATEGIC PLAN

1. INDUSTRY ROLE—The level of involvement a builder wants to assume in the multistep process of taking a project from raw land to prospective buyers.
2. EXPANSION—The desire to grow, which can be achieved by increasing market share, targeting new market segments, building in new geographic markets, or diversifying.
3. RATIONALIZATION—The flip side of expansion, the process of deciding when and how to change course or even abandon certain market segments or markets as a housing cycle heads down.
4. EFFICIENCY—Lowering production costs and speeding up the development process in response to the time value of money and big up-front costs associated with homebuilding.
5. ORGANIZATION—Most homebuilding firms are organized somewhere along a continuum that has project management at one end (one person has total responsibility for a project) to functional management (different people control different functions) at the other.

---

want to buy. A feeling of helplessness about external factors, particularly interest rates and housing demand, is the primary reason most builders have not bothered with strategic planning.

But if builders want to take as much control as possible over the direction of their companies, consciously developing a strategy is crucial. And perhaps more important, strategic planning can be a key to surviving economic recessions.

Builders who have developed strategic plans have come to understand that a homebuilder's strategy has five key components: industry role, expansion, rationalization, efficiency, and organization (see Figure B-1).

Industry Role. Industry role refers to the level of involvement a builder wants to assume when going from raw land to finished housing and then to the buyer (see Figure B-2). Some builders want to integrate fully, that is, stay deeply involved through the whole process. Others want to be more backwardly integrated, that is, to move away from the consumer and back toward land acquisition and development. The major benefits of backward integration are efficiency and control. Backward integration can be accomplished by hiring specialists to handle market research, architecture, planning, and financing, for example. Or it can take the form of hiring company crews or even erecting a factory for panelized construction.

The major drawback to backward integration is that it involves a larger overhead. And in an industry prone to extreme cycles, large overhead is a big danger during bad times. A builder can lay off staff, but that's disruptive. It's not easy to sell land or lease a housing factory or surplus office space for full value during a housing recession.

Many builders are backward integrating into land development or land speculation, new businesses that are completely different from homebuilding. Land development requires equity and the staying power to hold the land. Marketing is entirely different as well, and buyers often compete with the seller's homebuilding division. Finally, the value added in the land development, that is, the actual means of making money, is usually the ability to get proper zoning, water hookups, public access, and other approvals. Doing that requires far different skills from homebuilding.

Forward integration is good because it brings a builder closer to buyers. However, it can mean competing with companies that help builders and developers sell their products. For example, when land developers forward inte-

THE DEVELOPMENT PROCESS

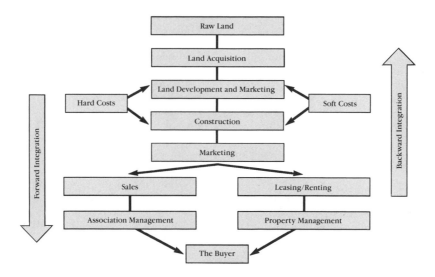

Some builders like to be forwardly integrated, that is, to be involved right through to the customer. Others prefer to be backwardly integrated, away from the consumer and back toward land acquisition and development.

Source: Robert Charles Lesser & Company.

grate into homebuilding, they can end up competing with the same builders who had been buying their lots. Or if builders decide to bring sales in-house, they may be competing with brokers who bring them buyers.

Expansion. Most builders want to grow. And when considering expansion, the second component of strategic planning, the question is always how to do it.

Basically, there are four ways of expanding a homebuilding business:
- Increase market share in an established market;
- Introduce products for new market segments;
- Establish operations in a new geographic market;
- Diversify, into nonresidential or multifamily rental products, for example.

The least risky of all methods of expansion, and one too often overlooked, is to increase share of market in a company's existing marketplace. Risk is relatively low because builders know (or should know) their own markets. While there are probably limits to how much builders can expand in their own markets before competing with themselves, in only a few

markets does any one local company control more than 10 percent of activity. (Ray Ellison, with a 45 percent share of the San Antonio market, and John Crosland Company, with a 25 percent share of the Charlotte market, dominate local markets like no other builders.)

Another low-risk method of expansion is to target new types of buyers. For example, a homebuilder who had been targeting first-time buyers could also seek move-up buyers.

The risk for this type of expansion increases as builders set their sights higher and higher. (It's always harder to please upper-income buyers.) It also is riskier to make the shift from detached to attached (or vice versa) because construction is different, as is marketing strategy. More specifically, builders of single-family housing usually don't have to build standing inventory. On the other hand, attached housing usually has to be built in relatively large phases and at the same time or before the sale of the units, radically altering the cost of carry and increasing the risk.

Moving into new geographic markets is a fairly common method of expansion, but it is considerably riskier than testing new market

457

segments in a builder's home market. Local decision making is an absolute necessity for a homebuilder, so a builder expanding to a new market must decide whether to have top management commute or to hire new managers for the new market site.

Long-time housing industry management consultant Lee Evans has a rule of thumb: a builder should never build more than an hour away from home base. That's especially limiting for a builder with no good markets close to home, but even if expansion is possible, the prospect of managing a decentralized organization is risky. If a builder is in two markets and both markets falter, and this inevitably will happen, the president of the company will have difficult and time-consuming decisions to make.

Diversifying into income-producing properties (apartments, retail space, offices, or mixed-use developments) is the final method of expansion and the riskiest. In essence, it involves learning a whole new business from scratch. A homebuilder first must understand the difference between for-sale and income real estate development. Then, there's potentially different building systems, financing sources, and marketing strategies.

Nonetheless, diversifying into a new business can be attractive. It's one way to build equity, obtain tax shelter, and carry homebuilding operations through bad times. So while it is risky, diversification is one of the best ways to build a stable company.

Diversification should be tried only on familiar territory. In other words, get your act together before you take it on the road. Entering a new market with essentially a new business poses an unacceptable chance of failure.

Finally, there is the question of how to grow. There are basically two methods: make growth and buy growth. "Making growth" means growing internally by increasing land holdings and financing, marketing, and construction capabilities. Making growth offers the advantage of quality control and the disadvantage of slow growth. There is a limit set by the time it takes to hire and train key staff, to how fast a company can grow—even with unlimited financial backing.

"Buying growth" means buying another company. It's riskier because nobody can know exactly what's being bought, no matter how much time is spent studying the acquisition. The major advantage is that growth can be achieved quickly enough to take advantage of perceived opportunities. Of course, there is a middle ground: joint venturing.

Rationalization. Rationalization is the third component of strategic planning, and in homebuilding its invariably the one that's least thought through. Rationalization is in essence the flip side of growth and refers to the process of deciding when and how to back off. It should be understood before the time when layoffs, land sales, and closing operations must be done in the midst of a crisis.

Instead, rationalization should be an integral part of strategic planning, especially in an industry like homebuilding, where what goes up always comes down. With downturns inevitable, planning for them during good times is essential.

As a flip side to expansion, rationalization involves figuring out when to leave a market and how to alter the approach to geographic markets, market segments, and/or products that a company either serves or builds.

It also may mean altering the roles the company plays in the housing industry. Perhaps a company will shift resources from building to land acquisition. Or the strategy may be to gear up to assist S&Ls and other financial institutions with the workouts that always occur when things slow down. Either pulling out of markets, dropping out of the production of certain nonessential products, or shifting away from certain market segments involves difficult decisions, but they're decisions that must be made.

Efficiency. Efficiency, the fourth component of strategic planning, involves lowering the costs of production and producing more quickly. Given the time value of money and the large up-front costs associated with homebuilding, efficiency is a key to the success of a company.

One of the major issues relating to efficiency is the ability to manage the conflict between marketing and construction. There will always be tension between marketing people, who demand new and different products, and construction superintendents, who are charged with controlling costs and balk at changes that drive up costs. But this tension can be managed, and, if managed properly, it's actually constructive.

There are a few ways to improve efficiency. Supply channels can be improved by shopping different sources. Standardized product specifications can be adopted. Working with subcontractors and suppliers to improve quality and delivery standards can drive down unit costs.

Another strategy is to shift to off-site factory construction of building components. In most cases, costs will drop and quality will improve, but given the heavy capital requirements of factory building and on-again, off-again housing cycles, this a high-risk strategy.

Controlling work flow—scheduling workers' time more judiciously and improving inventory control—is a third way to improve efficiency. This strategy involves only moderate investments (for a computer, for example), but it does require considerable management resources.

Organization. The final component of strategic planning involves figuring out how to organize a company. In the case of real estate development, there are many ways to organize, from project management on the one extreme, to functional management on the other.

With project management, in its purest form, one person has full responsibility for a project, from site acquisition through development, construction, and marketing.

With functional management, responsibility for each discrete function is assigned to separate individuals or departments. Of course, there are countless variations in between these two extremes.

Bringing the incentives of the company's managers in line with the goals of the company is the most important organizational strategy to implement. Also important is creating a work atmosphere that boosts morale and productivity companywide.

Economic Conditions. All strategic planning should be done of course in the context of prevailing economic conditions. For example, expansion strategies will be quite different during a slowdown than during an upturn.

For the purposes of planning, housing's economic cycles can be broken into three parts:

- A growing economy with demand increasing (upturn);
- A stable economy with demand leveling off (mature);
- A contracting economy with demand decreasing (downturn).

Each economic phase will affect a company's strategy profoundly. In fact, the strategic plan should be one step ahead of the cycle. In other words, the groundwork for an upturn should be laid during a downturn. Similarly, a builder's strategy during an upturn should anticipate the time when demand will level off.

During an upturn, the emphasis should be on growth and organization. Plans to grow should concentrate on products the company knows best and that have proven market acceptance. It is not the time to expand into new products, market segments, or geographic markets. While focus should be on building an organization capable of managing the growth, there should be little energy diverted to efficiency or rationalization. The return will be better on efforts devoted to increasing sales rather than attempts to improve efficiency, assuming reasonable margins are being achieved. However, potential areas for expansion should be studied in preparation for the mature phase of the economic cycle.

Once housing demand stabilizes, the emphasis shifts to a more complex set of issues. As sales and profits level off in base products, geographic markets, and market segments, consideration should be given to expansion to new products, markets, and segments. In addition, strong emphasis should be placed on improving efficiency, in turn to improve margins of the base business. The organizational emphasis should be placed on consolidating systems and improving personnel. Serious study of countercyclical businesses should be undertaken, as should a study of the staying power of the base business, during the coming economic downturn. At this point, rationalization strategies should be anticipated.

Once the economy turns down, it is time to batten down the hatches. The importance of good management becomes obvious and paramount. The rationalization strategies developed during the mature/stable cycle should now be implemented. The organization needs to be lean and mean, and there needs to be a continuous concentration on efficiency. The countercyclical sources of revenue should begin to offset the reduced sales volume of the base business.

Finally, the foundation of the upturn should be laid, including understanding changing demographics, considering new industry roles for the company, and, when possible, picking up land bargains. (Acquiring distressed property during bad times has been one of the prime reasons behind the success of many of the biggest names in homebuilding.)

Surviving—and thriving—during good times and bad requires a clear perception of economic reality and a well-formulated and -executed plan of action. That, in fact, is the essence of strategic planning.

Source: Christopher B. Leinberger, "Survival of the Fittest," *Builder*, March 1986, pp. 92-97. Used with permission.

Appendix C
Methods for Estimating Local Economic Change

Most local economic forecasts are based on some version of the economic base model, which is a simple multiplier model that relates employment in the sector that is exporting goods and services to the rest of the world (for example, manufacturing) to total employment in the area. Change in total employment is estimated from the predicted change in basic employment. The model derives from an accounting identity that equates local employment *(R)* plus basic employment *(B)* to total employment *(N)*. The multiplier is derived from a simple ratio of nonbasic or local employment to total employment. The model can thus be described:

$$N = R + B$$
$$R = aN$$
$$\text{then } N = (\frac{1}{1 - a}) B$$

After the level or change in basic employment is forecast, the export-base multiplier is used to predict the total amount or change in employment. Change in employment can be related to population or income (earnings) and used to forecast changes in population or income. This model of urban growth is the most common one encountered in market analysis that is used to gauge overall demand.

Basic employment reflects the functional specialization of a metropolitan area. Tradition-

ally, agriculture, mining, and manufacturing were viewed as basic and service sectors as nonbasic. Increasingly, the definition is refined to address more detailed sectors—for example, industries (four-digit standard industrial classifications) or industry groups (three-digit standard industrial classifications). With finer-grained analysis, some primary and secondary activities are oriented toward a local market (for example, quarries that supply materials for local road construction, or bakeries and other food processors). On the other hand, many business, professional, and financial services are exported beyond the metropolitan area. In fact, some of the more sophisticated are traded globally, such as specialized accounting or engineering services. Although retail trade and communications are primarily local, wholesale trade and distribution serve large market areas, especially in regional centers like Dallas, Minneapolis, or Seattle. Most public sectors are part of the local economy. Yet state or federal agencies, military installations, and universities are part of the export base.

The input-output model is a more refined multiplier model having one interindustry multiplier for each industry. The model relates changes in final demand to changes in total output or to total employment. It is very expensive to derive input-output models from information based on surveys, and, until recently, these models were too expensive for most areas. Fortunately, BEA has developed a method that gives reasonably consistent forecasts that should be better than economic base forecasts because they are more detailed. The model can be used to generate forecasts of total employment but also employment estimates in much more disaggregated form. BEA's model divides the economy into 30 or 40 industries. The multipliers are available from the BEA at a very reasonable cost for counties and metropolitan areas. Local planning agencies or councils of government may already have purchased this information.

The economic base and input-output models are short-term models of growth. If the time frame is under five years, the estimated multipliers can provide reasonably accurate forecasts. But for longer time periods, say 10 or 15 years, a conceptual shift is necessary. Concern for economic growth, which takes the structure of the local economy as given, should be replaced by a concern for economic development where the local economy's long-term viability is at issue. Long-term viability is becoming more and more important to real estate developers and investors, especially foreign real estate investors who are interested in long-term investments. Often such investors think in terms of 10, 20, or even longer holding periods. For these longer time frames, models of growth represent only a starting point. Questions of development, of changing economic structure in ways that promote long-term viability, become relevant. The key factors influencing an area's economic fundamentals in the United States are the composition and productivity of local industries, potential for innovation, centrality, diversity, and business climate.

Places with companies that can produce goods more cheaply than the global competition have a better future than ones that are less competitive. Places that have firms with the ability to create new products or open up new markets or access to new sources of supply have a better future than places that cannot. An innovative area supports the commercialization of technology and attracts companies with potential for growth. Livable areas have amenities, quality public education, reasonable living costs, and affordable housing. Central areas offer a range of high-quality professional and business services, adequate size and scale, and good access to national or global markets. Diverse areas have a good mix of industries and jobs. Long-term economic viability stands on two legs: the area's ability to make products efficiently (competitiveness) and its ability to make products well (innovativeness).

Appendix D

A Critical Review of a Residential Market Study: The Example of Fuqua Mills

A developer proposed the rehabilitation of Fuqua Mills, a vacant industrial structure in a medium-sized city adjacent to a major thoroughfare and close to state government offices and a small four-year college. The developer asked the market analyst to determine the feasibility of developing the space as rental housing for moderate-income elderly residents. The target market included people with household income above HUD's Section 8 threshold for subsidized housing but below the level needed to rent or purchase housing in more expensive developments. The analyst focused on annual income ranging from $10,000 to $30,000.

The study begins with a general description of growth in the metropolitan area. The description provides an excellent context for the study, but *it does not make a direct connection between overall demand and demand for the proposed product*. For example, it does not relate growing population to the elderly segment that would constitute the target market. Market studies often fail to relate an area's general strength to the specific advantages of the subject project. Although providing good contextual information on the market area is an admirable approach, the events occurring in the area must be shown to be related to demand for the project.[1] Projects can fail in very rapidly growing areas and succeed in stagnating or declining areas; therefore, documenting strong demand in an urban area does not imply excess

demand for the proposed project. Projects designed to house the elderly might be more feasible in stagnant markets than in growing markets, for example. Because the demand for housing for the elderly is driven by the aging of the population, growth in population or employment may have little bearing on demand. Even areas with net out-migration could have a strong demand for housing for the elderly, because it is the younger population that is migrating and because older people might seek greater association with others their own age in areas where younger members of their extended families are moving away. Furthermore, growth could increase the costs of food, clothing, and entertainment, leaving older people on fixed incomes with less disposable income for housing. Growth could increase land prices and construction costs, resulting in more expensive housing elderly individuals cannot afford.

It is not important to say that an area is growing and that it is a wonderful place to work and live without saying *how* the proposed project will exploit the area's attractive features. National, industrial, or demographic trends should be shown to support the need for the proposed project. Macroeconomic and macrodemographic trends should be clearly connected to the proposed project's design. The developer and design team could then use this information to specify features and functions of the project and its benefits to space users that will help sell the project. Effective communication between developer and market analyst is critical at this point. The market analyst can benefit from understanding the developer's preliminary analysis (stage two) in preparing the formal market study (stage three). For the Fuqua Mills project, the developer turned over his notes to the analyst, along with several key documents used in refining the idea.

The analyst next defines the target market as adults 55 and over interested in independent living but envisions no custodial-care or health-care facilities on the site. This market segment is too broad, for clear distinctions exist among the lifestyles, needs, and preferences of pre- or early retirees (ages 55 to 65), healthy retirees (65 to 75), and the elderly over 75. Without making these distinctions and gathering useful information on the health and needed health care of the elderly in the area, an analyst cannot properly segment demand. With no health facilities on site, the analyst should have focused on the younger, healthier elderly; otherwise, he has exaggerated demand and wasted time studying irrelevant market segments.

The projections of total elderly population in relation to the site were well done in terms of numbers and location by census tract. The adjacent census tracts did not contain a concentration of the elderly, because a college and a public housing project, both with very young populations, were located near the site. This situation creates a problem, because one critical assumption the analyst made was that the project would appeal to "older adults who wish to continue their independent lifestyle in a familiar neighborhood close to family, friends, and amenities." The analyst used secondary sources to support this assumption but did not go beyond these sources to check the validity of the assumption. He should have looked for similar successful projects in nearby neighborhoods or in similar cities to figure out the distance from which they drew residents. Would people relocate after they sold their houses, or would they stay in the area? A related key assumption was that elderly people would enjoy staying in the same rental complex. In fact, might they not be attracted to a residential environment with other elderly people? *Good marketing research requires corroboration of key assumptions*.

Another problem with the assumption regarding a familiar neighborhood was the isolation of the site. Access from only one direction was possible, because it was bordered on two sides by highways and on the third by well-maintained public housing and the college. How then could this rental residential project be integrated into a larger community to provide a familiar neighborhood for its elderly residents? An idea that sounded good when census tracts or neighborhoods were considered was not really feasible, given the characteristics of the specific site.

The analyst's estimates of demand for housing for the elderly, derived from a special study previously completed by HUD, were reasonable. The analyst made conservative assumptions about absorption and capture. But in using information that was based on a much broader survey of the elderly population, he lost the link to his argument that the project's proximity to the existing elderly population would be an important factor in determining demand for the units. And the inconsistency was never resolved. A good analyst should continually check assumptions and the logical flow of ideas, playing devil's advocate to test for consistency. In this case, one solution would have been to define a primary market area and estimate the number of prospective tenants from neighborhoods adjacent to the site.

The analysis of supply was well done; it identified a gap in the market for rental property in the targeted price range and noted that the few competitive projects were fully occupied. The analyst failed to determine, however, whether those projects had the potential for expansion that could increase future supply. Not only should he have considered planned supply; he should have anticipated the competition's other possible responses to the proposed project and suggested ways to meet such challenges.

The market study justified very well the overall capture of excess housing demand by those aged 55 to 75 with corresponding rent levels. The analyst proposed 68 units, which represented 12 percent of the projected excess demand. The relatively high capture rate was justified, because the expected supply was relatively modest. To renovate the building most efficiently, the plan proposed 48 one-bedroom units at $430 a month and 20 two-bedroom units at $500 a month. From the perspective of design, this mix was a logical way to convert Fuqua Mills. But the analyst presented no justification for that specific mix in the analysis of absorption and capture. He should have related market segments to demand for the proposed number of one-bedroom and two-bedroom units.

Given the carefully estimated schedule of absorption, the project's capture rate is necessarily subjective, but it should still be carefully thought through. In explaining why the expected capture rate can be achieved, the analyst should review the key factors that relate to the product's marketability, thereby clarifying the features, functions, and benefits that need to be incorporated in the project.

Market studies should be internally consistent, coherent, and logical, and to do so, the analyst should assume the role of an uninformed observer and review the research procedures. To enhance internal consistency, he should, whenever possible, use several different approaches to derive important estimates. Using several sources of information allows cross checking—for example, by comparing two or three sources of population estimates. If only one source is used, the analyst should base the choice on the quality of the sampling or research procedures, not on expediency. The market study is supposed to be comprehensive in scope but also correct in details. The analysis is likely to be correct if the analyses of demand, supply, absorption, and capture are tied together consistently and convincingly.

Assumptions are an inherent part of any market study, and good market analysts make them explicit. Explicit, carefully supported assumptions go a long way to increase the credibility of marketing research. In general, analysts can base initial key assumptions or standards on published sources, then use specific local estimates as a check on the original numbers. Often, market analysts seek local experts to improve the assumptions or standards—for example, to verify local construction practices and costs, to explain local tastes and preferences, to check recent trends in absorption of space, or to understand who the local players are. Focus groups can be helpful to learn consumers' reactions to a project's initial design. Although relatively expensive, they are much cheaper than building an unsuccessful project. Ultimately, market analysts should conduct primary research appropriate to the scope of the project, using the market study as a way to control risk and as a way to get commitments from some of the other players.

NOTE

1. David F. Haddow, "Making the City Overview Meaningful," *Appraisal Journal*, January 1984, pp. 48-52.

Appendix E

Applications of CPM Scheduling in Small Construction Projects

This appendix illustrates procedures applied to renovations and additions. For example, real estate professionals frequently deal with properties that need major structural modifications that potential buyers might be reluctant to consider. The uncertainties surrounding construction procedures could raise concerns among buyers. Familiarity with planning and scheduling small construction projects can better equip real estate professionals in marketing and in assisting clients. They can then advise prospective buyers how to understand and monitor construction activities through the use of the construction schedule, for buyers are more likely to purchase a property requiring improvements if they know how a building contractor organizes and controls a project through a schedule.

Regardless of size, a project's success depends upon an effective system of planning and control. Standardized schedules, such as CPM, are used extensively. A CPM schedule allows management to concentrate its attention on the project's *critical* activities, those upon which the project's completion *depends*. CPM scheduling accomplishes several tasks:

1. Clarifying objectives and intermediate goals;
2. Providing a realistic time frame from earliest finish to latest finish;
3. Detailing the sequence of tasks and their dependence on each other;

4. Determining critical activities;
5. Providing an effective instrument of control; and
6. Allowing modifications as the project progresses.

CPM is perhaps the most widely used scheduling system on large construction projects, but CPM concepts can be applied to smaller projects as well. CPM is a visual tool that allows a manager to follow day-to-day activities as they affect a project's long-range scheme. A Gantt bar chart (see Figure E-1) is another visual control system similar to CPM that is easier to compile but fails to clearly represent dependencies between activities.

The first step in compiling a schedule is to list all tasks, say from excavation to interior finishes. In planning the schedule, contractors break jobs into activities and durations and arrange activities in order of their dependence on each other. Tasks depend on others when the earlier element is required for support or connection, or when the earlier element establishes a dimension or will prevent installation of the following element. For example, the foundation must be in place before structural framing is installed, as the walls are connected to and supported by the foundation.

The sample of a Gantt chart and CPM network in Figure E-1 could represent the process of making a small addition to an existing structure. The CPM network depicts the flow of activities. The arrows represent an activity, and each node represents an event, typically the start or finish of an activity.

The following list contains some of the features of the CPM schedule and variations that are frequently seen:

1. Most activities depend on those immediately preceding them, those completed at the node where the next activity begins.

2. Overlapping activities are common, where one activity begins before the previous one is completed (for example, starting the structural frame after only half the foundation is poured). This technique can directly decrease the time required to complete the project.

3. The critical path is the path through the network with the longest duration. The length of the critical path is the sum of the individual activities on its path. These particular activities, if delayed, will affect overall time to complete the project.

4. Activities not on the critical path frequently can "float." For example, wiring must be completed when the wall is framed, within two time periods. Because wiring can be completed in one time period, it has a float time, or slack period, of one.

5. Structural substitutions may or may not affect the critical path. For example, replacing tilt-up construction (poured-in-place exterior walls lifted into position) for the structural frame and exterior finish will shorten the duration along this path. But because these activities are not on the critical path, the overall time to complete the project will not be shortened.

The schedule must be distributed to all participants for their review and commitments to be an effective instrument of control. Requiring rigid conformity to the schedule is impractical, because no project runs smoothly from be-

FIGURE E-1
GANTT BAR CHART

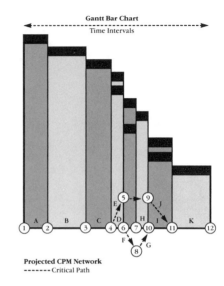

Projected CPM Network
------ Critical Path

ginning to end. With CPM, however, problems in scheduling can be identified quickly. Without the cooperation and dedication of the players, however, a schedule alone cannot be effective in controlling time. It does, however, simplify the task by providing clear goals and objectives for each player.

CPM has some shortcomings, emphasizing only certain activities, when in fact any element could become critical if it falls behind and affects the project's completion.

Source: "Applications of Critical Path Method Scheduling in Small Construction Projects," *Real Estate Indicators* (Los Angeles: Univ. of California–Los Angeles, Real Estate Center, 1986).

468

Appendix F

Real Estate as an Asset Class: A 25-Year Perspective

DEVELOPMENT OF A PARADIGM

In life, theory and fact are inextricably interwoven. Only with theory can we organize the sea of facts that surrounds us, and only with facts can we test theory to see whether it is useful, i.e., whether it should become the reigning paradigm. This productive interplay between theory and fact is depicted in Figure F-1.

In real estate investment, the interplay has provided insights over the last 25 years that are approaching the status of a paradigm. By looking at developments from real estate's Dark Ages, Renaissance, Modern, and Postmodern periods, we can appreciate the inevitability of the leap of faith that is currently transpiring and leading us to a new day of real estate investment strategies.

THE DARK AGES

In the early 1960s, European financial institutions were heavily involved in equity real estate investments that were developing considerable sophistication. In the United States, institutions tended to stay with investments they were comfortable with, which did not include real estate assets, dominated as they are by asymmetric information and heterogeneous products. As Steven Roulac later summarized, "Real estate is inherently different" (see Figure F-2) and therefore is not likely to be understood as

academics are coming to understand stocks and bonds. This left the investment in real estate to individuals who intuitively recognized the benefits of this asset class and did not require mathematical proof.

THE RENAISSANCE

Real estate investment was not left long with those who "knew real estate." In 1965, the great grandfather of real estate investment analysis, Paul Wendt, and his associate, S.N. Wong, produced the first ex post real estate return numbers, as shown in Figure F-3. Real estate offered higher mean returns than stocks over all periods tested. This posed a problem for the leading paradigm of the day, the CAPM (Capital Asset Pricing Model), because real estate appeared to be mispriced (unless real estate investments were far riskier than previously imagined). Based on Figure F-1, the interpretation was obvious. Wendt and Wong's results came from only one type of property studied over a short period of time and therefore were not generalizable.

In 1970, Professor H.C. Friedman produced another set of numbers (Figure F-4). His

Source: Mike Miles and David Hartzell, Salomon Brothers, 1988. Reproduced with permission.

THE EVOLUTION OF A PARADIGM

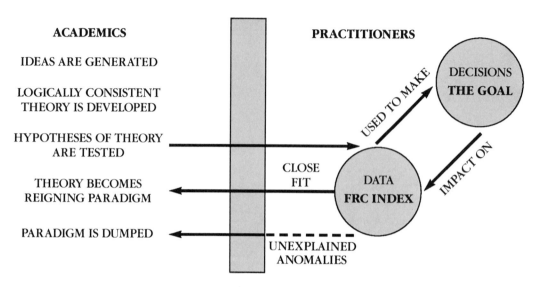

ACADEMICS

IDEAS ARE GENERATED

LOGICALLY CONSISTENT
THEORY IS DEVELOPED

HYPOTHESES OF THEORY
ARE TESTED

THEORY BECOMES
REIGNING PARADIGM

PARADIGM IS DUMPED

PRACTITIONERS

USED TO MAKE

DECISIONS
THE GOAL

CLOSE
FIT

DATA
FRC INDEX

IMPACT ON

UNEXPLAINED
ANOMALIES

Without theory, facts are unintelligible; without facts, theory is useless.

FIGURE F-2

THE DIFFICULTIES IN DEVELOPING A GENERALIZED PARADIGM FOR REAL ESTATE

I. The local orientation of the markets.
II. The infrequent trading of individual properties.
III. The uniqueness and lack of comparability of individual assets.
IV. The importance of tax and financing considerations.
V. The relative lack of sophistication of investors.[a]

---

[a]Roulac (1976) notes that securities markets became more efficient as institutional investors increased their level of participation and that increased efficiency should also come to the real estate market as these participants become more active.

FIGURE F-3

WENDT AND WONG'S RESULTS: AFTER-TAX RATES OF RETURN BETWEEN SAMPLE APARTMENT HOUSE PROPERTIES AND COMMON STOCKS

Investment Periods	1958–1962	1953–1962
Apartment Houses:		
Equity Capital	15.6%	9.4%
Common Stocks:		
Equity Capital	7.9	6.5

---

work picked up on the CAPM development in research on stocks and bonds and purported to show the performance of real estate in a modern portfolio setting. His findings support Wendt and Wong's result of high mean real estate returns and, in addition, indicate that real estate

FRIEDMAN'S RESULTS: CHARACTERISTICS AND COMPOSITION
OF MIXED-ASSET PORTFOLIOS

No Taxes			
Portfolio Composition		Expected Portfolio Percent Return (1963–1968)	Standard Deviation of Return
Common Stock	Real Estate		
100.0		48.2%	36.6
100.0		41.0	22.6
88.2	11.8	36.4	15.1
60.1	39.9	30.8	11.0
42.3	57.7	26.6	8.6
11.8	88.2	15.9	2.2
10.0	90.0	14.2	1.8
8.6	91.4	13.7	1.8
7.6	92.4	12.0	1.4
7.2	92.8	11.1	1.2
5.9	94.1	10.6	1.1
5.1	94.9	10.1	1.0
3.0	97.0	8.9	0.9
3.0	97.0	5.9	0.8

returns are blessed with low variances *and* low correlations with stock and bond returns.

This latter discovery implied even more underpricing for the real estate investment, as the real estate (which was itself low risk) could diversify the stock and bond portfolio (reduce the *portfolio's* variance) while at the same time improve the portfolio's return. Nothing could be that good, and Friedman's work was criticized because he obtained annual prices for the real estate by dividing five years worth of appreciation by five to get annual price changes. In spite of these problems, both of these articles were in leading academic journals, clearly suggesting that interest in real estate investment was undergoing a renaissance,[1] with the United States now leading the way.

THE MODERN PERIOD

The modern era of real estate investment analysis dawned with the work of a University of Chicago (now Yale) professor/consultant, Roger Ibbotson. In 1979, he published the first of what was to become a series entitled "The World Wealth and the U.S. Wealth Portfolios." Using publicly available statistics, Ibbotson's work indicated that real estate was a major portion of the world's and the United States's wealth (see Figure F-5)—proving that either real estate must fit in the investment portfolio, or else there were a lot of people out there making rather large mistakes.

While it was easy to quibble with Ibbotson's use of general statistics, his handling of overlapping asset classes (e.g., real estate owned by publicly traded companies), and the impossibility of institutions' investing in certain of his asset classes[2] (such as residential housing), this work marked the beginning of the modern era of real estate investment. A well-known stock and bond data producer had chosen to show real estate on equal footing with stocks and bonds—highlighting the point that real estate *is* another asset that competes for the investor's dollar with stocks and bonds.[3]

THE POSTMODERN PERIOD

With the focus now on the comparability of different asset classes, several authors of the postmodern period have sought to explain why the paradigm does not appear to be working. In fact, there were enough authors for Robert

ORIGINAL IBBOTSON AND FALL U.S. WEALTH PORTFOLIO:
U.S. CAPITAL MARKET TOTAL ANNUAL RETURNS, 1947–1978

	Total Value[a] 1978	Compound Return	Arithmetic Mean	Standard Deviation
Common Stocks				
NYSE	760	10.16%	11.56%	17.73%
OTC	73	12.63	14.79	21.79
Total	833	10.34	11.79	18.02
Fixed-Income Corporate Securities				
Preferred Stocks	25	2.92	3.31	9.20
Long-term Corporate Bonds	124	2.21	2.42	6.72
Intermediate Corporate Bonds	81	3.87	4.00	5.48
Commercial Paper	62	4.27	4.29	2.37
Total	292	2.89	3.03	5.53
Corporate Securities Total		8.19	9.07	13.84
Real Estate				
Farms	526	11.69	11.88	6.79
Residential Housing	1,635	6.88	6.93	3.28
Total	2,161	8.14	8.19	3.53
U.S. Government Securities				
U.S. Treasury Bills	161	3.51	3.53	2.11
U.S. Treasury Notes	239	3.65	3.73	3.71
U.S. Treasury Bonds	44	2.39	2.56	6.17
Agencies	159	4.00	4.08	3.42
Total	603	3.17	3.23	3.78
Municipal (State and Local) Bonds				
Short-term	19	2.44	2.45	1.37
Long-term	240	1.69	2.01	8.20
Total	259	1.75	2.02	7.62
MARKET TOTAL[b]	4,148	6.88	6.47	4.65

[a]In billions of dollars.
[b]Includes AMEX.

Zerbst and Barbara Cambon[4] to compile a summary of real estate investment research in 1984 (see Figure F-6). This summary clearly showed four basic "facts":

1. Real estate historically offers higher mean returns than stocks or bonds.
2. Real estate historically has lower variance of returns than stocks or bonds.
3. Real estate returns historically have low correlations with stock and bond returns (real estate has been a good diversifier).
4. Real estate returns historically have a high correlation with inflation (real estate has been a good inflation hedge).

Again, nothing could be this good. From Figure F-1, it was obvious that some new explanations were in order.

During the postmodern period, Ibbotson and Seigel developed the "New Equilibrium Theory" to try to explain why real estate looked "too good to be true." They posited that reported returns were overstated because of the higher

ZERBST AND CAMBON SUMMARY: COMPARISON OF RISK AND NOMINAL RETURNS ON REAL ESTATE STOCKS, BONDS, AND TREASURY BILLS

Study	Time Period	Real Estate	Common Stocks	Bonds	Treasury Bills	CPI
Ibbotson & Fall	1947–1978					
Percent Return		8.1	10.3	2.9	3.5	3.7
Standard Deviation		3.5	18.0	5.5	2.1	3.20
Coefficient of Variation[a]		0.43	1.75	1.90	0.60	
Robicheck, Cohn & Pringle	1951–1969					
Percent Return		9.5	11.9	1.3	3.0	2.2
Standard Deviation		4.5	17.4	5.0	1.5	1.8
Coefficient of Variation		0.47	1.46	3.85	0.50	
McMahan	1951–1978					
Percent Return		13.9	11.4	3.5	3.9	3.7
Standard Deviation		3.8	18.3	6.7	1.9	3.0
Coefficient of Variation		0.27	1.61	1.91	0.49	
————	1969–1978					
Percent Return		18.0	4.8	6.2	6.0	6.7
Standard Deviation		1.5	18.4	8.8	1.3	2.6
Coefficient of Variation		0.08	3.83	1.42	0.22	
Ricks[b]	1951–1978					
Percent Return		9.0	11.4	3.5	3.9	3.7
Standard Deviation		0.9	18.3	6.7	1.9	3.0
Coefficient of Variation		0.10	1.61	1.91	0.49	
————	1969–1978					
Percent Return		10.1	4.8	6.2	6.0	6.7
Standard Deviation		0.5	18.4	8.8	1.3	2.6
Coefficient of Variation		0.50	3.83	1.42	0.22	
Kelleher	1960–1973					
Percent Return		13.2	7.2	3.8	4.3	3.3
Standard Deviation		5.1	14.0	6.7	1.5	2.3
Coefficient of Variation		0.39	1.54	1.72	0.35	
Brachman	1970–1979					
Percent Return		10.3	4.7	5.6	6.3	7.4
Standard Deviation		4.9	19.6	8.0	1.8	3.4
Coefficient of Variation		0.48	4.17	1.43	0.29	
Smith—REITs	1965–1977					
Percent Return		9.8	4.6	4.2	5.4	5.4
Standard Deviation		22.1	18.4	8.7	1.3	2.8
Coefficient of Variation		2.26	4.00	2.07	0.24	
Burns & Epley	1970–1974					
Percent Return		3.0	-2.3	6.7	5.9	6.6
Standard Deviation		24.2	19.3	8.4	1.8	3.8

Study	Time Period	Real Estate	Common Stocks	Bonds	Treasury Bills	CPI
Burns & Epley	1975–1979					
Percent Return		37.4	14.8	5.8	6.7	8.2
Standard Deviation		29.5	16.9	9.9	2.2	3.2
——	1970–1979					
Percent Return		16.0	4.7	5.5	6.3	7.4
Standard Deviation		28.5	19.6	8.0	1.9	3.4
Coefficient of Variation		1.78	4.17	1.43	0.30	
Hoag	1973–1978					
Percent Return		14.2	3.7	6.4	6.2	8.1
Standard Deviation		27.2	20.2	8.0	1.0	1.2
Coefficient of Variation		1.21	5.62	1.25	0.16	
CREFs	1972–1981					
Percent Return		14.0	6.5	3.0	7.8	8.6
Standard Deviation		4.7	21.2	7.8	3.4	3.3
Coefficient of Variation		0.34	3.26	2.60	0.44	
Morguard[c]	1973–1981					
Percent Return		18.5	10.1	4.2	N/A	9.8
Standard Deviation		8.3	21.9	8.4	N/A	2.0
Coefficient of Variation		0.45	2.17	2.00		

Correlation of Real Estate Returns to Other Investment Classes

Study	Stocks	Bonds	Treasury Bills	CPI
Ibbotson & Fall	−.23	.02	.60	N/A
Robicheck, Cohn & Pringle	−.13	−.26	.06	N/A
McMahan	−.18	.08	.64	N/A
Sirmans & Webb	−.15	.53	.68	N/A
Miles & Rice	−.14	N/A	N/A	N/A
Hoag	−.07	−.31	.28	.50
Morguard[c]	−.44	−.46	N/A	.45

[a]The coefficient of variation measures the relative dispersion of the returns of the various investment classes and is calculated as follows:

$$\text{Coefficient of Variation} = \frac{\text{Standard Deviation}}{\text{Return}}$$

[b]Not calculated in original study but based on stated methodology, with the exception that capitalization rates were used as the proxy for income returns.
[c]All figures in Canadian dollars.

costs associated with real estate investment (i.e., information gathering, illiquidity, and management). If these costs were "netted out" of reported real estate returns, then real estate would "theoretically fit" in the investor's portfolio in roughly the same percentages as shown in the Market Wealth Portfolio. The idea had great intuitive appeal, but other researchers soon become discouraged with efforts to quantify the incremental costs of information, illiquidity, and management, and moved on to seek other explanations. This theory also failed to question the low variance and correlation numbers that practitioners found to be most questionable.

Numerous researchers concentrated on explanations for the unbelievably low variance numbers that were being reported. Hoag stressed the appraisal problem and constructed a return stream with substantially more variance than previously examined return streams. Fogler and friends tried a new theoretical development but couldn't test their theory directly. Hartzell et al. continued to work on appraisal-based returns and again documented superior (though tainted through the smoothing of the appraisal process) returns. In summary, Hoag's work seemed promising but couldn't be rigorously documented, Fogler's work was theoretically interesting but wasn't testable, and Hartzell documented a more sophisticated version.[5] Hartzell's results are presented in Figure F-7, once again indicating real estate offers higher returns, lower risk, and significantly negative correlations (with bonds). Journals published it and professional groups listened to it, but it surely was hard to believe.

FIGURE F-7

HARTZELL, HEKMAN, AND MILES RESULTS SHOWING QUARTERLY ASSET RETURNS COMPARISON FOR 40 QUARTERS: 1973–74 TO 1983–84

	S&P	Bonds	T-Bills	Inflation	REITs	Equal Weighted	Value Weighted
N	40	40	40	40	40	40	40
Mean	0.014	0.018	0.021	0.020	0.010	0.034	0.032
Median	0.002	0.012	0.020	0.020	0.019	0.028	0.027
Standard Deviation	0.093	0.075	0.008	0.010	0.114	0.025	0.018
Skewness	0.029	0.930	0.693	0.043	-0.184	2.183	0.957
Kurtosis	1.646	2.315	-0.544	-0.282	1.075	5.956	0.520
Coefficient of Variation[a]	-1329	-2374	35.36[b]	48.58[b]	-996.9	183.8	135.9

[a]Coefficient of variation calculated from excess returns.
[b]There are no excess returns on T-Bills and inflation.

Correlation with Other Assets

	Full Sample		S&P	Bonds	T-Bills	Inflation
	Equal Weighted	Value Weighted				
Equal Weighted	1.0					
Value Weighted	.7584 (.0001)	1.0				
S&P	-.0344 (.8332)	-.1159 (.4764)	1.0			
Bonds	-.3574 (.0236)	-.3949 (.0117)	.3074 (.0537)	1.0		
T-Bills	.2765 (.0842)	.5468 (.0003)	-.1072 (.5103)	-.0121 (.9412)	1.0	
Inflation	.2521 (.1166)	.5247 (.0005)	-.2889 (.0707)	-.3141 (.0484)	.2913 (.0682)	1.0

The number in parentheses is the probability that the true correlation coefficient is greater than $|R|$ under the null hypotheses of $R = 0$.

A NEW LOOK AT COMMERCIAL REAL ESTATE RETURNS: ASSET CLASS RETURN DISTRIBUTIONS

	Appraisal	Transaction
Real Estate		
N	20	20
Mean	.0267	.0274
Standard Deviation	.0105	.0508
Skewness	.8269	-.7873
Coefficient of Variation	39.186	185.30
Common Stocks		
N		20
Mean		.0490
Standard Deviation		.0771
Skewness		.0538
Coefficient of Variation		157.29
Corporate Bonds		
N		20
Mean		.0540
Standard Deviation		.0648
Skewness		.0807
Coefficient of Variation		119.96

	Appraisal	Transaction
Treasury Bills		
N		20
Mean		.0209
Standard Deviation		.00445
Skewness		.5024

Asset Return Correlations

	Real Estate (appraisal)	Real Estate (transaction)
Appraisal	1.000 (.000)	.0841 (.7244)
Transaction	.0841 (.7244)	1.000 (.000)
S&P500	-.311 (.1825)	-.0804 (.7362)
Corporate Bond	-.3930 (.0865)	-.0483 (.8397)
T-Bill	.3126 (.1796)	-.1703 (.4729)

An important development of the postmodern period was the continuing growth of the National Council of Real Estate Investment Fiduciaries (NCREIF).[6] In conjunction with the Frank Russell Company, NCREIF produces the FRC Index, which has become the standard for measuring real estate performance. This index is appraisal based, however, and may not be appropriate for portfolio decisions across broad classes of assets, i.e., determining how much real estate should go into a diversified portfolio.

LEAP OF FAITH

From the results shown in Figure F-7, it is clear that the insights to be gained from appraisal-based return series are limited. Sufficient work had been done during the postmodern period to suggest that something more was needed and that both researchers and professionals were going to have to be more flexible in their approach.

Henry Kaufman, the father of investment research at Salomon Brothers, pushed for a true market index and began a stream of investment research that is detailed in a Salomon publication, "Is a Transaction-Based Real Estate Index Possible?" Anticipating the logistical complexities that were destined to plague that effort, David Shulman suggested that the best approach to asset class comparability lay in capitalizing publicly traded companies' reported earnings at a market rate, and then comparing the resulting returns with appraisal-based real estate returns. It was a novel idea, but investors weren't ready to give up the transaction prices they had in stocks and bonds to achieve comparability.

The real leap of faith came when NCREIF, working with a group at the University of North

Carolina Business School, decided to use the sales from the FRC index to create a real estate return series that is at least "transactions driven." The methodology employed consists of estimating the value of different characteristics of a sample of sold properties, adjusting these estimated values by an amount consistent with the effect that the various characteristics have on the probability a property will be sold, and then applying these adjusted values to the characteristics of a sample of unsold properties. The results of this methodology appear in Figure F-8. These results are far more intuitively appealing than the appraisal-based results in Figure F-7, for while the risk-adjusted real estate returns are still attractive in a portfolio setting, they are not as unbelievably attractive as appraisal-based returns had previously made them appear.[7] With

Salomon's work terminating the hope for ever being able to construct a true transactions index and the Hartzell papers signaling the end of the line for appraisal work in this area, investors were provided with the push that was necessary for them to take a leap of faith.[8]

THE DAY OF INFINITE POSSIBILITIES

The new return series accomplishes two things. First, real estate is shown to fit (at least as well as stocks and bonds) with the reigning capital market paradigm. Although the fit isn't perfect, the paradigm has been found not to be perfect either, and now real estate can at least be examined comparably to alternative stock and bond investments. Second, the detail in the

---

FIGURE F-9

AN EARLY LOOK AT NEW DIVERSIFICATION STRATEGIES FOR REAL ESTATE INVESTMENT CATEGORIES

Category Name	Distinguishing Characteristics
Oil Sensitive	Properties located in Texas, Louisiana, Oklahoma, and Colorado.
Trade Deficit Reduction Expectation	Industrial properties (both warehouse and industrial/office/showroom) in counties with a greater-than-average concentration in manufacturing income.
Players' World	Properties that are not in the CBD, are less than five years old, are in counties with faster-than-median growth, and are not industrial warehouses.
Lifestyle	Garden office buildings (both office, three stories or less, and industrial/office/showroom) in counties with populations under 1 million.
Distribution	Industrial buildings (warehouse) located within one mile of the interstate highway in counties with above-mean wholesale income.
Yuppieland	All retail with less than 250,000 square feet in counties with income per capita greater than average—the logic that the "me generation" shops in specialty malls.
New South	All properties in Atlanta, Charlotte, and Raleigh/Durham.
Government Based	All office and industrial/office/showroom properties located in counties where government income per capita is above average.
Zoning Protected	All properties in Boston and San Francisco where zoning has *for several years* reduced overbuilding by constraining supply.

For the details behind this appraisal-driven effort, see Guilkey, Cole, and Miles (1988).

477

new data base allows for the testing of more specific real estate investment strategies.[9]

Several investment managers have been looking at specialized investment strategies in real estate.[10] Figure F-9 illustrates a few categories of real estate that can be analyzed with the expanded FRC data base. While serious investment managers would clearly want to do more rigorous background work, the categories in Figure F-9 provide interesting food for thought. So far, strategies of this type have been empirically tested only infrequently and then with appraisal-based data. Conversely, in stock mark investment management, the strategies are ingenious and highly varied. Tomorrow's real estate professional, at least the one who appreciates the concepts presented in this evolution, will have the data to use the past as one proxy for future expectations. The last two and one-half decades have seen a lot of blood on the real estate investment playing fields. But research is now better able to help focus on new strategies, and, consequently, those with the right new strategies should be shedding less blood in the future.

NOTES

1. The Wendt and Wong piece was in the *Journal of Finance*, while the Friedman piece appeared in the *Journal of Financial and Quantitative Analysis. Journal of Finance* has published only one other piece on real estate equity returns in a refereed edition since the Wendt and Wong article in 1965. Ricks in 1969 used ACLI (American Council of Life Insurers) data and "backed out" equity returns using a band-of-investment approach.

2. Salomon Brothers now estimates the level of investment-grade commercial real estate at $1.7 billion.

3. About this time, Miles and Rice pointed out that while real estate returns might not fit accepted financial theory, the testing of all financial theory was obviously flawed because the market proxies used did not include real estate. Miles and Rice's effort suggests that no general equilibrium financial theory will be completely acceptable until it can include real estate in the empirical testing.

4. The Zerbst and Cambon study was later updated by Sirmans and Sirmans in 1987. Zerbst himself is an interesting story of evolution. He became a professor during the renaissance, moved on to become a real estate investment consultant during the modern period, and then quit consulting to become an investment manager during the postmodern period.

5. Space precludes listing several other important authors of this period. A partial bibliography follows.

6. NCREIF includes nearly all of the major financial institutions involved in real estate investment research (insurance companies, trust departments, and private capital management firms).

7. For a full description of this methodology and a discussion of the results, see Guilkey et al. (1988).

8. Much of the early work on this methodology was supported by the Institute for Quantitative Research in Finance.

9. The series of Hartzell papers pointed the way toward more exacting categories of equity real estate investment by showing the relatively low levels of systematic risk found in broad geographic regions and major property types. Their work follows the Elton and Gruber methodology. For comparative purposes, the VM/VPI measure of systematic risk would be around .35 for a diversified stock portfolio and nearly .90 for high-grade bonds.

10. In a recent Salomon Brothers publication, Wurtzebach et al. suggest dividing real estate investments along the lines suggested by Garreau in his highly entertaining *Nine Nations of North America*.

BIBLIOGRAPHY

Andrews, R.B. *Urban Land Economics and Public Policy.* New York: Free Press, 1971.

Brinson, G.P., J.J. Diermeier, and L.R. Hood. *Multiple Market Index: A White Paper*. Chicago: First National Bank of Chicago, September 1982.

Brueggeman, W.B., A.H. Chen, and T.G. Thibodeau. "Real Estate Investment Funds: Performance and Portfolio Considerations." *AREUEA Journal.* Fall 1984.

Burns, W.L., and D.R. Epley. "The Performance of Portfolios of REITS and Stocks." *Journal of Portfolio Management*. Spring 1982.

Elton, E.J., and M.J. Gruber. "Risk Reduction and Portfolio Size: An Analytical Solution." *Journal of Business*. October 1977.

Estey A., and M. Miles. "How Well Do Real Estate Funds Perform?" *Journal of Portfolio Management*. Winter 1982.

Fogler, H.R. "A Mean/Variance Analysis of Real Estate." *Journal of Portfolio Management*. Winter 1983.

Fogler, H.R., M.R. Granito, and L.R. Smith. "A Theoretical Analysis of Real Estate Returns." *Journal of Finance*. July 1985.

Frank Russell Company and The National Council of Real Estate Investment Fiduciaries. *FRC*

Index. Washington, D.C.: ULI–the Urban Land Institute, quarterly.

Friedman, H.C. "Real Estate Investment and Portfolio Theory." *Journal of Financial and Quantitative Analysis*. April 1970.

Goldman Sachs & Company, Randall Zisler, and Robert A. Feldman. "Real Estate Report." New York: 1985.

Guilkey, David, Rebel Cole, and Mike Miles. "The Motivation for Institutional Real Estate." UNC Working Paper. Chapel Hill, N.C.: Univ. of North Carolina, 1988.

Harris, Robert S. "Return and Risk on Equity: Expectational Data and Equity Risk Premia." *Financial Management*. Spring 1986.

Hartzell, David, John Hekman, and Mike Miles. "Real Estate Returns and Inflation." *AREUEA Journal*. Winter 1987.

——. "Diversification Categories in Investment Real Estate." *AREUEA Journal*. Summer 1986.

Hartzell, D., D. Shulman, and C. Wurtzebach. "Discount Points, Effective Yield, and Mortgage Prepayments." *Journal of Real Estate Research*. Winter 1987.

Hoag, J.W. "Toward Indices of Real Estate Value and Return." *Journal of Finance*. May 1980.

Ibbotson, Roger G., J. Diermeier, and L. Seigel. "The Demand for Capital Market Returns: A New Equilibrium Theory." *Financial Analysts Journal*. January–February 1984.

Ibbotson R., and C.L. Fall. "The U.S. Market Wealth Portfolio." *Journal of Portfolio Management*. Fall 1979.

Ibbotson, R.G., and L.B. Seigel. "Real Estate Returns: A Comparison with Other Investments." *AREUEA Journal*. Fall 1984.

Kelleher, D. "How Real Estate Stacks Up to the S&P500." *Real Estate Review*. Summer 1976.

Markowitz, H. *Portfolio Selection*. New Haven: Yale Univ. Press, 1959.

Miles, Mike, and Tom McCue. "Commercial Real Estate Returns." *AREUEA Journal*. Fall 1984.

——. "Diversification in the Real Estate Portfolio." *Journal of Financial Research*. Spring 1984.

——. "Historic Return and Institutional Real Estate Portfolios." *AREUEA Journal*. Summer 1982.

Miles M., and M. Rice. "Toward a More Complete Investigation of the Correlation of Real Estate Investment Yield with the Rate Evidenced in the Money and Capital Market." *Real Estate Appraiser and Analyst*. November–December 1978.

National Council of Real Estate Investment Fiduciaries. "The NCREIF Report." Tacoma, Wash.: Frank Russell Company, quarterly.

Pensions & Investment Age. Chicago, Ill.: Crain Publications, 1987.

Ricks, R.B. "Imputed Equity Returns on Real Estate Financed with Life Insurance Company Loans." *Journal of Finance*. December 1969.

Robicheck, A.A., R. Cohn, and J. Pringle. "Returns on Alternative Investment Media and Implications for Portfolio Construction." *Journal of Business*. July 1972.

Ross, S., "The Arbitrage Theory of Capital Asset Pricing." *Journal of Economic Theory*. December 1976.

Ross, S., and R. Roll. "Regulation, the Capital Asset Pricing Model, and the Arbitrage Pricing Theory." *Public Utilities Fortnightly*. May 26, 1983.

Roulac, S. "Can Real Estate Returns Outperform Common Stocks?" *Journal of Portfolio Management*. Fall 1976.

——. "How to Structure Real Estate Investment Management." *Journal of Portfolio Management*. Fall 1981.

Salomon Brothers. "Real Estate Market Review." New York: Quarterly.

Sharpe, W.F. "Capital Asset Prices: A Theory of Market Equilibrium under Conditions of Risk." *Journal of Finance*. September 1964.

Sirmans, G.S., and C.F. Sirmans. "The Historical Perspective of Real Estate Returns." *Journal of Portfolio Management*. Spring 1987.

Smith, K.V., and D. Shulman. "The Performance of Equity Real Estate Investment Trusts." *Financial Analysts Journal*. September–October 1976.

Webb, J.R., and C.F. Sirmans. "Yields and Risk Measures for Real Estate, 1966–1977." *Journal of Portfolio Management*. Fall 1980.

Wendt, P.F., and S.N. Wong. "Investment Performance: Common Stocks vs. Apartment Houses." *Journal of Finance*. December 1965.

Zerbst, R.H., and B.R. Cambon. "Historical Returns on Real Estate Investment." *Journal of Portfolio Management*. Spring 1984.

Appendix G
Glossary

Absorption schedule. The estimated schedule or rate at which properties for sale or lease can be marketed in a given locality; usually used when preparing a forecast of the sales or leasing rate to substantiate a development plan and to obtain financing.

Agglomeration. Concentration of commercial activity within a given area, tending to have a synergetic effect increasing diversity, specialization, and overall business activity.

Amenity. Nonmonetary tangible or intangible benefit derived from real property (often offered to a lessee). Typically, swimming pools, parks, valets, and the like.

Appraisal. An opinion or estimate of value substantiated by various analyses.

Architect. A designer of buildings and supervisor of construction. All states require architects to be licensed under laws governing health, safety, and welfare.

Asset manager. A person who balances risk and reward in managing investment portfolios including, but not limited to, real property and improvements. Asset managers either oversee property management or are responsible for it themselves.

Attached housing. Two or more dwelling units constructed with party walls (for example, townhouses, cluster houses, stacked flats).

Binding constraint. Legally enforceable limit on the allowable development on a given site.

BOMA. Building Owners and Managers Association. A trade association of owners and managers of apartment and office buildings.

Bonding. A guarantee of completion or performance, typically issued by an insurance company that will back up the bonded party in any lawsuit. In real estate, contractors, for example, are often bonded as assurance that they will complete the work.

Broker. A person who, for a commission, acts as the agent of another in the process of buying, selling, leasing, or managing property rights.

Brokerage. The business of a broker that includes all the functions necessary to market a seller's property and represent the seller's (principal's) best interests.

Buildout. Construction of specific interior finishes to a tenant's specifications.

Build to suit. Construction of land improvements according to a tenant's or purchaser's specifications.

Capital. Money or property invested in an asset for the creation of wealth; alternatively, the surplus of production over consumption.

Capitalization. The process of estimating value by discounting stabilized net operating income at an appropriate rate.

Capital market. Financial marketplace in which savings (from individuals, companies, or pension funds) are aggregated by financial intermediaries and allocated to real investors.

Capture rate. Forecasted rate of absorption within a targeted market segment for a proposed project, based on an analysis of supply and demand.

Central business district (CBD). The center of commercial activity within a town or city; usually the largest and oldest concentration of such activity.

Commercial real estate. Improved real estate held for the production of income through leases for commercial or business use (for example, office buildings, retail shops, and shopping centers).

Comparable property. Another property to which a subject property can be compared to reach an estimate of market value.

Concession. Discount given to prospective tenants to induce them to sign a lease, typically in the form of some free rent, cash for improvements furnished by the tenant, and so on.

Condominium. A form of joint ownership and control of property in which specified volumes of air space (for example, apartments) are owned individually, while the common elements of the building (for example, outside walls) are jointly owned.

Construction lender. Entity or individual providing interim financing during the construction phase(s) of the real estate development process.

Construction loan. A loan made usually by a commercial bank to a builder to be used for the construction of improvements on real estate and usually running six months to two years.

Covenant. A restriction on real property that is binding, regardless of changes in ownership, because it is attached to the title. Used generally in covenants, conditions, and restrictions (CC&Rs).

Convenience goods. Items typically purchased at the most convenient locations. They are usually not very expensive or long-lasting, and their purchase involves little deliberation. Convenience goods are distinguished from shoppers goods (see glossary) when doing retail market studies.

Critical path method. A network analysis method that graphically displays the activities involved in completing a project and shows the relationship between the activities. This display can graphically show how a delay in one activity will affect other activities.

Debt service. Periodic payments on a loan, with a portion of the payment for interest and the balance for repayment (amortization) of principal.

Demand deposit. Shorter-term deposits, such as checking accounts, that banks typically put into relatively short-term investments.

Demographics. Information on population characteristics by location, including such aspects as age, employment, earnings, and expenditures.

Density. The level of concentration (high or low) of buildings, including their total volume, within a given area. Often expressed as a ratio, for example, dwelling units per acre or floor/area ratio.

Department of Housing and Urban Development (HUD). A cabinet-level federal department responsible for carrying out national housing programs, including Federal Housing Administration subsidy programs, home mortgage insurance, urban renewal, and urban planning assistance.

Detached housing. A freestanding dwelling unit, normally single family, situated on its own lot.

Developer. One who prepares raw land for improvement by installing roads, utilities, and so on; also, a builder (one who actually constructs improvements on real estate).

Development process. The process of preparing raw land so that it becomes suitable for the erection of buildings; generally involves clearing and grading land and installing roads and utility services.

Discounted cash flow. Present value of monies to be received in the future; determined by multiplying projected cash flows by the discount factor.

Downzoning. A change in the zoning for a given parcel that restricts the density to less than the previous maximum allowed.

Draw. The lender's release of construction loan funds in accordance with set procedures for providing portions of the total amount as each stage of construction is satisfactorily completed.

Due diligence. A forthright effort to investigate all reasonable considerations in a timely manner, as in the case of prior waste disposal on a parcel of land.

Eminent domain. The power of a public authority to condemn and take property for public use on payment of just compensation.

Enabling legislation. Legislation typically delegated to local government that specifies the police power the state is giving to the local government. Cities, counties, and other local governments undertake planning, zoning, and additional forms of development regulation according to state enabling statutes.

Enterprise concept. The idea that encouraging private enterprise will facilitate economic revitalization or other socioeconomic goals. Encourages owners to look at real estate as another type of private enterprise.

Entrepreneur. A venture capitalist; one who accepts personal financial risk in business ventures.

Equity. That portion of an ownership interest in real property or other securities that is owned outright, that is, above amounts financed.

Equity kicker. A provision in the loan terms that guarantees the lender a percentage of the property's appreciation over some specified time or a percentage of income from the property or both.

Escalation clause. A provision in a lease that permits a landlord to pass through increases in real estate taxes and operating expenses to tenants, with each tenant paying its prorated share. Also a mortgage clause that allows the lender to increase the interest rate based on terms of the note.

Exactions. Fee or payment-in-kind required of a developer by a local jurisdiction for approval of development plans, in accordance with state and local legislation regarding the provision of public facilities and amenities.

Fast-tracking. A method of project management in which construction of a project actually begins before all the details are finalized.

Feasibility study. A combination of a market study and an economic study that provides the investor with knowledge of the environment where the project exists and the expected returns from investment in it.

Fee simple absolute. The most extensive interest in land recognized by law. Absolute ownership but subject to the limitations of police power, taxation, eminent domain, escheat, and private restrictions of record.

Fee simple determinable. A fee simple ownership that terminates on the happening (or failure to happen) of a stated condition. Also referred to as a "defeasible fee."

Festival marketplace. A specialty retail center incorporating aspects of old marketplaces, including significant public spaces and a variety of activities. Concept developed by Boston architect Benjamin Thompson.

FIRE (fire/insurance/real estate). An employment classification used by the Department of Labor when analyzing the service industry.

Floor amount. Initial portion of a floor-to-ceiling mortgage loan, advanced when certain conditions—for example, construction of core and shell—are met.

Floor/area ratio. The ratio of floor area to land area, expressed as a percent or decimal, that is determined by dividing the total floor area of the building by the area of the lot; typically used as a formula to regulate building volume.

Floorplate. A metal plate set into a floor, sometimes fitted with slots to which equipment may be fastened.

Foreclosure. The legal process by which a mortgagee, in case of a mortgagor's default, forces sale of the mortgaged property to provide funds to pay off the loan.

Gantt chart. A horizontal bar chart used in the critical path method of analysis.

Garden apartments. Two- or three-story multifamily housing featuring low density, ample open space around buildings, and convenient on-site parking.

General contractor. Person or firm that supervises a construction project under a contract with the owner; also known as the "prime contractor."

Growth management. The public sector's control over the timing and location of real estate development by various means, including legislative and administrative.

Hard costs. Outlays for land, labor, and improvements.

Highest and best use. The property use that, at a given time, is deemed likely to produce the greatest net return in the foreseeable future, whether or not such use is the current use of the property.

High rise. Tall building, skyscraper, usually more than 10 stories.

HVAC. A building system supplying heating, ventilation, and air conditioning.

Impact fee. Charge levied (on developers) by local governments to pay for the cost of providing public facilities necessitated by a given development.

Income kicker. A provision in the loan terms that guarantees the lender's receiving a portion of gross income over an established minimum, for example, 10 percent of the first year's gross rent receipts.

Industrial park. A large tract of improved land used for a variety of light industrial and manufacturing uses. Users either purchase or lease individual sites.

Infrastructure. Services and facilities provided by a municipality, including roads, highways, water, sewerage, emergency services, parks and recreation, and so on. Can also be privately provided.

Institute of Real Estate Management (IREM). An affiliate of the National Association of Realtors whose purpose is to promote professionalism in the field of property management.

Internal rate of return (IRR). The discount rate at which investment has zero net present value (that is, the yield to the investor).

International Council of Shopping Centers (ICSC). A national trade association for owners, developers, and managers of shopping centers.

Joint venture. An association of two or more firms or individuals to carry on a single business enterprise for profit.

Junk bond. Any bond (a long-term debt obligation of a corporation or a government) with a relatively low rating. The lower the rating, the more speculative or risky the investment. Returns can be much higher than for a less speculative investment, however. Bonds are rated by credit-rating companies, the best known being Standard & Poor's.

Land planner. One who specializes in the art of subdividing land to combine maximum utility with such desirable amenities as scenic views and winding roads.

Lease. A contract that gives the lessor (the tenant) the right of possession for a period of time in return for paying rent to the lessee (the landlord).

Lease concession. A benefit to a tenant to induce him or her to enter into a lease; usually takes the form of one month of free rent.

Lease-up. Period during which a real estate rental property is marketed, leasing agreements are signed, and tenants begin to move in.

Leverage. The use of borrowed funds to finance a project.

Lien. The right to hold property as security until the debt that it secures is paid. A mortgage is one type of lien.

Limited partnership. A partnership that restricts the personal liability of the partners to the amount of their investment.

Linkage. Typically, a payment to a municipality for some needed development that is not necessarily profitable for a developer (say, low-income housing) in exchange for the right to develop more profitable, high-density buildings (say, commercial development).

Loan-to-value (LTV) ratio. The relationship between the amount of a mortgage loan and the value of the real estate securing it; the loan amount divided by market value.

Low rise. A multistory building, usually in outlying areas, with fewer than 10 stories.

Marketing research. The study of factors that will satisfy the needs of target customers and convince them to buy or rent.

Marketing study/marketability study. A study that determines the price or rent appropriate to market a project successfully.

Market niche. A particular subgroup within a market segment distinguishable, by certain characteristics, from the rest of the segment.

Market research. A study of the needs of groups of people to develop a product appropriate for an identifiable market niche.

Market study. An analysis of the general demand for a single real estate product for a particular project.

Mechanic's lien. A claim that attaches to real estate to protect the right to compensation of one who performs labor or provides materials in connection with construction.

Metropolitan statistical area (MSA). An urban area containing multiple political jurisdictions grouped together for purposes of counting individuals by the U.S. Bureau of the Census.

Miniperm loan. A short-term loan (usually five years) meant to be an interim loan between a construction loan and a permanent loan. A miniperm loan is usually securitized like any other loan; the interest rate could be less onerous than a construction loan but not as favorable as a permanent loan.

Miniwarehouse. A one-story building subdivided into numerous small cubicles intended to be used as storage by families or small businesses.

Mixed-use development. A development, in one building or several buildings, that combines at least three significant revenue-producing uses that are physically and functionally integrated and developed in conformance with a coherent plan. A mixed-use development might include, for example, retail space on the ground floor, offices on the middle floors, and condominiums on the top floors, with a garage on the lower levels.

Mortgage. An instrument used in some states (rather than a deed of trust) to make real estate security for a debt. A two-party instrument between a mortgagor (a borrower) and a mortgagee (a lender).

Mortgage banking. The process of originating real estate loans and then selling them to institutional lenders and other investors.

Mortgage loan constant. Percentage of the original loan balance represented by the constant periodic mortgage payment.

Move-up housing. Typically, larger, more expensive houses that homeowners buy as their incomes increase. First homes, or "starter houses," are generally modestly sized and priced. As purchasers' incomes increase, they "move up" into larger, more expensive housing.

Multifamily housing. Structures that house more than one family in separate units (apartments). Can be high rises, low rises, garden apartments, or townhouses.

National Association of Realtors (NAR). The largest real estate organization in the country and probably in the world. Members are entitled to use the designation "Realtor."

Neighborhood. A segment of a city or town having common features distinguishing it from adjoining areas.

Net operating income (NOI). Cash flow from rental income on a property after operating expenses are deducted from gross income.

Office building. A building or area of a building leased to tenants for the conduct of business or a profession, as distinguished from residential, commercial, or retail uses.

Operating budget. A budget, usually prepared a year in advance, listing projected costs of maintenance and repair for a building.

Operating expenses. Expenses directly related to the operation and maintenance of a property, including real estate taxes, mainte-nance and repair, insurance, payroll and management fees, supplies, and utilities. Do not include debt service on mortgages or depreciation.

Option. The right given by the owner of property (the optionor) to another (the optionee) to purchase or lease the property at a specific price within a set time.

Origination fee. A charge made by the lender at the inception of the loan to cover administrative costs.

Passive investor. An investor who seeks no active role in construction or operation of a building but merely seeks to invest funds to earn a return. Institutional investors, such as pension funds, are typically passive investors.

Pass-through. Lease provision whereby certain costs flow through directly to the tenant rather than to the owner (for example, property tax increases on a long-term lease).

Pass-through certificate. An investment instrument in which the periodic debt service payments on a package of mortgage loans are paid out (passed through) to the investors owning the instrument.

Pension fund. An institution that holds assets to be used for the payment of pensions to corporate or government employees, union members, and other groups.

Permanent lender. A financial institution undertaking a long-term loan on real estate subject to specified conditions (for example, the construction of improvements).

PERT. *P*rogram *e*valuation and *r*eview *t*echnique. A technique that provides project managers with a flowchart representing construction schedule times. Includes a critical path that indicates the activities that must be completed on time so as not to delay completion.

Planned unit development (PUD). Zoning classification created to accommodate master-planned developments that include mixed uses, varied housing types, and/or unconventional subdivision designs.

Portfolio. A collection of varied investments held by an individual or firm. Real estate is often among those investments.

Present value. The current value of an income-producing asset, estimated by discounting all expected future cash flows over the holding period.

Pro forma. A financial statement that projects gross income, operating expenses, and net operating income for a future period based on a set of specific assumptions.

Property manager. An individual or firm responsible for the operation of improved real estate. Management functions include leasing and maintenance.

Purchasing power. The financial means (including credit) that people possess to purchase durable and nondurable goods.

Rational nexus. A reasonable connection between impact fees and improvements that will be made with those fees. Jurisdictions must be able to justify the fees they charge developers by showing that the fees will be spent on improvements related to the development. For example, a fee of $25.00 per square foot charged for a shopping center might not be justifiable if it is to be used for building an addition to the local elementary school. It might be justified, however, if it will be used to improve roads near the shopping center because of the additional traffic that the shopping center is likely to generate.

Real estate investment trust (REIT). An ownership entity that provides limited liability, no tax on the entity, and liquidity. Ownership is evidenced by shares of beneficial interest similar to shares of common stock.

REALTOR®. A member of the National Association of Realtors. "Realtor" is also a generic term used to describe professionals who are involved in selling property.

Redevelopment. The redesign or rehabilitation of existing properties.

Reliability. The ability to remain consistent under repeated tests.

Resolution Trust Corporation. A mixed-ownership government corporation created by Congress to manage failed thrift institutions and their holdings.

Retainage. A portion of the amount due under a construction contract that the owner withholds until the job is completed in accordance with plans and specifications; usually a percentage of the total contract price.

Risk. The possibility that returns on an investment or loan will not be as high as expected.

Risk-control techniques. Stages in the development or construction process at which the developer can discontinue operations or modify them in light of new circumstances.

Savings and loan (S&L) association. A type of savings institution that is the primary source of financing for one- to four-family houses. Most S&Ls are mutual (nonstock) institutions.

Secondary mortgage market. The market in which existing mortgages are bought and sold: conventional loans by Freddie Mac and Fannie Mae, FHA and VA loans by Fannie Mae, and special assistance loans (HUD regulated) by Ginnie Mae.

Security. Evidence of ownership, such as stocks or bonds.

Setback. The part of zoning regulations restricting building within a specified distance from the property frontline or edge of the public street; thus, the structure must be set back a given number of feet from the frontline.

Shoppers goods. Items purchased after some degree of deliberation or shopping around. Generally, they are differentiated through brand identification, the retailer's image, or ambience of the shopping area. Such purchases are made less often, and the product is typically more durable and expensive.

Shopping center. Integrated and self-contained shopping area, usually in the suburbs. Classified as neighborhood (50,000 to 100,000 square feet and providing convenience goods and personal services), community (100,000 to 300,000 square feet and providing a wider range of goods), regional (about 400,000 square feet with one or two department store anchors), and super regional (1 million plus square feet with three or more department store anchors).

Single-family housing. Designed for use by one family.

Situs. The total urban environment in which a specific urban land use on a specific land parcel functions and with which it interacts at a specific time. More simply, location.

Smart building. A building that incorporates technologically advanced features to facilitate communications, information processing, energy conservation, and tenant services.

Soft costs. Outlays for interest, origination fees, appraisals, and other third-party charges associated with real estate development.

Strip mall. An enclosed shopping center located on a highway along which development has sprawled outward from a town or city center.

Subcontractor. An individual or company that performs a specific job for a construction project, pursuant to an agreement with the general contractor.

Subdivision. Division of a parcel of land into building lots that can also include streets, parks, schools, utilities, and other public facilities.

Suburbanization. The movement of development to the suburbs created by the overflow effect of cities and by the automobile, which improved accessibility to the inner city.

Syndication. The process of acquiring and combining equity investment from multiple sources (for example, syndicating units in a limited partnership).

Takeout commitment. The permanent loan commitment for a project to be constructed.

Tenant. One who rents from another.

Tenant allowance. A cash payment made by the developer to a tenant (usually in an income property) to enable the tenant, rather than the developer, to complete the interior work for the leased premises.

Tenant mix. The combination of various types of tenants in a leased building.

Title. Evidence of ownership of real property; often used synonymously with the term "ownership" to indicate a person's right to possess, use, and dispose of property.

Title company. A company that examines titles to real estate, determines whether they are valid and whether any limitations on the title exist, and, for a premium, insures the validity of the title to the owner or lender.

Townhouse. Single-family attached residence separated from another by party walls, usually on a narrow lot offering small front and rear yards.

Urban economics. Economic concepts applied in the context of a particular urban area.

Validity. Execution with proper legal authority.

Variance. In general, the difference between expected results and actual results. Statistically, "variance" refers to the square of the standard deviation. Can be used as a measure of risk.

Venture capital. Funds available for investment at risk i to a profit-seeking enterprise.

Warehouse. A building that is used for the storage of goods or merchandise and that can be occupied by the owner or leased to one or more tenants.

Workout. Negotiated arrangements between a lending institution and a developer unable to fulfill a loan agreement.

Writedown. A deliberate reduction in the book value of an asset, typically made because of changes in market conditions, deterioration of properties, loss of tenants, and the like.

Zoning. Classification and regulation of land by local governments according to use categories (zones); often includes density designations as well.

Index